AMERICA
and Its Peoples

SEED Warranted to Grow.

or order refilled gratis. I have sold vegetable and flower seed to over a million farmers and gardeners in the United States, perhaps some are your neighbors. If so ask them whether they are reliable. Mr. Thomas Henshall of Troy, Kansas, writes me: "For 28 years I have dealt with you. I have lived in Iowa, Missouri, Colorado, and Kansas, and no matter what the soil or climate, the result was always the same, to wit:—religiously honest and good." This is the kind of seed I raise and sell.
Hubbard and Marblehead Squash, Marblehead Corn, Marblehead Cabbages, Ohio Potato, Eclipse Beet, are some of the vegetables of which I was the original introducer. A fair with $10 in premiums. See my catalogue, free to all.
JAMES J. H. GREGORY, (Seed Grower,) Marblehead, Mass.

1885
GREGORY'S SEED CATALOGUE.
FREE

AGENTS WANTED FOR GEN. BEAUREGARD'S MILITARY OPERATIONS.

This work is regarded by the ablest reviewers, North and South, as the most valuable contribution to the history of the War from Southern steadily increasing in all

ALSO

THE WORLD'S O

AND

HOW TO US

GOLD PENS,
PENCILS, HOLDERS, CASES, &c.
THE CALLI-GRAPHIC PEN.
N and RUBBER HOLDER, containing
desk writer. Can be carried in the
try for a luxury for persons
ness, their individuality in writing,
TODD, A HARE
Liberty Sts., New York.
for Pricelistist
by FIRST-CLASS DEALERS.

EARL & WILSON'S
ENT "SHORT BAND" COLLARS
AND BEAD EDGE CUF
WAYS GIVE SATISFACTION

PATE

OR HO

SIMP

CHARLE
NO 16 FOURT

HARPER & B
Frank

$3 Printing

YOUMANS' HATS FOR GENTLEMEN

SPECIA

We are not

4TH EDITION

AMERICA
and Its Peoples

A Mosaic in the Making

Volume 1—to 1887

James Kirby Martin
University of Houston

Randy Roberts
Purdue University

Steven Mintz
University of Houston

Linda O. McMurry
North Carolina State University

James H. Jones
University of Arkansas

Longman

New York   Boston   San Francisco
London   Toronto   Sydney   Tokyo   Singapore   Madrid
Mexico City   Munich   Paris   Cape Town   Hong Kong   Montreal

Publisher: Priscilla McGeehon
Senior Acquisitions Editor: Jay O'Callaghan
Director of Development: Lisa Pinto
Development Manager: Betty Slack
Executive Marketing Manager: Sue Westmoreland
Supplements Editor: Jennifer Ackerman
Production Manager: Patti Brecht
Project Coordination, Text Design, and Electronic Page Makeup: Nesbitt Graphics, Inc.
Cover Designer/Manager: John Callahan
Cover Art: Collage by Michael Staats using the following images: Drawing of Native American by
John White, courtesy of the Trustees of the British Museum; Abigail Gerrish and grandmother, cour-
tesy of Peabody Essex Museum, Salem, MA; George Washington, The Metropolitan Museum of Art,
bequest of Grace Wilkes, 1922 (22.45.9); Joseph Brant, National Gallery of Canada, Ottawa; Thomas
Jefferson, The White House Collection, © White House Historical Association; Handkerchief for
William Henry Harrison campaign, New York Historical Society; Andrew Jackson, Memphis Brooks
Museum of Art, Memphis, TN, Memphis Park Commission Purchase 46.2; Sojourner Truth, Sophia
Smith Collection, Women's History Archive, Smith College, Northhampton, MA; Frederick
Douglass, Library of Congress; Paper continental currency ©AP/Wide World Photos; McCormick
reaper © Hulton Getty/Liaison Agency; Harriet Tubman, Library of Congress.
Maps: Mapping Specialists, Ltd.
Collage Art: Michael Staats
Photographer, Collage Art: Keith Tishken
Photo Researcher: Pearson Image Resource Center
Senior Print Buyer: Dennis J. Para
Printer and Binder: Quebecor World Taunton
Timeline Printer: Edison Lithographing and Printing Corp.
Cover Printer: The Lehigh Press, Inc.

For permission to use copyrighted material, grateful acknowledgment is made to the copyright holders on pages C-1–C-2, which are hereby made part of this copyright page.

Library of Congress Cataloging-in-Publication Data
America and its peoples : a mosaic in the making / James Kirby Martin ... [et al.].—4th ed.
    p. cm.
  Includes bibliographical references and index.
    ISBN 0-321-07985-X (v. 1)—ISBN 0-321-07984-1 (v.2)—ISBN 0-321-07910-8
  (single vol. edition)
    1. United States—History. I. Martin, James Kirby

E178.1.A4886 2000
973—dc21   00-040122

Please visit our website at http://www.awl.com/martin

ISBN 0-321-07910-8 (single volume)
ISBN 0-321-07985-X (volume 1)
ISBN 0-321-07984-1 (volume 2)

345678910—QWT—030201

FOR OUR STUDENTS

BRIEF *Contents*

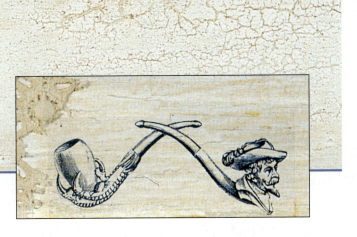

DETAILED *Contents*

7 THE FORMATIVE DECADE, 1790–1800   189

An "outrageous and wretched scandalmonger"

16 THE NATION RECONSTRUCTED: NORTH, SOUTH, AND THE WEST, 1865–1877   445

"I'd like tuh see any man put me outer dis house"

APPENDIX

MAPS

TABLES *and Figures*

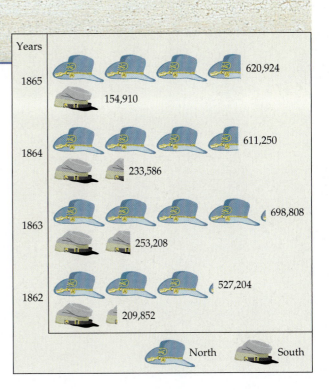

Years		
1865	North	620,924
	South	154,910
1864	North	611,250
	South	233,586
1863	North	698,808
	South	253,208
1862	North	527,204
	South	209,852

North   South

PREFACE

Americans are of two minds about history. Popular history fascinates them. Many of Hollywood's most popular films—from *Birth of a Nation* to *Titanic*—draw on history for their themes, characters, and drama. Nothing underscores this fascination with history better than the point that more Americans visit historical sites and museums like Colonial Williamsburg or the Smithsonian Institution on an annual basis than attend major league baseball games.

Academic history is much less popular, however. At colleges and universities, the number of history majors and enrollment in history courses has fallen at an alarming rate. At the high-school level, history requirements have increasingly been replaced by courses in social studies. A recent poll found that high school students consider history the least relevant subject that they study.

We have designed *America and Its Peoples* to convey American history's excitement and drama. The story that we tell is fraught with conflict, suspense, and controversy, and we have sought to recapture this excitement by writing a book built around vivid character sketches, colorful anecdotes, a strong narrative pulse, and a wide-angle view that allows us to examine such subjects as crime, disease, the family and sexuality, and sports.

A history textbook, in our view, need not be dull, humorless, or lifeless. Rather, it should bring the past back to life in all of its complexity, underscoring history's relevance to our daily lives. The issues addressed in this book—colonialism, revolution, the origins of racial prejudice, the costs and benefits of industrialization and urbanization—are anything but trivial. They remain very much a part of the human story today.

Nor do we think that a textbook should insulate readers from controversy. One of history's greatest benefits is that it allows us to "second guess" the decisions and choices made in the past, to reassess the meaning of past events, and to reevaluate real-life heroes and villains. History, we believe, is the ideal laboratory for critical thinking. By engaging the past, we can assess the roles of individuals and of social forces in producing historical transformations, and learn to evaluate conflicting interpretations of people and events. This textbook demonstrates that history is an arena of debate and contention as exciting as any other.

Each generation must produce a history that addresses the concerns of its own time. In writing *America and Its Peoples*, we have sought to fashion a history of the United States that speaks to the realities of a changing America. Today, the United States is the most ethnically diverse nation in the world. Over the past four centuries, 45 million people arrived in America from Africa, Asia, and Europe. In *America and Its Peoples* we recount the histories of the diverse ethnic, religious, and racial groups that have come to make up our society. We underscore the pivotal role that ethnicity, race, and religion have played in our nation's social, cultural, and political development. From its earliest settlement, America has been a multicultural society, and by placing ethnicity, race, gender, and class at the very heart of our narrative, we have sought to present a new perspective on how our multifaceted culture and politics functioned through time.

Contemporary American society perceives itself as beset by unprecedented problems—of ethnic and racial tension, economic stagnation and inequality, crime, family upheaval, and environmental degradation. In *America and Its Peoples*, we have made a special point of uncovering the historical roots of the problems confronting American society today. One of history's values is that it can show how previous generations confronted the controversial issues of their times, allowing us to assess their achievements as well as their failures.

Americans are an optimistic, forward-looking people who, in the course of everyday life, care little about the past. More than two centuries ago, Thomas Jefferson gave pointed expression to this attitude when he declared that "the earth belongs to the living and not the dead." But as the famous novelist William Faulkner once observed, "the past is never dead. It's not even past." We are convinced that the very worst forms of bigotry, fanaticism, and racism are ultimately grounded in historical ignorance and mythology. History reminds us that our values, our identities, and our most pressing social problems are rooted in our historical experience. Thus, in writing this book, we have not simply sought to create an encyclopedic compendium of names, dates, events, and concepts; we have conceived of United States history as a dramatic story: a story involving contention, struggle, compromise, and, above all, conflicting visions of the nation's dominant values.

Today, many Americans are wary about the future and uneasy about the state of their society. In *America and Its Peoples* we have written a textbook that emphasizes historical contingency—the idea that different decisions and choices in the past would have created a very different world today. Ours is a history that emphasizes the importance of personal choice and collective action; a history that stresses peoples' capacity to shape their own destiny. We believe that this is an inspiring historical lesson with profound implications for the nation's future.

FEATURES

Written by scholars who regularly teach the introductory U.S. history survey, *America and Its Peoples* is an exceptionally readable textbook that brings history to life through the stories of the women and men who shaped our history as a people. Highly sensitive to students' needs and interests, the authors place ethnicity, race, and gender at the core of the historical narrative, not as adjunct information. Carefully balancing cultural, diplomatic, economic, military, political, religious, and social history, the authors pay special attention to the clash of ideas and peoples that has shaped American history. Thoroughly revised and totally up-to-date, the fourth edition contains comprehensive coverage of the Clinton presidency.

America and Its Peoples is a textbook that students will genuinely enjoy reading. It thoroughly treats the history of all Americans, including extensive coverage of women, African Americans, Asian Americans, Hispanic Americans, and Native Americans. It offers exceptionally complete coverage of the areas that were originally colonized by Spain, to meet the special needs of students who live in the Sunbelt. An example of this coverage is the unique chapter (28) on the West and the South in the twentieth century, which examines the growing importance of these areas in our nation's recent history.

Concisely and vividly written, the textbook contains a wealth of special features designed to stimulate student interest in history and reinforce student learning.

NEW TO THIS EDITION

- *"The People Speak"* These excerpts from primary sources introduce students to critical documents in American history and allow them to hear the past speak in its own voice. Introductory headnotes provide the historical context for each document. One "People Speak" excerpt appears in each chapter.
- *Key Terms* In each chapter, 10 to 15 key terms are highlighted in boldface type to alert students to the principal concepts, events, and individuals discussed in the chapter. A page-referenced list of the key terms at the end of each chapter offers students the opportunity to review the main ideas and persons covered in the chapter.
- *Glossary* A thorough glossary at the end of the book provides definitions for each key terms and succinct identification of each key concept, individual, and event. Each glossary term is page referenced so that students can easily locate discussion of the term in its historical context.
- *Review Questions* End-of-the-chapter review questions allow students to examine how well they have absorbed the chapter content and invite them to think critically about the issues discussed in the chapter. The review questions can be used to spark class discussions or for written assignments.
- *Internet Resources* At the end of each chapter, guides to history resources on the World Wide Web direct students to sources of additional information that can be easily accessed online.
- *Comparative Chronology* A fold-out, illustrated timeline provides a thorough and accessible chronological reference guide for U.S. history. The timeline notes key events and trends in political, diplomatic, social, economic, and cultural history.

In addition to these new features, *America and Its Peoples,* Fourth Edition, includes a number of other components and pedagogical aids designed to engage students' interest and enhance their learning:

- Pictorial chapter-opening collages address students' capacity for visual learning by presenting images of the people, places, and events students will encounter in the chapter.
- Chapter-opening outlines help students organize their study by identifying the main topics and subtopics discussed in the chapter.

- Vignettes at the beginning of each chapter grab students' attention with a fascinating story of an individual or an event. The final paragraphs of the vignette succinctly introduce chapter themes and link the vignette to the chapter narrative.
- "The American Mosaic" essays, one in each chapter, offer an in-depth examination of some aspect of such high interest topics as crime, medicine, sports and other leisure-time activities, the experience of combat, and the reshaping of private life.
- Five full-page watercolor battlefield maps offer close examination of key battles in America's wars. An essay accompanying each battlefield map describes the battle in detail and explores its historical significance.
- "Road to War" tables summarize the key events that led up to the declaration of each of America's wars, providing students with a specialized chronology for these pivotal events in U.S. history.

SUPPLEMENTS

A comprehensive and up-to-date supplements package accompanies *America and Its Peoples*.

FOR QUALIFIED ADOPTERS

The History Place Web Site—Martin Special Edition (*www.awl.com/martin*)   This special edition of *The History Place* combines quality educational publishing with the immediacy and interactivity of the Internet. The Web site contains a continually updated source of maps, timelines, and other interactive learning activities. It also houses a rich collection of primary documents, news, and online quizzes that correspond to the text's organization. A free subscription to *The History Place—Martin Special Edition* is included with every new copy of the student text.

Martin Online (*www.awl.com/martin*)   Instructors can take advantage of the online course companion that supports this text. The instructor section of the Web site includes the instructor's manual, teaching links, animated maps, thematic timelines, narrated photo essays, and visual downloads. Additionally, instructors can take advantage of Syllabus Builder, our comprehensive course management system.

Instructor's Manual   This extensive resource by Mark Newman of the University of Illinois, Chicago, begins with essays on teaching history through maps, film, and primary sources. Each chapter contains a synopsis, sample discussion questions, lecture supplements, and instructional flowcharts. The manual includes a reproducible set of map exercises by James Conrad of Nichols College, designed to teach basic geographical literacy.

Test Bank   Written by Ken Weatherbie and Brian Hart of Del Mar College, the test bank contains multiple choice, true/false, and essay test items. The questions are keyed to topic, difficulty level, cognitive type, and relevant text page.

Computerized TestGen EQ Computerized Testing System   This flexible, easy-to-use computer test bank includes all the test items in the printed test bank. Available on dual platform CD-ROM and floppy disks, the software allows you to edit existing questions and add your own items. Tests can be printed in several different formats and can include graphs and tables.

Text Map Transparencies   A set of 40 four-color transparencies from the maps and figures in *America and Its Peoples*.

Comprehensive American History Transparency Set   This vast collection of American history transparencies is a necessary teaching aid. It includes over 200 maps covering social trends, wars, elections, immigrations, and demographics. Included is a set of reproducible map exercises.

Discovering American History Through Maps and Views Transparency Set   Created by Gerald Danzer of the University of Illinois at Chicago, the recipient of the AHA's 1990 James Harvey Robinson Prize for his work in the development of map transparencies, this set of 140 four-color acetates is a unique instructional tool. It contains an introduction on teaching history through maps and a detailed commentary on each transparency. The collection includes cartographic and pictorial maps, views and photos, urban plans, building diagrams, and works of art.

Discovering American History Through Film   Created by Randy Roberts of Purdue University, this guide provides instructors with a creative and practical tool for stimulating class discussions. The sections include "American Films: A Historian's Perspective," and a listing of "Films for Specific Periods in American History." The narrative film explains the connection between each film and the topics being studied.

Video Lecture Launchers   Prepared by Mark Newman of the University of Illinois at Chicago, these video lecture launchers (each two to five minutes in duration) cover key issues in American history from 1877 to the present. The launchers are accompanied by an instructor's manual.

American Impressions: A CD-ROM for American History   This unique, groundbreaking product for the U.S. Survey course is organized in a thematic framework that allows in-depth coverage of each topic. Hundreds of photos, maps, art, graphics, and historical film clips are organized into narrated vignettes and interactive activities to create a tool for both professors and students. Topics include "When Three Cultures Meet," "The Constitution," "Labor and Reform," and "Democracy and Diversity." It is available on Windows or Macintosh floppy disks.

This Is America Immigration Video   Produced by the Museum of Immigration, this video tells the story of immigrant America. By showing the personal stories and accomplishments of immigrants, it explores the contributions of millions of immigrants to America.

FOR STUDENTS

The History Place Web Site—Martin Special Edition *(www.ushistoryplace.com/martin)*   This special edition of *The History Place* combines quality educational publishing with the immediacy and interactivity of the Internet. The Web site contains a continually updated source of maps, timelines, and other interactive learning activities. It also houses a rich collection of primary documents, news, and online quizzes that correspond to the text's organization. A free subscription to *The History Place—Martin Special Edition* is included with every new copy of the student text.

Martin Online *(www.awl.com/martin)*   The online course companion provides a wealth of resources for students using *America and Its Peoples*. Students will find chapter summaries, practice test questions, interactive web exercises, animated maps, primary sources, thematic timelines, and more.

Interactive Edition CD-ROM for *America and Its Peoples*   This unique CD-ROM takes students beyond the printed page, offering them a complete multimedia learning experience. It contains the full text of the book on CD-ROM, with contextually placed media icons—audio, video, photos, figures, Web links, practice tests, primary sources, and more—that link students to additional content directly related to key concepts in the text. Free when packaged with the text.

StudyWizard Computerized Tutorial   Prepared by Ron Petrin of Oklahoma State University, this interactive program helps students learn major facts and concepts through drill and practice exercises and diagnostic feedback. Available on dual-platform CD-ROM and floppy disks, StudyWizard provides immediate correct answers and the text page number on which the material is discussed.

Study Guide   Designed to provide students with a comprehensive review of the text material and to encourage application and critical analysis of the material, this guide was prepared by Eddie Weller of San Jacinto College. Each chapter contains a chapter overview, learning objectives, important glossary terms, and multiple choice and essay questions.

Everything You Need to Know About Your History Course   Written by Sandra Mathews-Lamb of Nebraska Wesleyan University for first-year university students, this guide provides invaluable tips on how to study, use a textbook, write a good paper, take notes, read a map, graph, or bar chart, and review primary and secondary sources.

Longman American History Atlas   This four-color historical atlas includes 69 maps designed especially for this volume. This valuable reference tool is available shrink-wrapped with the text at a low cost.

Mapping American History: Student Activities   Written by Gerald Danzer of the University of Illinois at Chicago, this free map workbook for students features exercises designed to teach how to interpret and analyze cartographic materials as historical documents. The instructor is entitled to a free copy of the workbook for each copy of *America and Its Peoples* purchased from Longman.

Mapping America: A Guide to Historical Geography, Second Edition   Written by Ken Weatherbie of Del Mar College, this free two-volume workbook contains 35 exercises correlated to the text that review basic American historical geography and ask students to interpret the role geography has played in American history.

America Through the Eyes of Its People, Second Edition   This single-volume collection of primary documents reflects the rich and varied tapestry of American life. The revised edition includes more social history and enhanced pedagogy. It is available shrink-wrapped with *America and Its Peoples* at no charge.

Sources of the African-American Past   Edited by Roy Finkenbine of the University of Detroit at Mercy, this collection of primary sources covers the themes in the African American experience from the West African background to the present. Balanced between political and social history, it offers a vivid snapshot of the lives of African Americans in different historical periods, and includes documents representing women and different regions of the United States. Available at a minimum cost when bundled with the text.

Women and the National Experience   Edited by Ellen Skinner of Pace University, this primary source reader contains both classic and unusual documents describing the history of women in the United States. The documents provide dramatic evidence that outspoken women attained a public voice and participated in the development of national events and policies long before they could vote. Chronologically organized and balanced between social and political history, this reader offers a striking picture of the lives of women across American history. Available at a minimum cost when bundled with the text.

Reading the American West   Edited by Mitchel Roth of Sam Houston State University, this primary source reader uses letters, diary excerpts, speeches, interviews, and newspaper articles to let students experience how historians research and how history is written. Every document is accompanied by a contextual headnote and study questions. The book is divided into chapters with extensive introductions. Available at a minimum cost when bundled with the text.

Library of American Biography Series   Edited by Oscar Handlin of Harvard University, each of these interpretive biographies focuses on a figure whose actions and ideas significantly influenced the course of American history and national life. At the same time, each biography relates the life of its subject to the broader themes and developments of the era. Brief and inexpensive, they are ideal for any U.S. History course. New editions include *Abigail Adams: An American Woman*, Second Edition by Charles W. Akers; *Andrew Carnegie and the Rise of Big Business*, Second Edition by Harold C. Livesay; and *Eleanor*

Roosevelt: A Personal and Public Life, Second Edition by J. William T. Youngs.

A Short Guide to Writing About History   Written by Richard Marius of Harvard University, this short guide introduces students to the pleasures of historical research and discovery while teaching them how to write cogent history papers. Focusing on more than just the conventions of good writing, this supplement shows students first how to think about history, and then how to organize their thoughts into coherent essays.

Learning to Think Critically: Films and Myths About American History   In this guide, Randy Roberts and Robert May of Purdue University use well-know films such as *Gone With the Wind* and *Casablanca* to explore some common myths about America and its past. Many widely held assumptions of out country's past originate from, or are perpetuated by, popular films. Which are true? How can a student of history approach documents, sources, and textbooks with a critical and discerning eye? This short handbook scrutinizes some popular beliefs to help students develop a method of inquiry to approach the subject of history.

ACKNOWLEDGMENTS

Any textbook project is very much a team effort. Here we acknowledge with gratitude the assistance of the many talented historians who have served as reviewers and whose valuable critiques have greatly strengthened the final product.

Elizabeth Reilly Ansnes, San Jose State University; James Banks, Cuyahoga Community College; Robert A. Becker, Louisiana State University; Surendra Bhana, University of Kansas; Ballard Campbell, Northeastern University; Raymond W. Champagne, Jr., University of Scranton; Paul G. E. Clemens, Rutgers University; Kenton Clymer, University of Texas, El Paso; Roy E. Finkenbine, University of Detroit; Mark S. Foster, University of Colorado, Denver; J. David Hoeveler, University of Wisconsin, Milwaukee; Melissa M. Hovsepian, University of St. Thomas, Texas; Deborah M. Jones, Bristol Community College; Kathleen Kennedy, Western Washington University; Sterling J. Kernek, Western Illinois University; Stuart E. Knee, College of Charleston; Lee Bruce Kress, Rowan University; Thomas Lewis, Mount Senario College; Terrence Lindell, Wartburg College; James McCaffery, University of Houston, Downtown; M. Catherine Miller, Texas Tech University; Daniel Nelson, University of Akron; Mark Newell, Ramapo College; Peter L. Petersen, West Texas A&M University; Jon H. Roberts, University of Wisconsin, Stevens Point; David P. Shriver, Cuyhoga Community College; Jason H. Silverman, Winthrop University; Jason Tetzloff, Defiance College; Gary E. Thompson, Tulsa Junior College; Eddie Weller, San Jacinto College South; Larry Wilson, San Jacinto College Central.

Each author has received invaluable assistance from friends, colleagues, and family. James Kirby Martin thanks Don R. Gerlach, Joseph T. Glatthaar, Irene Guenther, Karen Guenther, Katie Harrison, J. Kent McGaughy, David M. Oshinsky, Cathy Patterson, Jeffrey T. Sammons, Halt T. Shelton, and Karen Martin, whose talents as an editor and critic are too often overlooked. Randy Roberts thanks Terry Bilhartz, Aram Goudsouzian, James S. Olson, and Joan Randall. Steven Mintz thanks Susan Kellogg for her encouragement, support, and counsel. Linda O. McMurry thanks Joseph P. Hobbs, John David Smith, Richard McMurry, and William C. Harris. James H. Jones thanks Laura Auwers, James S. Olson, Terry Rugeley, Kimberley Weathers, and especially Linda S. Auwers, who contributed both ideas and criticisms. All of the authors thank Gerard F. McCauley, whose infectious enthusiasm for this project has never wavered. And above all else, we wish to thank our students to whom we have dedicated this book.

The Authors

ABOUT *the Authors*

James Kirby Martin holds the rank of Distinguished University Professor of History at the University of Houston. His areas of special interest include early American history, including the era of the American Revolution, American military history through the years of the Civil War, and the history of such social-behavioral issues as drinking and smoking in America. He is the author, co-author, or editor of eleven books, including *Men in Rebellion* (1973), *In the Course of Human Events* (1979), *A Respectable Army: the Military Origins of the Republic* (1982), and *Drinking in America* (1982, revised edition 1987). His most recent book, *Benedict Arnold, Revolutionary Hero: An American Warrior Reconsidered* (1997) was the recipient of the Homer D. Babbidge, Jr. Award and was named by the *Los Angeles Times* to its list of the best 100 books published that year. Martin serves as general editor of the *American Social Experience* series, New York University Press. His many interests also include the study of ordinary persons and the ways in which their lives have shaped the course of American historical development. His capacity to present these lives in meaningful historical contexts helps explain why his students consistently rank him among the very best teachers in the department.

Randy Roberts earned his Ph.D. degree from Louisiana State University. His areas of special interest include modern U.S. history and the history of sports and films in America. He is a faculty member at Purdue University, where he has won both the Murphy Award for outstanding teaching and the Soci-

ety of Professional Journalists Teacher of the Year award. The books on which he is author or co-author include *Jack Dempsey: The Manassa Mauler* (1979, expanded edition, 1984), *Papa Jack: Jack Johnson and the Era of White Hopes* (1983), *Heavy Justice:* The State of Indiana *v.* Michael G. Tyson (1994), *My Lai: A Brief History with Documents* (1998), *John Wayne: American* (1995), *Where the Domino Fell: America in Vietnam, 1945–1990* (1990, revised edition 1996), and *Winning Is the Only Thing: Sports in America Since 1945* (1989). Roberts serves as the co-editor of the Sports and Society series, University of Illinois Press, and is on the editorial board of the *Journal of Sports History*.

Steven Mintz earned his Ph.D. degree at Yale University. One of the nation's leading authorities on the history of the family as well as a noted expert on slavery, social reform, and the history of film, Mintz is Professor of History, John and Rebecca Moores University Scholar, and Associate Dean at the University of Houston. His books include *The Boisterous Sea of Liberty* (with David Brion Davis, 1998), *Moralists & Modernizers: America's Pre-Civil War Reformers* (1995), *Domestic Revolutions: A Social History of American Family Life* (with Susan Kellogg, 1989), and *A Prison of Expectations: The Family in Victorian Culture* (1983). A pioneer in the integration of new computer and communication technologies in teaching and research, he moderates a scholarly discussion list on the history of slavery. Each summer, he team-teaches a seminar on "The Origins and Nature of New World Slavery" for high school teachers and National Park Service rangers at Yale University.

Linda O. McMurry is a member of the Department of History at North Carolina State University. Earning her Ph.D. degree from Auburn University, she specializes in African-American history. Her interest in personal perspectives and experiences of history has led her to write three biographies of African Americans: *To Keep the Waters Troubled: The Life of Ida B. Wells* (1998), *Recorder of the Black Experience: A Biography of Monroe Nathan Work* (1985), and *George Washington Carver: Scientist and Symbol* (1981). Both the Wells and Carver biographies are listed in the *New York Review of Books Readers' Catalog* of the best books in print. A recipient of a Rockefeller Foundation Humanities fellowship, McMurry has been active as a consultant and lecturer on topics relating to the black experience in America, appearing on such programs as NPR's "Morning Edition" and C-SPAN's "Booknotes." Although she enjoys research and writing, teaching has always been the top priority to McMurry, and she seeks to bring history alive for her students. She was pleased to win the top research award for her college in 1999, but was even more thrilled to win the college's top teaching award that same year.

James H. Jones earned his Ph.D. degree at Indiana University. His areas of specialization include modern U.S. history, the history of medical ethics and medicine, and the history of sexual behavior. The Distinguished Alumni Professor at the University of Arkansas, Jones is also on the advisory board of the Arkansas Center for Oral and Visual History. He has been a senior fellow of the National Endowment for the Humanities, a Kennedy fellow at Harvard University, a senior research fellow at the Kennedy Institute of Ethics, Georgetown University, and a Rockefeller fellow at the University of Texas Medical Branch, Galveston. His published works include *Bad Blood: The Tuskegee Syphilis Experiment, A Tragedy of Race and Medicine* (1981) revised edition (1993), which was named to the *New York Times Book Review* list of best books of 1981 and received the Arthur Viseltear prize for the Best Book in Public Health History. His most recent publication *Alfred C. Kinsey: A Public/Private Life* (1997) was a finalist for both the Pulitzer Prize in biography and for the Penn Center Award.

AMERICA
and Its Peoples

THE PEOPLING AND UNPEOPLING OF AMERICA

"A special instrument sent of God"

The Pilgrims called him Squanto, a corruption of his given name, Tisquantum. Each Thanksgiving Americans remember him as the valued native friend who saved the suffering Pilgrims from starvation. Few know the other ways in which Tisquantum's life reflected the disastrous collision of human beings that occurred in the wake of Christopher Columbus's first voyage of discovery to America in 1492. European explorers believed they had stumbled upon two empty continents, which they referred to as the "new world." In actuality, the new world was both very old and the home of millions of people. These Native Americans experienced chaos and death when they came into contact with the Europeans. A little more than 100 years after Columbus, at the time of the Pilgrims, the American Indian population had declined by as much as 90 percent. The tragic story of Tisquantum and his tribe, the Patuxets of eastern Massachusetts, vividly portrays what happened.

Born about 1590, Tisquantum acquired the values of his Algonquian-speaking elders before experiencing much contact with adventurers from overseas. Tribal fathers taught him that personal dignity came from respecting the bounties of nature and serving one's clan and village, not from acquiring material possessions. He also learned the importance of physical and mental endurance. To be accepted as an adult, he spent a harrowing winter surviving alone in the wilderness. When he returned the next spring, his Patuxet fathers fed him poisonous herbs for days on end, which he unflinchingly ate—and survived by forced vomiting. Having demonstrated his fortitude, tribal members declared him a man.

Living among 2000 souls in the Patuxet's principal village, located on the very spot where the Pilgrims settled in 1620, Tisquantum may well have foreseen trouble ahead when fair-skinned Europeans started visiting the region. First there were fishermen; then in 1605 the French explorer, Samuel de Champlain, stopped at Plymouth Bay. More fatefully, Captain John Smith, late of the Virginia colony, passed through in 1614. Smith's party treated the Patuxets with respect, but they viewed the natives as little more than wild beasts, to be exploited if necessary. Before sailing away, Smith ordered one of his lieutenants, Captain Thomas Hunt, to stay behind with a crew of mariners and gather up a rich harvest of fish. After completing his assignment, Hunt lured 20 Indians, among them Tisquantum, on board his vessel and, without warning, set his course for the slave market in Malaga, Spain.

Somehow Tisquantum avoided a lifetime of slavery. By 1617 he was in England, where he devoted himself to mastering the English tongue. One of his sponsors, Captain Thomas Dermer, who had been with Smith in 1614, asked Tisquantum to serve as an interpreter and guide for yet another New England expedition. Eager to return home, the native readily agreed and sailed back to America in 1619.

When Dermer's party put in at Plymouth Bay, a shocked Tisquantum discovered that nothing remained of his once-thriving village, except overgrown fields and rotting human bones. As if swept away by some unnamed force, the Patuxets had disappeared from the face of the earth. Trained to hide his emotions, Tisquantum grieved privately. Soon he learned about a disastrous epidemic. Thousands of natives had died in the Cape Cod vicinity of diseases heretofore unknown in New England—in this case probably chicken pox carried there from Europe by fishermen and explorers. When these microparasites struck, the native populace, lacking antibodies, had no way of fending them off.

Tisquantum soon left Dermer's party and went in search of possible survivors. He was living with the Pokanoket Indians when the Pilgrims stepped ashore in December 1620 at the site of his old village. The Pilgrims endured a terrible winter in which half their numbers died. Then in the early spring of 1621 a lone Indian, Samoset, appeared in Plymouth Colony. He spoke halting English and told of another who had actually lived in England. Within a

Tisquantum is best remembered for the assistance he gave the Pilgrims in providing for the necessities of life, but his own life—and death— illustrate the tensions and problems created by contact between Native American and European cultures.

week Tisquantum arrived and agreed to stay and help the Pilgrims produce the necessities of life.

Tisquantum taught them how to grow Indian corn (maize), a crop unknown in Europe, and how to catch great quantities of fish. His efforts resulted in an abundance of food, celebrated in the first Thanksgiving feast during the fall of 1621. To future Pilgrim Governor William Bradford, Squanto "was a special instrument sent of God for their good beyond their expectation."

The story does not have a pleasant ending. Contact with the English had changed Tisquantum, and he adopted some of their practices. In violation of his childhood training, he started to serve himself. As Bradford recorded, Squanto told neighboring Indian tribes that the Pilgrims would make war on them unless they gave him gifts. Further, he would unleash the plague, which the English "kept . . . buried in the ground, and could send it among whom they would." By the summer of 1622 Squanto had become a problem for the Pilgrims, who were eager for peace. Then he fell sick, "bleeding much at the nose," and died within a few days as yet another victim of some European disease.

As demonstrated by Tisquantum's life, white-Indian contacts did not point toward a fusing of Native American and European customs, values, and ideals. Rather, the westward movement of peoples destroyed Indian societies and replaced them with European-based communities. The history of the Americas (and of the United States) cannot be fully appreciated without considering the reasons that thousands of Europeans crossed the Atlantic Ocean and sought dominance over the American continents and their native peoples. Three groups in particular, the Spanish, French, and English, succeeded in this life-and-death struggle that changed forever the course of human history.

THE FIRST DISCOVERY OF AMERICA

The world was a much colder place 75,000 years ago. A great ice age, known as the Wisconsin glaciation, had begun. Year after year, water being drawn from the oceans formed into mighty ice caps, which in turn spread over vast reaches of land. This process dramatically lowered ocean levels. In the area of the Bering Straits, where today 56 miles of ocean separate Siberia from Alaska, a land bridge emerged. At times this link between Asia and America, *Beringia*,

may have been 1000 miles wide. Most experts believe it provided the pathway used by early humans to enter a new world.

These people, known as Paleo-Indians, were nomads and predators. With stone-tipped spears, they hunted mastodons, woolly mammoths, giant beavers, giant sloths, and bighorn bison, as well as many smaller animals. The mammals led prehistoric men and women to America up to 30,000 or more years ago. For generations, these humans roamed Alaska in small bands, gathering seeds and berries when not hunting the big game or attacking and killing one another.

Eventually, corridors opened through the Rocky Mountains as the ice started to recede. The migratory cycle began anew. Animals and humans trekked southward and eastward, reaching the bottom of South America and the east coast of North America by about 8000 B.C. This long journey covered thousands of miles and took several centuries to complete. In the process Paleo-Indians had become Native Americans.

A Diversity of Cultures

As these first Americans fanned out over two continents, they improved their weapons. They flaked and crafted such hard quartz stones as flint into sharper spear points, which allowed them to slaughter the big game more easily. Also, with the passing of time, the atmosphere began to warm as the ice age came to an end. Mammoths, mastodons, and other giant mammals did not survive the warming climate and needless overkilling.

The first Americans now faced a serious food crisis. Their solution was ingenious. Beginning in Central America between roughly 8000 and 5000 B.C., groups of humans started cultivating plant life as an alternative food source. They soon mastered the basic techniques of agriculture. They raked the earth with stone hoes and planted seeds that produced crops as varied as maize, potatoes, squashes, pumpkins, and tomatoes.

This agricultural revolution profoundly affected Native American life. Those who engaged in farming were no longer as nomadic. They constructed villages and ordered their religious beliefs around such elements of nature as the sun and rain. With dependable food supplies, they had more children, resulting in a population explosion. Work roles became differentiated by gender. Men still hunted and fished for game, but they also prepared the fields for crops. When not caring for children, women did the planting, weeding, and harvesting.

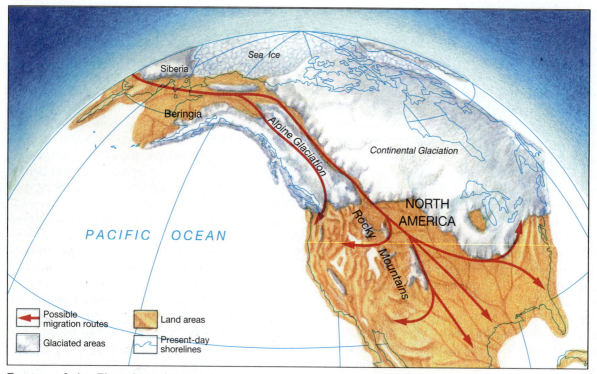

Routes of the First Americans

The Paleo-Indians migrated across the land bridge that once linked Asia and America. They then journeyed southward and eastward in populating North and South America.

Ultimately, out of these agriculturally oriented cultures evolved complex Native American societies, the most sophisticated of which appeared in Central America and the Ohio and Mississippi river valleys. Emerging before A.D. 300, the Mayas of Mexico and Guatemala based their civilization on abundant agricultural production. They also built elaborate cities and temples. Their craft workers produced jewelry of gold, silver, and other precious metals, and their merchants developed extensive trading networks. Their intellectuals devised forms of hieroglyphic writing, mathematical systems, and several calendars, one of which was the most accurate in the world at that time.

Powerful nobles and priests ruled over ordinary inhabitants in the highly stratified Maya social order. However, no strong central government existed, and warfare eventually broke out among the principal population centers. This internal strife so weakened the Mayas that after A.D. 1000 warlike peoples from the north began to overrun and conquer them. First came the Toltecs, then the Aztecs. The Aztecs called their principal city Tenochtitlán (the site of present-day Mexico City). At its zenith just before the Spanish conquistadores appeared in 1519, Tenochtitlán had a population of 300,000, making it one of the largest cities in the world at that time. The Aztecs imitated many aspects of Maya culture, and they brutally extracted tribute, both in wealth and lives, from subject tribes. Their priests reveled in human sacrifice, since Huitzilopochtli, the Aztec war god, voraciously craved human hearts. At one temple dedication, Aztec priests sacrificed some 20,000 subject peoples. Not surprisingly, these tribes hated their oppressors. Many later cooperated with the Spanish in destroying the Aztecs.

Other mighty civilizations also emerged, such as the Incas of Peru, who came into prominence after A.D. 1100. Settling in the Andes Mountains, the Incas developed a sophisticated food supply network. They trained all young males as warriors to protect the empire and their kings, whom they thought of as gods and to whom all riches belonged. The Incas were even wealthier than the Aztecs, and they particularly prized gold and silver, which they mined in huge quantities—and which made them a special target for Spanish conquerors.

In North America the Mound Builders (Adena and Hopewell peoples) appeared in the Ohio River valley around 1000 B.C. and lasted until A.D. 700.

The Aztecs, Mayas, and Incas

The Aztecs, Mayas, and Incas evolved from simple agriculturally based groups to become politically and socially complex civilizations.

Tlaloc (right), the Aztec rain god, represented fertility and emphasized the importance of water and moisture as a basis for agricultural prosperity. The mural below depicts the many facets of Maya civilization, which involved extensive agricultural production, far-reaching trading networks, complex architectural designs in urban centers, and the crafting of jewelry from rare metals.

These natives hunted and gathered food, but they obtained most of their diet from agriculture. They also raised such crops as tobacco for ceremonial functions. Their merchants traded far and wide. Fascinated with death, they built elaborate burial sites, such as the Great Serpent Mound in Ohio. In time they gave way to the Temple Mound Builders (Mississippian peoples), who were even more sedentary and agriculturally minded. They too were great traders, and they constructed large cities, including a huge site near Cahokia, Illinois, where as many as 75,000 people lived amid 85 large temple mounds.

For unknown reasons the Mississippian culture broke apart before European contact. Remnant groups may have included the Choctaws and Creeks of Mississippi and Alabama, as well as the Natchez Indians. In the rigidly stratified Natchez society the Great Sun was the all-powerful chief, and he ruled over nobles and commoners, the latter bearing the unpleasant name of "stinkards." As with their Mississippian forebears, when eminent individuals died, others gave up their lives so that central figures would have company as they passed into eternity. All but exterminated by the French in the 1730s, the Natchez were the last of the Mound Builders in North America.

The snake-shaped Great Serpent Mound, located in southern Ohio, is one of the lasting legacies of the Adena and Hopewell cultures. The mound is about 20 feet wide; uncoiled, its length would be more than 1300 feet.

The Myth of the "Virgin" Land

Beginning with the agricultural revolution, population in the Americas increased rapidly. Estimates vary widely. One authority has claimed a native populace of up to 120 million persons by the 1490s, whereas other experts suggest a figure of 50 to 80 million, with 5 to 8 million of these people inhabiting North America. Europe's population, by comparison, was roughly 75 million at the time of Columbus, which underscores the mistaken impression of European explorers that America was a "virgin" or "vacant" land.

Over several centuries the Native American populace developed as many as 2200 different languages, some 550 to 650 of which were in use in Central and North America at the time of Columbian contact. So many languages implied immense cultural diversity. Although sophisticated civilizations of enormous wealth did exist, most natives belonged to small, less complex groups in which families formed into clans—and clans into tribes.

Developing lifestyles to fit their environments, native groups varied greatly. Tribes in Oregon and Washington, such as the Chinooks, did some farming, but fishing for salmon was their primary means of subsistence. In the Great Plains region, Indians such as the Arapahos and Pawnees did not wander to the extent of their ancestors but pursued wild game within more or less fixed hunting zones. In the Southwest, the Hopi and Zuni tribes relied on agriculture, since edible plant and animal life was scarce in their desert environment. These natives even practiced irrigation. Perhaps they are best known for their flat-roofed, multitiered villages, which the Spanish called *pueblos.*

Eastern Indians on the Eve of Contact

In the East, where English explorers and settlers first made contact with Native Americans, dozens of small tribal groupings dotted the landscape. Southeastern Indians, including the Cherokees, Chickasaws, Creeks, Choctaws, and Seminoles, were more attuned to agriculture than to hunting because of lengthy growing seasons. Northeastern tribes, such as the Mahicans and Micmacs, placed more emphasis on hunting and gathering.

Eastern Woodland natives spoke several different languages but held many cultural traits in common. Perhaps linked to memories of the period of overkilling, they treated plant and animal life with respect. Essential to their religious values was the notion of an animate universe. They considered trees, plants, and animals to be spiritually alive (filled with *manitou*). As such, animals were not inferior to humans. They too organized themselves into nations, and through their "boss spirits" permitted some thinning of their numbers for humans to have food and survive. Boss spirits, however, would not tolerate overkilling. If tribes became gluttonous, animal nations could either leave the region or declare war, causing starvation and death.

The styles of Native American dwellings varied according to the particular group's customs, the climate in which they lived, and the materials readily available. Nomadic groups built temporary shelters of brush and bark, while Indians that engaged in farming constructed more permanent types of structures that might house one or several families.

Tribal *shamans,* or medicine men, communicated with the boss spirits and prescribed elaborate rules, or taboos, regarding the treatment of plants and animals. Indian parents, having mastered such customs, taught children like Tisquantum that nature contained the resources of life. Although intertribal trading was common, as was gift-giving in pottery, baskets, jewelry, furs, and wampum (conch and clam shells), religious values precluded tribal members from exploiting the landscape for the sake of acquiring great personal wealth.

Eastern Woodland parents introduced their children to many other concepts. Individual ownership of land was not known. Tribal boundaries consisted of geographic locales large enough to provide basic food supplies. Although individual dignity did matter, cooperation with tribal members rather than individual competitiveness was the essential ideal, even in sports. Eastern Woodland tribes enjoyed squaring off with one another in lacrosse matches, archery contests, and foot races. Betting and bragging occurred regularly, as did serious injuries in the heat of competition, but the matches had a decided group orientation. Individuals did not participate to gain personal glory but to bring accolades to their tribes.

The refinement of athletic skills also represented useful training for war. Intertribal warfare was sporadic and resulted from any number of factors, such as competition over valued hunting grounds. Skirmishes and the taking of a few lives by roving bands of warriors usually ended the conflict, but not necessarily the ill will, especially among different lan-guage groups. Festering tensions and language barriers worked against intertribal cooperation in repelling the Europeans.

Even though males served as warriors, they did not always control tribal decision making. Among the powerful Five Nations of Iroquois (Mohawks, Oneidas, Onondagas, Cayugas, and Senecas) in central New York, tribal organization was **matrilineal**. Women headed individual family units that in turn formed into clans. Clan leaders were also women, and they decided which males would sit on tribal councils charged with determining policies on diplomacy and war. Women held the power of removal as well, so males had no choice but to respect the authority of female clan heads. Among other Eastern Woodland Indians, women occasionally served as tribal *sachems* (chiefs), much to the shock of Europeans.

When European fishermen and explorers started making contact, an estimated 500,000 to 800,000 Indians inhabited the land between the North Atlantic coastline and the Appalachian Mountains. The Europeans, in a pattern that was essentially the same throughout the Americas, were initially curious as well as fearful in approaching the natives, but these feelings soon gave way to expressions of contempt. Judging all persons by their own cultural standards, Europeans came to regard the Indians as inferior. Native Americans looked and dressed differently. Their religious beliefs did not conform to European forms of Christianity. The men seemed lazy since women did the bulk of the farming, and they lacked a consuming drive to acquire personal wealth, leaving the mistaken impression of much "want in a land

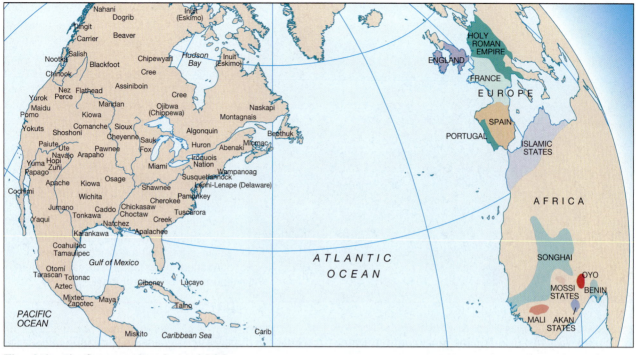

The Atlantic Community, Late 1400s

Native Americans, Europeans, and Africans made up a triad of peoples around the Atlantic Ocean.

of plenty," as one historian has summarized European perceptions.

To make matters worse, the native populace, as was the case with Tisquantum's Patuxet tribe, quickly began to die in huge numbers, further confirming European perceptions that Indian peoples were inferior rather than merely different. These native "savages," or so Europeans stated, were blocking the path of a more advanced civilization desirous of expansion. Thus commenced what historians have come to call the "invasion" of America.

PREPARING EUROPE FOR WESTWARD EXPANSION

Nearly 500 years before Columbus's initial westward voyage, Europeans made their first known contacts with North America. Around A.D. 1000, the Vikings (Scandinavians) explored barren regions of the North Atlantic. Eric the Red led an expedition of Vikings to Greenland, and one of his sons, Leif Ericson, continued exploring south and westward, stopping at Baffin Island, Labrador, and Newfoundland

(described as *Vinland*). There were some attempts at settlement, but none survived. The Viking voyages had no long-term impact because Europe was not yet ripe for westward expansion.

Changing Population Pressures

Most Europeans of the Middle Ages (approximately A.D. 500–1400) lived short, demanding lives. Many tilled the soil as peasants, owing allegiance to manor lords and eking out a meager subsistence. Their crops, grown on overworked soil, were not nutritious. Because they rarely ate fruits, they suffered from constipation and rickets among other diseases. These peasants worshipped as Roman Catholics, regularly attending church services that emphasized the importance of preparing for a better life after death. Meanwhile, the dominant concern was to survive long enough to help the next generation begin the cycle anew.

A variety of factors, including rapid population growth, gradually altered the established rhythms of life in the Middle Ages. Between A.D. 1000 and 1340, Europe's population doubled, reaching over 70 million people. Even with improved methods of

Vinland

Even though Leif Ericson made contact with North America about 500 years before Columbus, no permanent settlements resulted.

agricultural production, a new problem—overcrowding on the land—emerged. Overcrowding represents a condition in which too many individuals try to provide for themselves and their families on fixed parcels of farmland. To ease the pressure, manor lords forced some peasants off the land. These dispossessed persons struggled to avoid starvation. Some joined the growing class of beggars, or they became highway bandits. Others moved into the developing towns where they offered their labor for wages of any kind while seeking to acquire craft skills. Only a handful advanced beyond a marginal existence.

By 1340 Europe was bulging at the seams, but the knowledge and technology were not yet in place to facilitate the movement of people to distant regions. Then, suddenly, a frightening disaster relieved the population pressure. Italian merchant ships trading in Muslim ports in the eastern Mediterranean hauled rats as well as cargoes back to their home ports. These rats carried fleas infested with microbes that caused bubonic plague. The plague, or "Black Death," spread mercilessly through a populace already suffering less virulent maladies related to inadequate diet and un-

clean personal hygiene. When the plague struck the Italian city of Florence in 1348, for example, between half and two-thirds of the population of 85,000 died. More generally, between 1347 and 1353 about one-third of all Europeans died in a medical calamity not to be outdone until the plague and other killer diseases started wiping out Native Americans.

The unpeopling of Europe resulting from the Black Death temporarily checked any desire to find and inhabit new lands. In another two centuries rapid population growth, overcrowding, and consequent problems of destitution and starvation would again come to characterize life in Europe. By this time other factors were in place to facilitate the westward migration of peoples in search of new beginnings.

Crusades, Commerce, and the New Learning

Long before the Black Death, Europeans were gathering knowledge about previously unknown peoples and places. The Crusades, designed to oust the Muslim "infidels" from such Christian holy sites as Jerusalem, broadened their horizons. Sanctioned by the Roman Catholic church and begun in 1095, the Crusades lasted for two centuries. Although European warriors failed to break Muslim hegemony, they did discover that they could carry on trade with the Orient. They learned of spices that would preserve meats over long winters, fruits that would bring greater balance to diets, silk and velvet clothing, hand-crafted rugs, delicate glassware, and

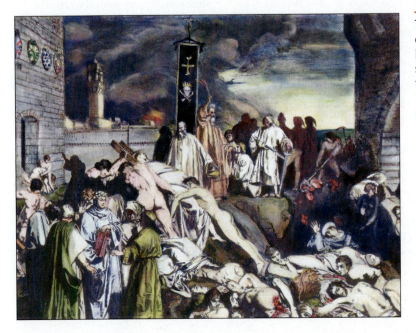

This engraving depicts the horrible destruction of the "Black Death" in Florence, a city visited by the plague sixteen times in the thirteenth and fourteenth centuries. Between 1347 and 1353, the plague claimed the lives of nearly 20 million Europeans.

Indian Scalping and European War Dogs

WHEN Native Americans and Europeans first came into contact, each seemed genuinely curious about the other. Curiosity, however, soon turned to mistrust, and mistrust to a state of unending warfare. Both sides employed "the tactics of remorseless terrorism" in their combat, as one student of early Indian-white relations has written, because both were fighting for control of the landscape—the natives to retain their ancient tribal homes and the Europeans to inhabit the same.

In their life-and-death struggle, Europeans and Indians drew upon long-accepted styles of waging combat. Neither showed much mercy toward the other. Europeans rationalized their acts of butchery by claiming they were dealing with "savages" who were at best "inhumanely cruel" and at worst "carnivorous beasts of the forest." Because of language barriers, the thoughts of Native Americans are not known, but they learned to fear and hate the invaders from across the ocean, and they too fought with a vengeance, although at times with more mercy than Europeans.

Long before the English first made contact, Eastern Woodland Indians regularly engaged in small-scale, intertribal wars. Their weapons included bows and arrows, knives, tomahawks, spears, and clubs. War parties did not attack in battle formations but used the forest as their cover as they ambushed enemies in surprise guerrilla-like raids. Employing hit-and-run tactics, intertribal combat rarely resulted in much bloodshed, since battles seldom lasted for more than a few minutes

before attacking warriors melted back into the forest.

When possible, Indian war parties celebrated their victories by the taking of enemy scalps, which for them were war trophies filled with religious meaning. Native Americans believed the piece of scalp and hair sliced from an enemy's head contained the victim's living spirit, which now belonged to the holder of the scalp. To take a scalp, then, was to gain control over that person's spirit (*manitou*). Even if victims survived scalping, which happened on occasion, they were spiritually dead, since they no longer possessed the essence of human life.

Because of their spiritual meaning and power, scalps were treated with great respect. Indians decorated them with jewelry and paint, and warriors kept them on display, even strapping them on their belts as symbols of individual prowess. In other instances warriors gave scalps to families who had lost relatives in battle. Since they contained life, scalps took the place of deceased tribal members.

When Europeans first saw scalps, they were not sure what to think. They certainly attached no spiritual significance to them. Frenchman Jacques Cartier, exploring along the St. Lawrence River in 1535, wrote about local Indians who showed him "the skins of five men's heads, stretched on hoops, like parchment." The local chief explained that the scalps were from Micmacs living to "the south, who waged war continually against his people." Just five years later in west Florida, natives killed two Spanish conquistadores ex-

ploring with Hernando de Soto. The Indians then "removed" the "head" of one victim, "or rather all around his skull—it is unknown with what skill they removed it with great ease—and carried it off as evidence of their deed."

Europeans quickly concluded that scalping was another barbarous practice of "savage" Native Americans. Also frightening was the way in which Indians conducted combat. They would not stand and fight in "civilized" fashion, holding to complex linear formations as Europeans did. Rather "they are always running and traversing from one place to another," complained de Soto, making it impossible for musket-wielding Europeans to shoot them down. Worse yet, an expert Indian bowman could easily "discharge three or four arrows" with great accuracy by the time musketeers went through the elaborate steps of preparing their cumbersome weapons for firing. This made combat with Native Americans particularly dangerous because, as de Soto concluded, an Indian bowman "seldom misses what he shoots at."

The Indian style of fighting caused a stream of negative commentary from various European New World adventurers. Natives did not fight fairly, they wrote, but used "cunning tricks" and "slippery designs" to defeat their adversaries. Rather than engaging in manly combat, they were "as greedy after their prey as a wolf," wanting above all else to mutilate their opponents by taking their scalps. The only effective way to deal with native tactics, reasoned these early adventurers, was to counter them with the most brutal

accepted methods for exacting terror, pain, and death. The Spanish conquistadores used war dogs to maim and kill their victims. The English, who during the sixteenth century reveled in horror stories about Spanish New World barbarities (the so-called Black Legend), thought of war dogs as a new low point in human warfare. Yet within a few years of founding their first settlements, the English likewise were training and unleashing war dogs on Native Americans.

Apparently the favored breed was the English mastiff. These were huge, ugly dogs, weighing up to 150 pounds and naturally protective of their masters. In sixteenth-century England their owners trained them to "bait the bear, to bait the bull and other such like cruel and bloody beasts." The next logical step was to turn these dogs loose on the "heavy beast" in America. In retaliation for Opechancanough's 1622 massacre of Virginians, surviving settlers used dogs, presumably mastiffs, to track down and kill local Indians. War dogs participated in the slaughter of Pequot Indians in Connecticut during 1637 and would perform similar duty throughout the colonial period.

If prospects of facing the scalping knife filled European New World settlers with horror, war dogs, whether on guard duty or on the attack, represented an "extreme terror to the Indians," as a New England minister wrote in the early eighteenth century. This clergyman wanted yet more dogs "trained up to hunt Indians as they do the bear." He understood the nature of "total war" between Indians and whites in the bloody contest for the Americas, and he wanted to survive.

forms of corporal punishment then known—and commonly used—in Europe.

In times of combat the Europeans treated Indians as if they were criminals. As such, natives, in various combinations, would be hanged, drawn and quartered, disemboweled, and like the "savage" and "wild" Irish, beheaded. Captain Miles Standish, charged with protecting the Pilgrims, killed one troublesome Indian and then carried his head back to Plymouth where he had it publicly displayed. When the Dutch in New Netherland went to war with local natives in the 1640s, they regularly beheaded their opponents and had their "gory heads . . . laid in the streets of New Amsterdam, where the governor's mother kicked them like footballs."

Such wanton cruelty, when measured by modern standards, recently resulted in claims from some students of Native American history that Indians, before making contact with Europeans, did not scalp their enemies. Scalping, they claimed, was modeled on beheading but was a more efficient means of gaining war trophies for highly mobile Indian warriors not wanting to carry the extra weight of human heads.

Seeking to demonstrate the "barbarous" influence of "civilized" Europeans expanding westward, this line of reasoning has been thoroughly refuted. Among other forms of evidence, Indian cultural traditions and the astonishment of explorers who first saw scalps support the conclusion that Europeans learned about scalping from Indians and soon incorporated the practice into their arsenal of punishments.

In at least one area, however, European adventurers reached beyond

dozens of other commodities that would make European lives more comfortable.

Italian merchants, living in independent city-states such as Venice and Genoa, took the lead in developing the Mediterranean trade. Other European cities mushroomed in size at key trading points when Oriental goods started making their way from Italy into Switzerland, France, and Germany. One benefit of this striking increase in commercial activity was to create work for dislocated peasants. Also of major consequence was the rise of great merchants who devoted themselves to securing scarce commodities—and selling them for handsome profits.

The new wealth displayed by the great merchants promoted a pervasive spirit of material acquisition. The merchants, however, did more than merely reinvest profits in additional trading ventures. They also underwrote a resurgence in learning, known as the **Renaissance**. Beginning in Italy, the Renaissance soon captivated much of Continental Europe. New probings took place in all subjects. Learned individuals rediscovered the writings of such ancient scholars as Ptolemy, who had mapped the Earth, and Eratosthenes, who had estimated the circumference of the planet. By the mid-fifteenth century educated Europeans knew the world was not flat. Indeed, early in 1492, just a few months before Columbus sailed, a German geographer, Martin Behaim, constructed a round globe for all to see.

Enhanced geographical knowledge went hand in hand with developments in naval science. Before the fifteenth century, Europeans risked their lives when they did not sail within sight of land. The Muslims provided knowledge about the astrolabe and sextant and their uses as basic navigational instruments. Contact with the Arabs also introduced Europeans to more advanced ship and sail designs. Europeans soon abandoned their outmoded square-rigged galleys, which required oarsmen to maneuver these craft against the wind, in favor of lateen-rigged caravels. These vessels were sleeker in design, making them faster. Since their triangular sails could also swivel, the caravels were more mobile. Tacking, or sailing at angles into the wind, was now possible. Such nautical breakthroughs heightened prospects for worldwide exploration in the ongoing search for valuable trading commodities.

The adventures of Marco Polo (1254?–1324?) underscored the new learning and exemplified its relationship to commerce and exploration. Late in the thirteenth century, this young Venetian trader traveled throughout the Orient. He recorded his findings and told of unbelievable wealth in Asian kingdoms such as Cathay (China). Around 1450, Johannes Gutenberg, a German printer, perfected movable type, making it possible to reprint limitless copies of manuscripts, heretofore laboriously copied by hand. The first printed edition of Marco Polo's *Journals* ap-

Ptolemy prepared his *Guide to Geography* in the second century A.D. He indicated that the world was round but underestimated the earth's circumference and imagined Asia as a larger continent than is actually the case. His work became part of Europe's new learning when widely republished after 1475.
Copyright © The British Museum.

peared in 1477. Merchants and explorers alike, among them Christopher Columbus, read Polo's *Journals*, which spurred them forward in their quest to gain complete access to Oriental riches.

Nation-States Support the First Explorations

Not all elements of European society embraced the new vitality. Powerful manor lords still controlled the countryside, and they made it difficult for merchants to move goods across their lands, unless traders paid heavy tolls. These nobles also sneered at monarchs wanting to collect taxes. Tapping into peasant manpower, manor lords quite often had stronger armies, leaving royal figures unable to enforce their will. Over time, merchants and monarchs started working together. Using mercantile capital, they formed armies that challenged the nobility.

The process of forming modern nation-states commenced during the fifteenth century. The marriage of Ferdinand of Aragon to Isabella of Castile in 1469 represented the beginnings of national unity in Spain. These joint monarchs hired mercenary soldiers to break the power of defiant nobles. In 1492 they also crushed the Muslims (Moors) inhabiting southern Spain, driving them as well as Jewish inhabitants out of the country. Working closely with the Roman Catholic church, Ferdinand and Isabella used inquisition torture chambers to break the will of those whose loyalty they doubted. By 1500 their subjects had become full-fledged Spaniards who expected to serve their nation with loyalty.

Portugal, France, and England also reckoned with the turbulent process of nation-making. John I led the way by consolidating Portugal in the 1380s. Louis XI, known as the "Spider King," was responsible for unifying France in the 1460s at the end of more than 100 years of intermittent but debilitating warfare with England. Two powerful English noble lines, the houses of York and Lancaster, fought endlessly and devastated themselves in the Wars of the Roses (1455–1485). Henry Tudor, who became Henry VII (reigned 1485–1509), arose from the chaos, worked to crush forever the power of the nobility, and initiated a lengthy internal unification process that set the stage for England's westward expansion.

Unification was critical to focusing national efforts on exploration, as demonstrated by Portugal. Secure in his throne, King John I was able to support his son, Prince Henry (1394–1460), called "the Navigator," in the latter's efforts to learn more about the world. Henry set up a school of navigation at Sagres on the rocky southwestern coast of Portugal. With official state support, he sent out ships on exploratory missions. When the crews returned, they worked to improve maps, sailing techniques, navigational procedures, and ship designs.

Initially, the emphasis was on learning, but then it shifted to a quest for valuable trade goods. Henry's mariners conquered such islands as the Azores and brought back raw wealth (gold, silver, and ivory) from the west coast of Africa. During the 1420s trading ties developed with Africans, including the first dealings in black slaves by early modern Europeans. The lure of wealth drove Portuguese ships farther south along the African coast. Bartholomeu Dias made it to the Cape of Good Hope in 1487. Ten years later, Vasco da Gama took a small flotilla around the lower tip of Africa and on to the riches of India.

Besides returning a 400 percent profit, da Gama's expedition led to the development of Portugal's Far Eastern empire. It also proved that the Muslim world, with its heavy trade tolls, could be circumvented in getting European hands on Oriental riches. None of this would have been possible without a unified Portuguese government able to tax the populace and thus sponsor Prince Henry's attempts to probe the boundaries of the unknown.

Ferdinand and Isabella were intensely aware of Portugal's triumphs when a young Genoese mariner, Christopher Columbus (1451–1506), asked them to underwrite his dream of sailing west to reach the Orient. Consumed by their struggle for internal unification, they refused him, but Columbus persisted. He had already contacted King John II of Portugal, who rebuffed him as "a big talker and boastful." Columbus also turned to France and England but gained no sponsorship. Ultimately, Queen Isabella reconsidered. She met Columbus's terms, which included 10 percent of all profits from his discoveries, and proclaimed him "Admiral of the Ocean Sea." Her decision, made possible by Spain's unification, had monumental consequences.

On August 3, 1492, Columbus and some 90 mariners set sail from Palos, Spain, in the *Niña*, *Pinta*, and *Santa María*. Using faulty calculations, the admiral estimated Asia to be no more than 4500 miles to the west (the actual distance is closer to 12,000 miles). Some 3000 miles out, his crew became fearful and almost rebelled. They wanted to return home, but he persuaded them to keep sailing west. Just two days later, on October 12, they landed on a small island in the Bahamas, which Columbus named San Salvador (holy savior). There they found hospitable natives, the Arawaks, whom Columbus described as "a loving people without covetous-

Columbus first landed on the Bahamian island that he named San Salvador. He described the local natives as peaceful and generous, an image that changed rapidly as conquistadores swept over the native populace in their rush to tap into the riches of the Americas.

ness." He called them Indians, a misnomer that stuck, because he believed he was near Asia (the Indies). Proceeding on, Columbus landed on Cuba, which he thought was Japan, and then on Hispaniola, where he traded for gold-laden native jewelry. In 1493 Columbus and his crew returned home to a hero's welcome and to funding for three more expeditions to America.

EXPLORERS, CONQUERORS, AND THE MAKING OF NEW SPAIN

A fearless explorer, Columbus proved to be an ineffective administrator and a poor geographer. He ended up in debtors' prison, and to his dying day in 1506 he never admitted to locating a world unknown to Europeans. Geographers named the western continents after another mariner, Amerigo Vespucci, a merchant from Florence who participated in a Portuguese expedition to South America in 1501. In a widely reprinted letter, Vespucci insisted that a new world had been found. His first name soon became associated with the two continents.

Columbus's significance lay elsewhere. His 1492 venture garnered enough extractable wealth to exhilarate the Spanish monarchs. They did not care whether Columbus had reached Asia, only that further exploratory voyages might produce unimagin-

able riches. Because they feared Portuguese interference, Ferdinand and Isabella moved quickly to validate their interests. They went to Pope Alexander VI, who issued a papal bull, *Inter Caetera,* that divided the unknown world between Portugal and Spain.

In 1494 the Spanish monarchs worked out a formal agreement with Portugal in the Treaty of Tordesillas, drawing a line some 1100 miles west of the Cape Verde Islands. All undiscovered lands to the west of the demarcation line belonged to Spain. Those to the east were Portugal's. Inadvertently, Ferdinand and Isabella had given away the easternmost portion of South America. In 1500 a Portuguese mariner, Pedro Alvares Cabral, laid claim to this territory, which came to be known as Brazil. Spain claimed title to everything else, which of course left nothing for emerging nation-states such as France and England.

The Spanish monarchs used their strong army, seasoned by the struggle for unification, as a weapon to conquer the Americas. These *conquistadores* did so with relish. Befitting their crusader's ideology, they agreed to subdue the natives and, with the support of church leaders, to convert them to Roman Catholicism. Bravery and courage, these warriors believed, would bring distinction to themselves and to Spain. Further, they could gain much personal wealth, even if shared with the Crown. Gold, glory, and the gospel formed a triad of factors motivating the Spanish conquistadores, and their efforts resulted in a far-flung American empire known as New Spain.

Conquistadores Overrun Native Americans

Before 1510 the Spanish confined their explorations and settlements to the Caribbean islands. The conquistadores parleyed with Indians, searched diligently for rare metals and spices, and listened to tales of fabulous cities of gold somewhere over the horizon. Most natives remained friendly, but they were hostile in some locales, such as the Lesser Antilles where the cannibalistic Caribs dined on more than one Spanish warrior.

Unwittingly, the conquistadores with their microbial weapons retaliated against all Indians—friend and foe alike. Natives on all the islands lacked the antibodies to fend off European diseases. Smallpox, typhoid, diphtheria, the measles, and various plagues and fevers took a rapid toll. In 1492, for example, more than 200,000 Indians inhabited Hispaniola. Just 20 years later, fewer than 30,000 were alive.

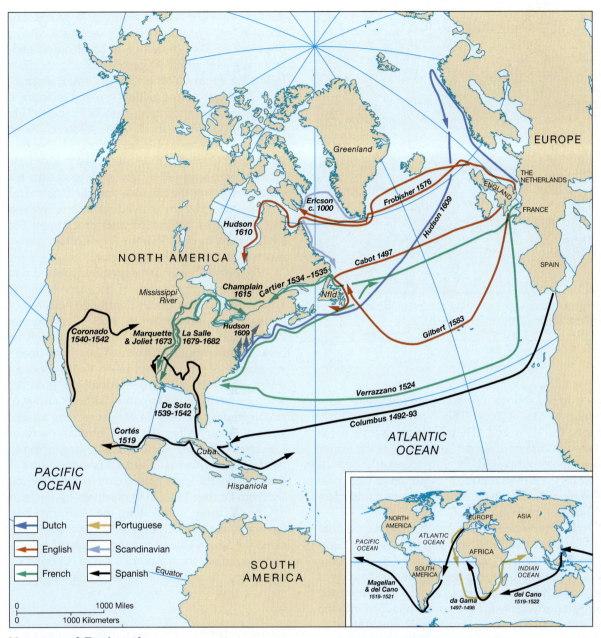

EUROPE

Greenland

THE NETHERLANDS

ENGLAND

FRANCE

SPAIN

Ericson c. 1000

Frobisher 1576

Hudson 1609

Cabot 1497

Hudson 1610

NORTH AMERICA

Champlain 1615   Cartier 1534–1535

Mississippi River

Nfld.

Coronado 1540-1542   Marquette & Joliet 1673   La Salle 1679-1682   Hudson 1609

Gilbert 1583

Verrazzano 1524

De Soto 1539-1542

Columbus 1492-93

ATLANTIC OCEAN

Cortés 1519

Cuba

Hispaniola

PACIFIC OCEAN

SOUTH AMERICA   *Equator*

	Dutch		Portuguese
	English		Scandinavian
	French		Spanish

0   1000 Miles
0   1000 Kilometers

NORTH AMERICA   EUROPE   ASIA

PACIFIC OCEAN   ATLANTIC OCEAN   AFRICA   INDIAN OCEAN

SOUTH AMERICA

Magellan & del Cano 1519-1521   da Gama 1497-1498   del Cano 1519-1522

Voyages of Exploration

The European exploration of the Americas came in waves after Columbus's initial voyages in the late 1400s. In the 1500s Spain's American empire took shape, and in the early 1600s England, France, Holland, and Sweden located settlements north of New Spain along the Atlantic coast.

After 1510 the conquistadores moved onto the mainland. Vasco Núñez de Balboa reached Panama in 1513. He organized an exploratory expedition, cut across the isthmus, and became the first European to see the Pacific Ocean, which he dutifully claimed for Spain. The same year Juan Ponce de León, governor of Puerto Rico, led a party to Florida in search of gold

and a rumored fountain of youth. Although disappointed on both counts, he claimed Florida for Spain.

Then in 1519 Hernán Cortés (1485–1547), a leader of great bravado, mounted his dramatic expedition against the Aztecs. Landing on the Mexican coast with 600 soldiers, his party began a difficult overland march toward Tenochtitlán. Along the

This Aztec drawing presumably represents Cortés's conquest of Tenochtitlán in 1519–1522.

way Cortés won to his side various tribes subservient to the Aztecs. These natives may have thought Cortés a god. They certainly admired his horses—unknown in America—as well as the armor and weapons of his soldiers. Still, so small an invading force, even if well armed, could never have prevailed over thousands of Aztec warriors if other factors had not intervened.

Aztec emperor Montezuma II, who feared that Cortés was the old Toltec war god Quetzalcoatl coming back to destroy the Aztecs, tried to keep the Spaniards out of Tenochtitlán. He offered mounds of gold and silver, but this gesture only intensified the conquistadores' greed. They boldly marched into the city and took Montezuma prisoner. The Aztecs finally drove off Cortés's army in 1520, but not before smallpox had broken out. Less than a year later, the Spaniards retook Tenochtitlán and claimed all Aztec wealth and political authority as their prize.

Carried away with success, Cortés's soldiers razed the city and boasted of their great prowess as warriors and the superiority of their weapons and knowledge of warfare. They even claimed that God had willed their victory. However, the microbes they brought with them were the true victors. As a participant wrote, when they reentered Tenochtitlán, "the streets, squares, houses, and courts were filled with bodies, so that it was almost impossible to pass. Even Cortés was sick from the stench in his nostrils."

European diseases resulted in at least 17 major epidemics in the Americas during the sixteenth century; there were 14 in Europe. One of these 17 epidemics broke the Aztecs' ability to keep resisting the Spanish. As additional epidemics struck, the native populace of 20 to 25 million in Mexico declined dramatically—by about 90 percent during the 50 years following the invasion of Cortés's small army.

Cortés's stunning victory spurred on many other conquistadores, such as aggressive Francisco Pizarro (1470–1541). With about 180 soldiers, he overwhelmed thousands of Incas in Peru, seizing the capital city of Cuzco in 1533 after hardly any fighting. Inca rulers, paralyzed by fear, provided little leadership in resisting the Spanish and their powerful microbial allies. Pizarro showed no mercy; he executed the great chief Atahualpa and proclaimed Spain's sovereignty. By the 1550s the Spanish had conquered much of the rest of South America.

To the north, various expeditions found nothing comparable to the wealth of the Aztecs and Incas. Four hundred men under Pánfilo de Narváez began a disastrous adventure in 1528. They landed in Florida and searched the Gulf Coast region before being shipwrecked in Texas. Only four men survived, one of whom, Cabeza de Vaca, wrote a tract telling of seven great cities laden with gold. Vaca's writings stimulated Hernando de Soto and 600 others, beginning in 1539, to investigate the lower Mississippi River valley. In 1540 another party under Francisco Vásquez de Coronado began exploring parts of New Mexico, Texas, Oklahoma, and Kansas. They were the first Europeans to see the Grand Canyon. During 1542–1543 mariners under Juan Rodríguez Cabrillo sailed along the California coast as far north as Oregon. None of these groups ever located the fabled cities, but they advanced geographic knowledge of North America while claiming everything they came in contact with for Spain.

Constructing the Spanish Empire

To keep out intruders and to maintain order in New Spain, the Spanish Crown set up two home-based administrative agencies in Madrid. The House of Trade formulated economic policies and provided for annual convoys of galleons, called plate fleets, to haul extractable forms of American wealth back to Spain. The Council for the Indies controlled all political matters in what became an autocratic, rigidly managed empire for the exclusive benefit of the parent state.

The Council for the Indies ruled through viceroys that headed four regional areas of administration. Viceroys, in turn, consulted with *audiencias* (appointed councils) on matters of local concern, but there were no popularly based representative assemblies. Normally, only pure-blooded Spaniards could influence local decision making—and only if they

Most of the Spanish colonists to the Americas were adventurers in search of fame and fortune or missionaries who hoped to convert the Native Americans to Christianity. Both groups used Indians as laborers to work the land, tend livestock, and process raw materials to help support the Spanish settlements.

had ties to councilors or viceroys. Those who questioned their political superiors soon learned there was little tolerance for divergent opinions.

During the sixteenth century the incentive to resettle in New Spain was lacking. Work was plentiful at home, and Spain's population was in decline, reflecting the government's constant warfare in Europe. Consequently, only about 200,000 Spaniards, a modest number, migrated to New Spain. Most migrants were young males looking for adventure and material riches. They did not find much of either, but a few became wealthy as manor holders, ranchers, miners, and government officials.

From the very outset, Spanish migrants complained about a shortage of laborers in America. One solution was the *encomienda* **system**, initially approved by the Crown to reward conquistadores for outstanding service. Favored warriors and settlers received land titles to Indian villages and the surrounding countryside. As *encomenderos,* or landlords, they agreed to educate the natives under their jurisdiction and to guarantee instruction in the Roman Catholic faith. In return, the landlords gained control of the labor of whole villages of people and received portions of annual crops and other forms of forced tribute in recognition of their efforts to "civilize" the native populace.

The *encomienda* system fostered serious problems. Landlords regularly abused the Indians, treating them like slave property. They maimed or put troublemakers to death and bought and sold many others as if they were commodities. The exploitation was so outrageous that one Dominican priest, Bartolomé de Las Casas (1474–1566), later a bishop in southern Mexico, repeatedly begged officials in Madrid to stop such barbarities.

In 1542 the Crown settled the issue by outlawing both the *encomienda* system and the enslavement of Indians. This ruling did not change matters that much. Governing officials continued to award pure-blooded Spaniards vast landed estates (*haciendas*), on which Indians lived in a state of peonage, cultivating the soil and sharing their crops with their landlords (*hacendados*).

Since the native populace also kept dying from European diseases, a second solution to the labor problem was to import Africans. In 1501 the Spanish Crown authorized the first shipment of slaves to the Caribbean islands, a small beginning to what became a vast, forced migration of some 10 million human beings to the Americas.

Slavery as it developed in New Spain was harsh. *Hacienda* owners and mine operators wanted only young adult males who could literally be worked to death, then replaced by new shiploads of Africans. On the other hand, Spanish law and Roman Catholic doctrine restrained some brutality. The Church believed that all souls should be saved, and it recognized marriage as a sacrament, meaning that slaves could wed and aspire to family life. Spanish law even permitted slaves to purchase their freedom. Such allowances were well beyond those made in future English-speaking colonies, and many blacks, particularly those who became artisans and house servants in the cities, did gain their independence.

Also easing slavery's harsh realities was the matter of skin color gradation: The lighter the skin, the greater the range of privileges. Pure-blooded natives of Spain (*peninsulares*) were at the apex of society. Next came the creoles (*criollos*), or whites born in New Spain. Since so many of the first Spanish migrants were males, they often intermarried with Indians, their children forming the *mestizo* class; or they intermarried with Africans, their children making up the *mulatto* class. The mixture of skin colors in New Spain helped Africans escape some of the racial contempt experienced by blacks in English North America, where legal restrictions against racial intermarriage resulted in less skin color variation.

Success Breeds Envy and Contempt

Still, most slaves and Indians lived in privation at the bottom of New Spain's society. Many church officials, as suggested by the pleas of Las Casas, worked to ease their burdens. Las Casas even went so far as to denounce the enslavement of Africans; but the Crown ignored him, realizing that without slavery Spain would receive fewer shipments of gold, silver, and other valuable commodities.

As Spanish authority spread north into New Mexico, Arizona, California, and other areas, Franciscan, Dominican, and Jesuit friars opened missions and offered protection to natives who would accept Roman Catholic beliefs. Quite often local Indians simply incorporated Catholic doctrines into their own belief systems.

When in the late 1660s and early 1670s a prolonged drought followed by a devastating epidemic ravaged Pueblos living in the upper Rio Grande valley of New Mexico, these natives openly questioned their new Catholic faith—and conquering masters. Spanish friars and magistrates reacted harshly and imprisoned some of the leading dissidents. The Pueblos eventually rallied around a native spiritual leader named Popé. In 1680 they rose in rebellion and killed or drove some 2500 Spanish inhabitants out of New Mexico. By 1700 Spanish soldiers had reconquered the region, maiming and killing hundreds of Pueblos in the process. With their numbers already in rapid decline, the Pueblos never again seriously challenged what seemed like the ever-expanding reach of Spanish authority.

As it took shape, then, the Spanish empire was more brutal than tolerant and contained many sharp contrasts. The construction of European-like cathedrals and the founding of great universities could not mask the terrible price in native lives lost, the endemic poverty of surviving Indian and *mestizo* villagers on *haciendas,* or the brutal treatment of slaves in gold and silver mines. These contrasts reflected the acquisitive beginnings of New Spain, which operated first and foremost as a treasure chest for the monarchs back in Madrid.

The flow of wealth made Spain the most powerful—and envied—nation in Europe during the sixteenth century. Such success also became a source of contempt. When Las Casas, for example, published *A Very Brief Relation of the Destruction of the Indies* (1552), he described the Indians as "patient, meek, and peaceful . . . lambs" whom bloodthirsty conquistadores had "cruelly and inhumanely butchered." Las Casas's listing of atrocities became the basis of the "Black Legend," a tale that other Europeans started to employ as a rationale for challenging Spain's New World supremacy. They promised to treat Native Americans more humanely, but in reality their primary motivation was to garner a share of America's riches for themselves.

CHALLENGERS FOR NORTH AMERICA: FRANCE AND ENGLAND

When Henry VII of England realized how successful Columbus had been, he chose to ignore the Treaty of Tordesillas. He underwrote another Italian explorer, Giovanni Caboto (John Cabot), to seek Cathay on behalf of the Tudor monarchy. Cabot's was the first exploratory expedition to touch North America since the Viking voyages. He landed on Newfoundland and Cape Breton Island in 1497. A second expedition in 1498 ended in misfortune when Cabot was lost at sea. Still, his voyages served as the basis for English claims to North America.

Soon France joined the exploration race. In 1524 King Francis I authorized yet another Italian mariner, Giovanni da Verrazzano, to sail westward. Verrazzano tracked along the American coast from North Carolina to Maine. Unfortunately, during another voyage in 1528 he died somewhere in the Lesser Antilles, where either Spaniards hanged him as an intruder or Caribs killed him. More important for later French claims, Jacques Cartier mounted three expeditions to the St. Lawrence River area, beginning in 1534. He scouted as far inland as modern-day Quebec and Montreal. Cartier even started a colony in 1541–1542, but too much political turmoil in France diverted the Crown from supporting trading stations or permanent settlements.

Verrazzano and Cartier were among the first to show interest in finding an all-water route—the **Northwest Passage**—through North America to the Orient. Seeking a northerly route was partially a response to the epic voyage of Ferdinand Magellan (1519–1522) under the Spanish flag. Magellan's party circumnavigated the globe by sailing around the southern tip of South America and proved, once and for all, that the world was round and that a vast ocean lay between America and Asia. The Northwest Passage, had it existed, would have allowed the English and French, among other Europeans, to avoid contact with New Spain while gaining access to Oriental wealth, since no one, as yet, had found readily extractable riches in North America. Searching for the passage was also a challenge to the worldwide ambitions of Portugal and Spain, especially after 1529 when these two powers extended their demarcation line down through the Pacific Ocean.

The Protestant Reformation Stirs Deep Tensions

Throughout the sixteenth century, the monarchs of England and France did not directly challenge Spain's supremacy in the Americas. They had too many problems at home, such as those related to religious strife. The **Protestant Reformation** shattered the unity of the Roman Catholic church, convulsed Europe, and provoked bloody wars. At the same time, the Reformation helped stimulate many Europeans, experiencing repression at home because of their newfound beliefs, to consider moving and resettling elsewhere. This was particularly the case in England.

The Roman Catholic church was the most powerful institution in medieval Europe. When dissenters spoke out, they were invariably punished, unless they publicly recanted their heretical views. Then in 1517, Martin Luther (1483–1546), an obscure friar of the Augustinian order and a professor of Scripture at the University of Wittenberg in Germany, tacked "Ninety-Five Theses" on a local church door. Luther was upset with what he thought were a number of unscriptural practices, particularly the selling of **indulgences** in the form of cash payments to the church to make amends for sins. As a form of penance, individuals could purchase indulgences for themselves or for others, such as deceased loved ones, to assure quick journeys through purgatory to heaven.

Luther found no biblical basis for indulgences. He could not understand why the church, which he described as "wealthiest of the wealthy," wanted money from hard-pressed peasants to help complete such building projects as St. Peter's Basilica in Rome. He also despised agents who were selling indulgences with clever sayings like: "As soon as coin in the coffer rings, the soul from purgatory springs." Luther had agonized for years over the ways to earn God's grace. He concluded that faith was all that mattered, not ritual or good works. The papacy demanded that Luther recant his heretical notions, but he refused, knowing full well that his penalty would be excommunication from the church.

Among other ideas, Luther contended that people did not need priests to interpret scriptures. All persons should have the right to read the Bible for themselves in cultivating their own faith in God. Luther thus advocated a "priesthood of all believers" in comprehending the mysteries of Christianity. In effect, he was attacking the widespread illiteracy of his era. Luther envisioned an educated populace capable of improving its lot in life. By the 1550s the doctrines of Lutheranism had taken firm hold in parts of Germany and the Scandinavian countries, often in the wake of enormous social turmoil and bloodshed.

Once under way, the Reformation, as this religious reform movement came to be known, gained rapid momentum. It also took many forms. In England politics rather than theology dictated the split with Rome. Henry VIII (reigned 1509–1547) prided

Martin Luther's ideas spread quickly among Europeans. His call for reform helped spur the Protestant Reformation in opposition to the Roman Catholic church and caused political and social upheaval throughout Europe.

Philadelphia Museum of Art, Johnson Collection.

FIGURE 1.1
The Tudor Monarchy of England

In England, the Protestant Reformation took root in Henry VIII's obsession with producing a male heir to secure the Tudor line. Henry did not accept the Pope's ruling that he should remain married to Catherine of Aragon, and he severed his ties with Rome. The Tudors reached their height under Elizabeth I, Henry's daughter by his second wife, Anne Boleyn.

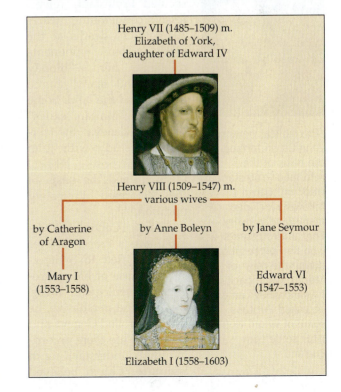

Henry VII (1485–1509) m. Elizabeth of York, daughter of Edward IV

Henry VIII (1509–1547) m.
— various wives —

by Catherine of Aragon   by Anne Boleyn   by Jane Seymour

Mary I (1553–1558)   Edward VI (1547–1553)

Elizabeth I (1558–1603)

himself on his devotion to Roman Catholicism. In 1521 he published a *Defense of the Seven Sacraments*, which berated Luther for arguing in favor of only two sacraments—baptism and communion. The Pope responded by awarding Henry a new title, "Defender of the Faith." At the same time, Henry worried about producing a male heir. His queen, Catherine of Aragon, daughter of Ferdinand and Isabella, bore him six children; but only one, a daughter named Mary, survived early childhood. Henry still wanted a male heir to ensure perpetuation of the Tudor line. In 1527 he asked Pope Clement VII to annul his marriage. When the Pope refused, Henry severed all ties with Rome.

Henry's actions were also spurred by his infatuation with Anne Boleyn, who bore him Elizabeth before being beheaded as an alleged adulteress. Through a series of parliamentary acts, Henry closed monasteries and seized church property. In the 1534 Act of Supremacy he formally repudiated the Pope and declared himself God's regent over England. Henceforth, all subjects would belong to the Anglican (English) church. The Church of England, unlike the Lutheran church, was similar to Catholicism in doctrine and ritual.

After his death Henry's reformation became a source of internal political chaos. When his daughter Mary I (reigned 1553–1558) came to the throne, she tried to return England to the Roman Catholic faith. Her government persecuted Protestants relentlessly, condemning nearly 300 to fiery deaths at the stake. Her opponents dubbed her "Bloody Mary," and many church leaders fled the land. Some of these "Marian exiles" went to Geneva, Switzerland, to study with John Calvin, whose Biblical ideas formed the basis of the Reformed Protestant tradition.

John Calvin (1509–1564) was a French lawyer who had fled to Switzerland because of his controversial theological ideas. Brilliant and persuasive, he soon controlled Geneva and reordered life there according to his understanding of Scripture. Calvin believed

The biblical views of John Calvin formed the basis of the reformed Protestant tradition. Calvin's followers included many Marian exiles—English Protestants who fled persecution during the reign of Mary I. Once back in England, they came to be called Puritans, some of whom would later settle New England.

God to be both all-powerful and wrathful. To avoid eternal damnation, persons had to gain God's grace through a conversion experience denoted by accepting Jesus Christ as their savior. All had to seek, insisted Calvin, even though God had already predestined who would be saved and who would be damned. Since no one could be sure which persons were God's chosen "saints," Calvin taught that correct moral behavior and outward prosperity—physical and mental as well as material—represented possible signs of divine favor.

Individuals disenchanted with Catholicism studied Calvin's famous *Institutes of the Christian Religion* (1536). Many, such as the Marian exiles, traveled to Geneva to learn more about the concepts that came to be known as **Calvinism**. Then they returned to their homelands eager to set up godly communities. Their numbers included founders of the German and Dutch Reformed churches, as well as Huguenots who eventually suffered from organized state persecution back in France. John Knox, another disciple of Calvin, established the Presbyterian church in Scotland.

The Marian exiles began reappearing in England after the death of Queen Mary. In time, they developed a large following and came to be known as "Puritans." They wanted to continue Henry's reformation, but now along theological lines. Fiercely dedicated to their beliefs, they had a startling impact on the course of English history, particularly after the time of Elizabeth I (reigned 1558–1603), when some of them moved to North America and others precipitated a civil war in England.

Defying the Supremacy of Spain

Spain's success in the Americas in combination with religious contention between Catholics and Protestants fostered unending turmoil among sixteenth-century nation-states. Some of the tension related to America, where French, Dutch, and English "sea dogs" attacked Spanish commerce or traded covertly within the empire. Some related to attempted Huguenot (French Protestant) settlements in South Carolina and Florida. Spain, cast as the primary defender of Roman Catholicism, fought back, using wealth extracted from America to pay for military forces capable of protecting its interests.

France remained overwhelmingly Roman Catholic but was at first tolerant of the Huguenots. The Crown, however, encouraged Huguenot emigration to America as a way to rid the realm of these zealous dissenters. Two attempts by Huguenots to settle in the Americas failed. Yet a third colonization undertaking occurred in 1564. These Huguenots located in northern Florida and called their settlement site Fort Caroline.

Spanish officials responded decisively. In 1565 they sent out a small army under Pedro Menéndez de Avilés, who first set up a garrison at San Augustín (the beginnings of St. Augustine, the oldest European-style city in North America), then turned on the Huguenots. Menéndez's troops massacred the Fort Caroline settlers, killing 132 of them but sparing about 50 women and children. To make sure other outsiders, especially Protestants, understood the danger of trying to colonize in Spanish territory, Menéndez ordered his soldiers to hack up the bodies before dumping the remains into a river. The butchery of Menéndez helped curtail sixteenth-century French settlement ventures.

Raids on Spanish treasure ships served as another source of tension. As early as the 1520s French freebooters started attacking Spanish vessels. The most daring of the sea dogs were Englishmen such as John Hawkins and Francis Drake. During the 1560s and 1570s Hawkins traded illegally and raided for booty in New Spain. Drake's adventures were even more dramatic. With private financial backing, including funds from Queen Elizabeth, he began a voyage in 1577 that took him around the world. Drake attacked wherever Spanish ports of call existed before returning home in 1580. Elizabeth gratefully dubbed him a knight, not only for being the first Englishman to circumnavigate the globe but also for securing a 4600 percent profit for his investors.

Elizabeth's professions of innocence to the contrary, King Philip II of Spain suspected her of actively supporting the sea dogs, whom he considered piratical scum. Further, he was furious with the English for giving military aid to the Protestant Dutch, who since 1567 had been fighting to free themselves from Spanish rule. Philip so despised Elizabeth that he conspired with her Catholic cousin Mary Stuart, Queen of Scots, to overthrow the English Protestant government. Wary of such plots, Elizabeth had Mary beheaded in 1587, at which point Philip decided to conquer the troublesome English heretics.

Philip and his military advisers pulled together an armada of Spanish vessels. They planned to sail 130 ships, including many hulking galleons, through the English Channel, pick up thousands of Spanish troops fighting the Dutch, and then invade England. The expedition ended in disaster for the Spanish when a flotilla of English ships, most of them smaller but far more maneuverable than the slow-moving galleons, appeared in the channel under Drake's command and offered battle. Then the famous "Protestant Wind" blew the Spanish Armada to bits. The war with Spain did not officially end until 1604; however, the destruction of the Armada in 1588 established England's rep-

utation as a naval power. It also demonstrated that little England, heretofore a minor kingdom, could prevail over Europe's mightiest nation, which caused some English subjects to press forward with plans to secure territories in North America.

England Prepares for Westward Expansion

Besides the diminished Spanish threat, other factors helped pave the way for England's westward expansion. None was more important than rapid population growth. During the sixteenth century, England's population doubled, reaching 4 million by the 1590s. Yet opportunities for employment and decent wages lagged behind the population explosion. The phenomenal growth of the woolen industry, for instance, forced peasants off the land as manor lords fenced in their fields to make pastures for sheep. Because of this **enclosure movement,** England in 1600 had three times as many sheep as people. Meanwhile, London and other cities exploded in size as persons displaced from the countryside poured in and subsisted as best they could under miserable conditions.

In addition, all Europeans faced the major problem of rapid inflation, a reflection of what has been called the **price revolution.** Between 1500 and 1600 the cost of goods and services spiraled upward by as much as 500 percent. The principal inflationary culprit was an overabundance of precious metal, mostly Spanish silver mined in America (7 million pounds in weight by about 1650) and then pumped into the European economy in exchange for various commodities. The amount of money in circulation expanded more quickly than did the supply of goods or services. As a result, prices jumped dramatically.

In England, even farmers who owned their own land struggled to make ends meet. What they had to pay for necessities rose faster than what they received in the marketplace for their agricultural produce. A prolonged decline in real income on top of heavy taxes under the Tudors left many independent farmers destitute. In time, the abundant land of America attracted great numbers of England's failing yeoman farmers and permanently poor (sometimes called "sturdy beggars").

Apparent overpopulation and so much poverty and suffering became powerful arguments for westward expansion. As the eminent Elizabethan expansionist Richard Hakluyt wrote in his influential *Discourse of Western Planting* (1584), "infinite numbers may be set to work" in America, "to the unburdening of the realm . . . at home." Hakluyt also viewed American settlements as the key to achieving national greatness, since colonies could serve as sources of valuable commodities. They would likewise stimulate England's shipbuilding industry. They would help "enlarge the glory of the gospel" by offering the Indians "sincere religion" in the form of the Protestant Anglican faith. Further, argued Hakluyt, no one, certainly not the native populace, could enjoy "humanity, courtesy, and freedom" in America unless England challenged Spain's tyrannical sway by planting true "liberty" in its overseas settlements.

As with other New World colonizers, the English viewed their motives as above reproach on all counts. Certainly Queen Elizabeth recognized the merits of Richard Hakluyt's arguments, especially as they related to increasing the power of her realm. Still, she was a tightfisted monarch who refused to plunge vast sums of royal funds into highly speculative American ventures. She preferred having her favored courtiers, such as those then subduing Ireland, expend their own capital and energies in the quest for riches across the Atlantic Ocean.

JOINING IN THE INVASION OF AMERICA

England's path to America lay through Ireland. Off and on over four centuries the English had conducted sporadic raids on the "wild" Irish, as they thought of their Gaelic-speaking neighbors. During Elizabeth's reign, these forays became routine. The goal was to gain political control of Ireland and to establish agricultural colonies, since ample food supplies had become a problem at home with the spread of the enclosure movement.

Elizabeth named as governor one of her court favorites, Sir Humphrey Gilbert (1539?–1583), and instructed him to subdue the Irish. Gilbert did so with a vengeance, operating as if the only good Irish subject was one who had been beheaded. The Irish, a million strong, fought back relentlessly, causing the English "plantations" there to exist precariously as military outposts in an alien environment.

For Elizabethan courtiers, Ireland became a laboratory for learning how to crush one's adversaries.

Sir Humphrey Gilbert's patent for founding the North American colonies established important guidelines for England's westward expansion.

Assumptions of cultural superiority abetted the English onslaught. The conquerors condemned the Irish, who were Roman Catholics, as religious heathens. They faulted them for using the land improperly, since the Irish were not sedentary farmers but people of migratory habits who tilled the soil only when they needed food. England's expansionists held these same attitudes when they began their American settlements. This time, however, the Indians would be the wild, unkempt, "savage" peoples in need of subjugation or eradication.

The Roanoke Disaster

Sir Humphrey Gilbert was as intolerant and contemptuous of the Spanish as he was of the Irish. He resented their pretensions to everything in America. He dreamed of finding the Northwest Passage to facilitate a flow of Oriental riches back to England, and he was willing to risk his personal fortune in that quest. Gilbert had other visions as well, including the effective occupation of North America and the founding of American colonies. He appealed to Elizabeth for exclusive rights to carry out his plans, and she acceded in 1578.

Gilbert's patent represented an important statement with respect to future guidelines for England's westward expansion. On the monarch's authority, he could occupy "heathen and barbarous lands . . . not actually possessed of any Christian prince or people." He would share in profits from extractable wealth, as would the Crown. Even more significant, prospective settlers would be assured the same rights of Englishmen "as if they were born and personally resident" at home. Not guaranteeing fundamental liberties would have inhibited the development of American colonies.

Gilbert did not live to see his dreams fulfilled. He disappeared in a North Atlantic storm after searching for the Northwest Passage. In 1584 his half-brother, Sir Walter Raleigh (1552?–1618), requested permission to carry on Gilbert's work. Elizabeth agreed, and Raleigh took quick action. He sent out a reconnoitering party, which explored the North Carolina coast and surveyed Roanoke Island. Then in 1585 Raleigh sponsored an expedition of 600 men, many of them veterans of the Irish wars. After some raiding for booty in New Spain, Raleigh's adventurers sailed north and dropped off 107 men under Governor Ralph Lane at the chosen site.

Lane's party found the local Croatoan and Roanoak Indians to be friendly. Then diseases struck. "That people," an eyewitness exclaimed, "began to die very fast, and many in short space." In the spring

Roanoke Island

The fate of the lost colony of Roanoke Island may never be known. The settlement was too small and underfinanced to survive disease and continued strife with local natives.

of 1586 a local chief, Wingina, probably trying to protect his tribe from an illness "so strange that they neither knew what it was, nor how to cure it," moved inland. Ralph Lane went after the natives and ordered an attack, during which one of his men beheaded Wingina in the tradition of dealing with the "wild" Irish. Fortunately for Lane, Sir Francis Drake appeared and carried the English party away before the Indians counterattacked.

Raleigh persisted. He decided to send out families in 1587, with John White, a capable, gentle person, as their governor. White had been on the 1585 expedition. Besides preparing many famous drawings of native life in the Roanoke area, he had spoken out against butchering the Indians. White and the other 114 settlers arrived at Roanoke Island in late July. In mid-August his daughter Elinor gave birth to Virginia Dare, the first English subject born in America. A few days later, White sailed back to England to obtain additional supplies. The outbreak of warfare between Spain and England delayed his return, and he did not get back to Roanoke until 1590. Nothing was left, except the word CROATOAN carved on a tree.

What happened to the lost colony may never be known. No European saw the settlers again. Local Indians either killed or absorbed them into their tribes. As for Raleigh, he had ruined himself financially, proving that funding overseas ventures lay beyond the means of any one person. All that he had left was a patent that he gave up in the 1590s, a sense that colonizing in America was a hazardous undertaking at best, and a name, Virginia, which Raleigh had offered in thanks to his patron, Elizabeth, the Virgin Queen.

Merchant Capitalists Sponsor the Founding of Virginia

A few sixteenth-century English subjects did prosper in the wake of economic dislocation and spiraling inflation. Among these fortunate few were manufacturers of woolen goods and merchants who made Europe a major marketplace for English cloth. With their profits, these gentlemen of capital gained social respectability. Many purchased landed estates, and some even married into England's titled nobility. As members of the gentry class, they started pooling their capital and sponsoring risky overseas business ventures by investing in **joint-stock trading companies.**

In 1555 the Crown chartered the Muscovy Company, giving that business venture the exclusive right to develop England's trade with Russia. Having a monopoly made the enterprise more attractive to potential stockholders. Although they hoped to make handsome profits, they would lose no more than the money they had subscribed. Meanwhile, the company could draw on a large pool of working capital to underwrite its activities. Queen Elizabeth liked this model of business organization, which depended on private capital rather than royal funds to finance England's economic—and eventually political—expansion abroad. The Crown, of course, was to share in any profits.

The Muscovy Company was a success, and other joint-stock undertakings followed, such as the East India Company, chartered in 1600 to develop England's Far Eastern interests. Then in 1606 a charter for the Vir-

A *Festive Dance* is one of John White's drawings depicting life among the Native Americans in the village of Secoton, near the Roanoke settlement.

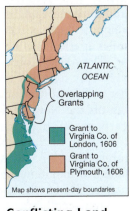

Overlapping Grants

■ Grant to Virginia Co. of London, 1606

■ Grant to Virginia Co. of Plymouth, 1606

Map shows present-day boundaries

Conflicting Land Claims

ginia Company received royal approval. Ironically, even though this business enterprise failed its stockholders, company activities produced England's first enduring settlement in North America.

During the 1590s, English courtiers and merchant capitalists did not pick up on Raleigh's failed efforts. The ongoing war with Spain took precedence, and profits came easily from capturing Spanish vessels on the high seas. When peace returned, influential merchants stood ready to pool their capital, spread the financial risk, and pursue Raleigh's patent. They took their case to the new king, the Stuart monarch James I (reigned 1603–1625), who willingly granted them a generous trading company charter.

Initially, the Virginia Company had two sets of investors. The first, a group of London merchants, held Raleigh's patent. They had earned bountiful profits from other joint-stock ventures and were ready to take further risks. Foolishly, they dreamed of heaping piles of gold and silver. More realistically, they hoped to trade for valuable commodities with the native populace and to plant vineyards and silk-producing mulberry trees. The London merchants had first claim to all land between the Cape Fear River in southern North Carolina and present-day New York City.

In December 1606, they sent out 144 adventurers under Captain Christopher Newport aboard the *Susan Constant*, *Godspeed*, and *Discovery*. The crossing was difficult, and 39 men died. In May 1607 the survivors located on an island some 30 miles up the James River off Chesapeake Bay. They called their settlement, really meant as a trading post, Jamestown.

The second set of investors were from such West Country port towns as Plymouth. In response to bitter complaints over the years about London's dominance of joint-stock ventures, the Virginia Company granted the West Country merchants lands lying between the mouth of the Potomac River and northern Maine. Thus the charter allowed for an overlapping middle zone that both investor groups could develop, so long as their settlements were at least 100 miles apart.

The West Country merchants hoped to reap profits by harvesting great stands of American timber and from fur trading with the Indians and fishing off the New England coast. They dispatched a party in 1607 that located at Sagadahoc, Maine, near the mouth of the Kennebec River. These 44 adventurers squabbled incessantly among themselves and failed to maintain harmonious relations with local natives. Those who survived the first winter gave up and returned home in 1608. The Plymouth investors refused to expend more funds, and their patent fell dormant.

As with the Irish invasion, both groups of adventurers came forth in military fashion. They built forts to protect themselves from unfriendly Indians and Spanish raiding parties. In its early days, Jamestown functioned as an outpost in another alien environment. The early participants were not settlers. They wanted to get in, gain access to easy forms of wealth, and get out before losing their lives.

Struggling Jamestown Survives

That Jamestown survived is amazing. Newport's adventurers were miscast for the American wilderness. Many were second and third sons of English noblemen. Because of primogeniture and entail (laws that specified that only firstborn male heirs could inherit landed estates and family titles), these younger sons had to choose alternate careers. Many became lawyers, clergymen, or high-ranking military officers, but none toiled in the fields, as farming was hardly a gentleman's calling. When Jamestown ran short of food, these company adventurers still avoided agricultural work, preferring to search for gold, silver, or the Northwest Passage. Some starved to death as a result.

Besides gentleman-adventurers, other equally ill-prepared individuals, such as valets and footmen, joined the expedition. Their duties extended only to waiting on their aristocratic masters. Also present were goldsmiths and jewelers, plus a collection of ne'er-do-wells who knew no occupation but apparently functioned as soldiers under gentleman-officers in dealings with the natives.

The social and economic characteristics of these first adventurers suggest that the London investors may have modeled the expedition after the early Spanish conquests—with the idea of forcing local Indians to become agricultural workers as peons or slaves. As matters turned out, the natives supplied food, but even with their assistance, only 38 Englishmen were still alive by the early spring of 1608.

Another problem was the settlement site. Company directors had ordered the adventurers to locate on high ground far enough in-

Powhatan's Confederacy

Powhatan's Confederacy, established for defense against aggressive neighbors, consisted of some 30 coastal tribes.

This imaginative drawing shows Native Americans sharing food with the Jamestown colonists. In fact, relations between the Indians and the English settlers were often quite thorny and several times erupted into open conflict.

land so as to go undetected by the Spanish. Jamestown Island met the second requirement, but it was a low, swampy place lying at a point on the James River where salt and fresh water mingled. The brackish water was "full of slime and filth," as one observer noted. The water could cause salt poisoning and was also a breeding ground for malaria, typhoid fever, and dysentery.

Several factors saved the Jamestown settlement. The local Indians under Powhatan, an Algonquian-speaking Pamunkey, initially offered sustenance. Powhatan had organized a confederacy of some 30 coastal tribes, numbering about 20,000 people, to defend themselves against aggressive interior neighbors. Powhatan tried to stay clear of the Jamestown adventurers, but when he was around them, he could not help but notice their large ships, gaudy body armor, and noisy firearms. He viewed the English as potential allies in warfare with interior tribes, a faulty assessment but one that kept him from wiping out the weakened adventurers.

At the same time, Company investors in London refused to quit. They kept sending out supplies and adventurers, as many as 800 more young men plus a few women in 1608 and 1609. Upon their arrival, however, many quickly died of malaria and other diseases. Others, debilitated from illnesses, were unable to work. They became a drain on Jamestown's precarious food supply.

In these early days the dynamic and ruthless local leadership of Captain John Smith (1580?–1631) kept the Jamestown outpost from totally collapsing. Smith had crossed the Atlantic with the original adventurers. Once in Jamestown, he emerged as a virtual dictator. Smith helped save many lives by imposing discipline and forcing everyone—gentleman or servant, sick or well—to adhere to one rule: "He who works not, eats not."

In October 1609 Smith returned to England after suffering severe burns from an accidental explosion of gunpowder. Lacking authoritarian leadership, the adventurers experienced a tragic "starving time" during the winter of 1609–1610. Hundreds died as food supplies, described as "moldy, rotten, full of cobwebs and maggots," gave out. Only about 60 persons survived by eating everything from rats to snakes, and there was even an alleged instance of cannibalism. One man completely lost his mind; he murdered his wife, then "powdered [salted] her up to eat her, for which he was burned" at the stake.

Smith's presence might not have averted the disaster. Too often, he, like the other early adventurers, had treated the Indians with contempt. Bad relations caused Powhatan to cut off food supplies. For some reason, however, the native leader did not seize the opportunity to wipe out Jamestown. Perhaps still hoping for an alliance, he simply allowed the feeble English to die on their own.

THE PEOPLE SPEAK

Powhatan Pleads for Peace and Harmony (1609)

The aging Chief Powhatan hoped to befriend the English adventurers who began appearing in the midst of his Confederacy in 1607. However, he quickly learned that they were just as likely to maim and kill his followers as to respond gratefully for the food that he was supplying them. Skeptics among the native populace started warning Powhatan that the English had but one goal—to kill them all and take their lands. In 1609, Powhatan, still hoping for peace, met with Captain John Smith and warned him of grave consequences should the English persist in their belligerent ways. The Jamestown adventurers did not listen. Powhatan cut off their food supplies, which resulted in the "starving time" of 1609–1610 and protracted warfare in the years ahead. Smith recorded the text of Powhatan's speech as follows:

> Captaine Smith, . . . I knowe the difference of peace and warre better than any in my Countrie. But now I am old, and ere long must die. My brethren, namely Opichapam, Opechankanough, and Kekataugh, my two sisters, and their two daughters, are distinctly each others successours. I wish their experience no lesse then mine, and your love to them, no less then mine to you: but this brute [rumor] from Nansamund, that you are come to destroy my Countrie, so much affrighteth all my people, as they dare not visit you. What will it availe you to take that perforce you may quietly have with love, or to destroy them that provide you food? What can you get by war, when we can hide our provision and flie to the woodes, whereby you must famish, by wronging us your friends? And whie are you thus jealous of our loves, seeing us unarmed, and both doe, and are willing still to feed you with that you cannot get but by our labours? Think you I am so simple not to knowe it is better to eate good meate, lie well, and sleepe quietly with my women and children, laugh, and be merrie with you, have copper, hatchets, or what I want being your friend; then bee forced to flie from all, to lie cold in the woods, feed upon acorns roots and such trash, and be so hunted by you that I can neither rest eat nor sleepe, but my tired men must watch, and if a twig but breake, everie one crie, there comes Captaine Smith: then must I flie I knowe not whether and thus with miserable feare end my miserable life, leaving my pleasures to such youths as you, which, through your rash unadvisednesse, may quickly as miserably ende, for want of that you never knowe how to find? Let this therefore assure you of our loves, and everie yeare our friendly trade shall furnish you with corn; and now also if you would come in friendly manner to us, and not thus with your gunnes and swords, as to invade your foes.

Source: Samuel G. Drake, *Biography and History of the Indians of North America* (Boston, 1841), 353.

Back in England, Virginia Company stockholders refused to concede defeat. By 1610 they realized that mineral wealth was an illusion, but still they sent out more people. One of them, John Rolfe, experimented with local tobacco plants, which produced a harsh-tasting crop. Rolfe, like the company, persisted. He procured some plants from Trinidad in the West Indies and grew a milder, more flavorful leaf. Tobacco soon became Virginia's gold and silver. The colony now had a valuable trading commodity, and settlements quickly spread along the banks of the James River. Englishmen had found an economic reason to stay in the Americas.

Dutch and French Adventurers

In the early 1600s the Spanish contented themselves with drawing wealth from their Caribbean basin empire. They did not challenge various European interlopers seeking to stake North American claims. Ultimately, Dutch settlements in New York were seized by the English, but France's efforts resulted in a Canadian empire capable of rivaling those of Spain and England.

Once fully liberated from Spanish domination at home, the Dutch grabbed at a portion of North America. In 1609 they sent out an English sea captain, Henry Hudson, to search for the Northwest Passage. He explored Delaware Bay, then the New York waterway that bears his name. Hudson made contact with the Iroquois Indians, probably the Mohawks, and talked of trade in furs. Broad-brimmed beaver hats were then the fashion rage in Europe, but fur supplies were dwindling. North America could become a new source of pelts, if the natives would cooperate. The Dutch established trading stations on Manhattan Island (later called New Amsterdam) and Albany (Fort Orange) in 1624. The Iroquois did their part in delivering furs, and the colony of New Netherland took hold under the auspices of the Dutch West India Company.

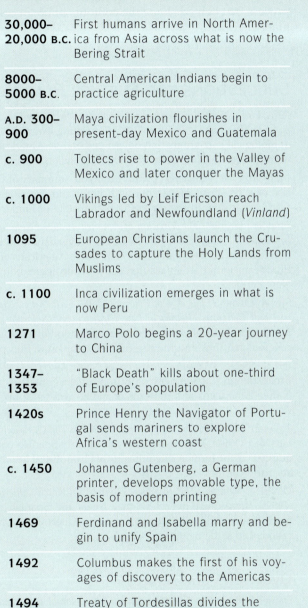

Chronology
OF KEY EVENTS

30,000– 20,000 B.C.	First humans arrive in North America from Asia across what is now the Bering Strait
8000– 5000 B.C.	Central American Indians begin to practice agriculture
A.D. 300– 900	Maya civilization flourishes in present-day Mexico and Guatemala
c. 900	Toltecs rise to power in the Valley of Mexico and later conquer the Mayas
c. 1000	Vikings led by Leif Ericson reach Labrador and Newfoundland (*Vinland*)
1095	European Christians launch the Crusades to capture the Holy Lands from Muslims
c. 1100	Inca civilization emerges in what is now Peru
1271	Marco Polo begins a 20-year journey to China
1347– 1353	"Black Death" kills about one-third of Europe's population
1420s	Prince Henry the Navigator of Portugal sends mariners to explore Africa's western coast
c. 1450	Johannes Gutenberg, a German printer, develops movable type, the basis of modern printing
1469	Ferdinand and Isabella marry and begin to unify Spain
1492	Columbus makes the first of his voyages of discovery to the Americas
1494	Treaty of Tordesillas divides the known world between Portugal and Spain
1497– 1498	John Cabot's two voyages to Newfoundland and Cape Breton Island lay the basis for English claims to North America
1501	Spain authorizes the first shipment of African slaves to the Caribbean islands
1517	Martin Luther's public protests against the sale of indulgences (pardons of punishment in Purgatory) mark the beginning of the Protestant Reformation
1519	Hernán Cortés and 600 Spanish conquistadores begin the conquest of the Aztec empire
1527	Henry VIII of England begins to sever ties with the Roman Catholic church
1531	Francisco Pizarro and 180 Spanish soldiers start the conquest of the Inca empire
1534	Jacques Cartier explores the St. Lawrence River and claims the region for France
1542	Spain outlaws the *encomienda* system and the enslavement of Indians
1585– 1587	Sir Walter Raleigh sponsors England's first North American settlement at Roanoke Island in present-day North Carolina
1607	English adventurers establish the first permanent English settlement at Jamestown in present-day Virginia

Profits from furs also helped motivate the French. In 1608 Samuel de Champlain set up an outpost at Quebec on the St. Lawrence River, and he found local Indians ready to trade. Quebec was the base from which New France spread. Yet only after 1663, when the Crown took control of managing the colony, did the French population in Canada grow significantly, reaching 10,000 people by the 1680s.

The French Canadians were energetic. Following Champlain's lead, they explored everywhere and claimed everything in sight. They established harmonious relations with dozens of different Indian nations, and they even joined in native wars as a way of solidifying trading ties. The French, with their small numbers, could not completely impose their cultural values. They did use the natives for their own purposes, especially in relation to the fur trade. At the same time, they also showed respect, which paid off handsomely when their many Indian allies willingly fought beside them in a series of imperial wars that beset America beginning in 1689.

CONCLUSION

Except in Canada, the Europeans who explored the Americas and began colonies after 1492 acted as foreign invaders. Although a few were at first curious, they generally viewed the natives as their adversaries, describing them as "worse than those beasts which are of the most wild and savage nature." Judgments of cultural superiority seemed to justify the destruction of Native Americans.

Still, there was a **Columbian exchange** of sorts. The Indians taught the Europeans about tobacco, corn, potatoes, varieties of beans, peanuts, tomatoes, and many other crops then unknown in Europe. In return, Europeans introduced the native populace to wheat, oats, barley, and rice, as well as to grapes for wine and various melons. The Europeans also brought with them domesticated animals, including horses, pigs, sheep, goats, and cattle. Horses proved to be important, particularly for Great Plains Indians, who used them in fighting against future generations of white settlers, just as tobacco production in the Chesapeake area had the unintended effect of attracting enough Europeans to end native control of that area.

Perhaps more than anything else, killer diseases served to unbalance the exchange. From the first moments of contact, great civilizations like the Aztecs and more humble groups like Tisquantum's Patuxets faced devastation. In some cases the Indians who survived, as in New Spain, had to accept the status of peons. Along the Atlantic coastline, survivors were drawn into the European trading network. In exchange for furs, the Indians wanted firearms to kill yet more animals whose pelts could be traded for still more guns and for alcohol to help them forget, even for a moment, what was happening to their way of life in the wake of European westward expansion.

The English would eventually send the most settlers. They left home for various reasons. Some, like the Pilgrims, crossed the Atlantic to avoid further religious persecution. Others, such as the Puritans, sought to build a holy community that would shine as a light upon Europe. Still others, including

colonists in the Chesapeake Bay area, desired land for growing tobacco. The latter group wanted laborers to help them raise their crops. Unable to enslave the Indians, they ultimately borrowed from the Spanish model and enslaved Africans. In so doing, they forced blacks to enter their settlements in chains and to become a part of a peopling and unpeopling process that helped shape the contours of life in colonial America.

SUGGESTIONS FOR FURTHER READING

Alfred W. Crosby, *Ecological Imperialism: The Biological Expansion of Europe, 900–1900* (1986). Revealing examination of biological encounters that devastated Native Americans in the process of European westward expansion.

John Guy, *Tudor England* (1990). Admirable summary of the rise of a powerful monarchy, with implications for westward expansion, in the emerging nation-state of England.

Francis Jennings, *The Invasion of America: Indians, Colonialism, and the Cant of Conquest* (1976). Controversial introduction to discordant relations between Native Americans and Europeans with particular reference to white aggression in New England.

Steven Ozment, *The Age of Reform (1250–1550): An Intellectual and Religious History of Late Medieval and Reformation Europe* (1980). Balanced, readable investigation of growing religious tensions and the rise of Protestantism in Europe.

Ian K. Steele, *Warpaths: Invasions of North America* (1994). Broad-ranging assessment of European encounters with Native Americans and patterns of Indian resistance up to the 1760s.

Tzvetan Todorov, *The Conquest of America: The Question of the Other* (1992). Engrossing analysis of early Spanish conquests and the human dilemmas posed by cultural intolerance and conflict.

David J. Weber, *The Spanish Frontier in North America* (1992). Revisionist overview that treats the Spanish as much more than plunderers in their American explorations and settlements.

Overviews and Surveys

Daniel J. Boorstin, *The Americans: The Colonial Experience* (1958); Stephen Greenblatt, *Marvelous Possessions: The Wonder of the New World* (1992); James A. Henretta and Gregory H. Nobles, *Evolution and Revolution: American Society, 1600–1820* (1987); Alvin M. Josephy, Jr., *The Indian Heritage of America* (1991); D. W. Meinig, *The Shaping of America,* Vol. I: *Atlantic America, 1492–1800* (1986); Richard Middleton, *Colonial America: A History, 1585–1776,* 2d ed. (1996); Gary B. Nash, *Red, White, and Black: The Peoples of Early America,* 4th ed. (2000); Anthony Pagden, *European Encounters with the New World: From Renaissance to Romanticism* (1992); Jerome R. Reich, *Colonial America,* 2d ed. (1989);

Richard C. Simmons, *The American Colonies: From Settlement to Independence* (1981); David E. Stannard, *American Holocaust: Columbus and the Conquest of the New World* (1992); Wilcomb E. Washburn, *The Indian in America* (1975).

The First Discovery of America

James Axtell, *After Columbus: Essays in the Ethnohistory of Colonial North America* (1988), *The European and the Indian: Essays in the Ethnohistory of Colonial North America* (1981), and *The Invasion Within: The Contest of Cultures in Colonial North America* (1985); Henry W. Bowden, *American Indians and Christian Missions: Studies in Cultural Conflict* (1981); William Cronon, *Changes in the Land: Indians, Colonists, and the Ecology of New England* (1983); Alfred W. Crosby, *The Columbian Exchange: Biological and Cultural Consequences of 1492* (1972); William N. Denevan, ed., *The Native Population of the Americas in 1492* (1992); Henry F. Dobyns, *Their Number Become Thinned: Native American Population Dynamics in Eastern North America* (1983); Harold E. Driver, *The Indians of North America*, 2d ed. (1969); Brian M. Fagan, *The Great Journey: The Peopling of Ancient America* (1987); John S. Henderson, *The World of the Ancient Maya* (1981); Francis Jennings, *The Ambiguous Iroquois Empire: The Covenant Chain Confederation of Indian Tribes with English Colonies From Its Beginnings to the Lancaster Treaty of 1744* (1984), and *The Founders of America* (1993); Alvin M. Josephy, Jr., ed., *America in 1492* (1992); Yasuhide Kawashima, *Puritan Justice and the Indian: White Man's Law and Massachusetts, 1630–1763* (1986); Shepard Krech, III, ed., *Indians, Animals, and the Fur Trade: A Critique of Keepers of the Game* (1981); Peter C. Mancall, *Deadly Medicine: Indians and Alcohol in Early America* (1995); Calvin Martin, ed., *The American Indian and the Problem of History* (1987); James H. Merrell, *The Indians' New World: Catawbas and Their Neighbors From European Contact Through the Era of Removal* (1989); Paul C. Phillips and J. W. Smurr, *The Fur Trade*, 2 vols. (1960); Daniel K. Richter, *The Ordeal of the Longhouse: The Peoples of the Iroquois League in the Era of European Colonization* (1992); Neal Salisbury, *Manitou and Providence: Indians, Europeans, and the Making of New England, 1500–1643* (1982); Bernard Sheehan, *Savagism and Civility: Indians and Englishmen in Colonial Virginia* (1980); Timothy Silver, *A New Face on the Countryside: Indians, Colonists, and Slaves in South Atlantic Forests, 1500–1800* (1990); Margaret C. Szasz, *Indian Education in the American Colonies, 1607–1783* (1988); Alden T. Vaughan, *The New England Frontier: Puritans and Indians, 1620–1675*, rev. ed. (1995); J. Leitch Wright, Jr., *The Only Land They Knew: The Tragic Story of American Indians in the Old South* (1981).

Preparing Europe for Westward Expansion

Paul H. Chapman, *The Norse Discovery of America* (1981); Carlo M. Cipolla, *Guns, Sails, and Empires: Technological Innovation and the Early Phases of European Expansion, 1400–1700* (1985); Felipe Fernandez-Armesto, *Before Columbus: Exploration and Colonization From the Mediterranean to the Atlantic, 1229–1492* (1987); Valerie Flint, *The Imaginative Landscape of Christopher Columbus* (1992); E. L. Jones, *The European Miracle: Environments, Economies, and Geopolitics in the History of Europe and Asia*, 2d ed. (1987); William H. McNeill, *The Rise of the West: A History of the Human Community* (1991), and *Plagues and Peoples* (1976); Frederick J. Pohl, *The Viking Settlements of North America* (1972); Robert L. Reynolds, *Europe Emerges: Transition Toward an Industrial World-Wide Society, 600–1750* (1961).

Explorers, Conquerors, and the Making of New Spain

Charles R. Boxer, *The Portuguese Seaborne Empire, 1415–1825* (1969); David Carrasco, *Quetzalcoatl and the Irony of Empire: Myths and Prophecies in the Aztec Tradition* (1982); Inga Clendinnen, *Aztecs: An Interpretation* (1991); J. H. Elliott, *Imperial Spain, 1469–1716* (1963), and *The Old World and the New, 1492–1650* (1970); Charles Gibson, *The Aztecs Under Spanish Rule: A History of the Indians of the Valley of Mexico* (1964), and *Spain in America* (1966); J. R. Hale, *Renaissance Exploration* (1968); Clarence H. Haring, *The Spanish Empire in America* (1947); James Lockhart and Stuart B. Schwartz, *Early Latin America: A History of Colonial Spanish America and Brazil* (1983); Samuel E. Morison, *The European Discovery of America: The Southern Voyages*, A.D. *1492–1616* (1979); J. H. Parry, *The Age of Reconnaissance* (1963), *The Spanish Seaborne Empire* (1966), and *The Discovery of South America* (1979); Daniel Peters, *The Incas* (1991); G. V. Scammell, *The World Encompassed: The First European Maritime Empires* (1981); Nathan Wachtel, *The Vision of the Vanquished: The Spanish Conquest of Peru Through Indian Eyes, 1530–1570* (1977); Silvio Zavala, *New Viewpoints on the Spanish Colonization of America* (1943).

Challengers for North America: France and England

Kenneth R. Andrews, *Trade, Plunder, and Settlement: The Genesis of the British Empire, 1480–1630* (1984); Carl Bridenbaugh, *Vexed and Troubled Englishmen, 1590–1642* (1967); Mildred Campbell, *The English Yeoman Under Elizabeth and the Early Stuarts* (1942); Patrick Collinson, *The Elizabethan Puritan Movement* (1967); G. R. Elton, *Reform and Reformation: England, 1509–1558* (1977); C. H. and Katherine George, *The Protestant Mind of the English Reformation* (1961); Peter Laslett, *The World We Have Lost, Further Explored*, 3d ed. (1984); Samuel E. Morison, *The European Discovery of America: The Northern Voyages*, A.D. *500–1600* (1971); Wallace Notestein, *The English People on the Eve of Colonization, 1603–1630* (1954); Theodore K. Rabb, *Enterprise & Empire: Merchant and Gentry Investment in the Expansion of England, 1575–1630* (1967); Lacey Baldwin Smith, *This Realm of England, 1399–1688*, 3d ed. (1988); Lewis Spitz, *The Protestant Reformation, 1517–1559* (1985); Lawrence Stone, *The Crisis of the Aristocracy, 1558–1641* (1979); Michael Walzer, *The Revolution of the Saints: A Study in the Origins of Radical Politics* (1965); Keith Wrightson, *English Society, 1580–1680* (1982).

Joining in the Invasion of America

Charles R. Boxer, *The Dutch Seaborne Empire, 1600–1800* (1988); Carl Bridenbaugh, *Jamestown, 1544–1699* (1980); Nicholas P. Canny, *The Elizabethan Conquest of Ireland: A Pattern Established, 1565–76* (1976); Ralph Davis, *The Rise of the Atlantic Economies* (1973); W. J. Eccles, *The Canadian Frontier, 1534–1760,* rev. ed. (1983), and *France in America,* rev. ed. (1990); Paul E. Hoffman, *A New Andalucia and a Way to the Orient: The American Southeast During the Sixteenth Century* (1990); Alice P. Kenney, *Stubborn for Liberty: The Dutch in New York* (1975); Karen O. Kupperman, *Settling with the Indians: The Meeting of English and Indian Cultures in America, 1580–1640* (1980), and *Roanoke: The Abandoned Colony* (1984); James Lang, *Conquest and Commerce: Spain and England in the Americas* (1975); David B. Quinn, *The Elizabethans and the Irish* (1966), *North America from Earliest Discovery to First Settlements: The Norse Voyages to 1612* (1977), and *Set Fair for Roanoke: Voyages and Colonies, 1584–1606* (1985); Helen C. Rountree, *Pocahontas's People: The Powhatan Indians of Virginia Through Four Centuries* (1990); A. L. Rowse, *The Expansion of Elizabethan England* (1955), and *The Elizabethans and America* (1959); George L. Smith, *Religion and Trade in New Netherland: Dutch Origins and American Development* (1973); Allen W. Trelease, *Indian Affairs in Colonial New York: The Sixteenth Century* (1960).

Biographies

William J. Bouwsma, *John Calvin: A Sixteenth Century Portrait* (1988); Carolly Erickson, *The First Elizabeth* (1983); Erik H. Erikson, *Young Man Luther: A Study in Psychoanalysis and History* (1993); Felipe Fernandez-Armesto, *Columbus* (1991); Richard Marius, *Martin Luther* (1991); Samuel E. Morison, *Samuel de Champlain* (1972), and *Christopher Columbus, Mariner* (1955); Theodore K. Rabb, *Jacobean Gentleman: Sir Edwin Sandys, 1561–1629*; Kirkpatrick Sale, *The Conquest of Paradise: Christopher Columbus and the Columbian Legacy* (1992); Andrew Sinclair, *Sir Walter Raleigh and the Age of Discovery* (1984); Alden T. Vaughan, *American Genesis: Captain John Smith and the Founding of Virginia* (1991).

INTERNET RESOURCES

Index of Native American Resources on the Internet
http://hanksville.phast.umass.edu/misc/
NAresources.html
A comprehensive source for Native American history and art.

Vikings in the New World
http://www.anthro.mankato.msus.edu/prehistory/
vikings/vikhome.html
This site explores the history of some of the earliest European visitors to America.

Sir Francis Drake
http://www.mcn.org/2/oseeler/drake.htm
This comprehensive site covers much of Drake's life and voyages.

1492: An Ongoing Voyage
http://metalab.unc.edu/expo/1492.exhibit/Intro.html
An exhibit of the Library of Congress, Washington, D.C., with brief essays and images about early civilizations and contact in the Americas.

The Computerized Information Retrieval System on Columbus and the Age of Discovery
http://marauder.millersv.edu/~columbus/
The History Department and Academic Computing Services of Millersville University of Pennsylvania provide this text retrieval system containing over 1000 text articles from various magazines, journals, newspapers, speeches, official calendars, and other sources relating to various encounter themes.

Cahokia Mounds
http://medicine.wustl.edu/~mckinney/cahokia/
cahokia.html
The Cahokia Mounds State Historical Site gives information about a fascinating pre-Columbian culture in North America.

Mexico Pre-Columbian History
http://www.mexonline.com/precolum.htm
This site provides information on the Aztecs, Maya, Mexica, Olmecs, Toltec, Zapotecs, and other pre-European cultures, as well as information on museums, archeology, language, and education.

The European Voyages of Exploration
http://www.acs.ucalgary.ca/HIST/tutor/eurvoya/
This University of Calgary site has images and texts for nearly every facet of European exploration.

The Discoverers' Web
http://www.win.tue.nl/cs/fm/engels/discovery/
Andre Engels maintains this most complete collection of information on the various efforts at exploration.

KEY TERMS

Matrilineal (p. 9)

Renaissance (p. 14)

Encomienda System (p. 19)

Northwest Passage (p. 20)

Protestant Reformation (p. 21)

Indulgences (p. 21)

Calvinism (p. 22)

Enclosure Movement (p. 23)

Price Revolution (p. 23)

Joint-Stock Trading Companies (p. 25)

Columbia Exchange (p. 30)

REVIEW QUESTIONS

1. Describe the principal regions of the Americas, and discuss how factors such as climate and the environment affected the economic and social development of various Native American peoples before the time of Columbus. Why did Native Americans not offer more resistance to the first European explorers and settlers?

2. What factors were in place by the late fifteenth century that facilitated European exploration and, ultimately, expansion into the Americas? Why were Portugal and Spain the first to become involved in these exploratory ventures?

3. How did the European Renaissance and Protestant Reformation affect the process of European westward expansion? Was one more important than the other? If so, why?

4. Compare and contrast the Spanish colonial system and its organization and objectives to those of the English, French, and Dutch. What elements did they have in common? What were the most significant differences, if any?

5. Why did Native Americans fail in their attempts to live in harmony with or drive off the Europeans? What else could they have done to maintain rather than lose control of their ancient tribal lands? Was the Columbian exchange, then, a failure for the original inhabitants of the Americas?

Plan of a Slave-Ship.

Section of a Slave-Ship.

By the Honourable Sir William Johnson Bart. His Majesty's sole Agent and Super-Intendant of Indian Affairs for the Northern Depart.

2

PLANTATIONS AND CITIES UPON A HILL, 1620–1700

"Slaves excepted"

John Punch wanted his freedom. He was a black indentured servant who joined two white servants and tried to flee Virginia in 1640, only to be caught by local residents and brought before the governor's council, the colony's highest court. The judges ordered the flogging of each runaway— 30 lashes well laid on. Then in a telling ruling, these officials revealed their thinking about the future status of blacks in England's North American colonies. The two whites had their terms of service extended by four years, but they ordered John Punch to "serve his said master . . . for the time of his natural life here or elsewhere."

Persons of African heritage were first transported to Virginia in 1619. In August of that year a Dutch vessel sailed north from the West Indies, where it had been trading or, more likely, stealing slaves from the Spanish. The Dutch ship entered Chesapeake Bay and sold some 20 "Negars," as John Rolfe described the human cargo, to settlers caught up in the early tobacco boom.

Virginia's first white settlers did not automatically assume that transplanted Africans were permanently unfree. They treated some blacks as indentured servants, a status that conveyed the prospect of personal freedom after four to seven years of laboring for someone else. English law did not recognize human slavery. The key phrase was *in favorem libertatis* (in favor of liberty), and the central tenet, wrote a contemporary legal authority, held that no person should ever "make or keep his brother in Christ, servile, bond, and underling forever unto him, as a beast rather than as a man."

Into the 1630s some black Virginians did gain their personal freedom. Others not only owned land but held servants of African origin as well, proof that permanent, inheritable slavery for blacks was a concept not yet fully developed in the Chesapeake Bay region.

By the 1640s, however, blacks faced a deteriorating legal status, ultimately leaving them outside the bounds of English liberty. In 1639 the new colony of Maryland guaranteed "all . . . Christians (slaves excepted)" the same "rights, liberties, . . . and free customs" as enjoyed by "any natural born subject of England." Worried about sporadic Indian raids, the Virginia assembly in 1640 ordered planters to arm themselves and "all those of their families which be capable of [bearing] arms . . . (excepting Negroes)." In 1643 the same assembly decreed that black women, like all adult males, would henceforth be "tithables"— those counted for local taxes because they worked in the fields. Black female servants planted, tended, and harvested tobacco crops while white female servants mainly performed household work—further evidence of discrimination based on skin color.

Local laws were catching up with the growing reality of lifetime slavery for blacks, as compared to

An African slave trader marches a group of yoked and chained captives— including women and children—from the interior of Africa to a trading post on the coast. There the captives awaited transport to the Americas.

temporary servitude for whites. In 1640 the Virginia council considered other runaway cases, besides that of John Punch. One of these involved a black named Emmanuel, who ran away with several whites. The judges handed out severe penalties, including whippings and extended terms of service for the whites. The leader of the group endured branding with an "R" on his face and had one of his legs shackled in irons for a year. Emmanuel received the same penalty, but the court made no mention of an extension of service. Apparently Emmanuel was already a slave for life.

Between 1640 and 1670 the distinction between short-term servitude for whites and permanent, inheritable slavery for blacks became firmly fixed. In appearance and by cultural and religious tradition, Africans were not like the English. As with the "wild" Irish and Indian "savages," noticeable differences translated into assumptions of inferiority, and blacks became "beastly heathens," not quite human.

Such thinking helped justify the mixing of words like "black" and "slave," so that by the 1690s slavery in the English colonies had emerged as a caste status for blacks only. Now fully excluded from the tradition of English liberty, local law defined Africans as chattels (movable property), and their masters held absolute control over their lives.

John Punch and Emmanuel were among those first African Americans in the Chesapeake Bay area who felt the stinging transition from servitude to slavery. They were also among the thousands of Europeans and Africans who helped settle England's North American colonies between 1620 and 1700. The societies and lifestyles of these migrants had many differences, as comparisons between the founding of the northern and southern colonies demonstrate. A common point for all migrants, regardless of status or condition, however, was their titanic struggle to survive in an alien land. Although thousands died, some 250,000 settlers inhabited England's mainland colonies by 1700, which resulted in the formation of another powerful European empire in the Americas.

FROM SETTLEMENTS TO SOCIETIES IN THE SOUTH

Smoking tobacco, wrote King James I, was "loathsome to the eye, hateful to the nose, harmful to the brain, [and] dangerous to the lungs." Despite the king's admonition, John Rolfe's experiments saved the Virginia Company—at least temporarily—by providing the struggling colony with an economic base. Early migrants grew tobacco with enthusiasm. The first exports occurred in 1617. By the mid-1630s Virginians were selling a million pounds a year, and by the mid-1660s annual tobacco crops for export reached 15 million pounds.

Company directors did not initially encourage the tobacco boom. Wanting a diversified economy, they sent out workers knowledgeable in the production of such commodities as silk, wine, glass, and iron, but all these efforts failed. Virginia's climate and soil were ideal for raising tobacco. Also, new land for cultivation was plentiful, since the "stinking weed" quickly depleted the soil of its minerals. Accepting reality, the London investors soon hailed tobacco as the savior of their venture. Other difficulties, however, cost the directors their charter, but not before company activities laid the basis for England's first enduring colony in North America.

Searching for Laborers

Life in early Virginia presented constant hardships. Migrants quickly succumbed to diseases such as malaria, typhoid fever, and dysentery. Survival, it seemed, depended upon "seasoning," or getting used to an inhospitable climate. Bad relations with Powhatan's Indians also was a source of mayhem and death, since the English and Native Americans fought in many isolated clashes. All told, the company convinced nearly 14,000 persons to attempt new lives in America. Only about 1150 were still alive and residing in the James River area in 1624, the year the company lost its charter.

Trying to overcome "a slaughter house" reputation, company leaders pursued various policies. Sir Thomas Smythe, a wealthy London merchant, used his boundless energy to keep the venture going. He tied company fortunes to England's potential for national greatness. His influence at court resulted in more generous charter rights in 1609 and 1612, the latter of which expanded company boundaries to include the island of Bermuda—soon a source of profitable cash crops. Also under Smythe's guidance, the company secured a steady supply of laborers. It also managed affairs in Virginia with an iron hand while attempting to improve Indian relations. Each activity was crucial to long-term development.

To encourage prospective laborers, company directors mounted publicity campaigns. These efforts helped neutralize Virginia's reputation as a death-

LONDON'S VIRGINIA.

The rise of the tobacco industry in the colonies spurred tobacco consumption in England.

trap. More successful in securing workers was the development of the system of **indentured servitude,** modeled along the lines of contractual farm service. During early Stuart times, between one-fourth and one-third of England's families had servants. Many young men and women, having no access to land, made agreements to work for a year or more as farm laborers in return for food, lodging, and modest wages. They had few other prospects for employment and virtually no chance of gaining title to their own freehold farms.

In theory, Virginia held out the opportunity of potential economic independence for rapidly growing numbers of landless farm servants and the urban poor. As early as 1609, the mayor of London asked the company "to ease the city and suburbs of a swarm of unnecessary inmates." The challenge was to get these struggling poor to America. Persons without money needed only to sign bonded contracts, or indentures, in which they legally exchanged up to seven years of labor in return for passage costs. After completing their terms of service, their masters owed them "freedom dues," including clothing, farm

tools, and in some cases land on which to begin anew as free persons.

The system of indentured servitude slowly took shape after 1609. At first, the company offered free passage along with shares of stock to those who signed up for seven years of labor. When terms were up, workers were to gain title to 100 acres of land as well as any stock dividends. The bait was eventual economic freedom, but even with so many unemployed persons in England, few applied. Getting by marginally or facing a hangman's noose remained more attractive than an early—and often brutal—death in America.

Some venturesome souls, mostly young, unattached males, signed on as company-managed laborers. To make sure these servants would take orders and work, Sir Thomas Smythe and his advisers gave dictatorial powers to their governors in Virginia. Lord De La Warr, a veteran of the Irish wars who arrived in 1610, organized the colony along military lines. He ruled by martial law, as did his surrogates, Sir Thomas Gates and Sir Thomas Dale, once he returned to England. Their *Lawes Divine, Moral, and Martiall* (1612) provided harsh penalties for even the smallest offenses.

Company servants were an undisciplined lot, less interested in work than in "bowling in the streets" of Jamestown, as an observer described their attitudes. When caught loafing, they paid with bloodied backs from public floggings, and when some laborers stole boats and tried to escape in 1612, Deputy Governor Gates showed no mercy. Their sentences included death by firing squad, hanging, or breaking upon the wheel, all as a warning to others with ideas of violating company contracts.

To Be Like English Subjects at Home

Stories of brutal treatment and high mortality rates undercut company efforts to secure a steady supply of laborers. Changes had to be made, and that process culminated when a reform-minded faction led by Sir Edwin Sandys prepared new instructions, since known as the "great charter" of 1618. The overriding goal was to frame incentives that would make risking settlement more attractive. Key provisions included an end to martial rule and a declaration assuring Virginians government "by those free laws which his Majesty's subjects live under in England." The charter promised a local representative assembly, which came to be known as the House of Burgesses. Its first deliberations took place in July 1619, a small cornerstone gathering pointing toward governments with a popular voice in England's North American colonies.

Besides guaranteeing political rights, the charter addressed economic incentives, including the notion of "private plantations" and **headrights.** Heretofore, the company controlled all acreage, but now potential settlers could purchase land without first serving as company laborers. Fifty acres per person would be given to those who migrated or those who paid for the passage of others to Virginia. Headrights would permit English families with funds to relocate and get title to enough property to grow tobacco and, perhaps, prosper. After all, Virginia had land in abundance but very few laborers, whereas England had a shortage of land and an oversupply of workers.

Even with these reforms, Virginia's unhealthful reputation kept families from migrating. English merchants and sea captains, however, developed a booming trade in indentured servants. They made substantial profits from delivering servants to labor-hungry planters and from headright patents, which they accumulated and sold to others with enough capital to purchase large tracts of land before migrating. In a few cases, buying up headrights resulted in the establishment of large plantations; still, three-fourths of all English settlers entering seventeenth-century Virginia were indentured servants.

The vast bulk of these migrants were single males under the age of 25 with no employment prospects in England. The unbalanced sex ratio concerned company officials. Wanting to give Virginia a "more settled" feeling, they contracted with 90 "uncorrupt" young women in 1619 to go to Jamestown and be sold as wives. The plan worked well, but because of other problems the company sent over only one more shipment of women. Stable family life was not a characteristic of the rough-and-tumble society of early Virginia.

Crushing Powhatan's Confederacy

Bickering, bloodshed, and death denoted relations with Powhatan's Indians as the English planted tobacco farms along the James River. John Rolfe's marriage to Powhatan's daughter, Pocahontas, in 1614, which implied a political alliance of sorts, eased tensions—but only briefly. Rolfe soon took Pocahontas to England, where she became an instant celebrity, and both of them encouraged settlement in Virginia. Unfortunately, while preparing to return home in 1616, Pocahontas contracted smallpox and died.

Two years later, Powhatan also died, leaving his more militant half-brother Opechancanough in

charge of the Confederacy. Watching the growing English presence with misgivings, Opechancanough decided that slaughtering the intruders was the only means left to save his people. On Good Friday, March 22, 1622, his warriors struck everywhere. Before the massacre was over, the Indians killed 347 settlers, or about 30 percent of the English colonists, including John Rolfe. Opechancanough, however, had failed to exterminate the enemy, and in many ways the massacre of 1622 was the beginning of the end for Virginia's coastal natives. White settlers, now more convinced than ever that Indians were savages, took vengeance whenever they could.

Retreating inland, Opechancanough waited 22 years before striking again. The attack came in April 1644, and another 400 or more colonists died (about 5 percent of the white population). The 1644 massacre was a last desperate gasp by Virginia's coastal natives. The numbers of whites were now too overwhelming for total destruction. As for Opechancanough, the settlers took him prisoner. A white

This sketch of a Virginia native appeared in about 1645, shortly after Virginia's coastal Indians failed in their second attempt to drive out the white settlers.
Copyright © The British Museum

guard, seeking personal vengeance, shot the old, enfeebled native leader to death in 1646. That same year, Confederacy chiefs signed a treaty agreeing to submit to English rule. The survivors of Powhatan's once-mighty league eventually accepted life on a reservation, as many other remnant Indian peoples would be forced to do as Europeans pushed westward across the North American continent.

A Model for Other Royal Colonies

The massacre of 1622 was one of two fatal blows to the Virginia Company. James I had started to dream about huge sums of money flowing into the royal treasury from taxes on tobacco. Company leaders, trying to stabilize their debt-ridden interests after the massacre, negotiated an exclusive contract with the Crown to deliver tobacco to England with the king receiving tax revenues on every pound shipped. However, a rumor spread that company leaders intended to charge exorbitant fees for handling the tobacco. The Crown, as a second fatal blow, quickly voided the tobacco contract. Then the king's advisers used court proceedings to revoke the company charter, thereby dissolving the enterprise in 1624.

King James next declared Virginia a royal colony and sent out his own governor. He did not promise basic political rights to the settlers and canceled the privilege of a local assembly. In a virtual throwback to the days of martial law, the king authorized his officials to rule absolutely.

Neither James nor his son, King Charles I (reigned 1625–1649), were advocates of popular rights or representative forms of government. Rather, they adhered to **divine right** theories of kingship, which meant that monarchs were literally God's political stewards on earth.

Virginia's planters, however, would not be denied a voice in government, and the royal governors shrewdly called upon locally prominent men to serve as advisory councilors. The governors also began authorizing assemblies, conveniently referred to as conventions, to deal with local problems. Still, relations between royal governors and colonists could become turbulent. In 1634 one governor, Sir John Harvey, known as a "choleric and impatient" man, got into a fist fight with one of his councilors. He punched out his opponent's teeth and threatened to hang the other councilors. In response, the councilors had Harvey arrested and sent him back to England in chains.

In 1639 King Charles, facing popular dissent at home because of his high-handed rule, finally relieved some of the pressure by granting Virginians a representative assembly, thereby assuring some local participation in colony-related decision making. Unlike the Spanish and French, English subjects had refused to accede to political domination by a far-off parent nation. They would share in the decision making affecting their lives as colonists in America.

Proprietary Maryland and the Carolinas

Charles's concession suggests the expediency with which the Stuart kings viewed colonization. Assuring basic rights did attract more settlers, which in turn meant larger tobacco crops and more tax revenues for the Crown. Founding additional colonies, moreover, would enhance England's stature among the nations of Europe. These same settlements could be used as dumping grounds for troublesome groups in England, such as the Puritans. Vast stretches of territory could also be granted to court favorites. The Stuarts had the power to make wealthy men even wealthier by awarding them huge "proprietary" estates in America, which would foster loyalty among powerful gentlemen at court who might otherwise choose, at some point, to challenge the authority of the Crown.

Sir George Calvert, described as a "forward and knowing person," was one such favored courtier. Serving as James I's secretary of state, he took charge of dissolving the Virginia Company. A year later he converted to Roman Catholicism and had to leave the government. To reward his loyal service, however, the king named Calvert the first Lord Baltimore and granted him permission to colonize Newfoundland, an effort that failed. Then in 1632 Charles I awarded Calvert title to 10 million acres surrounding the northern end of Chesapeake Bay. The king named the territory "Maryland" after his own Catholic wife, Queen Henrietta Maria, and he named Calvert lord proprietor over these lands.

When Calvert died, his son Cecilius, the second Lord Baltimore, took charge and sent out the first settlement parties. The idea was for Maryland to function as a haven for persecuted Roman Catholics. Those Catholics who migrated received substantial personal estates in return for annual quitrents, or land taxes, paid to Lord Baltimore. Many more Protestants than Catholics secured land patents, also with quitrents. The colony soon bore a striking similarity to its Chesapeake neighbor Virginia, since Marylanders also devoted themselves to cultivating tobacco.

The Maryland charter granted the Baltimore proprietors absolute political authority, but in 1635 Cecilius Calvert, hoping to induce further settlements,

Chesapeake Settlements, 1650

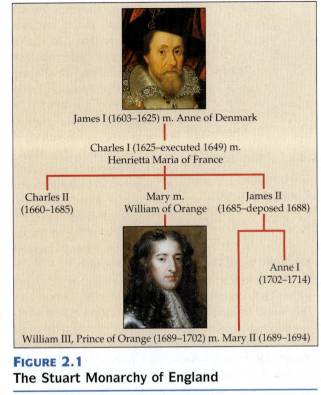

FIGURE 2.1
The Stuart Monarchy of England

The Stuart monarchs adhered to divine right theories of kingship. They only reluctantly granted basic political rights to English settlers in America.

granted a representative assembly. As the colony grew, Catholics and Protestants dueled bitterly over control of local politics. In an attempt to protect the minority Catholics, Calvert proposed an Act of Religious Toleration in 1649, which guaranteed all adult males voting or officeholding rights, so long as they subscribed to the doctrine of the Trinity. Although not full toleration, this act, which the assembly approved, was a key step toward liberty of conscience. Still, bickering between Maryland's Catholic and Protestant settlers continued for several decades.

Religious warfare, meanwhile, convulsed England. During the 1640s civil war turned English subjects against one another. Puritan "Roundheads" rose up against the "Cavalier" supporters of Charles I, who had refused to let Parliament meet for several years. In 1649 the victorious Puritans showed willful contempt for divine right theories of kingship by beheading Charles. Oliver Cromwell, the leader of Puritan military forces, then took political control of England as Lord Protector. After Cromwell's death and a brief, disastrous period of rule by his son, Parliament invited Charles I's exiled son to reestablish the Stuart monarchy—in exchange for promises to assemble Parliament regularly and to support the Anglican church.

The restoration of Charles II (reigned 1660–1685) left the new king with many political debts. In 1663 he paid off eight powerful gentlemen by awarding them title to all lands lying south of Virginia and north of Spanish Florida. The region was already known as Carolus, the Latin equivalent of Charles. The new proprietors quickly set about the task of finding settlers for the Carolinas, which proved difficult because of a dramatic new boom in England's economy—and a consequent decrease in the numbers of unemployed subjects.

Trying to spark the settlement process, one of the proprietors, Sir Anthony Ashley Cooper, assisted by his brilliant secretary, political philosopher John Locke, produced the "Fundamental Constitutions for Carolina" (1669). This document spelled out unworkable plans for a complex social order in which "landgraves" and "caciques" held vast estates and functioned as an American nobility, but shared the responsibilities of local government with smaller landholders. More important, the proprietors offered attractive headright provisions of up to 150 acres per person, guarantees of a representative assembly and religious toleration, and a fateful promise that free persons "shall have absolute power and authority over . . . negro slaves."

Barbadian Connection

Even with such generous terms, the Carolinas grew slowly. The Albemarle region of northeastern North Carolina developed as settlers spilled over from Virginia. William Byrd II, a prominent Virginia planter of the early eighteenth century, described the Albemarle inhabitants as having a "disposition to laziness for their whole lives." Most inhabitants subsisted marginally by exporting tobacco and various timber-derived products, including pitch, tar, and potash.

The proprietors focused on settling South Carolina. They contacted small-scale English farmers on the island of Barbados who were selling out to well-capitalized gentlemen building large sugar plantations. In 1670 a group of these Barbadians founded Charleston (then known as Charles Town), and a steady trade in deerskins and horsehides soon developed with interior natives. A few greedy migrants even dealt in humans by getting local Indians to capture tribal enemies, who were then sold off as slaves to the West Indies.

Picking up on the proprietors' promise, Barbadian migrants who owned slaves brought their chattels with them. Unlike in the Chesapeake area, slavery existed from the outset in South Carolina and took even firmer hold when rice production became the mainstay of economic activity after 1690. By the end of the seventeenth century, English colonists in the southern colonies had constructed their lives around the exportation of cash crops, particularly tobacco and rice, supported increasingly by black slave labor. Over time the institution of slavery gave white southerners a common identity—with serious long-term consequences.

RELIGIOUS DISSENTERS COLONIZE NEW ENGLAND

English men and women migrated to America for many reasons. Certainly the hope of economic betterment was a prime motivating factor, but in New England the initial emphasis reflected more directly on a communal desire to provide a hospitable environment for Calvinist religious values. Beginning in the 1620s New England emerged as a haven for religious dissenters of two types: **separatists,** such as the Pilgrims, and **nonseparatists,** such as the Puritans.

Separatists believed the Church of England to be so corrupt that it could not be salvaged. So as not to compromise their beliefs, their only course was to sever all ties with the Anglican church and establish their own religious communities of like-minded believers.

The dauntless band known as the Pilgrims were separatists from Scrooby Manor, a village in northeastern England. Facing official harassment, they fled to the Netherlands in 1608 but found it difficult to make a decent living there. Furthermore, they worried about their children, who not only were losing their sense of identity as English persons but also appeared "to degenerate and be corrupted" by frequent exposure to various worldly pleasures. As a result, Pilgrim leaders sought a land grant to settle in America, where they could set up their own religious community and worship as they pleased.

In September 1620 the first party of Pilgrims sailed west on the *Mayflower* under a land patent of the Virginia Company. Only one-third of the 102 migrants aboard were Pilgrims. The rest were employees of the London merchant Thomas Weston, who financed the venture in return for an exclusive seven-year monopoly over all trading commodities sent back to England. After surviving nine harrowing, storm-tossed weeks at sea, the *Mayflower* made first landfall on the northern tip of Cape Cod.

Knowing they were well to the north of Virginia territory and outnumbered by "strangers," the Pilgrims drafted a plan of government, called the Mayflower Compact, before proceeding to the mainland in December 1620 and selecting the site of Tisquantum's old Patuxet village for their permanent settlement. The Compact guaranteed settlers the right to elect governing officials to a representative assembly, but only Pilgrim "saints"—those who were church members—could vote. The Pilgrims would tolerate "strangers" in their midst and encourage them to seek God's grace—the basis of church membership—as long as they showed "due submission and obedience" to the authority of the congregation of church members. In this sense the Compact was not an advanced statement of popular government; its purpose was to assure the Pilgrims full political control of Plymouth Colony.

Plymouth Plantation struggled to survive. Under the effective, persistent leadership of Governor William Bradford, the settlers overcame all obstacles. Besides a deadly first winter, the Pilgrims had to reckon with no clear title to their land. In 1621 they obtained a proper patent, but several years passed before they fulfilled their financial obligations to Weston and a variety of other sponsors. They did so mostly by shipping fish and furs back to England.

English Barbadians settled Charleston, South Carolina. The local economy would develop around crops, such as rice, produced by slave labor.

At the outset the Pilgrims worked hard to maintain peace with local Indians. Under Miles Standish, the one professional soldier in their midst, they also trained for war, should serious discord with the natives develop. They certainly did not hesitate to discipline other whites in the region, such as the rowdy band of men at Thomas Morton's "Merry Mount" trading post not far from Plymouth. Not only was Morton selling alcohol and firearms, but his traders were regularly "dancing and frisking together" with native women around a maypole, in addition to "worse practices," according to Bradford. Morton's arming of the natives, as well as the lustful scenes at Merry Mount, incensed the Pilgrims. Above all else, they did not want to face the kind of massacre that had occurred in Virginia during 1622. With Standish in the lead, they closed down the Merry Mount post in 1628 and sent Morton packing off to England.

Slowly but surely the Pilgrim colony began to prosper, as recorded in Bradford's valuable account, *History Of Plymouth Plantation,* which covers the first 26 years of the colony's history. Through all of their adventures and travails, the Pilgrims never lost sight of their original purpose—freedom to worship God according to their own understanding of scripture. Their numbers increased to 7000 persons by 1691, the year they accepted annexation to the much more populous Puritan colony of Massachusetts Bay.

The Rise of Puritan Dissenters at Home

Far more numerous in England were nonseparatists, who wanted to "purify" rather than separate from the Church of England. The Puritans, as these dissenters were known, have often been characterized as prudish, ignorant bigots who hated the thought of having a good time. Modern historical research, however, has shattered this stereotype. The Puritans were reformers who, as recipients of John Calvin's legacy, took Biblical matters seriously. They believed that God's word should order the steps of every person's life. What troubled them most was their conviction that the Protestant Reformation in England had not gone far enough. They viewed the Church of England as "corrupt" in organization and guided by unscriptural doctrine; they longed for far-reaching institutional change that would rid the Anglican church of its imperfections. When church and state leaders harassed them, they responded in various ways, including the planting of a model utopian society—Massachusetts Bay Colony—in New England.

In the early 1600s the Puritans numbered in the hundreds of thousands. Their emphasis upon reading Scripture particularly appealed to literate members of the middle classes and lesser gentry—merchants, skilled craft workers, professionals, and freehold farmers. The Puritans prided themselves on hard work and the pursuit of one's "calling" as a way to glorify the Almighty. They also searched for signs of having earned God's saving grace through a personal conversion experience. The goal was to become one of God's "visible saints" on earth. To be a visible saint meant that a person was fit for church membership.

By comparison, the Church of England, as a state-supported institution, claimed all citizens, regardless of their spiritual nature, as church members. Besides this problem, the Anglican church, from the Puritan perspective, put too much emphasis on ritual. Its elaborate hierarchy of church officials did not include enough educated ministers who understood the Bible, let alone the need to teach parishioners to seek God's grace; rather, Anglican clergymen were the friends and relatives of the well connected. They were like "Mr. Atkins, curate of Romford, thrice presented for a drunkard," "Mr. Goldringe, parson of Laingdon Hills, . . . convicted of fornication," and "Mr. Cuckson, vicar of Linsell, . . . a pilferer, of scandalous life."

In his youth in Scotland, James Stuart, who became King James I, had regular dealings with John

A plaster statue of Governor William Bradford by Cyrus E. Dallin. There is no extant portrait of Bradford.

gland. Laud was particularly adept at persecuting his opponents. In response, the Puritans pushed a bill through Parliament denouncing "popish" practices in church and state. Finally, Charles used his royal prerogatives to disband Parliament and tried to rule by himself between 1629 and 1640, thus contributing to the advent of the bloody English Civil War.

In the late 1620s the Puritans were not ready for rebellion, but some in their numbers had decided upon an "errand into the wilderness." In 1629 they secured a joint-stock charter for the Massachusetts Bay Company. Investors knew they were underwriting the peopling of a utopian religious experiment in America. As for King Charles, the prospect of ridding the realm of thousands of Puritans was incentive enough to give royal approval to the Bay Company charter.

Godly Mission to New England

The Puritans organized their venture carefully. They placed their settlement effort under John Winthrop (1588–1649), a prominent lawyer and landholder. In 1630 some 700 Puritans crowded onto 11 ships and joined Winthrop in sailing to Massachusetts. They were the vanguard of what became the *Great Migration,* or the movement of an estimated 20,000 persons to New England by 1642. These men and women left not as indentured servants but as families fleeing the religious repression and worsening economic conditions of Charles I's England.

More than any other person, John Winthrop worked tirelessly to promote the Puritan mission. Before landing in Massachusetts Bay, he delivered a sermon entitled "A Model of Christian Charity," in which he asserted: "We must consider that we shall be as a **city upon a hill;** the eyes of all people are upon us." The Puritans' mission was to order human existence in the Bay Colony according to God's word. Their example, Winthrop and other company leaders hoped, would inspire England and the rest of Europe to change, thereby causing the full realization of the Protestant Reformation.

Curious events back in England facilitated attempts to build a model society in the wilderness.

John Winthrop led the Puritans to New England, where he served several terms as governor of the Massachusetts Bay Colony.

Knox and his Presbyterian (Scottish Puritan) followers. He developed a decided distaste for religious dissenters. "I will harry them out of the land," James boldly proclaimed after becoming king of England, "or else do worse." Like Queen Elizabeth before him, however, he endured the Puritans. He never felt secure enough in his own authority to test his will against their rapidly expanding influence.

During King James's reign, the Puritans moved aggressively to realize their goals. They built a political base from which to demand church reform by winning elections for seats in Parliament. James put up with their protests, but his son, Charles I, was more confrontational. He named William Laud, whom the Puritans considered a Roman Catholic in Anglican garb, as archbishop of the Church of En-

THE PEOPLE SPEAK

William Bradford's *History of Plymouth Plantation*

William Bradford (1590–1657) was a humble person who served several terms as the governor of Plymouth Plantation. In his spare moments he wrote vivid passages about what he and other Pilgrims experienced in crossing the Atlantic Ocean and building a new colony in the American wilderness. Scholars today regard Bradford's history, which was almost lost to posterity and was not published until the mid-nineteenth century, as a valuable source of information about the Pilgrims' quest to construct a godly society unfettered by Old World corruptions. Bradford's interpretive framework was providential in character. Like his fellow Pilgrims, he believed in an interventionist God who could either protect or destroy human beings. In the two passages that follow, Bradford describes how the Pilgrims survived both their harrowing voyage to America aboard the *Mayflower* and their terrible first winter in New England. For Bradford, God had saved them from destruction, which was proof that their quest to found a new society was a blessed undertaking.

[Aboard the *Mayflower*]

September 6 [1620]. These troubles being blown over, and now all being compact together in one ship, they put to sea again with a prosperous wind, which continued divers days together, which was some encouragement unto them; yet, according to the usual manner, many were afflicted with seasickness. And I may not omit here a special work of God's providence. There was a proud and very profane young man, one of the seamen, of a lusty, able body, which made him the more haughty; he would always be contemning the poor people in their sickness and cursing them daily with grievous execrations; and did not let to tell them that he hoped to help to cast half of them overboard before they came to their journey's end, and to make merry with what they had; and if he were by any gently reproved, he would curse and swear most bitterly. But it pleased God before they came half seas over, to smite this young man with a grievous disease, of which he died in a desperate manner, and so was himself the first that was thrown overboard. Thus his curses light on his own head, and it was an astonishment to all his fellows for they noted it to be the just hand of God upon him.

After they had enjoyed fair winds and weather for a season, they were encountered many times with cross winds and met with many fierce storms with which the ship was shroudly shaken, and her upper works made very leaky; and one of the main beams in the midships was bowed and cracked, which put them in some fear that the ship could not be able to perform the voyage. . . .

But in examining of all opinions, the master and others affirmed they knew the ship to be strong and firm under water; and for the buckling of the main beam, there was a great iron screw the passengers brought out of Holland, which would raise the beam into his place; the which being done, the carpenter and master affirmed that with a post put under it, set firm in the lower deck and otherways bound, he would make it sufficient. . . . So they committed themselves to the will of God and resolved to proceed.

[Disastrous First Winter]

But that which was most sad and lamentable was, that in two or three months' time half of their company died, especially in January and February, being the depth of winter, and wanting houses and other comforts; being infected with the scurvy and other diseases which this long voyage and their inaccommodate condition had brought upon them. So as there died some times two or three of a day in the foresaid time, that of 100 and odd persons, scarce fifty remained. And of these, in the time of most distress, there was but six or seven sound persons who to their great commendations, be it spoken, spared no pains night nor day, but with abundance of toil and hazard of their own health, fetched them wood, made them fires, dressed them meat, made their beds, washed their loathsome clothes, clothed and unclothed them. In a word, did all the homely and necessary offices for them which dainty and queasy stomachs cannot endure to hear named; and all this willingly and cheerfully, without any grudging in the least, showing herein their true love unto their friends and brethren; . . . And yet the Lord so upheld these persons as in this general calamity they were not at all infected either with sickness or lameness. . . .

But I may not here pass by another remarkable passage not to be forgotten. As this calamity fell among the passengers that were to be left here to plant, and were hasted ashore and made to drink water that the seamen might have the more beer, and one in his sickness desiring but a small can of beer, it was answered that if he were their own father he should have none. The disease began to fall amongst them also, so as almost half of their company died before they went away, and many of their officers and lustiest men, as the boatswain, gunner, three quartermasters, the cook and others. At which the Master was something strucken and sent to the sick ashore and told the Governor he should send for beer for them that had need of it, though he drunk water homeward bound. . . .

Source: William Bradford, *Of Plymouth Plantation, 1620–1647,* ed. with introduction by Samuel Eliot Morrison (New York, 1952), 58–59, 77–78.

The Bay Colony charter served as the basis for government in Massachusetts until 1684, when the Crown had the charter nullified because settlers refused to stop acting so independently of England's authority.

For some reason, perhaps because of a well-placed bribe, the Bay Company charter did not specify a location for stockholder (General Court) meetings. Seizing the opportunity, Winthrop and others drafted the Cambridge Agreement in August 1629; they decided to carry the charter with them and hold all stockholder meetings in New England—3000 miles from meddlesome king's officials. Of the stockholders who migrated, all were fervent Puritans, which meant that decision making for the colony would be controlled in General Court sessions by a handful of men fully committed to the Puritan mission.

Once in Massachusetts, the stockholders soon faced challenges to their all-inclusive authority. Typical was a protest in 1632 by settlers who refused to pay taxes under the "bondage" of no voice in government. The solution was to create a category of citizenship known as "freeman." Freemen would be like stockholders; they could participate in government. As with the Pilgrims, however, only male church members gained full citizenship status as voters. The leaders assumed that these visible saints would not subvert the colony's mission.

The government of Massachusetts developed out of this arrangement. As the colony grew, the General Court became an elective assembly with freemen (full church members) from each town sending delegates to Boston to represent local concerns. The governorship, too, was elective on an annual basis, and John Winthrop dominated the office until his death in 1649. Ministers were not eligible for political offices, so the government was not technically a theocracy. Clergymen, however, met occasionally in synods and offered written advice to colony leaders

regarding religious issues, which did affect political decision making.

Initially, Winthrop wanted all settlers to live in towns close to Boston, but with migrants pouring into the colony, that proved impossible. The General Court started to issue town charters, and settlements fanned out in semicircular fashion from Boston into the interior.

Designated proprietors guided the establishment of Puritan towns, emphasizing community control over individual lives. A 1635 law—later repealed—stated that inhabitants had to live within a half mile of the town church. Each family received a house lot near the village green, farmland away from the center of town, and access to pasture land and woodlots. Some towns perpetuated the European open-field system. Families gained title to strips of land in several fields and worked in common with other townspeople to bring in yearly crops. In other towns, families had all their farmland concentrated in one area.

These property arrangements reflected English patterns of land distribution as well as the desire to promote godly behavior, especially since some first-generation settlers were not Puritans. Village life was not wholly restrictive, however, so long as families viewed the Bay Colony, in the words of the Reverend John Cotton, as "the setting forth of God's house, which is His church."

Town leaders promoted harmonious living conditions. They set off lots for taverns, schools, and meeting houses. Taverns served as community centers in which people socialized and cheerfully drank alcohol, which they believed was essential to good health. School lots satisfied concerns about education. The Puritans advocated literacy so that everyone could read Scripture and "understand the principles of religion and . . . laws of the country." (The desire to have a learned clergy led to the founding of Harvard College in 1636.) Beginning in the 1640s, the General Court ordered each town to tax inhabitants to pay for formal schooling in reading and writing for all children. The meeting house was the gathering place for town meetings and church services. Church members had the duty to encourage non-Puritans in their midst to study the Bible, pray fervently, and seek God's grace so that they might also enjoy political and religious rights—as well as eternal salvation.

Testing the Limits of Toleration

The first generation of Puritans worked hard and prospered. Farming was the primary means of gaining a livelihood, although some coastal inhabitants took to shipbuilding, fishing, and mercantile activity. Prosperity did not stand in the way of serious internal controversies. These disagreements suggested how the Puritan system functioned on behalf of orthodoxy—and against diverse opinions—to assure adherence to the wilderness mission.

No Puritan was purer than Roger Williams (1603?–1683). When this well-educated clergyman arrived in Boston in 1631 and announced that "Bishop Laud pursued me out of the land," John Winthrop graciously welcomed him. Soon Williams received an offer to teach in the Boston church, but he refused because of rules about mandatory worship. To hold services with the unconverted in attendance was to

Charged and convicted of spreading "dangerous opinions," Roger Williams was banished from Massachusetts Bay Colony in October 1635.

be no purer than the Church of England. It "stinks in God's nostrils," Williams proclaimed.

So off Williams went, first to Salem and then to Plymouth Colony, where Governor William Bradford and the Pilgrims embraced him. Only the visible saints attended church services in Plymouth. The Pilgrims soon dismissed Williams for "strange opinions" having to do with questions of land ownership. He had become friendly with local Indians and had concluded that any Crown-based land patent was fraudulent—and that Puritans and Pilgrims alike were thieves because they had not purchased their land from the natives. Moving back to Salem, Williams next denounced Bay Colony leaders who meddled in church affairs. So long as churches were subject in any way to political influences, they would be as corrupt as the Church of England.

John Winthrop remained Williams's friend and kept advising him to keep his opinions to himself, but other Puritan leaders had endured enough. Orthodox adherence to the Puritan mission meant that this contentious young minister, no matter how logical in his criticisms, could not be tolerated. With Winthrop's reluctant approval, the General Court banished Williams in October 1635. To avoid being sent back to England, Williams fled to the Narragansett Indians, with whom he spent the winter and from whom he eventually purchased land for a new community—Providence, Rhode Island.

Partly because of Roger Williams's influence, the colony of Rhode Island took form as a center of religious toleration. Settlers there welcomed all faiths, including Judaism, and the government stayed out of matters of personal conscience. Personal conscience was truly sacred, Williams thought, which made him an advance agent for such concepts as religious freedom and separation of church and state.

Meanwhile, others such as Anne Hutchinson (1591–1643), also tested the limits of orthodoxy. Hutchinson was a woman of powerful mind and commanding presence who frightened leaders like John Winthrop. Hutchinson, the mother of 13 children, moved with her family to Boston in 1634, where she served as a midwife. She also spoke openly about her religious views, which had a strong mystical element. Once humans experienced saving grace, she believed, the "Holy Spirit illumines the heart," and God would offer direct revelation. This meant that his true saints no longer needed the church or the state to help order their daily existence.

Such ideas gained the label **Antinomian,** which Puritans defined as against the laws of human governance. To Winthrop, Hutchinson appeared as an ad-

Tried for her controversial religious ideas before the General Court, Anne Hutchinson refused to recant. The court banished her from the Bay Colony.

vocate of social anarchy. She was threatening to ruin the Puritan mission, since human institutions of any kind would have no purpose, except to control the unregenerate. Winthrop viewed the Antinomian crisis as very serious, especially since the movement came to involve large numbers of people.

With Antinomian thinking spreading so rapidly, orthodox Puritans girded themselves for battle. In 1637 Bay Colony clergymen assembled in a synod and denounced Antinomianism as "blasphemous." They also insisted that Hutchinson's brother-in-law, the Reverend John Wheelwright, recant his Antinomian views. Wheelwright held his ground, and he was banished. He and his followers went off to found Exeter, New Hampshire.

Now the target was Hutchinson. Ordered to appear before the General Court, she masterfully defended herself for two days, only to be declared guilty of sedition for dishonoring her spiritual parents, Winthrop and the other magistrates. As "a woman not fit for our society," she too was ban-

ished. In the spring of 1638 she migrated to Rhode Island where she helped establish the community of Portsmouth.

"Hivings Out" Provoke Bloody Indian Relations

For those who accepted mainstream Puritan orthodoxy, Massachusetts was paradise compared to England. But for dissidents like the Antinomians, Bay Colony leaders seemed just as intolerant as Charles I or Archbishop Laud. As a result, they felt compelled to locate elsewhere, and that is how Rhode Island began. Eventually settlers there pulled themselves together into a confederation and, thanks to Roger Williams, gained a separate patent from Parliament in 1644. Then in 1663 King Charles II granted a more generous charter. Local political offices, even including the governorship, were to be elective, and the Crown also declared that no person should ever be "molested, . . . [or] punished for any differences of opinion in matters of religion." This clause made Rhode Island a unique haven for religious freedom in Puritan New England.

Even before John Wheelwright's exodus to New Hampshire, a few hardy settlers had located in that region. Others established themselves along the coast of Maine. Massachusetts tried to maintain control of both areas, but in 1681 New Hampshire became a separate royal colony. The Bay Colony did sustain its authority over Maine by purchasing the land patents of rival claimants. This territory remained a thinly settled appendage of Massachusetts until it gained statehood in 1820.

Connecticut also started to emerge as a Puritan colony during the 1630s. The Reverend Thomas Hooker, who viewed John Winthrop as too dictatorial, led 100 settlers into the Connecticut River Valley in May 1636. By year's end, another 700 Puritans had followed Hooker's path, resulting in the founding of such towns as Hartford, Wethersfield, and Windsor. John Davenport guided a party of London Puritans to Boston in 1637 but after a few months decided that Winthrop was not dictatorial enough. He led his flock to the mouth of the Quinnipiac River, where they established New Haven.

In 1639 the three Connecticut river towns founded by Hooker adopted a plan of general government, known as the Fundamental Orders of Connecticut. Although based on the Bay Colony's political organization, this plan did permit all adult male property holders, not just church members, to vote, a step toward more inclusive franchise rights. Eventually, all the Connecticut settlements came together to form one political unit and gained a Crown charter (1662) as generous as Rhode Island's. Connecticut

Puritans, however, had little interest in encouraging religious diversity; as in Massachusetts, the Congregational church dominated spiritual life.

These "hivings out" from Massachusetts, as Winthrop called them, adversely affected relations with the native populace. A devastating smallpox epidemic in 1633 temporarily delayed Indian resistance. When Hooker's followers moved into the Connecticut River valley, they settled on land claimed by the Pequots, who decided to resist and struck at Wethersfield in April 1637, killing several people. A force of Puritans and Narragansett Indians, who hated the Pequots, retaliated a month later by surrounding and setting fire to the main Pequot village on the Mystic River. Some 400 men, women, and children died in the flames. "Horrible was the stink and scent thereof," wrote one Puritan, but destroying the Pequots "seemed a sweet sacrifice" to assure the peace and safety of those seeking to plant themselves on fertile Connecticut lands.

The Puritans were no worse than Virginians or Carolinians in their treatment of Native Americans. In some ways they tried to be better. The Bay Colony charter mandated that Indians be brought "to the knowledge . . . of the only true God and . . . the Christian faith." Most Puritans ignored this mandate, but the Reverend John Eliot devoted his ministry to converting the natives. Besides translating the Bible into an Algonquian tongue, he established four towns for "praying Indians," which by 1650 held a population of over 1000. Most of these natives did not actually seek conversion. They were remnant members of once vital tribes, and they were trying to survive while retaining as much of their cultural heritage as possible in the face of what had become an irreversible European tide of westward migration.

John Eliot was known as the Puritan Apostle to the Indians. Also shown below is the title page from the Bible as translated by Eliot into an Algonquian tongue.

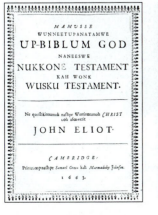

New England Colonies, 1650

FAMILIES, INDIVIDUALS, AND COMMUNITIES: SURVIVING IN EARLY AMERICA

Just as Opechancanough tried to wipe out the Virginians, Metacomet, better known to the Puritans as King Philip, attempted the same in New England. The son of Massasoit, a Wampanoag chieftain who, like Tisquantum, had aided the early Pilgrims, Metacomet felt threatened by the spread of white settlements. In 1671 the Pilgrims hauled him into court on the grounds of plotting against their colony and extracted a statement of submission to English authority. Thoroughly humiliated, Metacomet swore revenge.

The life-and-death struggle known as King Philip's War began during the summer of 1675 when various Indian tribes joined Metacomet's warriors in raiding towns along the Massachusetts-Connecticut frontier. Taking advantage of the settlers' habits, the natives often struck during Sunday church meetings. By early 1676 much of New England was in chaos. Metacomet's forces even attacked towns within 20 miles of Boston, but there were too many Puritans (around 50,000) and not enough Indians (fewer than 12,000) to annihilate the whites. When a "praying" Indian shot and killed Metacomet, King Philip's War rapidly lost its momentum.

Metacomet's warriors had leveled or done substantial damage to several towns, and around 2000 Puritan settlers died in the war. Roughly twice as many Indians lost their lives in what proved to be a futile effort to drive away the ever-expansive English. Still, King Philip's War was not the Indians' last gasp. In a few years remnant native groups started receiving support from the French in Canada and once again began attacking New England's frontier towns.

King Philip's War was very bloody. However, surviving in New England was less difficult than surviving in the Chesapeake region, as comparative experiences graphically reveal.

Life and Death, North and South

During the seventeenth century New England's population grew steadily by natural increase. Most of the 25,000 migrants crossed the ocean before the outbreak of England's civil war in the 1640s; yet by the end of the century some 93,000 colonists inhabited New England. In the Chesapeake, by comparison, as many as 100,000 persons had attempted settlement, but only about 85,000 were living in Virginia and Maryland in 1700. Had these two colonies not had a steady influx of new migrants, they might have ceased to exist altogether.

The Chesapeake colonists experienced shorter, less fertile lives than their New England counterparts. In 1640, for example, Chesapeake migrants had no more than a 50 percent chance of surviving their first year in America. Hot, steamy summers fostered repeated outbreaks of malaria and typhoid fever, which, along with dysentery and poisoning from brackish drinking water, killed thousands. New England's drinking water was safer, although Puritans generally preferred home-brewed beer, and the harsher winter climate helped kill off deadly germs. As a result, the Puritans enjoyed longer, healthier lives.

In New England 20 percent of all Puritan males who survived infancy lived into their seventies. Even with the hazards of childbirth, Puritan women lived almost as long. In Virginia and Maryland, men who survived into their early twenties had reached middle age; on the average, they would not live beyond

Population Comparison of New England and Chesapeake, Mid-1600s

Virulent disease and brackish water in the Chesapeake Bay region resulted in shorter life spans than in New England.

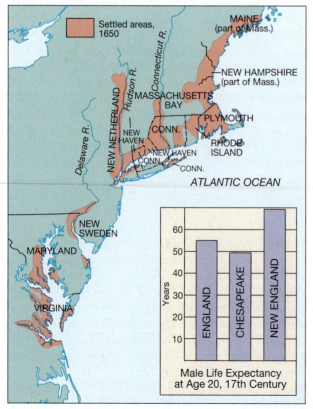

Living grandparents were a unique characteristic of New England families, as illustrated by this portrait of Abigail Gerrish and her grandmother.

their mid-forties. Women in their early twenties could not expect to survive too far beyond their late thirties. Given an average life expectancy of 50 to 55 years back in England, the Chesapeake region deserved its reputation as a human graveyard. In comparison early New England represented a utopian health environment.

Good health sustained life and meant longer marriages and more children. Men in New England were usually in their mid-twenties when they married, and their wives were only two to three years younger. Marriages lasted an average of 25 years before one or the other spouse died. Longevity also resulted in large families, averaging seven to eight children per household. In some locales, nine out of ten children survived infant diseases and grew to adulthood knowing not only their parents but their grandparents as well. Families with living grandparents were a unique characteristic of Puritan New England, reflecting life spans more typical of modern America than early modern Europe.

From a demographic perspective, then, New England families were far more stable and secure than those of the Chesapeake. Because Puritans crossed the Atlantic in family units, the ratio of women to men was more evenly balanced than in Virginia or Maryland, where most migrants were not married. Planters seeking laborers for their tobacco fields preferred young males, which skewed the gender ratio against women and retarded the development of family life. Before 1640 only one woman migrated to the Chesapeake for every six men; and as late as 1700, males still outnumbered females by a ratio of more than three to two.

The system of indentured servitude also affected population patterns. Servants could not marry until they had completed their terms. Typically, women were in their mid-twenties before they first wed, which in combination with short adult life expectancies curbed the numbers of children they could bear. Seventeenth-century Chesapeake families averaged only two to three children, and a quarter of them did not survive their first year of life. Marriages lasted an average of seven years before one or the other spouse died. Two-thirds of all surviving children lost one parent by the age of 18, and one-third lost both. Rarely did children know grandparents. Death was as much a daily reality as life for Chesapeake families, at least until the early eighteenth century when killer diseases stopped wreaking such havoc.

Roles for Men, Women, and Children

The early Puritans looked at their mission as a family undertaking, and they referred to families as "little commonwealths." Not only were families to "be fruitful and multiply," but they also served as agencies of education and religious instruction as well as centers of vocational training and social welfare. Families cared for the destitute and elderly; they took in orphans; and they housed servants and apprentices—all under one roof and subject to the authority of the father.

The Puritans carried **patriarchal** values across the Atlantic and planted them in America. New England law, reflecting its English base, subscribed to the doctrine of **coverture,** or subordinating the legal identity of women to their husbands, who were the undisputed heads of households. Unless there were prenuptial agreements, all property brought by women to marriages belonged to their mates. Husbands were responsible for assuring decency and good order in family life. They also represented their families in all community political, economic, and religious activities.

Wives also had major family responsibilities. "For though the husband be the head of the wife," the Reverend Samuel Willard explained, "yet she is the head of the family." The particular calling of mothers was to nurture their children in godly living, as well as to perform many other tasks—tending gardens, brewing beer, raising chickens, cooking, spinning, and sewing—when not helping in the planting and harvesting of crops.

Most Puritan marriages functioned in at least outward harmony. If serious problems arose, local churches and courts intervened to end the turmoil. Puritan law, again reflecting English precedent, made divorce quite difficult. The only legal grounds were bigamy, desertion, and adultery, and the process required the petitioning of assemblies for bills of separation. A handful of women, most likely battered or abandoned wives, effected their own divorces by setting up separate residences. On occasion the courts brought abusive husbands under control, such as a Maine man who brutally clubbed his wife for refusing to feed the family pig. Some instances occurred when wives defied patriarchalism, including one case involving a Massachusetts woman who faced community censure for beating her husband and even "egging her children to help her, bidding them knock him in the head."

Family friction arose from other sources as well, some of which stemmed from the absolute control that fathers exercised over property and inheritances. If sons wanted to marry and establish separate households, they had to conform to the will of their fathers, who controlled the land. Family patriarchs normally delayed the passing of property until sons had reached their mid-twenties and selected mates acceptable to their parents. Since parents also bestowed dowries on daughters as their contributions to new family units, romantic love had less to

Childbirth in Early America

WHEN the *Mayflower* left Plymouth, England, September 16, 1620, on its historic voyage to the New World, 3 of its 102 passengers were pregnant. Elizabeth Hopkins and Susanna White were each in their seventh month of pregnancy. Mary Norris Allerton was in her second or third month.

Their pregnancies must have been excruciatingly difficult. After a few days of clear weather, the *Mayflower* ran into "fierce storms" that lasted for six of the voyage's nine and a half weeks. For days on end, passengers were confined to the low spaces between decks, while high winds blew away clothing and supplies and the ship tossed and rolled on the heavy seas.

While the ship was still at sea, Elizabeth Hopkins gave birth to a baby boy named Oceanus after his birthplace. Two weeks later, while the Mayflower was anchored off Cape Cod, Susanna White also had a baby boy. He was christened Peregrine, a name that means "pilgrim." Peregrine White would live into his eighties, but Oceanus Hopkins died during the Pilgrims' first winter in Plymouth. In the spring of 1621, Mary Norris Allerton died in childbirth; her baby was stillborn.

Childbirth in colonial America was a difficult and sometimes dangerous experience for women. During the seventeenth and eighteenth centuries, between 1 and 1.5 percent of all births ended in the mother's death—as a result of exhaustion, dehydration, infection, hemorrhage, or convulsions. Since the typical mother gave birth to between five and eight children, her lifetime chances of dying in childbirth ran as high as one in eight. This meant that if a woman had eight female friends, it was likely that one would die in childbirth.

Understandably, many colonial women regarded pregnancy with dread. In their letters, women often referred to childbirth as "the Dreaded apparition," "the greatest of earthly miserys," or "that evel hour I loock forward to with dread." Many, like New England poet Ann Bradstreet, approached childbirth with a fear of impending death. In a poem entitled "Before the Birth of One of Her Children," Bradstreet wrote,

How soon, my Dear, death may my
 steps attend,
How soon't may be thy lot to lose thy
 friend.

In addition to her anxieties about pregnancy, an expectant mother was filled with apprehensions about the survival of her newborn child. The death of a child in infancy was far more common than it is today. In the healthiest seventeenth-century communities, 1 infant in 10 died before the age of 5. In less healthy environments, 3 children in 10 died before their fifth birthday. Puritan minister Cotton Mather saw 8 of his 15 children die before reaching the age of 2. "We have our children taken from us," Mather cried out, "the Desire of our Eyes taken away with a stroke."

Given the high risk of birth complications and infant death, it is not surprising to learn that pregnancy was surrounded by superstitions. It was widely believed that if a mother-to-be looked upon a "horrible spectre" or was startled by a loud noise her child would be disfigured. If a hare jumped in front of her, her child was in danger of suffering a harelip.

There was also fear that if the mother looked at the moon, her child might become a lunatic or sleepwalker. A mother's ungratified longings, it was thought, could cause a miscarriage or leave a mark imprinted on her child's body. At the same time, however, women were expected to continue to perform work until the onset of labor, since hard work supposedly made for an easier labor. Pregnant women regularly spun thread, wove fabric on looms, performed heavy lifting and carrying, milked cows, and slaughtered and salted down meat.

Today, most women give birth in hospitals under close medical supervision. If they wish, women can take anesthetics to relieve labor pangs. During the seventeenth and eighteenth centuries, the process of childbirth was almost wholly different. In colonial America, the typical woman gave birth to her children at home, while female kin and neighbors clustered at her bedside to offer support and encouragement. When the daughter of Samuel Sewall, a Puritan magistrate, gave birth to her first child on the last day of January 1701, at least eight other women were present at her bedside, including her mother, her mother-in-law, a midwife, a nurse, and at least four other neighbors.

Most women were assisted in childbirth not by a doctor but by a midwife. Most midwives were older women who relied on practical experience in delivering children. One midwife, Martha Ballard, who practiced in Augusta, Maine, delivered 996 babies with only 4 recorded fatalities. Skilled midwives were highly valued. Communities tried to attract experienced midwives by offering a

salary or a rent-free house. In addition to assisting in childbirth, midwives helped deliver the offspring of animals, attended the baptisms and burials of infants, and testified in court in cases of bastardy.

During labor, midwives administered no painkillers, except for alcohol. Pain in childbirth was considered God's punishment for Eve's sin of eating the forbidden fruit in the Garden of Eden. Women were merely advised to "arm themselves with patience" and prayer and to try, during labor, to restrain "those dreadful groans and cries which do so much discourage their friends and relations that are near them."

After delivery, new mothers were often treated to a banquet. At one such event, visitors feasted on "boil'd pork, beef, fowls, very good roast beef, turkey-pye, [and] tarts." Women from well-to-do families were then expected to spend three to four weeks in bed convalescing. Their attendants kept the fireplace burning and wrapped them in a heavy blanket in order to help them sweat out "poisons." Women from poorer families were generally back at work in one or two days.

During the second half of the eighteenth century, customs of childbirth began to change. One early sign of change was the growing insistence among women from well-to-do urban families that their children be delivered by male midwives and doctors. Many upper-class families assumed that in a difficult birth trained physicians would make childbirth safer and less painful. In order to justify their presence, physicians tended to take an active role in the birth process. They were much more likely than midwives to intervene in labor with forceps and drugs.

Another important change was the introduction in 1847 of two drugs—ether and chloroform—to relieve pain in childbirth. By the 1920s, the use of anesthesia in childbirth was almost universal. The practice of putting women to sleep during labor contributed to a shift from having children at home to having children in hospitals. In 1900, over 90 percent of all births occurred in the mother's home. But by 1940, over half took place in hospitals and by 1950, the figure had reached 90 percent.

The substitution of doctors for midwives and of hospital delivery for home delivery did little in itself to reduce mortality rates for mothers. It was not until around 1935, when antibiotics and transfusions were introduced, that a sharp reduction in the maternal mortality rate occurred. In 1900 maternal mortality was about 65 times higher than it is today, and not much lower than it had been in the mid-nineteenth century. By World War II, however, death in childbirth had been cut to its present low level.

In recent years, a reaction has occurred against the sterile impersonality of modern hospital delivery. Women today are much more likely than their mothers or grandmothers to want a "natural childbirth." Beginning in the 1960s, a growing number of women elected to bear their children without anesthesia, so that they could be fully conscious during childbirth. Many women also chose to have their husbands or a relative or a friend present during labor and delivery and to bear their children in special "birthing rooms" that provide a homelike environment. In these ways, many contemporary women have sought to recapture the broader support network that characterized childbearing in the colonial past, without sacrificing the tremendous advances that have been made in maternal and infant health.

do with mate selection than parental desires to unite particular family names and estates.

Puritans expected brides and grooms to learn to love one another as they went about their duty of conceiving and raising the next generation of children. In most cases spouses did develop lasting affection for one another, as captured by the gifted Puritan poet Anne Bradstreet in 1666 when she wrote to her "Dear and loving Husband":

> If ever two were one, then surely we.
> If ever man were lov'd by wife, then thee;
> If ever wife was happy in a man,
> Compare with me the women if you can.

Young adults who openly defied patriarchal authority were rare. Also unusual were instances of illegitimate children, despite the lengthy gap between puberty and marriage. As measured by illegitimate births, premarital sex could not have been that common in early New England. This is not a surprising finding among people living in closely controlled communities and seeking to honor the Almighty by reforming human society.

The experiences of seventeenth-century Chesapeake colonists were very different. The system of indentured servitude was open to abuse. Free planters ruled as patriarchs but with no sense of nurturing the next generation; rather, they presumed they were dealing with "simple people" who "professed idleness and will rather beg than work," as a contemporary claimed. The goal was to get as much labor as possible out of servants, since 40 percent died before completing their contracts. Disease was the major killer, but hard-driving planters also contributed to many early deaths.

Servants responded to cruel treatment in various ways. A few committed suicide. Others, like John Punch, ran away. Some killed farm animals, set buildings on fire, or broke tools. Local laws, as drafted by freeholding planters, specified harsh penalties. Besides floggings and brandings, resisting servants faced long extensions of service, as one unfortunate man learned after he killed three pigs belonging to his master. The court added six years to his term of service.

Indentured servitude also inhibited family life. Since servants could not marry, the likelihood of illicit sexual activity increased. Quite frequently, women became the unwilling sexual partners of lustful masters or male servants. Margerie Goold, for example, warded off attempted rape by her master in 1663, but another servant, Elizabeth Wild, was less successful. The planter, however, helped her induce an abortion. One-fifth of Maryland's indentured females faced charges of "bastardy," reflecting both a shortage of women and a labor system controlled by all-powerful masters. Finally in 1692, Virginia officials tried to improve the situation by adopting a statute that mandated harsh penalties for "dissolute masters" getting "their maids with child."

Widows and widowers in colonial America often remarried quickly, in the process creating households of persons of varying ages, many of whom might have no blood relation to one another.

Still, the fate of female and male servants was not always abuse or death. Some survived, gained title to land, and enjoyed, however briefly, personal freedom in America. A few women, usually widows, acquired influence. Margaret Brent, for example, controlled over 1000 acres in Maryland and served as the executor of Governor Leonard Calvert's estate in 1647. She even dared to demand the right to vote, a plea dismissed by male legislators.

Brent's case suggests that high death rates in combination with an unbalanced sex ratio may have, at least temporarily, enhanced the status of some Chesapeake women. English and colonial law recognized the category of *femes sole*, which permitted single, adult women and widows to own and manage property and households for themselves. Chesapeake women who outlived two or three husbands could acquire significant holdings through inheritances and then maintain control by requiring prenuptial contracts from future spouses. Once married, however, any property not so protected fell to new husbands because of *coverture*.

Since widowed mothers could presume they would outlive new husbands, most prenuptial contracts protected property for children by previous marriages. Indeed, few children grew to adulthood without burying one or both parents, and there were extreme cases like that of Agatha Vause, a Virginia child whose father, two stepfathers, mother, and guardian uncle all died before she was 11 years old.

The fragility of Chesapeake life resulted in complex family genealogies with some households containing children from three or four marriages. In some instances local Orphans' Courts had to take charge because all adult relatives had died. Because parents did not live that long, children quite often received their inheritances by their late teens, much earlier than in New England. This advantage meant only that economic independence, like death, came earlier in life.

COMMERCIAL VALUES AND THE RISE OF CHATTEL SLAVERY

By 1650 signs were abundant that the Puritan mission was in trouble. From the outset many non-Puritan settlers, including merchants in Boston, had shunned the religious values of the Bay Colony's founders. By the 1660s children and grandchildren of the migrating generation displayed less zeal about earning God's grace; they were becoming more like southern settlers in their eagerness to get ahead economically. By 1700 their search for worldly prosperity even brought some New Englanders into the international slave trade.

Declension in New England

Declension, or movement away from the ideals of the Bay Colony's founding fathers, resulted in tensions between settlers adhering to the original mission and those attracted to rising commercial values. Clergymen proposed a major compromise known as the **Half-Way Covenant** in 1662. The Covenant recognized that many children were not preparing for salvation, a necessary condition for full church membership, as their parents had done. The question was how to keep them—and their offspring—aspiring toward a spiritual life. The solution was half-way membership, which permitted the baptism of the children and grandchildren of professing saints. If still in the church, ministers and full members could continue to urge them to focus their lives on seeking God's eternal rewards.

Many communities disdained the Half-Way Covenant because of what it implied about changing values. As one minister wrote, too many individuals were acting "as if the Lord had no further work for his people to do but every bird to feather his own nest." With the passage of time, however, most accepted the covenant to help preserve some semblance of a godly society in New England.

Spreading commercial values took hold for many reasons, including the natural abundance of the New England environment and an inability to sustain fervency of purpose among American-born offspring who had not personally felt the religious repression of early Stuart England. Also, Puritans back in England, after overthrowing Charles I, generally ignored the model society in America, which left the impression that the mission had been futile, that no one back in Europe really cared.

The transition in values occurred gradually, as shown in various towns where families bought and sold common field strips so that all of their landholdings were in one place. The next step was to build homes on these sites and become "outlivers," certainly a more efficient way to practice agriculture, yet also a statement that making one's living was more important than daily participation in village life—with its emphasis on laboring together in God's love.

In Boston and other port towns, such as Salem, merchants gained increasing community stature because of their wealth. By the early eighteenth century some of them were earning profits by participating in the African slave trade. Retinues of household servants or, more properly, slaves taken from Africa, symbolized their newfound status.

Clergymen disapproved of these trends. Their sermons took on the tone of "jeremiads," modeled on the prophet Jeremiah who kept urging Israel to return to the path of godliness. In Calvinist fashion, they warned of divine retribution or "afflictions" from the Almighty, and they pointed to events like King Philip's War as proof that Jehovah was punishing New England. In 1679 the ministers met in another synod and listed several problems, everything from working on the Sabbath to swearing in public and sleeping during sermons. Human competitiveness and contention, they sadly concluded, were in ascendance. Worse yet, the populace, in its rush to garner worldly riches, showed little concern that Winthrop's "city upon a hill" was becoming the home of the acquisitive Yankee trader.

Stabilizing Life in the Chesapeake Region

By 1675 certain trends indicated that life in Maryland and Virginia could be something more than brief and unkind. The death rate was dropping; more children were surviving; the gender ratio was starting to balance out; and life expectancy was rising. By the early 1700s Chesapeake residents were living well into their fifties. This figure was comparable to longevity estimates for England but still 10 to 15 years shorter than that of New England. The patterns also indicate greater family stability, as shown by longer marriages and more children.

Not only did life become more stable, but also an elite group of families, controlling significant property and wealth, had begun to emerge. By 1700 the great tidewater families—the Byrds, Carters, Fitzhughs, Lees, and Randolphs, among others—were making their presence felt and had started to dominate social and political affairs in the Chesapeake area. These gentleman-planters aped the lifestyle of England's rural gentry class. They constructed lavish manor houses from which they ruled over their plantation estates, dispensing hospitality and wisdom as the most illustrious and powerful residents of their tobacco-producing region.

Such a person was William Byrd II (1674–1744), who inherited 26,000 fertile acres along the James River in 1705. He built the magnificent Westover plantation, raised a large family, served on the governor's council, and assumed, as he wrote to an English correspondent, that he was "one of the patriarchs" of Virginia society. By the time of his death, Byrd had holdings of 180,000 acres, and he owned at least 200 slaves.

Lavish estates like Westover plantation, built by William Byrd II on the James River, illustrate the wealth and social dominance of rising gentleman-planters in Virginia.

Byrd read widely, put together an impressive personal library, and wrote extensively on any subject that interested him. His "secret" diaries describe how he treated others, including his wife, Lucy Parke Byrd. When they argued, Byrd on occasion demonstrated his presumed masculine superiority with sexual bravado. In 1710 "a little quarrel" was "reconciled with a flourish . . . performed on the billiard table." Byrd's behavior was part of his assertive, self-confident manner. He was the master of everything on his magnificent plantation, making him a patriarch of the realm of Virginia.

For every great planter, there were dozens of small farmers who lacked the wealth to obtain land, slaves, and high status in society. Most eked out bare livings, yet they dreamed of the day when they, or their children, might live in the style of a William Byrd. Meanwhile, they deferred to their "betters" among the planter elite, who in turn "treated" them to large quantities of alcohol on election days and expressed gentlemanly concern about the welfare of their families. Such behavior was part of an ongoing bonding ritual among white inhabitants who, no matter how high or low in status, considered themselves superior to black slaves—whose numbers were now growing rapidly on the bottom rung of Maryland and Virginia society.

The Beginnings of American Slavery

The system of **perpetual servitude** that shaped the lives of persons of African heritage like John Punch and Emmanuel had ancient roots. However, slavery was dying out in much of Europe by the fifteenth century. Then the Portuguese mariners of Prince Henry started coasting along sub-Saharan Africa, making contact with various peoples and cultures, some of whom were willing to barter in human flesh as well as in gold and ivory. The first Portuguese expeditions represented the small beginnings of a trade that forcibly relocated an estimated 10 million Africans to the Americas during the next 350 years.

Africa, a continent of immense geographical diversity with vast deserts, grassy plains, and tropical rain forests, had a population of about 50 million people at the time of Columbus. Mighty kingdoms like Ghana had flourished in West Africa but had been overrun by Muslims from the north during the eleventh century, resulting in the empire of Mali and its magnificent trading and learning center, Timbuktu. Farther to the south in Guinea were smaller kingdoms such as Benin in which the populace farmed or worked at such crafts as pottery making, weaving, and metalworking. These cultures valued family life and were mostly matrilineal in the organization of kinship networks. They also had well-developed political systems and legal codes.

In addition, these kingdoms thrived on elaborate regional trading networks, which the Portuguese and other Europeans, offering guns and various iron products, tapped into easily. As time passed Europeans came to identify certain coastal areas with particular commodities. Upper Guinea contained the rice and grain coasts, and Lower Guinea the ivory, gold, and slave coasts.

Early modern European traders learned that some Africans held slaves—mainly individuals captured in tribal wars—who had the status of family members. The Portuguese found that coastal chiefs were willing to trade humans for European firearms, which they could use when attacking interior kingdoms. A new objective of this tribal warfare became the capturing of peoples who would then be transported back to the coast and sold into slavery in exchange for yet more European goods.

Once this vicious slave trading cycle began, it expanded rapidly. Decade after decade, thousands of Africans experienced the agony of being shackled in collars and ankle chains; marched in gangs, or *coffles*, to the coast; thrown into *barracoons*, or slave pens; and then packed aboard waiting European ships destined for ports of call in the Americas. One slave, Olaudah Equiano, who made the voyage during the eighteenth century, recalled the "loathsomeness of the stench" from overcrowded conditions, which made him "so sick and low" that he neither was "able to eat, nor had . . . the desire to taste anything."

Some Africans resisted by refusing to eat and starved to death. In response the Europeans made tools to break jaws and pry open mouths so that food could be jammed down unwilling throats. Other re-

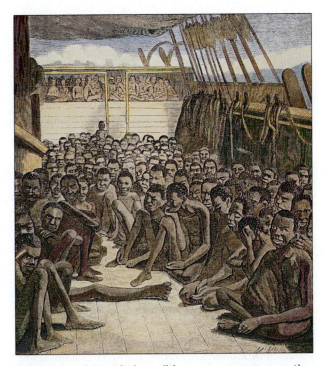

Cramped and crowded conditions were common on the decks of slave vessels. As shown here, slaves invariably became emaciated from deficient food during their passage across the Atlantic.

sisters jumped overboard and drowned, but the Europeans soon placed large nets on the sides of their vessels. About 15 percent of those Africans forced onto slave ships did not survive. Those who did had to reckon with the frightening realization of having lost everything familiar in their lives—with no knowledge of what might happen next.

During the sixteenth century the Spanish and Portuguese started pouring Africans into their colonies. These slaves were not thought of as family members, but as disposable beings whose energy was to be used up in mining or agricultural operations. High mortality rates among the migrants did not seem to bother their European masters because more slave ships kept appearing on the horizon. As a result, areas such as Brazil and the West Indian sugar islands earned deserved reputations as centers of human exploitation and death.

Shifting to Slavery in Maryland and Virginia

The English North American colonies existed at the outer edge of the African slave trade until the very end of the seventeenth century. In 1650 the popula-

West African Kingdoms, Late 1400s

European and Portuguese traders in the late 1400s found the West African kingdoms rich with rice, gold, and slaves.

tion of Virginia approached 15,000 settlers, including only 500 persons of African descent. By comparison, the English sugar colony of Barbados already held 10,000 slaves, a majority of the population. English Barbadians had started to model their economy on that of other Caribbean sugar islands, whereas Virginians, with a steady supply of indentured servants, had not yet made the transition to slave labor.

Factors supporting a shift, however, were present by the 1640s, as evidenced in laws discriminating against Africans and court cases involving blacks like John Punch and Emmanuel. During the same decade, a few Chesapeake planters started to invest in Africans. Governor Leonard Calvert of Maryland, for example, asked "John Skinner mariner" to ship him "fourteen negro-men-slaves and three women-slaves." Planters like Calvert were ahead of their time because slaves cost significantly more to purchase than indentured servants. Yet for those who invested, they owned their laborers for their lifetimes and did not have to pay "freedom dues." Moreover, they soon discovered that Africans, having built up immunities to tropical diseases like malaria and typhoid fever, generally lived longer than white servants. Resistance to such diseases made Africans a better long-term investment, at least for well-capitalized planters.

Then in the 1660s two additional factors spurred on the shift toward slave labor. First, Virginia legislators in 1662 decreed that slavery was an inheritable status, "according to the condition of the mother." The law made yet unborn generations subject to slavery, a powerful incentive for risking an initial investment in human chattels. If slaves kept reproducing, planters would control a never-ending supply of laborers. Second, the numbers of new indentured servants began to shrink as economic conditions improved in England. With expanded opportunities for work, poorer citizens were less willing to risk life and limb for a chance at economic independence in America.

Also assisting the shift was the chartering of the Royal African Company in 1672 to develop England's role in the slave trade. Royal African vessels soon made regular visits to Chesapeake Bay. As the supply of slaves increased, asking prices started to drop—at the very time that the cost of buying indentured servants began to climb. In 1698 the company lost its monopoly, which spurred some New England traders to engage actively in the slave trade. Yankee merchants now had something in common with Chesapeake planters besides English roots and language. Both were profiting from the international traffic in human beings.

Population figures explain the rest. In 1670 Virginia contained about 40,000 settlers, which included an estimated 6000 white servants and 2000 black slaves. By 1700 the number of slaves had grown to 16,000, and by 1750 white Virginians owned 120,000 slaves—about 40 percent of the total population. The same general pattern characterized Maryland, where by 1750 there were 40,000 slaves—some 30 percent of the populace. In the Chesapeake area, indentured servitude was by then a moribund institution. White planters, great and small, now measured their wealth and status in terms of plantations and slaves owned and managed.

The World the Slaves Made

Historians once argued that slavery in English North America was harsher than the Spanish-American version. They pointed to the moderating influence of the Roman Catholic church, which mandated legal recognition of slave marriages as a sacramental right, and ancient legal precedents influencing Spanish law, which meant that slaves could earn wages for their labor in off hours and buy their freedom. Although Spanish laws may have been more humane, daily working and living conditions were not. Most slaves destined for Caribbean or South American settlements did not survive long enough to marry or enjoy other legal rights. By contrast, in North America, where early deaths were not as pervasive among migrants, slaves more easily reconstructed meaningful lives for themselves.

About 10 percent of those Africans coming to the colonies entered northern port towns like Boston and became domestic servants, craft workers, or in rare cases, farmhands out in the countryside. The rest labored in the South, mostly on small plantations where field work dominated their existence. These slaves had little chance for family life, at least in the early years, because planters purchased an average of three males for every female. In addition, southern law did not recognize slave marriages—in case masters wanted to sell off some of their chattels. Anglican church leaders accepted the situation. In New England, by comparison, the Congregational church insisted that slave marriages be recognized and respected by masters.

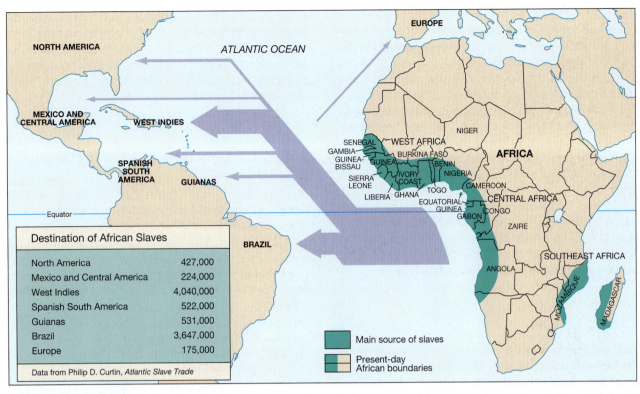

Destination of African Slaves	
North America	427,000
Mexico and Central America	224,000
West Indies	4,040,000
Spanish South America	522,000
Guianas	531,000
Brazil	3,647,000
Europe	175,000

Data from Philip D. Curtin, *Atlantic Slave Trade*

■ Main source of slaves

Present-day African boundaries

African Slave Trade

Central and South America represented the most common destination for slaves traded to the Americas between 1520 and 1810.

Facing a loss of personal freedom and pervasive racism, southern slaves made separate lives for themselves, particularly on large plantations where their substantial numbers allowed them to form their own communities in the slave quarters. Here they maintained African cultural traditions and developed distinctive forms of music. In South Carolina's sea island region, slaves continued to give their children African names, and they worked out a distinct dialect, known as *Gullah*, to communicate with one another in a unique combination of African and English sounds. In many places, female slaves managed slave quarter life, thus maintaining the matrilineal nature of African kinship ties.

Contrary to white owners' contentions, most slaves did not engage in promiscuous sexual relations. Whenever possible, they selected mates and had large families, even if slave quarter marriages had no standing in law. As a consequence, the ratio of men to women balanced itself out over time and in turn sped up natural population growth. Large families became a source of slave community pride. Natural increase also undercut the need to continue heavy importation of chattels. As a result, only 5 percent—an estimated 399,000 persons—of all imported Africans ended up in English North America.

Such comparisons are relative. Nowhere in the Americas did slavery function in an uplifting fashion. Although blacks on large southern plantations carried on traditional cultural practices, they still had to face masters or overseers who might whip them, sell off their children, or maim or kill them if they tried to run

The drawing *Old Plantation* shows that slaves, even though defined as property and without legal rights, succeeded in making meaningful lives for themselves in their own quarters.

away. Always present was the realization that whites considered them to be a subhuman species of property, which left scant room for human dignity in life beyond the slave quarters.

Despite the oppression, Africans made substantial contributions to colonial life. In South Carolina, for example, many early slave migrants were expert at raising and herding animals, and they helped develop and support a thriving trade in cattle. Others who came from the rice coast region of Africa used their agricultural skills in fostering South Carolina's emergence as a major center of rice production. These and many other contributions went unrecognized in the rush for profits in the maturing commercial world of the American colonies, except in the ironic sense of creating further demand among white settlers for additional black laborers.

CONCLUSION

Although most Africans adapted to slavery, some remained defiant. They stole food, broke farm tools, or in a few cases poisoned their masters. In rare instances they resorted to rebellion. In September 1739 twenty slaves in the Stono River area of South Carolina rose up, seized some weapons, killed a few whites, and started marching toward Spanish Florida. Within a few days frightened planters rallied together and crushed the Stono uprising by shooting or hanging the rebels.

The South Carolina legislature soon approved a more repressive slave code, which all but restricted the movement of blacks from their home plantations. No legislator gave thought to the other possibility, which was to abandon the institution of slavery. Even though long in development, slavery now supported southern plantation agriculture and the production of such cash crops as tobacco and rice.

Just as the southern colonies had made a fateful shift from servitude to slavery, New Englanders experienced another kind of transition. Slowly but surely, they had forsaken their utopian, religiously oriented mission into the wilderness. Service to mammon had started to replace loyalty to God and community. The religious side would remain, but the fervor of a nobler spiritual mission was in rapid decline by 1700. Material gain was now a quality shared by white English colonists in America— North and South.

Prosperity, which had come after so much travail and death, promoted a sense of unlimited opportunity in profiting from the abundance of the American environment. Other realities, however, were also tak-

ing shape. The colonists had learned that Crown officials now expected them to conform to new laws governing the emerging English empire. Because of these imperial rules, much turmoil lay ahead for the diversity of peoples now inhabiting English North America.

SUGGESTIONS FOR FURTHER READING

Ira Berlin, *Many Thousands Gone: The First Two Centuries of Slavery in North America* (1998). Detailed, highly readable account of the diverse and complex experiences of slaves during the colonial period and beyond.

David Hackett Fischer, *Albion's Seed: Four British Folkways in America* (1989). Broad-ranging investigation of the implantation of traditional cultural values and practices in North America by distinct groups of English-speaking colonists.

David D. Hall, *Worlds of Wonder, Days of Judgment: Popular Religious Belief in Early New England* (1990). Probing analysis of the mentality of ordinary Puritan settlers in relation to the publicly enunciated ideals of their leaders.

James Horn, *Adapting to a New World: English Society in the Seventeenth-Century Chesapeake* (1994). Comprehensive examination of migratory patterns and the construction of English society in the Chesapeake Bay region.

Jill Lepore, *The Name of War: King Philip's War and the Origins of American Identity* (1998). An evocative study of recollections and understanding of one of the bloodiest wars to take place on American soil.

Edmund S. Morgan, *American Slavery, American Freedom: The Ordeal of Colonial Virginia* (1975). Valuable discussion of the emergence of slavery in Virginia and the paradoxical evolution of freedom and slavery in British North America.

———, *The Puritan Dilemma: The Story of John Winthrop*, 2d ed. (1999). Classic introduction to Puritan religious beliefs and their implementation in the structure of life in Massachusetts Bay Colony.

Mary Beth Norton, *Founding Mothers and Fathers: Gendered Power and the Forming of American Society* (1996). A probing analysis of the evolution of gender relations in New England and the Chesapeake Bay region during the seventeenth century.

Peter H. Wood, *Black Majority: Negroes in Colonial South Carolina from 1670 Through the Stono Rebellion* (1974). Influential exploration of the lives and contributions of African-American slaves in the development of this Deep South colony.

Overviews and Surveys

Sydney E. Ahlstrom, *A Religious History of the American People* (1972); Bernard Bailyn, *Education in the Forming of American Society* (1960); Thomas Bender, *Community and*

Chronology
OF KEY EVENTS

1608 Pilgrims flee to Holland to avoid religious persecution in England

1617 Virginia begins to export tobacco

1619 The first persons of African descent arrive in Virginia; first representative assembly in English North America meets in Jamestown

1620 Pilgrims arrive at Cape Cod on the *Mayflower* and establish Plymouth Colony

1622 Opechancanough's Indians fail in an attempt to massacre all English settlers in Virginia

1624 English Crown takes control of Virginia; the Dutch begin to settle New York and name their colony New Netherland

1630 Puritans establish the Massachusetts Bay Colony

1632 Maryland becomes the first proprietary colony

1635 Leaders in Massachusetts Bay Colony banish Roger Williams

1636 Harvard College is founded; first permanent English settlements established in Connecticut and Rhode Island

1637–1638 Anne Hutchinson is convicted of heresy in Massachusetts and flees to Rhode Island

1640s Legal status of African Americans in the Chesapeake Bay region deteriorates

1644 Second attempted Native American massacre of Virginia colonists fails

1646 Powhatan's Confederacy accepts English rule

1647 Massachusetts Bay Colony adopts the first public school law in the colonies

1649 Maryland's Act of Toleration affirms religious freedom for Christians in the colony; Charles I of England is beheaded

1660 Charles II is restored to the English throne

1664 English conquer New Netherland and rename the colony New York

1675–1676 King Philip's (Metacomet's) War inflicts heavy casualties on New Englanders

1681–1682 William Penn founds Pennsylvania as a "holy experiment" in which diverse groups of people can live together harmoniously

1688 Glorious Revolution drives James II from England

1732 Georgia is founded as a haven for debtors and a buffer colony against Spanish Florida

1739 Stono slave uprising occurs in South Carolina

Social Change in America (1978); Rowland Berthoff, *An Unsettled People: Social Order and Disorder in American History* (1971); Richard D. Brown, *Modernization: The Transformation of American Life, 1600–1865* (1976); David Brion Davis, *The Problem of Slavery in Western Culture* (1988), and *Slavery and Human Progress* (1984); John Hope Franklin and Alfred A. Moss, Jr., *From Slavery to Freedom: A History of African Americans,* 7th ed. (1994); Philip Greven, *The Protestant Temperament: Patterns of Child-Rearing, Religious Experience, and the Self in Early America* (1977); E. Brooks Holifield, *Era of Persuasion: American Thought and Culture, 1521–1680* (1989); Nathan I. Huggins, *Black Odyssey: The Afro-American Ordeal in Slavery* (1977); Steven Mintz and Susan Kellogg, *Domestic Revolutions: A Social History of American Family Life* (1988); Edwin J. Perkins, *The Economy of Colonial America,* 2d ed. (1988); John E. Pomfret and Floyd M. Shumway, *Founding the American Colonies, 1583–1660* (1970); Helena M. Wall, *Fierce Communion; Fam-*

ily and Community in Early America (1990); Robert V. Wells, *The Population of the British Colonies in America before 1776: A Survey of Census Data* (1975).

From Settlements to Societies in the South

Carl Bridenbaugh, *Myths and Realities: Societies of the Colonial South* (1952); Paul G. E. Clemens, *The Atlantic Economy and Colonial Maryland's Eastern Shore: From Tobacco to Grain* (1980); Converse D. Clowse, *Economic Beginnings of Colonial South Carolina, 1670–1730* (1971); Wesley Frank Craven, *The Southern Colonies in the Seventeenth Century, 1607–1689* (1949); David Galenson, *White Servitude in Colonial America: An Economic Analysis* (1981); David W. Jordan, *Foundations of Representative Government in Maryland, 1632–1715* (1987); Aubrey C. Land et al., eds., *Law, Society, and Politics in Early Maryland* (1977); Richard L. Morton, *Colonial Virginia*, 2 vols. (1960); James R. Perry, *The Formation of a Society on Virginia's Eastern Shore, 1615–1655* (1990); David B. Quinn, ed., *Early Maryland in a Wider World* (1982); M. Eugene Sirmans, *Colonial South Carolina, A Political History, 1663–1763* (1966); Abbot E. Smith, *Colonists in Bondage: White Servitude and Convict Labor in America, 1607–1776* (1971).

Religious Dissenters Colonize New England

David Grayson Allen, *In English Ways: The Movement of Societies and the Transferal of English Local Law and Custom to Massachusetts Bay in the Seventeenth Century* (1981); Bernard Bailyn, *The New England Merchants in the Seventeenth Century* (1955); Francis J. Bremer, *The Puritan Experiment* (1995); Charles E. Clark, *The Eastern Frontier: The Settlement of Northern New England, 1610–1763* (1970); Charles L. Cohen, *God's Caress: The Psychology of Puritan Relgious Experience* (1986); Andrew Delbanco, *The Puritan Ordeal* (1989); Kai T. Erikson, *Wayward Puritans: A Study in the Sociology of Deviance* (1966); Stephen Foster, *The Long Argument: English Puritanism and the Shaping of New England Culture, 1570–1700* (1991), and *Their Solitary Way: The Puritan Social Ethic in the First Century of Settlement in New England* (1971); Richard P. Gildrie, *The Profane, the Civil, & the Godly: The Reformation of Manners in Orthodox New England, 1679–1749* (1994); Philip F. Gura, *A Glimpse of Sion's Glory: Puritan Radicalism in New England, 1620–1660* (1984); David D. Hall, *The Faithful Shepherd; A History of the New England Ministry in the Seventeenth Century* (1972); James Holstun, *A Rational Millennium: Puritan Utopias of Seventeenth-Century England and America* (1987); Stephen Innes, *Creating the Commonwealth: The Economic Culture of Puritan New England* (1995); Sydney V. James, *Colonial Rhode Island: A History* (1975); Lyle Koehler, *A Search for Power: The "Weaker Sex" in Seventeenth-Century New England* (1980); David Konig, *Law and Society in Puritan Massachusetts: Essex County, 1629–1692* (1979); George D. Langdon, Jr., *Pilgrim Colony: A History of New Plymouth 1620–1691* (1966); John Frederick Martin, *Profits in the Wilderness: Entre-*

preneurship and the Founding of New England Towns in the Seventeenth Century (1991); Perry Miller, *Orthodoxy in Massachusetts, 1630–1650* (1961), *The New England Mind: The Seventeenth Century* (1953), and *The New England Mind: From Colony to Province* (1982); Edmund S. Morgan, *Visible Saints: The History of a Puritan Idea* (1963); Darrett B. Rutman, *American Puritanism: Faith and Practice* (1970); William K. B. Stoever, *A Faire and Easie Way to Heaven: Covenant Theology and Antinomianism in Early Massachusetts* (1988); Harry S. Stout, *The New England Soul: Preaching and Religious Culture in Colonial New England* (1986); Laurel Thatcher Ulrich, *Good Wives: Image and Reality in the Lives of Women in Northern New England, 1650–1750* (1982); David E. Van Deventer, *The Emergence of Provincial New Hampshire, 1623–1741* (1976); Robert E. Wall, Jr., *Massachusetts Bay: The Crucial Decade, 1640–1650* (1972).

Families, Individuals, and Communities: Surviving in Early America

Lois Green Carr et al., eds., *Colonial Chesapeake Society* (1988), and Carr et al., *Robert Cole's World: Agriculture and Society in Early Maryland* (1991); Wesley Frank Craven, *White, Red, and Black: The Seventeenth-Century Virginian* (1971); John Demos, *A Little Commonwealth: Family Life in Plymouth Colony* (1970); Philip J. Greven, Jr., *Four Generations: Population, Land, and Family in Colonial Andover, Massachusetts* (1970); Stephen Innes, *Labor in a New Land: Economy and Society in Seventeenth-Century Springfield* (1983); Douglas E. Leach, *Flintlock and Tomahawk: New England in King Philip's War* (1958); Judith Walzer Leavitt, *Brought to Bed: Childbearing in America, 1750–1950* (1986); Kenneth A. Lockridge, *A New England Town: The First Hundred Years, Dedham, Massachusetts, 1636–1736*, rev. ed. (1985); Paul R. Lucas, *Valley of Discord: Church and Society Along the Connecticut River, 1636–1725* (1976); Gloria L. Main, *Tobacco Colony: Life in Early Maryland, 1650–1720* (1982); Sally G. McMillen, *Motherhood in the Old South: Pregnancy, Childbirth, and Infant Rearing* (1990); Edmund S. Morgan, *The Puritan Family: Religion and Domestic Relations in Seventeenth-Century New England*, rev. ed. (1966); Darrett B. Rutman, *Winthrop's Boston: Portrait of a Puritan Town, 1630–1649* (1965), and with Anita H. Rutman, *A Place in Time: Middlesex County, Virginia, 1650–1750*, 2 vols. (1984); Catherine M. Scholten, *Childbearing in American Society* (1985); David E. Stannard, *The Puritan Way of Death* (1977); Thad W. Tate and David L. Ammerman, eds., *The Chesapeake in the Seventeenth Century: Essays on Anglo-American Society* (1979); Roger Thompson, *Sex in Middlesex: Popular Mores in a Massachusetts County, 1649–1699* (1986); Robert V. Wells, *Revolutions in Americans' Lives: A Demographic Perspective on the History of Americans, Their Families, and Their Society* (1982).

Commercial Values and the Rise of Chattel Slavery

T. H. Breen and Stephen Innes, *"Myne Owne Ground": Race and Freedom on Virginia's Eastern Shore, 1640–1676* (1980); Jay Coughtry, *The Notorious Triangle: Rhode Island and the*

African Slave Trade 1700–1807 (1981); Basil Davidson, *The African Genius: An Introduction to African Cultural and Social History* (1969); Richard S. Dunn, *Sugar and Slaves: The Rise of the Planter Class in the English West Indies, 1624–1713* (1972); Winthrop D. Jordan, *White over Black: American Attitudes Toward the Negro, 1550–1812* (1968); Herbert S. Klein, *Slavery in the Americas: A Comparative Study of Virginia and Cuba* (1967), and *The Middle Passage: Comparative Studies in the Atlantic Slave Trade* (1978); Allan Kulikoff, *Tobacco and Slaves: The Development of Southern Cultures in the Chesapeake, 1680–1800* (1986); Daniel C. Littlefield, *Rice and Slaves: Ethnicity and the Slave Trade in Colonial South Carolina* (1981); Edgar J. McManus, *Black Bondage in the North* (1973); Gerald W. Mullin, *Flight and Rebellion: Slave Resistance in Eighteenth-Century Virginia* (1972); Michael Mullin, *Africa in America: Slave Acculturation and Resistance in the American South and the British Caribbean, 1736–1831* (1992); Richard Olaniyan, ed., *African History and Culture* (1982); James Rawley, *The Transatlantic Slave Trade: A History* (1981); Daniel Blake Smith, *Inside the Great House: Planter Family Life in Eighteenth-Century Chesapeake Society* (1980); Hugh Thomas, *The Slave Trade: The Atlantic Slave Trade, 1440–1870* (1997); Donald R. Wright, *African Americans in the Colonial Era: From African Origins through the American Revolution* (1990).

Biographies

Kenneth A. Lockridge, *The Diary, and Life, of William Byrd II of Virginia, 1674–1744* (1987); Robert Middlekauff, *The Mathers: Three Generations of Puritan Intellectuals, 1596–1728* (1971); Edmund S. Morgan, *Roger Williams: The Church and the State* (1967); Bradford Smith, *Bradford of Plymouth* (1951).

INTERNET RESOURCES

The Plymouth Colony Archive Project at the University of Virginia
http://www.people.virginia.edu/~jfd3a/
This site contains fairly extensive information about late seventeenth century Plymouth Colony.

DPLS Archive: Slave Movement During the 18th and 19th Centuries (Wisconsin)
http://dpls.dacc.wisc.edu/slavedata/index.html
This site explores the slave ships and the slave trade that carried thousands of Africans to the Americas.

Excerpts from Slave Narratives
http://vi.uh.edu/pages/mintz/primary.htm
The seventeenth- through nineteenth-century accounts of slavery housed in this site speak volumes about the many impacts of slavery.

KEY TERMS

Indentured Servitude (p. 38)
Headright (p. 39)
Divine Right (p. 40)
Separatists (p. 42)
Nonseparatists (p. 42)
"City upon a Hill" (p. 44)
Antinomian (p. 47)
Patriarchal (p. 51)
Coverture (p. 51)
Declension (p. 55)
Half-Way Covenant (p. 55)
Perpetual Servitude (p. 56)

REVIEW QUESTIONS

1. What were the major difficulties that early English settlers in the area of Jamestown had to overcome? What developments allowed the Virginia colony to survive and endure?

2. Compare and contrast Indian-white relations in the Chesapeake and New England colonies. What were the differences and similarities? Did they matter in the end?

3. Describe the original mission of the Puritans who settled in New England. How did the Puritans attempt to implement their mission in the organization of their society? How successful were they in fulfilling their mission?

4. Compare and contrast the characteristics of living in New England and the Chesapeake colonies during the seventeenth century. Why did life seem so much harsher in the Chesapeake region than in New England?

5. What were the differences between indentured servitude and chattel slavery? What factors supported the shift from indentured servitude to slavery and the enslavement of Africans in the southern colonies?

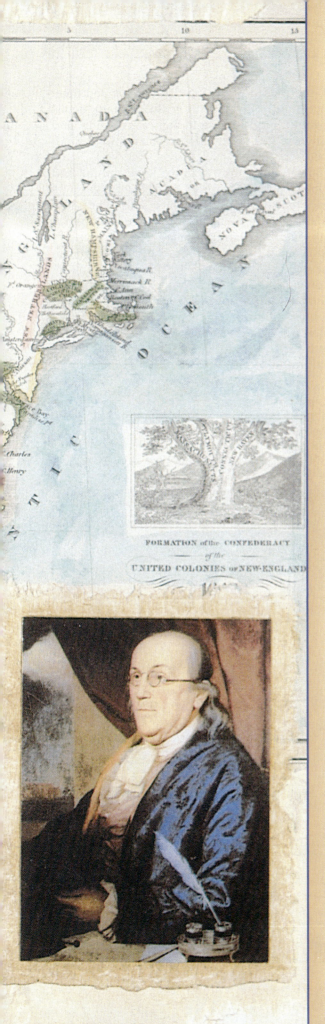

3

PROVINCIAL AMERICA IN UPHEAVAL, 1660–1760

"Stripped and scourged and run the gauntlet"

Hannah Dustan (1657–1736) and Eliza Lucas (1722–1793) never knew one another. Dustan lived in the town of Haverhill on the Massachusetts frontier, and Lucas spent her adult years in the vicinity of Charleston, South Carolina. Even though of different generations, both were inhabitants of England's developing North American empire. Along with so many other colonists, perpetual imperial warfare profoundly affected their lives as England, France, and Spain repeatedly battled for supremacy in Europe and America between 1689 and 1763.

During the 1690s, as part of a war involving England and France, frontier New Englanders experienced devastating raids by Indian parties from French Canada. On the morning of March 15, 1697, a band of Abenakis struck Haverhill. Hannah Dustan's husband and seven of her children saved themselves by racing for the community's blockhouse. Hannah, who had just given birth a few days before, was not so fortunate. The Abenakis captured her, as well as her baby and midwife Mary Neff.

After some discussion, the natives "dashed out the brains of the infant against a tree," the well-known Puritan minister, the Reverend Cotton Mather, later wrote; but they decided to spare Hannah and Mary along with a few other captives. Their plan was to march these residents to the principal Abenaki village in Canada where they would "be stripped and scourged and [made to] run the gauntlet through the whole army of Indians." If they survived, they would be adopted into the tribe, literally to become white Indians.

The Abenakis split up their captives. Two male warriors, three women, and seven children escorted Hannah, Mary, and a young boy named Samuel Lenorson. Hannah, although still in a state of shock, maintained her composure as the party walked northward day after day. She prayed fervently for some means of escape.

Just before dawn one morning, she awoke to find all her captors sound asleep. Seizing the mo-

ment, she roused Mary and Samuel, handed them hatchets, and told them to crush as many skulls as possible. Suddenly the Indians were dying, and only two, a badly wounded woman and a child, escaped.

Hannah then took a scalping knife and finished the bloody work. When she and the other captives got back to Haverhill, they had ten scalps, for which the Massachusetts General Court awarded them a bounty of £50 in local currency. New Englanders hailed Hannah Dustan as a true heroine—a woman whose courage overcame the French and Indian enemies of England's empire in America.

Cotton Mather spread Dustan's story far and wide, hoping to rekindle the faith of New England's founders. If citizens would just "humble" themselves before God, he argued, the Almighty would stop afflicting society with the horrors of war and

This heroic statue of Hannah Dustan in Haverhill, Massachusetts, shows her with the hatchet she used to escape from her captors. Dustan brought the scalps back with her to Haverhill to prove her story and collect a bounty.

provide for the "quick extirpation" of all "bloody and crafty" enemies. Mather's jeremiad had little effect. The war soon ended, and New Englanders devoted themselves more than ever before to acquiring personal wealth.

After a long and full life, Hannah Dustan died in 1736. Two years later, George Lucas, a prosperous Antigua planter who was also an officer in the British army, moved to South Carolina, where he owned three rice plantations. He wanted to get his family away from the Caribbean region, since hostilities were brewing with Spain.

When war did come a year later, Lucas returned to Antigua to resume his military duties. Leaving an ailing wife, he placed his 17-year-old daughter Eliza in charge of his Carolina properties. The responsibility did not faze her; she wrote regularly to her "Dear Papa" for advice, and the plantations prospered. The war, however, disrupted rice trading routes into the West Indies, and planters needed other cash crops to be sold elsewhere. George Lucas was aware of the problem and sent Eliza seeds for indigo plants, the source of a valued deep-blue dye, to see whether indigo could be grown profitably in South Carolina.

With the help of knowledgeable slaves, Eliza conducted successful experiments. In 1744 a major dye broker in England tested her product "against some of the best French" indigo and rated it "in his opinion . . . as good." Just 22 years old, Eliza had pioneered a cash crop that brought additional wealth to Carolina's planters and became a major trading staple of the British empire.

Had Eliza chosen to marry before this time, she could have lost the legal independence to conduct her experiments; but she favored no suitor until she met and wed Charles Pinckney, a widower of great wealth and high social standing. In later life she took pride in the success of her children. Charles Cotesworth Pinckney (b. 1746) was a powerful voice in the Constitutional Convention of 1787, and Thomas Pinckney (b. 1750) represented President Washington during 1795 in negotiating an agreement called Pinckney's Treaty (see p. 202), which resolved western boundary questions with Spain.

A heralded woman of her generation, Eliza Lucas Pinckney died at the end of the revolutionary era, nearly 140 years after the birth of Hannah Dustan. Dustan's life paralleled the years in which England laid the foundations for a mighty empire in America. Between 1660 and 1700, the colonists offered resistance but had to adjust to new imperial laws governing their lives. Then a series of wars with France and Spain that affected both Dustan and Pinckney caused yet more turbulence. Even with so much upheaval, the colonies grew and prospered. After 1760 provin-

cial Americans were in a position to question their subordinate relationship with England. The coming of the American Revolution cannot be appreciated without looking at the development of the English empire in America—and how that experience related to the lives of passing generations of colonists like Hannah Dustan and Eliza Lucas Pinckney.

DESIGNING ENGLAND'S NORTH AMERICAN EMPIRE

During the 1760s Benjamin Franklin tried to explain why relations between England and the colonies had turned sour. He blamed British trade policies designed to control American commerce. "Most of the statutes, or acts, . . . of parliaments . . . for regulating, directing, or restraining of trade," Franklin declared, "have been . . . political blunders . . . for private advantage, under pretense of public good." The trade system, he believed, had become both oppressive and corrupt.

Little more than a hundred years before, the colonists had traded as they pleased. After 1650, however, Oliver Cromwell and then the restored Stuart monarch Charles II (reigned 1660–1685) worked closely with Parliament to design trade policies that exerted greater control over the activities of the American colonists.

To Benefit the Parent Nation

Certain key ideas underlay the new, more restrictive policies. Most important was the concept of **mercantilism**, a term not invented until the late eighteenth century but one that describes what England's leaders set out to accomplish. Their goal was national greatness and, as one courtier told Charles II, the challenge was to develop "trade and commerce" so that it "draws [a] store of wealth" into England.

Mercantilist thinkers believed the world's supply of wealth was not infinite but fixed in quantity. Any nation that gained wealth automatically did so at the expense of another. In economic dealings, then, the most powerful nations always maintained a favorable balance of trade by exporting a greater value of goods than they imported. To square accounts, hard money in the form of gold and silver would flow into creditor nations. Governments controlling the most precious metals would be the most self-sufficient. They could use such wealth to stimulate internal economic development as well as to strengthen military forces, both of which were critical to economic survival and ascendancy over other nations.

Mercantilist theory also demonstrated how colonies could best serve their parent nations. Gold and silver extracted from Central and South America had underwritten Spain's rise to great power and glory in the sixteenth century. Although such easy wealth did not exist in eastern North America, the colonies could contribute to a favorable trade balance for England by producing such staple crops as tobacco, rice, and sugar, thus ending any need to import these goods from other countries.

The American provinces, in addition, could supply valuable raw materials—for example, timber products. England had plundered its own forests to have winter fuel and construct a strong naval fleet, making it necessary to import wood from the Baltic region. Now the colonies could help fill timber demands, again reducing foreign imports while supplying a commodity vital to national security. Great stands of American timber could also be fashioned into fine furniture and sold back to the colonists. Ideally, England's overseas colonies would serve as a source of raw materials and staple crops as well as a marketplace for manufactured goods.

Mercantilist thinking affirmed the principle that the colonies existed to benefit and strengthen the parent nation. As such, provincial economic and political activities required close management. To effect these goals, Parliament passed a series of Navigation Acts (1651, 1660, 1663, and 1673), which formed the cornerstone of England's commercial relations with the colonies and the rest of the world. The acts banned foreign merchants and vessels from participating in the colonial trade; proclaimed that certain **enumerated goods** could be shipped only to England or other colonies (the first list included dyewoods, indigo, sugar, and tobacco, and furs, molasses, rice, and wood products such as masts, pitch, and tar were added later); and specified that European goods destined for America had to pass through England.

Through the **Navigation System,** England became the central trading hub of its empire, which resulted in a great economic boom at home. Before 1660, for example, the Dutch operated the largest merchant fleet in Europe and dominated the colonial tobacco trade. With stimulus from the Navigation Acts, the shipbuilding industry began to boom in England as never before. By the late 1690s the English merchant fleet had outdistanced all competitors, including the Dutch, which seemed to bear out mercantilist ideas regarding one nation's strength coming at another's expense.

The ship's carpenter was typical of colonists who benefited from a thriving imperial economy. The colonies produced one-fourth or more of all English-registered vessels.

In the colonies the Navigation Acts had mixed effects. New Englanders, taking advantage of local timber supplies, bolstered their economy by heavy involvement in shipbuilding. By the early 1700s Americans were constructing one-fourth or more of all English merchant vessels. In the Chesapeake Bay region, however, the enumeration of tobacco resulted in economic problems. By the 1660s planters were producing too much tobacco for consumption in the British Isles alone. Because of the costs of merchandising the crop through England, the final market price was too high to support large sales in Europe. Consequently, the tobacco glut in England caused wholesale prices to decline, resulting in hard times in the Chesapeake region and much furor among planters.

Seizing Dutch New Netherland

Charles II learned from his father's mistakes. He never claimed divine authority in decision making; and so as not to appear too power hungry, he passed himself off at court as a sensuous, lazy, vulgar man whose major objectives were to attend horse races, tell bawdy jokes, and seduce women. His mistresses, like Nell Gwynn, became national celebrities and bore him at least 14 illegitimate children. When asked about his lustful ways, he replied, as if mocking the Puritans who had beheaded his father, "God will not damn a man for taking a little unregular pleasure by the way."

Charles often played the foppish fool, but he was an intelligent person with a vision for England's greatness. Besides urging Parliament to legislate the Navigation System, Charles pursued other plans for enhancing England's imperial power. None was more important than challenging Dutch supremacy over the Hudson and Delaware river valleys.

The precedent for attacking territory claimed by England's imperial rivals came in 1654 when Cromwell launched a fleet with 8000 troops to strike at the heart of New Spain. Cromwell's "Western Design" expedition failed to conquer the primary targets of Puerto Rico, Hispaniola, or the port city of Cartagena (located in modern-day Colombia). The fleet, however, seized the island of Jamaica, which in time became a center for illegal commerce with New Spain as well as a major slave trade marketing center.

Charles hated everything about Cromwell, which he proved by having the Lord Protector's corpse exhumed and hanged in public before a cheering crowd. Yet Charles borrowed freely from Cromwell's precedents. New Netherland, a colony having the geographic misfortune of lying between New England and the southern colonies, was an obvious target, especially since Dutch sea captains used New Amsterdam as a base for illegal trade with English settlers. To enforce the Navigation Acts, reasoned Charles and his advisers, the Dutch colony had to be conquered.

New Netherland was the handiwork of the Dutch West India Company, a joint-stock venture chartered in 1621. The company soon sent out a governor and employees to the Hudson River area to develop the fur trade with local Indians, particularly the Five Nations of Iroquois inhabiting upper New York west of Fort Orange (Albany).

Initially the company showed little interest in settlement, but its leaders had to reckon with food shortages. To encourage local agricultural production, the com-

Iroquois Nations

The Dutch West India Company developed the fur trade primarily with the Five Nations of Iroquois.

pany announced in 1629 that vast landed estates, known as *patroonships,* would be made available to wealthy individuals who transported at least 50 families to New Netherland. The migrants would become tenant farmers for their masters, or *patroons,* who hoped to live like medieval lords on manorial estates. With the Dutch home economy booming, few subjects accepted these less-than-generous terms.

The New Netherland colony was also internally weak and unstable. The governors were a sorry lot, typified by Wouter van Twiller (served 1633–1638), who was pleasant, claimed a contemporary, only "as long as there is any wine." In 1643 his successor, William Kieft, started a war with natives around New Amsterdam (New York City) that devastated the colony's settlers. Facing bankruptcy in 1647, company directors called on Peter Stuyvesant to save the venture. Stuyvesant, however, became embroiled in many disputes with the settlers, whom he repeatedly infuriated with his highhanded policies.

Despite everything, New Netherland's population pushed toward 8000 by 1660, counting Puritans who had settled on Long Island. New Amsterdam was home to people from all over Europe, as well as many African slaves. The unpopularity of Stuyvesant, the absence of any voice in government, and the denial of freedom of worship separate from the Dutch Reformed church all combined to favor a possible English takeover.

In the early days of his monarchy, Charles II strengthened his political base at home by making generous land grants in America, such as rewarding eight loyal court favorites with the Carolinas patent (see p. 41). In 1664 the king gave his brother, James, the Duke of York, title to all Dutch lands in North America, on the obvious condition that they be conquered. James quickly hired Colonel Richard Nicolls to organize a small invasion fleet. When the flotilla appeared before New Amsterdam in August 1664, Stuyvesant could not rally the populace. With hardly an exchange of shots, New Netherland became the Duke of York's English province of New York.

Proprietary Difficulties in New York and New Jersey

Unlike his older brother, James was an inflexible person. Although hard-working, he was a humorless autocrat. He even treated his mistresses coldly, as if they were "given him by priests for penance," wrote one court wag. Nor was James sensitive to the political trends of his time. He hated Parliament for having executed his father and was intolerant of representative government.

James's proprietary charter had no clause mandating a popular assembly for his colony, and he instructed Nicolls to make no concessions. As an adept administrator, Nicolls maneuvered around the issue by granting other rights. In his Articles of Capitulation, he confirmed the land titles of all inhabitants, including the Dutch. Next Nicolls announced the Duke's Laws, which provided for local government and guaranteed such basic liberties as trial by jury and religious toleration, so long as settlers belonged to and supported some church.

The Long Island Puritans kept pressing for a popularly elected assembly. They refused to pay local taxes, arguing that they were "enslaved under an arbitrary power." The absence of an assembly for New York's colonists remained a source of friction for several years. Finally, James conceded the point, and an assembly met for the first time in 1683. Once he became king in 1685, however, James disavowed further assembly meetings.

Making matters more confusing, in 1664 James turned over all his proprietary lands between the Hudson and Delaware rivers to John, Lord Berkeley, and Sir George Carteret, two court favorites who were also Carolina proprietors. Nicolls, however, did not learn of this grant until after he had offered some Puritans land patents in the eastern portion of what became the colony of New Jersey.

Until the end of the century, questions regarding proprietary ownership of New Jersey plagued the colony's development. Settlement proceeded slowly, with the population moving toward 15,000 by 1700. Most New Jersey colonists engaged in commercial farming and raised grain crops, which they marketed through New York City and Philadelphia, the two port towns that would dominate the region. Because of endless bickering over land titles and proprietary political authority, the Crown declared in 1702 that New Jersey would henceforth be a royal province.

Planting William Penn's "Holy Experiment"

During the English Civil War of the 1640s a number of radical religious sects—Ranters, Seekers, and Quakers among them—began to appear in England. Each represented a small band of fervent believers determined to recast human society in the mold of a particular religious vision. George Fox founded the Society of Friends. His followers came to be called "Quakers," because Fox, who went to jail many times, warned one judge to "tremble at the word of the Lord."

The Quakers adhered to many controversial ideas. They believed that all persons had a divine spark, or "inner light," which, when fully nurtured, allowed them to commune directly with God. Like Anne Hutchinson before them, they saw little need for human institutions. They had no ordained ministers and downplayed the importance of the Bible, since they could order their lives according to revelation received directly from God.

In addition, the Quakers held a unique social vision. All humans, they argued, were equal in the sight of God. Thus they wore unadorned black clothing and refused to remove their broad-brimmed hats when social superiors passed by them. Women had full access to leadership positions and could serve as preachers and missionaries. Members of the sect also refused to take legal oaths, which they considered a form of swearing, and they were pacifists, believing that warfare would never solve human problems. In time, Quakers became antislavery advocates, arguing that God did not hold some persons inferior because of skin color.

Early English Quakers were intensely fervent, and during the 1650s and 1660s they sent many witnesses of their faith to America. These individuals, about half of them women, fared poorly in the colonies. Puritan magistrates in Massachusetts told them of their "free liberty to keep away from us" and threw them out. Two Quaker males were so persistent in coming back to Boston that officials finally hanged them in 1659, and they gave a third witness, Mary Dyer, a gallows reprieve. Dyer, however, returned the next year, was hanged, and became a martyr to her vision of a more harmonious world.

William Penn (1644–1718) first became a Quaker in the early 1660s while a college student at Oxford. Hoping to cure his son's zealousness, Penn's father sent William on a tour of the Continent. Penn returned in a more worldly frame of mind, but he soon readopted Quaker beliefs. He was so outspoken that he even spent time in jail, but his father's high standing at court—he had supported the Stuart restoration—assured the family access to Charles II.

During the 1670s George Fox traveled to America, hoping to find a haven for his followers. He also encouraged William Penn to use his family connections to obtain a land grant. King Charles acceded to Penn's request for a proprietary charter in 1681, stating that the purpose was to "enlarge our British empire" and pay off a £16,000 debt long since due the estate of Penn's father. Years later, Penn claimed that Charles's real motivation was "to be rid of" the Quakers "at so cheap a rate" by conveying to him title to "a desert [wilderness] three thousand miles off."

Pennsylvania, which means Penn's woods, was hardly a desert. The tract was bountiful, and Penn tried to make the most of it, both as a sanctuary for oppressed religious groups and as a source of personal income from quitrents. He laid his plans carefully, making large grants to English Quakers, and he drew up a blueprint for a commercial center—Philadelphia, or the City of Brotherly Love. Penn sent agents to Europe in search of settlers, offering generous land packages with low annual quitrents. He also wrote his First Frame of Government (1682), which guaranteed a legislative assembly and full freedom of religion.

Like the Puritans before him, Penn had a utopian vision, in this case captured by the phrase **holy experiment.** Unlike the Puritans, Penn wanted to mold a society in which peoples of diverse back grounds and religious beliefs lived together harmoniously— a bold idea in an era not known for its toleration.

Determined to succeed, Penn sailed to America in 1682, landing first in the area known as the Three Lower Counties, later to become the colony of Delaware. He had purchased this strip of land from the Duke of York to assure an easy exit for commerce flowing out of Philadelphia to Atlantic trade routes. Until 1701, Delaware existed as an appendage of Pennsylvania, but then Penn granted the colonists there a separate assembly. Until the Revolution, however, the proprietary governors of Pennsylvania also headed Delaware's government.

Penn next journeyed upriver to lay out Philadelphia. Some settlers were already present, and during the next few years others migrated from England as well as from Wales, Scotland, Ireland, Holland, Germany, and Switzerland. Typical were Germans from the Rhineland who followed their religious leader, Francis Daniel Pastorius, and founded Germantown to the north of Philadelphia. From the very outset, Pennsylvania developed along pluralist lines, an early sign of what later characterized the cultural ideal of the United States as a whole.

Penn envisioned a "peaceable kingdom" and sought cordial relations with local Indians. Before traveling to America, he wrote to the Delawares, the dominant tribe in the region, explaining that the king of England "hath given me a great province." He asked that "we may always live together as neighbors and friends." True to his word, Penn met with the Delawares and told them that he would not take land from them unless sanctioned by tribal chieftains. What emerged was the "walking purchase" system in which the natives sold land based on the distance that a person could travel on foot in a day. Even though the system was open to abuse, Penn's goal was honest dealing, which had rarely been the case in other colonies.

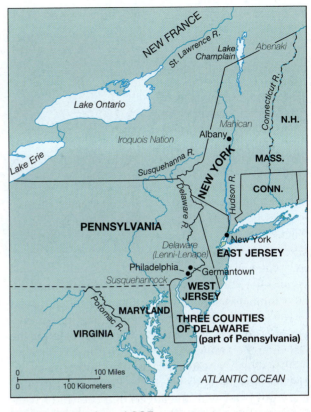

Middle Colonies, 1685

Completing these and other tasks, Penn returned to England in 1684 to encourage further settlement. That was no problem. Pennsylvania was very attractive, particularly for dissenter religious groups. By the early 1700s the population exceeded 20,000. Colonists poured through the booming port of Philadelphia and then fanned out into the fertile countryside. There they established family farms, raising livestock and growing abundant grain crops, which they marketed to the West Indies and Europe. The settlers prospered, and Pennsylvania gained a reputation as "one of the best poor man's countries in the world."

Still, not all was perfect in the peaceable kingdom. Religious sects segregated themselves, wanting little to do with one another. To Penn's dismay, life in Philadelphia was more raucous than pious. Drinking establishments and brothels sprang up in large numbers, and endless bickering characterized local politics. Quakers dominated the government but fought endlessly over the prerogatives of power. Penn thought these "brutish, . . . scurvy quarrels" were a "disgrace" to the colony, but his pleas for harmony went unheeded. Equally disturbing from his point of view, settlers refused to pay quitrents "to supply me with bread," yet he kept funding the colony's development.

In his dealings with Native Americans, William Penn sought to negotiate land rights fairly. However, Pennsylvania's settlers and Penn's own officials were not so scrupulous. They used many underhanded means to push the native populace off ancient tribal lands as rapidly as possible.

Hoping to solve such problems, Penn returned in 1699. His presence had a moderating influence—but only so long as he stayed. Before leaving for the last time, he announced a new Charter of Liberties (1701), which placed all legislative authority in an elective assembly, to be checked only by a proprietary governor with the advice of a council of well-to-do local gentlemen. The charter served as the basis of Pennsylvania's unicameral government until the Revolution.

Peace, prosperity, pluralism, and religious toleration were the hallmarks of Penn's utopian vision. In his old age, however, he considered the "holy experiment" a failure. He concluded that peaceable kingdoms on earth lay beyond human reach. Having even spent time in prison for debts contracted on behalf of his colony, Penn died an embittered man in 1718. Still, by seeking a better life for all peoples, he helped infuse the American experience with a profound sense of social purpose.

In this idealized drawing of Quaker farmer David Twining's Pennsylvania homestead, the emphasis is on harmonious and peaceful relations.

DEFYING THE IMPERIAL WILL: PROVINCIAL CONVULSIONS AND REBELLIONS

Establishing the Middle Colonies was an integral part of England's imperial expansion within the framework of mercantilist thinking. Certainly the Dutch understood this, and they fought two wars with England (1664–1667 and 1672–1674), hoping to recoup their losses. In the second war they recaptured New York, only to renounce all claims in the peace settlement. After that time, the Dutch focused their activities on other parts of the world, even though some of their mariners continued to trade illegally with the English North American colonists.

Besides reckoning with the Dutch, Charles II and his advisers endeavored to shape the emerging empire in other ways. Crown representatives crossed the Atlantic to determine whether the colonists were cooperating with the Navigation System. Also traveling to America were the first customs officers, who were to collect duties on enumerated goods being traded between colonies—and then to foreign ports. Increasingly the Americans felt England's constraining hand, which in some locales resulted in violent confrontations.

Bacon's Bloody Rebellion in Virginia

With tobacco glutting the market in England, Virginia's economy went into a tailspin during the 1660s. The planters blamed the Navigation Acts, which stopped them from dealing directly with such foreign merchants as the Dutch. The planters' mood did not improve when, in 1667, Dutch war vessels captured nearly the whole English merchant fleet hauling the annual tobacco crop out of Chesapeake Bay, resulting in the virtual loss of a year's worth of labor, harvest, and income.

Besides economic woes, other problems existed. Some Virginians thought their long-time royal governor, Sir William Berkeley (1606–1677), had become a tyrant. Berkeley handed out patronage jobs to a few favored planters, known as the "Green Spring" faction (named after Berkeley's plantation). Such favors allowed the governor to dominate the assembly and levy heavy taxes at a time when settlers were suffering economically. As a consequence, some planters lost their property, and young males just completing terms of indentured service saw few prospects for ever gaining title to land and achieving economic independence. In 1670 Berkeley and the assembly approved a 50-acre property holding requirement for voting privileges. This action fed suspicions that the governor and his cronies were out to amass all power for themselves.

In 1674 young Nathaniel Bacon (1647–1676) jumped into the simmering pot. From a wealthy English family and educated at Cambridge, he had squandered his inheritance before reaching his mid-twenties. Bacon's despairing father sent him to Virginia with a stipend to start a plantation, hoping the experience would force his son to grow up. When Bacon arrived, Berkeley greeted him warmly, stating that "gentlemen of your quality come very rarely into this country."

Bacon was ambitious, and he sought acceptance among Berkeley's favored friends, who controlled the lucrative Indian trade. He asked the governor for a trading license, but Berkeley denied the request, feeling that the young man had not yet proven his worth. Incensed by his rejection, Bacon started opposing Berkeley at every turn. He organized other substantial planters—also not favored by Berkeley—into his own "Castle" faction (the name of his plantation), and he appealed to Virginia's growing numbers of propertyless poor for support.

Stirrings among native peoples made matters worse. Far to the north in New York, the Five Nations of Iroquois had become more aggressive in their quest for furs. They started pushing other tribes southward toward Virginia, and some groups spilled onto frontier plantations, resulting in a few killings.

Bacon demanded reprisals, but Berkeley urged caution. A war, he stressed, would only add to Virginia's tax burdens. Bacon asked for a military commission, stating that he would organize an army of volunteers. The governor refused, at which point Bacon charged his adversary with being more interested in protecting profits from his Indian trading monopoly than in saving settlers' lives. Bacon pulled together a force of over 1000 men, described as "the scum of the country" by Berkeley's supporters, and indiscriminately started killing local natives.

In response, Berkeley declared Bacon "the greatest rebel that ever was in Virginia" and sent out militiamen to corral the volunteers, but Bacon's force eluded them. The governor also called a new assembly, which met at Jamestown in June 1676. Among reforms designed to pacify the "mutineers," the burgesses restored voting rights to all adult freemen, even if they did not own property. Events had gone too far, however, and a shooting war broke out. Before the fighting ceased, Bacon's force burned Jamestown to the ground, and Berkeley fled across Chesapeake Bay. What finally precipitated an end to the struggle was Bacon's death from dysentery in October 1676.

As the Salem witchcraft trials unfolded, the young "afflicted" girls became more bold in their accusations. They often fell into fits and shouted that the accused had cast evil satanic spells over them.

lives, the girls had asked Tituba, a local slave woman from the West Indies, to tell them their fortunes. She did so. Soon thereafter the girls started acting hysterically, observers claimed, as if possessed by Satan's demons. When asked to name possible witches, the girls did not stop with Tituba.

Before the hysteria ended, the "afflicted" girls made hundreds of accusations before a special court appointed to root the devil out of Massachusetts. With increasing frequency they pointed to more urbane, prospering citizens like those of Salem Town. The penalty for practicing witchcraft was death. Some 50 defendants, among them Tituba, saved themselves by admitting their guilt; but 20 men and women were executed (19 by hanging and 1 by the crushing weight of stones) after steadfastly refusing to admit that they had practiced witchcraft.

By the end of 1692 the craze was over, probably because too many citizens of rank and influence, including the wife of the new royal governor, Sir William Phips, had been accused of doing the devil's work. In time, most participants in the Salem witchcraft trials admitted to being deluded. While victims could not be brought back to life, the episode stood as a warning in the colonies about the dangers of mass hysteria at a time when Europeans were still actively ferreting out and prosecuting alleged witches. The playing out of events also helped sustain New England's transition to a commercial society by making traditional folk beliefs—and those who espoused them—appear foolish.

Settling Anglo-American Differences

In 1691 William and Mary began to address colonial issues. As constitutional monarchs, they were not afraid of popularly elected assemblies. In the case of Massachusetts they approved a royal charter that gave the Crown the authority to name royal governors and stated that all male property holders, not just church members, had the right to vote. On the other hand, the monarchs did not tamper with the established Congregational church, thereby reassuring old-line Puritans that conforming to the Church of England was not necessary so long as Bay Colony residents supported England's imperial aspirations.

New York also became a royal colony in 1691, complete with a local representative assembly. Henry Sloughter, the governor, delivered the news; but Jacob Leisler hesitated to step aside, fearing that Sloughter might be an agent of King James. Leisler's obstinacy led to his arrest and hasty trial for treason. His enemies gave all the testimony that the court needed to sentence him to a ghastly death by hanging, disemboweling, drawing and quartering and, if that were not enough, decapitation. It was little solace to Leisler's followers that Parliament, in later reviewing the evidence, declared him innocent of treason.

In Maryland's case the Calverts lost political control in 1692 in favor of royal government, although they still held title to the land and could collect quitrents. Shortly thereafter, a Protestant assembly banned Roman Catholics from political office. Not

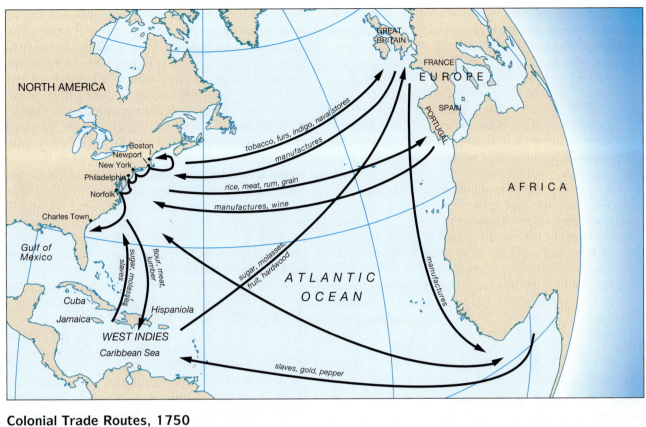

Colonial Trade Routes, 1750

until 1715 did the Calverts regain political control. By then the proprietary family had converted to Anglicanism and was no longer a threat to Protestant sensibilities.

The transformation revealed a movement toward the royal model of government in which the colonies established legislative assemblies to express and defend their local concerns. Crown-appointed governors, in turn, pledged themselves to enforce the Navigation Acts and other imperial laws. So long as the colonists cooperated, they would not face autocratic forms of government. Nor would the Crown permit the kind of loose freedom of earlier times, because in gaining basic rights, the colonists also accepted responsibility for conducting their daily affairs within the imperial framework. The Glorious Revolution and its reverberations in America had made this compromise possible.

Maintaining the delicate balance between imperial authority and local autonomy was the major challenge of the eighteenth century. Until the 1760s both sides succeeded in doing so. The Crown, for example, adopted the Navigation Act of 1696, which set up the Board of Trade and Plantations as an administrative agency to advise England's leaders on colonial issues. This act also mandated the establishment of vice-admiralty courts in America to punish with stiff penalties smugglers and others who violated the rules of trade.

The Board of Trade generally acted with discretion, even in recommending a few acts to restrain colonial manufacturers competing with home industries. Parliament in 1699 adopted legislation (the Woolen Act) that outlawed any exportation of woolen products from America or from one colony to another. The intent was to get the colonists to buy finished woolens from English manufacturers rather than develop their own industry. In 1732 the Hat Act barred the colonial production of beaver and felt hats. Then in 1750 Parliament passed the Iron Act, which forbade the colonists from building new facilities or expanding old ones for the manufacture of finished iron or steel products. On the other hand, the act encouraged them to keep preparing raw iron for final processing in England. As a whole, these acts had little adverse effect on the provincial economy. They simply reinforced fundamental mercantile notions regarding colonies as sources of raw materials and as markets for finished goods.

Occasionally, imperial leaders went too far, such as with the Molasses Act of 1733. In support of a thriving rum industry based mostly in New England, colonial merchants roamed the Caribbean for molasses, which cost less on French and Dutch West Indian islands. To placate British West Indian planters, Parliament tried to redirect the trade with a heavy duty (6 pence per gallon) on foreign molasses transported into the colonies. Enforcing the trade duty could have ruined the booming North American rum industry, but customs officers wisely ignored collecting the duty, a sensible solution to a potentially inflammatory issue.

As the eighteenth century progressed, imperial officials tried hard not to be overbearing. In certain instances they even stimulated provincial economic development by offering large cash bounties for raising indigo plants. (Thus, Eliza Lucas's efforts held the long-term potential to challenge France's dominant position in the production of that valued dye.) Caught up as the empire was in warfare with France and Spain, home leaders did not want to tamper with a system that, by and large, worked. The colonists, in turn, gladly accepted the relative autonomy that characterized their lives during the so-called era of **salutary neglect.**

MATURING COLONIAL SOCIETIES IN UNSETTLED TIMES

Stable relations with the parent nation and other factors nourished the maturing of the American provinces after 1700. Certainly a rapidly expanding population that nearly doubled every 20 years strengthened the colonies, as did widespread eco-nomic prosperity, even though it was not shared evenly among the populace. In times of internal social turmoil, such as during the religious upheaval known as the Great Awakening, the colonists disagreed heatedly among themselves but did not lose sight of the need for mutual respect and cooperation in further building their communities. Finally, participation in a series of imperial wars, in which the colonists contributed greatly to Britain's military success while also wresting yet more land for themselves from the native populace, underpinned a growing sense of self-confidence. By the 1760s, however, many colonists had come to doubt whether the home government truly appreciated what they had accomplished for the expanding British empire—portending an end to the long period of stable relations.

An Exploding Population Base

Between 1700 and 1760 the colonial population mushroomed from 250,000 to 1.6 million persons—and to 2.5 million by 1775. Natural population increase—predicated upon abundant land, early marriages, and high fertility rates—was only one source of the population explosion. Equally significant was the introduction of non-English peoples. Between 1700 and 1775 the British North American slave trade reached its peak, resulting in the involuntary entry of an estimated 250,000 Africans into the colonies. The black population grew from 28,000 in 1700 to over 500,000 in 1775, with most living as chattel slaves in the South. At least 40 to 50 percent of the African population increase in the colonies was attributable to the booming slave trade.

Among European groups, Scots-Irish and Germans predominated, although a smattering of French Huguenot, Swiss, Scottish, Irish, and Jewish migrants joined the westward stream. The Scots-Irish had endured many privations. Originally Presbyterian lowlanders from Scotland, they had migrated to Ulster (northern Ireland) in the seventeenth century at the invitation of the Crown. Once there, they harassed the Catholic Irish with a vengeance, only to face discrimination themselves when a new Parliamentary law, the Test Act of 1704, stripped non-Anglicans of political rights. During the next several years they also endured crop failures and huge rent increases from their English landlords.

In a series of waves between 1725 and 1775 over 100,000 Scots-Irish descended on North America, lured by reports of "a rich, fine soil before them, laying as loose . . . as the best bed in the garden." Philadelphia was their main port of entry. They then moved out into the backcountry where they squatted

TABLE 3.1
Colonial Population Growth, 1660–1780

Year	White	Black	Total
1660	70,200	2900	73,100*
1680	138,100	7000	145,100
1700	223,100	27,800	250,900
1720	397,300	68,900	466,200
1740	755,500	150,000	905,500
1760	1,267,800	325,800	1,593,600
1780	2,111,100	566,700	2,677,800

Note: All estimates rounded to the nearest hundred.

*Includes the population of New Netherland.

Source: The American Colonies: From Settlement to Independence by R. C. Simmons. Copyright © 1976 by R. C. Simmons. Reprinted by permission of Harold Matson, Inc.

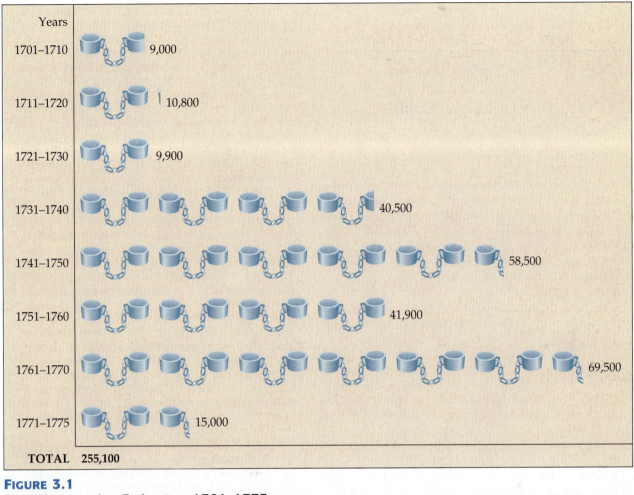

Years		
1701–1710		9,000
1711–1720		10,800
1721–1730		9,900
1731–1740		40,500
1741–1750		58,500
1751–1760		41,900
1761–1770		69,500
1771–1775		15,000
TOTAL	255,100	

FIGURE 3.1
Slave Importation Estimates, 1701–1775

Source: R. C. Simmons, *The American Colonies: From Settlement to Independence.* Copyright © 1976 by R. C. Simmons. Reprinted by permission of Harold Matson Company.

on open land and earned reputations as bloodthirsty Indian fighters. In time, the Scots-Irish took the Great Wagon Road through the Shenandoah Valley and started filling in the southern backcountry.

Even before the first Scots-Irish wave, Germans from the area of the upper Rhine River began streaming into the Middle Colonies. Some, like Amish, Moravian, and Mennonite sectarians, fled religious persecution; others escaped from crushing economic circumstances caused by overpopulation, crop failures, and heavy local taxes. So many Germans came through Philadelphia that Benjamin Franklin questioned whether "Pennsylvania . . . [will] become a colony of aliens, who will shortly be so numerous as to Germanize us, instead of our Anglifying them." Franklin's worries could not stop the German migrants, whose numbers exceeded 100,000 by 1775.

Many destitute Germans crossed the Atlantic as **redemptioners.** This system was similar to inden-

tured servitude, except that families migrated together and shippers promised heads of households a few days' time, upon arrival in America, to locate some person or group to pay for the family's passage in return for a set number of years of labor (usually three to six years per family member). If they failed, then ship captains held auctions at market with the expectation of making tidy profits. The redemptioner system was full of abuses, such as packing passengers on vessels like cattle and serving them worm-infested food. Hundreds died before seeing America. For those who survived, the dream of prospering someday as free colonists remained viable.

One reason for such optimism was that more settlers were enjoying longer life spans, as reflected in higher birth and lower death rates. Estimates indicate that post-1700 Americans were dying at an average of 20 to 25 per 1000 annually, but births numbered 45 to 50 per 1000 settlers.

THE PEOPLE SPEAK

Olaudah Equiano on His Ship Passage as a Slave to America

For free persons of great wealth, migrating to America in the eighteenth century was invariably an unpleasant undertaking. For unfree persons such as Olaudah Equiano (c. 1745–1797), the experience was truly mortifying. Stolen from his village in Nigeria by Africans involved in the slave trade, 11-year-old Equiano had to face the unknown with no sense of what his prospects were for the future. He had become one of about 250,000 Africans forced into migrating to the British North American colonies between 1700 and 1775. As events for young Equiano turned out, he was among the luckier slaves. A British naval officer purchased him in Virginia and later sold him to a Quaker merchant in the West Indies. This gentleman allowed Equiano the opportunity to trade on his own, enough so that he was able to purchase his freedom in 1766. For much of the rest of his life, Equiano lived in England and worked to halt the slave trade. His *Narrative* was part of his effort to bring an end to such human exploitation, as these passages about what he experienced on a slave ship attest.

> The first object which saluted my eyes when I arrived on the coast was the sea, and a slave ship, which was then riding at anchor, and waiting for its cargo.

These filled me with astonishment, which was soon converted into terror, which I am yet at a loss to describe, nor the then feelings of my mind. When I was carried on board I was immediately handled, and tossed up, to see if I were sound, by some of the crew; and I was now persuaded that I had got into a world of bad spirits, and that they were going to kill me. Their complexions too differing so much from ours, their long hair, and the language they spoke, which was very different from any I had every heard, united to confirm me in this belief. . . . When I looked round the ship too, and saw a large furnace or copper boiling, and a multitude of black people of every description chained together, every one of our countenances expressing dejection and sorrow, I no longer doubted of my fate; and, quite overpowered with horror and anguish, I fell motionless on the deck and fainted.

When I recovered a little, I found some black people about me, who I believed were some of those who brought me on board, and had been receiving their pay; they talked to me in order to cheer me, but all in vain. I asked them if we were not to be eaten by those white men with horrible looks, red faces, and long hair. They told me I was not. . . .

I was not long suffered to indulge my grief; I was soon put down under the decks, and there I received such a salutation in my nostrils as I had never experienced in my life; so that, with the loathsomeness of the stench, and crying together, I became so sick and low that I was not able to eat, nor had I the least desire to taste any thing. I now wished for the last friend, death, to relieve me; but soon, to my grief, two of the white men offered me eatables; and, on my refusing to eat, one of them held me fast by the hands, and laid me across, I think, the windlass, and tied my feet while the other flogged me severely. I had never experienced any thing of this kind before. . . .

Longer lives reflected improved health and agricultural abundance. Colonists had plentiful supplies of food. Nutritious diets led to better overall health, making it easier for Americans to fight virulent diseases. Even the poorest people, claimed a New England doctor, had regular meals of "salt pork and beans, with bread of Indian corn meal," as well as ample quantities of home-brewed beer and distilled spirits. In the same period, food supplies in Europe were dangerously sparse. Thousands of western Europeans starved to death between 1740 and 1743 because of widespread crop failures.

The "Europeanizing" of America

Compared to Europe, America was a land of boundless prosperity. To be sure, however, the colonists accepted wide disparities in wealth, rank, and privilege as part of the natural order of life. They did so because of the pervasive influence of European values, such as the need for hierarchy and deference in social and political relations. The eighteenth century was still an era in which individuals believed in three distinct social orders—the monarchy, the aristocracy, and the "democracy" of common citizens. All persons had an identifiable place in society, fixed at birth; and to try to improve one's lot was to risk instability in the established rhythms of the universe.

These notions, dating back to Aristotle and other ancient thinkers, helped justify the highly stratified world of early modern Europe, featuring monarchical families such as the Tudors and Stuarts and bloodline aristocrats who passed hereditary titles from one generation to the next. Among those threatening Europe's established social order were ambitious commoners

In a little time after, amongst the poor chained men, I found some of my own nation, which in a small degree gave ease to my mind. I inquired of them what was to be done with us? They gave me to understand we were to be carried to these white people's country to work for them. I then was a little revived, and thought, if it were no worse than working, my situation was not so desperate; but still I feared I should be put to than working, my situation was not so desperate; but still I feared I should be put to death, the white people looked and acted, as I thought, in so savage a manner; for I had never seen among any people such instances of brutal cruelty; and this not only shown toward us blacks, but also to some of the whites themselves. . . .

At last, when the ship we were in had got in all her cargo, they made ready with many fearful noises, and we were all put under deck. . . . The stench of the hold . . . became absolutely pestilential. The closeness of the place, and the heat of the climate, added to the number in the ship, which was so crowded that each had scarcely room to turn himself, almost suffocated us. This produced copious perspirations, so that the air soon became unfit for respiration, from a variety of loathsome smells, and brought on a sickness amongst the slaves, of which many died, thus falling victims to the improvident avarice, as I may call it, of their purchasers. This wretched situation was again aggravated by the galling of the chains, now become insupportable; and the filth of the necessary tubs, into which the children often fell, and were almost suffocated. The shrieks of the women, and the groans of the dying, rendered the whole scene of horror almost inconceivable. Happily perhaps for myself I was soon reduced so low here that it was thought necessary to keep me almost always on deck; and from my extreme youth I was not put in fetters.

In this situation I expected every hour to share the fate of my companions, some of whom were almost daily brought upon deck at the point of death, which I began to hope would soon put an end to my miseries. Often did I think many of the inhabitants of the deep much more happy than myself; I envied them the freedom they enjoyed, and as often wished I could change my condition for theirs. . . .

One day, when we had a smooth sea, and moderate wind, two of my wearied countrymen, who were chained together (I was near them at the time), preferring death to such a life of misery, somehow made through the nettings, and jumped into the sea; immediately another quite dejected fellow, who, on account of his illness, was suffered to be out of irons, also followed their example; and I believe many more would very soon have done the same, if they had not been prevented by the ship's crew, who were instantly alarmed. Those of us that were the most active were in a moment put down under the deck; and there was such a noise and confusion amongst the people of the ship as I never heard before, to stop her, and get the boat out to go after the slaves. However, two of the wretches were drowned, but they got the other, and afterwards flogged him unmercifully, for thus attempting to prefer death to slavery. In this manner we continued to undergo more hardships than I can now relate; hardships which are inseparable from this accursed trade. Many a time we were near suffocation, from the want of fresh air, which we were often without for whole days together. This, and the stench of the necessary tubs, carried off many. . . .

Source: Olaudah Equiano, *The Interesting Narrative of the Life of Olaudah Equiano or Gustavus Vassa, the African* (New York, 1791).

who had acquired great wealth through commerce. They too craved public recognition and high status, and they tried to earn a place for themselves at the top of the social pyramid by aping the manners and customs of those born into privileged social stations.

The same could be said for wealthy elite families that had emerged in America by the early eighteenth century. In Virginia names like Byrd, Carter, and Lee were of the first rank; the Pinckneys and Rutledges dominated South Carolina; in New York the Livingstons and Schuylers were among the favored few with great estates along the Hudson River; and in Massachusetts those of major consequence included merchant families like the Hutchinsons and Olivers.

Elite families set themselves apart from the rest of colonial society by imitating English aristocratic lifestyles. Wealthy southern gentlemen used gangs of slaves to produce the staple crops that generated the

income to construct lavish manor houses with elaborate formal gardens. Northern merchants built large residences of Georgian design and filled them with fashionable Hepplewhite or Chippendale furniture. Together, they thought of themselves as the "better sort," and they expected the "lower sort" (also described as the "common herd" or "rabble") to defer to their judgment in social and political decision making.

One characteristic, then, of the "Europeanizing" of colonial society was growing economic stratification, with extremes of wealth and poverty becoming more visible. In Chester County, Pennsylvania, where commercial farming was predominant, the wealthiest 10 percent of the people owned 24 percent of the taxable property in the 1690s, which jumped to 34 percent by 1760. Their gain came at the expense of the bottom 30 percent, who held 17 percent in the

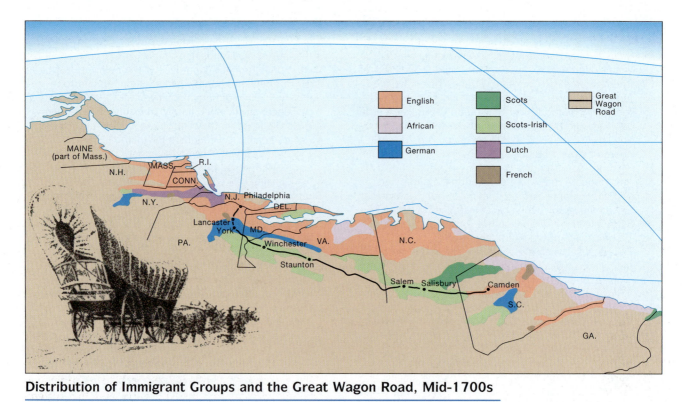

Distribution of Immigrant Groups and the Great Wagon Road, Mid-1700s

Many settlers carried their possessions in Conestoga wagons as they migrated south from Pennsylvania along the Great Wagon Road in search of new homesteads.

1690s but only 6 percent in 1760. The pattern was even more striking in urban areas like Boston and Philadelphia. By 1760 the top 10 percent controlled over 60 percent of the available wealth; the bottom 30 percent owned less than 2 percent.

Nevertheless, the colonies featured a large middle class, and it was still possible to get ahead in provincial America. Over 90 percent of the people lived in the countryside and engaged in some form of agricultural production. By European standards, property ownership was widespread, yet poverty was also common. Some of the worst instances were among urban dwellers, many of whom eked out the barest of livelihoods as unskilled day laborers or merchant seamen. These individuals at least enjoyed some personal freedom, which placed them above those persons trapped in slavery, who formed 20 percent of the populace but enjoyed none of its prosperity or political rights.

With colonial wealth concentrated in fewer and fewer hands, a second "Europeanizing" trend was toward the hardening of class lines. Elite families increasingly intermarried, and they spoke openly of an assumed right to serve as political stewards for the people. As one Virginia gentleman proclaimed in the 1760s, "men of *birth and fortune*, in every government

that is free, should be invested with power, and enjoy higher honors than the people. If it were otherwise, their privileges would be less, and they would not enjoy an equal degree of liberty with the people."

Here was a classic statement of "deferential" thinking. Although widespread property holding allowed substantial numbers of free white males to vote, they most often chose among members of the elite to represent them in elective offices, particularly in colonial assemblies. Once elected, these stewards regularly contested with Crown-appointed governors and councilors in upper houses over the prerogatives of decision making. In colony after colony during the eighteenth century, elite leaders chipped away at royal authority, arguing that the assemblies were "little parliaments" with the same legislative rights in their respective territorial spheres as Parliament had over all British subjects.

More often than not, governors had only feeble backing from the home government and lost these disputes. Consequently, the assemblies gained many prerogatives, including the right to initiate all provincial money and taxation bills. Because governors depended on the assemblies for their salaries, they often approved local legislation not in the best interests of the Crown in exchange for bills appropri-

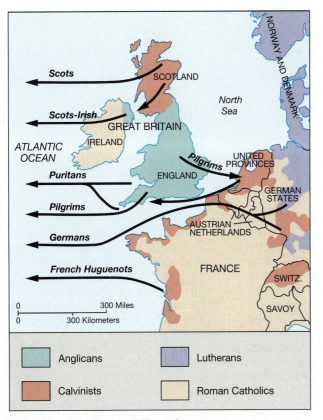

Western European Migration

Western Europeans, escaping religious persecution and dwindling food supplies, migrated in great numbers to North America.

Well-to-do colonists built stately homes and furnished them with fashionable furniture, in conscious imitation of the English aristocratic life-style.

Intellectual and Religious Awakening

Besides politics, colonial leaders paid close attention to Europe's dawning Age of Reason, also called the **Enlightenment.** The new approach to learning was secular, based on scientific inquiry and the systematic collection of information. A major goal was to unlock the physical laws of nature, as the great English physicist Sir Isaac Newton (1642–1727), often considered the father of the Enlightenment, had done in explaining how the force of gravity held the universe together (*Principia Mathematica*, 1687).

Europe's intellectuals, heavily influenced by the English political thinker John Locke (1632–1704), tried to identify laws governing human behavior. In his *Essay Concerning Human Understanding* (1690), Locke described the human mind as a blank sheet (*tabula rasa*) at birth waiting to be influenced by the experiences of life. If people followed the insights of reason, social and political ills could be reduced or eliminated from society, and each person, as well as humanity as a whole, could advance toward greater harmony and perfection. As such, the key watchword of the Enlightenment was **rationalism,** meaning a firm trust in the ability of the human mind to solve earthly problems—with much less faith in the centrality of God as an active, judgmental force in the universe.

Like their counterparts in Europe, educated colonists pursued all forms of knowledge. Naturalists John Bartram of Pennsylvania and Dr. Alexander Garden of Charleston, South Carolina, were among those who systematically collected and classified American plants. The wealthy merchant James Logan of Philadelphia was a skilled mathematician who also conducted experiments in botany that revealed how pollen functioned as a fertilizing agent in corn.

ating their annual salaries. By the 1760s the colonial assemblies had thus emerged as powerful agencies of government.

As self-conscious, assertive elite leaders, colonial gentlemen also read widely and kept themselves informed about European political activities. They were particularly attracted to the writings of a band of "radical" Whig pamphleteers in England who repeatedly warned of ministerial officials who would use every corrupting device to grab all power and authority as potential tyrants at home. The radical Whigs spoke of the delicate fabric of liberty; and provincial leaders, viewing themselves as the protectors of American rights, were increasingly on guard, in case the Crown became too oppressive, as it had been during the 1680s in demanding conformity to the imperial will.

These colonial leaders took challenges to their local autonomy seriously. At least some in their number were ready to mobilize and lead the populace in resisting any new wave of perceived imperial tyranny, should a time ever come when the parent nation attempted to return to arbitrary government.

Colonial Pastimes

FOR much of the past 300 years, Puritans have been the subject of considerable bad press. Novelists and historians have pictured them as dour, sour individuals, dressed in black with faces cast in a permanently disapproving expression. H. L. Mencken, the twentieth-century opponent of what he saw as the Puritan legacy in America, defined Puritanism as "the haunting fear that some one, some where, may be happy." Thomas Babington Macaulay, the nineteenth-century English writer, perhaps best set the tone for Mencken. "The Puritan," Macaulay noted, "hated bearbaiting, not because it gave pain to the bear, but because it gave pleasure to the spectators."

Is there any truth to such broadbrushed stereotyping? What was the Puritans' attitude toward games, sports, and amusements? And how did their attitudes differ from southern Americans? The answers to such questions indicate the differences between Americans North and South.

Commenting on Puritan religious leaders Increase and Cotton Mather, one historian observed, "Though father and son walked the streets of Boston at noonday, they were only twilight figures, communing with ghosts, building with shadows." Certainly, as the quote suggests, the Puritan clergy were sober figures. They looked askance at frivolous behavior. Into this category they lumped sports, games, and amusements played for the pure joy of play. In 1647 the Massachusetts Bay Colony outlawed shuffleboard. A ban against bowling followed in 1650. Football and other sports were similarly treated.

Puritan leaders were opposed to any Sabbath amusements. Sunday was a day for worship—not work, and certainly not play. Remaining true to the teachings of the Prophet Isaiah, Cotton Mather condemned those who tried to justify Sabbath sports: "Never did anything sound more sorrowfully or odious since the day the World was first bless'd with such a day." Those who broke the Sabbath were punished. They were denied food, publicly whipped, or placed in stocks.

Nor did Puritans condone pit sports which matched animal against animal. Before the eighteenth century, pit sports (or blood sports) were popular and commonplace in Europe and the American South. People would travel long distances to watch dogs fight bulls, bears, badgers, or other dogs. Cockfighting was equally popular. Were these spectators cruel? Perhaps not. The "bloodied animals," noted a historian of humanitarianism, "were probably not victims of cruelty. Cruelty implies a desire to inflict pain and thus presupposes an empathic appreciation of the suffering of the object of cruelty. Empathy, however, seems not to have been a highly developed trait in premodern Europe."

Unlike Europeans and southerners, Puritans condemned such activity. They did empathize with the animals. "What Christen [*sic*] heart," wrote Puritan Philip Stubbes, "can take pleasure to see one poor beast to rent, teare, and kill another, and all for his foolish pleasure?"

Although Puritans outlawed pit sports and insisted on the strict observance of the Sabbath, they did not oppose all sports and games. They supported such activities as walking, archery, running, wrestling, fencing, hunting, fishing, and hawking—as long as they were engaged in at a proper time and in a proper manner. Moderate recreation devoid of gambling, drunkenness, idleness, and frivolousness could refresh the body and spirit and thus serve the greater glory of God. This last point was the most important for the Puritans. Recreations had to help men and women better serve God; they were never to be ends in themselves.

Different attitudes toward sports and games emerged in the southern colonies. Almost from the time of settlement, southerners exhibited an interest—oftentimes bordering on a passion—for various sports. They were particularly attracted to sports that involved opportunities for betting and demonstrations of physical prowess.

Cockfights attracted southerners from every class. The matches were advertised in newspapers and eagerly anticipated; at important events thousands of dollars in bets would change hands. For northern observers the entire affair attracted only scorn and disgust. Elkanah Watson, who traveled to the South in the mid-1800s, was upset to see "men of character and intelligence giving their countenance to an amusement so frivolous and scandalous, so abhorrent to every feeling of humanity, and so injurious in its moral influence."

Horse racing surpassed even cockfighting as a favorite southern pastime. Wealthy southerners liked to trace their ancestry to the English aristocracy, and they viewed horse racing and horse breeding as aristocratic occupations. In fact, by the eighteenth century the ownership of horses had taken on a cultural significance. As one student of the subject explained, "By the turn of the century possession of . . . these animals had become a social necessity. Without a horse, a planter felt despised, an object of ridicule. Owning even a slow footed saddle horse made the common planter more of a man in his own eyes as well as those of his neighbors."

Horse races matched owner against owner, planter against planter, in contests where large sums of money and sense of personal worth often rode on the outcome. In most races planters rode their own horses, making the outcome even more important. Intensely competitive men, planters sometimes cheated to win, and many races ended in legal courts rather than on the racetrack.

If planters willingly battled each other on the racetrack, they did not ride against their social inferiors. When James Bullocke, a tailor, challenged Mr. Mathew Slader to a race in 1674, the county court informed the tailor that it was "contrary to Law for a Labourer to make a race being a Sport for Gentlemen." For his efforts, the court fined Bullocke 200 pounds of tobacco and cask. Although labor-

ers and slaves watched the contests, and even bet among each other, they did not mix socially with the gentry.

Unlike the Puritans who believed sports should serve God, southerners participated in sports as an outlet for their very secular materialistic, individualistic, and competitive urges. But neither North nor South had a modern concept of sports. Colonial Americans seldom kept records, respected equality of competition, established sports bureaucracies, standardized rules, or quantified results—all hallmarks of modern sports. Yet each section engaged in leisure activities that reflected their social and religious outlooks.

Benjamin Franklin epitomized Enlightenment thinking in the colonies. As a student of science he wanted to unlock the mysterious laws of nature, such as in his lightning experiments. Franklin was also a printer, inventor, philosopher, and statesman.

Courtesy of Mr. and Mrs. Wharton Sinkler Collection/Philadelphia Musem of Art.

Benjamin Franklin (1706–1790) became the best-known colonial student of science. In the early 1720s he organized the Junto, a club in Philadelphia devoted to exploring useful knowledge. In 1743 he helped found the American Philosophical Society, which focused on compiling scientific knowledge that would help "multiply the conveniences and pleasures of life." Flying his famous kite, Franklin himself performed experiments with lightning, seeking to reveal the mysteries of electrical energy. After publishing his *Experiments and Observations on Electricity* (1751), Franklin's fame spread throughout the Western world. The next year he invented the lightning rod (1752), which he first developed to protect his own home from the destructive energy contained in flashes of lightning.

Franklin was very much a man of secular learning. So were some clergymen, such as Boston's Cotton Mather, who dabbled in science without forsaking strongly held religious beliefs. During a deadly New England smallpox epidemic in 1720 and 1721, Mather was outspokenly in favor of inoculation, which involved purposely inducing slight infections. Many thought inoculations would only spread the disease, but Mather collected statistics that proved the procedure's preventive effects. Whereas 15 percent of uninoculated smallpox victims did not survive, just 3 percent died as a result of inoculation.

Mather conducted his experiment in the face of strong public opposition. Even local physicians railed against him, and one irate citizen threw a rock through the window of his home with the message: "Mather, you dog; damn you: I'll enoculate you with this, with a pox to you." Years would pass before most provincial Americans accepted inoculation as a sensible medical procedure for controlling deadly smallpox epidemics.

Unlike Mather, many ministers viewed the Enlightenment with great suspicion. Rationalism seemed to undermine orthodox religious values by reducing God to a prime mover who had set the universe in motion only to leave humans to chart their own destiny. (This system of thought was known as Deism.) Others perceived a decline in religious faith, as the populace rushed to achieve material rather than spiritual abundance. For some clergymen, the time was at hand for a renewed emphasis on vital religion.

During the 1720s and 1730s in Europe and America, some ministers started holding revivals. They did so in the face of dwindling church attendance in many locales. The first colonial outpouring of rejuvenated faith occurred during the mid-1720s in New Jersey and eastern Pennsylvania, where the determined Dutch Reformed minister, Theodorus Frelinghuysen, and his Presbyterian counterpart, Gilbert Tennent, attacked what the latter called the "presumptuous security" of his parishioners. Delivering impassioned sermons, these two ministers exhorted great numbers of people to seek after God's saving grace. Theirs was the first in a succession of revival "harvests" known collectively as the **Great Awakening.**

The next harvest came in New England. With each passing year fewer descendants of the Puritans showed interest in seeking God's grace and gaining full church membership. Attempting to reverse matters in the early eighteenth century, the longtime Congregational minister, Solomon Stoddard (c. 1643–1729) of Northampton, Massachusetts, threw open the doors of his church and encouraged everyone to join in communion services—the hallmark of full church membership. Stoddard's method worked, and he temporarily reversed the slide.

Then in 1734 Jonathan Edwards (1703–1758), who had succeeded Stoddard, his grandfather, in the

Jonathan Edwards (1703–1758) entered Yale before he was 13 years old, graduated in 1720, and was licensed to preach at the age of 19. In "Sinners in the Hands of an Angry God," he admonished his listeners to acknowledge their own sinfulness and thus take the necessary first step toward spiritual reawakening.

Although George Whitefield failed to convert Benjamin Franklin, the evangelist's eloquence moved Franklin to make a generous contribution to the preacher's collection.

Northampton pulpit, initiated a series of revival meetings aimed at young persons. Edwards was a learned student of the Enlightenment who argued that experiencing God's grace was essential to the full appreciation of the universe and its laws. Like his grandfather before him, he joyously preached about seeking redemption and salvation, soon noting that Northampton's inhabitants, both young and old, were now "full of love."

In 1741 Edwards delivered his best known sermon, "Sinners in the Hands of an Angry God." Preaching fervently, he reminded his listeners of the "manifold . . . abominations of your life," vividly picturing how each of them was "wallowing in sensual filthiness, as swine in mire." He also dangled his audience over "the abyss of *hell*" as a jarring reminder to place God at the center of human existence. Appealing to the senses more than to rational inquiry, Edwards felt, was the surest way to uplift individual lives, win souls for God, and improve society as a whole.

Such local revivals did not become broad and general until after the dynamic English preacher, George Whitefield (1714–1770), arrived in America. Whitefield was a disciple of John Wesley, the founder of the revival-oriented Methodist movement

in England. Possessing a booming voice and charismatic presence, he preached with great simplicity, always stressing the essentials of God's "free gift" of grace for those seeking conversion. Even Benjamin Franklin, a confirmed skeptic, felt moved when Whitefield appeared in Philadelphia. He went to the meeting determined to give no money but relented in the end: Franklin confessed, "I emptied my pocket wholly into the collector's dish, gold and all."

Whitefield, known as the "grand itinerant," made seven preaching tours to the colonies, traveled thousands of miles, and delivered hundreds of sermons. Perhaps his most dramatic tour was to New England in the autumn of 1740. In Boston alone over 20,000 persons heard him preach in a three-day period. Concluding his tour in less than a month, Whitefield left behind churches full of congregants anxious to experience conversion and bask in the glow of their newfound fellowship with God.

The Awakening soon became a source of much contention, splitting America's religious community into **new** and **old light** camps. When in 1740 Gilbert

This observation was essentially correct. With the boom in colonial population, leading planters in Virginia were among those casting a covetous eye on the development of the Ohio valley. With the backing of London merchants one group formed the Ohio Company in 1747 and two years later secured a grant of 200,000 acres from the Crown. Should the company settle 200 families in the valley within seven years, its investors would receive a patent to an additional 300,000 acres.

Determined to secure the region against encroaching Anglo-American traders and land speculators, the French in the early 1750s started constructing a chain of forts in a line running southward from Lake Erie in western Pennsylvania. They decided to locate their principal fortress—and trading station—at the strategic point where the Monongahela and Allegheny rivers join to form the Ohio River (the site of modern-day Pittsburgh).

By 1753 the British ministry knew of these plans and ordered colonial governors to challenge the French advance and "repel force by force" if necessary. Virginia's Governor Robert Dinwiddie, an investor in the Ohio Company, acted quickly. He sent a young major of militia, 21-year-old **George Washington,** whose older half-brother Lawrence was also an Ohio Company investor, to northwestern Pennsylvania with a message to get out. Politely, the French declined.

In the spring of 1754 Washington led 200 Virginia soldiers toward the forks of the Ohio River and learned that the French were already there constructing Fort Duquesne. Foolishly, he skirmished with a French party, killing 10 and capturing 21. Washington then hastily retreated and constructed Fort Necessity, but a superior French and Indian force attacked on July 3. Facing extermination, Washington surrendered and signed articles of capitulation on July 4, 1754, which permitted him to lead his troops back to Virginia as prisoners of war. Out of these circumstances erupted a world war that cost France the whole of its North American empire.

At the very time (June 1754) that Washington was preparing to defend Fort Necessity, delegates from seven colonies had gathered in Albany, New York, to plan for their defense in case of war and to secure active support from the powerful Iroquois Confederacy. The Indian chiefs readily accepted 30 wagons loaded with gifts but did not promise to turn their warriors loose on the French. So as not to get caught on the losing side and face eviction from their ancient tribal lands in New York, the Iroquois assumed a posture of neutrality, waiting to see which side was winning the war. Some Senecas did fight for

JOIN, or DIE.

This woodcut, displayed in the *Pennsylvania Gazette*, failed to overcome long-standing jealousies that thwarted attempts at intercolonial cooperation.

the French; but when the tide shifted in favor of the English after 1758, the Iroquois helped crush the French.

In other major business at the conference, delegates Benjamin Franklin and Thomas Hutchinson proposed an intercolonial plan of government, known as the Albany Plan of Union. The idea was to have a "grand council" made up of representatives from each colony who would meet with a "president general" appointed by the Crown to plan for defense, and even to tax the provinces on an equitable basis, in keeping the North American colonies secure from external enemies. The Plan of Union stirred little interest at the time, since the provincial assemblies were not anxious to share their prerogatives, especially that of taxation, with anyone. The plan's significance lay in its attempt to effect intercolonial cooperation against a common enemy—an important precedent for later years.

Leaders in England ignored the Albany Plan of Union, but the Fort Necessity debacle resulted in a fateful decision to send Major General Edward Braddock, an unimaginative 60-year-old officer who had never commanded troops in battle, to Virginia. Braddock arrived in February 1755 with two regiments of redcoats and orders to raise additional troops among the Americans. He eventually got his army of 3000 moving—Washington came along as a volunteer officer—toward Fort Duquesne. On July 9, about eight miles from the French fort, a much smaller French and Indian force nearly destroyed the British column, leaving two-thirds of Braddock's soldiers dead or wounded.

General Edward Braddock's failure to understand the nature of forest warfare and his underestimation of his opponents' abilities led to his disastrous defeat at Fort Duquesne. Braddock and his troops were ambushed by a force of French and Indian Warriors numbering less than half the size of the English group. The General was wounded in the attack and died three days later.

Washington, appalled by one of the worst defeats in British military history, spoke of being "most scandalously beaten by a trifling body of men." Braddock himself sustained mortal wounds; but before he died, he stated wryly: "We shall better know how to deal with them another time."

Braddock's defeat was an international embarrassment, yet King George II and his advisers hesitated to plunge into full-scale war. They knew the financial burden would be immense. Finally, a formal declaration of war came in May 1756. The Seven Years' War (1756–1763), later referred to in America as the French and Indian War, more accurately should be called "the great war for the empire." Certainly William Pitt (1708–1778), the king's new chief minister, viewed North America as the place "where England and Europe are to be fought for." Not a modest man, Pitt stated categorically that he alone could "save England and no one else can."

Pitt's strategic plan was straightforward. Letting King Frederick the Great of Prussia, Britain's ally, bear the brunt of warfare in Europe, Pitt placed the bulk of England's military resources in America with the intent of eradicating New France. He also advanced a group of talented young officers, such as General James Wolfe, over the heads of less capable men. His plans paid off in a series of carefully orchestrated military advances that saw Quebec fall in September 1759 to the forces of General Wolfe. Then in September 1760 with hardly an exchange of musket fire, Montreal surrendered to the army of General Jeffrey Amherst.

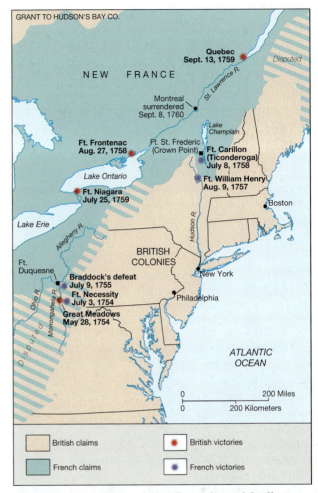

Significant Battles of the French and Indian War, 1756–1763

Allies as Enemies: Making War on the Cherokees

Unlike the Six Nations of Iroquois in New York, the four most powerful southern Indian nations—the Cherokees, Chickasaws, Choctaws, and Creeks—lacked unity of purpose when dealing with Europeans. The Choctaws, residing north and east of New Orleans, became heavily involved in trade with the French, who did not discourage them from engaging in warfare with the Chickasaws of northern Mississippi. The Creeks, who inhabited lands running north from Florida into central Alabama and western Georgia, successfully played off English, French, and Spanish trading interests in maintaining their territorial integrity. Sporadic warfare, however, denoted Creek relations with the Cherokees, whose territory encompassed the western portions of Virginia, North Carolina, and South Carolina as well as eastern Tennessee.

Chronology
OF KEY EVENTS

1651–1673 Parliament passes Navigation Acts to ensure that the colonies trade within the emerging English empire

1664 Dutch settlers in New Netherland surrender to the English, who rename the colony New York

1676 Bacon's Rebellion occurs in Virginia

1681–1682 William Penn founds Pennsylvania as a "holy experiment" in which diverse groups of people all live together homogeneously

1682 La Salle claims the Louisiana country for France

1684–1688 England revokes the Massachusetts Bay Colony charter and eliminates representative assemblies in all colonies east of New Jersey

1686 The Crown establishes the Dominion of New England

1688–1689 The English drive James II from the throne in the Glorious Revolution and replace him with William and Mary

1689 Massachusetts successfully rebels against the Dominion of New England; Leisler's Rebellion occurs in New York; Coode's uprising disrupts Maryland's government

1692 Witchcraft scare in Salem, Massachusetts, results in the execution of 20 women and men

1699 Parliament prohibits the export of woolen products from America

1733 Parliament passes the Molasses Act, which requires colonies to pay a high duty on molasses or rum imported from the foreign West Indies

1739–1740 George Whitefield begins preaching tours that turn local revivals into the Great Awakening

1749 Ohio Company obtains from the British government a 200,000-acre grant to western territory

1750 Parliament passes the Iron Act, which prohibits colonists from expanding the production of finished iron or steel products

1754 Albany Congress draws up a plan to unite the 13 colonies under a single government; George Washington defends Fort Necessity and helps to bring on the Seven Years' War

1759 British forces under General James Wolfe conquer Quebec; warfare erupts along the southern frontier between the Cherokee Nation and English settlers

1763 Treaty of Paris ends the Seven Years' War

At the time of the Seven Years' War, the Cherokees found themselves in a very vulnerable position. A devastating smallpox epidemic during the late 1730s had reduced their numbers by as much as 50 percent to about 10,000 persons. In seeking to restabilize themselves, the Cherokees drew closer to the English. They strengthened trading ties and generally ignored the ominous appearance of frontier settlers, among them many Scots-Irish, who were beginning to squat and farm in the easternmost portions of their tribal lands. After Braddock's defeat, the Cherokees even agreed to help fight the French, hoping in return to get lower prices for British trade goods along with increased supplies of gunpowder.

Then in 1758 a handful of Cherokee warriors coming home from service in the British ranks fell to fighting with western Virginia militiamen and settlers. Both sides lifted scalps, and two years of bloody combat ensued. The Cherokee War of 1759–1761 cost many lives and did not end until an expeditionary force of 2800 British regulars and frontier militiamen, accompanied by Indian support units, among them some Chickasaws, marched into the heart of Cherokee territory and destroyed at least 15 principal villages and hundreds of acres of crops. In the peace settlement that followed in December 1761, the Cherokees made land concessions along the eastern edge of their territory, based on the soon-to-be-broken promise that white settlers would not push beyond this boundary.

A determined people, the Cherokees eventually recovered from the devastation rained upon them in the midst of the Seven Years' War by their English allies. They would keep resisting, but in another seventy years they would have to accept, as would other Native Americans of the Southeast, resettlement in designated enclaves across the Mississippi River (see Chapter 10). Whether this long-term outcome would have been different had the southern nations found the means to rally together in some form of pan-Indian resistance movement will never be known.

CONCLUSION

The fall of the French empire in North America took place in the face of mounting antagonism between British military leaders and the colonists. Americans enlisted in provincial regiments and fought beside British redcoats, but most did not care for the experience. They found the king's regulars to be rough, crude, and morally delinquent. They viewed the king's officers as needlessly overbearing and aristocratic. They resented being treated as inferiors by the British.

Young George Washington explained how Virginia's recruits "behaved like men, and died like soldiers" during Braddock's defeat, as compared to the British regulars, who "behaved with more cowardice than it is possible to conceive." On the other hand, General James Wolfe later described provincial troops as "the dirtiest most contemptible cowardly dogs that you can conceive." The provincials, concluded another British officer, were a "naturally obstinate and ungovernable people, . . . utterly unacquainted with the nature of subordination in general."

The Americans were proud of their contributions to the triumphant British empire. They hoped the Crown would begin treating them with greater respect. Home government leaders, however, thought more like the British military officers in America. They believed that the colonists had done more to serve themselves than the British empire during the Seven Years' War. Because of so many problems related to the war, the Crown would soon prove to be less indulgent toward the "obstinate and ungovernable" American colonists.

Apparently the king's ministers had learned little from the previous 100 years of British-American history. Before 1690, when the laws by which the empire operated became too restrictive, colonial resistance ensued. After 1690, during the so-called era of salutary neglect, an accommodation of differences assured the Americans of basic rights and some local autonomy, so long as they supported the empire's economic and political objectives. Now more self-assertive than ever before, provincial Americans would once again resist imperial plans to make them more fully subordinate to the will of the parent nation. This time they would even challenge the bonds of empire.

SUGGESTIONS FOR FURTHER READING

Fred Anderson, *A People's Army: Massachusetts Soldiers and Society in the Seven Years' War* (1984). Prize-winning examination of colonists who went to war and came home disillusioned with the attitudes and values of their British comrades in arms.

Patricia U. Bonomi, *Under the Cope of Heaven: Religion, Society, and Politics in Colonial America* (1986). Balanced account of the Great Awakening in the framework of the firm commitment to religious beliefs among passing generations of English settlers.

John Demos, *The Unredeemed Captive: A Family Story from Early America* (1994). Fascinating study of a Puritan family captured by Indians during Queen Anne's War and one daughter's crossing of cultural boundaries by embracing the Mohawk way of life.

Carol F. Karlsen, *The Devil in the Shape of a Woman: Witchcraft in New England* (1987). Informative investigation that probes the meaning of witchcraft cases in assessing the constrained status of women in colonial society.

Douglas E. Leach, *Roots of Conflict: British Armed Forces and Colonial Americans, 1677–1763* (1986). Suggestive appraisal of the mounting mistrust between British regulars and American colonists that provoked imperial disunity pointing toward rebellion.

Philip D. Morgan, *Slave Counterpoint: Black Life and Culture in the Eighteenth-Century Chesapeake and Lowcountry* (1998). Thoroughly researched comparative study of the social, economic, and cultural interactions between black and white populations in Virginia and South Carolina.

Stephen S. Webb, *1676: The End of American Independence* (1984). Engaging analysis of Bacon's Rebellion, King Philip's War, and the long-term evolution of white-Indian and colonial-imperial relations.

Esmond Wright, *Franklin of Philadelphia* (1986). Highly readable biography about the amazingly talented Benjamin Franklin.

Overviews and Surveys

Wesley Frank Craven, *The Colonies in Transition, 1660–1713* (1968); Lawrence A. Cremin, *American Education, 1607–1783* (1970); John Morgan Dederer, *War in America to 1775: Before Yankee Doodle* (1990); John E. Ferling, *A Wilderness of Miseries: War and Warriors in Early America* (1980); Lawrence H. Gipson, *The British Empire Before the American Revolution*, 15 vols. (1936–1970); Jack P. Greene and J. R. Pole, eds., *Colonial British America* (1984), and Greene, *Peripheries and Center: Constitutional Development in the British Empire and the United States, 1607–1788* (1986); Richard Hofstadter, *America at 1750: A Social Portrait* (1971); Douglas E. Leach, *Arms for Empire: A Military History of the Colonies, 1607–1763* (1973); David S. Lovejoy, *Religious Enthusiasm in the New World* (1985); John J. McCusker and Russell R. Menard, *The Economy of British America, 1607–1789*, rev. ed. (1991); Alison G. Olson, *Anglo-American Politics, 1660–1775* (1973); Richard Slotkin, *Regeneration Through Violence: The Mythology of the American Frontier, 1600–1860* (1973); Gary M. Walton and James F. Shepherd, *The Economic Rise of Early America* (1979).

Designing England's North American Empire

Joyce O. Appleby, *Economic Thought and Ideology in Seventeenth-Century England* (1978); Thomas J. Condon, *New York Beginnings: The Commercial Origins of New Netherland* (1968); Wesley Frank Craven, *New Jersey and the English Colonization of North America* (1964); J. William Frost, *The Quaker Family in Colonial America* (1973); Joyce D. Goodfriend, *Before the Melting Pot: Society and Culture in New York City, 1664–1730* (1991); Joseph E. Illick, *Colonial Pennsylvania: A History* (1976); Michael Kammen, *Empire and Interest: The American Colonies and the Politics of Mercantilism* (1970); James T. Lemon, *The Best Poor Man's Country: A Geographical Study of Early Pennsylvania* (1972); Barry Levy, *Quakers and the American Family* (1988); Donna Merwick, *Possessing Albany, 1630–1710* (1990); Gary B. Nash, *Quakers and Politics: Pennsylvania, 1681–1726* (1968); Robert C. Ritchie, *The Duke's Province: Politics and Society in New York, 1660–1691* (1977); Sharon V. Salinger, *"To Serve Well and Faithfully": Labor and Indentured Servants in Pennsylvania, 1682–1800* (1987); Sally Schwartz, *"Mixed Multitude": The Struggle for Toleration in Colonial Pennsylvania* (1987); Jack M. Sosin, *English America and the Restoration Monarchy of Charles II* (1981); Stephen S. Webb, *The Governors-General: The English Army and the Definition of Empire, 1569–1681* (1979); Stephanie G. Wolf, *Urban Village: Germantown, Pennsylvania, 1683–1800* (1976); Arthur J. Worrall, *Quakers in the Colonial Northeast* (1980).

Defying the Imperial Will: Provincial Convulsions and Rebellions

Thomas J. Archdeacon, *New York City, 1664–1710: Conquest and Change* (1976); Paul Boyer and Stephen Nissenbaum, *Salem Possessed: The Social Origins of Witchcraft* (1974); Laurie Winn Carlson, *A Fever in Salem: The New England Witch Trials* (1999); Lois Green Carr and David W. Jordan, *Maryland's Revolution of Government, 1689–1692* (1974); John Putnam Demos, *Entertaining Satan: Witchcraft and the Culture of Early New England* (1982); Phillip S. Haffenden, *New England in the English Nation, 1689–1713* (1974); Chadwick Hansen, *Witchcraft at Salem* (1969); Peter Hoffer, *The Devil's Disciples: Makers of the Salem Witchcraft Trials* (1998); Richard R. Johnson, *Adjustment to Empire: The New England Colonies, 1675–1715* (1981); David S. Lovejoy, *The Glorious Revolution in America* (1972); Jerome R. Reich, *Leisler's Rebellion, 1664–1720* (1953); William L. Shea, *The Virginia Militia in the Seventeenth Century* (1983); Jack M. Sosin, *English America and the Revolution of 1688* (1982); Ian K. Steele, *The English Atlantic, 1675–1740: Communication and*

Community (1986); Wilcomb E. Washburn, *The Governor and the Rebel: A History of Bacon's Rebellion* (1957).

Maturing Colonial Societies in Unsettled Times

Richard Aquila, *The Iroquois Restoration, 1701–1754* (1983); Bernard Bailyn, *The Origins of American Politics* (1968), *The Peopling of British North America* (1986), and *Voyagers to the West* (1986); Patricia U. Bonomi, *A Factious People: Politics and Society in Colonial New York* (1971), and *The Lord Cornbury Scandal: The Politics of Reputation in British America* (1998); J. M. Bumsted and John E. Van De Wetering, *What Must I Do to Be Saved? The Great Awakening* (1976); Richard L. Bushman, *From Puritan to Yankee: Character and the Social Order in Connecticut, 1690–1765* (1967), and *The Refinement of America: Persons, Houses, Cities* (1992); Kenneth Coleman, *Colonial Georgia: A History* (1976); Bruce C. Daniels, ed., *Power and Status: Officeholding in Colonial America* (1986); Robert J. Dinkin, *Voting in Provincial America, 1689–1776* (1977); A. Roger Ekirch, *Bound for America: The Transportation of British Convicts to the Colonies, 1718–1775* (1987); Edwin S. Gaustad, *The Great Awakening in New England* (1957); Jack P. Greene, *The Quest for Power: The Lower Houses of Assembly in the Southern Colonies, 1689–1776* (1963); Nathan O. Hatch and Harry S. Stout, eds., *Jonathan Edwards and the American Experience* (1988); Tom Hatley, *The Dividing Paths: Cherokees and South Carolinians Through the Revolution* (1993); Alan Heimert, *Religion and the American Mind: From the Great Awakening to the Revolution* (1966); James A. Henretta, *"Salutary Neglect": Colonial Administration Under the Duke of Newcastle* (1972); Christine Leigh Heyrman, *Commerce and Culture: The Maritime Communities of Massachusetts, 1690–1750* (1984); Rhys Isaac, *The Transformation of Virginia, 1740–1790* (1982); Francis Jennings, *Empire of Fortune: Crown, Colonies, and Tribes in the Seven Years' War* (1988); Stanley N. Katz, *Newcastle's New York, 1732–1753* (1968); Sung Bok Kim, *Landlord and Tenant in Colonial New York, 1664–1775* (1978); Frank Lambert, *Inventing the "Great Awakening"* (1999); Ned Landsman, *Scotland and Its First American Colony, 1683–1760* (1985); Henry F. May, *The Enlightenment in America* (1976); Richard Middleton, *The Bells of Victory: The Pitt-Newcastle Ministry and the Conduct of the Seven Years' War* (1985); Edmund S. Morgan, *Inventing the People: The Rise of Popular Sovereignty in England and America* (1988); Robert C. Newbold, *The Albany Congress* (1955); Howard H. Peckham, *The Colonial Wars, 1689–1762* (1964); William Pencak, *War, Politics, and Revolution in Massachusetts* (1981); William D. Piersen, *Black Yankees: Afro-American Subculture in Eighteenth-Century New England* (1988); J. R. Pole, *The Gift of Government: Political Responsibility from the Restoration to Independence* (1983); Thomas L. Purvis, *Proprietors, Patronage, and Money: New Jersey, 1703–1786* (1986); Alan Rogers, *Empire and Liberty: American Resistance to British Authority, 1755–1763* (1974); Harold E. Selesky, *War and Society in Colonial Connecticut* (1990); Timothy J. Shannon, *Indians and Colonists at the Crossroads of Empire: The Albany Congress of 1754* (2000); Mechal Sobel, *The World They Made Together: Black and White Values in Eighteenth-Century Virginia* (1987); Donna J. Spindel, *Crime and Society in North Carolina, 1663–1776* (1989); Carl E. Swanson, *Predators and Prizes: American Privateering and Imperial Warfare, 1739–1748* (1991);

James Titus, *The Old Dominion at War: Late Colonial Virginia* (1991); Alan Tully, *William Penn's Legacy: Pennsylvania, 1726–1755* (1977); Richard White, *The Middle Ground: Indians, Empires, and Republics in the Great Lakes Region, 1650–1815* (1991); Michael Zuckerman, *Peaceable Kingdoms: New England Towns in the Eighteenth Century* (1970).

Biographies

Elaine G. Breslaw, *Tituba, Reluctant Witch of Salem* (1996); Mary Maples Dunn, *William Penn: Politics and Conscience* (1967); Melvin B. Endy, Jr., *William Penn and Early Quakerism* (1973); Michael G. Hall, *Edward Randolph and the American Colonies* (1960), and *The Last American Puritan: Increase Mather, 1639–1723* (1988); Christopher M. Jedrey, *The World of John Cleaveland: Family and Community in New England* (1979); Paul E. Kopperman, *Braddock at the Monongahela* (1977); Franklin T. Lambert, *"Pedlar in Divinity": George Whitefield, 1737–1770* (1994); William G. McLoughlin, *Isaac Backus and the American Pietistic Tradition* (1967); Kenneth Silverman, *The Life and Times of Cotton Mather* (1984); Phinizy Spalding, *Oglethorpe in America* (1977); Patricia J. Tracy, *Jonathan Edwards, Pastor* (1980).

INTERNET RESOURCES

William Penn, Visionary Proprietor
http://xroads.virginia.edu/~CAP/PENN/pnhome.html
William Penn had an interesting life, and this site is a good introduction to the man and some of his achievements.

Witchcraft in Salem Village
http://etext.virginia.edu/salem/witchcraft/
Extensive archive of the 1692 trials and life in late seventeenth-century Massachusetts.

The Search for La Salle's Ship *La Belle*
http://www.thc.state.tx.us/Belle/index.html
This site covers the archaeological dig to recover the ship of one of America's famous early explorers.

Salem Witchcraft Trials (1692)
http://www.law.umkc.edu/faculty/projects/ftrials/salem/salem.htm
Images, chronology, court, and official documents from the University of Missouri—Kansas City Law School.

Colonial Documents
http://www.yale.edu/lawweb/avalon/18th.htm
The key documents of the Colonial Era are reproduced here, as are some of the important documents from earlier and later time periods in American History.

History Buff's Reference Library
http://www.historybuff.com/library/refseventeen.html
Brief journalistic essays on newspaper coverage of sixteenth- to eighteenth-century American history.

Benjamin Franklin Documentary History Web Site
http://www.english.udel.edu/lemay/franklin/
University of Delaware professor J. A. Leo LeMay tells the story of Franklin's varied life in seven parts on this intriguing site.

Jonathan Edwards
http://www.jonathanedwards.com/
Speeches by this famous minister of the Great Awakening are on this site.

The French and Indian War
http://digitalhistory.org
Digital History LTD provides extensive archives in this site, not intended for an exclusively academic audience.

The French and Indian War
http://web.syr.edu/~laroux/
This site is about French soldiers who came to New France between 1755 and 1760 to fight in the French and Indian War.

KEY TERMS

Mercantilism   (p. 67)
Enumerated Goods   (p. 68)
Navigation System   (p. 68)
"Holy Experiment"   (p. 71)
Salutary Neglect   (p. 78)
Redemptioners   (p. 79)
Enlightenment   (p. 83)
Rationalism   (p. 83)
Great Awakening   (p. 86)
New Lights   (p. 87)
Old Lights   (p. 87)
George Washington   (p. 92)

REVIEW QUESTIONS

1. Define *mercantilism* and trace its implementation in relation to England's North American colonies after 1650. Were the Navigation Acts a burden or a benefit to these colonies?

2. Compare and contrast the factors that led to the establishment of the Middle Colonies (New York, New Jersey, Pennsylvania, and Delaware) in relation to those that resulted in the founding of the New England and southern colonies. What were the most important differences and similarities?

3. What were the major reasons for the political and social upheavals in Virginia, Massachusetts, New York, and Maryland during the 1670s and 1680s? What impact did all of this turmoil have on the long-term development of the colonies?

4. What were the Enlightenment and the Great Awakening, and how did they affect colonial society, culture, and politics? How did these movements relate to the "Europeanizing" of the colonies?

5. Describe the ongoing military conflict among the British, French, and Spanish in the Americas from the 1690s through the 1750s. What competing interests were at stake, and why did the British ultimately emerge triumphant in 1763.

TEA PARTY

J. New York Vol^{rs}
Loyal Amer^{ns}
Emmerick Chas^{rs}
52. Reg.
Reg.

FORT
MONTGOMERY
300 Feet
above the
River

Peleaps
Kill.

Boom

Chain

Galleys burnt.

Frigate burnt.

Sloop taken.

FORT CLINTON
323 Feet above
the River

Pond

HUDSON or NORTH RIVER

Lith. of R. H. Tea

BOSTON MASSACRE

4

BREAKING THE BONDS OF EMPIRE, 1760–1775

"Truly the man of the Revolution"

Samuel Adams (shown here in an engraving by Paul Revere) believed that royalist leaders in Massachusetts wanted to destroy American liberties. He was an organizer of Boston's Sons of Liberty, a vigorous opponent of the Stamp Act, and eventually a leader in the movement for independence. Later he served as governor of Massachusetts.

Samuel Adams (1722–1803) was "truly the *man of the Revolution*," wrote Thomas Jefferson. In the port city of Boston, Massachusetts, Adams was the prime instigator of protest against the new wave of imperial policies adopted by King and Parliament after the Seven Years' War. He was an authentic popular leader, but he preferred to operate as anonymously as possible in guiding the resistance movement. Adams was by nature a secretive person who late in life destroyed many personal records relating to his revolutionary political activities. Perhaps he had something to hide.

"The great Mr. Adams," as one contemporary referred to him during the 1760s, had grown up with many advantages in life. His father, "Deacon" Samuel, was a prospering maltster (manufacturer of malt, a basic ingredient in beer and distilled spirits). The deacon wanted his son to become a Congregational minister, so he sent him off to Harvard College. In 1740 Samuel emerged with a bachelor's degree, a reputation for free spending and excessive drinking, for which he once paid a heavy fine, and little desire to become a clergyman. Always proud of his Puritan heritage, Adams remained a lifelong student of Scripture, but his primary career interest was politics.

The year 1740 turned out to be disastrous for Adams's father. As a community leader the deacon had become deeply involved in a plan to provide individuals with paper currency for local business transactions. The deacon and others established a "land bank" that would lend out money to persons who put up collateral in the form of real estate. The bank's paper money could then be used to purchase goods and services—and even pay debts as legal tender.

The directors of the Massachusetts Land Bank believed they were performing a public service. Wealthy merchants, however, thought otherwise. They viewed such paper currencies with great skepticism. Only money properly backed by **specie,** such as gold or silver, they argued, could hold its value in the marketplace. Under the leadership of a powerful local merchant, Thomas Hutchinson (1711–1780), they appealed to the royal governor, who declared the land bank illegal, a position sustained in 1741 by Parliament.

The crushing of the land bank cost Deacon Adams large sums of money that he had invested to help underwrite the venture. As a bank director, he became a defendant in lawsuits from others trying to regain funds. He never recovered financially. When the deacon died in 1748, he left his son a legacy of bitterness toward arbitrary royal authority and Crown favorites, such as Thomas Hutchinson, whose actions had ravaged his family's prosperity. In addition, the deacon left Samuel a bequest of lawsuits rather than a handsome patrimony.

Samuel Adams considered his father's ruin an instructive lesson in high-handed, oppressive government, a matter very much on his mind when he accepted an M.A. degree at Harvard's commencement in 1743. Although Samuel did not address those in attendance, his printed topic was "whether it be lawful to resist the supreme magistrate, if the commonwealth cannot be otherwise preserved?" Five years later he helped found a short-lived newspaper, the *Independent Advertiser*, in which he repeatedly warned his readers to be on guard against power-hungry royal officials, men under whose authority "our liberties must needs degenerate."

Having no desire to continue his father's business, Samuel barely kept his own family in food and clothing. What little income he earned came from a number of minor political offices. In 1746 he won election as a clerk of the Boston market; in 1753 he became town scavenger; and in 1756 he assumed duties as a collector of local taxes for the town government. He held the latter post until declining reelection in 1765. Samuel had no other choice, since he was £8000 behind in his tax collections and facing legal prosecution to produce the delinquent sum.

Samuel Adams had not taken the money for himself. He simply had not collected taxes from hard-pressed Bostonians who, like himself, were struggling to make ends meet. Adams regularly accepted any good explanation—the outbreak of illness in some families and the loss of jobs in others. Boston's economy was stagnant, and unskilled workers were especially hard pressed. As Adams was also aware, each time he did not enforce a collection he made a friend. By the early 1760s he had built up a loyal following of admirers who considered him a good and decent man committed to protecting their interests.

Even as he earned the gratitude of Boston's ordinary citizens, Adams did not lose sight of his adversaries. He particularly loathed Thomas Hutchinson, whose stature as a wealthy merchant with wide-ranging imperial connections had helped him gain a number of prominent offices. In 1758 Hutchinson secured a Crown appointment as the Bay Colony's lieutenant governor. He was already holding a local probate judgeship, was the ranking local militia officer, and was serving as an elected member of the governor's council (the upper house of the General Court). Then in 1760 Hutchinson received appointment to the post of chief judge of the superior court. His combined annual salary from these offices was around £400 sterling, ten times the amount of an average family's yearly income.

Samuel Adams worried about having so much power placed in the hands of one favored plural officeholder, especially Hutchinson, the very person he held most responsible for wrecking the land bank and his father's finances. In the days ahead when Hutchinson and other royal officials in Massachusetts tried to implement the new imperial policies, Adams was ready to protest and resist. His allies in the streets would be the ordinary people, and they set a particularly defiant example for the broader resistance movement throughout the 13 provinces. Whether Adams acted out of personal rancor toward Hutchinson or purely to defend American liberties was one of the secrets he carried to his grave, even as contemporaries remembered him both in Europe and America as "one of the prime movers of the late Revolution."

The outbreak of the American Revolution can be traced directly to the year 1763 when British leaders began to tighten the imperial reins. The colonists protested vigorously, and communications started to break down, so much so that a permanent rupture of political affections began to take place. No one in 1763 had any idea the developing crisis would shatter the bonds of empire. That, however, is exactly what took place when the American colonists, after a dozen years of bitter contention with their parent nation, finally proceeded to open rebellion in 1775.

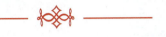

PROVOKING AN IMPERIAL CRISIS

In 1763 British subjects everywhere toasted the Treaty of Paris which ended the Seven Years' War. The empire had gained territorial jurisdiction over French Canada and all territory east of the Mississippi River, except for a tiny strip of land around New Orleans that France deeded to Spain. The Spanish, in turn, who also took over French territory west of the Mississippi River, had to cede the Floridas to Britain to regain the Philippines and Cuba, the latter having fallen to a combined Anglo-American force in 1762. The British likewise made substantial gains in India. From the colonists' perspective, eradicating the French "menace" from North America was a cause for jubilation that should have signaled a new era of imperial harmony. Such was not to be the case.

A Legacy of War-Related Problems

For the chief ministers in Great Britain under the vigorous new monarch George III (reigned 1760–1820), who was 25 years old in 1763, the most pressing issue was Britain's national debt. During the Seven Years' War it had skyrocketed from £75 million to £137 million sterling. Annual interest payments on the debt amounted to £5 million alone. Advisers to the Crown worried about ways to get the debt under control, a most difficult problem considering the newly won territories that the home government now had to govern.

Closely linked to the debt issue was the question of American smuggling activity. Many colonial merchants, eager for profits of any kind, had traded illegally with the enemy during the war. Even though the Royal Navy had blockaded French and Spanish ports in the Caribbean, traders from New England

North America, 1763

British   French   Spanish
Dutch   Russian

North America, 1763

With the signing of the Treaty of Paris, Great Britain received almost all of France's holdings in North America.

King George III, shown here in his coronation robes, was 22 when he acceded to the English throne in 1760.

and elsewhere used various pretexts to effect business deals. Some claimed to sail on missions of benevolence and exchanged prisoners of war to cover up illegal trading operations. These wily merchants and seamen carried more goods than prisoners, and the products they traded helped sustain the French and Spanish war efforts.

When chief war minister William Pitt, normally an advocate of American interests, learned in 1760 that 100 or more colonial vessels flying British flags were in the Spanish port of Montecristi, he sputtered with rage and ordered customs officers in North America to search inbound vessels with greater rigor. The minister was furious about such quasi-treasonous activity and was ready in 1763 to tighten controls on colonial commerce.

A host of issues relating to newly won territories to the north and west of the Anglo-American settlements also concerned the king's ministers. They es-

pecially worried about the financial burden of prolonged warfare on the frontier, should land-hungry white settlers keep pushing into Indian hunting grounds. The vacuum created by the end of French authority greatly concerned Native Americans. They had little reason to trust British traders and settlers. Trade goods, they soon found out, were suddenly more expensive in the absence of French competition. Furthermore, British officials hesitated to deal in firearms and gunpowder. Also aggravating relations were tribal suspicions that royal military officers had given them diseased blankets—taken from soldiers who had died of smallpox—during recent wartime parleys.

Native American prophets, among them Neolin, a Delaware Indian, started traveling among western tribes and arguing for resistance. Neolin urged a return to earlier tribal cultural practices and called for an alliance to drive the English from western forts. Pontiac, an Ottawa war chief who feared the loss of yet more land in the absence of French support, believed Neolin's words. He built a pan-Indian alliance that included Chippewas, Delawares, Hurons, Mingoes, Potawatomis, and Shawnees. Pontiac's initial targets were former French forts that the British now occupied and for which they refused to pay rents—as the French had regularly done in recognition of tribal ownership of the land.

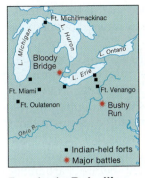

Pontiac's Rebellion

Pontiac, an Ottawa war chief, rebelled against white settlers who were moving onto tribal lands.

Beginning in May 1763, Pontiac's warriors struck with a vengeance at these posts, putting the major fortress at Detroit under heavy siege and attacking white settlements running in a southwesterly arc from New York through western Pennsylvania to Virginia. Only a severe drubbing at Bushy Run, Pennsylvania, in August 1763 turned the tide of bloody frontier warfare against the Indians. By autumn Pontiac's allies began drifting back to their villages, and they also lifted their siege of Detroit. When the final toll was taken, Pontiac's uprising had cost frontier white settlers some 2000 lives; a similar number of Native Americans died as well.

It fell to George Grenville (1712–1770), brother-in-law of William Pitt and a powerful leader in England, to solve these imperial problems. George III personally despised the humorless Grenville, but he needed the votes of Grenville's sizable following in Parliament, which was large enough to secure majorities for pressing legislative issues.

Grenville, who held strong anti-American feelings, became the king's chief minister in April 1763. In the common metaphor of the times, he viewed the provincials as spoiled children in need of a good spanking. As Grenville proclaimed before Parliament, "Great Britain protects America; America is bound to yield obedience." An ominous moment in British-American relations was at hand.

Getting Tough with the Americans

Grenville was not a rash man. A mercantilist in his thinking, he believed the colonists had forgotten their subordinate status in the empire. They needed to be reminded of their essential purpose, that of serving the parent nation. Having studied the issues carefully, Grenville struck hard on various fronts, leaving no doubt that a new era had dawned in Britain's administration of the American provinces.

Grenville made his first moves in early October 1763 through two administrative orders, each approved by the king's cabinet. The first, known as the Orders in Council of 1763, stationed British naval vessels in American waters with the intent of running down and seizing all colonial merchant ships suspected of illegal trading activity. Should juryless

This folk art painting depicts a well-to-do German farmer. The stock around his neck, his coat, and his walking stick all identify him with middle-class status.

Anderson, Elmer G. (American, active c. 1935). Pa. German Painted Wooden Box, c. 1937, watercolor and graphite on paper, .463 x .369 (18 $\frac{1}{4}$ x 14 $\frac{1}{2}$). Index of American Design, © 2000 Board of Trustees, National Gallery of Art, Washington.

vice-admiralty courts condemn these vessels on charges of smuggling, British naval captains and crews would share in profits from the public sales of both the erring colonial ships and their cargoes. The goal was to put an end to American smuggling while compelling the colonists to start paying more trade duties into royal coffers.

The second order, known as the Proclamation of 1763, dealt with the West. It addressed matters of government for the new British territories, including the temporary organization of such provinces as Quebec. It also mandated that a line be drawn from north to south along "the heads or sources of any of the rivers which fell into the Atlantic Ocean from the west and northwest." Deeply concerned by the news of Pontiac's uprising, the ministry's objective was to stop white incursions onto native lands. As such, territory west of the Proclamation line was forever to be "reserved to the Indians."

The Proclamation policy may have reflected some desire for humane treatment of Native Ameri-

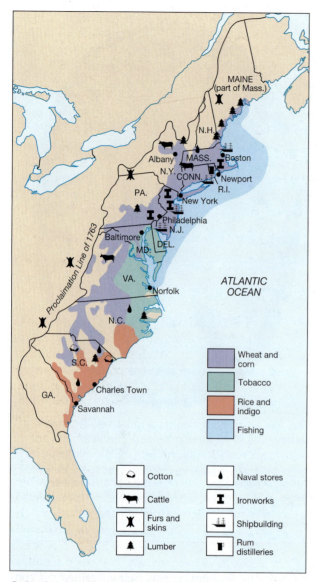

MAINE
(part of Mass.)

N.H.

Albany •   **MASS.**   Boston

N.Y.   **CONN.**   Newport

R.I.

PA.   New York

Philadelphia
N.J.

Baltimore
DEL.

MD.

VA.

Norfolk

N.C.

S.C.

Charles Town

GA.

Savannah

Proclamation Line of 1763

*ATLANTIC
OCEAN*

▬	Wheat and corn
▬	Tobacco
▬	Rice and indigo
▬	Fishing

🐚 Cotton		⬧	Naval stores
🐄 Cattle		I	Ironworks
⚔ Furs and skins		⚓	Shipbuilding
🌲 Lumber		₣	Rum distilleries

Colonial Products in the Mid-1700s

Proclamation policy determined that, at least initially, some of these redcoats would be ordered out onto the frontier.

The most critical matter was who would pay for these redcoats, an issue with the potential to provoke a serious imperial crisis if King and Parliament decided the colonists should assume that responsibility. Grenville had received estimates that the military force would cost at least £250,000 a year. Given the imposing home government debt, the chief minister soon went before Parliament with plans to tax His Majesty's subjects in America.

Grenville warmed to his task during 1764. He contacted the colonial agents who represented provincial interests in England and asked them for ideas about taxing the colonists. Not surprisingly, they had few thoughts. Nevertheless, fully intent on taxing the colonists, Grenville proceeded with Parliamentary legislation to do just that.

The Revenue Act of April 1764, usually called the Sugar Act, embodied a series of complex regulations relating to the loading and unloading of trading vessels. The purpose was to aid customs collectors in ferreting out smugglers. Even more important, the Sugar Act placed trade duties on a number of foreign goods—coffee, indigo, sugar, and wine—regularly purchased by the colonists. The bill also lowered the trade duty on foreign molasses from 6 to 3 pence per gallon (Parliament further reduced this duty to 1 penny in 1766.) The aim of revising downward the Molasses Act duty of 1733 (see p. 78) was to make the fee more collectible and to collect it—in contrast to the earlier period of lax enforcement.

Grenville projected initial annual revenue from the Sugar Act at £40,000. His stated objective was to help offset the costs of imperial administration, in this case only a portion of the sum needed to maintain British regulars in America. From the colonists' perspective, that was the problem with this legislation. The home government's purpose was something more than adopting slight trade duties that would adjust the flow of commerce in the imperial interest. In 1763, for instance, the colonists had paid only an estimated £1800 in imperial trade duties. (The Crown actually spent £8000 that year to operate the customs service in America.) A projected £40,000 in yearly revenue, by comparison, was a sure sign the home government intended to tax the Americans—and much more heavily than had ever been the case heretofore.

Taxation was what Grenville had most in mind; but he also had other concerns, as embodied in Parliament's passage in April of the Currency Act of 1764. This act represented an expansion of legislation directed against New England in 1751. Now the paper money of the colonial governments could no

cans; however, the cabinet's primary concern was to avoid costly Indian wars. Some cabinet leaders, furthermore, did not relish the prospect of American settlements spreading too far inland from the Atlantic coastline. If the colonists built communities across the mountains and out of the reach of the imperial trading network, they would of necessity begin manufacturing all sorts of products—and might, in time, compete with the British Isles for control of seaboard markets. From the imperial perspective, the parent nation's best interest lay in keeping the colonists on the eastern side of the Appalachian Mountains.

The Proclamation of 1763 also related to another policy decision of pivotal consequence. To keep control over both white settlers and Indians, the cabinet had already decided to garrison up to 10,000 British regulars in North America. Pontiac's uprising and the

longer be used as legal tender in payment of private debts. Nor could these governments issue any new paper bills, and the Crown expected them to retire what money they had in circulation within a reasonable time frame.

The logic behind this act was little different than that of wealthy merchants like Thomas Hutchinson when he denounced the Massachusetts Land Bank of 1740. Paper currencies could be highly inflationary, and wealthy creditors were invariably peevish about having to accept depreciated local money for debts. They only wanted to deal in hard coin. In 1764, unfortunately, the colonies were in the midst of a severe postwar depression. Reducing the provincial money supply only worsened conditions by forcing colonists to scramble in obtaining money to conduct business—let alone pay increased taxes. If nothing else, the timing of the Currency Act was terrible; it made the Crown appear incredibly insensitive about promoting the economic welfare of the colonies.

Parliament Endorses Direct Taxes

George Grenville was indifferent about the opinions of the colonists. His major goal was to raise a substantial tax revenue in the colonies. He finally got what he wanted with the Stamp Act of March 1765, the capstone of his imperial program. Through the Stamp Act, Parliament asserted for the first time ever its full authority to lay *direct* taxes, as opposed to *indirect* (or hidden taxes, such as trade duties) on the colonists.

The Stamp Act was not very subtle. To take effect on November 1, 1765, this legislation required Americans to pay for stamps attached to some 50 items, everything from newspapers, pamphlets, almanacs, and playing cards to port clearance papers for ships, land deeds, wills, and college diplomas. The price of the stamps varied according to the value of the particular items. Grenville estimated the tax would yield about £100,000 per year. All stamps would have to be paid for in hard currency, a virtual impossibility since specie (hard money) continually flowed to Britain to pay for imported goods. Also, violators could be prosecuted in juryless vice-admiralty courts, as well as in regular criminal courts.

George Grenville knew the colonists would not like the Stamp Act, but he justified the plan by declaring that "the [parent] nation has run itself into an immense debt to give them protection." The time had come for Americans to pay for the benefits of being part of the mightiest empire in the western world. Grenville was not asking the colonists to help reduce the home debt, only to assist in meeting the actual costs of imperial administration. For that reason, Parliament earmarked Stamp Act revenues for maintaining the redcoats in America.

Grenville used three lines of reasoning in arguing for the Stamp Act. First, citizens in England had been paying stamp taxes for years. Second, the colonial public debt amounted to only £2.6 million, as compared to £137 million in England. On a per capita basis, each person living in Britain owed approximately 20 times as much as each American (£18 as compared to 18 shillings). With such a light per capita public debt load, the colonists could afford a heavier tax burden. Third, to counter arguments about taxation without representation, Grenville employed the concept of **virtual representation.** He maintained that all English subjects, regardless of where they resided in the empire, enjoyed representation in Parliament. His assertion was that members of Parliament (M.P.s), when they made legislative decisions, did not just represent particular constituents at home but every imperial subject, including all colonial Americans.

Testaments to virtual representation found favor in Parliament, where little pro-American sentiment existed, but proved unconvincing to the colonists. Grenville's thinking, moreover, did not encompass the whole picture. From an economic point of view, if from no other, the colonies were invaluable to the British empire. The provinces so stimulated the home economy, particularly with regard to buying manufactured goods, that a serious trade deficit had developed for the colonists. They had gotten into the habit of importing much more from the British Isles than they exported in return. The trade deficit amounted to £1.6 million for the year 1760. By the early 1770s provincial Americans owed more than £4 million to English and Scottish creditors. This was a major reason that hard money was so difficult to come by in America. It was being drained off constantly to pay these debts.

By only looking at specific governmental costs, Grenville had missed an essential point. Provincial subjects were not just taking from the empire; they also provided a ready, indeed, captive market for British-manufactured commodities. In this sense the Americans were paying a significant price, as measured by the trade deficit, in support of the parent nation.

A few members of Parliament appreciated the inherent value of the provinces and did not think of the colonists as overindulged children. Colonel Isaac Barré, who had served under General James Wolfe at Quebec, was one such person. "They grew by your neglect of them," he stated sharply during the Stamp Act debates in Parliament. Now, the tightening imperial grip would cause "the blood of those *sons of liberty* to recoil within them. . . . And remember I this day told you so, that same spirit of freedom which actuated that people at first, will accompany them still." Barré's words were prophetic. The Stamp Act would truly arouse the Americans.

"LIBERTY, PROPERTY, AND NO STAMPS"

Certainly the colonists were not plotting independence in 1763. They were proud to be subjects of the far-flung British empire, stretching as it did from India in the East across the globe to some 30 American colonies in the West, including such Caribbean islands as Barbados and Jamaica. With the elimination of the French threat in North America, mainland colonists were also experiencing a buoyant new sensation of freedom. Paradoxically, the toughened imperial program came at the very time when the colonists, now needing much less government protection from across the ocean, hoped for a continuation if not expansion of the local autonomy to which they had become accustomed. Psychologically, they were ready for anything but new imperial constraints on their lives.

Emerging Patterns of Resistance

As the Grenville program took shape, the colonists evidenced various emotions. Dismay gave way to disappointment and anger. Initial reactions involved petitioning King and Parliament for a redress of grievances. By the summer of 1765 colonial protest took an extralegal turn as Americans resorted to such tactics of resistance as crowd intimidation and violence, economic boycott, and outright defiance of imperial law. The colonists did not think of themselves as Britain's children. Through their tactics of resistance they were asking to be treated more like adults. Few British officials, however, comprehended this message.

The first statements of protest were quite mild, expressed in a flurry of petitions and pamphlets that laid out an American position with respect to essential political rights. In reaction to the Sugar Act of 1764, Stephen Hopkins of Rhode Island expressed the sentiments of many in his widely read pamphlet, *The Rights of Colonies Examined*. He stated that "British subjects are governed only agreeable to laws to which [they] themselves have [in] some way consented." Hopkins then warned his fellow colonists: "Those who are governed at the will ... of others, and whose property may be taken from them by taxes, or otherwise, without their own consent, and against their will, are in the miserable condition of slaves." Hopkins's words may be summarized in the phrase "no taxation without representation"—the core argument against Parliamentary taxation.

In many ways protest by pamphlet and petition was so mild in tone during 1764 that George Grenville did not hesitate to argue for more comprehensive taxation plans. The intensity of American ill feeling in reaction to the Stamp Act thus shocked the home government.

First news of the Stamp Act arrived in the provinces during April 1765, which left ample time to organize resistance before its November 1 effective date. Colonial protest soon became very turbulent, with Samuel Adams's Boston taking the lead in the use of more confrontational forms of resistance.

In Massachusetts, as in many other provinces, a small number of royal officials enjoyed the parent nation's political patronage. This group held the most prominent offices in colonial government, and they were known as the "royalist" or "court" political faction. Besides Lieutenant Governor and Chief Justice Thomas Hutchinson, other leading members of the royalist faction were Governor Francis Bernard, Secretary and Councilor Andrew Oliver, and Associate Justice and Councilor Peter Oliver (Andrew's younger brother). Hutchinson and the Oliver brothers were natives of New England and had all graduated from Harvard College. They were interrelated by marriage, and they were among the wealthiest citizens in America.

Even though these gentlemen were at the apex of provincial society, their opponents in the "popular" or "country" faction did not defer to them. Besides Samuel Adams, another local leader, the brilliant

The Stamp Act, which required Americans to purchase stamps for everything from playing cards to marriage licenses, provoked intense colonial protest. Some newspaper printers expressed their outrage by using a skull and crossbones to mark the spot where the stamp was to be embossed, as shown here in the October 31, 1765, issue of the *Pennsylvania Journal* and *Weekly Advertiser*.

Thomas Hutchinson was key leader of the royalist political faction in Massachusetts.

lawyer James Otis, Jr., viewed the likes of Hutchinson and the Oliver brothers with contempt. In 1760 when Bernard became governor and appointed Hutchinson to the chief judgeship, he ignored the claims of assembly speaker James Otis, Sr., who had been promised this post by an earlier governor. Enraged by Bernard's slight to his father, Otis stated that he would "kindle such a fire in the province as shall singe the governor, though I myself perish in the flames."

Otis was soon speaking out on behalf of American rights and against royal appointees charged with enforcing imperial laws in Massachusetts. Before the end of 1760, for instance, customs collectors in the Bay Colony had started to use blanket search warrants, known as **writs of assistance,** to catch suspected smugglers, particularly those rumored to be trading with the enemy. The writs did not require any form of prior evidence to justify searches; as such, many respected attorneys in England questioned their legality, since they violated the fundamentals of due process in cases of search and seizure.

In 1761 on behalf of merchants in Boston, some number of whom were certainly smugglers, Otis argued against the writs in a well-publicized case before the Massachusetts superior court. Chief Justice Hutchinson ruled in favor of the writs, politely explaining how they were also then in use in England.

In turn, Otis declared that the power of King and Parliament had specified boundaries, implying that only tyrants would uphold the use of writs.

Otis and the merchants may have lost, but they had put Hutchinson in an embarrassing position. They portrayed him as a person blinded to the protection of fundamental legal rights because of his insatiable lust for offices and power. Unfortunately for Otis, he would in a few years lose his mental stability. As a consequence, after the mid-1760s Samuel Adams assumed overall leadership of the popular rights faction in Massachusetts politics.

Adams won his first term to the Assembly in 1765 as a representative from Boston. The emerging Stamp Act crisis gave him an opportunity to launch a simultaneous attack on both unacceptable imperial policies and his old political adversaries. The combined assault commenced in August 1765, shortly after citizens learned that none other than Andrew Oliver was the Bay Colony's proposed Stamp Act distributor.

Protest Takes a Violent Turn

Samuel Adams did not participate directly in crowd actions, nor did the informal popular rights governing body, known as the **Loyal Nine.** (Adams and Otis were not members of this group but were the principal guides in directing the politics of defiance.) The Loyal Nine communicated specific protest plans to men like Ebenezer Mackintosh, a shoemaker living in the South End of town, and Henry Swift, a cobbler from the North End. Before 1765 these two craft workers were leaders of "leather apron" gangs (workers' associations) from their respective districts. The North End and South End gangs, as the "better sort" of citizens called them, were in reality fraternal organizations providing fellowship for artisans, apprentices, and day laborers.

Each year these leather apron workers looked forward to November 5, known as Pope's Day—referring to an alleged plot in 1605 by Guy Fawkes, a Roman Catholic, to blow up Parliament. November 5 was a traditional anti-Catholic holiday during which leaders like Swift and Mackintosh, holding high crude effigies of the devil and the pope, led throngs of North and South End workers in a march through the streets. These working people vented their anti-Catholic emotions and their fears of satanic influences as they marched; they also readied themselves for the annual fistfight that invariably took place after the two groups converged on the center of Boston. The fighting was so vicious in 1764 that at least one person died.

During the summer of 1765 Samuel Adams and the Loyal Nine convinced the North and South End associators to stop fighting among themselves and to unite in defense of essential political liberties. This juncture proved a critical step in ending any attempted implementation of the Stamp Act in Massachusetts.

On the morning of August 14, 1765, the local populace awoke to find an effigy of Peter Oliver (and a boot, representing Lord Bute, Grenville's predecessor) hanging in an elm tree—later called the Liberty Tree—in the South End of Boston. An appalled Governor Bernard demanded removal of the figures; but no one touched them, knowing they were under the protection of the associators—in time called the Sons of Liberty. That evening Ebenezer Mackintosh, who soon gained the title "Captain General of Liberty Tree," solemnly removed the effigies and exhorted the thousands of Bostonians present to join in a march through the streets. Holding the effigies high on a staff, Mackintosh and Swift led what was an orderly procession. As they marched, the people shouted: "Liberty, Property, and No Stamps."

The crowd worked its way to the dockyards, where the Sons of Liberty ripped apart a warehouse recently constructed by Andrew Oliver. Rumor had it that Oliver intended to store his quota of stamps there. Next, the crowd moved toward Oliver's stately home, which the family had fled. Some of the Sons of Liberty tore up the fence, ransacked the first floor, and imbibed from the well-stocked wine cellar. Others gathered on a hill behind the Oliver residence. Materials from Oliver's warehouse as well as his wooden fence provided kindling for a huge bonfire that ultimately consumed the effigies even as the working men and women of Boston cheered enthusiastically. This crucial crowd action was over by midnight.

Early the next morning, as Hutchinson later wrote, the thoroughly intimidated Oliver "despairing of protection, and finding his family in terror and distress, ... came to the sudden resolution to resign his office before another night." Mackintosh's crowd, rather than Crown officials, now were in control of Boston. After this action of August 14, moreover, no one thought at all about assuming Oliver's stamp distributorship. Intimidating threats and selective property destruction had preserved the interests of the community over those of the Crown.

Had Boston's Sons of Liberty and their leaders been solely concerned with rendering the Stamp Act unenforceable, they would have ceased their rioting after Oliver's resignation; however, they had other accounts to settle. A misleading rumor began circulating through the streets, claiming that Thomas Hutchinson was very much in favor of the Stamp Act, indeed had even helped write the tax plan. As a result, the Sons of Liberty appeared again on the evening of August 26. After a few other intimidating stops, the crowd descended upon Hutchinson's opulent home, one of the most magnificent in the province. They ripped it apart. As the lieutenant governor later described the scene, "they continued their possession until daylight" and "demolished every part of it, except for walls, as lay in their power."

Who started the rumor remains a moot point, but Hutchinson's political enemies were well known. Further, some Bostonians may have vented their frustrations with the depressed local economy by ransacking the property of a well-placed person with key imperial connections who was prospering during difficult times. Whatever the explanation, royal author-

Crowds protesting imperial policies—in this case burning tax officials in effigy—were normally made up of ordinary citizens, particularly the working poor.

ity in the Bay Colony had suffered another setback. The looming threat of crowd violence gave Samuel Adams and his popular rights faction a powerful presence that Hutchinson and other royalist officials never overcame.

Resistance Spreads Across the Landscape

By rendering the office of stamp distributor powerless, Boston had established a prototype for resistance. Colonists elsewhere were quick to act. Before the end of the month Augustus Johnston, Rhode Island's stamp distributor-designate, had been cowed into submission. In September Maryland's distributor, Zachariah Hood, not only resigned but fled the province after a crowd destroyed his home. Jared Ingersoll was the victim in Connecticut. The local Sons of Liberty met him on the road to Hartford, surrounded him, and demanded his resignation. They then rode with him to Hartford where the staid Ingersoll renounced the office in public, threw his periwig in the air, and cheered for liberty—to the delight of a menacing crowd. By November 1 virtually no one was foolish or bold enough to distribute stamps in America. Only Georgians experienced a short-lived implementation of the despised tax.

While the colonists employed intimidation and violence, they also petitioned King and Parliament. Assembly after assembly prepared remonstrances stating that taxation without representation was a fundamental violation of the rights of English subjects. Patrick Henry, a young and aggressive backcountry Virginia lawyer, had a profound influence on these official petitions. Henry first appeared in the Virginia House of Burgesses (lower house of the Assembly) in mid-May 1765. The session, meeting in Williamsburg, was coming to a close. Only a handful of burgesses were still present when Henry proposed seven resolutions. They endorsed the first four, which reiterated the no taxation without representation theme, but rejected the fifth as too categorical a denial of Parliament's authority. Henry did not bother to present his remaining two resolutions.

Some newspapers in other provinces reprinted all seven resolutions. The fifth stated that the Virginia Assembly held "the only exclusive right and power to lay taxes and impositions upon the inhabitants of this colony." The sixth asserted that Virginians were "not bound to yield obedience to any law" not approved by their own assembly. The seventh indicated that anyone thinking otherwise would "be deemed an enemy by His Majesty's colony."

Patrick Henry first served in the Virginia House of Burgesses in May 1765 and presented a series of resolutions condemning the Stamp Act.

These three resolutions read as if the Virginia burgesses had denied King and Parliament all legislative power over the American provinces. They seemed to advocate some form of dual sovereignty in which the American assemblies held final authority over legislative matters in America—comparable in scope to Parliament's authority over the British Isles. This was a radical concept, indeed too radical for the Virginia burgesses. Still, the reprinting of all seven of the Virginia Resolutions, as they came to be known, encouraged other assemblies to prepare strongly worded petitions during the summer and fall of 1765.

An important example of intercolonial unity, also bearing on the petitioning process, was the **Stamp Act Congress,** held in New York City during October 1765. At the urging of James Otis, Jr., the Massachusetts General Court called for an intercolonial congress to draft a joint statement of grievances. Nine colonies responded, and 27 delegates appeared in New York.

The delegates to the Stamp Act Congress were mostly cautious gentlemen from the upper ranks of

Those Hated Customs Informers

BENEDICT Arnold, who later became famous for turning against the American cause of liberty, was a prospering merchant in New Haven, Connecticut, before the Revolution. One of Arnold's trading vessels returned from the West Indies during January 1766 and managed to unload its cargo of rum and molasses without paying the required trade duties. Like hundreds of other colonial merchants, Arnold thought nothing of evading imperial customs collectors in American port towns. The economy was depressed, and many merchants were struggling to avoid bankruptcy. In addition, many argued that not paying duties at a time when the colonists were demanding repeal of the Stamp Act was a justifiable form of protest against the willfulness of the home government.

In attempting to stop colonial smuggling, British customs officers were in regular contact with informers, or local inhabitants who listened for rumors in the streets and secretly provided evidence about merchants evading the law. Informers expected cash payments for their services, and if vice-admiralty courts ruled against an offending merchant, informers sometimes shared in profits gained from the sale of confiscated cargoes. To be an informer could be lucrative, but it also assured the wrath of local citizens, should colonists caught smuggling find out who had broken the unwritten law of noncooperation with customs collectors.

Peter Boles was a seaman in the employ of Benedict Arnold who had helped to unload the smuggled cargo. Late in January he approached Arnold and asked for extra wages, implying that the money would help

keep him quiet. Arnold responded tersely that he did not hand out bribes. Boles went straight to the New Haven customs office. The chief collector was not there, so the informer announced his intention to return later with important information.

When Arnold learned of Boles's action, he sought out the mariner, "gave him a little chastisement," and told him to get out of New Haven. Boles agreed to leave, but two days later he was still in town. Arnold, now backed by a number of seamen, confronted Boles at a local tavern and forced him to sign a prepared confession. "Being instigated by the devil," Boles acknowledged that "I justly deserve a halter for my malicious and cruel intentions." He also promised "never to enter the same [town] again."

Four hours later, at 11 P.M., Boles was still tippling at the tavern. This time Arnold returned with yet more followers. The party grabbed Boles and dragged the informer to the town's whipping post, where he "received forty lashes with a small cord, and was conducted out of town." Peter Boles was not heard from again.

Boles's punishment outraged more law-abiding community leaders. Arnold and a few members of his crowd were arrested for disturbing the peace, which ultimately cost each of them a small fine. In response, Arnold organized a demonstration and parade. Dozens of citizens participated in this evening spectacle, which saw effigies of the local magistrates who had issued the arrest warrants carried through the streets on pretended gallows and then consumed in a huge bonfire. As Arnold wrote later, these magistrates had

acted as if they wanted to "vindicate, protect, and caress an informer," rather than stand up for American rights when colonial trade "is nearly ruined by the . . . detestable Stamp and other oppressive acts." Vigilante justice for "infamous informers" like Boles, Arnold maintained, was an effective way to loosen the stranglehold of imperial restrictions on provincial commerce and, at the same time, defend basic rights.

The whipping and banishment of Boles were relatively mild punishments. Angry crowds often covered informers with tar and feathers before strapping them onto wooden rails and "riding" them out of town. In some cases, such as that of Ebenezer Richardson of Boston, informers nearly lost their lives. A combative person and occasional employee of the customs office, Richardson provided damaging information about a prominent local merchant in 1766, for which this informer was " frequently abused by the people." Then in early 1770 Richardson gained the community's wrath by defying citizens enforcing Boston's nonimportation agreement protesting the Townshend Duties. Events got out of hand, and he became known as the greatest "monster of the times."

Since August 1768, when Bostonians accepted Samuel Adams's call for nonimportation, an informal group known as "the Body" directed the harassment of violators. Merchants who kept importing British goods endured much abuse as "importers." Roving bands of citizens struck at night, breaking windows and defacing importers' property; the damage included coating walls with a combination of mud and feces known

> O MURD'RER! RICHARDSON! with their latest breath
> Millions will curse you when you sleep in death!
> Infernal horrors sure will shake your soul
> When o'er your head the awful thunders roll.
> Earth cannot hide you, always will the cry
> Of Murder! Murder! haunt you 'till you die!
> To yonder grave! with trembling joints repair,
> Remember, SEIDER's corps lies mould'ring there;

as "Hillsborough treat." During the day, crowds moved from location to location, posting large wooden hands pointing toward the shops of offending merchants. As customers came and went, they received verbal abuse while dodging flying handfuls of Hillsborough treat.

On February 22, 1770, a crowd visited such a shop in Boston's North End, unfortunately across the street from Richardson's residence. The ever-belligerent informer suddenly appeared and, in the face of verbal taunts and flying debris, tried to remove the hand. Soon he retreated to his house with the crowd, including many boys, following close behind. "Come out, you damn son of a bitch," they shouted, and they started to break the windows. Inside, Richardson and another man loaded their muskets. When the crowd tried to enter the house, the informer first warned his assailants and then fired. He severely wounded an 11-year-old boy, Christopher Seider, who died several hours later. Only the intervention of well-known patriot gentlemen saved Richardson from being lynched.

Samuel Adams and other popular leaders in Boston took full advantage

of this ugly incident. They planned an elaborate funeral during which some 2500 mourners solemnly marched in front and back of Seider's coffin from Liberty Tree to the burial ground. Hundreds more lined the streets as the procession passed by. Popular rights advocate John Adams considered young Seider a martyr to the cause of liberty. Lieutenant Governor Thomas Hutchinson was less charitable. Had his political adversaries had the power to restore Seider's life, he declared, they "would not have done it, but would have chosen the grand funeral."

Christopher Seider's death and emotional funeral were signs of the tension filling the streets of Boston over such imperial legislation as the Townshend Duties. That British redcoats were present to help enforce imperial law and keep the populace under control only made matters worse. In the week following Seider's funeral, there was a dramatic increase in incidents of troop baiting, including the fight at John Gray's ropemaking establishment, all of which culminated in the Boston Massacre.

As for Ebenezer Richardson, he soon stood trial on the charge of willfully murdering Seider. His argu-

ment was self-defense. His wife and two daughters were in the house and had been struck by eggs, stones, and flying Hillsborough treat. The Superior Court judges realized that manslaughter was the proper charge, not "damn him—hang him—murder not manslaughter," the phrase enraged Bostonians shouted as the jurors left the courtroom to deliberate on a verdict.

The jury pronounced Richardson guilty of murder; however, the court, headed by Thomas Hutchinson, initiated a series of legal actions that in 1772 secured Richardson's freedom by king's pardon. Now an outcast, Boston's most notorious informer tried to find work, only to be reviled and sent on his way. Finally, he secured employment with the customs office in Philadelphia, but more than once he disappeared to avoid a coat of tar and feathers because everywhere colonists knew Richardson as the "execrable villain, . . . as yet unhanged" customs informer who had shot down young Christopher Seider.

TABLE 4.1

Estimated Population of Colonial Port Towns Compared to London, England (1775)

London	700,000
Philadelphia	28,000
New York City	23,000
Boston	16,000
Charleston	12,000
Newport	11,000
Baltimore	10,000

London, the capital of the British empire, had an enormous population by the standards of the largest cities in the colonies. The king's ministers were aware of this striking discrepancy, and they regarded American port towns like Boston as minor trading outposts in which a few well-trained redcoats could easily restore order among protesting colonists. Lord Hillsborough certainly believed so, but events proved him wrong.

predicated on Dickinson's widely reprinted pamphlet and his call for petitions. If the British ministry had ignored the Massachusetts document, nothing of consequence might have happened. However, Wills Hill, Lord Hillsborough (1718–1793), who had recently taken the new cabinet post of Secretary for American Affairs, overreacted and provoked needless conflict.

Hillsborough considered the Circular Letter insubordinate. He quickly fired off orders to Governor Bernard to confront the General Court and demand an apology. If the delegates refused (they did overwhelmingly), Bernard was to dissolve the assembly and call for new elections. In addition, Hillsborough sent his own circular letter to the other colonial governors, insisting that they not allow their assemblies "to receive or give any countenance to this seditious paper" from Massachusetts. If they did, such assemblies were also to be dissolved. The result of Hillsborough's actions actually strengthened the colonists' resolve when new elections swelled the ranks of delegates firmly committed to resisting any form of Parliamentary taxation.

Just as the Massachusetts Circular Letter infuriated Hillsborough, so did the rough treatment experienced by royal customs officials, particularly in Boston where the Crown had recently located a new five-man Board of Customs Commissioners. When members of the board, which was to coordinate all customs collections in America, arrived at the end of 1767, jeering crowds greeted them at the docks. The

commissioners found it virtually impossible to walk the streets or carry out their official duties without harassment.

More serious trouble erupted in June 1768 when a crowd attacked local customs collectors who had seized John Hancock's sloop *Liberty* on charges of smuggling in a cargo of Madeira wine. (Hancock was notorious for illegal trading.) For their personal safety, the new commissioners fled to Fort Castle William in Boston harbor. Even before the *Liberty* riots, they had sent reports to Hillsborough about the unruly behavior of Bostonians, and they had asked for military protection.

In the wake of the August 1765 Stamp Act riots, royalist political faction leaders had likewise talked in private about calling for military support. Governor Bernard demurred, thinking that the presence of redcoats might provoke even greater turmoil in the streets. Hillsborough, however, was not going to tolerate such abusive behavior from the Bostonians, even in the absence of a formal gubernatorial request for troops. Just before the *Liberty* riots took place, the American secretary issued orders for four regiments of redcoats to proceed to Boston. The troops were "to give every legal assistance to the civil magistrate in the preservation of the public peace; and to the officers of the revenue in the execution of the laws of trade and revenue."

When the first redcoats arrived in the fall of 1768 without serious incident, members of the royalist political faction went about their duties with newfound courage. Many inhabitants hoped that crowd rule, civil anarchy, and open harassment were tactics of the past.

Samuel Adams and the popular rights faction, however, kept demanding more resistance. On August 1, 1768, they convinced an enthusiastic town meeting to accept a nonimportation boycott of British goods. New Yorkers signed a similar agreement a few days later. Philadelphians refused at first to go along with their two northern neighbors, bowing to the pressure of influential merchants. Somewhat reluctantly, they finally joined the trade boycott in February 1769. Pressure from South Carolina's popular leader, Christopher Gadsden, backed by threats of crowd action, convinced Charleston merchants to come around in August 1769. A year had passed, but now all the major port cities had endorsed yet another trade boycott in defense of political liberties.

The colonists did more than boycott. In some communities talk was rife about producing manufactured goods, such as woolen cloth, in direct defiance of imperial restrictions. With the boycott in full force wealthier citizens could no longer get the most fashionable fabrics from London, and popular lead-

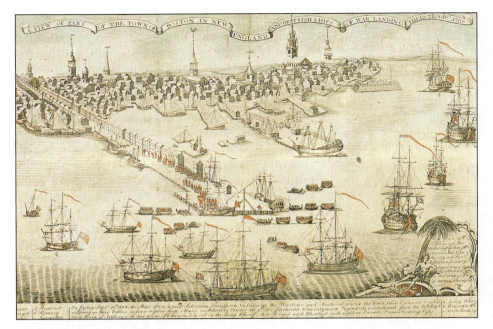

British redcoats landed at Boston's Long Wharf in 1768 with orders to put an end to ongoing political unrest in that port city.

ers encouraged them to join poorer colonists in wearing homespun cloth—a sign of personal sacrifice for the cause. Some leaders urged all "genteel ladies" to master the skills of spinning and weaving. The *Boston Gazette* asked "Daughters of Liberty" everywhere to:

> First then throw aside your high top knots of pride
> Wear none but your own country linen
> Of economy boast. Let your pride be the most
> To show clothes of your make and spinning.

Upper-class women, by and large, remained skeptical. They did not like the itchy feeling of homespun, and they considered spinning and weaving to be beneath their station in society. For poorer women, particularly those in the port cities, the trade boycott generated opportunities for piecemeal work in the production of homespun cloth. Such labor meant extra income, but there was virtually no long-term effect in improving the lot of the poor in America. Homespun was abundant, and the market price remained quite low. While wealthier women itched, complained, and worried about losing their status, poorer women were virtually donating their labor to the defense of American rights. For them the term "sacrifice" held a special meaning.

A "Bloody Massacre" in Boston

The citizens of Boston deeply resented the redcoats in their midst. When the king's troops had first debarked in October 1768, a concerned local minister

proclaimed: "Good God! What can be worse to a people who have tasted the sweets of liberty! Things have come to an unhappy crisis, . . . and the moment there is any bloodshed all affection will cease."

Besides symbolizing political tyranny, the redcoats also competed for scarce jobs because, when not on duty, their officers allowed them to work for extra wages on a piecemeal basis. As a result, the troops made hard economic times even harder for day laborers, semiskilled workers, and other poorer Bostonians already suffering from the prolonged economic depression besetting their community.

Throughout 1769 troop baiting by Boston's working men and women had resulted in fistfights and bloodied faces. Bad feelings continued to mount as winter snows covered the ground. Then on March 2, 1770, an ugly confrontation took place. A young off-duty soldier, Patrick Walker, entered John Gray's ropemaking establishment and asked for work. Seizing the opportunity to be insulting, one of Gray's workers snorted: "Well, then go and clean my shithouse." Taken aback, the soldier snapped in response: "Empty it yourself." Upset and angry, Walker fled amid taunts and threats from other laborers.

Walker told his story to comrades like Mathew Kilroy and William Warren of the 29th regiment. He convinced several of them to join him in teaching these workers a lesson. The soldiers soon appeared at Gray's, and a general brawl ensued before Gray's workers drove off the redcoats. This nasty fight would have been lost to history had it not been an important precursor to the so-called Boston Massacre three days later.

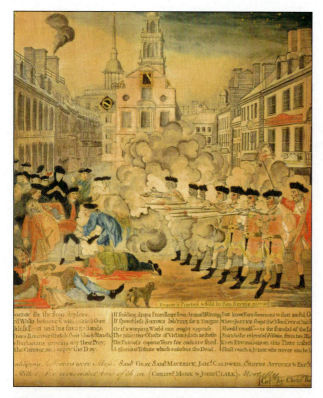

Effective propaganda, such as Paul Revere's engravings of the Boston Massacre, helped increase outrage over the event. Here, the British soldiers appear to be firing without provocation into an innocent-looking crowd.

Revere, Paul, Boston Massacre, 1770. U.S., 1735–1818. Engraving after Henry Pelham, hand-colored by Christian Remik (1726–after 1783) 10¼ x 8⅝ in. Gift of Watson Grant Cutter. Courtesy, Museum of Fine Arts, Boston.

Monday, March 5, was bitterly cold, but heated emotions among workers and soldiers could have melted the deep piles of snow in the streets. A number of isolated fights had occurred over the weekend, but an eerie calm pervaded on Monday because Boston's working people had decided to challenge the redcoats' continued presence in their community. Toward evening small parties of day laborers, apprentices, and merchant seamen began milling about in the streets, eventually moving toward King Street, the site of the Customs House. Here a lone redcoat was on guard duty, and the growing crowd pressed in on him.

Then a small detachment from the 29th regiment, including privates Kilroy and Warren, appeared. After rescuing their isolated comrade, the redcoats retreated to the steps of the customs house with the Boston crowd harassing them with mud, snowballs, and rocks every step of the way. Captain Thomas Preston tried to steady his squad, but one

of his soldiers, fearing for his life, panicked. He leveled his musket and shot into the crowd. Ignoring Preston's orders to stop, other soldiers also fired their weapons. Before the shooting was over, a number of civilians lay wounded and dying.

All told, five colonists lost their lives, including Samuel Gray, a relative of John Gray and a participant in the March 2 brawl; seventeen-year-old Samuel Maverick, brother-in-law of shoemaker Ebenezer Mackintosh; and Crispus Attucks, an unemployed mulatto merchant seaman. Bostonians would soon hail these men as martyred heroes in the struggle to defend American liberties.

Captain Preston and his troops faced trials for murder. The court found all but two of the redcoats innocent on the grounds of having been forced into a life-threatening situation by an enraged crowd of citizens. Private Kilroy and another soldier were declared guilty of manslaughter. By pleading benefit of clergy they had their thumbs seared with a hot branding iron before being sent back to their regiment.

Long before these verdicts, royal officials removed the hated redcoats from Boston. In this sense the working citizens of Boston had won—at the cost of five lives. They had freed their community of British regulars and unwanted economic competition. Just as important, the Boston Massacre caused colonists everywhere to ask just how far King and Parliament would go to sustain the imperial will. With lives now lost, Americans would be increasingly wary of British government actions that might result in some detestable form of political tyranny. In sum, the legacy of the Boston Massacre was even greater mistrust of the parent nation's intentions.

Parliament Backs Down Again

The colonists' trade boycott seriously hurt merchants and manufacturers in the British Isles. By the beginning of 1770 the Townshend program had netted only about £20,000 in revenue, a paltry sum when compared to the loss in American trade, estimated to be as high as £7 million. Once again, the colonists had found the means to get Parliament to reevaluate its position.

It may have been fortunate for Charles Townshend that he died unexpectedly in September 1767. He did not have to listen to the abuse that his infamous duties took before Parliament in early 1770. By that time the Pitt ministry had collapsed. In January 1770 George III asked amiable Lord Frederick North (1732–1792) to form a new cabinet and give some direction to drifting governmental affairs.

North, listening to the wrath of powerful merchants and manufacturers in the British Isles, moved quickly to settle differences with America. He went before Parliament on March 5, 1770 (ironically the same day as the Boston Massacre) and called for repeal of the Townshend Duties, except for the tax on tea, which was to stand as a face-saving, symbolic reminder of Parliament's right to tax and legislate for the Americans in all cases whatsoever. As with the Stamp Act confrontation, the colonial trade boycott of 1768–1770 most certainly had a telling effect. King and Parliament had backed down again—but for the last time.

THE RUPTURING OF IMPERIAL RELATIONS

Lord North was a sensible leader who wanted to avoid taxation schemes and other forms of legislation that could provoke more trouble. He understood that imperial relations had been strained almost to a breaking point by too many controversial policies thrown at the colonists in too short a time after so many years of salutary neglect. North carefully avoided challenging the Americans between 1770 and 1773. In turn, the colonial resistance movement clearly waned. For a while, then, there were no new issues to stir further conflict—only old problems needing resolution.

When Parliament stepped back from the Townshend Duties, most colonists wanted to end the boycott and return to normal trade relations, despite the irritating tax on tea. That duty, they knew, could be avoided by the continued smuggling of Dutch tea. Slowly, economic relations with Great Britain improved, and His Majesty's subjects in England and America enjoyed a brief period of mutually beneficial economic prosperity.

The Necessity of Vigilance

Political relations were not so resilient. Many colonists had become very suspicious of the intentions of home government officials. Provincial leaders tried to explain what had happened since 1763 by drawing on the thoughts of England's "radical" **whig** opposition writers of the early eighteenth century. Men such as John Trenchard and Thomas Gordon, who had penned an extended series of essays known as *Cato's Letters* (1720–1723), had repeatedly warned about corruption in government caused by high ministerial officials lusting after power. If such officials were not stopped, citizens like the colonists would find themselves stripped of all liberties and living in a state of tyranny (often described as **political slavery**).

What took firm hold during the 1760s was an American worldview, or ideology, that saw liberties

under attack by such grasping, power-hungry leaders as George Grenville and Charles Townshend in England and their royalist puppets in America, personified by such officials as Thomas Hutchinson and Andrew Oliver. Evidence of a conspiracy seemed overwhelming to those attempting to explain what had happened. Obvious signs included the hovering presence of British redcoats in such places as Boston and ships of the Royal Navy patrolling American waters, all during peacetime. The colonists had been cut off from frontier lands, and—perhaps worst of all from their perspective—they had experienced three willful attempts to tax them, literally to deprive them of property without any voice in the matter.

As never before, great numbers of colonists doubted the goodwill of the home government. Even if Lord North was behaving himself and keeping Parliament in check, many were sure that ministerial inaction was nothing more than a trick designed to lull Americans into a false sense of security while conspiring royal officials devised new and even more insidious plans to strip them of basic political rights.

Popular leaders exhorted the citizenry to be vigilant at all times. They employed various devices to ensure that the defense of liberties was not forgotten. In Boston Samuel Adams and his political lieutenants declared March 5 to be an annual commemorative holiday to honor the five fallen martyrs of the Massacre. Each year there was a large public meeting and grand oration to stir memories and to remind the populace of the possible dangers of a new ministerial assault.

Local confrontations also kept emotions stirred up. One such incident occurred in June 1772 and involved a Royal Naval vessel, the *Gaspée*, that regu-

Tension increased between British leaders and the American colonists when in June 1772 Rhode Islanders burned the *Gaspée*, a Royal Naval vessel charged with patrolling the area for smugglers.

THE PEOPLE SPEAK

Dr. Joseph Warren's Boston Massacre Oration (1772)

Just 31 years old in 1772, Joseph Warren was a seasoned veteran of the political struggles in Massachusetts between the popular rights faction of Samuel Adams and the royalist clique of Thomas Hutchinson. Warren graduated from Harvard College in 1759. He then turned to the study of medicine while also nurturing his political skills as an advocate of American rights. He became a favorite of Samuel Adams, who saw in Warren a keenly intelligent person who also possessed extraordinary speaking talent. On the second anniversary of the massacre, March 5, 1772, Warren stood before a huge assemblage in Boston and presented an oration about that terrible confrontation—and its larger meaning. He appealed to history in warning his audience about the dangers of standing armies, and he passionately described how much destruction the king's troops were so capable of producing. His words had a certain prophetic quality, at least for Warren himself. Just a little over three years later he died at the hands of British regulars in the midst of combat during the Battle of Bunker Hill.

The ruinous consequences of standing armies to free communities may be seen in the histories of Syracuse, Rome, and many other once flourishing states; some of which have now scarce a name! Their baneful influence is most suddenly felt when they are placed in populous cities; for, by a corruption of morals, the public happiness is immediately affected! . . . And this will be more especially the case when the troops are informed that the intention of their being stationed in any city is to overawe the inhabitants. That this was the avowed design of stationing an armed force in this town is sufficiently known; and we, my fellow citizens, have seen, we have felt the tragical effects! *The fatal fifth of March, 1770, can never be forgotten*. The horrors of *that dreadful night* are but too deeply impressed on our hearts. Language is too feeble to paint the emotion of our souls, when our streets were stained with the blood of our brethren—when our ears were wounded by the groans of the dying, and our eyes were tormented with the sight of the mangled bodies of the dead.

When our alarmed imagination presented to our view our houses wrapped in flames, our children subjected to the barbarous caprice of the raging soldiery, our beauteous virgins exposed to all the insolence of unbridled passion, our virtuous wives, endeared to us by every tender tie, falling sacrifice to worse than brutal violence, and perhaps like the famed Lucretia, distracted with anguish and despair, ending their wretched lives by their own fair hands. When we beheld the authors of our distress parading in our streets, or drawn up in a regular *battalia*, as though in a hostile city, our hearts beat to arms; we snatched our weapons, almost resolved by one decisive stroke to avenge the death of our slaughtered brethren, and to secure from future danger all that we held most dear: but propitious heaven forbade the bloody carnage and saved the threatened victims of our too keen resentment, not by their discipline, not by their regular array, no, it was royal George's livery that proved their shield—it was that which turned the pointed engines of destruction from their breasts. The thoughts of vengeance were soon buried in our inbred affection to Great Britain, and calm reason dictated a method of removing the troops more mild than an immediate resource to the sword. With united efforts you urged the immediate departure of the troops from the town—you urged it, with a resolution which ensured success—you obtained your wishes, and the removal of the troops was effected without one drop of their blood being shed by the inhabitants. . . .

Source: Merrill Jensen, ed., *English Historical Documents*, Vol. 9: *American Colonial Documents to 1776* (New York, 1969), 756–757.

larly patrolled for smugglers in the waters off Rhode Island. The ship's crew and its captain, William Dudingston, were very efficient. Finally, Rhode Islanders had endured enough. One day they sent out a sloop that purposely flaunted itself before the *Gaspée*. Suspecting illicit trading activity, Dudingston gave chase but ran aground as the smaller vessel swept close to shore. That evening, a crowd, disguised as Indians, descended upon the stranded ship and

burned it. One of the crowd delivered the supreme insult by firing a load of buckshot into Dudingston's buttocks.

Crown officials were furious about the *Gaspée's* destruction. They set up a royal commission of inquiry but never obtained any conclusive evidence regarding the perpetrators of this crowd action. Curiously, popular leaders, ignoring the reasons that the *Gaspée* was in American waters in the first place, set up a hue and cry about the royal commission. They feared that the intention was to send suspects to England for trial. Consequently, several provincial assemblies established **committees of correspondence** to communicate with one another, should home government leaders appear to jeopardize liberties of any kind—in this case holding trials of persons outside districts where they had allegedly committed crimes. These correspondence committees were soon writing back and forth regarding problems over tea.

The Tea Crisis of 1773

The final assault on American rights, as the colonists perceived reality, grew out of a rather inconspicuous piece of legislation known as the Tea Act of 1773. When Lord North proposed this bill, he had no idea that it would precipitate a disastrous sequence of events; indeed, he was hardly thinking about the American provinces. His primary concern was the East India Company, a joint-stock trading enterprise that dated back to the early seventeenth century whose officials ruled over British interests in India.

Once enormously prosperous, the company had descended into desperate economic straits by the early 1770s. One reason was that the recent colonial boycott had cost the company its place in the American tea market. With tea warehouses bulging, company directors sought marketing concessions from Parliament. They asked to have the authority to ship tea directly from India to America rather than through England, which would lower the final market price. In May 1773 King and Parliament acceded to this request and, in turn, forced the company to give up some of its political authority in India.

To reduce costs further, the company proceeded to name its own tea agents in the major American ports. The agents were to function as local distributors for 6 percent commissions. The net effect of these changes was to make company tea much more competitive with, if not cheaper than, smuggled Dutch blends—a fact that pleased Lord North very much.

North was even more pleased to have found a way, he thought, to get the Americans to accept the tea tax—and, symbolically at least, recognize Parliament's sovereignty. How could they refuse cheaper tea, even with the Townshend duty added to the price? The chief minister should have listened to the M.P. who warned him during the debates on the Tea Act that "if we don't take off the duty they won't take the tea."

In September 1773 the company dipped into its warehouses and readied its first American consignment of 600,000 pounds of tea worth £60,000. Vigilant Americans were waiting. Conditioned by years of warding off undesirable imperial legislation, they were looking for signs of further conspiratorial acts. A small economic saving meant nothing in the face of what they believed to be another, more insidious plot to reduce them to a state of political slavery. East India Company tea had to be resisted.

Once again, the port city of Boston became the focal point of significant protest. In early November a crowd took to the streets and tried to intimidate the tea agents (among them Thomas and Elisha Hutchinson, sons of Thomas who was now the royal governor) into resigning. The merchant agents, who had not received official commissions as yet, refused to submit; the crowd did not press the matter, waiting for a more timely moment to force resignations.

On November 28 the first tea ship, the *Dartmouth,* docked in Boston. The local customs collectors fled to Fort Castle William, and the local committee of correspondence, headed by Samuel Adams and his associates, put guards on the *Dartmouth* and two other tea ships entering the port within the next few days. Repeatedly the popular rights faction insisted that the three tea ships be sent back to England. But Governor Hutchinson refused. This native-son royal governor could be fair-minded but also stubborn, and this time Hutchinson decided that a showdown was necessary. He called on Royal Naval vessels in the vicinity to block off the port's entrance.

According to imperial law, unclaimed cargo had to be unloaded after 20 days in port and then sold at public auction. Since the tea ships could not escape the harbor, Hutchinson fully expected to have the vessels unloaded after the 20-day waiting period. Once the tea had been sold at auction, the Townshend duty would be paid from the revenues obtained, and the governor would have upheld the law of King and Parliament. Hutchinson's determination to stand firm on behalf of imperial authority—and against his troublesome, long-time local enemies—proved to be a bad idea.

The waiting period for the *Dartmouth* was over on December 16. That day a mass meeting of local citizens took place at Old South Church. The Samuel Adams faction made one last attempt to communicate the gravity of the situation to Hutchinson. They sent a messenger to him with a very clear message—remove the tea ships or else. Hutchinson refused again. Late in the day, Adams appeared before the huge gathering and reportedly shouted: "This meeting can do no more to save the country." The moment for crowd action had come. Several dozen artisans, apprentices, and day laborers, led by Ebenezer Mackintosh, went to the docks disguised as Indians. They clambered onto the tea ships and dumped 342 chests of tea valued at £10,000 into the harbor. It took them nearly three hours to complete the work of the Boston Tea Party.

Tea confrontations occurred later in other ports, but none were as destructive as that in Boston. Philadelphians used the threat of tar and feathers to convince local officials to send back the first tea ships to arrive there. The governor of South Carolina outmaneuvered the local populace and managed to get the tea landed, but the company product lay rotting in a warehouse and was never sold. New Yorkers had to wait until the spring of 1774 for tea ships to appear in their port. They jeered loudly at the docks, and an intelligent sea captain raised anchor and fled for the high seas. Once again, then, the Bostonians stood out for their bold defiance of imperial law.

Parliament Adopts the Coercive Acts

The Boston Tea Party shocked Lord North and other British leaders. North decided that the "rebellious" Bostonians had to be taught a lesson, and Parliament adopted a series of legislative bills, collectively known as the *Coercive Acts*. Although King and Parliament aimed these laws at Massachusetts, the Coercive Acts held implications for colonists elsewhere who believed that the tyrannical parent nation was using the Tea Party as a pretext for the final destruction of American liberties.

King George III signed the first act, known as the Boston Port Bill, into law at the end of March 1774. This act closed the port of Boston, making trade illegal until such time as local citizens paid for the tea. In May Parliament passed the Massachusetts Government Act and the Administration of Justice Act. The first suspended the colony's royal charter (which dated to 1691), vastly expanded the powers of the royal governor, abolished the elective council (upper house of the General Court), and replaced that body with appointed councilors of the Crown's choosing. Town meetings could be held only with the governor's permission, except for annual spring election gatherings.

Governor Hutchinson never exercised this vastly expanded range of authority. Distraught by the Tea

Quebec Act of 1774

By making the Ohio River the new southwest boundary of Quebec, the Quebec Act cut into land the colonists wanted for expansion.

Party, he asked for a leave of absence and traveled to England. The Crown replaced him with General Thomas Gage, Britain's North American military commander, who held the governorship until the final disruption of royal government in the Bay Colony.

The Administration of Justice Act provided greater protection for customs collectors and other imperial officials in Massachusetts. If they injured or killed anyone while carrying out their official duties, the governor would have the right to move trials to some other colony or to England. The assumption was that local juries were too biased to render fair judgments.

Finally, in early June 1774 Parliament sanctioned the fourth coercive bill, which was an amendment to the Quartering Act of 1765. The earlier law had outlined procedures relating to housing for the king's regulars and had specifically excluded the use of private dwellings of any kind. The 1774 amendment gave General Gage the power to billet his troops anywhere, including unoccupied private homes, so long as the army paid fair rental rates. Parliament passed this law because Gage was bringing several hundred troops to Boston with him.

The colonists also viewed the Quebec Act, approved in June 1774, as another piece of coercive legislation. Actually, this bill mainly concerned itself with the territorial administration of Canada by providing for a royal governor and a large appointed advisory council, but no popularly elected assembly. Roman Catholicism was to remain the established religion for the French-speaking populace. In addition, the Ohio River was to become the new southwestern boundary of Quebec.

Ever-vigilant colonial leaders viewed the Quebec Act as confirming all the worst tendencies of imperial rule over the past decade. Parliament had denied local representative government; it had ratified the establishment of a branch of the Christian faith that was repugnant to militantly Protestant Americans, especially New Englanders; and it had wiped out the claims of various colonial governments to millions of acres of western land, in this case all of the Ohio country. The latter decision particularly infuriated well-placed provincial land speculators, among them Benjamin Franklin and George Washington, who had fixed on this region for future development and population expansion. The Quebec Act, concluded thousands of Americans, smacked of abject political slavery.

Even without the Quebec Act, Lord North had made a tactical error by encouraging Parliament to pass so much legislation. The port bill punishing Boston was one thing; some Americans believed the Bostonians had gone too far and deserved some chastisement. The sum total of the Coercive Acts, however, caused widespread concern because they seemed to violate the sanctity of local political institutions, to distort normal judicial procedures, and to favor military over civil authority. For most colonists the acts resulted in feelings of solidarity with (rather than separateness from) the Bostonians, a critical factor in generating a unified resistance movement.

Hurling Back the Challenge: The First Continental Congress

News of the full array of Coercive Acts provoked an outburst of intercolonial activity, the most important expression of which was the calling of the **First Continental Congress.** This body began its deliberations in Philadelphia on September 5, 1774. Gentlemen of all political persuasions were in attendance (Georgia was the only colony not represented). Among the more radical delegates were Samuel Adams and his younger cousin John, as well as Patrick Henry. George Washington was present, mostly silent in debates but firmly committed to defending fundamental rights. Conservative delegates included Joseph Galloway of Pennsylvania and John Jay of New York. The core question was how confrontational the Congress should be. The more cautious delegates wanted to find some nonhostile means to settle differences with Britain, but the radicals believed that only a well-organized resistance effort would induce home government leaders to back down yet a third time.

As the largest American city and a central geographic point, Philadelphia was a logical location for delegates of the First Continental Congress to gather in 1774.

Political maneuvering for control of the Congress began even before the sessions got under way. Conservative delegates favored meeting in the Pennsylvania State House, a building symbolizing ties with British rule. The radicals argued in favor of Carpenter's Hall, a gathering place for Philadelphia's laborers. The delegates chose the latter building, thus seeming to identify with the people and their desire to preserve political liberties. Then the radicals insisted on naming Charles Thomson, a popular leader in Philadelphia, secretary for the Congress. Thomson gained the post and was able to design the minutes so that more confrontational actions stood out in the official record.

These signs foreshadowed what was to come. Accounts of the work of the First Continental Congress make clear that Samuel Adams, Patrick Henry, and others of their radical persuasion dominated the proceedings. Although they went along with the preparation of an elaborate petition to Parliament, known as the "The Declaration of Colonial Rights and Grievances," these experienced molders of the colonial protest movement demanded much more. They drew upon the old weapons of resistance that had caused King and Parliament to retreat before, and they added a new cudgel. Just in case they could not convince home government leaders to repeal the Coercive Acts, they argued that Americans should begin to prepare for war.

To ensure that Congress moved in the right direction, Samuel Adams and his political allies back in Massachusetts had done some careful planning. Their efforts came to light on September 9, 1774, when a convention of citizens in Suffolk County (Boston and environs) adopted a series of resolutions written by Dr. Joseph Warren. Once approved, Paul Revere, talented silversmith and active member of Adams's popular rights faction, rode hard for Philadelphia. Revere arrived in mid-September and laid the Suffolk Resolves before Congress. Not only did these statements strongly profess American rights, but they also called for a complete economic boycott and the rigorous training of local militia companies, just in case military action became necessary to defend lives, liberty, and property against the redcoats of Thomas Gage.

Congress approved the Suffolk Resolves—and with them the initial step in organization for a possible military showdown. The delegates also committed themselves to a plan of economic boycott, which became known as the Continental Association. The association represented a comprehensive plan mandating the nonimportation and nonconsumption of British goods, to be phased in over the next few months, as well as the nonexportation of

Chronology
OF KEY EVENTS

1760   George III becomes King of England

1763   Treaty of Paris ends the Seven Years' War (February); Pontiac begins an unsuccessful Indian rebellion on the western frontier (May); Orders in Council station Royal Naval vessels in American waters to run down smugglers (October); Proclamation of 1763 forbids white settlement west of the Appalachian Mountains (October)

1764   Sugar Act levies new trade duties on coffee, indigo, sugar, and wine (April); Currency Act prohibits colonial governments from issuing paper money and requires all debts to be paid in hard money (April)

1765   Stamp Act—which requires stamps to be affixed to all legal documents, almanacs, newspapers, pamphlets, and playing cards, among other items—provokes popular protests (March–December); Quartering Act directs colonists to provide barracks, candles, bedding, and beverages to soldiers stationed in their area (May); representatives from nine colonies at the Stamp Act Congress in New York City deny that Parliament has the right to tax the colonists (October)

1766   Parliament repeals the Stamp Act, but asserts its authority to tax the colonies in the Declaratory Act (March)

1767   Townshend Duties Act imposes taxes on imported glass, lead, paint, paper, and tea to defray the cost of colonial administration (June)

1768   British troops ordered to Boston (June); colonists begin to mount a trade boycott of British goods to protest the Townshend Duties (August)

1770   Boston Massacre leaves five colonists dead and others wounded (March)

1772   Rhode Island colonists attack and burn British naval vessel *Gaspée* (June)

1773   Tea Act allows the East India Company to sell tea directly to American retailers (May); Boston Tea Party occurs when a band of "Indians" boards three British vessels and dumps 342 chests of tea into Boston Harbor (December)

1774   Coercive Acts close the port of Boston (March), modify the Massachusetts charter (May), provide for trials outside colonies when royal officials are accused of serious crimes (May), and call for billeting of troops in unoccupied private homes (June); Quebec Act expands the boundaries of Quebec to the Mississippi and Ohio rivers (June); First Continental Congress, meeting in Philadelphia, protests oppressive Parliamentary legislation, votes to boycott trade with Britain, and defeats the Galloway Plan of Union (September–October)

---

colonial products should Parliament not retreat within a year.

The association also called on every American community to establish a local committee of observation and inspection charged with having all citizens subscribe to the boycott. In reality, the association was a loyalty test. Citizens who refused to sign were about to become outcasts from the cause of liberty. The term of derision applied to them was *tory*; however, they thought of themselves as *loyalists*—maintaining their allegiance to the Crown.

The only conciliatory countercharge of any consequence during the first Congress came from Joseph Galloway, a wealthy Philadelphia lawyer who had long served as Pennsylvania's speaker of the house. Galloway desperately wanted to maintain imperial ties because he feared what the "common sort" of citizens might do if that attachment should be irrevocably severed. He could imagine nothing but rioting, dissipation, and the confiscation of the property of economically successful colonists. For Galloway, the continuation of any kind of political and social order in America depended on the stabilizing influence of British rule.

Galloway drew from the Albany Plan of Union of 1754 (see p. 92) in proposing a central government based in America that would be superior to the provincial assemblies. This government would consist of a "grand council" elected by colonial assembly-men and a "president general" appointed by the Crown. Grand council legislation would have to gain Parliament's approval; at the same time imperial acts from King and Parliament would have to secure the assent of the grand council and president before becoming law.

Galloway's Plan of Union, as his blueprint came to be known, represented a structural alternative that would allow Americans a greater voice in imperial decisions affecting the colonies—and also foreshadowed the future commonwealth organization of the British empire. The more radical delegates, however, belittled it as an idea that would divert everyone from the task of the moment, which was to get King and Parliament to rescind the Coercive Acts. In a close vote the delegates remanded Galloway's plan to a committee, where it lay dormant for lack of majority support.

Later, at the urging of the radicals, Secretary Thomson expunged all references to Galloway's plan from the official minutes of Congress. He did so on the grounds of displaying full unity of purpose in resisting the home government. As for Galloway, he faced growing harassment as a loyalist in the months ahead and eventually fled to the British army for protection.

When the First Continental Congress ended its deliberations in late October 1774, its program was one of continued defiance. The delegates understood the course they had chosen. One of their last acts was to call for the Second Continental Congress, to convene in Philadelphia on May 10, 1775, "unless the redress of grievances, which we have desired, be obtained before that time."

As the fall of 1774 gave way to another cold winter, Americans awaited the verdict of King and Parliament. Would the Coercive Acts be repealed, or would the course of events lead to war? Local committees of observation and inspection were busily at work encouraging—and in some cases coercing—the populace to boycott British goods. Local militia companies were vigorously training. Even as they prepared for war, the colonists hoped that George III, Lord North, and Parliament would choose a less strident course. They would soon learn that imperial leaders had dismissed the work of the First Continental Congress, having decided the parent nation could not retreat a third time.

CONCLUSION

In September 1774 Lord North remarked: "The die is now cast, the colonies must either submit or triumph." Once-harmonious relations between Britain and America had become increasingly discordant between 1763 and the end of 1774. The colonists refused to accept undesirable imperial acts, and they successfully resisted such taxation plans as the Stamp Act and the Townshend Duties. In the process they came to believe that ministerial leaders in England were engaging in a deep-seated plot to deprive them of their fundamental liberties. When something as inconsequential as the Townshend duty on tea precipitated yet another crisis in 1773, neither side was willing to disengage. By early 1775 both had decided to show their resolve.

A small incident that well illustrates the deteriorating situation occurred in Boston during March 1774. At the state funeral of Andrew Oliver, the Bay Colony's most recent lieutenant governor and former stamp distributor-designate, a large gathering of ordinary citizens came out to watch the solemn procession. As Oliver's coffin was slowly lowered into the ground, these Bostonians, many of them veterans of the American resistance movement, suddenly burst into loud cheers.

This open expression of disaffection for the memory of so locally prominent a royalist leader epitomized the acute strain in British-American relations. Symbolically, the cheers almost seemed like a testament on behalf of the burial of imperial authority in America. Such striking changes in attitudes, over just a few years, pointed toward the fateful clash of arms known as the War for American Independence.

SUGGESTIONS FOR FURTHER READING

Bernard Bailyn, *The Ideological Origins of the American Revolution* (1967). Broadly influential, Pulitzer Prize-winning examination of the role of "radical" whig ideas in provoking the Revolution.

Ian R. Christie and Benjamin W. Labaree, *Empire or Independence, 1760–1776* (1976). Engaging appraisal of the reasons for revolution from the perspectives of British policymakers and ordinary American colonists.

Edmund S. and Helen M. Morgan, *The Stamp Act Crisis*, 3d ed. (1995). Classic account of the political, social, and constitutional aspects of the first major political confrontation pointing toward revolution.

Gary B. Nash, *The Urban Crucible: Social Change, Political Consciousness, and the Origins of the Revolution* (1979). Challenging analysis of the lives of ordinary persons in Boston, New York City, and Philadelphia, and the factors that propelled them toward revolution.

Gordon S. Wood, *The Radicalism of the American Revolution* (1992). Winner of a Pulitzer Prize focusing on pre-Revolutionary social and political values and the transformations wrought by the Revolution.

Alfred F. Young, *The Shoemaker and the Tea Party: Memory and the American Revolution* (1999). Fascinating account of an ordinary Bostonian who participated in key events pointing toward rebellion against the British.

Overviews and Surveys

Bernard Bailyn, *The Origins of American Politics* (1968); Colin Bonwick, *The American Revolution* (1991); Richard Maxwell Brown, *Strain of Violence: Historical Studies of American Violence and Vigilantism* (1975); Robert M. Calhoon, *Revolutionary America: An Interpretive Overview* (1976); Edward Countryman, *The American Revolution* (1985); Marc Egnal, *A Mighty Empire: The Origins of the Revolution* (1988); Lawrence Henry Gipson, *The Coming of the Revolution, 1763–1775* (1954); Merrill Jensen, *The Founding of a Nation, 1763–1776* (1968); Stephen G. Kurtz and James H. Hutson, eds., *Essays on the American Revolution* (1973); James Kirby Martin, *In the Course of Human Events: An Interpretive Exploration of the Revolution* (1979); Robert Middlekauff, *The Glorious Cause, 1763–1789* (1982); Edmund S. Morgan, *The Birth of the Republic, 1763–89*, 3d ed. (1993); Robert E. Shalhope, *The Roots of Democracy: American Thought and Culture, 1760–1800* (1990); Neil R. Stout, *The Perfect Crisis: The Beginning of the Revolutionary War* (1976); Harry M. Ward, *The American Revolution: Nationhood Achieved, 1763–1788* (1995); Esmond Wright, *Fabric of Freedom, 1763–1800*, rev. ed. (1978).

Provoking an Imperial Crisis

Robert A. Becker, *Revolution, Reform, and the Politics of American Taxation, 1763–1783* (1980); Colin Bonwick, *English Radicals and the American Revolution* (1977); John Brewer, *Party Ideology and Popular Politics at the Accession of George III* (1976); John L. Bullion, *A Great and Necessary Measure: George Grenville and the Genesis of the Stamp Act, 1763–1765* (1982); Ian R. Christie, *Crisis of Empire, 1754–1783* (1966); John Derry, *English Politics and the American Revolution* (1976); Joseph A. Ernst, *Money and Politics in America, 1755–1775* (1973); Daniel M. Friedenberg, *Life, Liberty, and the Pursuit of Land: The Plunder of Early America* (1992); Eric Hinderaker, *Elusive Empires: Constructing Colonialism in the Ohio Valley, 1673–1800* (1997); Michael Kammen, *A Rope of Sand: Colonial Agents, British Politics, and the Revolution* (1968); Lewis B. Namier, *England in the Age of the American Revolution*, rev. ed. (1961), and *The Structure of Politics at the Accession of George III*, rev. ed. (1957); Howard H. Peckham, *Pontiac and the Indian Uprising* (1947); Francis Philbrick, *The Rise of the West, 1754–1830* (1965); John Shy, *Toward Lexington: The Role of the British Army in the Coming of the Revolution* (1965); Jack M. Sosin, *Whitehall and the Wilderness: The Middle West in British Colonial Policy, 1760–1775* (1961), and *The Revolutionary Frontier, 1763–1783* (1967); Neil R. Stout, *The Royal Navy in America, 1760–1775* (1973); Robert W. Tucker and David C. Hendrickson, *The Fall of the First British Empire* (1982); Carl Ubbelohde, *The Vice-Admiralty Courts and the American Revolution* (1960); Franklin B. Wickwire, *British Subministers and Colonial America, 1763–1783* (1966).

"Liberty, Property, and No Stamps" and A Second Crisis: The Townshend Duties

Paul Gilje, *Road to Mobocracy: Popular Disorder in New York City, 1763–1834* (1987); Dirk Hoerder, *Crowd Action in Revolutionary Massachusetts, 1765–1780* (1977); Pauline R. Maier, *From Resistance to Revolution: Colonial Radicals and the Development of Opposition to Britain, 1765–1776* (1972), and *The Old Revolutionaries: Political Lives in the Age of Samuel Adams*, rev. ed. (1990); Charles S. Olton, *Artisans for Independence: Philadelphia Mechanics and the Revolution* (1975); Peter Shaw, *The Character of John Adams* (1976), and *American Patriots and the Rituals of Revolution* (1981); Peter D. G. Thomas, *British Politics and the Stamp Act Crisis* (1975), and *The Townshend Duties Crisis: The Second Phase of the Revolution, 1767–1773* (1987); John W. Tyler, *Smugglers and Patriots: Boston Merchants and the Advent of the Revolution* (1986); John J. Waters, Jr., *The Otis Family in Provincial and Revolutionary Massachusetts* (1968); Hiller B. Zobel, *The Boston Massacre* (1970).

The Rupturing of Imperial Relations

David Ammerman, *In the Common Cause: American Response to the Coercive Acts of 1774* (1974); Richard R. Beeman, *The Evolution of the Southern Backcountry: A Case Study of Lunenburg County, Virginia, 1746–1832* (1984); Ruth H. Bloch, *Visionary Republic: Millennial Themes in American Thought, 1756–1800* (1985); T. H. Breen, *Tobacco Culture: The Mentality of the Great Tidewater Planters* (1985); Richard D. Brown, *Revolutionary Politics in Massachusetts: The Boston Committee of Correspondence, 1772–1774* (1970); Edwin G. Burrows and Michael Wallace, "The Ideology and Psychology of National Liberation," *Perspectives in American History*, 6 (1972), pp. 167–306; Richard L. Bushman, *King and People in Provincial Massachusetts* (1985); H. Trevor Colbourn, *The Lamp of Experience: Whig History and the Intellectual Origins of the Revolution* (1965); Jere R. Daniell, *Experiment in Republicanism: New Hampshire Politics and the Revolution, 1741–1794* (1970); Bernard Donoughue, *British Politics and the American Revolution: The Path to War, 1733–1775* (1964); A. Roger Ekirch, *"Poor Carolina": Politics and Society in North Carolina, 1729–1776* (1981); Jay Fliegelman, *Prodigals and Pilgrims: The American Revolution Against Patriarchal Authority, 1750–1800* (1982); Larry R. Gerlach, *Prologue to Independence: New Jersey in the Coming of the Revolution* (1976); Ronald Hoffman, *A Spirit of Dissension: Economics, Politics, and the Revolution in Maryland* (1973); Woody Holton, *Forced Founders: Indians, Debtors, Slaves, and the Making of the Revolution in Virginia* (1999); Benjamin W. Labaree, *The Boston Tea Party* (1964); David S. Lovejoy, *Rhode Island Politics and the Revolution, 1760–1776* (1958); Stephen E. Lucas, *Portents of Rebellion: Rhetoric and Revolution in Philadelphia, 1765–1776* (1976); Bernard Mason, *The Road to Independence: The Revolutionary Movement in New York, 1773–1777* (1966); John A. Neuenschwander, *The Middle Colonies and the Coming of the American Revolution* (1973); Gregory H. Nobles, *Divisions Throughout the Whole: Politics and Society in Hampshire County, Massachusetts, 1740–1775*

(1983); J. G. A. Pocock, *The Machiavellian Moment: Florentine Political Thought and the Atlantic Republican Tradition* (1975); Bruce Ragsdale, *A Planter's Republic: The Search for Economic Independence in Virginia* (1996); Caroline Robbins, *The Eighteenth-Century Commonwealthman* (1959); Clinton Rossiter, *Seedtime of the Republic: The Origin of the American Tradition of Political Liberty* (1953); Richard A. Ryerson, *The Revolution Is Now Begun: The Radical Committees of Philadelphia, 1765–1776* (1978); David Curtis Skaggs, *Roots of Maryland Democracy, 1753–1776* (1973); Alan Taylor, *Liberty Men and Great Proprietors: The Maine Frontier, 1760–1820* (1990); Peter D. G. Thomas, *Tea Party to Independence: The Third Phase of the Revolution, 1773–1776* (1991).

Biographies

Bernard Bailyn, *The Ordeal of Thomas Hutchinson* (1974); Richard R. Beeman, *Patrick Henry* (1974); John Brooke, *King George III* (1972); John H. Cary, *Joseph Warren* (1961); Noble E. Cunningham, Jr., *In Pursuit of Reason: Thomas Jefferson* (1987); John Ferling, *The First of Men: George Washington* (1988), and *John Adams* (1992); William M. Fowler, Jr., *The Baron of Beacon Hill: John Hancock* (1979), and *Samuel Adams: Radical Puritan* (1997); Don R. Gerlach, *Philip Schuyler and the Revolution in New York, 1733–1777* (1964); E. Stanly Godbold, Jr., and Robert W. Woody, *Christopher Gadsden* (1982); David Freeman Hawke, *Franklin* (1976); Christopher Hibbert, *George III* (1999); James L. McKelvey, *George III and Lord Bute* (1973); John C. Miller, *Sam Adams: Pioneer in Propaganda* (1936); Lewis B. Namier and John Brooke, *Charles Townshend* (1964); Sheila Skemp, *William Franklin: Son of a Patriot, Servant of a King* (1990); Peter D. G. Thomas, *Lord North* (1976); Andrew S. Walmsley, *Thomas Hutchinson and the Origins of the American Revolution* (1999).

Internet Resources

The Leslie Brock Center for the Study of Colonial Currency
http://www.virginia.edu/~econ/brock.html
This site includes useful primary and secondary documents on early American currency.

Canada History
http://www.civilization.ca/index1e.html
Canada and the United States shared a colonial past but developed differently in the long run. This site is a part of the virtual museum of the Canadian Museum of Civilization Corporation.

Key Terms

Specie   (p. 100)

Vice-Admiralty Courts   (p. 103)

Virtual Representation   (p. 105)

Writs of Assistance   (p. 107)

Loyal Nine   (p. 107)

Stamp Act Congress   (p. 109)

Whigs   (p. 117)

Political Slavery   (p. 117)

Committees of Correspondence   (p. 119)

First Continental Congress   (p. 121)

Review Questions

1. How did Great Britain's overwhelming success in the Seven Years' War (the French and Indian War in America) help produce an imperial crisis with the English colonies in North America after 1763?

2. Why did the Stamp Act cause such immense fury among the colonists? What various nonviolent and violent tactics were employed by the colonists in resisting British policy actions? Which proved to be most effective, and why?

3. What motivated George Grenville, Charles Townshend, and Lord Frederick North to attempt to tax the Americans? Prepare a brief defense of British colonial policies between 1763 and 1774.

4. The Boston Massacre and the Boston Tea Party were pivotal events in the colonial resistance movement. Examine both events by considering their short-term and long-term causes as well as their wide-reaching consequences.

5. Why did the combination of the Coercive Acts and the Quebec Act prove to be a legislative tactical blunder for Lord North's administration? How did the colonists respond to these measures, and why did their response seem to imply rebellion?

TREATY
OF
AMITY, COMMERCE,
AND
NAVIGATION,
BETWEEN
His Britannic Majefty
AND
The United States of America,

CONDITIONALLY RATIFIED
BY THE SENATE OF THE UNITED STATES,
AT PHILADELPHIA, JUNE 24, 1795.

TO WHICH IS ANNEXED,

A Copious Appendix.

PHILADELPHIA.

PRINTED BY HENRY TUCKNISS,
FOR MATHEW CAREY, No. 118, MARKET-STREET.

Aug. 12, 1795.

PLURIBUS UNUM

5

THE TIMES THAT TRIED MANY SOULS, 1775–1783

"Starve, dissolve, or disperse"

Joseph Plumb Martin was a dedicated patriot soldier, one of 11,000 men and women who formed the backbone of General George Washington's Continental army. When that force entered its Valley Forge winter campsite in December 1777, the soldiers' trail could "be tracked by their blood upon the rough frozen ground," Martin recorded despondently. The Continentals were "now in a truly forlorn condition,—no clothing, no provisions, and as disheartened as need be." They had fought hard against British regulars and Hessians that summer and autumn but had not prevented the army of General Sir William Howe from taking Philadelphia, the rebel capital. Washington had chosen Valley Forge as a winter encampment because, as a hilly area, it represented an easily defensible position some 20 miles northwest of Philadelphia, should Howe's soldiers venture forth from their far more comfortable quarters.

Washington was very worried about the conditions facing his troops. If something was not done, and soon, he stated, "this army must inevitably . . . starve, dissolve, or disperse." Private Martin thought the same. The weather was bitterly cold, but the Continentals, using what energy they had left, constructed "little shanties" described as "scarcely gayer than dungeon cells."

Making matters even more grim was the lack of food and clothing. Martin claimed that, upon first entering Valley Forge, he went a full day and two nights without anything to eat, "save half a small pumpkin, which I cooked by placing it upon a rock, the skin side uppermost, and making fire upon it." His comrades fared no better. Within two days of moving into Valley Forge, a common grumble could be heard everywhere: "No Meat! No Meat!" By the first of January the words had become more ominous: "No bread, no soldier!"

Thus began a tragic winter of desperation for Washington's Continentals. Some 2500 soldiers, or nearly one fourth of the troops, perished before the army broke camp in June 1778. They died from exposure to the elements, malnutrition, and such viru-

lent diseases as typhus and smallpox. Not uncommonly, soldiers languished for days in their rudely constructed huts because they were too weak to drill or to participate in food-hunting expeditions. Sometimes for lack of straw and blankets, they simply froze to death in their beds. To add to the woes of the camp, more than 500 of the army's horses starved to death that winter. Their carcasses could not be buried in the frozen ground, which only magnified the deplorable sanitation conditions and the consequent spread of disease.

Under such forsaken circumstances, hundreds of soldiers deserted. If Washington had not let his troops leave camp to requisition food in the countryside or if there had not been an unusually early shad run in the Schuylkill River, which flowed behind the encampment, the army might well have perished.

Commentators have usually attributed the extreme suffering at Valley Forge to the severe weather and a complete breakdown of the army's supply system. Actually, weather conditions were no worse than in other years. Certainly a major reason for the deprivation at Valley Forge was widespread civilian indifference toward an army made up of the poor, the expendable, and the unfree in American society.

Joseph Plumb Martin clearly thought this was the case. He was a young man from Connecticut, without material resources, who had first enlisted during 1776 at the very peak of patriot enthusiasm for the war—sometimes called the **rage militaire.** He soon learned that soldiering had few glorious moments. Camp life was both dull and dangerous, given the many killer diseases that ravaged armies of the era, and battle was a frightening experience. Before 1776 was over, Martin had faced the hurtling musket balls and bloodied bayonets of British soldiers in the Continental army's futile attempt to defend New York City and vicinity. He did not renew his enlistment and returned to Connecticut.

For a poor, landless person, economic prospects at home were not much better than serving for promises of regular pay in the Continental army. So in 1777 Martin stepped forth again and agreed to enlist as a substitute for some local gentlemen being threatened by an attempted draft. For a specified sum of money (Martin "forgot the sum"), he became their substitute. As Martin later wrote, "they were now freed from further trouble, at least for the present, and I had become the scapegoat for them."

The experiences of Martin typified those of many others who performed long-term Continental service on behalf of the cause of liberty. After an initial rush to arms in defiance of British authority in 1775, the harsh realities of military life and pitched battles

George Washington led a bedraggled, half-starved army of 11,000 men and women into Valley Forge in December 1777.

dampened patriot enthusiasm to the point that by December 1776 the Continental army all but ceased to exist. Washington's major task became that of securing enough troop strength and material support to shape an army capable of standing up time after time to British forces.

The commander in chief found his long-term soldiers among the poor and deprived persons of revolutionary America. In addition, major European nations such as France, Spain, and Holland also came to the rescue with additional troops, supplies, and vital financial support. Working together, even in the face of so much popular indifference, these allies-in-arms outlasted the mighty land and sea forces of Great Britain, making possible a generous peace settlement in 1783 that guaranteed independence for the group of former British colonies that now called themselves the 13 United States.

RECONCILIATION OR INDEPENDENCE

Crown officials in England gave scant attention to the acts of the First Continental Congress. They believed the time had come to teach the American provincials a military lesson. George III explained why: The colonists, he asserted, "have boldly thrown off the mask and avowed nothing less than a total independence of the British legislature will satisfy them." The king's impression was inaccurate, but it lay behind the decision to turn the most powerful military machine in the western world, based on its record in recent wars, against the troublemakers in America and to crush resistance to British authority once and for all.

The Shooting War Starts

During the winter of 1774–1775 the king's ministers prepared for what they expected to be a brief but decisive demonstration of military force. General Gage received "secret" orders to employ the redcoats under his command "to arrest and imprison the principal actors and abettors" of rebellion; however, if the likes of Samuel Adams, John Hancock, and Joseph Warren could not be captured, then Gage was to challenge in any way he deemed appropriate "this rude [American] *rabble* without plan, without concert, and without conduct . . . unprepared to encounter with a regular force." Above all else, Gage was to strike hard with a crushing blow.

In a series of related showdown decisions, King and Parliament authorized funds for a larger force of regular troops in America and named three high-

ROAD TO WAR, 1763–1776

WAR FOR AMERICAN INDEPENDENCE

1763	**Orders in Council**	Places British naval vessels in American waters during peacetime to run down smugglers, thereby threatening highly profitable illegal trading activities.
	Proclamation of 1763	Denies colonists access to western lands with the purpose of avoiding frontier warfare with Native Americans; infuriates land-hungry settlers searching for tillable farmland.
1764	**Sugar Act**	Designed to collect trade duty on foreign molasses and toughen other trading regulations.
	Currency Act	Requires colonial governments to stop issuing paper currencies heretofore used to conduct local business transactions and pay private debts.
1765	**Stamp Act**	Unprecedented legislation to tax colonists directly; heavily resisted through crowd actions and the boycotting of British trade goods.
	Quartering Act	Shifts onto the colonists the financial burden of paying for the housing of imperial troops stationed in America.
1767	**Townshend Duties**	Another plan to tax the colonists, this time indirectly through a series of trade duties; provokes further resistance.
1770	**Boston Massacre**	Local crowd action against hated redcoats results in the death of five persons who are transformed into martyrs in the defense of American liberties.
1772	*Gaspée* **Affair**	Rhode Islanders destroy British naval vessel charged with seizing smugglers, thereby incensing the Crown.
	Committee organization	Colonial assemblies organize committees of correspondence to communicate about imperial policies; Massachusetts establishes local committees to be vigilant in relation to possible acts of tyranny.
1773	**Tea Act**	Colonists defy this plan to market cheaper tea with the Townshend duty attached; Boston Tea Party sets the tone of resistance.
1774	**Coercive Acts**	Crown closes port of Boston and makes various modifications in the Massachusetts government, actions that many colonists consider tyrannical.
	First Continental Congress	Offers something less than an olive branch in calling for a complete economic boycott of British trade goods and advising colonists to prepare for possible war.
1775	**Lexington and Concord**	Warfare breaks out when British regulars attempt to seize powder and arms at Concord.
	Lord Dunmore's Proclamation	Offers freedom to slaves and indentured servants in Virginia who who will fight for the Crown.
	Invasion of Canada	Patriot attempt to conquer Quebec Province as the fourteenth colony in rebellion does not succeed.

1776	*Common Sense*	Thomas Paine demands independence and denounces colonists too faint-hearted to break free of perceived British tyranny.
	Massive British buildup	Crown musters huge martial force, including Hessians, to put down the American rebellion.
	Declaration of Independence	Second Continental Congress proclaims American desire to become a separate nation.

ranking generals—William Howe, Henry Clinton, and "Gentleman Johnny" Burgoyne—to sail to Boston and join Gage. George III also declared Massachusetts to be in a state of rebellion, which permitted redcoats to shoot down suspected rebels on sight should that be necessary to quell opposition. Eventually this decree would be applied to all 13 provinces.

General Gage received the ministry's secret orders in mid-April 1775. Being on the scene, he was not quite as convinced as his superiors about American martial weakness. Gage had repeatedly urged caution in his reports to home officials, but now he had no choice; he had to act. Because the rebel leaders had already gotten word of the orders and fled to the countryside, Gage decided upon a reconnaissance in force mission. He would send a column of regulars to Concord, a town some 20 miles northwest of Boston that served as a storage point for patriot gunpowder and related military supplies. Once there, the troops were to seize or destroy as much weaponry and ammunition as possible. Gage hoped this maneuver could be effected without bloodshed; he feared the onset of full-scale warfare if patriot lives were lost.

After dark on April 18 some 700 British troops under Lieutenant Colonel Francis Smith moved out across Boston's back bay. Popular leaders monitored this deployment, and soon Paul Revere and William Dawes were riding through the countryside alerting the populace to what was happening. In Lexington, 5 miles east of Concord and on the road that the king's troops had taken, 70 militiamen, trained to respond at a moment's notice, gathered at the local tavern with their captain, John Parker. Samuel Adams and John Hancock were also present. Obviously outnumbered, the Minutemen debated possible actions. They decided to respond to the redcoats' provocative incursion into the countryside by acting as an army of observation.

Parker and his men lined up across the village green as the British column bore down on them at dawn (Adams and Hancock, as known enemies, fled into the woods). The Minutemen were not there to exchange shots, but to warn the regulars against trespassing on the property of free-born British subjects. As the redcoats came closer, Parker tried to shout out words to this effect. He could not be heard. A mysterious shot rang out just as the Minutemen, having made their protest, turned to leave the green. The shot caused troops at the front of the British column to level their arms and fire. Before order was restored, several of Parker's men lay wounded, mostly shot in their backs. Eight of them died in what was the opening volley of the War for American Independence.

The redcoats regrouped and continued their march to Concord. Once there, a detachment moved out to cross the Old North Bridge in search of weapons and gunpowder. Rallying militiamen repulsed them. Falling back to the center of town, the redcoats left behind three dead comrades. Now blood had been spilled on both sides.

Lieutenant Colonel Smith began to worry that his column might be cut to pieces by harassing citizen-soldiers, so he ordered a retreat. The rest of the day turned into a rout as an aroused citizenry fired away at the British from behind trees and stone fences. Only a relief column of some 1100 troops, which Gage had the foresight to send out, saved Smith's column. Final casualty figures showed 273 redcoats dead or wounded, as compared to 95 colonists. Lexington and Concord were clear blows to the notion of the invincibility of British arms and suggested that American citizens, when defending their own property, could and would hold their own against better-trained British soldiers.

As word of the bloodshed spread, New Englanders rallied to the patriot banner. Within days thousands of colonists poured into hastily assembled military camps surrounding Boston. Thomas Gage and his soldiers were now trapped, and they could only hope that promised reinforcements would soon reach them. The *rage militaire* was on. Everyone, it seemed, wanted to be a temporary soldier—and fire a few shots at a redcoat or two before returning home again.

This painting, based on an eyewitness sketch, shows British troops under Lieutenant Colonel Francis Smith marching into Concord to destroy patriot stores of gunpowder and military supplies.

Most colonists believed the ministry would soon regain its senses and quickly restore all American rights rather than engage in warfare. They did not realize that imperial leaders were irrevocably committed to eradicating all American resistance, or that the conflict would become a long and grueling war in which the fortitude to endure would determine the eventual winner.

Moderates Versus Radicals in Congress

The shadow of Lexington and Concord loomed heavily as the **Second Continental Congress** convened in Philadelphia in May 1775. Despite the recent bloodshed, very few delegates had become advocates of independence. New Englanders like Samuel and John Adams were leaning that way, but the vast majority held out hope for a resolution of differences. By the summer of 1775 two factions had emerged in Congress: the one led by New Englanders, favoring a formal declaration of independence, and the opposing reconciliationist or moderate faction, whose strength lay in the Middle Colonies and whose most influential leader was John Dickinson of Pennsylvania. The two factions debated every issue with regard to possible effects on the subject of independence. The moderates remained the dominant

faction into the spring of 1776, but then the weight of the spreading rebellion swung the pendulum decisively toward those favoring independence.

Early congressional wrangling centered on the organization of the Continental army. In mid-June 1775 the delegates, at the urging of the New Englanders, voted to adopt the patriot forces around Boston as a Continental military establishment. They asked the other colonies to supply additional troops and unanimously named wealthy Virginia planter George Washington, who had been appearing in Congress in his military uniform, to serve as commander in chief. Washington had qualifications for the job, including his combat experiences during the Seven Years' War. Also, he was a southerner. His presence at the head of the army was a way to involve the other colonies, at least symbolically, in what was still a localized conflict being fought by New Englanders.

Although the delegates agreed about the need for central military planning and coordination, the moderates worried about how British officials would view the formation of an independent American army. At the urging of John Dickinson, they wanted Congress to prepare a formal statement explaining this bold action. In early July the delegates approved the "Declaration of the Causes and Necessity for Taking up Arms," which they sent to England. The purpose of a Continental force, the "Declaration" stressed, was not "to dis-

George Washington, who regularly appeared in Congress in military uniform, was a natural choice to serve as the Continental army's commander in chief.
Metropolitan Museum of Art, Bequest of Grace Wilkes, 1922.

solve that union which has so long and so happily subsisted between us." Rather, Congress had formed the army to assure the defense of American lives, liberty, and property until "hostilities shall cease on the part of the aggressors, and all danger of their being renewed shall be removed, and not before." Given home government attitudes about American intentions, this document received scant ministerial attention.

The moderates were persons caught in a bind. Even though deeply concerned about American rights, they feared independence. Like many other colonists of substantial wealth, they envisioned internal chaos in the colonies without the stabilizing influence of British rule. They also doubted whether a weak, independent American nation could long survive among aggressive European powers.

The moderates thus tried to keep open the channels of communication with the British government. Characteristic of such attempts was John Dickinson's

"Olive Branch" petition, approved by Congress in July 1775. This document stated that "our breasts retain too tender a regard for the kingdom from which we derive our origin" to want independence. It implored George III to intercede with Parliament and find some means to preserve English liberties in America. Like so many other petitions, the Olive Branch had little impact in Britain. By the autumn of 1775 the home government was already mobilizing for full-scale war. This was one form of a response to the Olive Branch. The other was a public declaration that all the colonies were now in open rebellion.

The Expanding Martial Conflict

Congressional moderates accomplished little, except to delay a declaration of independence. The war kept spreading, making a formal renunciation of British allegiance seem almost anticlimactic. On May 10, 1775, citizen-soldiers under Vermont's Ethan Allen and Connecticut's Benedict Arnold seized the once-mighty fortress of Ticonderoga at the southern end of Lake Champlain. This action netted the Americans more than 100 serviceable artillery pieces that would eventually be deployed to help drive British forces from Boston.

Taking Ticonderoga raised the question of luring Canada into the rebellion. Many hoped that Quebec Province would become the fourteenth colony, so much so that Congress approved a two-pronged invasion in the late summer of 1775. One column under General Richard Montgomery, a former British officer who had resettled in America, traveled down Lake Champlain and seized Montreal. The second column under Colonel Benedict Arnold proceeded on a harrowing march through the woods of Maine and finally emerged before the walls of Quebec City. Early on the morning of December 31, 1775, combined forces under these two commanders boldly tried to take the city but were repulsed. Montgomery lost his life, Arnold was seriously wounded, and great numbers of patriot troops were killed or captured. The rebel attempt to seize Canada had failed. This effort, however, made it increasingly difficult to argue that the colonists were only interested in defending their homes and families until political differences with Britain could be resolved.

Back in Boston, meanwhile, generals Howe, Clinton, and Burgoyne arrived in May 1775 and urged General Gage to resume the offensive against the New Englanders. That opportunity came on June 17 just after patriot forces moved onto Charlestown peninsula north of Boston's back bay. The rebels planned to dig in on Bunker Hill but constructed the most extended portions of their line on Breed's Hill closer to Boston. After lengthy debate the British generals decided upon a frontal assault by some 2500 troops under William Howe's command to show the rebels the awesome power of concentrated British arms.

That afternoon, as citizens in Boston watched the misnamed Battle of Bunker Hill from rooftops, Howe's detachment made three separate charges, finally dislodging the patriots, who were running out of ammunition. This engagement was the bloodiest of the whole war. The British suffered 1054 casualties—40 percent of the redcoats engaged. American casualties amounted to 411, or 30 percent. Among those slain was Samuel Adams's close political associate, Dr. Joseph Warren, mourned by patriots everywhere.

The realization that patriot soldiers had been driven from the field undermined the euphoria that followed the rout of the redcoats at Lexington and Concord. Still, the British gained little advantage because they had failed to pursue the fleeing rebels. They remained trapped in Boston, surrounded by thousands of armed and angry colonists. Henry Clinton summarized matters best when he called Bunker Hill "a dear bought victory," adding dryly that "another such would have ruined us."

Lord Dunmore's Proclamation of Emancipation

New England and Canada did not long remain the only theaters of war. Before the end of 1775 fighting erupted in the South. In Virginia the protagonist was John Murray, Lord Dunmore, who was the last royal governor of the Old Dominion. In May 1774 Dunmore had dissolved the Assembly because the burgesses called for a day of fasting and prayer in support of the Bostonians. Incensed at Dunmore's arbitrary action, Virginia's gentleman-planters started meeting in provincial conventions, acting as if royal authority no longer existed.

Dunmore resented such impudence. In June 1775 he fled Williamsburg and announced that British subjects still loyal to the Crown should join him in bringing the planter elite to its senses. Very few citizens came forward. By autumn Dunmore, who used a naval vessel in Chesapeake Bay as his headquarters, had concluded that planter resistance could only be broken by turning Virginia's slaves against their masters. On November 7, 1775, he issued an emancipation proclamation. It read in part: "And I do hereby further declare all indentured servants, Negroes, or others . . . free, that are able and willing to bear arms."

LEXINGTON AND CONCORD

The Shot Heard 'Round the World

AFTER the bloody skirmish at Lexington, Lieutenant Colonel Francis Smith's redcoats marched toward their intended target, the village of Concord, which served as a central storage point for patriot powder and arms. Smith's troops were to "seize and destroy" these military goods.

Just east of Concord, Smith's column found the road blocked by 250 Minutemen under Major John Buttrick. Choosing not to fight, Buttrick ordered his citizen-soldiers to retreat. They did so in disciplined fashion, marching into Concord just ahead of the redcoats and then to higher ground a mile north of the village across Old North Bridge.

Colonel Smith soon had his troops out hunting for supplies. He sent six companies up to North Bridge to seize any powder and weapons stored at farms in that area. Once there, Captain Lawrence Parsons led three companies across the bridge, right past the patriot militia. Captain Walter Laurie secured the bridge with the remaining companies.

At this juncture, just a little before 10 A.M., Buttrick's Minutemen saw a cloud of smoke rising from the village. The British were burning Concord's liberty tree, along with some gun carriages. An alarmed patriot officer shouted, "Would you let them burn down our town?" Angered by this prospect, Buttrick's troops advanced and engaged Laurie's redcoats; both contingents fired at each other across the bridge. The British, sustaining several casualties, fell back to Concord in reacting to these shots "heard 'round the world."

By late morning, Smith realized that the local patriots, fearing an incursion, had earlier that week moved most of the military supplies to other locales. The redcoat mission was a failure. Worse yet, hundreds of militiamen, enraged by news of events at Lexington, were gathering behind trees and stone fences, just waiting for Smith's retreat.

Had General Gage not sent out a relief force under Hugh, Lord Percy, Smith's redcoats might have been exterminated. The two British columns linked up just east of Lexington. By sundown, they had reached Charlestown peninsula, just north of Boston, having barely survived the opening encounter of the War for American Independence.

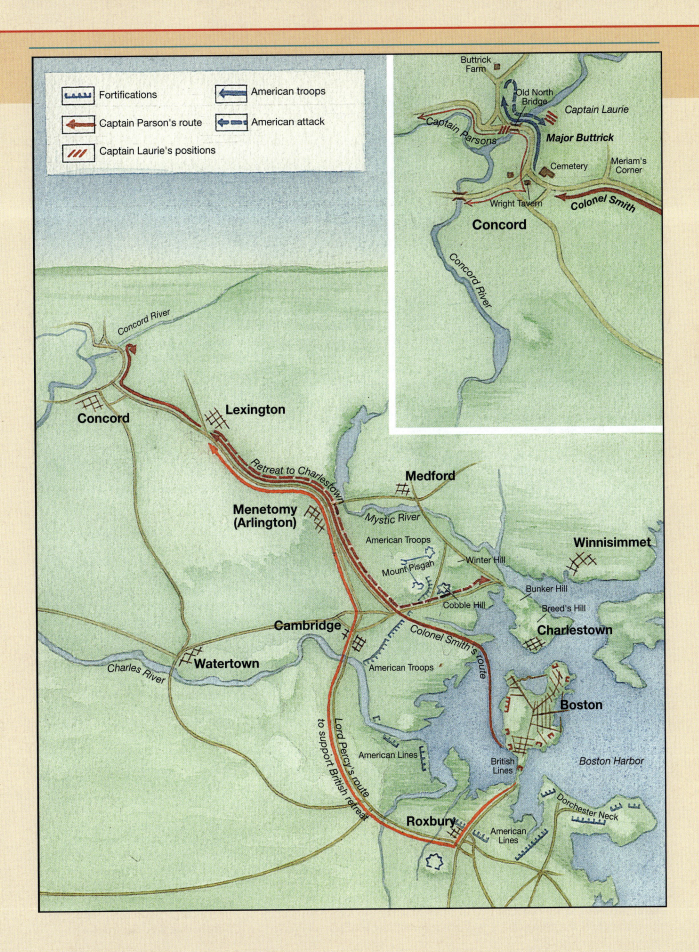

Fortifications

Captain Parson's route

Captain Laurie's positions

American troops

American attack

Buttrick Farm

Old North Bridge

Captain Laurie

Captain Parsons

Major Buttrick

Cemetery

Meriam's Corner

Wright Tavern

Colonel Smith

Concord

Concord River

Concord River

Concord

Lexington

Retreat to Charlestown

Medford

Menetomy (Arlington)

Mystic River

American Troops

Winter Hill

Mount Pisgah

Winnisimmet

Cobble Hill

Bunker Hill

Breed's Hill

Cambridge

Colonel Smith's route

Charlestown

American Troops

Watertown

Charles River

American Lines

British Lines

Boston

Lord Percy's route to support British retreat

Boston Harbor

Dorchester Neck

Roxbury

American Lines

The Battle of Bunker Hill

EARLY on Friday evening, June 16, 1775, rebel military leaders held an urgent meeting in Cambridge, Massachusetts. Intelligence had just reached them that redcoats under Lieutenant General Thomas Gage would soon attempt to break out of Boston. The British plan was to cross the body of water south of Boston, take Dorchester Heights, then sweep north through Cambridge, the patriot army command base, and send the rebels, now numbering well over 10,000 volunteers, reeling back into the countryside. The target date for this operation was Sunday, June 18.

The assembled rebel officers decided to divert the British from their plans by moving patriot lines yet closer to Boston. They gave orders to Colonel William Prescott to fortify Bunker Hill on Charlestown peninsula, just to the north of Boston. The rebels would now control terrain from which they could cannonade British vessels in the harbor and even the city, if necessary. Should the British attempt to dislodge the rebels, they would have to storm up a hill rising 130 feet above sea level into withering patriot fire.

Before midnight on June 16, Prescott, leading more than 1000 troops, reached Bunker Hill. At this point he called together the other officers, including Colonel Richard Gridley, an experienced military engineer, to discuss the placement of earthworks. As they studied the terrain around them, they could see another hill some 600 yards closer to Boston, which rose sharply to 75 feet above sea level. Gridley recommended a line of trenches and a redoubt on that site. Bunker Hill, the group concluded, should serve as a secondary line of defense.

Moving forward as quietly as possible, the Americans dug in rapidly on Breed's Hill, knowing that daylight would expose their activity. At dawn on Saturday, June 17, sailors on board a British war vessel in the harbor spied the new rebel position and opened up with artillery fire. The cannonade awoke everyone in the vicinity, including Gage, who soon met in a council of war with three other generals—William Howe, Henry Clinton, and John Burgoyne—all of whom had recently arrived in Boston.

Gage, despite his superior rank as commander of British military forces in North America, deferred to the three major generals in his presence. Since Gage had repeatedly urged caution in handling the rebels, many home leaders had started asking whether he was too timid for the task at hand. The appearance of Howe, Clinton, and Burgoyne, he knew, was hardly a vote of confidence.

During the imperial wars, British military officers had repeatedly characterized the colonists as fainthearted fighters. Reflecting this attitude, the three generals could not fathom how Gage had gotten his troops trapped in Boston by untrained, disorganized, and ill-disciplined rebels. The generals, not surprisingly, demanded an immediate offensive against Prescott's troops. They hoped for a victory so crushing that rebel resistance would disintegrate completely.

Then they debated tactics. Henry Clinton wanted to seize control of the narrow neck of land behind Bunker Hill connecting Charlestown peninsula to the mainland. That maneuver would trap Prescott's force, which then could be defeated and captured in detail. Howe and Burgoyne favored a direct frontal assault. The rebels would wither and run, they argued, in the face of concentrated, disciplined British arms. Gage reluctantly agreed to a frontal assault. He hoped the other generals were correct, that the Americans would flee rather than fight, but deep inside he expected heavy casualties.

British regulars were very well trained soldiers. They would rather stand up to furious enemy fire than to the wrath of their officers and the brutal military penalties for insubordination of any kind. Insolence toward an officer or attempted desertion resulted in punishments of up to 1000 lashes well laid on, which few persons could survive.

New soldiers received rigorous training in the basics of combat. When deployed in front of the enemy, they moved easily from column formations into three battle lines. After troops in the first line fired their smoothbore muskets, affectionately known as the "Brown Bess," they reloaded as their comrades in the next two lines stepped in front of them and fired their muskets in turn.

Smoothbore muskets were inaccurate weapons with an effective range of less than 80 yards. Experienced soldiers going through the steps of ramming powder and ball down the barrel could rarely get off more than two shots a minute. Thus most battle casualties came from bayonet wounds when competing armies, once having fired three or four

rounds at very close range, charged forward and engaged in hand-to-hand combat. The bayonet, fastened to the end of the musket, was the major killing weapon of eighteenth-century European-style warfare, and the proficient soldier more often stabbed than shot his opponent to death.

Knowing all of this, General Howe, whom Gage placed in charge of the assault, envisioned an overwhelming victory over a motley band of rebels. By 3 P.M., more than 2000 redcoats had been ferried across the bay and were ready to advance. Howe sent forward troops on his left under General Robert Pigot directly at Breed's Hill to divert the Americans. In turn, he led his column along the shore to break through a patriot line behind a rail fence. He expected to sweep these defenders aside in a classic flanking maneuver, then swing sharply to the left and cut Prescott's soldiers off from retreat as they dueled with Pigot's redcoats on their front. Bayonets would finish the expected rout.

Galling rebel fire frustrated the first British assault. The patriots held off shooting until the last possible moment, then unleashed a furious series of blasts. The redcoats staggered and fell back. Wrote one British officer with Howe, we "were served up in companies against the grass fence, without being able to penetrate. . . . Most of our grenadiers and light infantry, in presenting themselves, lost three-fourths, and many nine-tenths, of their men." Far to the left Pigot's soldiers also ran back from the blistering volleys of musket fire being laid down by Prescott's defenders.

Retreating on all fronts, the British regrouped and then tried to execute Howe's plan a second time. "It was surprising," wrote an observer, to watch the redcoats "step over . . . dead bodies, as though they had been logs of wood." Once again, exclaimed one British officer, "an incessant stream of fire" forced them back. From his vantage point in Boston, General Burgoyne described what was happening as "a complica-

tion of horror . . . more dreadfully terrible" than anything he had ever seen. He wondered whether "defeat" would bring on "a final loss to the British empire in America."

At this critical juncture, Howe, reinforced by 400 fresh troops, decided to throw everything against the redoubt, where, unknown to him, Prescott's troops were running out of ammunition. Now the British, with regimental pride at stake, shouted "push on, push on." Within minutes they overran the Americans, most of whom lacked bayonets to defend themselves. Prescott's coolness under heavy fire resulted in an orderly retreat, but most of the rebel casualties occurred among defenders who did not evacuate in time. Included among them was Samuel Adams's valued political associate, Dr. Joseph Warren, already wounded but who died from bayonet wounds inflicted by an enraged redcoat who apparently recognized him and cried out that agitators like Warren were responsible for such horrible carnage.

The misnamed Battle of Bunker Hill was over within little more than an hour. Most of the patriots did escape, having no way of knowing that they had participated in the bloodiest fight of the Revolutionary War. The figure of 1465 combined casualties shocked everyone in what General Clinton called "a dear bought victory." The British had really gained nothing of consequence, since the American patriots still controlled the countryside surrounding Boston and Charlestown peninsula.

Dunmore hoped that Virginia's slaves would break their chains and join with him in teaching their former masters that talk of liberty was a two-edged sword. The plan backfired. Irate planters suppressed copies of the proclamation and spread the rumor of a royal hoax designed to lure blacks into Dunmore's camp so that he could sell them to the owners of West Indian sugar plantations, where inhuman working conditions and very high mortality rates prevailed. Still, as many as 2000 slaves took their chances and escaped to the royal standard.

Those blacks who first fled became a part of **Dunmore's Ethiopian regiment,** which made the mistake of engaging Virginia militiamen in a battle at Great Bridge in December 1775. Having had no time for even the fundamentals of military training, the regiment took a drubbing. This battle ended any semblance of royal authority in Virginia. Dunmore and his following soon retreated to a flotilla of vessels in Chesapeake Bay. During the next few months the numbers of royalist adherents kept growing, but then smallpox struck, killing hundreds of people. In the summer of 1776 Dunmore sailed away, leaving behind planters who more closely guarded their human property while demanding independence from those in Britain whom they denounced as tyrants.

Resolving the Independence Question

Lord Dunmore's experiences highlighted the collapse of British political authority. Beginning in the summer of 1775, colony after colony witnessed an end to royal government. To fill the void, the patriots elected ad hoc provincial congresses. These bodies functioned as substitute legislatures and dealt with pressing local issues. They also took particular interest in suppressing suspected loyalists.

During that same summer Massachusetts asked the Continental Congress for permission to establish a more enduring government based on a written constitution. After ousting its royal governor, New Hampshire followed suit. These requests forced Congress to act. The delegates did so in early November, stating that Massachusetts, New Hampshire, and any others might adopt "such a form of government, as . . . will best produce the happiness of the people," yet only if written constitutions specified that these governments would exist until "the present dispute between Great Britain and the colonies" came to an end. The moderates realized that new state governments, as much if not more than a separate army, had the appearance of de facto independence. They did everything they could to prevent a total rejection of British political authority in America.

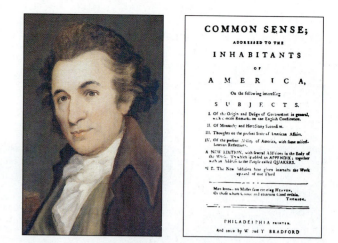

Thomas Paine's *Common Sense*, first published in January 1776, urged the colonists to embrace independence and a bold new world of political freedom.

John Dickinson led the campaign in Congress to suppress discussion of a declaration of independence. In early November 1775 he got the Pennsylvania Assembly to instruct its congressional delegates to "dissent from, and utterly reject, any propositions . . . that may cause or lead to a separation from our mother country." New York, Delaware, Maryland, and South Carolina soon adopted similar instructions. Thus there was to be no resolution of the independence question before 1776.

Events outside of Congress were about to overwhelm the moderates. In January 1776 Thomas Paine, a recent migrant from England who had once been a corsetmaker's apprentice, published a pamphlet entitled **Common Sense.** It became an instant best-seller, running through 25 editions and 120,000 copies over the next three months.

Common Sense electrified the populace with its dynamic, forceful language. Paine communicated a sense of urgency about moving toward independence. He attacked congressional moderates for not being bold enough to break with the past, and he likewise denounced the British monarchy, writing: "The folly of hereditary right in Kings, is that nature disapproves it . . . by giving mankind *an ass for a lion.*" He encouraged Americans to adopt republican forms of government, since "every spot of the old world is overrun with oppression." The fate of all humans everywhere, he concluded, hung in the balance. *Common Sense* put severe pressure on the moderates, but they held on doggedly, hoping against hope that Great Britain would turn from its belligerent course and begin serious negotiations with Congress.

At the end of February 1776 another significant incident took place in the form of a short, bloody battle between loyalists and patriot militia at Moore's Creek Bridge in North Carolina. This engagement resulted in more than a rout of local **tories.** Now facing a shooting war, North Carolina's provincial congress reversed instructions to its congressional delegates and allowed them to discuss independence and vote on a plan of national government. Soon thereafter the Virginians, furious about Lord Dunmore's activities, issued similar instructions. Then leaders in Rhode Island, impatient with everyone else, boldly declared their own independence in early May.

On June 7, 1776, Richard Henry Lee, speaking on behalf of the Virginia provincial convention, presented formal resolutions to Congress. Lee urged "that these United Colonies are, and of right ought to be, free and independent states, . . . and that all political connection between them and the State of Great Britain is, and ought to be, totally dissolved." The resolutions also called for the creation of a national government and the formation of alliances with foreign nations in support of the war effort.

Within a few days Congress established two committees, one headed by John Dickinson to produce a plan of central government and another to prepare a statement on independence. Thomas Jefferson (1743–1826), a tall, young Virginian, agreed to write a draft text on independence, which the committee laid before Congress on Friday, June 28. John Adams was expecting "the greatest debate of all" on Monday, July 1. In the session that day Dickinson spoke forcefully against a formal severance of ties with Great Britain. Americans, he argued, could not endure against superior British arms, especially "when we are in so wretched a state of preparation" for war. Nor did he think that significant foreign aid from France and other nations would be readily forthcoming. Moving forward with independence, he concluded, would be like reading "a little more in the Doomsday Book of America."

The delegates listened politely, but Dickinson was no longer in step with the mood of Congress. At the end of the day they voted on Lee's resolutions, and nine state delegations gave their assent. Political maneuvering produced what could be described as a unanimous vote the next day when 12 states voted affirmatively. New York's delegates had not yet received instructions from leaders back home, so they abstained, even though they were now personally in favor of independence. By so overwhelming a ratification of Lee's resolutions, Congress technically declared independence on Tuesday, July 2.

Congress next turned to the consideration of Jefferson's draft, which one delegate in a classic understatement called "a pretty good one." The delegates made only a few changes. They deleted a controversial statement blaming the slave trade on the king as well as a phrase repudiating friendship with the British people. By Thursday evening, July 4, 1776, everything was in place, and Congress unanimously adopted Jefferson's document, a masterful explanation of the reasons why the colonists were seeking independence.

The Declaration of Independence proclaimed to the world that Americans had been terribly mis-

Delegates to the Second Continental Congress formally debated whether to declare independence on July 1, 1776. After making minor modifications in Jefferson's draft, they unanimously approved the Declaration of Independence on July 4.

treated by their parent nation. Much of the text represents a summary list of grievances, ranging from misuse of a standing army of redcoats in the colonies and the abuse of the rightful powers of popularly elected colonial assemblies to the ultimate crime, starting an unjustified war against loyal subjects. The Declaration blamed George III for the pattern of tyranny. He had failed to control his ministers, thereby abandoning his role as a true servant of the people.

Besides grievances, the Declaration also offered a long-range vision. Jefferson believed the Revolution would succeed only if Americans acted with a clear and noble purpose. Since "all men are created equal" and have "certain unalienable rights," which Jefferson defined as "life, liberty, and the pursuit of happiness," Americans needed to dedicate themselves to the establishment of a whole new set of political relationships guaranteeing all citizens fundamental liberties. The great task facing the revolutionary generation would be to institute republican forms of government, based on the rule of law and human reason. Governments had "to effect" the "safety and happiness" of all persons in the name of human decency, and all persons would be obligated to work for the greater good of the whole community.

Through Jefferson's words, the patriots of 1776 committed themselves to uplifting humanity in what they viewed as a world overrun by greed, petty ambition, and political tyranny. They would not realize their lofty purpose, however, unless they found the means to defeat the huge British military force arriving in America at the very time that Congress was debating and approving the Declaration of Independence.

WITHOUT VISIBLE ALLIES: THE WAR IN THE NORTH

British officials had made a great blunder in 1775. Disdaining the colonists as "a set of upstart vagabonds, the dregs and scorn of the human species," they had woefully underestimated their opponent. Lexington and Concord drove home this reality. Although the king's civil and military leaders continued to presume their superiority, they became far more serious about waging war. They had come to realize that snuffing out the rebellion was a complex military assignment, given the sheer geographic size of the colonies and the absence of a strategically vital center, such as a national capital, that, if captured, would end the contest. They also understood that the use of an invading army was not the easiest way to regain the political allegiance of a people

no longer placing such great value on being British subjects.

Britain's Massive Military Buildup

Directing the imperial war effort were King George, Lord North, and Lord George Germain (1716–1785), who became the American secretary in 1775. Germain, who during the Seven Years' War had been court-martialed on charges of cowardice in battle and thrown out of the British army, was a surprisingly effective administrator. He proved adept at dealing with the bureaucratic and inefficient imperial military machine. His skills became evident in planning for the campaign of 1776—the largest land and sea offensive executed by any western nation until the Allied invasion of North Africa in 1942.

Step by step, Germain pulled the elements together. Of utmost importance was overall campaign strategy. It involved concentrating as many troops as possible on the port of New York City, where great numbers of loyalists lived, then subduing the surrounding countryside as a food and supply base. Loyalists would be used to reinstitute royal government, and the king's forces would engage and crush the rebel army. The American will to resist had to be shattered, and Germain hoped the king's forces could do so in only one campaign season. The longer the rebels lasted, he thought, the greater would be their prospects for success.

Next was the matter of assembling the military forces. It was not the practice in Britain, or elsewhere in Europe, to draw upon all able-bodied, adult males. By and large the middle classes were exempt from service because they were considered productive members of society. The rank and file would come from two sources. First would be the poorer, less productive subjects in the British Isles either recruited or dragooned into service. Since life in European armies was often brutal, it was not always possible to convince or coerce even the most destitute of subjects to sign enlistment papers.

A second source would be the principalities of Germany. Before the end of the war, six German states procured 30,000 soldiers. Some 17,000 came from Hesse-Cassel, where the local head of state coerced many unwilling subjects into service. In return, he received cash payments from the British Crown for each soldier supplied. **Hessians** and downtrodden Britons, including many Irish subjects, thus became the backbone of His Majesty's army.

Certainly as significant a matter as troop recruitment was military leadership. Home government leaders viewed General Gage as too timid and too respectful of Americans. The king recalled Gage in October 1775, naming William Howe (1729–1814) to replace him as commander in chief. William's brother Richard, Admiral Lord Howe (1726–1799), took charge of the naval flotilla that transported thousands of troops to America in 1776.

Lord Germain expected the Howe brothers to use their combined land and naval forces to smash and bayonet the rebels into submission. However, they did not turn out to be fearsome commanders. Politically, they identified with Whig leaders in England who believed the colonists had some legitimate grievances. They intended to move in careful steps, using the presence of so many well-trained regulars to persuade Americans to sign loyalty oaths and renounce the rebellion. In failing to achieve the strategic objective of wiping out patriot resistance in only one campaign season, the less than daring Howe brothers actually helped save the patriot cause from early extinction.

The Campaign for New York

Not yet aware of the scale of British mobilization, New Englanders cheered loudly in mid-March 1776 when William Howe took redcoats and loyalists in tow and fled by sea to Halifax, Nova Scotia. British control of Boston had become untenable because Washington placed the cannons captured at Ticonderoga on Dorchester Heights overlooking the city. Howe's choice was to retreat or be bombarded into submission. Washington, however, did not relax. For months he had predicted the British would strike at New York City. He was absolutely right.

The king's army soon converged on Staten Island, across the bay from Manhattan. William Howe, sailing south from Halifax, arrived with 10,000 soldiers at the end of June. During July, even as Americans learned about the Declaration of Independence, more and more British troops appeared, another 20,000 by mid-August. They came in some 400 transports escorted by 70 naval vessels and 13,000 sailors under Admiral Lord Howe's supervision. All told, the Howe brothers had some 43,000 well-supplied, well-trained, and well-armed combatants. By comparison, George Washington had 28,000 troops on his muster rolls, but only 19,000 were present and fit for duty in August. Even worse, the bulk of the rebel army lacked good weapons or supplies and was deficient in training and discipline.

The decision to defend New York, which the Continental Congress insisted upon and to which Washington acceded, was one of the great rebel blunders of the war. Completely outnumbered, the American commander unwisely divided his soldiers between Manhattan and Brooklyn Heights, separated by the East River. The Howe brothers responded on August 22 by landing troops at Gravesend, Long Island, thereby putting them in an excellent position to trap Washington's force in Brooklyn. For some inexplicable reason, however, Lord Howe chose not to move his naval vessels into the East River, which would have sealed off Washington's escape route. The rebels took a severe beating from the redcoats and Hessians, but they escaped back across the East River. Washington had been lucky, and he clearly learned from his error. Never again did he place his troops in so potentially disastrous a position.

Although Washington's officers wanted to burn New York City to keep the British from using this port city as a base for military operations, Congress vetoed the proposal. When a fire broke out on September 20, 1776, the British and the Americans accused one another of starting the conflagration.

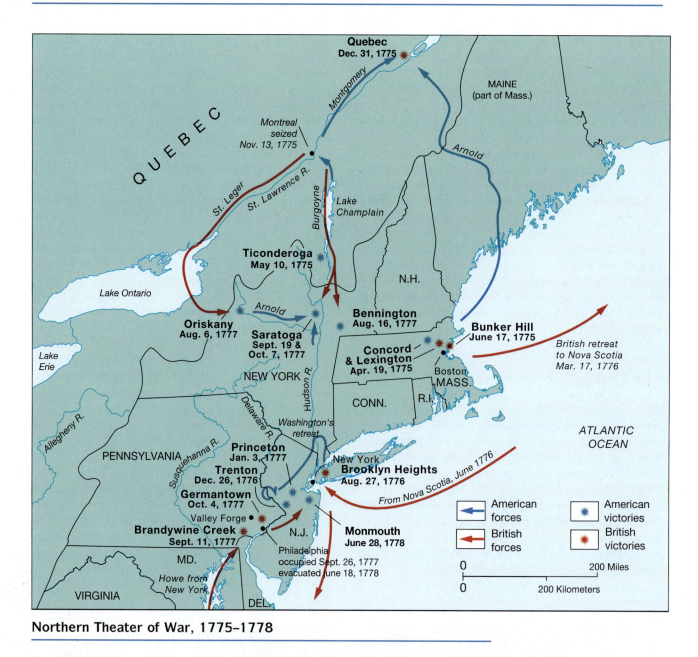

Northern Theater of War, 1775–1778

The Howe brothers moved along indecisively through the rest of the campaign season. Every time they had the advantage, they failed to destroy the rebel army. They drove Washington's forces northward out of Manhattan, then wheeled about and captured some 2000 rebels defending Fort Washington (November 16, 1776), located high on a bluff overlooking the Hudson River. Two days later a British column under Charles, Lord Cornwallis (1738–1805), nearly bagged another sizable patriot contingent at Fort Lee in New Jersey, across from Fort Washington. One of Washington's most talented field commanders, Nathanael Greene of Rhode Island, managed to extricate his force just in time.

Washington had already moved into New Jersey. He ordered a retreat, hoping to get his soldiers across the Delaware River and into Pennsylvania before the aggressive Cornwallis caught up with the dispirited rebel band. By early December 1776 what remained of Washington's army had reached Pennsylvania.

Saving the Cause at Trenton

As the half-starving, battle-wearied patriot troops fled, hundreds of them also deserted. They had learned that British muskets and bayonets could maim and kill. Others, ravaged by disease or wounded in battle, were left behind along the way with the hope of their receiving decent treatment from the enemy. The American army was on the verge of extinction. Washington wrote in mid-December, "I think the game is pretty near up. . . . No man, I believe, ever had a greater choice of difficulties and less means to extricate himself from them." Knowing he had virtually destroyed his prey, William Howe ordered his troops into winter camps and returned to New York City. He was sure mopping up operations could be easily completed in the spring of 1777.

At this juncture George Washington earned his credentials as an innovative commander. He assessed his desperate position and decided upon a bold counterstroke. The success of this maneuver might save his army; defeat would surely ruin it. With muster rolls showing only 6000 troops, Washington divided his soldiers into three groups and tried to recross the icy Delaware River on Christmas evening. Their targets were British outposts in New Jersey. Of the three contingents, only Washington's near-frozen band of 2400 troops accomplished this daring maneuver.

At dawn they reached Trenton, where Colonel Johann Rall's unsuspecting Hessians were still groggy with liquor from their Christmas celebration. The engagement was over in a moment. Four hundred enemy troops escaped, but the Continentals captured almost 1000 Hessians. Within another few days the elated Americans again outdueled British units at Princeton. Stunned by this flurry of rebel activity, Howe redeployed his New Jersey outposts in a semicircle much closer to New York.

Washington had done much more than regain lost ground. He had saved the Continental army from virtual extinction. Never again during the war would the British come so close to total victory—and all because of Howe's failure to demolish Washington's shattered forces when the opportunity was there.

Also of importance was Howe's decision to pull in his outposts. As the British army had marched across New Jersey, it lured thousands of neutrals and loyalists under its banner. These individuals signed loyalty oaths, thus identifying themselves publicly as enemies of the Revolution. As the British army drew back toward New York, the fury of local patriots descended on these tory neighbors whose true allegiance had been revealed.

Time and again throughout the war, British military commanders committed the error of not sustaining support for the king's friends in America. They rarely took advantage of the reservoir of loyal subjects, an estimated 20 percent of the populace, who stood ready to fight the rebels and to do anything else within reason to assure a continuation of British rule. Before the war was over an es-

Diversity of dress among American soldiers was common, but more common was the fact that few soldiers ever had the prescribed clothing.

timated 50,000 loyalists formed into nearly 70 regiments to help the British army regain control in America. British commanders, however, largely used this valuable source of troop strength ineffectively. They did not really trust loyalists or respect their fighting prowess. Their attitude was that loyalists were just colonists, a part of the "rude" American rabble. Such presumed superiority represented a major blindspot, when an essential military task involved regaining the allegiance of enough citizens to effect a complete revival of imperial political authority in America.

On the rebel side, the Trenton and Princeton victories did not result in a revived outpouring of popular support for Washington's army. When the Continentals were in flight across New Jersey, Thomas Paine stepped forth with his first *Crisis* paper. He begged the populace to rally at this moment of deep desperation. "These are the times that try men's souls," Paine stated forcefully. "The summer soldier and the sunshine patriot will, in this crisis, shrink from the service of his country; but he that stands it now, deserves the love and thanks of man and woman." Many read Paine's words, but the massive British campaign effort of 1776 had snuffed out the *rage militaire*.

The Real Continentals

One of the greatest problems facing Washington and the Continental Congress after 1776 was sustaining the rebel army's troop strength. In May 1777 the commander in chief had only 10,000 soldiers, of whom 7363 were present and fit for duty. This number increased substantially during the summer and fall, although only an estimated 11,000 Continentals entered Valley Forge. For the remainder of the war Washington's core of regulars rarely was more sizable. At times, as few as 5000 soldiers stood with him.

Certainly after his experiences in 1776, Washington understood that he must maintain "a respectable army" in the field, hoping ultimately to break Britain's will to continue the fight. He needed troops who would commit themselves to long-term service (three years or the duration), would submit to rigorous training and discipline, and would accept privation in the field. These were hardly glamorous prospects, especially when service often entailed death or dismemberment. Still, Washington, Congress, and the states could promise cash bounties for enlisting, as well as regular pay, decent clothing, adequate food, and even land at war's end. For people who had

nothing to lose, long-term service in the Continental army was at least worth considering.

After 1776 the rank and file of the Continental army came to be made up of economically hard pressed and unfree citizens. Private Joseph Plumb Martin was probably better off than most who enlisted—or were forced into service. The bulk were young (ranging in age from their early teens to mid-twenties), landless, unskilled, poverty-stricken males whose families were likewise quite poor. Also well represented were indentured servants and slaves who stood as substitutes for their masters in return for guarantees of personal freedom at the war's end.

In 1777 Massachusetts became the first state to authorize the enlistment of African Americans—both slaves and freemen. Rhode Island soon followed suit by raising two black regiments. Southern states were far more reluctant to allow slaves to substitute for their masters. Maryland and Virginia ultimately did so, which caused one patriot general to query why so many "sons of freedom" seemed so anxious "to trust their all to be defended by slaves." Add to these groups captured British soldiers and deserters, particularly Hessians and Irishmen, as well as tories and criminals who were often given a choice between military service or the gallows, and a composite portrait of the real Continental army begins to emerge.

Eighteenth-century armies also accepted women in the ranks. Like their male counterparts, they were invariably living on the margins of society. These women "on the ration" (more literally half rations) must be differentiated from so-called camp followers—those who marched along with their husbands or lovers or were prostitutes. Women in service performed various functions, ranging from caring for the sick and wounded, cooking, and mending clothes to scavenging battlefields for clothing and equipment and burying the dead. On occasion they became directly involved in combat. Such a person was hard-drinking Margaret "Dirty Kate" Corbin. Her husband, a cannoneer, was shot dead when British forces attacked and captured Fort Washington in November 1776. Kate Corbin stepped forth, took his place, and helped fire the artillery piece until she also sustained a serious

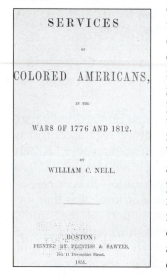

The title page of a first edition on the history of African-American soldiers.

Deborah Sampson served in the army under the name of Timothy Thayer.

THE PEOPLE SPEAK

Thomas Paine's *American Crisis I* (December 1776)

In 1774 Benjamin Franklin, then residing in England, urged Thomas Paine to resettle in America and make his living as a writer. Paine was 37 years old at the time and had failed at virtually everything. He had nothing to lose, so he sailed for Philadelphia, where he gained the opportunity to become one of the great pamphleteers of the Revolution. His *Common Sense* (January 1776) was a runaway bestseller and clearly helped push American patriots toward independence. "We have it in our power to begin the world over again," Paine wrote excitedly in *Common Sense,* but that possibility depended on beating the British militarily. By the end of 1776 the Continental army was struggling to survive, having been shoved by British forces all the way across New Jersey into Pennsylvania. Paine, traveling with the army, penned his first *Crisis* paper to assist in reviving patriot fervor for the cause of liberty. His words, though powerful, had little effect in getting more Americans to commit to long-term military service against the British, a chronic patriot problem after 1776.

These are the times that try men's souls. The summer soldier and the sun-shine patriot will, in this crisis, shrink from the service of his country: but he that stands it *now*, deserves the thanks of man and woman. Tyranny, like hell, is not easily conquered: yet we have this consolation with us, that the harder the conflict, the more glorious the triumph. What we obtain too cheap, we esteem too lightly: 'tis dearness only that gives every thing its value. Heaven knows how to set a proper price upon its goods; and it would be strange, indeed, if so celestial an article as freedom should not be highly rated. Britain, with an army to enforce her tyranny, has declared that she has a right, not only to tax, but 'to bind us in all cases whatsoever:' and if being bound in that manner is not slavery, there is not such a thing as slavery upon earth. Even the expression is impious: for so unlimited a power can belong only to God. . . .

I turn, with the warm ardour of a friend, to those who have nobly stood, and are yet determined to stand the matter out. I call not upon a few, but upon all; not on this state, or that state, but on every state. Up and help us. Lay your shoulders to the wheel. Better have too much force than too little, when so great an object is at stake. Let it be told to the future world, that in the depth of winter, when nothing but hope and virtue could survive, that the city and the country, alarmed at one common danger, came forth to meet and to repulse it. Say not that thousands are gone: turn out your tens of thousands: throw not the burden of the day upon providence, but show your faith by your good works, that God may bless you. It matters not where you live, or what rank of life you hold; the evil or the blessing will reach you all. The far and the near, the home counties and the back, the rich and the poor, shall suffer or rejoice alike. The heart that feels not now, is dead. The blood of his children shall curse his cowardice, who shrinks back at a time when a little might have saved the whole and made them happy. I love the man that can smile in trouble—that can gather strength from distress, and grow brave by reflection. It is the business of little minds to shrink; but he, whose heart is firm, and whose conscience approves his conduct, will pursue his principles unto death. My own line of reasoning is to myself, as strait and clear as a ray of light. Not all the treasures of the world, so far as I believe, could have induced me to support an offensive war; for I think it murder: but if a thief break into my house—burn and destroy my property, and kill, or threaten to kill me and those that are in it, and to 'bind me in all cases whatsoever,' to his absolute will, am I to suffer it? . . . Let them call me rebel, and welcome; I feel no concern from it; but I should suffer the misery of devils, were I to make a whore of my soul, by swearing allegiance to one whose character is that of a sottish, stupid, stubborn, worthless, brutish man. . . .

This is our situation—and who will, may know it. By perseverance and fortitude, we have the prospect of a glorious issue; by cowardice and submission, the sad choice of a variety of evils—a ravaged country—a depopulated city—habitations without safety—and slavery without hope—our homes turned into barracks and bawdy-houses for Hessians—and a future race to provide for, whose fathers we shall doubt of! Look on this picture, and weep over it! and if there yet remains one thoughtless wretch, who believes it not, let him suffer it unlamented.

December, 1776

Source: Thomas Paine, *American Crisis I* (December 1776).

The American victories at Saratoga thwarted the British plan to defeat the colonies by dividing them. Benedict Arnold led the Americans to victory but credit for the success went to General Horatio Gates. Frustrated by the lack of recognition he felt he deserved for his military service and leadership, Arnold eventually switched his allegiance to the British.

were to act as a diversionary force. Soon they had 750 desperate rebel defenders of Fort Schuyler under siege. Seemingly nothing could stop these two columns, which were to converge again in Albany.

After seizing Ticonderoga, Burgoyne became more tentative about his southward movement. Like William Howe in 1776, he did not take his opponent seriously enough. Under the leadership of General Philip Schuyler, the Continental army's Northern Department had started to rally. The rebels blocked Burgoyne's path by cutting down trees, ripping up bridges, and moving boulders into fording points on streams. Soon the British advance had been slowed to less than a mile a day. Then Congress confused matters by replacing Schuyler—New Englanders considered him too aristocratic in his behavior—with General Horatio Gates.

Burgoyne, meanwhile, was having problems controlling his Native-American allies. In late July a few of them murdered and scalped a young woman, Jane McCrea, who was betrothed to one of his loyalist officers. Burgoyne refused to punish the culprits, fearing he might drive off all his native allies. Despite his forbearance, the Indians found traveling with the slow moving British army tedious at best; most retreated back to Canada before the end of August. Moreover, not disciplining Jane McCrea's murderers conveyed a message of barbarism that helped convince at least some frontier New England militiamen, worried about shielding their own families from possible Indian depredations, to take up arms and come forward in support of the Continentals.

Just as bad for the British, St. Leger's diversionary force ran into trouble. Militiamen in the Mohawk Valley under General Nicholas Herkimer, in alliance with Oneidas and Tuscaroras of the Six Nations, tried to break through to Fort Schuyler. On August 6, 1777, they clashed with St. Leger's loyalists and Indians, among them Mohawks, Cayugas, and Senecas (also of the Six Nations) at the Battle of Oriskany. Herkimer and nearly half of his column were killed or wounded that day, one of the bloodiest of the war.

Oriskany represented the beginning of the end for the once mighty Iroquois nation, whose tribes were now hopelessly divided and consuming each other in combat. When war chieftain Joseph Brant (Thayendanegea) of the Mohawks led numerous bloody frontier raids for the British, a Continental army expedition under General John Sullivan marched into central New York in 1779 and destroyed every Iroquois village it came upon. After the Revolutionary War ended, the more aggressive Iroquois migrated north to Canada or west into the Ohio country, where they fought to keep out white settlers; others, less militant, moved onto reservations in western New York.

St. Leger's victory was temporary. Continentals under Benedict Arnold rushed west from the Albany area and drove off St. Leger without a second major fight. Arnold sent a dim-witted local loyalist into St. Leger's camp with fabricated news of thousands of rebel soldiers moving rapidly toward Fort Schuyler. The Indians, already upset by the loss of so many warriors at Oriskany, quickly broke camp and fled,

Joseph Brant (Thayendanegea), a Mohawk war chieftain, believed the Iroquois could not remain neutral and that their only chance was to side with the British.

most ashamed to be heard on such an occasion." Losing Burgoyne's army was an unnecessary disaster for Britain, caused primarily by William Howe's unwillingness to work in concert with Burgoyne and follow through on the Hudson Highlands strategy. The victory was a momentous triumph for the Americans and a key factor in convincing Vergennes that France could now commit itself publicly to the rebel cause.

On February 6, 1778, the French government signed two treaties with the American commissioners. The first, the Treaty of Amity and Commerce, recognized American independence and encouraged the development of close trading ties. For Vergennes the prospect of conducting—and perhaps even dominating—international trade with the Americans was another way to weaken the British. Still, trading concessions were really not enough to entice the French into an alliance. What Vergennes and Louis XVI really wanted was the opportunity to strike devastating military blows at the British. They knew the Treaty of Amity and Commerce would likely provoke Britain into an act of war with France, so they insisted upon a second agreement, the more entangling Treaty of Alliance, by which the young United States and France would stand as "good and faithful" allies in the event of such hostilities.

On March 20 Louis XVI formally greeted the American commissioners at court and announced that the new nation had gained France's diplomatic recognition. In June 1778 a naval battle in the English Channel involving British and French warships resulted in formal warfare between these two powers. The drum beat for British rule over the 13 states had now taken on the cadence of a death march.

leaving the British colonel no alternative but to retreat back into Canada.

Burgoyne had now lost his diversionary force. He suffered another major setback on August 16 when New Hampshire militiamen under General John Stark overwhelmed some 900 Hessians who were out raiding for supplies near Bennington in the Vermont territory. Burgoyne's army was all but entrapped some 30 miles north of Albany along the Hudson River. In two desperate battles (September 19 and October 7) the British force tried to find a way around the well-entrenched rebels, but the brilliant field generalship of Benedict Arnold inspired the Americans to victory. Burgoyne finally surrendered what remained of his army—some 5000 soldiers and auxiliaries—to General Gates on October 17, 1777.

According to one British soldier on the Saratoga surrender field, "we marched out, . . . with drums beating and the honors of war, but the drums seemed to have lost their former inspiring sounds, . . . as if al-

THE WORLD TURNED UPSIDE DOWN

When George Washington learned about the French alliance, he declared a holiday for "rejoicing throughout the whole army." On that spring day in early May 1778, the Continentals at Valley Forge thoroughly enjoyed themselves. They had much to celebrate. They had survived the winter, and they had also benefited from the rigorous field training of colorful Baron Friedrich von Steuben, a pretended Prussian nobleman who had volunteered to teach the soldiery how to fight in more disciplined fashion. Equally important was the announcement of open, direct aid from France, which would include not only land troops but critical naval support. Having gained the formal backing of a powerful European nation certainly enhanced prospects for actually beating the British. Washington, so elated by this turn in events, even winked at the issuance of "more than the common quantity of liquor" to his soldiers, which he knew would result in "some little drunkenness among them."

Revamping British Strategy

The American alliance with France changed the fundamental character of the War for Independence. British officials realized that they were no longer just contending with upstart rebels in America. They were getting themselves ensnared in a world war. France, with its well-trained army and highly mobile navy, had the ability to strike British territories anytime and anywhere it chose. While renouncing any desire to retake Canada, the French did have designs on the valuable British sugar islands in the Caribbean. They built up troop strength in the French West Indies and soon had a four-to-one advantage in that region.

The British military problem became even more complex in 1779 when Spain joined the war but only after signing a secret agreement with France—the Convention of Aranjuez—stipulating that Louis XVI's military forces were not to stop fighting until the Spanish regained the Rock of Gibraltar (lost to the British at the end of the War of the Spanish Succession in 1713). Then in late 1780 the British declared war on the Netherlands, partly so they could capture the Dutch Caribbean island of St. Eustatius, which served as a key point of exchange for American patriots in obtaining war supplies from Dutch merchants.

The dawning reality of world war threatened the British empire with major territorial losses across the globe. One result was a redesigned imperial war plan—the **Southern strategy**—for reconquering the rebellious American provinces. The assumption was that his Majesty's troops could no longer be massed against the American rebels; instead, they would have to be dispersed to threatened points, such as islands in the West Indies.

The first step came in May 1778 when General Sir Henry Clinton (1738?–1795), who had taken over as North American commander from a discredited William Howe, received orders to evacuate Philadelphia. In June Clinton's troops retreated to New York City, narrowly averting a disastrous defeat by Washington's pursuing Continentals at Monmouth Court House (June 28) in central New Jersey. Clinton was to hang on as best he could at the main British base, but he would have to accept a reduction in forces for

campaigns elsewhere. The process of dispersal began during the autumn of 1778. Sir Henry avoided major battles with Washington's army in the North while he implemented the Southern strategy.

Crown officials mistakenly assumed that, in the South, loyalists existed in far greater numbers than in the North. In a slight modification of the Hudson Highlands strategy, the idea was to employ the king's friends, primarily as substitutes for depleted British forces, in partisan (guerrilla) warfare. Bands of armed loyalists would operate in conjunction with a main redcoat army to break patriot resistance, beginning in Georgia and then moving in carefully planned steps northward. As soon as any rebel-dominated region had been fully resecured for the Crown, royal government would be reintroduced. Ultimately through attrition, the whole South would be brought back into the British fold, opening the way for eventual subjugation of the North.

The Southern strategy required patience as well as careful nurturing of loyalist sentiment. Both seemed very possible when a detachment of 3500 redcoats sailed south from New York City in November 1778 and quickly reconquered Georgia.

Until the French alliance the South was a secondary theater of war, marked mostly by sporadic partisan fighting between loyalists and rebel militia. Indian-white relations were bloodier. As in the North with Iroquois, both sides maneuvered to gain favor with the Cherokees, Chickasaws, Creeks, and Choctaws. These four nations had a total of about 10,000 warriors, compared to an estimated 2000 among the northern Iroquois.

John Stuart, Britain's Superintendent of Indian Affairs in the southern colonies, had a network of agents working among the native populace. Late in 1775 he focused on winning over the Cherokees and Creeks, who had the most warriors, urging them to fight in concert with loyalists. Stuart was particularly successful with the Cherokees, who had recovered somewhat from their losses during the Seven Years' War. Led by the Overhill chieftain Dragging Canoe (Chincohacina), Cherokee war parties in the summer of 1776 attacked frontier settlements from Virginia to South Carolina, massacring settlers who had unwisely moved onto traditional tribal hunting grounds.

Dragging Canoe's raids had two major effects. First, in September 1776 hundreds of Virginia and North Carolina frontiersmen came together as militia and wreaked mayhem on the most easterly Cherokee towns. During October the Virginians proceeded farther west to the Overhill Cherokee villages. Dragging Canoe and his warriors retreated, promising to foreswear further assistance to the British. This

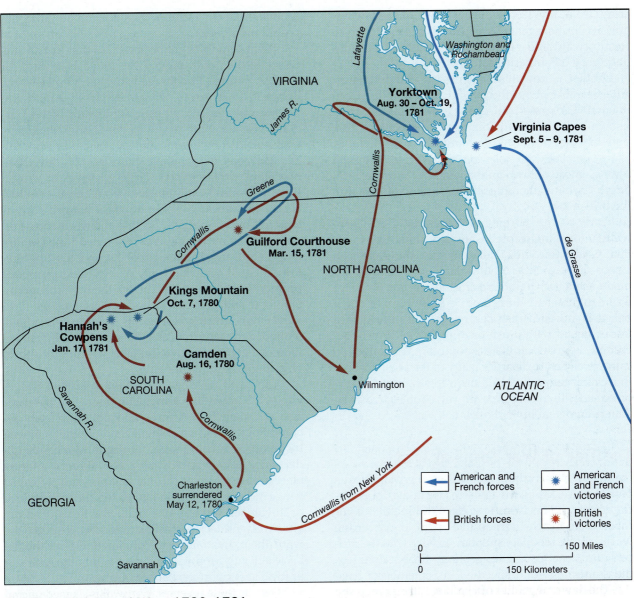

Southern Theater of War, 1780–1781

agreement took the Cherokees out of the war. Second, the other major nations, seeing what had happened, snubbed John Stuart's agents and backed off from the "family quarrel." By 1777 the southern Indians had been neutralized. Although a band of Creeks did support the British after their invasion of Georgia, Native Americans did not figure prominently in Britain's post-1778 strategy.

Sir Henry Clinton, who was probably less decisive than William Howe, was slow to expand on the redcoats' success in Georgia. Finally, in late 1779 he sailed with 7600 troops toward his target—Charleston, South Carolina. There General Benjamin Lincoln, with just 3000 Continental regulars and a

smattering of militia, found himself completely outnumbered and trapped when part of Clinton's force moved inland and cut off escape routes. Facing prospects of extermination, Lincoln surrendered without much of a fight on May 12, 1780. This was the only occasion during the war that the British captured an American army.

Clinton's victory at Charleston was the second success in the Southern strategy. The British commander sailed back to New York in high spirits, leaving behind Lord Cornwallis to secure all of South Carolina. Clinton had ordered Cornwallis to advance with careful steps, making sure that loyalist partisans always had firm control of territory behind his army. Ironically, Cornwallis was one of the few aggressive British generals in America. His desire to rush forward and get on with the fight helped undermine the Southern strategy.

At first, Cornwallis's boldness reaped dividends. After learning about the fall of Charleston, the Continental Congress ordered Horatio Gates, now known as the "hero of Saratoga," to proceed south, pull together a new army, and check Cornwallis. Gates botched the job completely. He gathered troops, mostly raw militiamen, in Virginia and North Carolina, then hastily rushed his soldiers into the British lair.

Early on the morning of August 16, 1780, Cornwallis's force intercepted Gates's column near Camden, South Carolina. Not only did the American troops lack training, but tainted provisions had made them sick. The evening before the Battle of Camden they had supped on "a hasty meal of quick baked bread and fresh beef, with a dessert of molasses, mixed with mush or dumplings," which, according to one of Gates's officers, "operated so cathartically as to disorder many of the men" just before the engagement. Cornwallis's army overwhelmed the rebel force in yet another crushing American defeat in the South.

The Tide of War Turns at Last

During 1780 everything seemed to go wrong for the patriot cause. Besides major setbacks in the South, officers and soldiers directly under Washington's command were increasingly restive about long overdue wages and inadequate supplies. In July 1780 the officers threatened mass resignations unless Congress did something—and speedily. In September a frustrated Benedict Arnold switched his allegiance to the British. By the end of 1780 Continental army troop strength fell below 6000. Then, as the new year dawned, Washington faced successive mutinies among his hardened veterans in the Pennsylvania and New Jersey lines. The Continental army seemed to be disintegrating, so much so that the commander in chief put aside plans for a possible strike against New York City. Even though French troops under the Comte de Rochambeau were now in the vicinity, his own Continental numbers were too few to pursue such an elaborate venture.

Quite simply, the British seemed to be winning the endurance contest of wills: One despondent Continental officer wrote, "It really gives me great pain to think of our public affairs; where is the public spirit of the year 1775? Where are those flaming *patriots* who were ready to sacrifice their lives, their fortunes, their all, for the public?" At no time during the war, except for those dark days just before Washington's

counterstrike at Trenton, had the rebel cause appeared more forlorn.

What could not yet be seen was that British successes in the South moved the redcoats toward far greater failure. Encouraged by its victories, the British southern army overreached itself. After Camden, Cornwallis started pushing toward North Carolina. His left wing under Major Patrick Ferguson, whose soldiers were mostly loyalists, was soon under the eye of growing numbers of "over-the-mountain" frontiersmen. Their goal was to protect their homesteads and families from Ferguson's loyalists, who repeatedly shot down or hanged patriots who fell into their path. Feeling their presence, Ferguson began retreating. When he spied Kings Mountain, Ferguson calculated that he and his 1100 followers could withstand any assault from atop that promontory. On October 7, 1780, the over-the-mountain force attacked from all sides. Ferguson fell mortally wounded; the rest of his column was killed, wounded, or captured; and the frontiersmen hanged nine of Ferguson's loyalists as a warning to others who might fight for the king.

The Battle of Kings Mountain destroyed the left wing of Cornwallis's army. Compounding the damage, the main British force had not completely secured South Carolina. Whenever Cornwallis moved his troops to a new locale, rebel guerrilla bands under such leaders as "Swamp Fox" Francis Marion emerged from their hiding places and wreaked vengeance on tories who had aided the British force or threatened rebels. Once again, the British had not effectively protected citizens favorably disposed toward them; this failing in combination with the debacle at Kings Mountain cut deeply into the reservoir of loyalist support available to Cornwallis.

Despite these reverses, Cornwallis seemed unconcerned. Like his fellow officers, he held Americans in contempt, believing it was only a matter of time until

Rebel guerrilla leaders like Francis Marion kept the patriot cause alive in South Carolina. In this scene, Marion is leading his troops across the Pee Dee River.

superior British arms would destroy the rebels. However, Cornwallis did not bargain on facing the likes of General Nathanael Greene (1742–1786), who replaced Gates as the Southern Department commander. Greene arrived in North Carolina during December 1780. Not surprisingly, very few troops were available for duty and, as Greene stated despondently, the "appearance" of those in camp "was wretched beyond description."

Greene was a military genius. Violating the military maxim of massing troop strength as much as possible, he decided to divide his soldiers into three small groups, one of which would work with partisan rebel bands. The idea was to let Cornwallis chase after the other two columns of just over 1000 each, until the redcoats were worn out. At that point Greene would stand and fight.

The aggressive Cornwallis took the bait. He went after Greene and sent a detached force after the other rebel column headed by shrewd, capable General Daniel Morgan of Virginia. Morgan's troops lured the onrushing British into a trap at Hannah's Cowpens in western South Carolina on January 17, 1781. Only 140 of the some 1100 British soldiers escaped being killed, captured, or wounded.

Meanwhile, Cornwallis relentlessly pursued Greene, who kept retreating northward before swinging back into central North Carolina. Then, on March 15, 1781, the rebels squared off for battle at Guilford Courthouse. The combatants fought throughout the afternoon, when the Americans abandoned the field. Greene's force had inflicted 506

casualties, as compared to taking 264 of their own. Cornwallis had gained a technical victory, but his troops were exhausted from Greene's game of "fox and hare," and the rebels were still very much in the field.

Franco-American Triumph at Yorktown

Cornwallis retreated to the seacoast to rest his army, then decided to take over British raiding operations in Virginia, which had begun in January 1781 under turncoat Benedict Arnold. In storming northward, Cornwallis totally abandoned the Southern strategy. Nathanael Greene was now free to reassert full patriot authority in the states south of Virginia.

Back in New York, General Clinton fumed. He wanted to discipline his subordinate but was too timid to do so. Instead, he sent Cornwallis orders in July to establish a defensive base in Virginia and to refrain from conducting any offensive operations until such time as Clinton issued further orders. A most reluctant Cornwallis selected Yorktown, with easy access to Chesapeake Bay.

At this juncture everything fell into place for the Americans. Washington learned from General Rochambeau that a French naval fleet would be making its way north from the West Indies. If that fleet could seal off the entrance to Chesapeake Bay and combined Franco-American land forces could surround Cornwallis's army, a major victory would be in the making.

The rebel commander seized the opportunity. Washington and Rochambeau began marching soldiers south from New York, leaving only enough troops behind to keep Clinton tied down. In early September the French fleet, after dueling with British warships, took control of Chesapeake Bay. As the month came to a close, some 7800 French troops and 9000 Continentals and militiamen surrounded the British army of 8500 at Yorktown. Cornwallis wrote Clinton: "If you cannot relieve me very soon you must expect to hear the worst."

Using traditional siege tactics, Washington and Rochambeau slowly squeezed Cornwallis into submission. On October 17 a lone British drummer marched toward the Franco-American lines with a white flag showing. Two days later, on a bright, sunny autumn afternoon, the army of Charles, Lord Cornwallis, marched out from its lines in solemn procession and laid down its arms. As these troops did so, their musicians played an appropriate song, "The World Turned Upside Down." The surrender at Yorktown was an emotional scene. A second British army had been captured in America, and the

With combined Franco-American forces, General Washington put Yorktown under siege in October 1781 and entrapped General Cornwallis's army.

lingering question was whether Great Britain still had the resolve to continue the war.

A Most Generous Peace Settlement

An accumulation of wounds, with the great Franco-American victory at Yorktown being the most damaging, brought the British to the peace table. As early as 1778 Britain had felt the effects of world war. Daring seaman John Paul Jones (1747–1792), known as the "father of the American navy," had conducted damaging raids along the English and Scottish coasts during that year. In 1779, while sailing in the North Sea, Jones lost his own warship, the *Bon Homme Richard*, but captured the British war frigate *Serapis* in a dramatic naval engagement, all within sight of England.

By 1781 French and Spanish warships were attacking British vessels at will in the English Channel, and French warships threatened British possessions in the West Indies. France and Spain were about to launch a major expedition against Gibraltar. In the spring of 1781 a Spanish force under Bernardo de Gálvez captured a sizable British garrison at Pensacola, Florida, and the British soon experienced defeats as far away as India. The allies had demonstrated they could carry the war anywhere, even to the shores of England, suggesting the possibility of much greater damage to the far-flung British empire than just the loss of 13 rebellious colonies in North America.

Keenly aware of these many setbacks, Lord North received the news about Yorktown "as he would have taken a [musket] ball in the breast." In March 1782 North's ministry collapsed, and a new cabinet opened negotiations with designated American peace commissioners—Benjamin Franklin, John Adams, and John Jay—in France. On November 30, 1782, the representatives agreed to preliminary peace terms, pending final ratification by both governments. The other belligerents also started coming to terms, largely because the naval war had turned

Chronology
OF KEY EVENTS

1775 The shot "heard 'round the world"—the first military clashes between British troops and colonists take place at Lexington and Concord (April); Second Continental Congress begins meeting in Philadelphia (May); fighting breaks out in New York, Massachusetts, and Canada (May–December); Continental army forms under the command of George Washington (June)

1776 Thomas Paine publishes *Common Sense* (January); Continental Congress adopts the Declaration of Independence (July); Virginia, North Carolina, and South Carolina frontiersmen neutralize southern Indians (July–November); British rout rebel soldiers in vicinity of New York City (August–November); American forces defeat British units at Trenton (December)

1777 Massachusetts begins enlisting free African Americans for Continental service (April); British forces seize Philadelphia after defeating Washington's troops at Brandywine Creek in Pennsylvania (September); American forces capture General Burgoyne's army at Saratoga (October)

1778 American patriots form an alliance with France (February–March); John Paul Jones raids along the British coastline (April–May); British troops invade the Deep South and conquer Savannah, Georgia (December)

1779 Spain joins the war against Britain

1780 British forces defeat American armies at Charleston (May) and Camden (August), South Carolina, but lose at Kings Mountain (October); Benedict Arnold, caught in his efforts to exchange West Point for a commission in the British army, flees to the British (September); British declare war on the Dutch (December)

1781 American forces defeat British soldiers at Hannah's Cowpens (January) in western South Carolina and fight to a draw at Guilford Courthouse (March) in central North Carolina; British surrender to combined Franco-American forces at Yorktown, Virginia (October)

1783 Treaty of Paris ends the War for American Independence

against France and Spain and British troops had saved Gibraltar. All parties signed the final peace accords at Paris on September 3, 1783.

The major European powers now recognized the 13 rebellious colonies as a separate nation. Further, the peace accords established the Mississippi River as the western boundary line of the new nation and 31° north latitude as the southern boundary. Based on Gálvez's success, Britain returned the lands south of this line, constituting Florida, to Spain.

Although the American commissioners failed to obtain Canada, they had gained title to the vast reserve of Indian territory lying between the Appalachian Mountains and the Mississippi River. The treaty was silent about the rights of Indians, whose interests the British ignored, despite repeated promises during the war to protect the lands of Native Americans who joined the king's cause. All told, effective bargaining by the American peace commissioners gave the former colonists a huge geographic base on which to build their new republic.

The peace settlement also contained other important provisions. Britain recognized American fishing rights off the coast of eastern Canada, thus sustaining a major New England industry. The British promised not to carry away slaves when evacuating their troops (which they did anyway). At the same time, they demanded that prewar American debts be paid in full to British creditors (few actually would be paid) and insisted upon the complete restoration of the rights and property of loyalists. The American commissioners agreed to have Congress make such a recommendation to the states (which they generally ignored). The peace treaty, then, both established American independence and laid the groundwork for future conflict.

CONCLUSION

The rebellious Americans came out remarkably well in 1783. They emerged victorious not only in war but at the peace table as well. The young republic had endured over its parent nation, Great Britain, and with invaluable assistance from foreign allies, particularly France, had earned its freedom from European monarchism and imperialism. On the other hand, no one knew for sure whether the young United States could sustain its independence or have much of a future as a separate nation, given the many internal problems facing the 13 sovereign states.

Among those who did not cheer heartily at the prospect of peace were the officers and soldiers of the Continental army. They had made great personal sacrifices and had every reason to be proud of their accomplishments; however, they deeply resented the lack of civilian support that had plagued their efforts throughout the long conflict. Even in leaving the service, wrote Private Joseph Plumb Martin, the Continentals were "turned adrift like old worn-out horses" without just financial compensation for their services. Still, they had the personal satisfaction of knowing that their pain and suffering had sustained the grand vision of 1776, which would only prevail if revolutionary Americans resolved among themselves their many differences—especially those relating to the process of implanting republican ideals in the social and political fabric of the new nation.

SUGGESTIONS FOR FURTHER READING

Colin G. Calloway, *The American Revolution in Indian Country: Crisis and Diversity in Native American Villages* (1995). Thoughtful presentation of the ways in which eight Indian communities dealt with the American Revolution, viewed from the native as opposed to the British-American perspective.

Stephen Conway, *The War of American Independence, 1775–1783* (1995). Suggestive study that depicts the contest with Britain as the first modern war, a description usually reserved for the French Revolutionary and Napoleonic wars of a later period.

Jonathan R. Dull, *A Diplomatic History of the American Revolution* (1985). Succinct, incisive treatment of the competing national interests and rivalries that affected the outcome of the Revolutionary War.

David Hackett Fischer, *Paul Revere's Ride* (1994). Engaging narrative of Revere's life and the battles of Lexington and Concord in the context of New England's folkways.

Pauline Maier, *American Scripture: Making the Declaration of Independence* (1997). Fresh evaluation of the factors that helped shape Thomas Jefferson's landmark document.

James Kirby Martin and Mark Edward Lender, *A Respectable Army: The Military Origins of the Republic, 1763–1789* (1982). Overview analysis of Revolutionary ideals in contact with the realities of who served in the Continental army, their reasons for fighting, and their contributions to the nation-making process.

Charles Royster, *A Revolutionary People at War: The Continental Army and American Character, 1775–1783* (1979). Widely read study of the ways in which the Revolutionary populace perceived their involvement in the martial contest with Britain.

John Shy, *A People Numerous and Armed: Reflections on the Military Struggle for American Independence*, rev. ed. (1990). Classic essays illuminating the nature of eighteenth-century military values and practices and how the Revolutionary War helped foster a sense of national identity.

Overviews and Surveys

John R. Alden, *The American Revolution, 1775–1783* (1954); Jeremy Black, *War for America: The Fight for Independence,*

1775–1783 (1991); Lawrence D. Cress, *Citizens in Arms: The Army and the Militia in American Society to the War of 1812* (1982); R. Ernest Dupuy, et al., *The American Revolution: A Global War* (1977); John Ferling, ed., *The World Turned Upside Down: The American Victory in the War of Independence* (1988); Sylvia R. Frey, *The British Soldier in America* (1981); Don Higginbotham, *The War of American Independence, 1763–1789* (1971), ed., *Reconsiderations on the Revolutionary War* (1978), and *War and Society in Revolutionary America* (1988); Ronald Hoffman and Peter J. Albert, eds., *Arms and Independence: The Military Character of the American Revolution* (1984); Piers Mackesy, *The War for America, 1775–1783* (1964); Holly A. Mayer, *Belonging to the Army: Camp Followers and Community during the Revolution* (1996); Charles P. Neimeyer, *America Goes to War: The Continental Army* (1996); Dave R. Palmer, *The Way of the Fox: American Strategy in the War for America, 1775–1783* (1975); Eric Robson, *The American Revolution in Its Political and Military Aspects, 1763–1783* (1955); Reginald C. Stuart, *War and American Thought: From the Revolution to the Monroe Doctrine* (1982); Robert K. Wright, Jr., *The Continental Army* (1984).

Reconciliation or Independence

Joseph L. Davis, *Sectionalism in American Politics, 1774–1787* (1977); H. James Henderson, *Party Politics in the Continental Congress* (1974); Merrill Jensen, *The Articles of Confederation: An Interpretation of the Social-Constitutional History of the American Revolution, 1774–1781* (1940); Jackson Turner Main, *The Sovereign States, 1775–1783* (1973); Jerrilyn Greene Marston, *King and Congress: The Transfer of Political Legitimacy, 1774–1776* (1987); Jack N. Rakove, *The Beginnings of National Politics: An Interpretive History of the Continental Congress* (1979).

Without Visible Allies: The War in the North

Rodney Atwood, *The Hessians* (1980); George A. Billias, ed., *George Washington's Generals* (1964), and ed., *George Washington's Opponents* (1969); Richard Buel, Jr., *Dear Liberty: Connecticut's Mobilization for the Revolutionary War* (1980); John C. Dann, ed., *The Revolution Remembered: Eyewitness Accounts of the War for Independence* (1980); Barbara Graymont, *The Iroquois in the American Revolution* (1972); Robert A. Gross, *The Minutemen and Their World* (1976); Robert McConnell Hatch, *Thrust for Canada: The American Attempt on Quebec in 1775–1776* (1979); Richard M. Ketchum, *The Winter Soldiers* (1973); James Kirby Martin, ed., *Ordinary Courage: The Revolutionary War Adventures of Joseph Plumb Martin,* 2d ed. (1999); Max M. Mintz, *Seeds of Empire: The American Revolutionary Conquest of the Iroquois* (1999); John S. Pancake, *1777: The Year of the Hangman* (1977); Gary Alexander Puckrein, *The Black Regiment in the American Revolution* (1978); Jonathan Gregory Rossie, *The Politics of Command in the American Revolution* (1975); Steven Rosswurm, *Arms, Country, and Class: The Philadelphia Militia and "Lower Sort" During the Revolution, 1775–1783* (1987); Paul H. Smith, *Loyalists and Redcoats: A Study in British Revolutionary Policy* (1964).

Rescuing the Patriots: Toward Global Conflict

Samuel F. Bemis, *The Diplomacy of the American Revolution,* rev. ed. (1957); Light Townsend Cummins, *Spanish Observers and the American Revolution, 1775–1783* (1992); Ronald Hoffman and Peter J. Albert, eds., *Diplomacy and Revolution: The Franco-American Alliance of 1778* (1981); Reginald Horsman, *The Diplomacy of the New Republic, 1776–1815* (1985); James H. Hutson, *John Adams and the Diplomacy of the American Revolution* (1980); Lawrence S. Kaplan, ed., *The American Revolution and "A Candid World"* (1977); Richard B. Morris, *The Peacemakers: The Great Powers and American Independence* (1965); Charles R. Ritcheson, *British Politics and the American Revolution* (1954); H. M. Scott, *British Foreign Policy in the Age of the American Revolution* (1991); William C. Stinchcombe, *The American Revolution and the French Alliance* (1969); Gerald Stourzh, *Benjamin Franklin and American Foreign Policy,* 2d ed. (1969); Richard W. Van Alstyne, *Empire and Independence: The International History of the American Revolution* (1965); Paul A. Varg, *Foreign Policies of the Founding Fathers* (1963).

The World Turned Upside Down

Lawrence E. Babits, *A Devil of a Whipping: The Battle of Cowpens* (1998); R. Arthur Bowler, *Logistics and the Failure of the British Army in America, 1775–1783* (1975); John Buchanan, *The Road to Guilford Courthouse* (1997); E. Wayne Carp, *To Starve the Army at Pleasure: Continental Army Administration and American Political Culture, 1775–1783* (1984); Jeffrey J. Crow and Larry E. Tise, eds., *The Southern Experience in the American Revolution* (1978); John Morgan Dederer, *Making Bricks Without Straw: Nathanael Greene's Southern Campaign and Mao Tse-Tung's Mobile War* (1983); Jonathan R. Dull, *The French Navy and American Independence, 1774–1787* (1975); William M. Fowler, Jr., *Rebels Under Sail: The American Navy During the Revolution* (1976); W. Robert Higgins, ed., *The Revolutionary War in the South* (1979); Ronald Hoffman, Thad W. Tate, and Peter J. Albert, eds., *An Uncivil War: The Southern Backcountry During the American Revolution* (1985); Lee Kennett, *The French Forces in America, 1780–1783* (1977); Henry Lumpkin, *From Savannah to Yorktown* (1981); George S. McCowen, Jr., *The British Occupation of Charleston, 1780–82* (1972); James H. O'Donnell, III, *Southern Indians in the American Revolution* (1973); John S. Pancake, *This Destructive War: The British Campaign in the Carolinas, 1780–1782* (1985); John E. Selby, *The Revolution in Virginia, 1775–1783* (1988); David Syrett, *The Royal Navy in American Waters* (1989), and *Shipping and the American War, 1775–83: A Study of British Transport Organization* (1970); John A. Tilley, *The British Navy and the American Revolution* (1987); Russell F. Weigley, *The Partisan War: The South Carolina Campaign of 1780–1782* (1970).

Biographies

Edward J. Cashin, *The King's Ranger: Thomas Brown and the Revolution on the Southern Frontier* (1989); Marcus Cunliffe, *George Washington: Man and Monument,* rev. ed. (1982); Don R. Gerlach, *Proud Patriot: Philip Schuyler and the War of Independence, 1775–1783* (1987); Louis R. Gottschalk, *Lafayette*

Joins the American Army (1937); Ira D. Gruber, *The Howe Brothers and the American Revolution* (1972); Richard J. Hargrove, Jr., *General John Burgoyne* (1983); Don Higginbotham, *Daniel Morgan* (1961), and *George Washington and the American Military Tradition* (1985); James Kirby Martin, *Benedict Arnold, Revolutionary Hero* (1997); David B. Mattern, *Benjamin Lincoln and the American Revolution* (1995); Max M. Mintz, *The Generals of Saratoga: John Burgoyne and Horatio Gates* (1990); Samuel E. Morison, *John Paul Jones* (1959); Orville T. Murphy, *Charles Gravier, Comte de Vergennes* (1982); Paul David Nelson, *General Horatio Gates* (1976), and *Anthony Wayne: Soldier of the Early Republic* (1985); Louis W. Potts, *Arthur Lee: A Virtuous Revolutionary* (1981); Hugh F. Rankin, *Francis Marion: The Swamp Fox* (1973); Thomas J. Schaeper, *France and America in the Revolutionary Era: Jacques-Donatien Leray de Chaumont, 1725–1803* (1995); Hal T. Shelton, *General Richard Montgomery: From Redcoat to Rebel* (1994); Willard M. Wallace, *Traitorous Hero: Benedict Arnold* (1954); Franklin B. and Mary Wickwire, *Cornwallis: The American Adventure* (1970); William B. Willcox, *Portrait of a General: Sir Henry Clinton in the War of Independence* (1964).

INTERNET RESOURCES

Exploring the West from Monticello: An Exhibition of Maps and Navigational Instruments
http://www.lib.virginia.edu/exhibits/lewis_clark/home.html
Maps and charts reveal knowledge and conceptions about the known and the unknown. This site includes a number of eighteenth century maps.

Georgia's Rare Map Collection
http://scarlett.libs.uga.edu/darchive/hargrett/maps/colamer.html
http://scarlett.libs.uga.edu/darchive/hargrett/maps/revamer.html
These two sites contain maps for Colonial and Revolutionary America.

LVA Colonial Records Project—Index of Digital Facsimiles of Documents on Early Virginia
http://eagle.vsla.edu/colonial/
This site contains numerous early documents, but it is unguided and a little difficult to use.

Thomas Paine National Historical Association
http://www.dpipc.com/cdadesign/paine/home.html
This official site contains a large archive of Paine's works and information about the Association.

Maryland Loyalists and the American Revolution
http://www.erols.com/candidus/index.htm
This look at Maryland's loyalists promotes the author's book, but it has good information about an underappreciated phenomenon, including loyalist songs and poems.

Revolution Era Documents
http://www.geocities.com:80/Athens/Forum/9061/USA/revolution/rev.html
The Historical Text Archive has numerous useful documents for the period of the Revolution.

The American Revolution
http://revolution.h-net.msu.edu/
This site accompanies the PBS series Revolution with essays and resource links.

KEY TERMS

Rage Militaire　(p. 128)

Second Continental Congress　(p. 132)

Dunmore's Ethiopian Regiment　(p. 138)

Common Sense　(p. 138)

Tory　(p. 139)

Hessians　(p. 140)

Roderigue Hortalez & Cie.　(p. 146)

Hudson Highlands Strategy　(p. 147)

Southern Strategy　(p. 150)

REVIEW QUESTIONS

1. What is meant by the concept *rage militaire*? What factors account for the widespread desire of the American colonists to challenge Great Britain militarily by the spring and summer of 1775?

2. Why were so many leaders in the Second Continental Congress so hesitant about moving toward formal independence? Discuss the text of the Declaration of Independence. How does the Declaration both summarize colonial grievances and provide a bold vision for the future of an independent American republic?

3. Examine the composition of British and American military forces. How did the Continental army change as the war progressed beyond 1775 and 1776? Who were the real Continentals, and what did they accomplish as the backbone of Washington's "respectable" army?

4. Assess the role of European powers such as the French, Spanish, and Dutch and the role of Native Americans in the colonists' fight for independence. Of these groups, did any seem to benefit from their support of the rebel cause? If so, how? If not, why not?

5. Why did the Americans emerge victorious in the Revolutionary War? Explain how all three of the following contributed to that final triumph—American strengths, British weaknesses, and the global diplomatic and strategic situation. How did these factors help secure a favorable peace settlement in 1783?

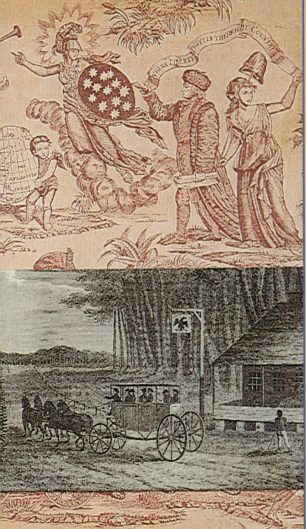

6

SECURING THE REPUBLIC AND ITS IDEALS, 1776–1789

"Others may never feel tyrannic sway"

Nancy Shippen was a product of Philadelphia's best lineage. Because she was born in 1763, the political turmoil leading to rebellion did not affect her early life. As a privileged daughter in an upper-class family, her duty was to blossom into a charming woman, admired for her beauty and social graces rather than her intellect. Nancy's education consisted of the refinement of skills that would please and entertain—dancing, cultivating her voice, playing musical instruments, painting on delicate china, and producing pieces of decorative needlework.

Had Nancy shown any interest in politics, an exclusively masculine preserve, she would have shocked everyone, including her father, William Shippen. Shippen was a noted local physician who espoused independence in 1776. That was his prerogative as paterfamilias; where he led, according to the customs of the time, his family followed. Indeed, he was a proud father in 1777 when, at his urging, Nancy displayed her patriotic virtue by sewing shirt ruffles for General Washington.

Three hundred miles away in Boston, another woman by the name of Phillis Wheatley was also reckoning with the American Revolution. Her life had been very different from Nancy's. Born on Africa's West Coast around 1753, she had been snatched from her parents by slave catchers. At the Boston slave market, Mrs. Susannah Wheatley, looking for a young female slave to train in domestic service, noticed her. In Phillis the Wheatley family got much more; their new slave yearned to express her thoughts and feelings through poetry.

Conventional wisdom dictated that slaves should not be educated. Exposure to reading and writing might make them resentful, perhaps even rebellious. Sensing Phillis's talents, the Wheatley family defied convention. She mastered English and Latin, even prepared translations of ancient writings. By 1770 some of her poems had been published, followed in 1773 by a collection entitled *Poems on Various Subjects, Religious and Moral*. In one verse addressed to Lord Dartmouth, Britain's secretary for American affairs, she queried:

> I young in life, by seeming cruel fate
> Was snatch'd from Afric's fancy'd seat:
> Such was my case. And can I then but pray
> Others may never feel tyrannic sway?

Experiencing the tyranny of slavery influenced Phillis's feelings about the presence of redcoats in Boston. Late in 1775 she sent a flattering poem to George Washington. He responded gratefully and called her words "striking proof of your great poetical talents."

Little as Phillis Wheatley and Nancy Shippen had in common, they lived during an era in which men thought of all women, regardless of their rank in society, as second-class human beings. Phillis carried the additional burden of being black in an openly racist society. Like other women in revolutionary America, they could only hope that the ideals of human liberty might someday apply to them.

Nancy Shippen had two male tyrants in her life. The first was her father William, who in 1781 forced her into marriage with Henry Beekman Livingston, a son of one of New York's most powerful and wealthy families. The man she truly loved had only "honorable expectations" of a respectable income. So her father insisted that Nancy wed Livingston. The rejected suitor wanted to know "for what reason in this *free* country a lady . . . must be married in a hurry and given up to a man whom she dislikes." None of the Shippens responded. In truth, the answer was that Nancy legally belonged to her father until she became the property of the second tyrant in her life—her husband Henry.

The marriage was a disaster, most likely because Henry was a philanderer. Nancy eventually took her baby daughter and moved back to her family. She wanted full custody of the child, who by law was the property of her husband. Henry made it clear that he would never give up his legal rights to his daughter, should Nancy embarrass him in public by seeking a bill of divorcement. Even if she had defied him, divorce bills were very hard to get because they involved proving adultery or desertion.

To keep actual custody of her daughter, Nancy accepted her entrapment. Several years later Henry relented and arranged for a divorce, but by that time Nancy's spirit was broken. This former belle of Philadelphia society lived on unhappily in hermit-like fashion until her death in 1841. Having been so favored at birth, her adult years were a personal tragedy, primarily because of her legal dependence on the will of men.

Although from different social and racial backgrounds, Nancy Shippen and Phillis Wheatley shared one characteristic: As women, they were second-class citizens in Revolutionary America.

Phillis Wheatley, by comparison, enjoyed some personal freedom before her untimely death in 1784. Mr. and Mrs. Wheatley died during the war period, and their will provided for Phillis's emancipation. She married John Peters, a free black man, and bore him three children. But John Peters was poor, and Phillis had scant time for poetry. Free blacks rarely got decent jobs, and Phillis struggled each day to help her family avoid destitution. She lived long enough to see slavery being challenged in the northern states; nevertheless, she died knowing that African Americans, even when free, invariably faced racial discrimination, which caused families like hers to exist on the margins of revolutionary society.

The experiences of Phillis Wheatley and Nancy Shippen raise basic questions about the character of the Revolution. Did the cause of liberty really change the lives of Americans? If it was truly a movement to end tyranny, secure human rights, and ensure equality of opportunity, then why did individuals like Wheatley and Shippen benefit so little? A major reason was that white, adult males of property and community standing put much greater emphasis on establishing an independent nation between 1776 and 1789 than on securing human rights. Still, the ideology of liberty could not be denied. Primarily, the revolutionary era saw the creation of a new na-

tion and the articulation of fundamental ideals regarding human freedom and dignity—ideals that have continued to shape the course of American historical development.

ESTABLISHING NEW REPUBLICAN GOVERNMENTS

Winning the war and working out a favorable peace settlement represented two of three crucial elements that made for a successful rebellion. The third centered on the formation of stable governments, certainly a challenging assignment because that process involved the careful definition of how governments should function to support life, liberty, and property (or happiness, as Jefferson framed the triad). A monarchical system, indeed any other capable of producing political tyranny, everyone agreed, was unacceptable. A second point of consensus was that governments should be republican in character. Sovereignty, or ultimate political authority, previously residing with King and Parliament, should be vested in the people. After all, political institutions presumably existed to serve them. As such, citizens should be governed by laws, not by power-hungry officials, and laws should be the product of the collective deliberations of representatives elected by the citizenry.

Defining the core ideals of **republicanism**—popular sovereignty, rule by law, and legislation by elected representatives—was not a source of disagreement. Revolutionary leaders, however, argued passionately about the organization and powers of new governments, both state and national, as well as the extent to which basic political rights should be put into practice. At the heart of the debate was the concept of **public virtue:** whether citizens were capable of subordinating their self-interest to the greater good of the whole community. Although some leaders answered in the affirmative, others did not. Their trust or distrust of the people directly affected how far they were willing to go in implementing republican ideals.

Leaders who believed that citizens could govern themselves and not abuse public privileges for private advantage were in the vanguard of political thinking in the western world. As such, they may be called radicals. They were willing to establish "the most democratic forms" of government, as Samuel Adams so aptly capsulized their thinking.

More cautious, elitist revolutionary leaders feared what the masses might do without the restraining hand of central political authority. As one of them wrote: "No one loves liberty more than I do, but of all tyranny I most dread that of the multitude." These leaders remained attached to traditional notions of hierarchy and deference in social and political relationships. They still thought that the "better sort" of citizens—men of education, wealth, and proven ability, whom they now defined as "natural aristocrats"—should be the stewards who guided the people. For such leaders the success of the Revolution depended on transferring power from the despoilers of liberty in Britain to "enlightened" gentlemen like themselves in America. As a precaution against a citizenry abusing liberties, they wanted a strong central government to replace King and Parliament, a government controlled by cautious revolutionaries in the interests of national political stability.

People Victorious: The New State Governments

In the wake of collapsing British authority during 1775 and 1776, **radical** and **cautious revolutionaries** squared off in constitutional conventions. Their heated debates produced ten new state constitutions

TABLE 6.1

Personal Wealth and Occupations of Approximately 900 Representatives Elected to Prewar and Postwar Assemblies (Expressed in Percentages)

	New Hampshire, New York, and New Jersey		Maryland, Virginia, and South Carolina	
	Prewar	Postwar	Prewar	Postwar
Property holdings				
Over £5000	36%	12%	52%	28%
£2000–£5000	47	26	36	42
Under £2000	17	62	12	30
Occupations				
Merchants and lawyers	43%	18%	23%	17%
Farmers*	23	55	12	26

Source: Derived from Jackson T. Main, "Government by the People: The American Revolution and the Democratization of the Legislatures," *William and mary Quarterly,* 3d ser., 23 (1966), p. 45.

*Plantation owners with slaves are not included with farmers.

by the end of 1777, plus a plan of national government written by the Continental Congress. Connecticut and Rhode Island kept their liberal colonial charters, which had provided for the popular election of executive officials, and simply deleted all references to British sovereignty; Massachusetts ratified a new state constitution in 1780.

The first constitutional settlement of the Revolution shows that leaders who had firm faith in the people prevailed over those who did not, based on three essential characteristics. First, there was general agreement that governments derive their authority from the consent of the governed. This principle of popular sovereignty has prevailed to this day. Second, although state constitution-makers varied in their commitment, free, white, adult male citizens (about 20 percent of the total population) gained expanded voting and office holding rights. The movement clearly was toward greater popular participation in governmental decision making. Third, the central government would not have the power to inhibit the state governments and the people in the management of the republic's political affairs.

Pennsylvanians produced the most democratic of the first state constitutions. Decision-making authority resided in an annually elected unicameral, or one-chamber, assembly. All white male citizens, with or without property, could now vote for legislators. By comparison, Maryland's constitution-framers were much less trusting. They maintained a three-tiered structure of government, reminiscent of that of King and two houses of Parliament. Potential voters had to meet modest propertyholding requirements (at least a £30 valuation in local currency). At a minimum, those elected to the lower house had to own a 50-acre freehold farm while those chosen for the upper house needed to demonstrate a net worth of £1000 in local currency. For the governor the requirement was £5000. In Pennsylvania ordinary citizens could control their own political destiny, but in Maryland wealthier citizens were to act as stewards for the people, hence continuing the tradition of deferential politics. The other state constitutions varied between these two extremes.

Only New Jersey defined the electorate without regard to gender. Its 1776 constitution gave the vote to "all free inhabitants" meeting minimal property qualifications. This permitted some women to vote. Since all property in marriage belonged to husbands, New Jersey had technically extended franchise rights only to widows and spinsters (very few divorced women were to be found anywhere in America). Nonetheless, great numbers of married women went to the polls regularly. Not until 1807 did New Jersey

TABLE 6.2

Family and Personal Wealth of Approximately 450 Executive Officials* in Late Colonial and Early Revolutionary Governments (Expressed in Percentages)

	Family Wealth†		Personal Wealth	
	1774	1777	1774	1777
Over £5000	40%	26%	65%	37%
£2000–£5000	34	33	29	52
Under £2000	26	41	6	11

Source: Derived from James Kirby Martin, *Men in Rebellion: Higher Governmental Leaders and the Coming of the American Revolution* (New Brunswick, NJ: Rutgers University Press, 1973).

*Officeholders included are governors, lieutenant governors, secretaries, treasurers, members of upper houses of assemblies (councilors before the Revolution), attorneys general, chief judges, and associate judges of the highest provincial and state courts.

†Refers to the wealth of parents. A higher percentage of late colonial leaders (74 percent) than early revolutionary leaders (59 percent) came from upper-class and upper-middle-class families.

disenfranchise females, on the alleged grounds that they were more easily manipulated by self-serving political candidates. For a brief time, then, at least one state regarded women—not just free, white, adult males—as a legitimate voice in government. Even though the experiment worked, this concept proved too radical for the customary male-dominated political culture of revolutionary America.

Because of the first state constitutions, male citizens with more ordinary family backgrounds, less personal wealth, and a greater diversity of occupations began to hold higher political offices after the Revolution started. As an excited citizen noted in late 1776, elected delegates to the new Virginia assembly were more "plain and of consequence, less disguised, but I believe to be full[y] as honest, less intriguing, more sincere." Not "so politely educated, nor so highly born," these delegates were "the people's men (and the people in general are right)." Radical leaders throughout the states heartily endorsed these sentiments.

New Jersey extended the right to vote to all free inhabitants until 1807 when a new state law specifically limited the franchise to free white male citizens.

The Articles of Confederation

In June 1776 the Continental Congress called for a plan of national government. John Dickinson, the well-known reluctant revolutionary who refused to vote for independence, took the lead. Concerned about losing the stabilizing influence of British authority, Dickinson proposed a muscular central government in the draft constitution his committee presented to Congress. The Confederacy was to be called "THE UNITED STATES OF AMERICA" and was to exist "for their common defense, the security of their liberties, and their mutual and general welfare." Not surprisingly, the states would have little authority. Each would retain only "as much of its present laws, rights and customs, as it may think fit . . . in all matters that shall not interfere with the Articles of this Confederation."

The exigencies of war kept interrupting congressional debate on Dickinson's draft. Furthermore, the radical revolutionaries who dominated Congress in late 1776 and 1777 did not like this plan. They feared power too far removed from the people. After all, they had rebelled against a distant government that they had perceived as tyrannical. When Congress fi-

nally completed revisions in November 1777, the delegates had turned Dickinson's draft inside out. The Articles now stated: "Each state retains its sovereignty, freedom and independence, and every power, jurisdiction and right, which is not . . . expressly delegated to the United States, in Congress assembled."

As a testament to the sovereignty of the 13 states, each had to ratify the Articles before this plan could go into full operation. At most the central government could coordinate activities among the states. It could manage the war, but it lacked taxation authority to support that effort. If Congress needed money (it obviously did), it could "requisition" the states. The states, however, would decide for themselves whether they would send funds to Congress.

Fundamentally penniless and powerless, the Confederation government represented the optimistic view that a virtuous citizenry did not require the constraining hand of central authority. This bold vision—fully in line with the rejection of King and Parliament as a remote, autocratic central government—pleased radicals like Samuel Adams, Thomas Paine, and Thomas Jefferson. Jefferson wrote glowingly of the "ease" with which the people "had deposited the monarchical and taken . . . republican government," as effortlessly as "throwing off an old and putting on a new suit of clothes." Cautious revolutionaries still harbored grave doubts, and events over the next few years convinced them that the first constitutional settlement had all but doomed the experiment in republicanism to failure.

CRISES OF THE CONFEDERATION

Internal difficulties soon beset the young American republic. Cautious revolutionaries viewed the years between 1776 and 1787 as a "critical period" because of problems encountered with the sovereign states and the people. These difficulties included ratifying the Articles of Confederation, establishing a national domain west of the Appalachian Mountains, finding some means to pay for the war, achieving stable diplomatic relations with foreign powers, and guarding against domestic upheavals.

Over time, those who advocated a strong central government formed an informal political alliance, and they have since come to be known as the **nationalists**. With each passing year the nationalists became more and more frustrated by the Confederation. In 1787 they finally overwhelmed their opposition by pressing for and getting a new plan of national government.

Struggle to Ratify the Articles

Given the wartime need for national unity in the face of a common enemy, Congress asked each state to approve the Articles of Confederation quickly. Overcoming much indifference, 12 states had finally ratified by January 1779—but Maryland still held out.

The propertied gentlemen who controlled Maryland's revolutionary government objected to one specific provision in the Articles. Although Dickinson's draft had designated all lands west of the Appalachians as a *national domain*, belonging to all the people for future settlement, the final version left these lands in the hands of states having sea-to-sea clauses in their colonial charters—a logical extension of the principle of state sovereignty. Maryland, having a fixed western boundary, had no such western claim. Nor did Rhode Island, New Jersey, Pennsylvania, or Delaware.

Maryland's leaders refused to be cut off from western development. In public they talked in terms of high principle. Citizens from "landless" states should have as much right to resettle in the West as inhabitants of "landed" states. Equal access was not the only issue, however. Many Maryland leaders had invested in pre-Revolution land companies trying to gain title to large parcels of western territory. They had done so by appealing to the Crown and by making purchases from individual Native Americans, who without tribal approval often "sold" rights in return for alcohol and other "gifts." Wanting to avoid costly frontier warfare, the Crown had promulgated the Proclamation of 1763 (see p. 103) and thereafter refused to recognize any such titles. After independence there was new hope for these land speculators, but only if the Continental Congress rather than some of the states controlled the West.

The Maryland Assembly adamantly refused ratification unless the landed states agreed to turn over their charter titles to Congress. Virginia, which had the largest claim, including the vast region north of the Ohio River that came to be known as the "Old Northwest," faced the most pressure. Forsaking local land speculators for the national interest, the Virginia Assembly broke the deadlock in January 1781 by agreeing to cede its claims to Congress.

Had self-interest not been involved, ratification would have followed quickly; however, covetous Maryland leaders still held out. They pronounced Virginia's grant unacceptable because of a condition not permitting Congress to award lands on the basis of Indian deeds. Fortunately for the republic, the war intervened. In early 1781, with the British raiding in the Chesapeake Bay region, Marylanders became quite anxious about their defense. Congressional leaders urged ratification in exchange for promises of Continental military support. All but cornered, the Maryland Assembly reluctantly gave in and approved the Articles of Confederation.

March 1, 1781, the day formal ratification ceremonies finally took place, elicited only muted celebrations. Some cheered "the union," at long last "indissolubly cemented," as an optimist wrote. Certainly, too, the prospect of a national domain for a rapidly expanding population pleased many citizens. The nationalists, on the other hand, believed that Maryland's behavior showed how self-interest could be masked as public virtue. With so many problems needing solutions, they wondered how long the republic could endure when any sovereign state had the capacity to thwart the will of the other 12.

Turmoil over Financing the War

From the outset financial problems plagued the new central government. Under the Articles, Congress had no power of taxation; it repeatedly asked the states to pay a fair proportion of war costs. The states, also hard pressed for funds, rarely sent in more than 50 percent of their requisitions. Meanwhile, soldiers like Joseph Plumb Martin endured shortages of food, clothing, camp equipment, and pay. As a result, with each passing month the army grew increasingly angry about its role as a creditor to the republic.

The lack of tax revenues forced Congress to resort to various expedient measures to meet war costs. Between 1775 and 1780 it issued some $220 million in paper money, or Continental dollars. Lacking any financial backing, these "Continentals" became so worthless by 1779 that irate army officers complained how "four months' pay of a private [soldier] will not procure his wretched wife and children a single bushel of wheat." In addition, Congress, largely to get military supplies, issued interest-bearing certificates of indebtedness. Because Congress lacked the means to pay interest, these certificates, which also circulated as money, rapidly lost value. In 1780 Congress attempted to refinance Continental dollars at a 40 to 1 ratio, but the plan failed. Had it not been for grants and loans from allies like France and the Netherlands, the war effort might well have floundered.

Deeply disturbed by these conditions, many nationalists in the Continental Congress acted forcefully to institute financial reform. Their leader was the wealthy Philadelphia merchant, Robert Morris (1734–1806), sometimes called the "financier of the Revolution," who became Congress's Superintendent of Finance in 1781. His assistant superintendent, Gouverneur Morris (no relation), a wealthy New Yorker

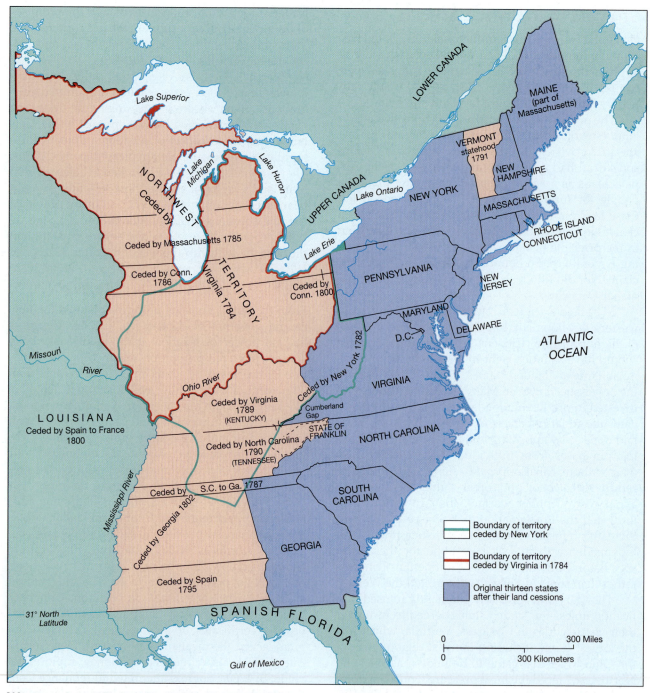

Western Land Claims Ceded by the States

The battle over conflicting state claims to western lands was a major issue facing the Continental Congress.

then practicing law in Philadelphia, was also critical to shaping the events that lay ahead, as were Alexander Hamilton of New York and James Madison of Virginia. Hamilton summarized their feelings this way: "The Confederation . . . gives the power of the purse too entirely to the state legislatures. . . . That power, which holds the purse strings absolutely, must rule."

At the urging of the nationalists, congressional delegates approved the Impost Plan of 1781. It called for import duties of 5 percent on all foreign trade goods entering the United States, the revenues to belong to Congress. These funds could be used to pay the army, to back a stable national currency, and, ultimately, to meet foreign loan obligations. Because

Gouverneur Morris (left) and Robert Morris (right) were key figures in the nationalist drive for financial reform.

the Plan would allow Congress some taxation authority, the delegates recommended it in the form of an amendment to the Articles. Amendments required the approval of all 13 states.

Reluctant as they were to share taxation powers with the central government, many state leaders agreed with Robert Morris, who had warned: "The political existence of America depends on the accomplishment of this [Impost] plan." Twelve states had ratified by the autumn of 1782. Only Rhode Island hesitated. With so little land to tax, the easiest way to fund its own war debt was to collect state import duties. If a choice had to be made, state interests came first. The Assembly voted against ratification. Once again local interests had prevailed; a single state had blocked the will of the other 12.

In this crucial matter the nationalists had allies. Most prominent were disgruntled officers in the Continental army. Rarely had the soldiers been paid, and in 1780 the officers had exacted from Congress a promise of half-pay postwar pensions as their price for staying in the service. Without a fixed source of revenue, Congress lacked the ability to meet these obligations.

After a group of high-ranking officers learned about Rhode Island's decision, they sent a menacing petition to Congress in December 1782. It stated; "We have borne all that men can bear—our property is expended—our private resources are at an end." With no likelihood of pensions being funded, they insisted upon five years of full pay when mustering out of the service. Even with British troops still on American soil, the angry officers warned Congress: "Any further experiments on their patience may have fatal effects."

Threatened Military Coup: The Newburgh Conspiracy

For years Continental officers and soldiers alike had complained about the ungenerous treatment they received from revolutionary leaders and civilians. Convinced that the general populace had lived well at home while the army endured privation, sickness, and death in the field, they spoke out passionately about the absence of citizen virtue. As one officer bluntly wrote, "I hate my countrymen."

After the British force at Yorktown surrendered, Washington moved 11,000 troops north to the vicinity of Newburgh, New York. From this campsite on the Hudson River, the Continental army waited for peace terms and kept its eye on British forces in New York City. As peace negotiations dragged on during 1782, officers and soldiers worried about being demobilized without back pay and promised pensions. When Rhode Island refused to ratify the Impost Plan, their worst fears seemed to be realized.

Curiously, when the congressional nationalists received the officers' hotly worded petition, they were more pleased than alarmed. They soon devised a scheme to use these threats to extort taxation authority from the states. If need be, they would encourage the army to go back into the field and threaten the civilian populace with a military uprising. The danger, of course, was that the army might get out of control, seize the reins of government, and push the Revolution toward some form of military dictatorship.

When the states refused to be bullied, the nationalists turned to George Washington in February 1783. As his former military aide, Alexander Hamilton (1757?–1804), wrote to him, the critical issue was "the establishment of general funds. . . . In this the influence of the army, properly directed, may cooperate." Washington refused to help; perhaps better than anyone in revolutionary America, he understood that military power had to remain subordinate to civilian authority, or the republic would never be free.

At this juncture, Robert Morris and other congressional nationalists began "conspiring" with General Horatio Gates, second in command at Newburgh, who had often dreamed of replacing Washington at the head of the Continental army. Gates made his move in early March. He authorized two Newburgh Addresses, both prepared by members of his staff. The addresses warned the officers to "suspect the man [Washington] who would advise to more moderation and forbearance." If peace comes, let nothing separate you "from your arms but death," or at least not until the army had realized financial justice. The first address instructed the officers to attend a meeting to vent grievances—and take action. Dismayed, Washington called this proposal "disorderly"; he nevertheless approved a meeting for March 15. He would not attend, he stated, but would let Gates chair the gathering.

Despite his promise, Washington appeared at this showdown meeting. He pleaded with the officers to temper their rage and not go back into the field. That would destroy everything the army had accomplished during eight long years of war. The officers appeared unmoved. Then preparing to read a letter, Washington reached into his pocket, pulled out spectacles, and put them on. The officers, never having seen their commander wear eyeglasses before, started to murmur. Sensing a mood shift, Washington calmly stated, "Gentlemen, you must pardon me. I have grown gray in your service and now find myself growing blind." These heartfelt words caught the angry officers off guard. They recalled that they, as exemplars of truly virtuous citizenship, likewise had offered their lives for a cause larger than any of them. Many openly wept, even as the threat of a possible mutiny, or worse, a military coup directed against the states and the people, suddenly came to an end.

Washington promised to do everything in his power to secure "complete and ample justice" for the army. He did send a circular letter to the states imploring them to give more power to Congress. He warned them that "the Union could not be of a long duration" with a central government lacking in the capacity "to regulate and govern the general concerns of the Confederated republic." The states ignored Washington's plea for a strengthened national government.

Even though British troops were still in New York City, Washington also started "furloughing" soldiers, so that further troublesome incidents would not occur. After leaving the army one angry group of Pennsylvania Continentals marched on Philadelphia in June 1783. They surrounded Independence Hall (the Pennsylvania State House), where Congress held its sessions. In threatening fashion these veterans refused to leave until they received back pay. The frightened delegates asked the Pennsylvania government to have local militia troops protect them, but state officials turned down their request. Amid the taunts and jeers of the angry soldiers, the delegates finally abandoned Independence Hall. They never came back.

Thoroughly humiliated by armed soldiers and a state government that would not defend them, the delegates first moved to Princeton, New Jersey, then to Annapolis, Maryland, and finally to New York City. One newspaper, in mocking the central government, spoke of "the itinerant genius of Congress," a body that would "float along from one end of the continent to the other" as would a hot-air balloon.

Many citizens did not seem to care much one way or the other, since Congress was so lacking in authority. Nationalist leaders, on the other hand, kept trying to redress the balance of power between the impotent central government and the sovereign states. They drafted the Impost Plan of 1783, but this proposal, too, failed to secure unanimous state ratification. The plan was still languishing in late 1786, but by that time the nationalists were pursuing other avenues of change.

Drifting Toward Disunion

Despite the Paris peace settlement and the final removal of British troops, most citizens were engaged in another battle beginning in late 1783—this one against a hard-hitting economic depression. It had many sources. Planters in the South had lost about 60,000 slaves, many of whom the British had carried off. In addition, crop yields for 1784 and 1785 were small, largely because of bad weather. Farmers in New England reeled from the effects of new British trade regulations—in essence turning the Navigation system against the independent Americans. The Orders in Council of 1783 prohibited the sale of many American agricultural products in the British West Indies, formerly a key market for New England goods, and required many commodities to be conveyed to and from the islands in British vessels. The orders represented a serious blow to New England's agricultural, shipping, and shipbuilding trades.

Making matters even worse, merchants in all the states rushed to reestablish old trading connections with their British counterparts. These overly optimistic traders quickly became oversupplied with British goods on easy credit terms. They soon discovered that they could not sell these commodities to citizens feeling the effects of the postwar depression. Many American merchants thus faced total economic ruin by 1785.

The central government could do little. Congress did send John Adams to Britain in 1785 as the first minister from the United States. Adams, however, made no headway in getting British officials to back off from the Orders in Council. He dejectedly reported to Congress: British leaders "rely upon our disunion" to avoid negotiations.

To add to these economic woes, significant postwar trading ties did not develop with France. In fact, American exports to France far exceeded the value of imports (by roughly $2 million a year during the 1780s). The same held true with the Dutch. Even though some venturesome merchants sent a trading vessel—the *Empress of China*—to the Far East in 1784, all the new activity was insignificant in comparison to the renewed American dependency on British manufactured goods. The former colonists stayed glued to the old imperial trading network; decades would pass before they would gain full economic independence.

Named in 1784 as secretary for foreign affairs, John Jay was unsuccessful in his efforts to negotiate trade accords with Spain.

Copyright © Collection of the New-York Historical Society.

Some merchants, primarily from the Middle Atlantic states, were anxious to break free of Britain's economic hold. An opportunity presented itself in 1784 after Congress named John Jay (1745–1829), one of the Paris peace commissioners, to be its secretary for foreign affairs. Jay soon started negotiations with Don Diego de Gardoqui, Spain's first minister to the United States. Gardoqui talked about his government's concern that Americans, now streaming into the trans-Appalachian west, would in time covet Spanish territory beyond the Mississippi River. To stem the tide, Gardoqui informed Congress that Spain would not allow the Mississippi to serve as an outlet for western agricultural goods. To ease possible bad feelings, Gardoqui offered an advantageous commercial treaty.

Jay and a number of powerful merchants from the Middle Atlantic states saw merit in the Spanish proposal. They viewed western development—settlements were sprouting in Kentucky and Tennessee—as a potential threat to eastern economic dominance. Meanwhile, Gardoqui had Spanish agents circulating through the west. They encouraged settlers to become Spanish subjects in return for trade access to the Mississippi River—a means to protect Spanish holdings beyond the Mississippi. Basically these agents did little more than stir up resentment, both toward Spain and eastern leaders like Jay, who appeared to be selling out western interests for a commercial treaty of undetermined value.

When Jay reported on his discussions to Congress in August 1786, tempers flared. The southern states voted as a bloc against any such treaty, which represented a mortal blow to the Jay-Gardoqui negotiations. Southerners and westerners remained suspicious that Jay and his eastern merchant allies would not hesitate to abandon them altogether for petty commercial

gains. Some leaders in Congress, as one delegate explained, began to speak "lightly of a separation and dissolution of the Confederation." Such talk helped galvanize the nationalists for dramatic action, as did a rebellion that now convulsed Massachusetts.

Daniel Shays's Rebellion

Postwar economic conditions were so bad in several states that citizens began demanding tax relief from their governments. In western Massachusetts desperate farmers complained about huge property tax increases by the state government to pay off the state's war debt. Taxes on land rose by more than 60 percent in the period from 1783 to 1786, exactly when a depressed postwar economy meant that farmers were getting little income from the sale of excess agricultural goods.

Local courts, in the absence of tax payments, started to seize the property of persons like Daniel Shays (1747?–1825), a revolutionary war veteran. Some lost their freehold farms, and in certain cases the courts remanded delinquent taxpayers to debtors' prison. Viewing their plight in terms of tyranny, the farmers of western Massachusetts believed they had the right to break the chains of political oppression, just as they had done in resisting British rule a few years before. This time, however, the perceived enemy was their own state government.

The **Shaysites,** as they came to be known, tried to resist in orderly fashion. They first met in impromptu conventions and sent petitions to the state assembly. Getting no relief, they turned to more confrontational means of resistance. In late August 1786 an estimated 1000 farmers poured into Northampton and shut down the county court. This crowd action represented the first of many such closures. By popular mandate citizens would no longer permit judges to seize property or condemn people to debtors' prison as the penalty for not paying taxes.

State leaders in Boston started to panic, fearing the "rebels" would soon descend upon them. Desperately, they conducted an emotional public appeal for funds. Frightened Bostonians opened their purses. They subscribed £5000 to pay for an eastern Massachusetts army headed by former Continental general Benjamin Lincoln. Lincoln's assignment was to march his army into western parts of the state and subdue the Shaysites.

The insurrection soon fizzled. Lacking weapons and suffering in bitterly cold weather, Daniel Shays and his followers lacked the essentials to sustain themselves. To get weapons, they attacked the federal arsenal at Springfield on January 25, 1787. A few well-placed cannon shots, which resulted in 24

Still, western lands remained a source of hope for economically downtrodden soldiers and civilians alike. In 1775 explorer Daniel Boone laid out the "Wilderness Road" to Kentucky. Others, like rugged Simon Kenton, scouted down the Ohio River from Pittsburgh. Where these frontiersmen went, thousands of land-hungry easterners soon followed. By 1790 Kentucky contained a population of 74,000, and Tennessee held 36,000. These settlers paid dearly for their invasion of Native-American lands. The Shawnees, Cherokees, and Chickasaws fought back in innumerable bloody clashes. The white death toll reached 1500. Besides losing ancient tribal lands, Native Americans also suffered considerable casualties.

White settlements in Kentucky and Tennessee generated pressure to open territory north of the Ohio River. After ceding the Old Northwest to the United States in 1783, however, the British did not abandon their military posts there. To maintain the lucrative fur trade, they bolstered the Miamis, Shawnees, Delawares, and remnant groups of the Iroquois nation with a steady supply of firearms. Americans foolish

First Territorial Survey

Thomas Hutchins, a native of New Jersey, directed the first survey of territorial lands.

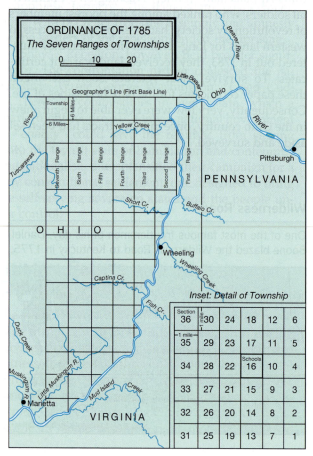

enough to venture north of the Ohio River rarely survived, and the region remained closed to large numbers of westward-moving settlers well into the 1790s.

Despite these circumstances, Congress was eager to open the Ohio country. With this goal in mind, the delegates approved three land ordinances. The 1784 Ordinance provided for territorial government and guaranteed settlers they would not remain in permanent colonial status. When enough people (later specified at 60,000) had moved in, a constitution could be written, state boundaries set, and admission to the union as a full partner would follow. The 1785 Ordinance called for orderly surveying of the region. Townships of 6 miles square were to be laid out in gridlike fashion—each township to contain 36 sections of 640 acres each with proceeds from the sale of the sixteenth section to be used to finance public education. The Northwest Ordinance of 1787 refined governmental arrangements, gave a bill of rights to prospective settlers, and proclaimed slavery forever banned north of the Ohio River—a prohibition that Thomas Jefferson had sought but failed to get included in the 1784 Ordinance. In providing for orderly development and eventual statehood, the land ordinances may well have been the most significant legislation of the Confederation-period Congress.

The ordinances, however, were not fully enlightened. Congress, in its continuing search for revenue, viewed the Old Northwest as a source of long-term income. The smallest parcel individual settlers could buy was 640 acres, priced at $1.00 per acre, and there were to be no purchases on credit. Families of modest means, let alone poorer ones, could not meet such terms. As a result, Congress dealt mainly with well-to-do land speculators—and even extended them deeds to millions of acres on credit no less! These decisions cut off the poorest citizens from the West, unless they were willing to squat on uninhabited land until driven off, which thousands did to survive economically.

Women Appeal for Fundamental Liberties

Like the poor, women experienced little success in improving their lot during the revolutionary era. Among their advocates was Abigail Adams. In the spring of 1776 she wrote to her husband John, then in Philadelphia arguing for independence, and admonished him to "remember the ladies, and be more generous and favorable to them than your ancestors."

As if joking with his wife, John Adams replied by asking whether American women were now working in league with the British ministry. Should political independence come, he wrote, "we know better than to repeal our masculine system," claim-

THE PEOPLE SPEAK

Abigail Adams Exhorts Her Husband to "Remember the Ladies" (1776)

In the spring of 1776 John Adams, who had become a staunch advocate of independence, was attending the Second Continental Congress in Philadelphia. His wife Abigail (1744–1818) was back in Massachusetts tending to the family homestead and their children. Abigail was a brilliant, insatiably curious person. She corresponded regularly with her husband, repeatedly asking him for news about the momentous events of the day. Moreover, she offered her own opinions, such as in late March 1776 when she wrote to John about the inferior status of women in American society. Should independence come about, Abigail wanted to see a real revolution as well that would include a vast expansion of social, political, and legal rights for women. In his reply, John was somewhat dismissive of Abigail's words. Her statement, however, did not go away but served as an important rallying cry for women as they struggled to obtain a full measure of equal rights for themselves over the next two centuries of United States history.

ABIGAIL TO JOHN ADAMS
Braintree March 31 1776

. . . I long to hear that you have declared an independancy—and by the way in the new Code of Laws which I suppose it will be necessary for you to make I desire you would Remember the Ladies, and be more generous and favourable to them than your ancestors. Do not put such unlimited power into the hands of the Husbands. Remember all Men would be tyrants if they could. If perticuliar care and attention is not paid to the Laidies we are determined to foment a Rebelion, and will not hold ourselves bound by any Laws in which we have no voice, or Representation.

That your Sex are Naturally Tyrannical is a Truth so thoroughly established as to admit of no dispute, but such of you as wish to be happy willingly give up the harsh title of Master for the more tender and endearing one of Friend. Why then, not put it out of the power of the vicious and the Lawless to use us with cruelty and indignity with impunity. Men of Sense in all Ages abhor those customs which treat us only as the vassals of your Sex. Regard us then as Beings placed by providence under your protection and in immitation of the Supreem Being make use of that power only for our happiness.

JOHN TO ABIGAIL ADAMS
Ap. 14. 1776

. . . As to your extraordinary Code of Laws, I cannot but laugh. We have been told that our Struggle has loosened the bands of Government every where. That Children and Apprentices were disobedient—that schools and Colledges were grown turbulent—that Indains slighted their Guardians and Negroes grew insolent to their Masters. But your Letter was the first Intimation that another Tribe more numerous and powerfull than all the rest were grown discontented.—This is rather too coarse a Compliment but you are so saucy, I wont blot it out.

Depend upon it, We know better than to repeal our Masculine systems. Altho they are in full Force, you know they are little more than Theory. We dare not exert our Power in its full Latitude. We are obliged to go fair, and softly, and in Practice you know We are the subjects. We have only the Name of Masters, and rather than give up this, which would compleatly subject Us to the Despotism of the Peticoat, I hope General Washington, and all our brave Heroes would fight. I am sure every good Politician would plot, as long as he would against Despotism, Empire, Monarchy, Aristocracy, Oligarchy, or Ochlocracy.—A fine Story indeed. I begin to think the Ministry as deep as they are wicked. After stirring up Tories, Landjobbers, Trimmers, Bigots, Canadians, Indians, Negroes, Hanoverians, Hessians, Russians, Irish Roman Catholicks, Scotch Renegadoes, at last they have stimulated the   to demand new Priviledges and threaten to rebell.

Source: L. H. Butterfield, et al., eds. *The Adams Papers*, Series II: *Adams Family Correspondence*, Vol 1: December 1761–May 1776 (New York, 1965), 369–371, 381–383.

ing that men "have only the name of masters." John Adams knew very well that by law and social practice, women were legally dependent on men, as the case of Nancy Shippen so vividly illustrates.

Women gained no significant political rights during the revolutionary period, except briefly in New Jersey. Yet they contributed enthusiastically to the cause. Some, like "The Association" headed by Esther DeBerdt Reed of Philadelphia, called themselves "daughters of liberty" and met regularly to make clothing for the Continental army. Others, such as Mary Ludwig Hays McCauly of Carlisle, Pennsyl-

THE
American Mosaic

Birth Control in the Early Republic

ONE of the most hotly debated questions in late eighteenth-century America and Europe was whether human beings were capable of improvement. Famous philosophers of the Enlightenment argued that people were naturally good and that all of society's problems could be solved by the application of reason. English philosopher William Godwin described the future in particularly glowing terms. He wrote that in the future "there would no longer be a handful of rich and a multitude of poor. . . . There will be no war, no crime, no administration of justice, as it is called, and no government. Beside this there will be no disease, anguish, melancholy, or resentment."

On the other side of the debate on human perfectibility was a young Anglican clergyman, Thomas Robert Malthus. Parson Malthus argued that human perfection was unattainable because human population growth would inevitably exceed the growth of the world's food supply. He asserted—on the basis of figures collected by Benjamin Franklin—that population tends to increase geometrically (1, 2, 4, 8) while subsistence only grows arithmetically (1, 2, 3, 4). Ultimately population would be held in check by famine, war, and disease.

Malthus's gloomy vision of the future failed to come true because large numbers of people began to limit the number of children through the use of birth control. Nowhere was the limitation of births more striking than in the United States. In 1800 the American birthrate was higher than the birthrate in any European nation. The typical American woman bore an average of 7 children. She had her first child around the age of 23 and proceeded to bear children at two-year intervals until her early forties. Had the American birthrate remained at this level, the nation's population would have reached 2 billion by 1990.

Late in the eighteenth century, however, Americans began to have fewer children. Between 1800 and 1900 the birthrate fell 40 percent and even more sharply among the middle and upper classes. Where the typical American mother bore 7 children in 1800, the average number of children had fallen to 3.5 in 1900. And instead of giving birth to her last child at the age of 40 or later, by 1900 the typical American woman bore her last child at the age of 33. The decline of the birthrate is such an important historical breakthrough that it has its own name: *the demographic transition.*

The sharp decline in birthrates is a phenomenon easier to describe than to explain. The drop in fertility was not the result of sudden improvements in contraceptive devices. The basic birth control techniques used before the Civil War—coitus interruptus (withdrawal), douching, and condoms—were known in ancient times. Ancient Egyptian papyri and the Old Testament describe cervical caps and spermicides, while ancient Greek physicians were aware of the contraceptive effects of douching. Contraception was not unknown in the past, it was simply used haphazardly and ineffectively. Nor was the imposition of limits on birthrates a result of urbanization. Although fertility fell earliest and most rapidly in the urban Northeast, the decline in fertility occurred in all parts of the country, in rural as well as urban areas and in the South and West as well as the Northeast.

What accounted for the declining birthrate? In part, the reduction in fertility reflected the growing realization among parents that in an increasingly commercial and industrial society children were no longer economic assets who could be productively employed in household industries or bound out as apprentices or servants. Instead, children required significant investment in the form of education to prepare them for respectable careers and marriages. The emergence of a self-conscious middle class concerned about social mobility and maintaining an acceptable standard of living also encouraged new limits on family size.

The shrinking size of families also reflected a growing desire among women to assert control over their lives. Much of the impetus behind birth control came from women who were weary of an unending cycle of pregnancy, birth, nursing, and new pregnancy. A letter written by a sister of Harriet Beecher Stowe suggests the desperation felt by many women who were single-handedly responsible for bearing and rearing a family's children. "Harriet," her sister observed, "has one baby put out for the winter, the other at home, and number three will be here the middle of January. Poor thing, she bears up wonderfully well. . . . She says she shall not have any more children, she knows for certain for one while."

How did Americans limit births? Periodic abstinence—or what is now known as the rhythm method—was the most widely advocated method of birth control. Unfortunately, knowledge about women's ovulation cycle, menstruation, and conception was largely inaccurate and most advice writers suggested that the "safe period" was the ten days halfway between menstrual periods—which is in fact the time when a woman is most likely to conceive.

Other principal methods of contraception included coitus interruptus—withdrawal prior to ejaculation—and douches of the vagina after intercourse. Less common was the insertion of a sponge soaked in a spermicidal fluid into the vagina. None of these methods, however, were especially effective in preventing conception since each of these techniques can still allow small amounts of semen to reach the fallopian tubes. Other popular forms of contraception were heavily influenced by superstition. These included ingestion of teas concocted out of fruitless plants; having a woman engage in violent movements immediately after intercourse; and having intercourse on an inclined plane in order to prevent the sperm from reaching the egg or to prevent the egg from leaving the ovary.

Charles Goodyear's discovery in 1839 of the vulcanization of rubber permitted the mass production of an inexpensive and effective birth control device, the condom. But during the nineteenth century condoms were mainly used for protection against venereal disease, not for birth control.

Given the ineffectiveness of other methods of contraception, it is not surprising to learn that abortion was a major method of population control. By 1860, according to one estimate, 20 percent of pregnancies were terminated by abortion, compared to 30 percent today. Some of the popular practices for inducing abortion included taking hot baths, jumping off tables, performing heavy exercises, having someone jump on a pregnant woman's belly, drinking nauseating concoctions, and poking sharp instruments into the uterus.

Why were abortions so widespread during the nineteenth century? In part, it reflected the general ignorance of the reproductive process. It was not until 1827 that the existence of the human egg was established. Before that time it was believed by many scientists that the human sperm constituted a miniature person that grew into a baby in the mother's womb. Thus there was no modern notion of a moment of conception when egg and sperm unite.

Furthermore, for most of the nineteenth century, it was difficult to determine whether a woman was pregnant or simply suffering menstrual irregularity. A woman only knew she was pregnant for sure when she could feel the child stir within her. This occurs around the fourth or fifth month of pregnancy and in most jurisdictions abortions prior to this time were not considered

crimes. It was not until the late nineteenth century that most jurisdictions in the United States declared abortions to be criminal offenses.

The decline in the birthrate carried far-reaching consequences for family life. First of all, motherhood and the strain of pregnancy ended earlier for women. They had an increasing number of years when young children were no longer their primary responsibility. It also meant that parents were free to invest more time, energy, and financial resources in each individual child.

still involved in the international slave trade. Maryland, Delaware, and Virginia passed laws making it easier for planters to manumit (free) individual slaves. George Washington was one among a few wealthy planters who took advantage of Virginia's **manumission** law. He referred to slavery as a "misfortune" that sullied revolutionary ideals, and in his will he made provision for the liberation of his slaves.

Washington was unusual. Far more typical was Thomas Jefferson. In his *Notes on the State of Virginia* (1785), he called slavery "a perpetual exercise" in "the most unremitting despotism." Fearing the worst should human bondage continue, he wrote: "I tremble for my country when I reflect that God is just." Such thinking led him to propose in Congress during 1784 that slavery never be allowed to spread north of the Ohio River. Jefferson, however, could not bring himself to free his own slaves. His chattels formed the economic base of his way of life. Their labor gave him the time that he needed for politics and, ironically, the time to work so persuasively on behalf of human liberty.

Support for his lifestyle was not the only reason Jefferson held back. He was representative of his times in believing blacks to be inherently inferior to whites. In his *Notes*, he made a number of comparisons of ability that were disparaging toward blacks, such as in the category of reasoning power. Trying to prove his point, Jefferson scoffed at the poems of Phillis Wheatley, which he described as "below the dignity of criticism." Jefferson thought, too, that the emancipation of African Americans would result in racial war and "the extermination of the one or the other race." Thus a man who labored so diligently for human rights in his own lifetime remained in bondage to the racist concepts of his era.

Negative racial attitudes were the norm in revolutionary America, as the growing number of freed African Americans learned again and again. Because of the general abolition and individual manumission movements, the free black population approached 60,000 by 1790 and 108,000 by 1800 (11 percent of the total African-American population). Like the some 5000 black Continental army veterans, Phillis Wheatley, and George Washington's former slaves, these individuals repeatedly had to struggle to survive in a hostile society.

Not only did they survive, but they led noteworthy lives. Benjamin Banneker (1731–1806) was such a person. He grew up in a free black family in Maryland, attended an interracial Quaker school, and became a talented mathematician, astronomer, and surveyor. During the 1790s he published a series of almanacs and also served on the commission that de-

Absalom Jones (top) established St. Thomas's African Episcopal Church of Philadelphia, while Richard Allen founded the African Methodist Episcopal Church in the United States (bottom).

signed the new federal city of Washington, D.C. Throughout his life Banneker successfully disproved, as he wrote to Jefferson in 1791, the "train of absurd and false ideas and opinions" regarding the innate intelligence of African Americans.

Unlike Banneker, who spent his whole life in Maryland, many free blacks moved to the large northern port cities, where slavery was a fading threat. They built their own neighborhoods, and skilled workers opened shops to serve one another. Other urban free blacks, including both males and females, performed domestic service at low wages for well-to-do white families, but they did so as free persons with the opportunity to fashion independent lives for themselves.

Free African Americans also established their own schools and churches. With the assistance of the New York Society for the Promotion of Manumission, blacks helped found the African Free School in New York City during 1787. At first the school faced opposition from whites, who worried about educating blacks. This school survived, however, and would train hundreds of students in the fundamentals of reading and mathematics. In Delaware, Richard Allen, who purchased his own freedom in 1777, became a powerful preacher within the Methodist ranks. After enduring incidents of intimidation from unfriendly whites, Allen moved to Philadelphia in 1786 where he became the founder of the African Methodist Episcopal Church. African Baptist and African Presbyterian denominations also developed in the northern port cities, and these churches provided opportunities for formal education, since African-American children were rarely welcome in white schools.

Whether in the North or the South, the reality most often was overt discrimination. As a group, free African Americans responded by providing for one another and believing in a better day when revolutionary ideals regarding human freedom and liberty would have full meaning in their lives. In this sense they still had much in common with their brethren in slavery.

SECOND NEW BEGINNING, NEW NATIONAL GOVERNMENT

In 1787 many revolutionary leaders were more concerned about internal political stability than securing human rights. With all the talk of breaking up the Confederation, with Shays's Rebellion not yet completely quelled, and with the states arguing endlessly about almost everything, political leaders believed that matters of government should take primacy, or the republican experiment might be forever lost. Certainly the nationalists felt this way, and they were pushing hard for a revision of the first constitutional settlement.

In September 1786 representatives from five states met briefly in Annapolis, Maryland, to discuss pressing interstate commercial problems. Those present included such strong nationalists as Alexander Hamilton, John Dickinson, and James Madison. Since so few states were represented, the delegates abandoned their agenda in favor of an urgent plea asking all the states to send delegates to a special constitutional convention for remedying "such defects as exist" in the Articles of Confederation.

This time the states responded, largely because of the specter of civil turmoil associated with Shays's Rebellion. Twelve states—Rhode Island refused to participate—named 74 delegates, 55 of whom would attend the Constitutional Convention in Philadelphia. As the Continental Congress instructed the delegates in February 1787, their purpose was to revise the Articles of Confederation, making them "adequate to the exigencies . . . of the union." Some nationalists, however, had other ideas. They wanted a whole new plan of national government. Their ideas would dominate the proceedings from beginning to end, and their determination produced the Constitution of 1787.

The Framers of the Constitution

The men who gathered in Philadelphia were successful lawyers, planters, and merchants of education, wealth, and wide-ranging accomplishments, not ordinary citizens. They represented particular states, but most of them thought in national terms, based on experiences like serving in the Continental Congress and the Continental army. They feared for the future

James Madison, a strong nationalist, has been called the "father of the Constitution" for his plan of national government. He became the nation's fourth president.

of the republic, unless the weak central government was strengthened as a means of containing the selfishness of particular states. They seized this opportunity for change and made the most of it.

Among those present during the lengthy proceedings, which stretched from May 25 to September 17, was the revered George Washington, who served as the convention's president. Other notable leaders included James Madison, Alexander Hamilton, Gouverneur and Robert Morris, and John Dickinson. Benjamin Franklin, at 81, was the oldest delegate. He offered his finely tuned diplomatic tact in working out compromises that kept the proceedings moving forward.

Although the delegates disagreed vehemently over particular issues, they never let their differences deflect them from their main purpose—to find the constitutional means for an enduring republic. The Constitution was not perfect, as Benjamin Franklin stated on the last day of the convention, but it did bring stability and energy to national government—and it has endured.

A Document Constructed by Compromises

Had the nationalists been doctrinaire, their deliberations would have collapsed. They held fast to their objective—providing for a strong central government—but were flexible about ways to achieve their goal. Thus they were able to compromise on critical issues. The first great points of difference dealt with the structure of government and whether states should be represented equally or according to population distribution. The eventual compromise required the abandonment of the Articles of Confederation.

Slight of build and reserved, James Madison of Virginia (1751–1836) has been called the "father of the Constitution." A diligent student of history and politics, he drafted a proposed plan of national government, then made arrangements to have it presented by Edmund Randolph, Virginia's governor and a more adept public speaker, at the outset of the convention. This strategy worked, and the delegates gave the "Virginia Plan" their undivided attention. The plan outlined a three-tiered structure with an executive branch and two houses of Congress. Madison also envisioned a separate judicial branch.

Delegates from the less populous, smaller states objected. Under the Virginia Plan representatives to the two chambers of Congress would be apportioned to the states according to population, whereas under the Articles, each state, regardless of population, had an equal voice in national government. For such delegates as lawyer William Paterson of New Jersey, the latter practice ensured that the interests of the smaller states would not be sacrificed to those of the more populous, larger states. Paterson countered with his "New Jersey Plan" on June 15. It retained equal voting in a unicameral national legislature, and it also vested far greater authority, including the powers of taxation and regulation of interstate and foreign commerce, in the central government. Paterson's plan was far more consistent with the convention's original charge—an argument in its favor.

On June 19 the delegates voted to adopt a three-tiered structure of government, but they did not resolve the question of how the states should be represented in the two new legislative branches. The convention had reached an impasse, and some delegates now threatened to leave. At the end of June Benjamin Franklin made one of his well-timed speeches. He urged everyone present to put aside "our little partial local interests" so that future generations would not "despair of establishing governments by human wisdom and leave it to chance, war, and conquest."

The advice of Franklin and others calling for unity of purpose helped ease tensions. By July 12 the delegates had hammered out a settlement. Central to the "Great Compromise," which saved the convention from dissolving, was an agreement providing for proportional representation in the lower house (favoring the more populous states) and equality of representation in the upper house (favoring the less populous states). In the upper house each state would have two senators. Although the senators could vote independently of each other, they could also operate in tandem to protect state interests.

Having passed this crucial hurdle, the convention turned to other issues, not the least of which was slavery. Delegates from the Deep South wanted guarantees that would prevent any national tampering with their chattel property. Some Northerners, however, including those who had supported abolition in their states, preferred constitutional restrictions on slavery.

For a while, compromise did not seem possible. In the heat of debate South Carolinian Pierce Butler blurted out that the North and the South were "as different as . . . Russia and Turkey." Later on, Pennsylvania delegate Gouverneur Morris, a firm antislavery advocate, suggested that it was impossible "to blend incompatible things." Finally, both sides made concessions for the sake of union. What they produced was the first major national compromise on the continuation of slavery (to be followed by others, including the Compromises of 1820 and 1850).

In the North-South compromise of 1787, the delegates left matters purposely vague. By mutual agreement, the Constitution neither endorsed nor condemned slavery, nor can that word be found in the text. It did guarantee Southerners that slaves would count as "three-fifths" of white persons for purposes of determining representation in the lower house. While this meant more congressional seats for the South, direct taxes would also be based on population, including "three-fifths of all other persons." Thus the South would also pay more in taxes. The delegates also agreed to prohibit any national legislation against the importation of slaves from abroad until 1808.

Although these clauses gave implicit recognition to slavery, it should be noted that the Northwest Land Ordinance of 1787, adopted by the Continental Congress in New York at the same time, forever barred slavery north of the Ohio River. The timing has led some historians to conclude that inhibiting the spread of slavery was also part of the compromise, representing a major concession to northern interests.

The North-South compromise kept the convention and the republic together by temporarily mollifying most delegates on an extremely divisive issue. Still, slavery was so remarkably inconsistent with the ideals of human liberty that the problem could not be sidestepped for long.

A third set of issues provoking compromise had to do with the office of president. Nobody seemed sure what range of authority the national executive should have, how long the term of office should be, or how the president should be elected. By early September the delegates, fatigued by endless debates and extremely hot weather during three months of meetings, settled these questions quickly. The office of the president was potentially powerful. Besides serving as commander in chief of military forces, the incumbent could fashion treaties with foreign powers, subject to ratification by a two-thirds vote of the Senate. The president could veto congressional legislation, which both houses of Congress could only override with two-thirds majorities. Congress, in turn, had an important check on the president. It could impeach the executive if presidential powers were abused. Four years seemed like a reasonable term of office, and reelection would be permitted.

To help insulate the president from manipulation by public opinion, the delegates made the office indirectly elective. They did so by creating the electoral college. Each state would have the same number of electors as representatives and senators. In states that permitted popular voting for the presidency, citizens would cast ballots for electors who favored particular candidates. In turn the electors would meet and vote for the person they favored. The candidate with a majority of electoral college votes would become president. The person with the second highest total would become vice president. Should the electors fail to reach a majority decision (this happened in the elections of 1800 and 1824), the election would be turned over to the House of Representatives, where each state would have one vote in choosing a president.

The subject of the presidency might have been more contentious had no person of George Washington's universally acclaimed stature been on the scene. Washington was the one authentic popular hero and symbol of national unity to emerge from the Revolution, and the delegates were already thinking of him as the first president. Since he was so fully trusted as a firm apostle of republican principles who had disdained the mantle of a military dictator, defining the mode of election and powers of the national executive were not insurmountable tasks.

The Ratification Struggle

Thirty-nine delegates affixed their signatures to the proposed Constitution on September 17, 1787. Benjamin Franklin hoped that more of the delegates would sign, and he echoed the thoughts of those who did so by indicating that "there are several parts of this Constitution which I do not at present approve. . . . It therefore astonishes me, Sir," he stated, "to find this system approaching so near to perfection as it does." Pointing toward a seal with a carving of the sun on the president's chair, Franklin concluded: "At length I have the happiness to know that it is a rising and not a setting sun."

The delegates who signed the Constitution of 1787 knew there would be significant opposition because their plan cut so heavily into state authority. So they made the shrewd move of agreeing that only nine states needed to ratify the Constitution—through special state conventions rather than through state legislatures—to allow the new central government to commence operations. The nationalists were not going to let one or two states destroy months of work—and what they viewed as the best last hope for a languishing republic.

In another astute move, the nationalists started referring to themselves as **Federalists**, and they disarmed their opponents by calling them **Antifederalists**. Actually, the Antifederalists were the real federalists; they wanted to continue the confederation of sovereign states, and they sought to keep power as close as possible to the people, mostly in the hands of state governments. This manipulation of terminology may have gotten some local Federalist candidates elected to state ratifying conventions, thus helping to secure victory for the Constitution.

George Washington (on the podium) presided at the Constitutional Convention in Philadelphia during the summer of 1787. Washington was a popular hero and a natural choice to serve as the first president of the United States.

The nationalists were also very effective in explaining the Convention's work. The essence of their argumentation appeared in **The Federalist Papers,** a series of 85 remarkably cogent newspaper essays written by James Madison, Alexander Hamilton, and John Jay on behalf of ratification in New York. Under the pseudonym "Publius," they discussed various aspects of the Constitution and tried to demonstrate how the document would ensure political stability and provide enlightened legislation.

The new government, they asserted, had been designed to protect the rights of all citizens. No one self-serving faction ("a landed interest, a manufacturing interest, a mercantile interest, a monied interest"), whether representing a minority or majority of citizens, could take power completely and deprive others of their liberties and property. The Constitution would check and balance these interest groups because basic powers (executive, legislative, judicial) would be divided among the various branches of government. Furthermore, the system was truly federal, they argued, because much decision-making authority remained with the states as a further protection against power-hungry, self-serving factional interest groups.

Beyond these advantages, the Constitution embodied the principle of representative republicanism, as Madison explained in *Federalist No. 10.* Large election districts for the House of Representatives would make it more difficult for particular interest groups to manipulate elections and send "unworthy candidates" to Congress. Citizens of true merit, hence, could rise up, emerge triumphant, and then meet in Congress to enact laws beneficial for all citizens of the republic.

The nationalists admitted they were overturning the first constitutional settlement of 1776. The emphasis would now be on a national government whose acts would be "the supreme law of the land." Federal leaders would be drawn from citizens of learning and wealth, many like those nationalists who had never fully trusted the people. From their perspective the people had failed the test of public virtue. They had shown more concern for their individual welfare than in making material or personal sacrifices to support the Continental war effort. They had formed into troublesome factions like the Maryland land speculators and the Massachusetts rebel followers of Daniel Shays, all to the detriment of the republic's political stability.

The nationalists, now expecting to function as the new nation's political stewards, did not repudiate the principle of popular sovereignty. Rather, they enshrined it in such concepts as representative republicanism. The people were to have a political voice, in the abstract at least, and they were to remain the constituent authority of American government. Their stewards, supposedly detached from selfish concerns, could now more easily check narrow interests inhibiting stable national development.

The Antifederalists understood, and they viewed this new settlement with grave alarm. One writer, "Centinel," stated that the Constitution would support "in practice a *permanent* ARISTOCRACY" of self-serving, wealthy citizens. Another, calling himself "Philadelphiensis," saw in the Constitution "a conspiracy against the liberties of his country, concerted by a few *tyrants,* whose views are to lord it over the rest of their fellow citizens."

These arguments, reminiscent of those that had stirred up revolutionary fervor in the 1760s and 1770s, lay at the heart of the Antifederalist critique of the proposed Constitution. Leading Antifederalists, among them Samuel Adams, Patrick Henry, and Richard Henry Lee, still had negative images of the distant British government, too far removed from the people to be checked in any effective way. Having rebelled against what they perceived as the tyranny of the British imperial government, they were not anxious to approve a plan for a new central government with enough power to threaten the states and the people with yet more political tyranny. They preferred life under the Articles of Confederation.

The Antifederalists failed to counter nationalist momentum. Close calls occurred in some ratifying conventions, such as in Massachusetts, New York, and Virginia. The well-organized nationalists were always ready to counter Antifederalist complaints. When some complained about the absence of a national bill of rights guaranteeing each citizen fundamental liberties, they promised that the first Congress would prepare one. When some demanded a second convention that would not overturn but modify the Articles of Confederation, they argued that the new government should first be given a chance. If it did not work, the nationalists stated, they would support another convention.

Once the New Hampshire convention voted to ratify on June 21, 1788, the necessary nine states had given their approval. The two large states of Virginia and New York were still not in the fold, however, so everyone hesitated. Virginia was the most populous state, and New York was fourth behind Pennsylvania and Massachusetts. In addition, both Virginia and New York were so strategically located that it would have been virtually impossible to operate the new national government without their involvement.

Promises of a bill of rights helped bring the Virginia convention around in a close vote (89 yeas to 79 nays) on June 25. A month later after much skillful Federalist maneuvering, including promises of a second constitutional convention should the 1787 plan fail to work, the dominant Antifederalists in New York's ratifying convention conceded enough votes for ratification to occur by the slim margin of 30 yeas to 27 nays. New York thus became the "eleventh pillar" of the union. Since the constitution did succeed, as demonstrated by George Washington's presidential administration, arguments for a second convention faded away.

TABLE 6.3
Ratification of the Constitution of 1787

State	Date	Vote Yes	Vote No
Delaware	December 7, 1787	30	0
Pennsylvania	December 12, 1787	46	23
New Jersey	December 18, 1787	38	0
Georgia	January 2, 1788	26	0
Connecticut	January 9, 1788	128	40
Massachusetts	February 6, 1788	187	168
Maryland	April 26, 1788	63	11
South Carolina	May 23, 1788	149	73
New Hampshire	June 21, 1788	57	47
Virginia	June 25, 1788	89	79
New York	July 26, 1788	30	27
North Carolina*	November 21, 1789	194	77
Rhode Island†	May 29, 1790	34	32

*On July 21, 1788, the first ratifying convention in North Carolina voted 184 to 84 not to consider approval of the Constitution. The vote recorded is that of the second convention.

†Rhode Island not only refused to participate in the Philadelphia Constitutional Convention but also decided not to call a state ratifying convention. Only after the United States Senate threatened to sever commercial ties with Rhode Island did the state government agree to a convention that reluctantly approved the Constitution.

Chronology
OF KEY EVENTS

1775 Daniel Boone blazes the "Wilderness Road" to Kentucky; Lord Dunmore calls for the emancipation of Virginia's slaves (November)

1775–1777 Ten states adopt new state constitutions

1776–1777 Congress drafts the Articles of Confederation

1780 Pennsylvania becomes the first state to provide for the emancipation of slaves

1781 Articles of Confederation are finally ratified by all the states

1782 Rhode Island refuses to ratify the Impost Plan to provide Congress a tax revenue, thereby precipitating the threat of a military coup—the Newburgh Conspiracy

1783 Washington defuses the threat of a military coup

1784 Land Ordinance of 1784 guarantees western settlers territorial government

1785 Land Ordinance of 1785 provides for the survey and sale of western lands

1786 Virginia adopts Jefferson's Statute of Religious Freedom separating church and state (January); Jay-Gardoquí negotiations fail to produce a trading alliance with Spain (August); Shays's Rebellion gains momentum (August–December); Annapolis Convention calls for a national constitutional convention (September)

1787 Constitutional Convention convenes in Philadelphia (May); Congress passes the Northwest Ordinance, forever barring slavery north of the Ohio River (July)

1788 Hamilton, Madison, and Jay publish 85 essays on behalf of the Constitution, known as *The Federalist Papers*; Constitution is ratified by the necessary number of states

CONCLUSION

In 1776 those radical revolutionaries who believed in a virtuous citizenry had sought to expand popular participation in government. By and large they succeeded. This first constitutional settlement proved to be unsatisfactory, however, largely because the weak central government under the Articles of Confederation lacked the authority to support even the minimal needs of the new nation. Blaming the states and the people, the nationalist leaders produced a second constitutional settlement in 1787 by drafting a plan for a more powerful central government. It was to be above the people and the states, strong enough to establish and preserve national unity and stability.

The new national government began functioning in April 1789. No sooner had these "diffusive and established" gentlemen started to govern, however, than they fell to fighting among themselves over a host of controversial issues. To gain allies, they turned back to the people. Against the wishes of many nationalists, some leaders started to organize political parties and urged the citizenry to support their candidates as a means of stopping the opposition. By the mid-1790s the people were emerging as much more than a token voice in national politics. Concepts of deference and stewardship were now in full retreat; common citizens were at last becoming the true foundation of what would one day be a system of political democracy.

The years between 1776 and 1789 thus secured the republic and republican ideals. On the other hand, notions regarding each American's right to enjoy life, liberty, happiness, and property in an equalitarian society fell far short of full implementation. Women remained second-class citizens, and the shackles of slavery and racist thinking still manacled African Americans. Even with the opening of the trans-Appalachian West, which came at the expense of thousands of Native Americans, poorer citizens found it difficult to gain access to farmland on which they could provide for themselves and secure their personal prosperity. Although future generations would argue and fight, even to the point of a bloody civil war, over how best to realize the full potential of republican ideals, there was no denying their rudimentary presence. In this sense the years before 1789 had witnessed a revolution in human expectations.

SUGGESTIONS FOR FURTHER READING

Gregory Evans Dowd, *A Spirited Resistance: The North American Indian Struggle for Unity, 1745–1815* (1992). Incisive account of militant Native-American resistance in reaction to white expansion into the trans-Appalachian West.

Sylvia R. Frey, *Water from the Rock: Black Resistance in a Revolutionary Age* (1991). Revisionist investigation of southern slaves and how they sought to make better lives for themselves out of the turmoil of the Revolutionary era.

Robert A. Gross, ed., *In Debt to Shays: The Bicentennial of an Agrarian Rebellion* (1993). Illuminating essays focusing on Shays's Rebellion and the many problems besetting ordinary citizens in late eighteenth-century America.

Merrill Jensen, *The New Nation, 1781–1789* (1950). Classic examination of "critical period" politics and the nationalist mind-set of the Founding Fathers.

Jean B. Lee, *The Price of Nationhood: The American Revolution in Charles County* (1994). Suggestive appraisal of the impact of the Revolution on the inhabitants of this Maryland county.

Mary Beth Norton, *Liberty's Daughters: The Revolutionary Experience of American Women, 1750–1800* (1980). Valuable study of ways in which the Revolution affected the roles women defined for themselves.

Jack N. Rakove, *Original Meanings: Politics and Ideas in the Making of the Constitution* (1996). Prize-winning analysis of the ideas, concerns, and intentions that both shaped and gave meaning to the Constitution of 1787.

Gordon S. Wood, *The Creation of the American Republic, 1776–1787* (1969). Influential analysis of changing conceptions of political thought and culture culminating in the Constitution of 1787 and a new national government.

Overviews and Surveys

Richard R. Beeman, et al., eds., *Beyond Confederation: Origins of the Constitution and American National Identity* (1987); Robert M. Calhoon, *Dominion and Liberty: Ideology in the Anglo-American World* (1994); Edward Countryman, *The American Revolution* (1985); Staughton Lynd, *Class Conflict, Slavery, and the United States Constitution* (1967); Forrest McDonald, *E Pluribus Unum: The Formation of the American Republic, 1776–1790* (1965); Edmund S. Morgan, *Inventing the People: The Rise of Popular Sovereignty in England and America* (1988); Richard B. Morris, *The Forging of the Union, 1781–1789* (1987); Alfred F. Young, ed., *The American Revolution: Explorations in the History of American Radicalism* (1976).

Establishing New Republican Governments

Willi Paul Adams, *The First American Constitutions* (1980); Edward Countryman, *A People in Revolution: Political Society in New York, 1760–1790* (1981); Robert J. Dinkin, *Voting in Revolutionary America* (1982); Jackson Turner Main, *The Upper House in Revolutionary America, 1763–1788* (1967), and *Political Parties Before the Constitution* (1973); James Kirby Martin, *Men in Rebellion: Higher Governmental Leaders and the Coming of the Revolution* (1973); Jerome J. Nadelhaft, *The Disorders of War: The Revolution in South Carolina* (1981); Stephen E. Patterson, *Political Parties in Revolutionary Massachusetts* (1973); J. R. Pole, *Political Representation in England and the Origins of the American Republic* (1966); Garry Wills, *Cincinnatus: George Washington and the Enlightenment* (1984).

Crises of the Confederation

John L. Brooke, *The Heart of the Commonwealth: Worcester County, Massachusetts, 1713–1861* (1989); Thomas Doerflinger, *A Vigorous Spirit of Enterprise: Merchants and Economic Development in Revolutionary Philadelphia* (1986); E. James Ferguson, *The Power of the Purse: American Public Finance, 1776–1790* (1961); Dall W. Forsythe, *Taxation and Political Change in the Young Nation, 1781–1833* (1977); Van Beck Hall, *Politics Without Parties: Massachusetts, 1780–1791* (1972); Ronald Hoffman and Peter J. Albert, eds., *Sovereign States in an Age of Uncertainty* (1981); Richard H. Kohn, *Eagle and Sword: The Federalists and Military Establishment in America, 1783–1802* (1975); Peter S. Onuf, *The Origins of the Federal Republic: Jurisdictional Controversies in the United States, 1775–1787* (1983), and *Statehood and Union: The Northwest Ordinance* (1987); Irwin H. Polishook, *Rhode Island and the Union, 1774–1795* (1969); Norman K. Risjord, *Chesapeake Politics, 1781–1800* (1978); Charles R. Ritcheson, *Aftermath of Revolution: British Policy, 1783–1795* (1969); Malcolm Rohrbough, *The Trans-Appalachian Frontier, 1775–1850* (1978); David Szatmary, *Shays' Rebellion* (1980); Robert J. Taylor, *Western Massachusetts in the Revolution* (1954); Alfred F. Young, *The Democratic-Republicans of New York, 1763–1797* (1967).

Human Rights and Social Change

John K. Alexander, *Render Them Submissive: Responses to Poverty in Philadelphia, 1760–1800* (1980); Lee L. Bean, et al., *Fertility Change on the American Frontier* (1990); Ira Berlin and Ronald Hoffman, eds., *Slavery and Freedom in the Age of the American Revolution* (1983); Wallace Brown, *The Good Americans* (1969); Joy Day Buel and Richard Buel, Jr., *The Way of Duty: A Woman and Her Family in Revolutionary America* (1984); Robert McCluer Calhoon, *The Loyalists in Revolutionary America, 1760–1781* (1973); David Brion Davis, *The Problem of Slavery in the Age of Revolution, 1770–1823* (1975); Carl N. Degler, *At Odds: Women and the Family in America from the Revolution to the Present* (1980); Linda Grant De-

Pauw and Conover Hunt, *"Remember the Ladies": Women in America, 1750–1815* (1976); Philip S. Foner, *Labor and the American Revolution* (1977); Linda Gordon, *Woman's Body, Woman's Right: Birth Control in America* (1976); Adele Hast, *Loyalism in Revolutionary Virginia* (1982); Norman Edwin Himes, *Medical History of Contraception* (1970); J. Franklin Jameson, *The American Revolution Considered as a Social Movement* (1926); Sidney and Emma N. Kaplan, *The Black Presence in the Era of the American Revolution*, rev. ed. (1989); Linda Kerber, *Women of the Republic: Intellect and Ideology in Revolutionary America* (1980); Allan Kulikoff, *The Agrarian Origins of American Capitalism* (1992); Duncan J. MacLeod, *Slavery, Race, and the American Revolution* (1974); Jackson Turner Main, *The Social Structure of Revolutionary America* (1965); John C. Miller, *The Wolf by the Ears: Thomas Jefferson and Slavery* (1977); James C. Mohr, *Abortion in America* (1978); Gary B. Nash, *Forging Freedom: Philadelphia's Black Community, 1720–1840* (1988), and *Race and Revolution* (1990); William H. Nelson, *The American Tory* (1961); Mary Beth Norton, *The British-Americans: The Loyalist Exiles in England, 1774–1789* (1972); Theda Perdue, *Slavery and the Evolution of Cherokee Society, 1540–1866* (1979); Merrill D. Peterson, *Thomas Jefferson and the New Nation* (1970); Janice Potter, *The Liberty We Seek: Loyalist Ideology in New York and Massachusetts* (1983); Benjamin Quarles, *The Negro in the American Revolution* (1961); Donald L. Robinson, *Slavery in the Structure of American Politics, 1765–1820* (1971); Marylynn Salmon, *Women and the Law of Property in Early America* (1986); Billy G. Smith, *The "Lower Sort": Philadelphia's Laboring People, 1750–1800* (1990); Merril D. Smith: *Breaking the Bonds: Marital Discord in Pennsylvania, 1730–1830* (1991); Gregory A. Stiverson, *Poverty in a Land of Plenty: Tenancy in Eighteenth-Century Maryland* (1977); James W. St. G. Walker, *The Black Loyalists: The Search for a Promised Land in Nova Scotia and Sierra Leone, 1783–1870* (1976); John Todd White, "The Truth About Molly Pitcher," in James Kirby Martin and Karen R. Stubaus, eds., *The American Revolution: Whose Revolution?* rev. ed. (1981), pp. 99–105; Shane White, *Somewhat More Independent: The End of Slavery in New York City, 1770–1810* (1991); Arthur Zilversmit, *The First Emancipation: The Abolition of Slavery in the North* (1967).

Second New Beginning, New National Government

John K. Alexander, *The Selling of the Constitutional Convention: A History of News Coverage* (1990); Charles A. Beard, *An Economic Interpretation of the Constitution of the United States* (1913); Stephen R. Boyd, *The Politics of Opposition: Antifederalists and the Acceptance of the Constitution* (1979); Christopher Collier and James L. Collier, *Decision in Philadelphia* (1986); Linda Grant DePauw, *The Eleventh Pillar: New York State and the Federal Constitution* (1966); Michael Kammen, *A Machine That Would Go by Itself: The Constitution in American Culture* (1986); Jackson Turner Main, *The Antifederalists: Critics of the Constitution, 1781–1788* (1961); Frederick W. Marks, III, *Independence on Trial: Foreign Affairs and the Constitution*, 2d ed. (1986); Forrest McDonald, *We the People: The Economic Origins of the Constitution* (1958), and *Novus*

Ordo Seclorum: The Intellectual Origins of the Constitution (1985); Clinton Rossiter, *1787: The Grand Convention* (1966); Robert A. Rutland, *The Ordeal of the Constitution: The Antifederalists and the Ratification Struggle of 1787–88* (1966); Garry Wills, *Explaining America: The Federalist* (1981).

Biographies

Lance Banning, *The Sacred Fire of Liberty: James Madison and the Founding of the Federal Republic* (1996); George A. Billias, *Elbridge Gerry* (1976); Fawn Brodie, *Thomas Jefferson: An Intimate History* (1974); Roger J. Champagne, *Alexander McDougall* (1975); Christopher Collier, *Roger Sherman's Connecticut: Yankee Politics and the Revolution* (1971); Jacob E. Cooke, *Alexander Hamilton* (1982); John Mack Faragher, *Daniel Boone* (1992); Eric Foner, *Tom Paine and Revolutionary America* (1976); John P. Kaminski, *George Clinton: Yeoman Politician of the New Republic* (1993); Elizabeth P. McCaughey, *From Loyalist to Founding Father: William Samuel Johnson* (1980); Merrill D. Peterson, *Thomas Jefferson and the New Nation* (1970); Jack N. Rakove, *James Madison and the Creation of the American Republic* (1990); C. Edward Skeen, *John Armstrong, Jr., 1758–1843* (1981); Sheila Skemp, *Judith Sargent Murray* (1998); Laurel Thatcher Ulrich, *A. Midwife's Tale: The Life of Martha Ballard, 1785–1812* (1990); Clarence L. Ver Steeg, *Robert Morris: Revolutionary Financier* (1954); Lynne Withey, *Dearest Friend: A Life of Abigail Adams* (1981); Rosemarie Zagarri, *A Woman's Dilemma: Mercy Otis Warren and the American Revolution* (1995).

INTERNET RESOURCES

Northwest Territory Alliance
http://www.nwta.com/main.html
This Revolutionary Era reenactment organization site contains several links and is an interesting look at historical reenactment.

Archiving Early America
http://earlyamerica.com/
Old newspapers are excellent windows into the issues of the past. This site includes the Keigwin and Matthews collection of historic newspapers.

Biographies of the Founding Fathers
http://www.colonialhall.com/
This site provides information about the men who signed the Declaration of Independence and includes a trivia section.

Religion and the Founding of the American Republic
http://lcweb.loc.gov/exhibits/religion/religion.html
This Library of Congress site is an online exhibit about religion and the creation of the United States.

Several Federalist Papers with Special Reference to the Government's Power to Tax
http://www.taxhistory.org/federalists/
The Federalist Papers, a series of 85 essays designed to encourage ratification of the United States Constitution, pro-

vide important insight about the history of U.S. federal taxation.

The Federalist Papers
http://www.law.emory.edu/FEDERAL/federalist/
A collection of the most important *Federalist Papers*, a series of documents designed to convince people to support the new Constitution.

The Constitution and the Amendments
http://www.law.emory.edu/FEDERAL/usconst.html
A searchable site to the Constitution, especially useful for its information about the Bill of Rights and other constitutional amendments.

Documents from the Continental Congress and the Constitutional Convention, 1774–1789
http://memory.loc.gov/ammem/bdsds/bdsdhome.html
The Continental Congress Broadside Collection (253 titles) and the Constitutional Convention Broadside Collection (21 titles) contain 274 documents relating to the work of Congress and the drafting and ratification of the Constitution. Items include extracts of the journals of Congress, resolutions, proclamations, committee reports, treaties, and early printed versions of the United States Constitution and the Declaration of Independence. Most broadsides are one page in length; others range from 2 to 28 pages.

KEY TERMS

Republicanism (p. 162)

Public Virtue (p. 162)

Radical Revolutionaries (p. 162)

Cautious Revolutionaries (p. 162)

Nationalists (p. 164)

Shaysites (p. 169)

Republican Motherhood (p. 174)

Manumission (p. 178)

Federalists (p. 181)

Antifederalists (p. 181)

The Federalist Papers (p. 182)

REVIEW QUESTIONS

1. Examine the major points of disagreement between radical and reluctant revolutionaries. What characterized their viewpoints regarding the concept of public virtue, and how did these differences affect constitution making during the Revolutionary era?

2. What were some of the numerous internal problems that plagued the early American republic? In what ways were these problems aggravated by having a weak national government under the Articles of Confederation and sovereign power granted to the states?

3. Compare and contrast the Newburgh Consipiracy of 1783 with Shays's Rebellion of 1786–1787. In what ways did these two events relate to the drive for a stronger national government, and what was their significance?

4. What were some of the contradictions between the Revolution's rhetoric of liberty and actual conditions faced by such groups as African Americans, women, and the propertyless poor? What effect, if any, did the rhetoric of liberty have on these groups during the Revolution and beyond?

5. Explain why the Constitution of 1787 might be described as a bundle of compromises? How did this plan of government address the major problems that had beset the struggling Confederation of states between 1776 and 1787? Why did the Constitution raise prospects for long-term political stability?

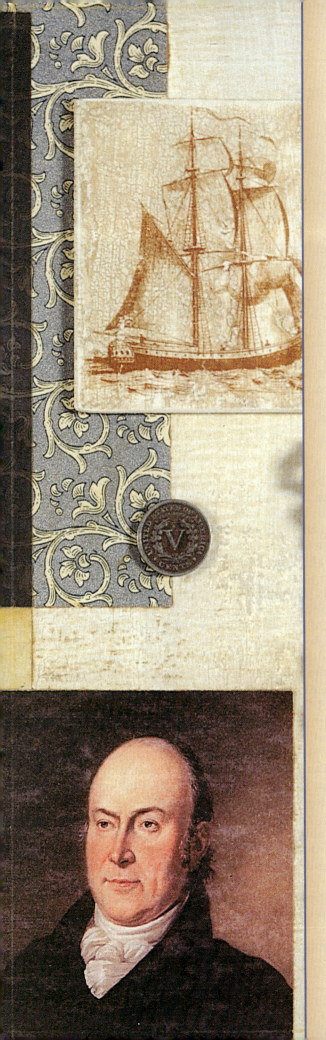

7

THE FORMATIVE DECADE, 1790–1800

An "outrageous and wretched scandalmonger"

Alexander Hamilton responded to journalist James Thomson Callender's charges that he had engaged in illegal financial speculations by publishing a detailed denial.

A critic called James Thomson Callender "the most outrageous and wretched scandalmonger of a scurrilous age." Callender, a pioneering muckraking journalist, during the 1790s published vicious attacks on George Washington, John Adams, Alexander Hamilton, and other leading political figures. Today, Callender is best known as the journalist who first published the story that Thomas Jefferson had a decades-long affair with one of his slaves.

Born in Scotland in 1758, Callender became a clerk and writer and an early proponent of Scottish independence from Britain. Indicted for sedition in 1793, he fled to Philadelphia, where he made a living as a congressional reporter and a political propagandist.

Profoundly suspicious of Treasury Secretary Alexander Hamilton's financial program and his pro-British views on foreign affairs, Callender used his pen to discredit Hamilton. In 1797 he published evidence—probably provided by supporters of Thomas Jefferson—that Hamilton had an adulterous extramarital affair with a woman named Maria Reynolds. Callender also accused Hamilton of involvement in illegal financial speculations with Reynolds's husband, an unsavory character who had been convicted of fraud and dealing in stolen goods. Hamilton acknowledged the affair, but denied the corruption charges, claiming that he was a victim of blackmail. Nevertheless, Hamilton's public reputation was hurt, and he never held public office again.

In 1798 Hamilton's political party, the Federalist party, pushed the Sedition Act through Congress, making it a crime to attack the government or the president with false, scandalous, or malicious statements. In 1800 Callender was one of several journalists indicted, tried, and convicted under the law. He was fined $200 and sentenced to nine months in prison, where he found himself "surrounded by thieves of every description."

By the time Callender was released, Thomas Jefferson had been elected president. Callender expected the new administration to refund his fine and appoint him to a government job. When repayment of the fine was delayed and Jefferson refused to appoint him as a postmaster, Callender struck back. In 1802, a year before his death, Callender publicly accused Jefferson of having a lifelong liaison with his slave Sally Hemings.

Sally Hemings was the half-sister of Jefferson's deceased wife Martha. Her mother had been impregnated by her master, John Wayles, the father of Martha Jefferson. Sally Hemings herself bore five mulatto children out of wedlock. Callender insisted that Jefferson fathered the children. Jefferson's defenders denied the assertion. In 1998 DNA testing indicated that Thomas Jefferson fathered at least one of Sally Hemings's children.

Despised by his critics as a "traitorous and truculent scoundrel," Callender defended himself on strikingly modern grounds: that the public had a right to know the moral character of people it elected to public office. Although he has often been dismissed as a "pen for hire," willing to defame anyone, Callender's work underscores one of the most radical consequences of the American Revolution. The revolution gave new meaning to the idea of popular sovereignty and ensured that ordinary Americans would be the ultimate arbiters of American politics. Passionately rejecting the notion that common people should express deference toward the educated and well-to-do, Callender aimed his political commentary at artisans and at immigrants who flocked to seaport towns during the 1790s. Scandal, sensation, and suspicion of the powerful were the appeals he used to attract readers.

Politically and economically, the 1790s was the nation's formative decade. During this time the United States implemented the new Constitution, adopted a bill of rights, created its first political parties, and built a new national capital city in Washington, D.C. The 1790s were also years of rapid economic and demographic growth, the time when the new United States established a strong and vigorous national government and a prosperous, growing economy.

The Constitution provided for a census every ten years. The first census, conducted in 1790, estimated the population of the United States at 3.9 million people. The jug, made in England after the 1790 census, shows the figures gathered in that census.

THE ROOTS OF AMERICAN ECONOMIC GROWTH

Early in August 1790, David Howe, an assistant federal marshal, began the difficult task of counting all the people who lived in Hancock County, Maine. One of 650 federal census takers, charged with making "a just and perfect enumeration and description of all persons" in the United States, he began by writing down his own name followed by his wife's and child's. He next listed the names of all the other people who lived in his hometown of Penobscot, then proceeded to crisscross the Maine coast, recording the names of 9549 residents. In March 1791 he submitted his findings: 2436 free white males, 16 and older; 4544 free white females; 2631 white children; and 38 "other free persons" (including Peter Williams, "a black," and his wife and child).

The United States was the first nation in history to institute a periodic national census. Since 1790, the country has tried to count each woman, man, and child every ten years. The first census asked just six simple questions, yet when supplemented by other statistical information, it provides a treasure chest of information about the social and economic life of the American people.

Taking the nation's first census was an extraordinarily difficult challenge. The nation's sheer physical size—stretching across 867,980 square miles from Georgia to Maine—made it impossible to make an accurate count. Many people refused to speak to census takers; some because they feared that this was

the first step toward enactment of new taxes, others because they believed that the Bible prohibited census taking. To make matters worse, census takers were abysmally paid; they received just $1 for every 150 rural residents and $1 for every 300 city dwellers counted. Indeed, the pay was so low that one judge found it difficult to find "any person whatever" to take the census.

What was the United States like in 1790? According to the first census, the United States contained just 3,929,214 people, about half living in the northern states, half in the South. At first glance, the population seems quite small (it was only about a quarter the size of England's and a sixth the size of France's), but it was growing extraordinarily rapidly. Just 1.17 million in 1750, the population would pass five million by 1800.

The 1790 census revealed a nation still overwhelmingly rural in character. In a population of nearly four million, only two cities had more than 25,000 people. Yet the urban population, while small, was growing extremely rapidly, especially in the West where frontier towns like Louisville started to sprout.

In 1790, most Americans still lived on the Atlantic coast. Nevertheless, the West was the most rapidly growing part of the nation. During the 1790s, the population of Kentucky and Tenessee increased nearly 300 percent, and by 1800, Kentucky had more people than five of the original 13 states.

The first census also revealed an extraordinarily youthful population, with half the people under the age of 16. Extraordinarily diverse, a fifth of the entire population was African American. Three-fifths of the white population was English in ancestry and another fifth was Scottish or Irish. The remainder was of German, Dutch, French, Swedish, or other background.

Records indicate that the American economy was still quite undeveloped. There were fewer than 100 newspapers in the entire country, three banks (with a total capital of less than $5 million), and three insurance companies; yet, the United States was perched on the edge of an extraordinary decade of growth.

Over the next ten years, American society made tremendous economic advances. During the 1790s, states chartered almost ten times more corporations, banks, and transportation companies than during the 1780s. Exports climbed from $29 million to $107 million; cotton production rose from 3000 bales to 73,000. Altogether, eleven mechanized mills were built in the country during the 1790s, laying the foundations of future economic growth.

In 1800, as in 1790, the United States remained a nation of farms, plantations, and small towns, of yeomen farmers, slaves, and artisans. Nevertheless, the nation was undergoing far-reaching social and economic transformations. Improvements in education were particularly striking. Between 1783 and 1800, Americans founded 17 new colleges and a large number of female academies.

Why did the United States experience such rapid growth during the 1790s? In part, the answer lies in European wars, pitting France against Britain, that increased demand for U.S. products and stimulated American shipping and trade. But the answer also lies in critical political developments, especially enactment of a financial program that secured the nation's credit.

IMPLEMENTING THE CONSTITUTION

The United States was the first modern nation to achieve independence through a successful revolution against colonial rule. Although many colonies in the nineteenth and twentieth centuries followed the example of the United States in winning independence through revolution, few were as successful in subsequent economic and political development.

Even the United States, however, struggled to establish itself in its first decade under the Constitution.

The new nation faced severe economic and foreign policy problems. A huge debt remained from the Revolution, and paper money issued during and after the war was virtually worthless. Along with these pressing economic problems were foreign threats to the new nation's independence. In violation of the peace treaty of 1783 ending the Revolutionary War, Britain continued to occupy forts in the Old Northwest, and Spain refused to recognize the new nation's southern and western boundaries. In 1790, economic problems, domestic political conflict, and foreign policy issues challenged the new nation in its efforts to establish a stable republic.

Establishing the Machinery of Government

The first task facing American leaders was to establish the machinery of government. The new United States government consisted of 75 post offices, a large debt, a small number of unpaid clerks, and an army of just 46 officers and 672 soldiers. There was no federal court system, no navy, and no system for collecting taxes.

It fell to Congress to take the initial steps toward putting the new national government into operation: To raise revenue, it passed a tariff on imported goods and an excise tax on liquor; to encourage American shipping, it imposed duties on foreign vessels; and to

In its first session, Congress organized a federal judicial system as part of the new national government. This depiction of an early courthouse was drawn in 1804 by Lewis Miller.

provide a structure for the executive branch of the government, it created departments of State, Treasury, and War. By the Judiciary Act of 1789, Congress organized a federal court system, which consisted of a Supreme Court with six justices, a district court in each state, and three appeals courts.

To strengthen popular support for the new government, Congress also approved a **Bill of Rights** in the form of ten amendments to the Constitution. These first amendments guaranteed the rights of free press, free speech, and free exercise of religion; the right to peaceful assembly; and the right to petition government. The Bill of Rights also ensured that the national government could not infringe on the right to trial by jury. In an effort to reassure Antifederalists that the powers of the new government were limited, the tenth amendment "reserved to the States respectively, or to the people" all powers not specified in the Constitution.

Defining the Presidency

The Constitution provided only a broad outline of the office and powers of the president. It would be up to George Washington, as the first president, to define the office, and to establish many precedents regarding the president's relationship with the other branches of government. It was unclear, for example, whether the president was personally to run the executive branch or, instead, act like a constitutional monarch and delegate responsibility to the vice president and executive officers, called the **cabinet.** Washington favored a strong and active role for the president. Modeling the executive branch along the lines of a general's staff, Washington consulted his cabinet officers and listened to them carefully, but he made the final decisions, just as he had done as commander in chief.

The relationship between the executive and legislative branches was also uncertain. Should a president, like Britain's prime minister, personally appear before Congress to defend administration policies? Should the Senate have sole power to dismiss executive officers? The answers to such questions were not clear. Washington insisted that the president could dismiss presidential appointees without the Senate's permission. A bitterly divided Senate approved this principle by a single vote.

With regard to foreign policy, Washington tried to follow the literal words of the Constitution, which stated that the president should negotiate treaties with the advice and consent of the Senate. He appeared before the Senate to discuss a pending Indian treaty. The senators, however, refused to provide immediate answers and referred the matter to a com-

This figurative drawing depicts President George Washington meeting with his first cabinet—Secretary of War Henry Knox, Secretary of State Thomas Jefferson, and Secretary of the Treasury Alexander Hamilton—at Washington's Mount Vernon home.

mittee. "This defeats every purpose of my coming here," Washington declared. In the future he negotiated treaties first and then sent them to the Senate for ratification.

The most difficult task that the president faced was deciding whom to nominate for public office. For secretary of war, Washington nominated Henry Knox, an old military comrade, who had held a similar position under the Articles of Confederation. As postmaster general, he named Samuel Osgood of Massachusetts, who carried out his tasks in a single room with the help of two clerks. For attorney general, he tapped fellow Virginian Edmund Randolph, and for chief justice of the Supreme Court, he selected New Yorker John Jay. Washington nominated another Virginian, Thomas Jefferson, for secretary of state. He named his former aide-de-camp, the 34-year-old Alexander Hamilton, to head the Treasury Department.

Alexander Hamilton's Financial Program

The most pressing problems facing the new government were economic. As a result of the revolution, the federal government had acquired a huge debt: $54 million including interest. The states owed another $25 million. Paper money issued under the

Continental Congresses and Articles of Confederation was worthless. Foreign credit was unavailable.

Ten days after **Alexander Hamilton** became Treasury Secretary, Congress asked him to report on ways to solve the nation's financial problems. Hamilton, a man of strong political convictions, immediately realized that he had an opportunity to create a financial program that would embody his political principles.

Hamilton believed that the nation's stability depended on an alliance between the government and citizens of wealth and influence. No society could succeed, he maintained, "which did not unite the interest and credit of rich individuals with those of the state." Unlike Thomas Jefferson, Hamilton doubted the capacity of common people to govern themselves. "The people are turbulent and changing," he maintained, "they seldom judge or determine right."

To keep the masses in check, Hamilton favored a strong national government. Born in the British West Indies, Hamilton never developed the intense loyalty to a state that was common among many Americans of the time. He wanted to create a unified nation and a powerful federal government, intending to use government fiscal policies to strengthen federal power at the expense of the states and "make it in the immediate interest of the moneyed men to cooperate with government in its support."

The paramount problem facing Hamilton was the national debt. Hamilton argued that it was vital for the nation to repay the debts in order to establish the credit of the federal government. He proposed that the government assume the entire indebtedness—principal and interest—of the federal government and the states. His plan was to retire the old depreciated obligations by borrowing new money at a lower interest rate.

This proposal ignited a firestorm of controversy, because states like Maryland, Pennsylvania, North Carolina, and Virginia had already paid off their war debts. They saw no reason why they should be taxed by the federal government to pay off the debts of states like Massachusetts and South Carolina. Others opposed the scheme because it would provide enormous profits to speculators who had bought bonds from revolutionary war veterans for as little as 10 or 15 cents on the dollar. Many of these financial speculators were associates of Hamilton or members of Congress who knew that Hamilton's report would recommend full payment of the debt.

For six months, a bitter debate raged in Congress. The nation's future seemed in jeopardy until a compromise orchestrated by James Madison and Thomas Jefferson secured passage of Hamilton's plan. In exchange for Southern votes in Congress, Hamilton promised his support for locating the future national capital on the banks of the Potomac River, the border between two southern states, Virginia and Maryland.

Hamilton's debt program was a remarkable success. Funding and assumption of the debt created pools of capital for business investment and firmly established the credit of the United States abroad. By demonstrating Americans' willingness to repay their debts, he made America a good credit risk attractive to foreign investors. European investment capital poured into the new nation in large amounts.

Hamilton's next objective was to create a Bank of the United States, modeled after the Bank of England, to issue currency, collect taxes, hold government funds, and make loans to the government and borrowers. This proposal, like his debt scheme, unleashed a storm of protest.

One criticism directed against the bank was that it threatened to undermine the nation's republican values. Banks—and the paper money they issued—would simply encourage speculation, paper shuffling, and corruption. Some opposed the bank on constitutional grounds. Adopting a position known as **strict construction,** Thomas Jefferson and James Madison charged that a national bank was unconstitutional since the Constitution did not specifically give Congress the power to create a bank. Other grounds for criticism were that the bank would subject America to foreign influences (because foreigners would have to purchase a high percentage of the bank's stock) and give a propertied elite disproportionate influence over the nation's fiscal policies (since private investors would control the bank's board of directors). Worse yet, the bank would increase the public debt, which, in turn, would add to the nation's tax burden. Under Hamilton's plan, the bank would raise capital by selling stock to private investors. Investors could pay for up to three-quarters of the bank stock they purchased with government bonds of indebtedness. The burden of financing the bank, therefore, would ultimately rest on the public treasury.

Hamilton responded to the charge that a bank was unconstitutional by formulating the doctrine of **implied powers.** He argued that Congress did have the power to create a bank since the Constitution granted the federal government authority to do anything "necessary and proper" to carry out its constitutional functions (in this case its fiscal duties). This represented the first attempt to defend a **loose interpretation** of the Constitution. Hamilton also defended his bank plan on another ground. He asserted that his plan would transform the public debt into a public good by using it to expand credit, finance business expansion, and provide a much needed pool of capital.

In 1791 Congress passed a bill creating a national bank for a term of 20 years, leaving the question of the bank's constitutionality up to President Washington. After listening to Madison, Jefferson, and Hamilton, the president reluctantly decided to sign the measure out of a conviction that a bank was necessary for the nation's financial well-being.

The first **Bank of the United States,** like Hamilton's debt plan, was a great success. It helped regulate the currency of private banks. It provided a reserve of capital on which the government and private investors drew. It helped attract foreign investment to the credit-short new nation. In 1811, however, the jealousy of private commercial banks convinced Congress to allow the bank, which had been chartered for a maximum of 20 years, to expire.

The final plank in Hamilton's economic program was a proposal to aid the nation's infant industries. In his *Report on Manufactures* (1791), Hamilton argued that the nation's long-term interests "will be advanced, rather than injured, by the due encouragement of manufactures." Through high tariffs designed to protect American industry from foreign competition, government bounties and subsidies, and internal improvements of transportation, he hoped to break Britain's manufacturing hold on America.

Opposition to Hamilton's proposal came from many quarters. Many Americans feared that the proposal would excessively cut federal revenues by discouraging imports. Shippers worried that the plan would reduce foreign trade. Farmers feared the proposal would lead foreign countries to impose retaliatory tariffs on agricultural products. Many southerners regarded the plan as a brazen attempt to promote northern industry and commerce at the South's expense, since it provided no assistance to agriculture.

The most eloquent opposition to Hamilton's proposals came from Thomas Jefferson, who believed that the growth of manufacturing threatened the values of an agrarian way of life. Hamilton's vision of America's future directly challenged Jefferson's ideal of a nation of freehold farmers, tilling the fields, communing with nature, and maintaining personal freedom by virtue of landownership. Manufacturing, Jefferson believed, should be left to European cities, which he considered to be cesspools of human corruption. Like slaves, factory workers would be manipulated by their masters, who not only would deny them satisfying lives but also would make it impossible for them to think and act as independent citizens.

Alexander Hamilton offered a remarkably modern economic vision based on investment, industry, and expanded commerce. Most strikingly, it was an economic vision that had no place for slavery. Before the 1790s, the American economy—North and South—was intimately tied to a transatlantic system of slavery. States south of Pennsylvania depended on slave labor to produce tobacco, rice, indigo, and cotton. The northern states conducted their most profitable trade with the slave colonies of the West Indies. A member of New York's first antislavery society, Hamilton wanted to reorient the American economy away from slavery and trade with the slave colonies of the Caribbean.

Congress rejected most of Hamilton's proposals to aid industry. Nevertheless, the debate over Hamilton's plan carried with it fateful consequences. Fundamental disagreements had arisen between Hamiltonians and Jeffersonians over the federal government's role, constitutional interpretation, and distinct visions of how the republic should develop. To resolve these fundamental differences, Americans would create modern political parties—parties the writers of the Constitution never wanted nor anticipated.

The National Bank of the United States, which opened in Philadelphia in 1791, was a key part of Alexander Hamilton's economic plan for a strong central government.

THE BIRTH OF POLITICAL PARTIES

When George Washington assembled his first cabinet, there were no national political parties in the United States. In selecting cabinet members, he paid no attention to partisan labels and simply chose the individuals he believed were best qualified to run the new nation. Similarly, the new Congress had no party divisions. In all the states, except Pennsylvania, politics was waged not between parties but rather between impermanent factions built around leading families, political managers, ethnic groups, or interest groups such as debtors and creditors.

By the time Washington retired from the presidency in 1797, the nature of the American political system had changed radically. The first president devoted part of his "Farewell Address" to denouncing "the baneful effects of the Spirit of Party," which had come to dominate American politics. Local and state factions had given way to two competing national parties, known as the **Federalists** and the **Republicans.** They nominated political candidates, managed electoral campaigns, and represented distinctive outlooks or ideologies. By 1796 the United States had produced its first modern party system.

The framers of the Constitution had not prepared their plan of government with political parties in mind. They associated parties with the political factions and interest groups that dominated the British government and hoped that in the United States the "better sort of citizens," rising above popular self-interest, would debate key issues and reach a harmonious consensus regarding how best to legislate for the nation's future. Thomas Jefferson reflected widespread sentiments when he declared in 1789, "If I could not go to heaven but with a party, I would not go there at all."

Yet despite a belief that parties were evil and posed a threat to enlightened government, political factions gradually coalesced into political parties during Washington's first administration. To build support for his financial program, Alexander Hamilton relied heavily on government patronage. Of 2000 federal officeholders appointed between 1789 and 1801, two-thirds were Federalist party activists, who used positions as postmasters, tax collectors, judges, and customs house officials to favor the interests of the Federalists. By 1794 Hamilton's faction had evolved into the first national political party in history capable of nominating candidates, coordinating votes in Congress, staging public meetings, organizing petition campaigns, and disseminating propaganda.

Hamilton's opponents struck back. James Madison and his ally Thomas Jefferson saw in Hamilton's program an effort to establish the kind of corrupt patronage society that existed in Britain; that is, one with a huge public debt, a standing army, high taxes, and government-subsidized monopolies. Hamilton's aim, declared Jefferson, was to assimilate "the American government to the form and spirit of the British monarchy."

World Events and Political Polarization

World events intensified partisan divisions. On July 14, 1789, the Bastille, a hated royal fortress, was stormed by 20,000 French men and women, an event that marked the beginning of the French Revolution. For three years France experimented with a constitutional monarchy. Then, in 1792, the revolution took a violent turn. In August Austrian and Prussian troops invaded France to put an end to the revolution. French revolutionaries responded by officially deposing King Louis XVI and placing him on trial. He was found guilty and, in January 1793, beheaded. France declared itself a republic and launched a reign of terror against counterrevolutionary elements in the population. Three hundred thousand suspects were arrested; 17,000 were executed. A general war erupted in Europe pitting revolutionary France against a coalition of European monarchies, led by Britain. With two brief interruptions, this war would last 23 years.

Many Americans reacted enthusiastically to the overthrow of the French king and the creation of a French republic. The French people appeared to have joined America in a historic struggle against royal absolutism and aristocratic privilege. More cautious observers expressed horror at the cataclysm sweeping France. The French Revolution, they feared, was not merely a rebellion against royal authority, but a mass assault against property and Christianity. Conservatives urged President Washington to support England in its war against France.

Washington believed that involvement in the European war would weaken the new nation before it had firmly established its own independence. He proposed to keep the country "free from political connections with every other country, to see them independent of all, and under the influence of none." The president, however, faced a problem. During the War for American Independence, The United States had signed an alliance with France (see pp. 149). Washington took the position that while the United States should continue to make payments on its war debts to France, it should refrain from directly supporting the new French republic. In April 1793 he issued a proclamation of neutrality, stating that the "conduct" of the United States would be "friendly and impartial toward the belligerent powers."

1793 and 1794: Years of Crisis

During 1793 and 1794 a series of explosive new controversies further divided the followers of Hamilton and Jefferson: Washington's administration confronted a French effort to entangle America in its war with England, an armed rebellion in western Pennsylvania, several Indian uprisings, and the threat of war with Britain. These controversies intensified party spirit and promoted an increase in voting along party lines in Congress.

Citizen Genêt Affair

In April 1793 "Citizen" Edmond Charles Genêt, minister of the French Republic, arrived in the United States. His mission was to persuade American citizens to join in France's "war of all peoples against all kings." Genêt proceeded to pass out military commissions as part of a plan to attack Spanish New Orleans, and letters authorizing Americans to attack British commercial vessels. Washington regarded these activities as clear violations of U.S. neutrality and demanded that France recall its hotheaded minister. Fearful that he would be executed if he returned to France, Genêt requested and was granted political asylum, bringing his ill-fated mission to an end. However, the Genêt affair did have an important effect—it intensified party feeling. From Vermont to South Carolina, citizens organized Democratic-Republican clubs to celebrate the triumphs of the French Revolution. Hamilton suspected that these societies really existed to stir up grass-roots opposition to the Washington administration. Jefferson hotly denied these accusations, but the practical consequence was to further divide followers of Hamilton and Jefferson.

Whiskey Rebellion

The outbreak of popular protests in western Pennsylvania against Hamilton's financial program further intensified political polarization. To help fund the nation's war debt, Congress in 1791 passed Hamilton's proposal for a whiskey excise tax. Frontier farmers objected to the tax on whiskey as unfair. On the frontier, because of high transportation costs, the only practical way to sell surplus corn was to distill it into whiskey. Thus, frontier farmers regarded a tax on whiskey in the same way as American colonists had regarded Britain's stamp tax.

By 1794 western Pennsylvanians had had enough. Like the Shaysites of 1786, they rose up in defense of their property and the fundamental right to earn a decent living. Some 7000 frontiersmen marched on Pittsburgh to stop collection of the tax. Determined to set a precedent for the federal government's authority, Washington gathered an army of 15,000 militiamen to disperse the rebels. In the face of this overwhelming force, the uprising collapsed. Two men were convicted of treason but later pardoned by the president. The new government had proved that it would enforce laws enacted by Congress.

Thomas Jefferson viewed the Whiskey Rebellion from quite a different perspective. He saw the fiendish hand of Hamilton in putting down what he called a rebellion that "could never be found." Hamilton had "pronounced and proclaimed and

President Washington is reviewing the troops at Fort Cumberland, Maryland. These troops formed part of the force of 15,000 militiamen Washington assembled to disperse the Whiskey Rebellion in western Pennsylvania, a protest against the whiskey excise tax.

Gift of Edgar William and Bernice Chrysler Garbisch, 1963, Metropolitan Museum of Art.

Yellow Fever in Philadelphia: Pills and Politics

DEATH stalked the streets of Philadelphia in 1793 in the form of a yellow fever epidemic. The first case appeared in August, and by the time the epidemic disappeared in November, yellow fever had killed 10 percent of the city's population, while another 45 percent had fled in terror. At the height of the epidemic, Philadelphia was a city under siege, with city services interrupted; communications impaired; the port closed; the economy in shambles; and people locked in their homes, afraid to venture beyond their doorsteps. To make matters worse, the city's leaders—unable to reach agreement on what caused the disease or what should be done to combat it—attacked each other in endless debates. The result was that Philadelphia, America's premiere city, all but shut down.

Philadelphia's plight is not hard to explain, for yellow fever is a pulverizing, terrifying disease. Caused by a virus, the disease is spread by the female mosquito. Yellow fever's early symptoms are nearly identical to those of malaria; the victim feels flush and then develops chills, followed by a sizzling fever, accompanied by a severe headache or backache. The fever lasts for two or three days, and then the patient usually enjoys a remission.

Mild cases of yellow fever stop here. For the less fortunate, however, remission soon gives way to jaundice (hence "yellow" fever), and the victim starts to hallucinate. Massive internal hemorrhaging follows, and the sufferer starts vomiting huge quantities of black blood. Next, the victim goes into a coma. A lucky few emerge from the coma to escape death, but the vast majority die from internal bleeding.

If any American city seemed well equipped to handle a medical crisis, it was Philadelphia. It was the nation's leading center of medicine, home to the prestigious College of Physicians, America's first medical school (1765), and to America's most famous physician, Dr. Benjamin Rush, a founder of the Pennsylvania Society for Promoting the Abolition of Slavery and a signer of the Declaration of Independence. The City of Brotherly Love could also point with pride to Franklin's Pennsylvania Hospital (1752), the first hospital in America and a model facility for the poor.

Yet for all of its luster, Philadelphia's medical community was no match for yellow fever. The basic problem was that doctors in 1793 could not agree on what caused the disease, how it spread, or how to treat it. Many physicians, including Dr. Rush, cited local factors. They blamed the disease on the decaying vegetation and rotting filth that littered Philadelphia's streets and docks, producing an atmospheric "miasma" that was carried by the wind, infecting anyone who breathed its noxious fumes. Rejecting local causes, other physicians argued that yellow fever was a contagious disease. It had been imported to Philadelphia, they insisted, by the 2000 French refugees who had fled the revolution (and a yellow fever epidemic!) in Haiti to seek political asylum in the United States.

Physicians in 1793 had no way of settling the dispute. Those who blamed the epidemic on dirty streets sounded just as believable as those who pointed an accusing finger at sickly foreigners. What made the controversy truly remarkable, however, was the extent to which it became embroiled in politics, for what began as a purely medical debate quickly degenerated into a raging political battle.

With very few exceptions, the doctors who insisted that yellow fever was contagious were Federalists, while the anticontagionists were almost all Jeffersonian Republicans. Taught by the French Revolution to be wary of free-thinking political ideas, Federalist doctors regarded yellow fever as just another unwanted French import. Ablaze with pro-French sympathies, anticontagionist Republicans saw the French refugees as honored friends who brought virtue rather than death. The source of the epidemic, they insisted, lay with unvirtuous filth at their doorsteps.

Partisan leaders tried desperately to bend this medical debate to their political advantage. To Federalists, the doctrine of importation demanded that the United States protect itself from the French menace. Therefore, trade with French West Indian islands should be suspended; French refugees who had gained entry to the United States should be quarantined and future refugees excluded. Republicans, by contrast, denounced these demands as a federal plot to ruin profitable trade with the West Indies and to infect Americans with a new disease—hatred of all things French. Nor was their concern unfounded, for public hysteria was definitely building. At one point, amid persistent rumors that the French had poisoned the public drinking wells in preparation for a full-scale invasion, Philadelphians threatened violence against the innocent refugees.

At the height of the turmoil, politics even influenced how physicians treated the victims of yellow fever. At the beginning of the epidemic, doctors were pretty evenly divided, without regard to politics, into two schools. One prescribed stimulants—quinine bark, wine, and cold baths; while the other recommended bleeding—drawing off huge quantities of the patient's blood. (Dr. Rush had long been an advocate of the bleeding treatment. He recommended removing about four-fifths of the patient's blood supply, more than enough to kill all but the unkillable!)

Alexander Hamilton was personally responsible for converting this medical squabbling into a political issue. After managing to survive an attack of yellow fever, he published a ringing testimonial to the life-saving properties of the bark and wine cure. The treatment had been prescribed, he declared, by Dr. Edward Stevens of Philadelphia, a longtime friend of Hamilton. Dr. Stevens was the only physician in the City of Brotherly Love who was a publicly confessed Federalist.

A few days after his testimonial appeared, Hamilton published a second article in which he ridiculed Dr. Rush's "new treatment." Hamilton's attack was immediately echoed by Federalist editors across the country, and in the wake of their articles, the public came to regard "bark" as the Federalist cure and "bleeding" as the Republican cure.

The controversy over yellow fever raged until the epidemic ended in the fall. Philadelphia's struggle against yellow fever was one of the many times that Americans would infuse their discussions of health problems with nonmedical concerns. In future epidemics, notions of class, race, individual virtue, and even gender would color public discussions of health, just as surely as politics enlivened the medical debate over yellow fever in Philadelphia in 1793 when the republic was young.

armed against" the people for the sheer pleasure of suppressing liberties. And further, Jefferson claimed, Hamilton had done so because westerners no longer supported Washington's administration. He had used the army to stifle legitimate opposition to unfair government policies.

Clearing the Ohio Country of Native Americans

The end of the American Revolution unleashed a mad rush of white settlers into frontier Georgia, Kentucky, Tennessee, Ohio, and western New York. To allow whites to occupy lands in central Georgia, the United States bribed a Creek leader, Alexander McGilvray, to sign a peace treaty in 1790. In New York, following the Revolution, large-scale land acquisitions by whites forced Native Americans to migrate (the Mohawk moved to Canada) or to settle (like the Seneca) on small, impoverished, and unproductive reservations. In Kentucky and Tennessee, clashes between Cherokees, Chickasaws, Shawnees, and frontier settlers between 1784 and 1790 left some 1500 whites dead or captured, but ultimately warfare forced many Native Americans to migrate north of the Ohio River.

To clear the Ohio country, President Washington dispatched three armies. Twice, a confederacy of eight tribes led by Little Turtle, chief of the Miamis, defeated American forces. But, in 1794, a third army defeated the Indian alliance. A 3000-man force under Anthony Wayne overwhelmed 1000 Native Americans at the Battle of Fallen Timbers in northwestern Ohio. Under the Treaty of Greenville (1795), Native Americans ceded much of the present state of Ohio in return for cash and a promise that the federal government would treat the Indian nations fairly in land dealings.

Native Americans responded to the loss of land and declining population in a variety of ways. One response was cultural renewal, the path taken by the Seneca, who lived in upstate New York. Displaced from their traditional lands and suffering the psychological and cultural disintegration brought on by epidemic disease, the Seneca revitalized their culture under the leadership of a prophet named Handsome Lake. Handsome Lake preached a new religion that blended Quaker and traditional Iroquois beliefs, which helped the Seneca adapt to a changing social environment while maintaining many traditional practices and religious tenets. Most strikingly, the prophet endorsed the demand of Quaker missionaries that the traditional Iroquois sexual division of labor emphasizing male hunting and female horticulture be replaced. Instead, men took up farming, even though this had been traditionally viewed as women's work.

Another response to cultural disruption was the formation of loosely knit Indian confederacies. In the Great Lakes region, the Shawnees, Delawares, and other Indian peoples banded together in an effort to resist white expansion, while across the Mississippi, the Chippewas, Fox, Kickapoos, Ottawas, Potawatomis, Sauks, and Sioux formed another confederation. But the ability of these confederacies to obstruct expansion depended on military support from Britain.

The Continuing Threat from Britain

The year 1794 brought a crisis in America's relations with Britain. For a decade, Britain had refused to evacuate forts in the Old Northwest as promised in the treaty ending the Revolution. Control of those forts impeded white settlement of the Great Lakes region and allowed the British to monopolize the fur trade. Frontiersmen believed that British officials at those posts sold firearms to Native Americans and incited uprisings against white settlers. War appeared imminent when British warships stopped 300 American ships carrying food supplies to France and to France's overseas possessions, seized their cargoes, and forced seamen suspected of deserting from British ships into the British navy.

Washington acted decisively to end the crisis. After Anthony Wayne's soldiers overwhelmed Indians at the Battle of Fallen Timbers, the president sent Chief Justice John Jay to London to seek a negotiated settlement with the British. The United States's strongest bargaining chip was a threat to join an alliance of European trading nations to resist British trade restrictions. Alexander Hamilton undercut Jay by secretly informing the British minister that the United States would not join the alliance.

Jay secured the best agreement he could under the circumstances. Britain agreed to evacuate its forts on American soil and promised to cease harassing American ships (provided the ships did not carry contraband to Britain's enemies). Britain agreed to pay damages for the ships it had seized, to permit trade with Indians, and to carry on restricted trade with the British West Indies; however, Jay failed to win concessions on a host of other American grievances, such as British incitement of the Indians and Britain's routine searching of American ships for escaping deserters.

As a result of the debate over Jay's Treaty, the first party system fully emerged. Publication of the terms of the treaty unleashed a storm of protest from the emerging Jeffersonian Republicans. Republican newspapers and pamphlets denounced the treaty as craven submission to British imperial power and to wealthy commercial, shipping, and trading interests.

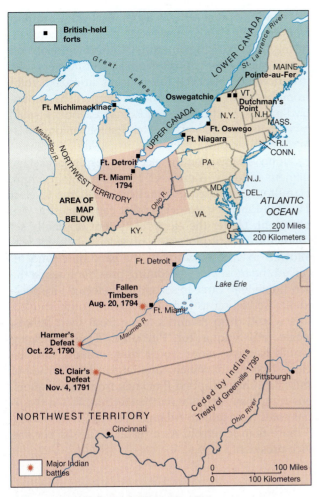

British-held forts

Great Lakes

LOWER CANADA

St. Lawrence River

MAINE

Pointe-au-Fer

Oswegatchie

Ft. Michlimackinac

UPPER CANADA

VT.
Dutchman's Point

N.Y.

N.H.

Ft. Oswego
Ft. Niagara

MASS.

R.I.
CONN.

Ft. Detroit

Ft. Miami
1794

PA.

N.J.

NORTHWEST TERRITORY

Mississippi R.

Ohio R.

MD.

DEL.

ATLANTIC OCEAN

AREA OF MAP BELOW

VA.

KY.

0   200 Miles
0   200 Kilometers

Ft. Detroit

Lake Erie

**Fallen Timbers
Aug. 20, 1794**

Ft. Miami

Maumee R.

**Harmer's Defeat
Oct. 22, 1790**

**St. Clair's Defeat
Nov. 4, 1791**

Pittsburgh

Ceded by Indians
Treaty of Greenville 1795

Ohio River

NORTHWEST TERRITORY

Cincinnati

Major Indian battles

0   100 Miles
0   100 Kilometers

British Posts and Indian Battles

Because Americans still felt threatened by the continuing British refusal to evacuate forts and by Native American uprisings in the Northwest, John Jay, the first chief justice of the United States, was sent to negotiate a treaty with Great Britain.

In New York, a mob pelted Alexander Hamilton with stones. In Boston, graffiti appeared on a wall: "Damn John Jay! Damn everyone who won't damn John Jay!! Damn everyone that won't put lights in his windows and sit up all night damning John Jay!!!"

Washington never anticipated the wave of outrage that greeted his decision to sign the treaty. Republicans accused him of forming an Anglo-American alliance, and they made his last years in office miserable by attacking him for conducting himself like a "tyrant." James Thomson Callender denounced Washington in particularly negative terms: "If ever a nation was debauched by a man, the American Nation has been debauched by Washington. . . . If ever a nation has been deceived by a man,

Angry Republicans denounced John Jay's treaty as submission to British power and hanged his effigy in Charleston, South Carolina.

the American Nation has been deceived by Washington." It was even suggested that he should be impeached because he had overdrawn his $25,000 salary. Privately, Washington complained that he was being compared to the Roman emperor "Nero" and to a "common pickpocket."

They sought to kill the treaty in the House of Representatives by refusing to appropriate the funds necessary to carry out the treaty's terms unless the president submitted all documents relating to the treaty negotiations. Washington refused to comply with the House's request for information, thereby establishing the principle of executive privilege. This precedent gives the chief executive authority to withhold information from Congress on grounds of national security. In the end, fear that rejection of the Jay Treaty would result in disunion or war convinced the House to approve the needed appropriations.

Washington's popularity returned within a few months when he was able to announce that a treaty had been negotiated with Spain opening up the Mississippi River to American trade. Spain, fearing joint British and American action against its American colonies, recognized the Mississippi River as the new nation's western boundary and the 31st parallel (the northern border of Florida) as America's southern boundary. In addition, Pinckney's Treaty (1795)—also known as the Treaty of San Lorenzo—granted Americans the right to navigate the Mississippi River as well as the right to export goods, duty free, through New Orleans, which was still a Spanish city.

Washington Retires

President Washington was now in a position to retire gracefully. He had avoided war, crushed the Native Americans, pushed the British out of western forts, established trade with selected parts of Asia, and opened the Northwest Territory to settlement. In his **Farewell Address,** published in a Philadelphia newspaper in September 1796, Washington warned his countrymen against the growth of partisan divisions. In foreign affairs, he warned against long-term alliances. Declaring the "primary interests" of America and Europe to be fundamentally different, he argued that "it is our true policy to steer clear of permanent alliance with any portion of the foreign world."

A NEW PRESIDENT AND NEW CHALLENGES

Washington's decision to retire set the stage for one of the most critical presidential elections in American history. The election of 1796 was the first in which voters could choose between competing political parties; it was also the first election in which candidates were nominated for the vice presidency. It was a critical test of whether the nation could transfer power through a contested election.

The Federalists chose John Adams, the first vice president, as their presidential candidate, and the Republicans selected Thomas Jefferson. In an effort to attract southern support, the Federalists named Thomas Pinckney of South Carolina as Adams's running mate. The Republicans, hoping to win votes in New York and New England, chose Aaron Burr of New York as their vice presidential nominee.

Both parties appealed directly to the people, rallying supporters through the use of posters, handbills, and mass rallies. Republicans portrayed their candidate as "a firm Republican" while they depicted his opponent as "the champion of rank, titles, and hereditary distinctions." Federalists countered by condemning Jefferson as the leader of a "French faction" intent on undermining religion and morality.

In the popular voting, Federalists drew support from New England; commercial, shipping, manufacturing, and banking interests; Congregational and Episcopalian clergy; professionals; and farmers who produced for markets. Republicans attracted votes from the South and from smaller planters; backcountry Baptists, Methodists, and Roman Catholics; small merchants, tradesmen, and craftsmen; and subsistence farmers.

John Adams won the election, despite backstage maneuvering by Alexander Hamilton against him. Hamilton developed a complicated scheme to elect Thomas Pinckney, the Federalist candidate for vice president. Under the electoral system originally set up by the Constitution, each presidential elector was allowed to vote twice, with the candidate who received the most votes becoming president, while the candidate who came in second was elected vice president. According to Hamilton's plan, southern electors would drop Adams's name from their ballots, while still voting for Pinckney. Thus Pinckney would receive more votes than Adams and be elected president. When New Englanders learned of this plan, they dropped Pinckney from their ballots, ensuring that Adams won the election. When the final votes were tallied, Adams received 71 votes, only 3 more than Jefferson. As a result, Jefferson became vice president.

The Presidency of John Adams

The new president was a 61-year-old Harvard-educated lawyer who had been an early leader in the struggle for independence. Short, bald, overweight, and vain (he was known, behind his back, as "His Rotundity"), **John Adams** had found the vice presidency extremely frustrating. He complained to his wife Abigail: "My country has contrived for me the most insignificant office that ever the invention of man contrived or his imagination conceived."

His presidency also proved frustrating. He had failed to win a decisive electoral mandate and was saddled with the opposition leader as his vice president. He faced intense challenges within his own party and continuing problems from France throughout his four years in office. He avoided outright war with France, but he destroyed his political career in the process.

A New National Capital

John Adams was the first president to live in what would later be called the White House. In 1800 the national capital moved to Washington, D.C., from

John Adams was elected the second president of the United States by only three electoral votes. During his presidency, he strengthened the military and averted war with France.

Philadelphia (in 1790 it had moved to Philadelphia from New York).

In planning the city of Washington, the architect Benjamin Latrobe hoped that "the days of Greece may be revived in the woods of America." Like many other late-eighteenth-century Americans, he hoped to build a country that would emulate the spirit of the ancient Greek and Roman republics.

The White House and the Capitol were designed along classical lines. Greek Revival architecture became the dominant style, influencing the design not only of government buildings but also houses. Many new towns received classical names, such as Syracuse and Troy. Government institutions, like the Senate, also acquired classical names.

When John Adams moved into the unfinished executive mansion, only 6 of the structure's 30 rooms were plastered; the main staircases were not installed for another four years. The mansion's grounds were cluttered with workers' shanties, privies, and stagnant pools of water. The president's wife, Abigail, hung laundry to dry in the East Room.

The nation's Capitol was also uncompleted. Construction of the building's central portion had not even begun. All that stood were the House and Senate wings connected by a covered boardwalk.

The city of Washington consisted of a brewery, a half-finished hotel, an abandoned canal, an empty warehouse and wharf, and 372 "habitable" dwellings, "most of them small miserable huts." Cows and hogs ran freely in the capital's streets, and snakes frequented the city's many bogs and marshes. A bridge, supported by an arch of 13 stones—symbolizing the first 13 states—had collapsed. The entire population consisted of 500 families and some 300 members of government. A visitor saw "no fences, gardens, nor the least appearance of business."

The Quasi War with France

A decade after the Constitution was written, the United States faced its most serious international crisis: an undeclared naval war with France. In Jay's Treaty, France perceived an American tilt toward Britain, especially in the provision permitting the British to seize French goods from American ships in exchange for financial compensation. France retaliated by launching an aggressive campaign against American shipping, particularly in the West Indies, capturing hundreds of vessels flying the United States flag.

Adams attempted to negotiate with France, but the French government refused to receive the American envoy and suspended commercial relations. Adams then called Congress into special session. Determined not to permit the United States to be "humiliated under a colonial spirit of fear and a sense of inferiority," he recommended that Congress arm American merchant ships, purchase new naval vessels, fortify harbors, and expand the artillery and cavalry. To pay for it all, Adams recommended a series of new taxes. By a single vote, a bitterly divided House of Representatives authorized the president to arm American merchant ships, but it postponed consideration of the other defense measures.

Adams then sent three commissioners to France to try to negotiate a settlement. Charles Maurice de Talleyrand, the French foreign minister, continually postponed official negotiations. In the meantime, three emissaries of the French minister (known later simply as X, Y, and Z) said that the only way the Americans could see the minister was to pay a bribe of $250,000 and provide a $10 million loan. The indignant American commissioners refused. When word of the "XYZ affair" became known in the United States, it aroused a popular demand for war. The popular slogan was "millions for defense, but

Abigail Adams supervises the work of a maidservant hanging laundry in the East Room of the White House.

not one cent for tribute." The Federalist-controlled Congress authorized a standing army of 20,000 troops, established a 30,000-man reserve army, and created the nation's first navy department. It also unilaterally abrogated America's 1778 treaty with France.

Adams named George Washington commanding general of the United States Army, and, at Washington's insistence, designated Alexander Hamilton second in command. During the winter of 1798, 14 American warships backed by some 200 armed merchant ships captured some 80 French vessels and forced French warships out of American waters and back to bases in the West Indies. But the president refused to ask Congress for an official declaration of war. Thus, this conflict is known as the quasi war.

Despite intense pressure to declare war against France or to seize territory belonging to France's ally, Spain, President Adams managed to avert a full-scale war and achieve a peaceful settlement. Early in 1799, with the backing of moderate Federalists and Republicans, Adams proposed reestablishing diplomatic relations with France. When more extreme Federalists refused to go along with the plan, Adams threatened to resign and leave the presidency in the hands of Vice President Jefferson.

In 1800, after seven months of wearisome negotiations, negotiators worked out an agreement known as the Convention of 1800. The agreement freed the United States from its alliance with France; in exchange, America forgave $20 million in damages caused by the illegal seizure of American merchant ships during the 1790s.

Adams kept the peace, but at the cost of a second term as president. The more extreme Federalists reacted furiously to the negotiated settlement. Hamil-

ton vowed to destroy Adams: "If we must have an enemy at the head of Government, let it be one whom we can oppose, and for whom we are not responsible."

The Alien and Sedition Acts

During the quasi war, the Federalist-controlled Congress attempted to suppress political opposition and stamp out sympathy for revolutionary France by enacting four laws in 1798 known as the **Alien and Sedition acts.** The Naturalization Act lengthened the period necessary before immigrants could receive citizenship from 5 to 14 years. The Alien Act gave the president the power to imprison or deport any foreigner believed to be dangerous to the United States. The Alien Enemies Act allowed the president to deport enemy aliens in time of war. Finally, the Sedition Act made it a crime to attack the government with "false, scandalous, or malicious" statements or writings. Adams, bitterly unhappy with the "spirit of falsehood and malignity" that threatened to undermine loyalty to the government, signed the measures.

The Alien acts were so broadly written that hundreds of foreign refugees—French intellectuals, Irish nationalists, and English radicals—fled to Europe fearing detention. But it was the Sedition Act that produced the greatest fear within the Republican opposition. Federalist prosecutors and judges used the Sedition Act to attack leading Republican newspapers, securing indictments against 25 people, mainly Republican editors and printers. Ten people were eventually convicted, one a Republican Representative from Vermont.

One of the most notorious uses of the law to suppress dissent took place in July 1798. Luther Bald-

In the early days of the Republic, political dissent sometimes escalated into physical violence. This fight between Republican Matthew Lyon and Federalist Roger Griswold took place on the floor of Congress on February 15, 1798. Lyon was later arrested for violating the Sedition Act by publishing in his newspaper a letter attacking the government.

THE PEOPLE SPEAK

Gabriel's Revolt

In 1800 a group of slaves in Virginia plotted to seize the city of Richmond. Led by a man known as Gabriel, the insurrection was inspired in part by the slave revolt that began in the French colony of St. Domingue (Haiti) in 1791. It was also motivated by the ideals of liberty and natural rights that had led the American colonists to revolt against Britain. About 30 of the accused conspirators were executed, and many others were sold as slaves to Spanish and Portuguese colonies. Here, a visitor to Virginia describes why one of the slaves had decided to participate in Gabriel's revolt.

> In the afternoon I passed by a field in which several poor slaves had lately been executed, on the charge of having an intention to rise against their masters. A lawyer who was present at their trials at Richmond, informed me that on one of them being asked, what he had to say to the court on his defence, he replied, in a manly tone of voice: "I have nothing more to offer than what General Washington would have had to offer, had he been taken by the British and put to trial by them. I have adventured my life in endeavouring to obtain the liberty of my countrymen, and am a willing sacrifice in their cause: and I beg, as a favour, that I may be immediately led to execution. I know that you have pre-determined to shed my blood, why then all this mockery of a trial?"

Source: Robert Sutcliff, *Travels in Some Parts of North America in the Years 1804, 1805, & 1806* (Philadelphia: B. & T. Kite, 1812).

win, the pilot of a garbage scow, was arrested in a Newark, New Jersey, tavern on charges of criminal sedition. While cannons roared through Newark's streets to celebrate a presidential visit to the city, Baldwin was overheard saying "that he did not care if they fired through [the president's] arse." For his drunken remark, Baldwin was arrested, locked up for two months, and fined.

Republicans accused the Federalists of conspiring to subvert fundamental liberties. In Virginia, the state legislature adopted a resolution written by James Madison that advanced the idea that states have the right to determine the constitutionality of federal law, and pronounced the Alien and Sedition acts unconstitutional. Kentucky's state legislature went even further, adopting a resolution written by Thomas Jefferson that declared the Alien and Sedition acts "void and of no force." The Kentucky resolution raised an issue that would grow increasingly important in American politics in the years before the Civil War: Did states have the power to declare acts of Congress null and void? In 1799, however, no other states were willing to go as far as Kentucky and Virginia.

With the Union in danger, violence erupted. In the spring of 1799 German settlers in eastern Pennsylvania rose up in defiance of federal tax collectors. President Adams called out federal troops to suppress the so-called Fries Rebellion. The leader of the rebellion, an auctioneer named John Fries, was captured, convicted of treason, and sentenced to be hanged. Adams followed Washington's example in the Whiskey Rebellion and pardoned Fries, but Republicans feared that the Federalists were prepared to use the nation's army to suppress dissent.

THE REVOLUTION OF 1800

In 1800 the young republic faced another critical test: Could national leadership pass peacefully from one political party to another? Once again, the nation had a choice between John Adams and **Thomas Jefferson.** But this election was more than a contest between two men; it was also a real party contest for control of the national government. Deep substantive and ideological issues divided the two parties and partisan feelings ran deep. Federalists feared that Jefferson would reverse all the accomplishments of the preceding 12 years. A Republican president, they thought, would overthrow the Constitution by returning power to the states, dismantling the army and navy, and overturning Hamilton's financial system.

The Republicans charged that the Federalists, by creating a large standing army, imposing heavy taxes, and using federal troops and the federal courts to suppress dissent, had shown contempt for the liberties of the American people. They worried that the Federalists' ultimate goal was to centralize power in the national government and involve the United States in the European war on the side of Britain.

The contest was one of the most vigorous in American history; emotions ran high. Federalist opponents called Jefferson an "atheist in religion, and a fanatic in politics." They claimed he was a drunkard, an enemy of religion, and the father of numerous mulatto children. Timothy Dwight, the president of Yale, predicted that a Jefferson administration would see "our wives and daughters the victims of legal prostitution; soberly dishonored; speciously polluted."

Jefferson's supporters responded by charging that President Adams was a warmonger, a spendthrift, and a monarchist who longed to reunite Britain with its former colonies. Republicans even claimed that the president had sent General Thomas Pinckney to England to procure four mistresses, two for himself and two for Adams. Adam's response: "I do declare if this be true, General Pinckney has kept them all for himself and cheated me out of my two."

The election was extremely close. The Federalists won all of New England's electoral votes, while the Republicans dominated the South and West. The final outcome hinged on the results in New York. Rural New York supported the Federalists, and Republican fortunes therefore depended on the voting in New York City. There, Jefferson's running mate, **Aaron Burr,** had created the most successful political organization the country had yet seen. Burr organized rallies, established ward committees, and promoted loyal supporters for public office. Burr's efforts paid off; Re-

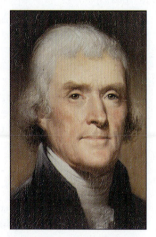

Thomas Jefferson described his election as president in 1800 as a "revolution." His goal was to reverse the centralizing policies of the Federalists.

TABLE 7.1 Election of 1800		
Candidate	**Party**	**Electoral Vote**
T. Jefferson	Republican	73
J. Adams	Federalist	65

publicans won a majority in New York's legislature, thus giving the state's 12 electoral votes to Jefferson and Burr. Declared one Republican: The election "has been conducted . . . in so miraculous a manner that I cannot account for it but from the intervention of a Supreme Power and our friend Burr the agent."

Jefferson appeared to have won by a margin of eight electoral votes. But a complication soon arose. Because each Republican elector had cast one ballot for Jefferson and one for Burr, the two men received exactly the same number of electoral votes.

Under the Constitution, the election was now thrown into the Federalist-controlled House of Representatives. Instead of emphatically declaring that he would not accept the presidency, Burr failed to say anything. So the Federalists faced a choice. They could help elect the hated Jefferson—whom they had called "a brandy-soaked defamer of churches," "a contemptible hypocrite"—or they could throw their support to the opportunistic Burr—considered by Federalists to be "a profligate," "a voluptuary." Hamilton disliked Jefferson, but he believed he was a far more honorable man than Burr, whose "public principles have no other spring or aim than his own aggrandizement." Most other Federalists supported the New Yorker.

As the stalemate persisted, Virginia and Pennsylvania mobilized their state militias. Recognizing "the certainty that a legislative usurpation would be resisted by arms," as Jefferson noted, the Federalists finally backed down. On February 17, 1801, after six days of balloting and 36 ballots, the House of Representatives finally elected Thomas Jefferson the third president of the United States. And as a result of the election, Congress adopted the Twelfth Amendment to the Constitution, by which electors in the Electoral College cast one ballot for president and a separate and distinct ballot for vice president.

CONCLUSION

Sometime between 2:00 A.M. and 3:00 A.M., on December 13, 1799, George Washington woke his wife,

Chronology
OF KEY EVENTS

1789 First session of Congress meets; Electoral College names George Washington the first president; Washington selects the first cabinet; Federal Judiciary Act establishes federal court system; French Revolution begins

1790 Congress adopts Hamilton's proposal to fund the national debt at full value and to assume all state debts from the Revolutionary War

1791 Bank of the United States is established; Congress adopts an excise tax on distilled liquors; the Bill of Rights becomes part of the Constitution

1793 King Louis XVI of France is beheaded and war breaks out in Europe; Washington issues the Proclamation of Neutrality; Citizen Genêt affair

1794 Jay's Treaty with Britain; Whiskey Rebellion in western Pennsylvania; General Anthony Wayne defeats an Indian alliance at the Battle of Fallen Timbers in Ohio

1795 Treaty of Greenville opens Ohio to white settlement; Pinckney's Treaty is negotiated with Spain

1796 Washington issues Farewell Address warning against political factionalism and foreign entanglements

1797 John Adams is inaugurated as second president

1798 Adams reports XYZ Affair to Congress; undeclared naval war with France begins; Alien and Sedition acts give the president the power to imprison or deport dangerous foreigners and make it a crime to attack the government with "malicious" statements or writings; Virginia and Kentucky resolutions, drawn up by Jefferson and Madison, declare the Alien and Sedition acts unconstitutional

1800 Washington, D.C., replaces Philadelphia as the nation's capital; Convention of 1800 supplants treaties of 1778 with France

1801 House of Representatives elects Thomas Jefferson as third president

complaining of severe pains. Martha Washington called for an overseer, who inserted a lancet in the former president's arm and drew blood. Over the course of that day and the next, doctors arrived and attempted to ease General Washington's pain by applying blisters, administering purges, and additional bloodletting—eventually removing perhaps four pints of Washington's blood. Medical historians generally agree that Washington needed a tracheotomy (a surgical operation into the air passages), but this was too new a technique to be risked on the former president, who died on December 14.

During the early weeks of 1800 every city in the United States commemorated the death of the former leader. In Philadelphia, an empty coffin, a riderless horse, and a funeral cortege moved through the city streets. In Boston, business was suspended, cannons roared, bells pealed, and 6000 people—a fifth of the city's population—stood in the streets to express their last respects for the fallen general. In Washington, Richard Henry Lee delivered the most famous eulogy: "First in war, first in peace, and first in the hearts of his countrymen."

In 1789 it was an open question whether the Constitution was a workable plan of government. It was still unclear whether the new nation could establish a strong and vigorous national government or win the respect of foreign nations. For a decade, the new nation battled threats to its existence. It faced bitter party conflict, threats of secession, and foreign interference with American shipping and commerce.

By any standard, the new nation's achievements were impressive. During the first decade under the Constitution, the country adopted a bill of rights, protecting the rights of the individual against the power of the central government; enacted a financial program that secured the government's credit and stimulated the economy; and created the first political parties that directly involved the enfranchised segment of the population in national politics. In the face of intense partisan conflict, the United States became the first nation to transfer peacefully political power from one party to another as a result of an election. A nation, strong and viable, had emerged from its baptism by fire.

Suggestions for Further Reading

Stanley Elkins and Eric McKitrick, *The Age of Federalism: The Early American Republic, 1788–1800* (1993). Examines the major political and diplomatic controversies of the period from the beginning of the U.S. government under the Constitution to Thomas Jefferson's election as president.

James Roger Sharp, *American Politics in the Early Republic: The New Nation in Crisis* (1993). Vividly recaptures the atmosphere of passion, suspicion, and fear that marked the country's first 12 years under the new Constitution.

Overviews and Surveys

Jacob E. Cooke, "The Federalist Age: A Reappraisal," in George A. Billias and Gerald N. Grob, eds., *American History: Retrospect and Prospect* (1971); John R. Howe, *From the Revolution Through the Age of Jackson* (1973); Seymour M. Lipset, *The First New Nation: The United States in Perspective* (1963); John C. Miller, *The Federalist Era, 1789–1801* (1960); Robert E. Shalhope, *The Roots of Democracy: American Thought and Culture, 1760–1800* (1990).

Implementing the Constitution

Margo J. Anderson, *The American Census: A Social History* (1988); Richard R. Beeman, *The Old Dominion and the New Nation, 1788–1801* (1972); Thomas E. Cronin, ed., *Inventing the American Presidency* (1989); Noble Cunningham, Jr., *The United States in 1800: Henry Adams Revisited* (1988); Richard H. Kohn, *Eagle and Sword: The Federalists and the Creation of the Military Establishment in America, 1783–1802* (1975); Forrest McDonald, *The Presidency of George Washington* (1974); Carl Prince, *The Federalists and the Origins of the U.S. Civil Service* (1977); John Rhodehamel, *The Great Experiment: George Washington and the American Republic* (1998); Robert A. Rutland, *The Birth of the Bill of Rights, 1776–1791* (1955); Barry Schwartz, *George Washington: The Making of an American Symbol* (1987); Bernard Schwartz, *The Great Rights of Mankind: A History of the American Bill of Rights* (1977); Gerald Stourzh, *Alexander Hamilton and the Idea of Republican Government* (1970); Leonard D. White, *The Federalists: A Study in Administrative History* (1948).

The Birth of Political Parties

Harry Ammon, *The Genêt Mission* (1973); Joyce Appleby, *Capitalism and a New Social Order: The Republican Vision of the 1790s* (1984); James M. Banner, *To the Hartford Convention: The Federalists and the Origins of Party Politics in Massachusetts, 1789–1815* (1970); Lance Banning, *The Jeffersonian Persuasion* (1978); Richard Beeman, *The Old Dominion and the New Nation, 1788–1801* (1972); Samuel Flagg Bemis, *Jay's Treaty* (1923), and *Pinckney's Treaty* (1926); Doron Ben-Atar and Barbara B. Oberg, *Federalists Reconsidered* (1998); Steven R. Boyd, ed., *The Whiskey Rebellion* (1985); Richard Buel, Jr., *Securing the Revolution: Ideology in American Politics, 1789–1815* (1972); William N. Chambers, *Political Parties in a New Nation* (1963); Joseph Charles, *The Origins of the American Party System* (1956); Jerald A. Combs, *The Jay Treaty* (1970); Noble E. Cunningham, Jr., *The Jeffersonian Republicans: The Formation of Party Organization, 1789–1801* (1957); David Brion Davis, *Revolutions: Reflections on American Equality and Foreign Liberations* (1990); Alexander De Conde, *Entangling Alliance: Politics and Diplomacy Under George Washington* (1958); Felix Gilbert, *To the Farewell Address* (1961); Paul Goodman, *The Democratic-Republicans of Massachusetts* (1964); Sanford W. Higginbotham, *The Keystone in the Democratic Arch: Pennsylvania Politics, 1800–1816* (1952); John F. Hoadley, *Origins of American Political Parties, 1789–1803* (1986); Ronald Hoffman and Peter J. Albert, eds., *Launching the "Extended Republic": The Federalist Era* (1996); Richard Hofstadter, *The Idea of a Party System: The Rise of Legitimate Opposition in the United States, 1780–1840* (1969); Lawrence S. Kaplan, *Jefferson and France: An Essay on Politics and Political Ideas* (1967); Eugene P. Link, *Democratic-Republican Societies, 1790–1800* (1942); Gilbert L. Lycan, *Alexander Hamilton and American Foreign Policy: A Design for Greatness* (1970); Conor Cruise O'Brien, *The Long Affair: Thomas Jefferson and the French Revolution* (1996); Carl E. Prince, *New Jersey's Jeffersonian Republicans* (1967); Norman Risjord, *Chesapeake Politics, 1781–1800* (1978); Arthur M. Schlesinger, Jr., ed., *History of United States Political Parties, Volume I: 1798–1860: From Factions to Parties* (1973); Bernard Schwartz, *The Great Rights of Mankind: A History of the American Bill of Rights* (1977); Louis M. Sears, *George Washington and the French Revolution* (1960); Thomas P. Slaughter, *The Whiskey Rebellion* (1986); James Morton Smith, *Freedom's Fetters: The Alien and Sedition Laws and American Civil Liberties* (1956); Paul A. Varg, *Foreign Policies of the Founding Fathers* (1963); Patricia Watlington, *The Partisan Spirit* (1972); Alfred F. Young, *The Democratic Republicans of New York* (1967); John Zvesper, *Political Philosophy and Rhetoric: A Study of the Origins of American Party Politics* (1977).

A New President and New Challenges

Ralph Adams Brown, *The Presidency of John Adams* (1975); Manning J. Dauer, *The Adams Federalists* (1953); Alexander De Conde, *The Quasi-War: Politics and Diplomacy of the Undeclared War with France, 1797–1801* (1966); John R. Howe, *The Changing Political Thought of John Adams* (1966); Lawrence S. Kaplan, *Colonies into Nation: American Diplo-*

macy, 1763–1801 (1972); Stephen G. Kurtz, *The Presidency of John Adams: The Collapse of Federalism, 1795–1800* (1957); Leonard W. Levy, *Legacy of Suppression: Freedom of Speech and Press in Early American History* (1960); John C. Miller, *Crisis in Freedom: The Alien and Sedition Acts* (1951); John R. Nelson, *Liberty and Property: Political Economy and Policymaking in the New Nation* (1987); Bradford Perkins, *The First Rapprochement: England and the United States, 1795–1805* (1955); Peter Shaw, *The Character of John Adams* (1976); William Stinchcombe, *The XYZ Affair* (1980).

The Revolution of 1800

David Hackett Fischer, *The Revolution of American Conservatism: The Federalist Party in the Era of Jeffersonian Democracy* (1965); Robert M. Johnstone, Jr., *Jefferson and the Presidency: Leadership in the Young Republic* (1978); Linda K. Kerber, *Federalists in Dissent* (1970); A. M. Schlesinger, Jr., and Fred L. Israel, eds., *History of American Presidential Elections, 1789–1968* (1971); Daniel Sisson, *The American Revolution of 1800* (1974).

Biographies

Charles Akers, *Abigail Adams: An American Woman* (1980); Irving Brant, *James Madison*, 6 vols. (1941–1961); Fawn M. Brodie, *Thomas Jefferson: An Intimate History* (1974); Richard Brookhiser, *Alexander Hamilton* (1999), and *Founding Father: Rediscovering George Washington* (1996); Jacob Ernest Cooke, *Alexander Hamilton* (1982); Marcus Cunliffe, *George Washington: Man and Monument* (1958); Noble E. Cunningham, Jr., *In Pursuit of Reason: The Life of Thomas Jefferson* (1987); James Thomas Flexner, *George Washington*, 4 vols. (1965–1972); Douglas Southall Freeman, *George Washington: A Biography*, 7 vols. (1948–1957); Ralph Ketcham, *James Madison* (1971); Phyllis Lee Levin, *Abigail Adams* (1987); Milton Lomask, *Aaron Burr*, 2 vols. (1979–1982); Paul K. Longmore, *Invention of George Washington* (1988); Dumas Malone, *Jefferson and His Time*, 6 vols. (1948–1981); John C. Miller, *Alexander Hamilton* (1959); Broadus Mitchell, *Alexander Hamilton*, 2 vols. (1957–1962); Merrill Peterson, *The Jefferson Image in the American Mind* (1960), and *Thomas Jefferson and the New Nation* (1970); William M. S. Rasmussen and Robert S. Tilton, *George Washington* (1999); Lynne Withey, *Dearest Friend: A Life of Abigail Adams* (1981).

INTERNET RESOURCES

The Electoral College
http://www.nara.gov/fedreg/ec-hmpge.html
This National Archives and Records Administration site explains how the electoral college works.

George Washington Papers
http://www.virginia.edu/~gwpapers/
Information on the publishing project, with selected documents, essays, and an index of the published volumes.

George Washington at Home
http://www.mountvernon.org/
Pictures and documents of Mount Vernon, the home of the first president, George Washington.

George Washington Papers at the Library of Congress, 1741–1799
http://memory.loc.gov/ammem/gwhtml/gwhome.html
This site, "the complete George Washington Papers from the Manuscript Division at the Library of Congress consists of approximately 65,000 documents. This is the largest collection of original Washington documents in the world."

White House Historical Association
http://www.whitehousehistory.org/whha/default.asp
This site contains a timeline of the history of the White House and several interesting photos and links.

John Adams
http://www.whitehouse.gov/WH/glimpse/presidents/html/ja2.html
This site contains biographical information about the second president, his inaugural address, and links to his more quotable phrases.

KEY TERMS

Bill of Rights   (p. 193)
Cabinet   (p. 193)
Alexander Hamilton   (p. 194)
Strict Construction   (p. 194)
Implied Powers   (p. 194)
Loose Interpretation   (p. 194)
Bank of the United States   (p. 195)
Federalists   (p. 196)
Republicans   (p. 196)
Farewell Address   (p. 202)
John Adams   (p. 202)
Alien and Sedition Acts   (p. 204)
Thomas Jefferson   (p. 205)
Aaron Burr   (p. 206)

REVIEW QUESTIONS

1. What were the most serious problems facing the new nation when George Washington became president?

2. What strengths and skills did George Washington bring to the presidency?

3. What measures did Alexander Hamilton propose to create a strong central government and a prospering economy? Why did his opponents oppose these measures?

4. Which set of ideas and programs—Alexander Hamilton's or Thomas Jefferson's—best addressed the new country's needs?

5. Why did George Washington warn against permanent alliances and party divisions in his Farewell Address?

6. Why did Congress enact the Alien and Sedition Acts? Why did the Jeffersonians oppose these measures?

REPUBLICANS

Turn out, turn out and save your Country from ruin !

From an *Emperor*—from a *King*—from the iron grasp of a *British Tory Faction*—an unprincipled banditti of British speculators. The hireling tools and emissaries of his majesty king George the 3d have thronged our city and diffused the poison of principles among us.

DOWN WITH THE TORIES, DOWN WITH THE BRITISH FACTION,

Before they have it in their power to enslave you, and reduce your families to distress by heavy taxation. Republicans want no Tribute-liars—they want no ship Ocean-liars—they want no Rufus King's for Lords —they want no Varick to lord it over them—they want no Jones for senator, who fought with the British against the Americans in time of the war.—But they want in their places such men as

Jefferson & Clinton,

who fought their Country's Battles in the year '76

8

THE JEFFERSONIANS IN POWER, 1800–1815

"A dangerous man"

On the morning of June 18, 1804, a visitor handed a package to former treasury secretary Alexander Hamilton. Inside was a newspaper clipping and a terse three-sentence letter. The clipping said that Hamilton had called Vice President Aaron Burr "a dangerous man, and one who ought not to be trusted with the reins of government." It went on to say that Hamilton had "expressed" a "still more despicable opinion" of Burr—apparently a bitter personal attack on Burr's public and private morality, not merely a political criticism. The letter, signed by Burr, demanded a "prompt and unqualified" denial or an immediate apology.

Hamilton and Burr had sparred verbally for decades. Hamilton regarded Burr as an unscrupulous man and considered him partly responsible for a duel in 1801 that had left his son Philip dead. Burr, in turn, blamed Hamilton for his defeat in the race for governor of New York earlier in the year. When, after three weeks, Hamilton had failed to respond to his letter satisfactorily, Burr insisted that they settle the dispute according to the code of honor.

Shortly after 7 A.M., on July 11, 1804, Burr and Hamilton met on the wooded heights of Weehawken, New Jersey, a customary dueling ground directly across the Hudson River from New York. Hamilton's son died there in a duel in 1801.

Hamilton's second handed Burr one of two pistols equipped with hair-spring triggers. After he and Burr took their positions ten paces apart, Hamilton raised his pistol on the command to "Present!" and fired. His shot struck a tree a few feet to Burr's side. Then Burr fired. His shot struck Hamilton in the right side and passed through his liver. Hamilton died the following day.

The popular view was that Hamilton had intentionally fired to one side, while Burr had slain the Federalist leader in an act of cold-blooded murder. In fact, historians do not know whether Burr was guilty of willful murder. Burr had no way of knowing whether Hamilton had purposely missed. Hamilton, after all, had accepted the challenge, raised his pistol, and fired. According to the code of honor, if Burr missed on his first try, Hamilton would have a second chance to shoot.

The states of New York and New Jersey wanted to try Burr for murder; New Jersey actually indicted him. The vice president fled through New Jersey by foot and wagon to Philadelphia, then took refuge in Georgia and South Carolina, until the indictments were quashed and he could finish his term in office.

The Jeffersonian era—the period stretching from 1800 to 1815—was rife with conflict, partisan passion, and larger-than-life personalities. On the domestic front, a new political party, the Republicans, came to office for the first time and a former vice president was charged with treason against his coun-

On July 11, 1804, Vice President Aaron Burr critically wounded Alexander Hamilton in a duel.

try. The era was also marked by foreign policy challenges. Pirates, operating from bases on the coast of North Africa, harassed American shipping and enslaved American sailors. Britain and France interfered with American shipping. Finally, the United States once again waged war with Britain, the world's strongest power. These developments raised profound questions: Could the country peacefully transfer political power from one party to another? Could the country preserve political stability? And most important of all, could the nation preserve its neutral rights and national honor in the face of grave threats from Britain and France?

Republicans celebrated Thomas Jefferson's victory in the election of 1800 with a flag inscribed: "T. Jefferson President . . . John Adams no more."

JEFFERSON TAKES COMMAND

Thomas Jefferson's goal as president was to restore the principles of the American Revolution. In his view, a decade of Federalist party rule had threatened republican government. Not only had the Federalists levied oppressive taxes, stretched the provisions of the Constitution, and established a bastion of wealth and special privilege in the creation of a national bank, they also had subverted civil liberties and expanded the powers of the central government at the expense of the states. A new revolution was necessary, "as real a revolution in the principles of our government as that of 1776 was in its form." What was needed was a return to basic republican principles.

Beginning with his very first day in office, Jefferson sought to demonstrate his administration's commitment to republican principles. At noon, March 4, 1801, Jefferson, clad in clothes of plain cloth, walked from a nearby boardinghouse to the new United States Capitol in Washington. Without ceremony, he entered the Senate chamber and took the presidential oath of office. In his inaugural address Jefferson sought to allay fear that he planned a Republican reign of terror. "We are all Republicans," he said, "we are all Federalists." Echoing George Washington's Farewell Address, he asked his listeners to set aside partisan and sectional differences and remember that "every difference of opinion is not a difference of principle." He also laid out the principles that would guide his presidency: a frugal, limited government; reduction of the public debt; respect for states' rights; encouragement of agriculture; and a limited role for government in peoples' lives. He committed his administration to repealing oppressive taxes,

slashing government expenses, cutting military expenditures, and paying off the public debt.

Who Was Thomas Jefferson?

In 1962 President John F. Kennedy hosted a White House dinner for America's Nobel Laureates. He told the assemblage that this was "probably the greatest concentration of talent and genius in this house except perhaps for those times when Thomas Jefferson ate alone."

Thomas Jefferson, the nation's third president, was a man of many talents. Though best known for his political accomplishments, he was also an architect, inventor, philosopher, planter, scientist, and talented violinist. Jefferson was an extremely complex man, and his life was filled with apparent inconsistencies. An idealist who repeatedly denounced slavery, the "Apostle of Liberty" owned 200 slaves when he wrote the Declaration of Independence and freed only five slaves at the time of his death. A vigorous opponent of all forms of human tyranny and staunch defender of human equality, he adopted a patronizing attitude toward women, declaring that their proper role was to "soothe and clam the minds of their husbands." Yet Jefferson remains this country's most eloquent exponent of democratic principles. A product of the Enlightenment, Jefferson was a stalwart defender of political freedom, equality, and re-

THE PEOPLE SPEAK

Religion in the Early Republic

During the late eighteenth and early nineteenth centuries, America's churches were deprived of state tax support. Nevertheless, church membership soared, largely due to the success of religious revivals in converting thousands of Americans. Peter Cartwright (1785–1872), a Methodist minister in frontier Kentucky, Tennessee, and Illinois, describes the revival at Cane Ridge, Kentucky, which touched off a wave of revivals that continued until the Civil War. In 1846, Cartwright ran for Congress in Illinois but was defeated by a young Springfield attorney named Abraham Lincoln.

> Somewhere between 1800 and 1801, in the upper part of Kentucky, at a memorable place called "Cane Ridge," there was appointed a sacramental meeting by some of the Presbyterian ministers, at which meeting, seemingly unexpected by ministers or people, the mighty power of God was displayed in a very extraordinary manner; many were moved to tears, and bitter and loud crying for mercy. The meeting was protracted for weeks. Ministers of almost all denominations flocked in from far and near.

The meeting was kept up by night and day. Thousands heard of the mighty work, and came on foot, on horseback, in carriages and wagons. It was supposed that there were in attendance at times during the meeting from twelve to twenty-five thousand people. Hundreds fell prostrate under the mighty power of God, as men slain in battle. Stands were erected in the woods from which preachers of different Churches proclaimed repentance toward God and faith in our Lord Jesus Christ, and it was supposed, by eye and ear witnesses, that between one and two thousand souls were happily and powerfully converted to God during the meeting. It was not unusual for one, two, three, and four to seven preachers to be addressing the listening thousands at the same time from the different stands erected for the purpose. The heavenly fire spread in almost every direction. It was said, by truthful witnesses, that at times more than one thousand persons broke into loud shouting all at once, and that the shouts could be heard for miles around.

From this camp-meeting, for so it ought to be called, the news spread through all the Churches, and through all the land, and it excited great wonder and surprise; but it kindled a religious flame that spread all over Kentucky and through many other states. And I may here be permitted to say, that this was the first camp-meeting ever held in the United States, and here our camp-meetings took their rise.

Source: W. P. Strickland, ed., *Autobiography of Peter Cartwright, The Backwoods Preacher* (New York: Carlton & Porter, 1856), 30–33.

ligious and intellectual freedom. He was convinced that the yeoman farmer, who worked the land, provided the backbone of democracy. He popularized the idea that a democratic republic required an enlightened and educated citizenry and that government has a duty to assist in the education of a meritocracy based on talent and ability.

Jefferson's Goal: To Restore Republican Government

As president, Jefferson strove to return the nation to republican values. Through his personal conduct and public policies he sought to return the country to the principles of democratic simplicity, economy, and limited government. He took a number of steps to rid the White House of aristocratic customs that had prevailed during the administrations of Washington and Adams. He introduced the custom of having guests shake hands instead of bowing stiffly; he also placed dinner guests at a round table, so that no individual would sit in a more important place than any other. In an effort to discourage a "cult of personality," he refused to sanction public celebrations of his birthday declaring, "The only birthday I ever commemorate is that of our Independence, the Fourth of July." Jefferson also repudiated certain "monarchical practices" that had marked the Washington and Adams presidencies. Jefferson refused to ride in an elegant coach or host elegant dinner parties and balls and wore clothes made of homespun cloth. To dramatize his disdain for pomp and pageantry, he received the British minister in his dressing gown and slippers.

Jefferson believed that presidents should not try to impose their will on Congress, and consequently he refused on policy grounds to initiate legislation openly or to veto congressional bills. Convinced that presidents Washington and Adams had acted like British monarchs by personally appearing before Congress and requesting legislation, Jefferson simply sent Congress written messages. Not until the presi-

One of Thomas Jefferson's inventions was this polygraph machine, which made copies of Jefferson's letters as he wrote them.

ment officials, Jefferson ordered publication of a register of all federal employees.

In one area Jefferson felt his hands were tied. He considered the Bank of the United States "the most deadly" institution to republican government. But Hamilton's bank had been legally chartered for 20 years and Jefferson's secretary of the treasury, Albert Gallatin, said that the bank was needed to provide credit for the nation's growing economy. So Jefferson allowed the bank to continue to operate, but he weakened its influence by distributing the federal government's deposits among 21 state banks. "What is practicable," Jefferson commented, "must often control pure theory."

Contemporaries were astonished by the sight of a president who had renounced all the practical tools of government: an army, a navy, and taxes. Jefferson's actions promised, said a British observer, "a sort of Millennium in government." Jefferson's goal was, indeed, to create a new kind of government, a republican government wholly unlike the centralized, corrupt, patronage-ridden one against which Americans had rebelled in 1776.

Reforming the Federal Government

Jefferson thought that one of the major obstacles to restoring republican government was the 3000 Federalist officeholders. Of the first 600 political appointees named to federal office by presidents Washington and Adams, all but 6 were Federalists. Even after learning of his defeat, Adams appointed Federalists to every vacant government position. His most dramatic postelection appointment was naming **John Marshall,** a Federalist, chief justice of the Supreme Court.

Jefferson was committed to the idea that government office should be filled on the basis of merit, not political connections. Only government officeholders guilty of malfeasance or incompetence should be fired. Nothing more should be asked of government officials, he felt, than that they be honest, able, and loyal to the Constitution. Jefferson wholly rejected the idea that a victorious political party had a right to fill public offices with loyal party supporters.

Although many Republicans felt that Federalists should be replaced by loyal Republicans, Jefferson declared that he would remove only "midnight" appointees who had been named to office by President Adams after he learned of his electoral defeat.

War on the Judiciary

When Thomas Jefferson took office, not a single Republican was serving as a federal judge. In Jeffer-

dency of Woodrow Wilson would another president publicly address Congress and call for legislation.

Jefferson matched his commitment to republican simplicity with an emphasis on economy in government. His ideal was "a wise and frugal Government, which shall . . . leave [Americans] free to regulate their own pursuits of industry and improvement." He slashed army and navy expenditures, cut the budget, eliminated taxes on whiskey, houses, and slaves, and fired all federal tax collectors. He reduced the army to 3000 soldiers and 172 officers, the navy to 6 frigates, and foreign legations to 3—in Britain, France, and Spain. His budget cuts allowed him to cut the federal debt by a third, despite the elimination of all internal taxes.

Jefferson did not conceive of government in entirely negative terms. Convinced that ownership of land and honest labor in the earth were the firmest bases of political stability, Jefferson persuaded Congress to cut the price of public lands and extend credit to purchasers in order to encourage landownership and rapid western settlement. A firm believer in the idea that America should be the "asylum" for "oppressed humanity," he moved Congress to reduce the residence requirement for citizenship from 14 to 5 years. In the interest of protecting civil liberties, he allowed the Sedition Act to expire in 1801, freed all people imprisoned under the act, and refunded their fines. And finally, to ensure that the public knew the names and number of all govern-

son's view, the Federalists had prostituted the federal judiciary into a branch of their political party and intended to use the courts to frustrate Republican plans. "From that battery," said Jefferson, "all the works of republicanism are to be beaten down and erased."

The first major political battle of Jefferson's presidency involved his effort to weaken Federalist control of the federal judiciary. The specific issue that provoked Republican anger was the **Judiciary Act of 1801,** which was passed by Congress five days before Adams's term expired. The law created 16 new federal judgeships, positions which Adams promptly filled with Federalists. Even more damaging from a Republican perspective, the act strengthened the power of the central government by extending the jurisdiction of the federal courts over bankruptcy and land disputes, which were previously the exclusive domain of state courts. Finally, the act reduced the number of Supreme Court justices effective with the next vacancy, delaying Jefferson's opportunity to name a new Supreme Court justice.

Jefferson's supporters in Congress repealed the Judiciary Act, but the war over control of the federal courts continued. One of Adams's "midnight appointments" to a judgeship was William Marbury, a loyal Federalist. Although approved by the Senate, Marbury never received his letter of appointment from Adams. When Jefferson became president, Marbury demanded that the new secretary of state, James Madison, issue the commission. Madison refused and Marbury sued, claiming that under section 13 of the Judiciary Act of 1789, the Supreme Court had the power to issue a court order that would compel Madison to give him his judgeship.

The case threatened to provoke a direct confrontation between the judiciary on the one hand and the executive and legislative branches of the federal government on the other. If the Supreme Court ordered Madison to give Marbury his judgeship, the secretary of state was likely to ignore the Court, and Jeffersonians in Congress might try to limit the high court's power. This is precisely what had happened in 1793 when the Supreme Court had ruled that a state might be sued in federal court by nonresidents. Congress had retaliated by initiating the Eleventh Amendment, which restricted such suits.

In his opinion in **_Marbury_ v. _Madison,_** John Marshall, the new chief justice of the Supreme Court, ingeniously expanded the court's power without directly provoking the Jeffersonians. Marshall conceded that Marbury had a right to his appointment but ruled the Court had no authority to order the secretary of state to act, since the section of the Judiciary Act that gave the Court the power to issue an order was unconstitutional. "A law repugnant to the constitution is void," Marshall declared. "It is emphatically the province and duty of the judicial department to say what the law is." For the first time, the Supreme Court had declared an act of Congress unconstitutional.

Marbury v. _Madison_ was a landmark in American constitutional history. The decision firmly established the power of the federal courts to review the constitutionality of federal laws and to invalidate acts of Congress when they are determined to conflict with the Constitution. This power, known as **judicial review,** provides the basis for the important place that the Supreme Court occupies in American life today.

John Marshall, the fourth chief justice of the United States, expanded the Court's power in _Marbury_ v. _Madison_ by establishing the right of judicial review. He thus gave the federal courts the power to determine the constitutionality of federal laws and congressional acts.

Marshall's decision in _Marbury_ v. _Madison_ intensified Republican party distrust of the courts. Impeachment, Jefferson and his followers believed, was the only way to be rid of judges they considered unfit or overly partisan and make the courts responsive to the public will. "We shall see who is master of the ship," declared one Jeffersonian. "Whether men appointed for life or the immediate representatives of the people . . . are to give laws to the community." Federalists responded by accusing the administration of endangering the independence of the federal judiciary.

Three weeks before the Court handed down its decision in _Marbury_ v. _Madison,_ congressional Republicans launched impeachment proceedings against Federal District Judge John Pickering of New Hampshire. An alcoholic, who may have been insane, Pickering was convicted and removed from office.

On the day of Pickering's conviction, the House voted to impeach Supreme Court Justice Samuel Chase, a staunch Federalist and a signer of the Declaration of Independence. From the bench, he had openly denounced equal rights and universal suffrage and accused the Jeffersonians of atheism and being power hungry. Undoubtedly, Chase was guilty of unrestrained partisanship and injudicious statements. An irate President Jefferson called for Chase's impeachment.

Chase was put on trial for holding opinions "hurtful to the welfare of the country." But the real issue was whether Chase had committed an impeachable offense, since the Constitution specified that a judge could be removed from office only for "treason, bribery, or other high crimes" and not for partisanship or judicial misconduct. In a historic decision that helped to guarantee the independence of the judiciary, the Senate voted to acquit Chase. Although a majority of the Senate found Chase guilty, seven Republicans broke ranks and denied Jefferson the two-thirds majority needed for a conviction. "Impeachment is a farce which will not be tried again," Jefferson commented.

Chase's acquittal had momentous consequences for the future. If the Jeffersonians had succeeded in removing Chase, they would probably have removed other Federalist judges from the federal bench. However, since Chase's acquittal, no further attempts have ever been made to remove federal judges solely on the grounds of partisanship or to reshape the federal courts through impeachment. Despite the Republicans' active hostility toward an independent judiciary, the Supreme Court had emerged as a vigorous third branch of government.

International Conflict

In his inaugural address, Thomas Jefferson declared that his fondest wish was for peace. "Peace is my passion," he repeatedly insisted. As president, however, Jefferson was unable to realize his wish. Like Washington and Adams before him, Jefferson faced the difficult task of preserving American independence and neutrality in a world torn by war and revolution.

The Barbary Pirates

Jefferson's first major foreign policy crisis came from the "Barbary pirates" who preyed on American shipping off the coast of North Africa. In 1785, Algerian pirates boarded an American merchant schooner sailing off the coast of Portugal, took its 21-member crew to Algeria, and enslaved them for twelve years. During the next eight years, 100 more American hostages were seized from American ships. In 1795 Congress approved a $1 million ransom for their release, and by 1800, one-fifth of all federal revenues went to the North African states as tribute.

Early in Jefferson's first term, he refused to pay additional tribute. Determined to end the humiliating demands, he sent warships to the Mediterranean to enforce a blockade of Tripoli. The result was a pro-

Barbary States

Thomas Jefferson's first foreign policy crisis occurred when he refused to pay tribute to the Barbary States for the release of hostages captured by Algerian pirates. Instead, he sent eight ships to enforce a blockade of Tripoli.

Burning of the *Philadelphia*

To avenge the capture of 307 crew members of the U.S. frigate *Philadelphia*, Lt. Stephen Decatur, Jr., and a small band of sailors boarded the ship and set it afire in 1804.

The American Flag was raised over New Orleans in 1803 after the Louisiana Purchase.

tracted conflict with Tripoli, which lasted until 1805. Tripoli eventually agreed to make peace, though the United States continued to pay other Barbary states until 1816.

The Louisiana Purchase

At the same time that conflict raged with the Barbary pirates, a more serious crisis loomed on the Mississippi River. In 1795 Spain granted western farmers the right to ship their produce down the Mississippi River to New Orleans, where their cargoes of corn, whiskey, and pork were loaded aboard ships bound for the east coast and foreign ports. In 1800 Spain secretly ceded the Louisiana territory to France and closed the port of New Orleans to American farmers. Westerners, left without a port from which to export their goods, exploded with anger. Many demanded war.

The prospect of French control of the Mississippi alarmed Jefferson. Spain had held only a weak and tenuous grip on the Mississippi, but France was a much stronger power. Jefferson feared the establishment of a French colonial empire in North America blocking American expansion. The United States appeared to have only two options: diplomacy or war.

The president sent James Monroe to join Robert Livingston, the American minister to France, with instructions to purchase New Orleans and as much of the Gulf Coast as they could for $2 million. Circumstances played into American hands when France failed to suppress a slave rebellion in Haiti. One hundred thousand slaves, inspired by the French Revolution, had revolted, destroying 1200 coffee and 200 sugar plantations. In 1800 France sent troops to crush the insurrection and reconquer Haiti, but they met a determined resistance led by a former slave named **Toussaint Louverture.** Then, they were wiped out by mosquitoes carrying yellow fever. "Damn sugar, damn coffee, damn colonies," Napoleon exclaimed. Without Haiti, which he regarded as the centerpiece of an American empire, Napoleon had little interest in keeping Louisiana.

Two days after Monroe's arrival, the French finance minister unexpectedly announced that France was willing to sell not just New Orleans but all of Louisiana Province, a territory extending from Canada to the Gulf of Mexico and westward as far as the Rocky Mountains. The American negotiators agreed on a price of $15 million, or about 4 cents an acre.

Since the Constitution did not give the president specific authorization to purchase land, Jefferson considered asking for a constitutional amendment empowering the government to acquire territory. In Congress, Federalists bitterly denounced the purchase, fearing that the creation of new western states

On his expedition with Meriwether Lewis to explore the Louisiana Territory, William Clark kept a detailed journal of field notes and drawings. This drawing shows how the Chinook Indians flattened their infants' heads by binding them between two boards.

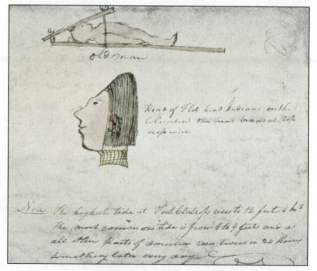

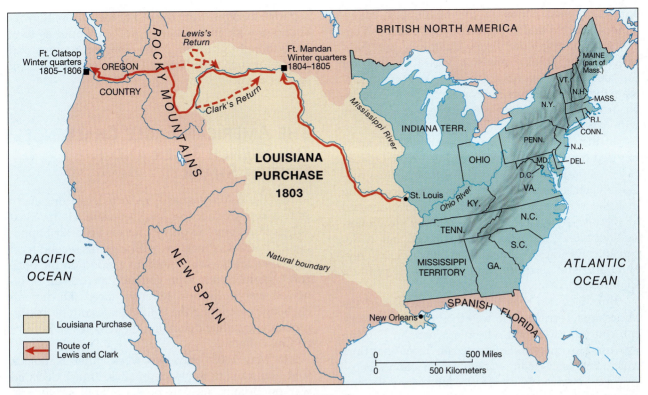

The Louisiana Purchase and Route of Lewis and Clark

No one realized how much territory Jefferson had acquired through the Louisiana Purchase until Lewis and Clark explored the far West.

would weaken the influence of their party. In the end Jefferson, fearing that Napoleon might change his mind, simply sent the agreement to the Senate, which ratified it. "The less said about any constitutional difficulty, the better," he stated. In a single stroke, Jefferson had doubled the size of the country.

To gather information about the geography, natural resources, wildlife, and peoples of Louisiana, President Jefferson dispatched an expedition led by his private secretary Meriwether Lewis and William Clark, a Virginia-born military officer. For 2 years Lewis and Clark led some 30 soldiers and 10 civilians up the Missouri River as far as present-day central North Dakota and then west to the Pacific.

Disunionist Conspiracies

Anger over the acquisition of Louisiana led some Federalists to consider secession as a last resort to restore their party's former dominance. One group of Federalist congressmen plotted to establish a "Northern Confederacy," which would consist of New Jersey, New York, the New England states, and Canada.

Alexander Hamilton repudiated this scheme, and the conspirators turned to Vice President Aaron Burr. In return for Federalist support in his campaign for the governorship of New York, Burr was to swing New York into the Northern Confederacy. Burr was badly beaten, in part because of Hamilton's opposition. Incensed and irate, Burr challenged Hamilton to the duel described at the beginning of this chapter.

The duel ruined Burr's career as a politician and made him a fugitive from the law. The Republican party stripped away his control over political patronage in New York. In debt, disgraced, on the edge of bankruptcy, the desperate Burr became involved in a conspiracy for which he would be put on trial for treason.

During the spring of 1805 Burr traveled to the West, where he and an old friend, James Wilkinson, commander of United States forces in the Southwest and military governor of Louisiana, hatched an adventurous scheme. It is still uncertain what the conspirators' goal was, since Burr, in his efforts to attract support, told different stories to different people. Spain's minister believed that Burr planned to set up an independent nation in the Mississippi Valley. Others reported that he planned to seize Spanish territory in what is now Texas, California, and New Mexico. The British minister was told that for $500,000 and British naval support, Burr would separate the states and territories west of the Appalachians from the rest of the Union and create an empire with himself as its head.

In the fall of 1806 Burr and some 60 schemers traveled down the Ohio River toward New Orleans to assess possibilities and perhaps to incite disgruntled French settlers to revolt. Wilkinson, recognizing that the scheme was doomed to failure, decided to betray Burr. He wrote a letter to Jefferson describing a "deep, dark, wicked, and widespread conspiracy, . . . to seize on New Orleans, revolutionize the territory, and carry an expedition against Mexico."

Burr fled, but was finally apprehended in the Mississippi Territory. He was then taken to the circuit court in Richmond, Virginia, where, in 1807, he was tried for treason. Jefferson, convinced that Burr was a dangerous man, wanted a conviction regardless of the evidence. Chief Justice John Marshall, who presided over the trial, was equally eager to discredit Jefferson. Ultimately, Burr was acquitted. The reason for the acquittal was the Constitution's very strict definition of treason as "levying war against the United States" or "giving . . . aid and comfort" to the nation's enemies. In addition, each overt act of treason had to be attested to by two witnesses. The prosecution was unable to meet this strict standard; as a result of Burr's acquittal, few cases of treason have ever been tried in the United States.

Was Burr guilty of conspiring to destabilize the United States and separate the West by force? Probably not. The prosecution's case rested largely on the unreliable testimony of co-conspirator James Wilkinson, who was a spy in the pay of Spain while also a U.S. army commander and governor of Louisiana. What, then, was the purpose of Burr's mysterious scheming? It appears likely that the former vice president was planning a filibuster expedition—an unauthorized military attack—on Mexico, which was then controlled by Spain. The dream of creating a western republic in Mexico, Florida, or Louisiana appealed to many early nineteenth-century Americans—especially to those who feared that a European power might seize Spain's New World colonies unless America launched a preemptive strike. Alexander Hamilton himself, back in 1798, had proposed a plan to conquer Louisiana and the Floridas.

To the end of his life, Burr denied that he had plotted treason against the United States. Asked by one of his closest friends whether he had sought to separate the West from the rest of the nation, Burr responded with an emphatic "No!" "I would as soon have thought of taking possession of the moon and informing my friends that I intended to divide it among them."

THE AMERICAN EAGLE CHALLENGES THE FRENCH TIGER AND THE BRITISH SHARK

In 1804, Jefferson was easily reelected, carrying every state except Connecticut and Delaware. He received 162 electoral votes to only 14 for his Federalist opponent, Charles C. Pinckney. Although his second term began, he later wrote, "without a cloud on the horizon," storm clouds soon gathered as a result of renewed war in Europe. Jefferson faced the difficult challenge of keeping the United States out of the European war, while defending the nation's rights as a neutral country.

In May 1803, only two weeks after Napoleon sold Louisiana to the United States, France declared war on Britain. As part of his overall strategy to bring Britain to its knees, Napoleon instituted the "Continental System," a policy of economic warfare that closed European ports to British goods and ordered the seizure of any neutral vessel that carried British goods or stopped in a British port. Britain retaliated in 1807 by issuing Orders in Council, which required all neutral ships to land at a British port to obtain a trading license and pay a tariff. Britain threatened to seize any ship that failed to obey the Orders in Council. United States shipping was

In the election of 1804, Thomas Jefferson dropped Aaron Burr from the Republican ticket and replaced him with another New Yorker, George Clinton.

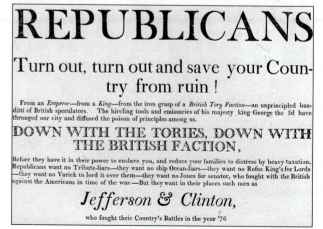

caught in the crossfire. By 1807 France had seized 500 ships and Britain nearly 1000.

The most outrageous violation of America's neutral rights was the British practice of **impressment.** The British navy desperately needed sailors. Unable to procure sufficient volunteers, the British navy resorted to seizing—impressing—men on streets, in taverns, and on British merchant ships. When these efforts failed to muster sufficient men, the British began to stop foreign ships and remove seamen alleged to be British subjects. By 1811 nearly 10,000 American sailors had been forced into the British navy, although an undetermined number were actually deserters from British ships who made more money sailing on U.S. ships.

Outrage over impressment reached a fever pitch in 1807 when the British man-of-war *Leopard* fired three broadsides at the American naval frigate *Chesapeake* as the American crew had refused to allow British officers to search the American ship for Royal Navy deserters. The blasts killed 3 American sailors and wounded 18 more. British authorities then boarded the American ship and removed 4 sailors, only 1 of whom was really a British subject.

"Dambargo"

In a desperate attempt to stave off war, for which it was ill-prepared, and to win respect for America's neutral rights, the United States imposed an **embargo** on foreign trade. Convinced that American trade was vital to European industry, Jefferson persuaded Congress in late 1807 to adopt a policy of "peaceable coercion": a ban on all foreign shipping and exports.

Jefferson regarded the embargo as an idealistic experiment—a moral alternative to war. Jefferson was not a doctrinaire pacifist, but he had long advocated economic coercion as an instrument of diplomacy. Now he had a chance to put his ideas into practice.

The embargo was an unpopular and costly failure. It hurt the American economy far more than it did the British or French and resulted in widespread smuggling. Without the European export market, harbors filled with idle ships, and nearly 30,000 sailors found themselves jobless. The embargo resuscitated the Federalist party, which regained power in several New England states and made substantial gains in the Congressional elections of 1808. "Would to God," said one American, "that the embargo had done as little evil to ourselves as it has done to foreign nations!"

Jefferson believed that Americans would cooperate with the embargo out of a sense of patriotism. Instead, evasions of the embargo were widespread,

and smuggling flourished, particularly through Canada, and early in 1809, just three days before Jefferson left office, Congress repealed the embargo. In effect for 15 months, the embargo exacted no political concessions from either France or Britain. But it had produced economic hardship, evasion of the law, and political dissension at home. Upset by the failure of his policies, the 65-year-old Jefferson looked forward to his retirement: "Never did a prisoner, released from his chains, feel such relief as I shall on shaking off the shackles of power."

The problem of American neutrality now fell to Jefferson's hand-picked successor, **James Madison.** "The Father of the Constitution" was small in stature and frail in health. A quiet and scholarly man, who secretly suffered from epilepsy, Madison brought a keen intellect and a wealth of experience to the presidency. At the Constitutional Convention, he had played a leading role in formulating the principles of federalism and separation of powers that underlie the American system of government. As a member of Congress, he had sponsored the Bill of Rights and founded the Republican party. As Jefferson's secretary of state, he had kept the United States out of the Napoleonic wars and was committed to using economic coercion to force Britain and France to respect America's neutral rights.

In 1809 Congress replaced the failed embargo with the **Non-Intercourse Act,** which reopened trade with all nations except Britain and France.

Violations of American neutrality continued, and a year later Congress replaced the Non-Intercourse Act with a new measure, **Macon's Bill No. 2.** This policy reopened trade with France and Britain. It stated, however, that if either Britain or France agreed to respect America's neutral rights, the United States would immediately stop trade with the other nation. Napoleon seized on this new policy in an effort to entangle the United States in his war with Britain. In the summer of 1810, he announced repeal of all French restrictions on American trade. Even though France continued to seize American ships and cargoes, President Madison snapped at the bait. In early 1811 he cut off trade with Britain and recalled the American minister.

For 19 months the British went without American trade, but gradually economic coercion worked. Food shortages, mounting unemployment, and increasing inventories of unsold manufactured goods led the British to end its trade restrictions (though not the British navy's policy of impressment). Unfortunately, Prime Minister Perceval was assassinated before he actually revoked the restrictions. When the restrictions were finally suspended on June 16, it was too late. President Madison had asked Congress for a declaration of war on June 1. A divided House and Senate concurred. The House voted to declare war on Britain by a vote of 79 to 49; the Senate by a vote of 19 to 13.

A Second War of Independence

Why did the United States declare war on Britain in 1812? Resentment at British interference with American rights on the high seas was certainly the most loudly voiced grievance. British trade restrictions, impressment of thousands of American seamen, and British blockades humiliated the country and undercut America's national honor and neutral rights.

But if British harassment of American shipping was the primary motivation for war, why then did the prowar majority in Congress come largely from the South, the West, and the frontier, and not from northeastern shipowners and sailors? The vote to declare war on Britain divided along sharp regional lines. Representatives from western, southern, and frontier states voted 65 to 15 for war, while representatives from New England, New York, and New Jersey, states with strong shipping interests, voted 34 to 14 against war.

Northeastern Federalists and a handful of Republicans from coastal regions of the South regarded war with Britain as a grave mistake. The United

At the Battle of Tippecanoe, U.S. troops led by General William Henry Harrison routed the small force of Native Americans under the Shawnee Prophet, Tenskwatawa.

States, they insisted, could not hope to challenge successfully British supremacy on the seas, and the government could not finance a war without bankrupting the country. Southerners and westerners, in contrast, were eager to avenge British insults against American honor and British actions that mocked American sovereignty on land and sea. Many southerners and westerners blamed British trade policies for depressing agricultural prices and producing an economic depression. War with Britain also offered another incentive: the possibility of clearing western

THE ROAD TO WAR

1807	*Leopard-Chesapeake* Affair	British man-of-war H.M.S. *Leopard* fires upon the American warship U.S.S. *Chesapeake*, killing three; then the British forcibly remove four alleged deserters, bringing the United Sates and Great Britain to the brink of war.
	Embargo Act	Prohibits all American trade with foreign nations.
1809	The Non-Intercourse Act	Reopens overseas commerce except to Britain and France; trade with these countries is to be reinstituted if they halt interference with American shipping.
1810	Macon's Bill No. 2	Restores trade with Britain and France but stipulates that if either country lifts its restrictions on neutral trade, the United States would terminate trade with the other.
	Trade Disputes	France informs the United States that it will repeal its trade restrictions if the United States halts trade with Britain; United States forbids trade with Britain.
	Congressional Elections	Voters sweep the "War Hawks" into Congress.
1811	The Battle of Tippecanoe	Battle in Indiana Territory shatters the influence of the Shawnee Prophet, Tenskwatawa.
1812	Declaration of War	Congress declares war against Britain on grounds of British impressment of American seamen, interference with trade, and blockading of American ports.

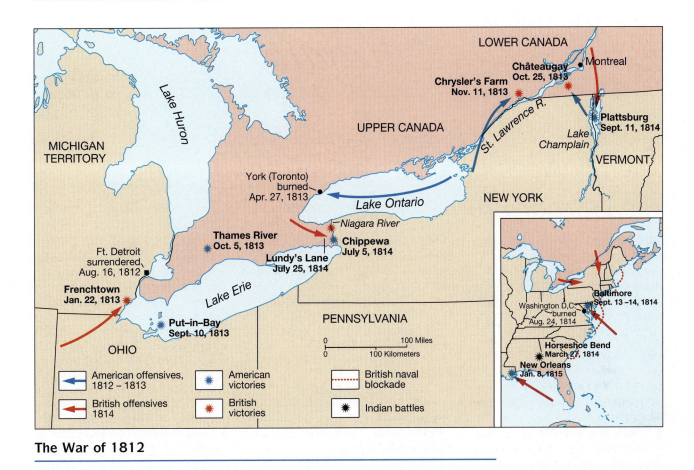

The War of 1812

lands of Indians by removing the Indians' strongest ally—the British. And finally, many westerners and southerners had their eye on expansion, viewing war as an opportunity to add Canada and Spanish-held Florida to the United States.

Weary of Jefferson and Madison's patient and pacifist policy of economic coercion, voters swept 63 of the 142 representatives out of Congress in 1810 and replaced them with young Republicans that Federalists dubbed "War Hawks." These second-generation Republicans avidly supported national expansion and national honor. They elected Henry Clay, a representative from frontier Kentucky, Speaker of the House on his very first day in Congress. Clay then assigned other young Republicans, such as John C. Calhoun, a freshman representative from South Carolina, to key House committees.

Staunchly nationalist and rabidly anti-British, eager for territorial expansion and economic growth, the young Republicans regarded the Napoleonic Wars in Europe as an unparalleled opportunity to defend national honor, assert American interests, and conquer Canada and Florida.

Further contributing to their prowar fervor was the belief that the British incited Native Americans

on the frontier to attack. Anti-British feeling soared in November 1811, when General William Henry Harrison precipitated a fight with a Native-American alliance led by the Shawnee Prophet, Tenskwatawa, at Tippecanoe Creek in Indiana. More than 60 American soldiers were killed and 100 were wounded. Since British guns were found on the battlefield, young Republicans concluded that the British were responsible for the incident.

Early Defeats

Although Congress voted strongly in favor of war, the country entered the conflict deeply divided. Not only would many New Englanders refuse to subscribe to war loans, some merchants would actually ship provisions that Britain needed to support its army, which was fighting Napoleon in Europe. Moreover, the United States was woefully unprepared for war. The army consisted of fewer than 7000 soldiers and the navy was grotesquely overmatched.

The American strategy called for a three-pronged invasion of Canada and heavy harassment of British shipping. The attack on Canada, however, was a disastrous failure. At Detroit, 2000 American troops surrendered to a much smaller British and Native-American

The Shawnee Prophet Tenskwatawa and His Warrior Brother Tecumseh

DURING the last years of the eighteenth century, defeat, disease, and death were the bitter lot of Native Americans living in the Northwest Territory. In 1794 an American expeditionary force led by Major General "Mad" Anthony Wayne crushed an opposing Indian army at the Battle of Fallen Timbers near present-day Toledo, Ohio. This decisive victory eventually forced Native Americans to give up 25,000 square miles of land north of the Ohio River.

Forty-five thousand land-hungry white settlers poured into the Ohio Country during the next six years. They spread a variety of killer diseases, including smallpox, influenza, and measles, in their wake. Whole villages succumbed, and hundreds of natives died. High Indian mortality rates did not bother the intruding whites, who also considered the arbitrary "murdering of the Indians in the highest degree meritorious," according to William Henry Harrison, the territorial governor. Aggressive frontier settlers likewise infringed on Indian hunting grounds and rapidly killed off wild game that provided the natives with basic sustenance. Deprived of their ancestral homelands, faced with severe food shortages, and enduring a drastic loss of population, Native Americans in the Old Northwest saw the fabric of their society coming apart. Tribal unity eroded, villages broke apart, and violent disputes became widespread. To escape from their problems, some natives turned to alcohol for the mind-numbing relief it provided them.

One of the Native Americans who suffered from the breakdown of Indian society was a Shawnee youth named Laulewasika. A few months before he was born in 1774, white frontiersmen—they had crossed into the Ohio Country in violation of a recent treaty—killed his father, a respected Shawnee warrior chief. Shortly thereafter, his despondent mother, a Creek, fled westward, leaving behind her children to be raised by relatives.

As a young man Laulewasika lacked direction. He became a dissolute, drunken idler, known only for the handkerchief he wore to cover up the facial disfigurement he suffered when he lost an eye during an accident. Then in 1805 in the midst of a frightening epidemic, Laulewasika underwent a powerful transformation. Overcome by images of his own wickedness, he fell into a deep trance during which he met the Indian Master of Life. On the basis of this mystical experience, Laulewasika embarked on a crusade "to reclaim the Indians from bad habits." Adopting the name Tenskwatawa, meaning "the open door," he first called upon Indians everywhere to stop drinking the white traders' alcohol. He soon broadened his appeals. Like other Native-American revitalization prophets before and after him, Tenskwatawa vigorously demanded an end to intertribal fighting, a return to ancestral ways, and a complete rejection of all aspects of white civilization. His central message was native unity as the key to blocking further white encroachments on ancient tribal lands.

Tenskwatawa's reputation reached a high point in 1806 after Governor William Henry Harrison demanded the performance of a miracle. "If he is a prophet," an almost mocking Harrison said to some Indians, "ask him to cause the sun to stand still, the moon to alter its course, . . . or the dead to rise from their graves. If he does these things, you may then believe he has been sent from God." Tenskwatawa obliged. Most likely learning from the British about an upcoming solar eclipse, he pronounced that he would make the sun disappear on the morning of June 16. When the shadow of the moon darkened the rays of the sun that day, the prophet's fame and message of unity spread far and wide among Native Americans.

The doctrines of Tenskwatawa were not solely his own. His older brother, the famed Shawnee war chief Tecumseh (1768–1813), had come to recognize the futility of fighting piecemeal against the whites. He also emerged as a firm advocate of a broad-based Indian alliance. In conjunction with the Shawnee Prophet, he struggled to convince Native Americans as far north as Wisconsin, as far west as Arkansas, and as far south as Florida to join together in blocking white expansion.

Besides working to build an alliance, Tecumseh's immediate goal was to save Indiana territory, or "the country of Indians," for the native populace. In 1808 he and Tenskwatawa relocated their tribal village in northwestern Indiana along the shoreline of the Tippecanoe River where it flowed into the Wabash River. The presence of the so-called Prophet's Town greatly worried Governor Harrison, since it served as a mecca for Indian unification. In reaction Harrison directly challenged

war loa
ber 181.
Hartforc
series o
power c
and adr
one-terr
ginians
fifths c
clout of
not get

The
came pt
of the T
the Batt
end led
tors. Th
disappe

CON(

Early in
sloop F
York H
ing the
through
boomec
carrying
and thr
Britain
Niles' I
"Who v
public!

Bet
cans ha
lands to
respect
war a
Louisia
dian co
evicted
emerge
and un

SUG(

Donald
the War

Drew M
fersonian
Madison
informa

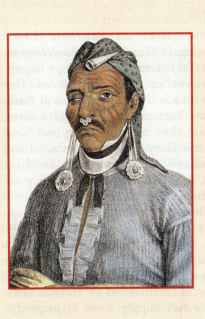

The Field Museum, Neg# A93851, Chicago.

the growing influence of the Shawnee brothers. He conducted negotiations with friendly local chiefs and plied them with alcohol until they turned over title to 3 million acres in Indiana for the paltry sum of $7000 and an annuity of $1750. This precipitous act put Harrison on a collision course with Tecumseh and Tenskwatawa.

Harrison eventually held a meeting with the outraged Shawnee brothers. The governor told them they could surely place their faith in treaties with the United States, but not before Tecumseh, a spellbinding orator, had queried: "How can we have confidence in the white people? When Jesus Christ came upon the earth, you killed Him and nailed Him to a cross. You thought He was dead, but you were mistaken." Harrison did not miss the point. Tecumseh and Tenskwatawa intended to revitalize Native Americans so that they too would regain life as a united nation of peoples and put an end to legalized land grabbing as provided for in such treaties as the one recently negotiated by Harrison.

Tecumseh needed time to build his alliance, and he soon set off on another of his journeys to convince his native brethren to put aside their petty tribal squabbles and prepare to rise up as one to resist the whites. He warned Tenskwatawa to avoid any conflict with Harrison, but the prophet did not listen. In November 1811, while Tecumseh was away in the south attempting to rally support, Harrison approached the Prophet's Town with an army of nearly 1000 men. Tenskwatawa rose to the bait and allowed some 450 warriors to attack the Americans. What followed was a rout. As the battle raged, the prophet called upon the Master of Life to protect his native fighters. His prayer failed. Harrison's troops drove off the warriors and then sacked and burned the village. In so doing, they destroyed the prophet's credibility and prestige. They also inadvertently gave Harrison the kind of impressive military victory that helped him successfully secure the presidency of the United States in 1840. "Tippecanoe and Tyler Too" was Harrison's catchy electioneering slogan.

Tecumseh returned home from his trip a few months later. He was in an optimistic frame of mind, believing the grand native alliance could yet become reality. Then he saw the devastated village. Shocked and enraged that his brother had challenged Harrison's force, he angrily denounced Tenskwatawa and sent him packing westward into obscurity. In frustration Tecumseh likewise abandoned his dream of a pan-Indian alliance, since he now doubted whether his native brethren had the patience to plan and work together. Then, in his own words, he "swore . . . eternal hatred—the hatred of an avenger" against white settlers everywhere. He would rally what warriors he could and fight with all his strength in the name of his way of life until death relieved him of the anguish he felt for the collapsing world of his native brethren.

When the War of 1812 broke out, Tecumseh allied himself with the British in his final effort to halt American expansion. In October 1813, after U.S. forces compelled the British to retreat from the area around Detroit, the Shawnee warrior and an army consisting of Indian and British troops tried to halt the American advance at the Thames River in the eastern part of Canada's Ontario Province. The day before the climactic encounter, Tecumseh told his native followers: "Brother warriors, we are about to enter an engagement from which I shall not return. My body will remain on the field of battle." Tecumseh's premonition was correct. The next afternoon he died from multiple wounds in combat. With his demise the vision of pan-Indian resistance to white encroachment on native lands in the Middle West also perished.

No
Sou
the
the
lan
we:

rela
low
wit
siss

9

NATIONALISM, ECONOMIC GROWTH, AND THE ROOTS OF SECTIONAL CONFLICT, 1815–1824

John Marshall established many basic principles of constitutional law in the 34 years he served as chief justice of the United States. Marshall and the six other members of the Supreme Court appear on the podium in this 1822 painting of the House of Representatives by Samuel F. B. Morse.

powers to do whatever was "necessary and proper" to carry out its constitutional powers—in this case, the power to manage a currency. In a classic statement of "broad" or "loose" construction of the Constitution, Marshall said, "Let the end be legitimate, let it be within the scope of the Constitution, and all means which are plainly adapted to that end, which are not prohibited, but consistent with the letter and spirit of the Constitution, are constitutional."

The second question raised was whether a state had the power to tax a branch of the Bank of the United States. In answer to this question, the Court said no. The Constitution, the Court asserted, created a new government with sovereign power over the states. "The power to tax involves the power to destroy," the Court declared, and the states do not have the right to exert an independent check on the authority of the federal government.

During the postwar period, the Supreme Court also encouraged economic competition and development. In **Dartmouth v. Woodward** (1819) the Court promoted business growth by establishing the principle of sanctity of contracts. The case involved the efforts of the New Hampshire legislature to alter the charter of Dartmouth College, which had been granted by George III in 1769. The Court held that a charter was a valid contract protected by the Constitution and that states do not have the power to alter contracts unilaterally.

In *Gibbons* v. *Ogden* (1824), the Court broadened federal power over interstate commerce. The Court overturned a New York law that had awarded a monopoly over steamboat traffic on the Hudson River, ruling that the Constitution had specifically given Congress the power to regulate commerce.

Under John Marshall, the Supreme Court became the final arbiter of the constitutionality of federal and state laws. The Court's role in shifting sovereign power from the states to the federal government was an important development. It would become increasingly difficult in the future to argue that the union was a creation of the states, that states could exert an independent check on federal government authority, or that Congress's powers were limited to those specifically conferred by the Constitution.

Defending American Interests in Foreign Affairs

The War of 1812 stirred a new nationalistic spirit in foreign affairs. In 1815, this spirit resulted in a decision to end the raids by the Barbary pirates on American commercial shipping in the Mediterranean. For 17 years the United States had paid tribute to the ruler of Algiers. In March 1815, Captain Stephen Decatur and a fleet of ten ships sailed into the Mediterranean, where they captured two Algerian gunboats, towed the ships into Algiers harbor, and threatened to bombard the city. As a result, all the North African states agreed to treaties releasing American prisoners without ransom, ending all demands for American tribute, and providing compensation for American vessels that had been seized.

After successfully defending American interests in North Africa, Monroe acted to settle old grievances with the British. Britain and the United States had left a host of issues unresolved in the peace treaty ending the War of 1812, including disputes over boundaries, trading and fishing rights, and rival claims to the Oregon region. The two governments moved quickly to settle these issues. The Rush-Bagot Agreement (1817) removed most military ships from the Great Lakes. In 1818, Britain granted American fishermen the right to fish in eastern Canadian waters, agreed to the 49th parallel as the boundary between the United States and Canada from Minnesota to the Rocky Mountains, and consented to joint occupation of the Oregon region.

The critical foreign policy issue facing the United States after the War of 1812 was the fate of Spain's crumbling New World empire. A source of particular concern was Florida, which was still under Spanish control. Pirates, fugitive slaves, and Native Americans used Florida as a sanctuary and as a jumping off point for raids on settlements in Georgia. In December 1817, to end these incursions, Monroe authorized General Andrew Jackson to lead a punitive expedition against the Seminole Indians in Florida. Jackson not only attacked the Seminoles and destroyed their villages but overthrew the Spanish governor. He also court-martialed and executed two British citizens whom he accused of inciting the Seminoles to commit atrocities against Americans.

Jackson's actions provoked a furor in Washington. Spain protested Jackson's acts and demanded that he be punished. Secretary of War John C. Calhoun and other members of Monroe's cabinet urged the president to reprimand Jackson for acting without specific authorization. In Congress, Henry Clay called for Jackson's censure. Secretary of State Adams, however, saw in Jackson's actions an opportunity to wrest Florida from Spain.

Instead of apologizing for Jackson's conduct, Adams declared that the Florida raid was a legitimate act of self-defense. Adams informed the Spanish government that it would either have to police Florida effectively or cede it to the United States. Convinced that American annexation was inevitable, Spain ceded Florida to the United States in the Adams-Onís Treaty of 1819. In return, the United States agreed to honor $5 million in damage claims by Americans against Spain, and renounced, at least temporarily, its claims to Texas.

At the same time, European intervention in the Pacific Northwest and Latin America threatened to become a new source of anxiety for American leaders. In 1821, Russia claimed control of the entire Pacific coast from Alaska to Oregon and closed the area to foreign shipping. This development coincided with rumors that Spain, with the help of its European allies, was planning to reconquer its former colonies in Latin America. European intervention threatened British as well as American interests. Not only did Britain have a flourishing trade with Latin America, which would decline if Spain regained its New World colonies, but it also occupied the Oregon region jointly with the United States. In 1823, British Foreign Minister George Canning proposed that the United States and Britain jointly announce their opposition to further European intervention in the Americas.

Monroe initially regarded the British proposal favorably. But his secretary of state, John Quincy Adams, opposed a joint Anglo-American declaration. Secure in the knowledge that the British would use their fleet to support the American position, Adams convinced President Monroe to make an independent declaration of American policy. In his annual message to Congress in 1823, Monroe outlined the principles that have become known as the **Monroe Doctrine.** He announced that the Western Hemisphere was henceforth closed to any further European colonization, declaring that the United States would regard any attempt by European nations "to extend their system to any portion of this hemisphere as dangerous to our peace and safety." European countries with possessions in the hemisphere—Britain, France, the Netherlands, and Spain—were warned not to attempt expansion. Monroe also said that the United States would not interfere in internal European affairs.

For the American people, the Monroe Doctrine was the proud symbol of American hegemony in the Western Hemisphere. Unilaterally, the United States had defined its rights and interests in the New World. It is true that during the first half of the nineteenth century the United States lacked the military power to enforce the Monroe Doctrine and depended on the British navy to deter European intervention in the Americas, but the nation had clearly warned the European powers that any threat to American security would provoke American retaliation.

THE GROWTH OF THE AMERICAN ECONOMY

At the beginning of the nineteenth century, the United States was an overwhelmingly rural and agricultural nation. Most Americans lived on farms or in villages with fewer than 2500 inhabitants. The nation's population was small and scattered over a vast

remove the garbage and refuse, many cities allowed packs of dogs, goats, and pigs to scavenge freely.

Although elite urbanites began to enjoy such amenities as indoor toilets, the cities' poorest inhabitants lived in slums. On New York's lower east side, many men, women, and children were crowded into damp, unlighted, ill-ventilated cellars with 6 to 20 persons living in a single room. Despite growing public awareness of the problems of slums and urban poverty, conditions remained unchanged for several generations.

THE GROWTH OF POLITICAL FACTIONALISM AND SECTIONALISM

The Era of Good Feelings began with a burst of nationalistic fervor. The economic program adopted by Congress, including a national bank and a protective tariff, reflected the growing feeling of national unity. The Supreme Court promoted the spirit of nationalism by establishing the principle of federal supremacy. Industrialization and improvements in transportation also added to the sense of national unity by contributing to the nation's economic strength and independence and by linking the West and the East together.

But this same period also witnessed the emergence of growing factional divisions in politics, including a deepening sectional split between the North and South. A severe economic depression between 1819 and 1822 provoked bitter division over questions of banking and tariffs. Geographic expansion exposed latent tensions over the morality of slavery and the balance of economic power. Political issues that arose during the Era of Good Feelings dominated American politics for the next 40 years.

The Panic of 1819

In 1819 a financial panic swept across the country. The growth in trade that followed the War of 1812 came to an abrupt halt. Unemployment mounted, banks failed, mortgages were foreclosed, and agricultural prices fell by half. Investment in western lands collapsed.

In Richmond, property values fell by half. In Philadelphia, 1808 individuals were committed to debtors' prison. In Boston, the figure was 3500.

For the first time in American history, the problem of urban poverty commanded public attention. In New York in 1819, the Society for the Prevention of Pauperism counted 8000 paupers out of a population of 120,000. The next year, the figure climbed to

13,000. Fifty thousand people were unemployed or irregularly employed in New York, Philadelphia, and Baltimore, and one foreign observer estimated that half a million people were jobless nationwide. To address the problem of destitution, newspapers appealed for old clothes and shoes for the poor, and churches and municipal governments distributed soup. Baltimore set up 12 soup kitchens in 1820 to give food to the poor.

The panic had several causes, including a dramatic decline in cotton prices, a contraction of credit by the Bank of the United States designed to curb inflation, an 1817 congressional order requiring hard-currency payments for land purchases, and the closing of many factories due to foreign competition.

The panic unleashed a storm of popular protest. Many debtors agitated for "stay laws" to provide relief from debts as well as the abolition of debtors' prisons. Manufacturing interests called for increased protection from foreign imports, but a growing number of southerners believed that high protective tariffs, which raised the cost of imported goods and reduced the flow of international trade, were the root of their troubles. Many people clamored for a reduction in the cost of government and pressed for sharp reductions in federal and state budgets. Others, particularly in the South and West, blamed the panic on the nation's banks and particularly the tight-money policies of the Bank of the United States.

By 1823 the panic was over. But it left a lasting imprint on American politics. The panic led to demands for the democratization of state constitutions, an end to restrictions on voting and officeholding, and heightened hostility toward banks and other "privileged" corporations and monopolies. The panic also exacerbated tensions within the Republican party and aggravated sectional tensions as Northerners pressed for higher tariffs while Southerners abandoned their support of nationalistic economic programs.

The Missouri Crisis

In the midst of the panic, a crisis over slavery erupted with stunning suddenness. It was, Thomas Jefferson wrote, like "a firebell in the night." Missouri's application for statehood ignited the crisis, and the issue raised involved the status of slavery west of the Mississippi River.

East of the Mississippi, the Mason-Dixon line and the Ohio River formed a boundary between the North and South. States south of this line were slave states; states north of this line had either abolished slavery or adopted gradual emancipation policies.

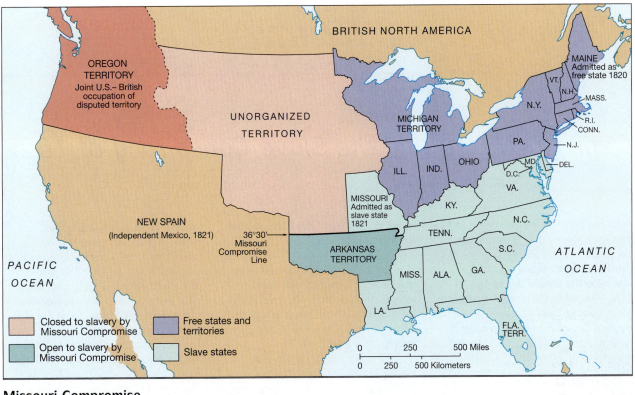

Missouri Compromise

The agreement reached in the Missouri Compromise temporarily settled the argument over slavery in the territories.

West of the Mississippi, however, no clear line demarcated the boundary between free and slave territory.

Representative James Tallmadge, a New York Republican, provoked the crisis in February 1819 by introducing an amendment to restrict slavery in Missouri as a condition of statehood. The amendment prohibited the further introduction of slaves into Missouri and provided for emancipation of all children of slaves at the age of 25. Voting along ominously sectional lines, the House approved the Tallmadge Amendment, but the amendment was defeated in the Senate.

Southern and Northern politicians alike responded with fury. Southerners condemned the Tallmadge proposal as part of a northeastern plot to dominate the government. They declared the United States to be a union of equals, claiming that Congress had no power to place special restrictions upon a state.

Talk of disunion and civil war was rife. Senator Freeman Walker of Georgia envisioned "civil war . . . a brother's sword crimsoned with a brother's blood." Northern politicians responded with equal vehemence. Said Representative Tallmadge, "If blood is necessary to extinguish any fire which I have assisted to kindle, I can assure you gentlemen, while I regret the necessity, I shall not forbear to contribute my mite." Northern leaders argued that national policy, enshrined in the Northwest Ordinance, committed the government to halt the expansion of the institution of slavery. They warned that the extension of slavery into the West would inevitably increase the pressures to reopen the African slave trade.

Mass meetings convened in a number of cities in the Northeast. The vehemence of anti-Missouri feeling is apparent in an editorial that appeared in the New York *Advertiser:* "THIS QUESTION INVOLVES NOT ONLY THE FUTURE CHARACTER OF OUR NATION, BUT THE FUTURE WEIGHT AND INFLUENCE OF THE FREE STATES. IF NOW LOST— IT IS LOST FOREVER." Never before had passions over the issue of slavery been so heated or sectional antagonisms so overt.

Compromise ultimately resolved the crisis. In 1820, the Senate narrowly voted to admit Missouri as a slave state. To preserve the sectional balance, it also voted to admit Maine, which had previously been a part of Massachusetts, as a free state, and to prohibit the formation of any further slave states from the territory of the Louisiana Purchase north of 36°30' north latitude. Henry Clay then skillfully steered the compromise through the House, where a handful of anti-

Denmark Vesey and the Slave Conspiracy of 1822

"DO not open your lips! Die silent, as you shall see me do." Speaking from the gallows, Peter Poyas soon met his death with stoic dignity—as did five others on the second day of July in 1822. Among the five was Denmark Vesey, whose quiet composure at death reflected the steely courage with which he had led blacks in and around Charleston, South Carolina, in plotting insurrection. As their trials revealed, for over a year Vesey and his lieutenants had planned, re-cruited, and hoarded the provisions for the fight. Only betrayal by a few slaves had prevented what could well have become the bloodiest slave revolt in America's history.

Many whites were surprised at the revelation of Vesey's leadership. In their eyes he seemed to have few grievances. Born in the late 1760s in either Africa or the Caribbean, he served as a slave to Captain Joseph Vesey, a Bermuda slave trader who settled in Charleston in 1783 as a slave broker and ship merchandiser. In 1800 Denmark Vesey won $1500 in the East Bay Lottery. He then pur-chased his freedom for $600 and opened a carpentry shop; by 1817 he had amassed savings of several thou-sand dollars. He was literate and well traveled. He had once been offered the opportunity to return to Africa as a free man and rejected it. "What did he have to be upset about?" many whites must have asked. Well, for one thing, his wife and several of his chil-dren were still in bondage. He also deeply resented white interference in the lives of free blacks as well as slaves.

Vesey was a proud man and fre-quently rebuked friends who acqui-esced to such traditional displays of deference as bowing to whites on the street. One remembered Vesey telling him "all men were born equal, and that he was surprised that anyone would degrade himself by such con-duct; that he would never cringe to whites, nor ought any who had the feelings of a man."

As in cities throughout the nation, blacks in Charleston were meeting oppression by forging their own institutions and creating self-affirming communities. A key part of this process was religious indepen-dence. At the close of the War of 1812 black Methodists in Charleston out-numbered white ones ten to one. Af-ter an unsuccessful attempt by blacks to control their destinies within the white church, Morris Brown went to Philadelphia and was ordained by the African Methodist Episcopal church. In 1818, following a dispute over a burial ground, more than three-fourths of the 6000 black Methodists of Charleston withdrew from the white-led churches. Morris Brown was appointed bishop, and the African Church of Charleston was established.

White authorities regarded such independent churches as possible seedbeds of radicalism. Thus they ha-rassed church meetings and jailed church leaders. Beginning in 1820 legislation was passed to reduce the free black population of South Car-olina. Finally, in 1821, the city of Charleston closed the Hampstead Church, which had been the leader of the independent church movement—and which included Denmark Vesey among its members. That closing be-came the spark that ignited Vesey to action. He began holding meetings, often in his own home, with other members of the congregation, includ-ing Rolla Bennett, "Gullah Jack" Pritchard, Monday Gell, and Ned and Peter Poyas. They became the nucleus of what came to be called the Vesey Conspiracy.

Later testimony indicates that Vesey was well aware of several re-cent events that convinced him that the tide of history was changing. Foremost was the successful slave re-bellion in Haiti that began in 1791. Vesey "was in the habit of reading to me all the passages in the newspapers that related to St. Domingo, and ap-parently every pamphlet he could lay his hands on that had any connection with slavery," one rebel testified. Vesey was also knowledgeable about the debates over Missouri statehood; the same rebel reported, "He one day brought me a speech which he told me had been delivered in congress by a Mr. [Rufus] King on the subject of slavery; he told me this Mr. King was the black man's friend, that he, Mr. King, had declared . . . that slavery was a great disgrace to the country."

Vesey used religion as a potent force to spur blacks to join him in armed rebellion. At almost every meeting he "read to us from the Bible, how the children of Israel were delivered out of Egypt from bondage." He also frequently used the passage: "Behold the day of the Lord cometh, and thy spoil shall be divided in the midst of thee. For I shall gather all nations against Jerusalem to battle; and the city shall be taken." In addition, "Gullah Jack," born in Africa, was known as a powerful conjurer, and many were

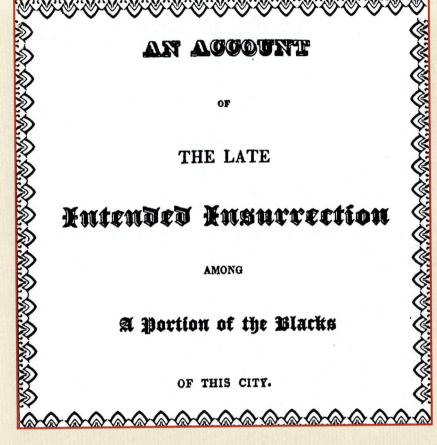

AN ACCOUNT

OF

THE LATE

Intended Insurrection

AMONG

A Portion of the Blacks

OF THIS CITY.

convinced his power could protect them from harm.

There was a distinctly Pan-African cast to the conspiracy. A number of the leaders had lived in either Africa or the Caribbean. One of them, Monday Gell, had apparently corresponded with the president of Haiti. Charleston blacks were told that "Santo Domingo and Africa will assist us to get our liberty, if we will only make the motion first." The motion they planned was bold indeed. They were to attack the city at seven different points, capture weapons at the arsenal, set fire to the city, and kill all whites they encountered.

The plan was bold but not rashly undertaken. They prepared for a deadline in the second week of July 1822. Large numbers were needed and available. Blacks outnumbered whites ten to one in the area surrounding Charleston, and recruiting extended to plantations as far away as 80 miles. The big problem was a shortage of arms until the arsenal was taken. So blacksmiths began making bayonets and spikes. Anything that could be used as a weapon was hoarded, along with gunpowder. Draymen, caters, and butchers were recruited to supply horses. Hundreds of blacks from all classes and occupations were contacted, but the nucleus remained skilled artisans, free and slave, from Charleston.

The dangers of advance planning and a widespread network were leaks and betrayal. For months luck held, but in late May 1822 a slave reported an attempt to recruit him to the insurrection. As authorities began to investigate, the betrayals escalated, and the authorities deployed military force to quash the rebellion before it had a chance to get started. Ten slaves were arrested on June 17 and 18, and the court began hearings. On June 22 Vesey was captured and stood trial the next day, while "Gullah Jack," the only major leader still free, tried to continue the revolt. Three days after the July 2 executions "Gullah Jack" was arrested. By August 9 more than 30 blacks had been hanged and many more deported.

White retaliation was swift and sure. So was white hysteria. The executions were public, and blacks were forbidden to dress in black or wear black crepe to mourn the dead. Examples were also made of the informers, who were freed and granted lifetime annuities. Finally, whites responded to Vesey's conspiracy with further antiblack legislation.

On the surface little good came from Denmark Vesey's bold plan. Its chances of success were meager at best. During Vesey's sentencing, the presiding magistrate told him, "It is difficult to imagine what *infatuation* could have prompted you to attempt an enterprise so wild and visionary. You were a free man; were comparatively wealthy; and enjoyed every comfort, compatible with your situation. You had therefore, much to risk and little to gain. From your age and experience you *ought* to have known, that success was impracticable." Nevertheless, Vesey took his indomitable stand. While recruiting for the Union army, the great black abolitionist Frederick Douglass called upon blacks "to remember Denmark Vesey."

Chronology OF KEY EVENTS

1785 Oliver Evans opens the first automated flour mill

1786 Samuel Fitch demonstrates his first steamboat

1793 Samuel Slater opens the first American textile mill at Pawtucket, Rhode Island; Eli Whitney invents the cotton gin

1807 Robert Fulton's *Clermont* demonstrates practicality of steam-powered navigation

1814 First factory to turn raw cotton into cotton cloth opens in Waltham, Massachusetts

1815 Congress declares war on Algiers

1816 Second Bank of the United States is chartered; Protective Tariff is passed; James Monroe is elected fifth president

1817– 1818 General Andrew Jackson invades Florida; Rush-Bagot convention between Britain and United States establishes American fishing rights and U.S.-Canadian boundary

1819 Panic of 1819; Spain cedes Florida to the United States and recognizes the western limits of the Louisiana Purchase in the Adams-Onis Treaty; *Dartmouth* v. *Woodward* upholds the sanctity of contracts; *McCulloch* v. *Maryland* upholds the constitutionality of the second Bank of the United States

1820 Missouri Compromise prohibits slavery in the northern half of the Louisiana Purchase; Missouri enters the union as a slave state and Maine as a free state

1822 Denmark Vesey's slave insurrection in South Carolina is exposed

1823 President James Monroe opposes any further European colonization or interference in the Americas, establishing the principle now known as the Monroe Doctrine

1824 *Gibbons* v. *Ogden* broadens federal power over interstate commerce

1825 Erie Canal opens

---

slavery representatives, fearful of the threat to the Union, threw their support behind the proposals.

Southerners won a victory in 1820, but they paid a high price. While many states would eventually be organized from the Louisiana Purchase area north of the compromise line, only two (Arkansas and part of Oklahoma) would be formed from the southern portion. If the South was to defend its political power against an antislavery majority, it had but two options in the future. It would either have to forge new political alliances with the North and West, or it would have to acquire new territory in the Southwest. The latter would inevitably reignite northern opposition to the further expansion of slavery.

The Era of Good Feelings ended on a note of foreboding. Although compromise had been achieved, it was clear that sectional conflict had not been resolved, only postponed. Sectional antagonism, Jefferson wrote, "is hushed, indeed, for the moment. But

this is a reprieve only, not a final sentence. A geographical line, coinciding with a marked principle, moral and political, once conceived and held up to the angry passions of men, will never be obliterated; and every new irritation will mark it deeper and deeper." John Quincy Adams agreed. The Missouri crisis, he wrote, is only the "title page to a great tragic volume."

CONCLUSION

The Era of Good Feelings came to a formal close on March 4, 1825, the day that John Quincy Adams was inaugurated as the nation's sixth president. Adams, who had served eight years as his predecessor's secretary of state, believed that James Monroe's terms in office would be regarded by future generations of Americans as a "golden age." In his inaugural address, he spoke with pride of the nation's achievements since the War of 1812. A strong spirit of nationalism pervaded the nation and the country stood united under a single political party, the Republicans. The nation had settled its most serious disputes with England and Spain, extended its boundaries to the Pacific, asserted its diplomatic independence, encouraged the wars for national independence in Latin America, had developed a strong manufacturing system, and had begun to create a system of transportation adequate to a great nation.

The Era of Good Feelings marked a period of dramatic growth and intense nationalism, but it also witnessed the emergence of new political divisions as well as growing sectional animosities. The period following the War of 1812 brought rapid growth to cities, manufacturing, and the factory system in the North, while the South's economy remained centered on slavery and cotton. These two great sections were developing along diverging lines. Whether the spirit of nationalism or the spirit of sectionalism would triumph was the great question that would dominate American politics over the next four decades.

Suggestions for Further Reading

Jeremy Atack and Peter Passell, *A New Economic View of American History*, 2nd ed. (1994) and Charles Sellers, *The Market Revolution, 1815–1846* (1991). Analyze thoroughly American economic development after 1815.

William Barney, *The Passage of the Republic* (1987). Offers a highly informative overview of the period.

Ernest R. May, *The Making of the Monroe Doctrine* (1975). Examines American foreign policy during this period.

Overviews and Surveys

William Barney, *The Passage of the Republic: An Interdisciplinary History of Nineteenth-Century America* (1987); W. Elliot Brownlee, *Dynamics of Ascent: A History of the American Economy*, 2d ed. (1988); Stuart Bruchey, *The Roots of American Economic Growth, 1607–1861* (1965); George Dangerfield, *The Awakening of American Nationalism* (1965), and *The Era of Good Feelings* (1952); Robert Heilbroner, *The Economic Transformation of America*, 2d ed. (1984); John R. Howe, *From the Revolution Through the Age of Jackson* (1973); John Mayfield, *The New Nation, 1800–1845*, rev. ed. (1982); Douglas C. North, *The Economic Growth of the United States, 1790–1860* (1961); Sidney Ratner, James H. Soltow, and Richard Sylla, *The Evolution of the American Economy* (1979).

The Growth of American Nationalism

Samuel Flagg Bemis, ed., *The American Secretaries of State and Their Diplomacy*, vol. 4 (1928); Edward M. Burns, *The American Idea of Mission: Concepts of National Purpose and Destiny* (1957); Robert K. Faulkner, *The Jurisprudence of John Marshall* (1968); Lloyd C. Gardner et al., *Creation of the American Empire: U.S. Diplomatic History* (1973); C. C. Griffin, *The United States and the Disruption of the Spanish Empire* (1937); George Lee Haskins and Herbert A. Johnson, *History of the Supreme Court of the United States*, vol. 2, *Foundations of Power: John Marshall, 1801–1815* (1981); Ernest R. May, *The Making of the Monroe Doctrine* (1975); Frederick W. Merk, *Manifest Destiny and Mission in American History: A Reinterpretation* (1963), and *The Monroe Doctrine and American Expansionism, 1843–1849* (1966); Paul C. Nagel, *One Nation Indivisible: The Union in American Thought, 1776–1861* (1964); Dexter Perkins, *The Monroe Doctrine* (1927); Gregg Russell, *John Quincy Adams and the Public Virtues of Diplomacy* (1995).

The Growth of the American Economy

Richard A. Bartlett, *The New Country: A Social History of the American Frontier, 1776–1890* (1974); Alfred D. Chandler, Jr., ed., *The Railroads: The Nation's First Big Business* (1965), and *The Visible Hand* (1977); Howard Chudacoff, *The Evolution of American Urban Society* (1975); Victor S. Clark, *History of Manufactures in the United States, 1607–1860*, 2 vols. (1916–1928); Thomas C. Cochran, *Frontiers of Change: Early Industrialism in America* (1981); Robert F. Dalzell, Jr., *Enterprising Elite: The Boston Associates and the World They Made* (1987); Clarence H. Danhof, *Change in Agriculture: The Northern United States, 1820–1870* (1969); Paul David, *Technical Choice, Innovation and Economic Growth* (1975); Lance Davis et al., *American Economic Growth: An Economist's History of the United States* (1972); Everett Dick, *The Lure of the Land: A Social History of the Public Lands* (1970); Joseph A. Durrenberger, *Turnpikes: A Study of the Toll Road Movement* (1968); John Faragher, *Sugar Creek* (1986); Albert Fishlow, *American Railroads and the Transformation of the Antebellum Economy* (1965); Paul W. Gates, *The Farmer's Age: Agriculture, 1815–1860* (1960); Sigfried Giedion, *Mechanization Takes Command* (1948); Carter Goodrich, ed., *Canals and American Economic Development* (1961), and *Government Promotion of American Canals and Railroads, 1800–1890* (1960); Ralph D. Gray, *The National Waterway: A History of the Chesapeake and Delaware Canal*, 2d ed. (1989); Erik F. Haites, James Mak, and Gary M. Walton, *Western River Transportation: The Era of Early Internal Development, 1810–1860* (1975); David Hamer, *New Towns in the New World: Images and Perceptions of the Nineteenth-Century Urban Frontier* (1990); Oscar and Mary Handlin, *Commonwealth: A Study of the Role of Government in the American Economy*, rev. ed. (1969); Louis Hartz, *Economic Policy and Democratic Thought* (1948); Morton Horwitz, *The Transformation of American Law, 1780–1860* (1977); David A. Hounshell, *From the American System to Mass Production* (1984); Louis C. Hunter, *Steamboats on the Western Rivers* (1949); James Willard Hurst, *Law and the Conditions of Freedom in the Nineteenth-Century United States* (1956), and *The Legitimacy of the Business Corporation in the Law of the United States, 1780–1970* (1970); David J. Jeremy, *Transatlantic In-*

dustrial Revolution: The Diffusion of Textile Technologies Between Britain and America, 1790–1830s (1981); Arthur M. Johnson and Barry Supple, Boston Capitalists and Western Railroads: A Study in the Nineteenth Century Railroad Investment Process (1967); John F. Kasson, Civilizing the Machine: Technology and Republican Values in America, 1776–1900 (1976); Darwin P. Kelsey, ed., Farming in the New Nation (1972); Susan Previant Lee and Peter Passell, A New Economic View of American History (1979); Leonard W. Levy, The Law of the Commonwealth and Chief Justice Shaw (1957); Timothy R. Mahoney, River Towns in the Great West: The Structure of Provincial Urbanization in the American Midwest, 1820–1870 (1990); Blake McKelvey, American Urbanization: A Comparative History (1973); Nathan Miller, The Enterprise of a Free People: Aspects of Economic Development in New York State During the Canal Period, 1792–1838 (1962); Zane Miller, The Urbanization of America (1973); Eric H. Monkkonen, America Becomes Urban: The Development of U.S. Cities and Towns (1988); William Nelson, The Americanization of the Common Law: The Impact of Legal Change on Massachusetts Society, 1760–1830 (1975); James D. Norris, R. G. Dun and Co., 1841–1900 (1978); Douglas C. North, Growth and Welfare in the American Past, 2d ed. (1974); F. S. Philbrick, The Rise of the West, 1754–1830 (1965); Glenn Porter and Harold C. Livesay, Merchants and Manufacturers: Studies in the Changing Structure of Nineteenth-Century Marketing (1971); J. Potter, "The Growth of Population in America, 1700–1860" in D. V. Glass and D. E. C. Eversley, eds., Population in History (1965); Allan R. Pred, Urban Growth and the Circulation of Information (1973); Malcolm J. Rohrbough, The Land Office Business (1960), and The Trans-Appalachian Frontier (1978); Nathan Rosenberg, Technology and American Economic Growth (1972); Harry Scheiber, Ohio Canal Era: A Case Study of Government and the Economy, 1820–1861 (1969); Leo F. Schnore, ed., The New Urban History: Quantitative Explorations by American Historians (1975); Ronald E. Shaw, Canals for a Nation: The Canal Era in the United States (1990), and Erie Water West: A History of the Erie Canal, 1792–1854 (1966); Carl Siracusa, A Mechanical People: Perceptions of the Industrial Order in Massachusetts, 1815–1880 (1979); Merritt Roe Smith, Harpers Ferry Armory and the New Technology (1977); John R. Stilgoe, Borderland: Origins of the American Suburb (1988); John F. Stover, Iron Road to the West: American Railroads in the 1850s (1978), and The Life and Decline of the American Railroad (1970); Alan Taylor, William Cooper's Town (1995); George Rogers Taylor, The Transportation Revolution (1951); Jon C. Teaford, The Municipal Revolution in America: Origins of Modern Urban Government, 1650–1825 (1975); Peter Temin, Causal Factors in American Economic Growth in the Nineteenth Century (1975), and Iron and Steel in Nineteenth Century America (1964); Stephan Thernstrom and Richard Sennett, eds., Nineteenth-Century Cities: Essays in the New Urban History (1969); Robert L. Thompson, Wiring a Continent: The History of the Telegraph Industry in the United States, 1832–1866 (1947); Dale Van Every, The Final Challenge: The American Frontier, 1804–1845 (1964); Richard C. Wade, The Urban Frontier (1959); Caroline F. Ware, The Early New England Cotton Manufacture (1931); Sam Bass Warner, Jr., The Private City: Philadelphia in Three Periods of Its Growth (1968), and The Urban Wilderness (1972); James W. Whitaker, ed., Farming in the Midwest, 1840–1900 (1974).

The Growth of Political Factionalism and Sectionalism

David Brion Davis, The Problem of Slavery in the Age of Revolution, 1770–1823 (1975); Don E. Fehrenbacher, The South and Three Sectional Crises (1980); Staughton Lynd, Class Conflict, Slavery and the United States Constitution (1967); Duncan J. MacLeod, Slavery, Race, and the American Revolution (1974); Glover Moore, The Missouri Controversy (1953); D. L. Robinson, Slavery in the Structure of American Politics, 1765–1820 (1971); Murray N. Rothbard, The Panic of 1819: Reactions and Policies (1962).

Biographies

Harry Ammon, James Monroe: The Quest for National Identity (1971); Leonard Baker, John Marshall: A Life in Law (1974); Samuel Flagg Bemis, John Quincy Adams and the Foundations of American Foreign Policy (1949), and John Quincy Adams and the Union (1956); Evan Cornog, The Birth of Empire: Dewitt Clinton and the American Experience, 1769–1828 (1998); Richard Current, Daniel Webster and the Rise of National Conservatism (1955); Gerald T. Dunne, Justice Joseph Story and the Rise of the Supreme Court (1970); Clement Eaton, Henry Clay and the Art of American Politics (1957); Mary W. M. Hargreaves, The Presidency of John Quincy Adams (1985); John Horton, James Kent: A Study in Conservatism (1939); George A. Lipsky, John Quincy Adams: His Theory and Ideas (1950); J. H. Powell, Richard Rush: Republican Diplomat (1942); F. N. Stites, John Marshall: Defender of the Constitution (1981); Barbara M. Tucker, Samuel Slater and the Origins of the American Textile Industry, 1790–1860 (1984); Glyndon G. Van Deusen, The Life of Henry Clay (1937); Charles M. Wiltse, John C. Calhoun: Nationalist, 1782–1828 (1944).

INTERNET RESOURCES

Prairietown, Indiana
http://www.indianapolis.in.us/cp/stories.html
This fictional model of a town and its inhabitants on the early frontier says much about America's movement westward and the everyday lives of Americans.

The Seminole Indians of Florida
http://www.seminoletribes.com/
Before he was president, Andrew Jackson began a war against the Seminole Indians.

Whole Cloth: Discovering Science and Technology Through American Textile History
http://www.si.edu/lemelson/centerpieces/whole_cloth/
The Jerome and Dorothy Lemelson Center for the Study of Invention and Innovation/Society for the History of Tech-

nology put together this site, which includes excellent activities and sources concerning early American manufacturing and industry.

The National Road
http://www.connerprairie.org/ntlroad.html
The National Road was a hot political topic in the early republic and was part of the beginning of the development of America's infrastructure.

Nineteenth Century Scientific American Online
http://www.history.rochester.edu/Scientific_American/
Magazines and journals are windows through which we can view society. This site provides online editions of one of the more interesting nineteenth-century journals.

KEY TERMS

Era of Good Feelings   (p. 234)

James Monroe   (p. 235)

Henry Clay   (p. 236)

John C. Calhoun   (p. 236)

Daniel Webster   (p. 236)

McCullough v. *Maryland*   (p. 239)

Dartmouth v. *Woodward*   (p. 240)

Monroe Doctrine   (p. 241)

American System of Production   (p. 245)

Eli Whitney   (p. 245)

REVIEW QUESTIONS

1. Why is the period following the War of 1812 called the "Era of Good Feelings"? What political, social, and economic developments contributed to a growing sense of nationalism after the conflict?

2. In what ways did the Supreme Court strengthen the authority of the national government?

3. What problems had to be overcome for the United States to develop a vigorous economy? How did the United States overcome the problems of scarce labor and poor transportation and communication?

4. Identify the main provisions of the Monroe Doctrine.

5. Explain how the Panic of 1819 and the Missouri Crisis ended the "Era of Good Feelings" and helped produce new sectional and party divisions.

GW

CHE

AS BOUDINOTT.   CONST

DARRIS,

A GOOD CONSCIENCE.

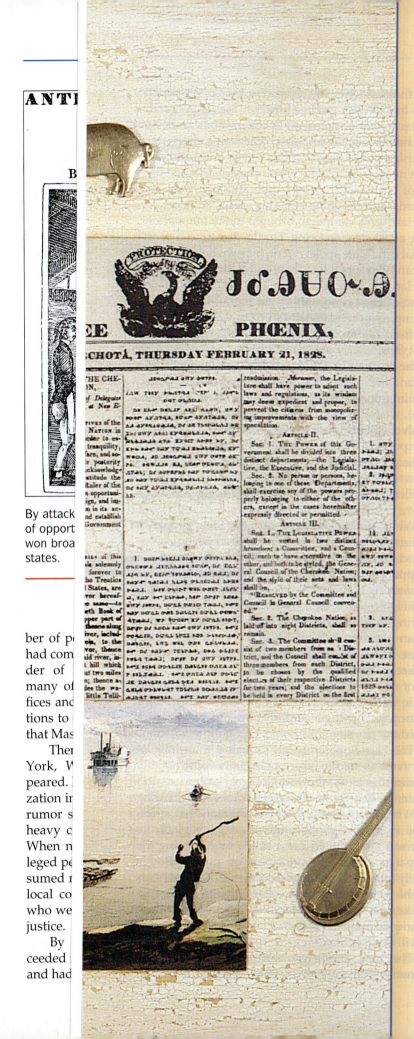

By attack
of opport
won broa
states.

ber of p
had com
der of
many of
fices and
tions to
that Mas
    Ther
York, W
peared. I
zation in
rumor s
heavy c
When r
leged pe
sumed r
local co
who we
justice.
    By
ceeded :
and had

10

POWER AND POLITICS IN JACKSON'S AMERICA

THE American Mosaic

The Cholera Epidemic of 1832: Sinners and Saints

IN the spring of 1832, Americans braced themselves for an attack by cholera—what one historian has called "the classic epidemic disease of the nineteenth century." They knew it was coming. Throughout the preceding year, newspapers had reported with alarm the disease's escape from its Asian homeland and its westward march across Europe. The press had turned shrill when cholera crossed the Atlantic Ocean—the last great barrier that shielded the Americas from this horrible plague—and struck Canada in June 1832. Despite the certainty that the disease would soon reach the United States, however, neither the federal, state, nor local governments did much to prevent or even prepare for an epidemic.

Nothing in their inventory of illnesses, not even the ravages of smallpox or malaria, had prepared Americans for the terror that seized them when cholera finally appeared. Their fear is easily understood: Cholera killed approximately half of those who contracted it, and it struck with unbelievable rapidity. A New Yorker who survived the 1832 epidemic testified that he was walking down the street when he suddenly fell forward on his face "as if knocked down with an axe."

Cholera's symptoms, which mimic those of severe arsenic poisoning, are indeed spectacular. The onset of the disease is marked by acute diarrhea, uncontrollable vomiting, and violent abdominal cramps. Within hours, this sudden and massive loss of fluids causes dehydration, and the victim's extremities feel cold, the face turns blue, and the feet and hands

appear dark and swollen. Unless proper medical treatment is provided, death can follow within a few hours after the first symptoms appear, or, at most, within a few days. Even more than its devastating symptoms, it was the disease's ability to kill so swiftly that terrorized the public. "To see individuals well in the morning & buried before night, retiring apparently well & dead in the morning is something which is appalling to the boldest heart," exclaimed another survivor of America's first cholera epidemic.

The cause of cholera was not discovered until 1883 when Robert Koch, the famous scientist, led a commission to Egypt that isolated *Vibrio comma*, the guilty bacterium. These deadly germs settle in the intestines of their victims, following a journey along any one of several pathways that lead to the human digestive tract. Although dirty hands or raw fruits and vegetables often transmit the disease, most cholera epidemics are spread by polluted drinking water from sewage-contaminated water systems.

Unfortunately, America's cities in 1832 harbored more than enough filth to nurture an epidemic. New York was especially dirty. Residents were required by law to pile their garbage in the gutter in front of their homes for removal by the city, but it seldom got collected. (With their characteristic sense of humor, New Yorkers dubbed these piles of stinking, decomposing garbage "corporation pie.") The only effective "sanitary engineers" in New York were

the thousands of swine that roamed the streets gorging themselves on the refuse.

Thanks to this filth, cholera unleashed a great plague of death when it reached New York. Thousands died in the epidemic, producing so many bodies that the undertakers could not keep up with the volume and had to stack corpses in warehouses and public buildings to await burial. In short, cholera hit New York with the same force with which yellow fever had knocked Philadelphia to its knees in 1793 (see pp. 198–199).

In the midst of their suffering, New Yorkers could not help but wonder why some people contracted the disease while others escaped it. To answer this question, America's physicians espoused a doctrine of predisposing causes. People who kept God's laws, they explained, had nothing to fear, but the intemperate and the filthy stood at great risk. In fact, physicians elaborated their warnings about "predisposing" or "exciting" causes into a jeremiad against sin. Impiety, imprudence, idleness, drunkenness, gluttony, and sexual excess all left their devotees weakened and "artificially stimulated" their bodies to be vulnerable to cholera.

Because the disease was "decidedly vulgar," physicians predicted that it would confine itself largely to the lower classes—specifically, to blacks and to the Irish, who were thought by upper-class individuals to be the most intemperate and debauched members of society. Here, then, was a classic example of how the medical profession appropriated

their water was an excellent purgative, they might as well have called it "liquid death" when cholera swept the land.

Once cholera struck, physicians found that none of the traditional remedies of heroic medicine worked. In addition to bloodletting, they treated their patients with laudanum (the main ingredient of which was opium), tobacco smoke, enemas, and huge doses of calomel, a chalky mercury compound employed as a cathartic. In desperation, one of New York's leading physicians (a practical thinker) even recommended plugging the patient's rectum with beeswax to halt the diarrhea.

Many Americans turned to quacks or treated themselves with home remedies. It made no difference. Those who survived the epidemic did so in spite of the medical care they received, not because of it.

Cholera receded from the land almost as quickly as it had come. By the fall of 1832 the epidemic had spent its fury, and by the winter it was gone. When it struck again in 1866, Americans had learned how to battle the disease. They no longer talked about cholera in moral terms as God's vengeance on the poor and the wicked. Instead, they approached it as a social problem amenable to human intervention. They imposed quarantines, opened emergency hospitals, increased the powers of health authorities, removed the trash and garbage from city streets, and cleaned up municipal water supplies. The contrast between 1832 and 1866 could not have been more complete.

Within the span of two generations, the public changed the way it viewed disease. American physicians became more scientific in handling and treating the sick—eloquent testimony to the medical advances in a modernizing society.

social attitudes regarding class and race to blame the victims of disease for their suffering.

The doctors appeared to be right, but for the wrong reasons. Cholera was indeed a "poor man's plague"; sin, however, was not the explanation. The upper classes suffered less because they fled the cities for country homes and lodges where pure water and low population density prevented infection. The poor, by contrast, could not afford to leave: they had to remain and take their chances.

Most of New York's lower classes lived in tiny, unvented apartments where entire families (and perhaps a boarder or two) occupied a single room; the most wretched subsisted in unfurnished cellars whose walls glistened with sewage and slime every time it rained. Instead of pure water imported in hogsheads from fresh water springs in the countryside (the only water the wealthy would touch), the poor drew their drinking water from the river or from contaminated shallow wells. Though New Yorkers had long joked that

disagreed with probusiness interests, which called for the extension of credit, higher tariffs to protect infant industries, and government-financed transportation improvements to reduce the cost of trade.

A second source of political division was southern alarm over the slavery debates in Congress in 1819 and 1820. Many southern leaders feared that the Missouri crisis (see pp. 248–249, 252) might spark a realignment in national politics along sectional lines. Such a development, John Quincy Adams wrote, was "terrible to the South—threatening in its progress the emancipation of all their slaves, threatening in its immediate effect that Southern domination which has swayed the Union for the last twenty years." Anxiety over the slavery debates in 1819 and 1820 induced many southerners to seek political alliances with the North. As early as 1821, Old Republicans in the South—who opposed high tariffs, a national bank, and federally funded internal improvements—had begun to form a loose alliance with Senator Martin Van Buren of New York and the Republican party faction he commanded.

The third major source of political division was the selection of presidential candidates. The "Virginia dynasty" of presidents, a chain that had begun with George Washington and included Thomas Jefferson, James Madison, and James Monroe, was at its end by 1824. Traditionally, a caucus of the Republican party's members of Congress selected the Republican party's candidate. At the 1824 caucus, the members met in closed session and chose William Crawford, Monroe's secretary of the Treasury, as the party's candidate. Not all Republicans, however, supported this method of nominating candidates and therefore refused to participate.

When Crawford suffered a stroke and was left partially disabled, four other candidates emerged: Secretary of State John Quincy Adams, the son of the nation's second president and the only candidate from the North; John C. Calhoun, Monroe's secretary

of war, who had little support outside of his native South Carolina; Henry Clay, the Speaker of the House; and General Andrew Jackson, the hero of the Battle of New Orleans and victor over the Creek and Seminole Indians. About the latter, Thomas Jefferson commented dryly, one might as well try "to make a soldier of a goose as a President of Andrew Jackson."

In the election of 1824, Jackson received the greatest number of votes both at the polls and in the electoral college, followed (in electoral votes) by Adams, Crawford, and then Clay. But he failed to receive the constitutionally required majority of the electoral votes. As provided by the Twelfth Amendment of the Constitution, the election was therefore thrown into the House of Representatives, which was required to choose from among the top three vote-getters in the electoral college. There, Henry Clay persuaded his supporters to vote for Adams, commenting acidly that he did not believe "that killing two thousand five hundred Englishmen at New Orleans" was a proper qualification for the presidency. Adams was elected on the first ballot.

The Philadelphia *Observer* charged that Adams had made a secret deal to obtain Clay's support. Three days later, Adams's nomination of Clay as secretary of state seemed to confirm the charges of a "corrupt bargain." Jackson was outraged, since he could legitimately argue that he was the popular favorite. The general exclaimed, "The Judas of the West has closed the contract and will receive the thirty pieces of silver."

The Presidency of John Quincy Adams

John Quincy Adams was one of the most brilliant and well-qualified men ever to occupy the White House. A deeply religious, intensely scholarly man, he read Biblical passages at least three times a day—once in English, once in German, and once in French. He was fluent in seven foreign languages, including Greek and Latin. During his remarkable career as a diplomat and secretary of state, he negotiated the treaty that ended the War of 1812, acquired the Floridas, and conceived the Monroe Doctrine.

But Adams lacked the political skills and personality necessary to create support for his program. Like his father, Adams lacked personal warmth. His adversaries mockingly described him as a "chip off the old iceberg."

Adams's problems as president did not arise exclusively from his temperament. His misfortune was to serve as president at a time of growing partisan

TABLE 10.1
Election of 1824

Candidate	Party	Popular Vote	Electoral Vote
J. Q. Adams	No party	113,122	84
Jackson	designations	151,271	99
Clay		47,531	37
Crawford		40,856	41

divisions. The Republican party had split into two distinct camps. Adams and his supporters, known as National Republicans, favored a vigorous role for the central government in promoting national economic growth, while the Jacksonian Democrats demanded a limited government and strict adherence to laissez-faire principles.

As the only president to lose both the popular vote and the electoral vote, Adams faced hostility from the start. Jackson and his supporters accused the new president of "corruptions and intrigues" to gain Henry Clay's support. Acutely aware of the fact that "two-thirds of the whole people [were] averse" to his election as president, Adams promised in his inaugural address to make up for this with "intentions upright and pure; a heart devoted to the welfare of our country." A staunch nationalist, Adams proposed an extraordinary program of federal support for scientific and economic development that included a national university, astronomical observatories ("lighthouses of the skies"), federal funding of roads and canals, and exploration of the country's territory—all to be financed by a high tariff.

Adams's advocacy of a strong federal government and a high tariff enraged defenders of slavery and states' rights advocates who clung to traditional Jeffersonian principles of limited government and strict construction of the Constitution. They feared that any expansion of federal authority might set a precedent for interference with slavery. Thomas Jefferson himself condemned Adams's proposals, declaring in a stinging statement that they would undermine the states and create a national elite—"an aristocracy . . . riding and ruling over the plundered ploughman and beggarded yeomanry."

Adams met with further frustration because he was unwilling to adapt to the practical demands of politics. Adams made no effort to use his patronage powers to build support for his proposals and refused to fire federal officeholders who openly opposed his policies. During his entire term in office he

John Quincy Adams won the election of 1824 in the House of Representatives even though Andrew Jackson received the most popular votes.

removed just 12 incumbents, and these only for gross incompetence. He justified his actions by saying that he did not want to make "government a perpetual and unremitting scramble for office."

Adams's Indian policies also cost him supporters. Although he, like his predecessor Monroe, wanted to remove Native Americans in the south to an area west of the Mississippi River, he believed that the state and federal governments had a duty to abide by Indian treaties and to purchase, not merely annex, Indian lands. Adams's decision to repudiate and renegotiate a fraudulent treaty that stripped the Georgia Creek Indians of their land outraged land-hungry southerners and westerners.

Even in the realm of foreign policy, his strong suit prior to the presidency, Adams encountered difficulties. His attempts to acquire Texas from Mexico through peaceful means failed, as did his efforts to persuade Britain to permit more American trade with the British West Indies.

The "American System" and the "Tariff of Abominations"

President Adams was committed to using the federal government to promote national economic development. His program included a high protective tariff to promote industry, the sale of public lands at low prices to encourage western settlement, federally financed transportation improvements, expanded markets for western grain and southern cotton, and a strong national bank to regulate the economy.

Adams's secretary of state, Henry Clay, called this economic program the **American system** because it was supposed to promote growth in all parts of the country. But the program infuriated southerners who believed that it favored Northeastern industrial interests at their region's expense. Southerners particularly disliked a protective tariff, since it raised the cost of manufactured goods, which they did not produce.

Andrew Jackson's supporters in Congress sought to exploit the tariff question in order to embarrass Adams and help Jackson win the presidency in 1828. They framed a bill, which became known as the **Tariff of Abominations,** to win support for Jackson in Kentucky, Missouri, New York, Ohio, and Pennsylvania while weakening the Adams administration in New England. The bill raised duties on iron, hemp, and flax (which would benefit westerners), while lowering the tariff on woolen goods (to the detriment of New England textile manufacturers). John Randolph of Virginia accurately described

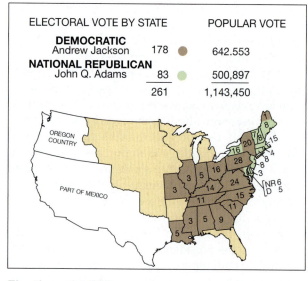

ELECTORAL VOTE BY STATE   POPULAR VOTE

DEMOCRATIC
Andrew Jackson   178 ● 642.553

NATIONAL REPUBLICAN
John Q. Adams   83 ● 500,897

        261   1,143,450

Election of 1828

the object of the bill as an effort to encourage "manufactures of no sort or kind, except the manufacture of a President of the United States."

The Tariff of Abominations created a political uproar in the South, where it was denounced as unconstitutional and discriminatory. The tariff, southerners insisted, was essentially a tax on their region to assist northern manufacturers. South Carolina expressed the loudest outcry against the tariff. At a public meeting in Charleston, protesters declared that a tariff was designed to benefit "one class of citizens [manufacturers] at the expense of every other class." Some South Carolinians called for revolutionary defiance of the national government.

Vice President John C. Calhoun, a skilled logician well versed in political theory, offered a theoretical framework for Southern discontent. Retreating from his early nationalistic position, the South Carolinian anonymously published the "South Carolina Exposition," an essay that advanced the principle of **nullification.** A single state, Calhoun maintained, might overrule or "nullify" a federal law within its own territory, until three-quarters of the states had upheld the law as constitutional. In 1828 the state of South Carolina decided not to implement this doctrine but rather to wait and see what attitude the next president would adopt toward the tariff.

The Election of 1828

"J. Q. Adams who can write" squared off against "Andy Jackson who can fight" in the election of 1828, one of the most bitter campaigns in American history. Jackson's followers repeated the charge that Adams was an "aristocrat" who had obtained office

as a result of a "corrupt bargain." The Jackson forces also alleged that the president had used public funds to buy personal luxuries and had installed gaming tables in the White House. They even charged that Mrs. Adams had been born out of wedlock.

Adams's supporters countered by digging up an old story that Jackson had begun living with his wife before she was legally divorced from her first husband (which was technically true, although neither Jackson nor his wife Rachel knew her first husband was still living). They called the general a slave trader, a gambler, and a backwoods buffoon who could not spell more than one word out of four correctly. One Philadelphia editor published a handbill picturing the coffins of 12 men allegedly murdered by Jackson in numerous duels.

The Jackson campaign in 1828 was the first to appeal directly for voter support through a professional political organization. Skilled political organizers, like Martin Van Buren of New York, Amos Kendall of Kentucky, and Thomas Ritchie of Virginia, created an extensive network of campaign committees and subcommittees to organize mass rallies, parades, and barbecues, and to erect hickory poles, Jackson's symbol.

For the first time in American history, a presidential election was the focus of public attention, and voter participation increased dramatically. Twice as many voters cast ballots in the election of 1828 as in 1824, four times as many as in 1820. As in most previous elections, the vote divided along sectional lines. Jackson swept every state in the South and West and Adams won the electoral votes of every state in the North except Pennsylvania and part of New York.

Contemporaries interpreted Jackson's resounding victory as a triumph for political democracy. Jackson's supporters called the vote a victory for the "farmers and mechanics of the country" over the "rich and well born." Even Jackson's opponents agreed that the election marked a watershed in the nation's political history, signaling the beginning of a new democratic age. One Adams supporter said bluntly, "a great revolution has taken place."

ANDREW JACKSON: THE POLITICS OF EGALITARIANISM

Supporters of Adams regarded Jackson's victory with deep pessimism. A justice of the Supreme Court declared, "The reign of King 'Mob' seems triumphant." But enthusiasts greeted Jackson's victory as a great triumph for the people. At the inaugural, a cable stretched in front of the east portico of the Capitol to keep back the throngs snapped under the pres-

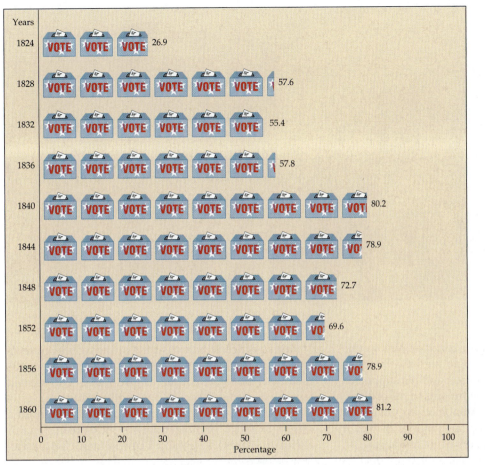

Years		
1824	VOTE VOTE VOTE	26.9
1828	VOTE VOTE VOTE VOTE VOTE VOTE	57.6
1832	VOTE VOTE VOTE VOTE VOTE VOTE	55.4
1836	VOTE VOTE VOTE VOTE VOTE VOTE	57.8
1840	VOTE VOTE VOTE VOTE VOTE VOTE VOTE VOTE VOT	80.2
1844	VOTE VOTE VOTE VOTE VOTE VOTE VOTE VOTE VO	78.9
1848	VOTE VOTE VOTE VOTE VOTE VOTE VOTE VOTE	72.7
1852	VOTE VOTE VOTE VOTE VOTE VOTE VOTE VO	69.6
1856	VOTE VOTE VOTE VOTE VOTE VOTE VOTE VOTE VO	78.9
1860	VOTE VOTE VOTE VOTE VOTE VOTE VOTE VOTE VOTE	81.2

0   10   20   30   40   50   60   70   80   90   100
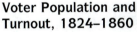
Percentage

Voter Population and Turnout, 1824–1860

sure of the surging crowd. As many as 20,000 well-wishers attended a White House reception to honor the new president, muddying rugs, breaking furniture, and damaging china and glassware. "It was a proud day for the people," commented one Kentucky newspaperman. "General Jackson is their own President."

In certain respects, Jackson was truly a self-made man. Born in 1767 in a frontier region along the North and South Carolina border, he was the first president to be born in a log cabin. His father, a poor farmer from northern Ireland, died two weeks before his birth, while his mother and two brothers died during the American Revolution. At the age of 13, Jackson volunteered to fight in the American Revolution. He was taken prisoner and a British officer severely slashed Jackson's hand and head when the boy refused to shine the officer's shoes.

Jackson soon rose from poverty to a career in law and politics, becoming Tennessee's first congressman, a senator, and judge on the state supreme court. Although he would later gain a reputation as the champion of the common people, in Tennessee he was allied by marriage, business, and political ties to the state's elite. As a land speculator, cotton planter, and attorney, he accumulated a large personal fortune and acquired more than 100 slaves. His candidacy for the presidency was initially promoted by speculators, creditors, and elite leaders in Tennessee who hoped to exploit Jackson's popularity in order to combat antibanking sentiment and fend off challenges to their dominance of state politics.

Expanding the Powers of the Presidency

In office, Jackson greatly enhanced the power and prestige of the presidency. While each member of Congress represented a specific regional constituency, only the president, Jackson declared, represented all the people of the United States.

Jackson convinced many Americans that their votes mattered. He espoused a political ideology of "democratic republicanism" that stressed the common peoples' virtue, intelligence, and capacity for self-government. He also expressed a deep disdain for the "better classes," which claimed a "more enlightened wisdom" than common men and women.

Twenty thousand people attended a reception for President Jackson at the White House, trampling rugs, breaking furniture, and damaging china.

Endorsing the view that a fundamental conflict existed between working people and the "nonproducing" classes of society, Jackson and his supporters promised to remove any impediments to the ordinary citizen's opportunities for economic improvement. According to the Jacksonians, inequalities of wealth and power were the direct result of monopoly, favoritism, and special privileges, which made "the rich richer and the powerful more potent." Only free competition in an open marketplace would ensure that wealth would be distributed in accordance with each person's "industry, economy, enterprise, and prudence." The goal of the Jacksonians was to remove all obstacles that prevented farmers, artisans, and small shopkeepers from earning a greater share of the nation's wealth.

Nowhere was the Jacksonian ideal of openness made more concrete than in Jackson's theory of rotation in office, known as the **spoils system.** In his first annual message to Congress, Jackson defended the principle that public offices should be rotated among party supporters in order to help the nation achieve its republican ideals. Performance in public office, Jackson maintained, required no special intelligence or training, and ro-

Known as a champion of the common people, President Jackson greatly expanded the powers of the presidency.

tation in office would ensure that the federal government did not develop a class of corrupt civil servants set apart from the people. His supporters advocated the spoils system on practical political grounds, viewing it as a way to reward party loyalists and build a stronger party organization. As Jacksonian Senator William Marcy of New York proclaimed, "To the victor belongs the spoils."

The spoils system opened government positions to many of Jackson's supporters, but the practice was neither as new nor as democratic as it appeared. During his first 18 months in office, Jackson replaced fewer than 1000 of the nation's 10,000 civil servants on political grounds, and fewer than 20 percent of federal officeholders were removed during his administration. Moreover, many of the men Jackson appointed to office had backgrounds of wealth and social eminence. Further, Jackson did not originate the spoils system. By the time he took office, a number of states, including New York and Pennsylvania, practiced political patronage.

Clearing the Land of Indians

The first major political controversy of Jackson's presidency involved Indian policy. At the time Jackson took office, 125,000 Native Americans still lived east of the Mississippi River. Cherokee, Choctaw, Chickasaw, and Creek Indians—60,000 strong—held millions of acres in what would become the southern cotton kingdom stretching across Georgia, Alabama, and Mississippi. The key political issues were whether these Native-American groups would be permitted to block white expansion and whether the U.S. government and its citizens would abide by previously made treaties.

Since Jefferson's presidency, two conflicting policies, assimilation and removal, had governed the treatment of Native Americans. Assimilation encouraged Indians to adopt the customs and economic practices of white Americans. The government provided financial assistance to missionaries in order to Christianize and educate Native Americans and convince them to adopt single-family farms. Proponents defended assimilation as the only way Native Americans would be able to survive in a white-dominated society.

By the 1820s, the Cherokee had demonstrated the ability of Native Americans to adapt to changing conditions while maintaining their tribal heritage. Sequoyah, a leader of these people, had developed a written alphabet. Soon the Cherokee opened schools, established churches, built roads, operated printing presses, and even adopted a constitution.

The other policy—**removal**—was first suggested by Thomas Jefferson as the only way to ensure the survival of Native American cultures. The goal of this policy was to encourage the voluntary migration of Indians westward to tracts of land where they could live free from white harassment. As early as 1817, James Monroe declared that the nation's security depended on rapid settlement along the Southern coast and that it was in the best interests of Native Americans to move westward. In 1825 he set before Congress a plan to resettle all eastern Indians on tracts in the West where whites would not be allowed to live.

After initially supporting both policies, Jackson favored removal as the solution to the controversy. This shift in federal Indian policy came partly as a result of a controversy between the Cherokee nation and the state of Georgia. The Cherokee people had adopted a constitution asserting sovereignty over their land. The state responded by abolishing tribal rule and claiming that the Cherokee fell under its jurisdiction. The discovery of gold on Cherokee land triggered a land rush, and the Cherokee nation sued to keep white settlers from encroaching on their territory. In two important cases, *Cherokee Nation* v. *Georgia* in 1831 and *Worcester* v. *Georgia* in 1832, the Supreme Court ruled that states could not pass laws conflicting with federal Indian treaties and that the federal government had an obligation to exclude white intruders from Indian lands. Angered, Jackson is said to have exclaimed: "John Marshall has made his decision; now let him enforce it."

The primary thrust of Jackson's removal policy was to encourage Native Americans to sell their homelands in exchange for new lands in Oklahoma and Arkansas. Such a policy, the president maintained, would open new farmland to whites while offering Indians a haven where they would be free to develop at their own pace. "There," he wrote, "your white brothers will not trouble you, they will have

In 1809 a Cherokee named Sequoyah began to devise an alphabet consisting of letters based on English, Greek, and Hebrew. The Cherokee nation's weekly newspaper, the *Cherokee Phoenix*, was printed with this alphabet.

no claims to the land, and you can live upon it, you and all your children, as long as the grass grows or the water runs, in peace and plenty."

Pushmataha, a Choctaw chieftain, called on his people to reject Jackson's offer. Far from being a "country of tall trees, many water courses, rich lands and high grass abounding in games of all kinds," the promised preserve in the West was simply a barren desert. Jackson responded by warning that if the Choctaw refused to move west, he would destroy their nation.

During the winter of 1831, the Choctaw became the first tribe to walk the "Trail of Tears" westward. Promised government assistance failed to arrive, and malnutrition, exposure, and a cholera epidemic killed many members of the nation. Then, in 1836, the Creek suffered the hardships of removal. About 3500 of the tribe's 15,000 members died along the westward trek. Those who resisted removal were bound in chains and marched in double file.

Emboldened by the Supreme Court decisions declaring that Georgia law had no force on Indian territory, the Cherokees resisted removal. Fifteen thousand Cherokee joined in a protest against Jackson's policy: "Little did [we] anticipate that when taught to think and feel as the American citizen ... [we] were to be despoiled by [our] guardian, to become strangers and wanderers in the land of [our] fathers, forced to return to the savage life, and to seek a new home in the wilds of the far west, and that without [our] consent." The federal government bribed a faction of the tribe to leave the land in exchange for transportation costs and $5 million, but most Cherokees held out until 1838, when the army evicted them from their land. All told, 4000 of the 15,000 Cherokee died along the trail to Indian territory in what is now Oklahoma.

A number of other tribes also organized resistance against removal. In the Old Northwest, the Sauk and Fox Indians fought the Black Hawk War (1832) to re-

Trail of Tears (Indian Removal)

Andrew Jackson's Indian removal policy was known to many Native Americans as the Trail of Tears. Native Americans were herded westward off their lands in order to open the territory for expansion. The trek brought death to perhaps one-fourth of those who set out.

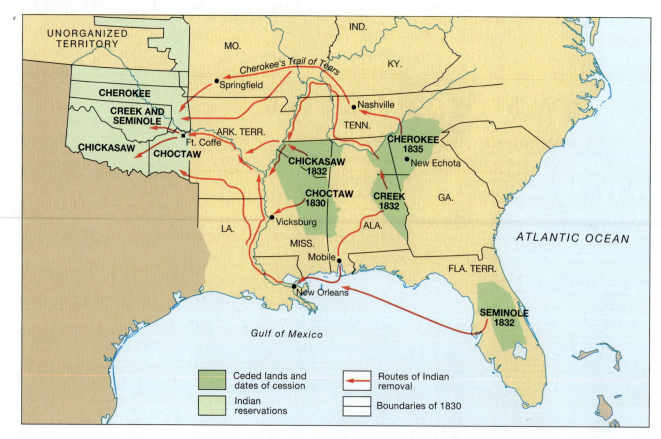

Black Hawk War

The Sauk and Fox resisted removal and fought the Black Hawk War to recover ceded lands in Illinois and Wisconsin. The U.S. army and the Illinois state militia ruthlessly suppressed the Native Americans.

cover ceded tribal lands in Illinois and Wisconsin. The Indians claimed that when they had signed the treaty transferring title to their land, they had not understood the implications of the action. "I touched the goose quill to the treaty," said Chief Black Hawk, "not knowing, however, that by that act I consented to give away my village." The United States army and the Illinois state militia ended the resistance by wantonly killing nearly 500 Sauk and Fox men, women, and children who were trying to retreat across the Mississippi River. In Florida, the military spent seven years putting down Seminole resistance at a cost of $20 million and 1500 casualties, and even then succeeding only after the treacherous act of kidnapping the Seminole leader Osceola during peace talks.

By twentieth-century standards, Jackson's Indian policy was both callous and inhumane. Despite the semblance of legality—94 treaties were signed with Indians during Jackson's presidency—Native-American migrations to the West almost always occurred under the threat of government coercion. Even before Jackson's death in 1845, it was obvious that tribal lands in the West were no more secure than Indian lands had been in the East. In 1851 Congress passed the Indian Appropriations Act, which sought to concentrate the western Native-American population on reservations.

Why were such morally indefensible policies adopted? Because many white Americans regarded Indian control of land and other natural resources as a serious obstacle to their desire for expansion and as a potential threat to the nation's security. Even had the federal government wanted to, it probably lacked the resources and military means necessary to protect the eastern Indians from encroaching white farmers, squatters, traders, and speculators. By the 1830s, a growing number of missionaries and humanitarians agreed with Jackson that Indians needed to be resettled westward for their own protection. Removal failed in large part because of the nation's commitment to limited government and its lack of

THE PEOPLE SPEAK

The Cherokee Nation Protests Against Jackson's Removal Policy (1836)

The Cherokee nation did not respond passively to President Andrew Jackson's efforts to evict them from their land. They challenged the removal policy in court. In 1836, 15,000 members of the nation submitted a protest to Congress, denouncing the evils of the removal policy and declaring that the agreements that supposedly justified their removal from their homelands had been obtained by fraud.

It will be seen, from the numerous subsisting treaties . . . that . . . in consideration of valuable concessions made by the Cherokee nation, the United States solemnly guaranteed to said nation all their lands . . . and pledged the faith of the government, that "all white people who have intruded, or may hereafter intrude on the lands reserved for the Cherokees, shall be removed by the United States. . . ." The Cherokees were happy and prosperous under a scrupulous observance of treaty stipulations by the government of the United States, and from the fostering hand extended over them, they made rapid advance in civilization, morals, and the arts and sciences. Little did they anticipate, that when taught to think and feel as the American citizen, and to have with him a common interest, they were to be *despoiled by their guardian*, to become strangers and wanderers in the land of their fathers, forced to return to the savage life, and to seek a new home in the wilds of the far west, and that without their consent. An instrument purporting to be a treaty with the Cherokee people, has recently been made public by the President of the United States, that will have such an operation if carried into effect. This instrument, the delegation aver before the civilized world, and in the presence of Almighty God, is fraudulent, false upon its face, made by unauthorized individuals, without the sanction, and against the wishes, of the great body of the Cherokee people. Upwards of fifteen thousand of those people have protested against it, solemnly declaring they will never acquiesce. . . .

Source: "Memorial and Protest of the Cherokee Nation," June 22, 1836, Exec. Doc. No. 286, 24th Cong., 1st sess., pp. 1–2.

experience with social welfare programs. Contracts for food, clothing, and transportation were awarded to the lowest bidders, many of whom failed to fulfill their contractual responsibilities. Indians were resettled on semiarid lands, unsuited for intensive farming. The tragic outcome was readily foreseeable.

The problem of preserving native cultures in the face of an expanding nation was not confined to the United States. Jackson's removal policy can only be properly understood when seen as part of a broader process: the political and economic conquest of frontier regions by expanding nation states. During the early decades of the nineteenth century, Western nations were penetrating into many frontier areas, including the steppes of Russia, the pampas of Argentina, the veldt of South Africa, the outback of Australia, and the American West. In each of these regions, national expansion was justified on the grounds of strategic interest (to preempt settlement by other powers) or in the name of opening valuable land to white settlement and development. And in each case, expansion was accompanied by the removal or wholesale killing of native peoples.

Sectional Disputes over Public Lands and Nullification

Bitter sectional disputes arose during Jackson's presidency over public lands and the tariff. After the Revolutionary War, the federal government owned one-quarter billion acres of public land; the Louisiana Purchase added another half-billion acres to the public domain. These public lands constituted the federal government's single greatest resource.

In 1820, to promote the establishment of farms, Congress encouraged the rapid sale of public land by reducing the minimum land purchase from 160 to just 80 acres at a price of $1.25 per acre. Still, a variety of groups favored even easier terms for land sales. Squatters, for example, who violated federal laws that forbade settlement prior to the completion of public surveys, pressured Congress to adopt preemption acts that would permit them to buy the land they occupied at the minimum price of $1.25 when it came up for sale. Urban workingmen—agitating under the slogan "Vote Yourself a Farm"—demanded free homesteads for any American who would settle the public domain. Transportation companies, which built roads, canals, and later railroads, called for grants of public land to help fund their projects.

In Congress, two proposals—"distribution" and "graduation"—competed for support. Under the distribution proposal, which was identified with Henry Clay, Congress would distribute the proceeds from the sale of public lands to the states, which would use it to finance transportation improvements. Senator Thomas Hart Benton of Missouri offered an alternative proposal, graduation. He proposed that Congress gradually reduce the price of unsold government land and finally freely give away unpurchased land.

At the end of 1829, a Connecticut senator proposed a cessation of public land sales. This transformed the debate over public lands into a sectional battle over the nature of the union. Senator Benton denounced the proposal as a brazen attempt by manufacturers to keep laborers from settling the West, fearing that westward migration would reduce the size of the urban workforce and therefore raise their wage costs.

Benton's speech prompted Robert Y. Hayne, a supporter of John C. Calhoun, to propose an alliance of southern and western interests based on a low tariff and cheap land. Affirming the principle of nullification, he called on the two sections to unite against attempts by the Northeast to stengthen the powers of the federal government.

Daniel Webster of Massachusetts answered Hayne in one of the most famous speeches in American history. The United States, Webster proclaimed, was not simply a compact of the states. It was a creation of the people, who had invested the Constitution and the national government with ultimate sovereignty. If a state disagreed with an action of the federal government, it had a right to sue in federal court or seek to amend the Constitution, but it had no right to nullify a federal law. That would inevitably lead to anarchy and civil war. It was delusion and folly to think that Americans could have "Liberty first and Union afterwards," Webster declared. "Liberty and Union, now and forever, one and inseparable."

Jackson revealed his position on the questions of states' rights and nullification at a Jefferson Day dinner on April 13, 1830. Fixing his eyes on Vice President John C. Calhoun, Jackson expressed his sentiments with the toast: "Our Union: It must be preserved." Calhoun responded to Jackson's challenge and offered the next toast: "The Union, next to our liberty, most dear. May we always remember that it can only be preserved by distributing equally the benefits and burdens of the Union."

Relations between Jackson and Calhoun had grown increasingly strained. Jackson had learned that when Calhoun was secretary of war under Monroe he had called for Jackson's court-martial for his conduct during the military occupation of Florida in 1818. Jackson was also angry because Mrs. Calhoun had snubbed the wife of Secretary of War John H. Eaton, because Mrs. Eaton was the twice-married

In his famous oration, Senator Daniel Webster answered Senator Robert Hayne's call for states' rights, proclaiming, "Liberty and Union, now and forever, one and inseparable."

daughter of a tavernkeeper. Because Jackson's own late wife Rachel had been snubbed by society (partly because she smoked a pipe, partly because she had unknowingly married Jackson before a divorce from her first husband was final), the president had empathy for young Peggy Eaton. In 1831, Jackson reorganized his cabinet and forced Calhoun's supporters out. The next year, Calhoun became the first vice president to resign his office, when he became a senator from South Carolina.

In 1832, in an effort to conciliate the South, Jackson proposed a lower tariff. Revenue from the existing tariff (together with the sale of public lands) was so high that the federal debt was quickly being paid off; in fact on January 1, 1835, the United States Treasury had a balance of $440,000, not a penny of which was owed to anyone—the only time in U.S. history when the government was completely free of debt. The new tariff adopted in 1832 was somewhat lower than the Tariff of 1828 but still maintained the principle of protection. In protest, South Carolina's fiery "states' righters" declared both the Tariff of 1832 and the Tariff of 1828 null and void. To defend nullification, the state legislature voted to raise an army.

Jackson responded by declaring nullification illegal and then asked Congress to empower him to use force to execute federal law. Congress promptly enacted a Force Act. Privately, Jackson threatened to "hang every leader . . . of that infatuated people, sir, by martial law, irrespective of his name, or political or social position." He also dispatched a fleet of eight ships and a shipment of 5000 muskets to Fort Pinckney, a federal installation in Charleston harbor.

In Congress, Henry Clay, the "great compromiser" who had engineered the Missouri Compromise of 1820, worked feverishly to reduce South Carolina's sense of grievance. "He who loves the Union must desire to see this agitating question brought to a termination," he said. In less than a month, he persuaded Congress to enact a compromise tariff with lower levels of protection. South Carolinians backed down, rescinding the ordinance nullifying the federal tariff. As a final gesture of defiance, however, the state adopted an ordinance nullifying the Force Act.

In 1830 and 1831 South Carolina stood alone. No other southern state yet shared South Carolina's fear of federal power or its militant desire to assert the doctrine of states' rights. South Carolina's anxiety had many causes. By 1831 declining cotton prices and growing concern about the future of slavery had turned the state from a staunch supporter of economic nationalism into the nation's most aggressive advocate of states' rights. Increasingly, economic grievances fused with concerns over slavery. In 1832, the Palmetto State was one of just two states the majority of whose population was made up of slaves. By that year events throughout the hemisphere made South Carolinians desperately uneasy about the future of slavery. In 1831 and 1832 militant abolitionism had erupted in the North, slave insurrections had occurred in Southampton County, Virginia, and Jamaica, and Britain was moving to emancipate all slaves in the British Caribbean.

By using the federal tariff as the focus of their grievances, South Carolinians found an ideal way of debating the question of state sovereignty without debating the morality of slavery. Following the Missouri Compromise debates, a slave insurrection led by Denmark Vesey had been uncovered in Charleston in 1822. By 1832 South Carolinians did not want to stage debates in Congress that might bring the explosive slavery issue to the fore and possibly incite another slave revolt.

The Bank War

The major political issue of Jackson's presidency was his war against the second Bank of the United States. The banking system at the time Jackson assumed the presidency was completely different than it is today. At that time, the federal government coined only a limited supply of hard money and printed no paper money at all. The principal source of circulating currency—paper bank notes—was private commercial banks (of which there were 329 in 1829), chartered by the various states. These private, state-chartered banks supplied the credit necessary to finance land purchases, business operations, and economic growth. The notes they issued were promises to pay in gold or silver, but they were backed by a limited amount of precious metal and they fluctuated greatly in value.

In 1816, the federal government had chartered the **second Bank of the United States** partly in an effort to control the notes issued by state banks. By demanding payment in gold or silver, the national bank could discipline overspeculative private banks. But the very idea of a national bank was unpopular for various reasons. Many people blamed it for causing the Panic of 1819. Others resented its political influence. For example, Senator Daniel Webster was both the bank's chief lobbyist and a director of the bank's Boston branch. Wage earners and small-business owners blamed it for economic fluctuations and loan restrictions. Private banks resented its privileged position in the banking industry.

In 1832, Henry Clay, Daniel Webster, and other Jackson opponents in Congress, seeking an issue for that year's presidential election, passed a bill rechartering the second Bank of the United States. The bank's charter was not due to expire until 1836, but Clay and Webster wanted to force Jackson to take a clear probank or antibank position. Jackson had frequently attacked the bank as an agency through which speculators, monopolists, and other seekers after economic privilege cheated honest farmers and mechanics. Now, his adversaries wanted to force him either to sign the bill for recharter, alienating voters hostile to the bank, or veto it, antagonizing conservative voters who favored a sound banking system.

Jackson vetoed the bill in a forceful message that condemned the bank as a privileged "monopoly" created to make "rich men . . . richer by act of Congress." The bank, he declared, was "unauthorized by the Constitution, subversive of the rights of the States, and dangerous to the liberties of the people." In the presidential campaign of 1832, Henry Clay tried to make an issue of Jackson's bank veto, but Jackson swept to an easy second-term victory, defeating Clay by 219 electoral votes to 49.

Jackson interpreted his reelection as a mandate to undermine the bank still further. In September 1833, he ordered his Treasury secretary to divert federal revenues from the Bank of the United States to selected state banks, which came to be known as "pet" banks. The secretary of the Treasury and his assistant resigned rather than carry out the president's order. It was only after Jackson appointed a second new secretary that his order was implemented. Jackson's decision to divert federal deposits from the national bank prompted his adversaries in the Senate to formally censure the president's actions as arbitrary and unconstitutional. The bank's president, Nicholas Biddle, responded to Jackson's actions by reducing loans and calling in debts. "This worthy President," said Biddle, "thinks that because he has scalped Indians and imprisoned Judges he is to have his way with the Bank. He is mistaken." Jackson retorted: "The Bank . . . is trying to kill me, but I will kill it."

Jackson's decision to divert funds drew strong support from many conservative businesspeople who believed that the bank's destruction would increase the availability of credit and open up new business opportunities. Jackson, however, hated all banks, and believed that the only sound currencies were gold and silver. Having crippled the Bank of the United States, he promptly launched a crusade to replace all bank notes with hard money. Denouncing "the power which the moneyed interest derives from a paper currency," the president prohibited banks that received federal deposits from issuing bills valued at less than $5. Then, in the Specie Circular of 1836, Jackson prohibited payment for public lands in anything but gold or silver. That same year, in another antibanking measure, Congress voted to deprive pet banks of federal deposits. Instead, nearly $35 million in surplus funds was distributed to the states to help finance internal improvements.

To Jackson's supporters, the presidential veto of the bank bill was a principled assault on a bastion of wealth and special privilege. His efforts to curtail the circulation of bank notes was an effort to rid the country of a tool used by commercial interests to exploit farmers and working men and women. To his critics, the veto was an act of economic ignorance that destroyed a valuable institution that promoted monetary stability, eased the long-distance transfer of funds, provided a reserve of capital on which

As this anti-Jackson cartoon illustrates, defenders of the second Bank of the United States regarded Jackson's banking policies as a threat to the nation's economic health.

other banks drew, and helped regulate the bank notes issued by private banks. Jackson's effort to limit the circulation of bank notes was a misguided act of a "backward-looking" president, who failed to understand the role of a banking system in a modern economy.

The effect of Jackson's banking policies remains a subject of debate. Initially, land sales, canal construction, cotton production, and manufacturing boomed following Jackson's decision to divert fed-

eral funds from the bank. At the same time, however, state debts rose sharply and inflation increased dramatically. Prices climbed 28 percent in just three years. Then in 1837, just after the election of Jackson's successor Democrat Martin Van Buren, a deep financial depression struck the nation. Cotton prices fell by half. In New York City, 50,000 people were thrown out of work and 200,000 lacked adequate means of support. Hungry mobs broke into the city's flour warehouse. From across the country came "ru-

This anti-Democratic cartoon lays the blame for the Panic of 1837 on Jackson and his fiscal policies. His Specie Circular of 1836 has led to a run on the bank as panicked citizens try to exchange their paper bills for gold and silver. Debtors, unable to pay the soaring prices for food and other necessities, are being herded into the sheriff's office. A woman and her child are forced to beg for alms, while workers, idled by unemployment, hold the tools of their trade or slump in discouragement. Other targets of the cartoonist's criticism are the immigrants and drunkards pictured on the left side of the cartoon.

mor after rumor of riot, insurrection, and tumult." Not until the mid-1840s would the country fully pull out of the depression.

Who was to blame for the **Panic of 1837**? One school of thought holds Jackson responsible, arguing that his banking policies removed a vital check on the activities of state-chartered banks. Freed from the regulation of the second Bank of the United States, private banks rapidly expanded the volume of bank notes in circulation, contributing to the rapid increase in inflation. Jackson's Specie Circular of 1836, which sought to curb inflation by requiring that public land payments be made in hard currency, forced many Americans to exchange paper bills for gold and silver. Many private banks lacked sufficient reserves of hard currency and were forced to close their doors, triggering a financial crisis.

Another school of thought blames the panic on factors outside of Jackson's control. A surplus of cotton on the world market caused the price of cotton to drop sharply, throwing many southern and western cotton farmers into bankruptcy. Meanwhile, in 1836, Britain suddenly raised interest rates, which drastically reduced investment in the American economy and forced a number of states to default on loans from foreign investors.

If Jackson's policies did not necessarily cause the panic, they certainly made recovery more difficult. Jackson's hand-picked successor, Martin Van Buren, responded to the economic depression in an extremely doctrinaire way. A firm believer in the Jeffersonian principle of limited government, Van Buren refused to provide government aid to business.

Fearful that the federal government might lose funds it had deposited in private banks, Van Buren convinced Congress in 1840 to adopt an independent treasury system. Under this proposal, federal funds were locked up in insulated subtreasuries, which were totally divorced from the banking system. As a result the banking system was deprived of funds that might have aided recovery.

The Jacksonian Court

Presidents' judicial appointments represent one of their most enduring legacies. In his two terms as president, Andrew Jackson appointed five of the seven justices on the Supreme Court. To replace Chief Justice John Marshall, who died in 1835, Jackson selected his Treasury secretary, Roger B. Taney, who would lead the court for nearly three decades. Under Taney, the first chief justice to wear trousers instead of knee breeches, the Court broke with tradition and sought to extend Jacksonian principles of promoting individual opportunity by removing tra-

ditional restraints on competition in the marketplace. The Taney Court upheld the doctrine of limited liability for corporations and provided legal sanction to state subsidies for canals, turnpikes, and railroads. Taken together, the decisions of the Taney Court played a vital role in the emergence of the American system of free enterprise.

One case in particular, that of *Charles River Bridge* v. *Warren Bridge*, raised an issue fundamental to the nation's future economic growth: whether state-granted monopolies would be allowed to block competition from new enterprises. In 1828, the state of Massachusetts chartered a company to build a bridge connecting Boston and neighboring Charlestown. The owners of an existing bridge sued, claiming that their 1785 charter included an implied right to a monopoly.

In its decision, the Court ensured that monopolistic privileges granted in the past would not be allowed to interfere with public welfare. The Court held that contracts conferred only explicitly stated rights. Any ambiguity in wording should be construed in the public interest. The decision epitomized the ideals of Jacksonian democracy: a commitment to removing artificial barriers to opportunity and an emphasis upon free competition in an open marketplace.

Jackson's Legacy

Andrew Jackson was one of the nation's most resourceful and effective presidents. In the face of hostile majorities in Congress, he carried out his most important policies, affecting banking, internal improvements, Native Americans, and tariffs. As president, Jackson used the veto power more often than had all earlier presidents together during the preceding 40 years, and used it in such a way that he succeeded in representing himself as the champion of the people against special interests in Congress. In addition, his skillful use of patronage and party organization and his successful manipulation of public symbols helped create the nation's first modern political party with truly national appeal.

And yet, despite his popular appeal, Jackson's legacy is a matter of great dispute among historians. His Indian policies continue to arouse passionate criticism, while his economic policies, contrary to his reputation as the president of the common man, did little to help small farmers, artisans, and working people. In fact, his policies actually weakened the ability of the federal government to regulate the nation's economy. Indeed, many historians now believe that slaveholders—not small farmers or working people—benefited most. His Indian policy helped to open new lands for slaveowners, and his view of limited government forestalled federal interference with slavery.

RISE OF A POLITICAL OPPOSITION

Although it took a number of years for Jackson's opponents to coalesce into an effective national political organization, by the mid-1830s the Whig party, as the opposition came to be known, was able to battle the Democratic party on almost equal terms throughout the country.

A Party Formed by Coalition

The party was formed in 1834 as a coalition of National Republicans, Anti-Masons, and disgruntled Democrats, who were united by their hatred of "King Andrew" Jackson and his "usurpations" of congressional and judicial authority, came together in 1834 to form the **Whig party.** The party took its name from the seventeenth-century British Whig group that had defended English liberties against the usurpations of pro-Catholic Stuart Kings.

In 1836 the Whigs mounted their first presidential campaign, running three regional candidates against Martin Van Buren: Daniel Webster, the senator from Massachusetts who had substantial appeal in New England; Hugh Lawson White, who had appeal in the South; and William Henry Harrison, who fought an Indian alliance at the Battle of Tippecanoe and appealed to the West and to Anti-Masons in Pennsylvania and Vermont. The party strategy was to throw the election into the House of Representatives, where the Whigs would unite behind a single candidate. Van Buren easily defeated all his Whig opponents, winning 170 electoral votes to just 73 for his closest rival.

Following his strong showing in the election of 1836, William Henry Harrison received the united support of the Whig party in 1840. Benefiting from the Panic of 1837 and from a host of colorful campaign innovations as described at the beginning of this chapter, Harrison easily defeated Van Buren by a vote of 234 to 60 in the electoral college.

Unfortunately, the 68-year-old Harrison caught cold while delivering a two-hour inaugural address in the freezing rain. Barely a month later he died of pneumonia, the first president to die in office. His successor, John Tyler of Virginia, was an ardent defender of slavery, a staunch advocate of states' rights, and a former Democrat, whom the Whigs had nominated in order to attract Democratic support to the Whig ticket.

A firm believer in the principle that the federal government should exercise no powers other than those expressly enumerated in the Constitution, Tyler rejected the entire Whig legislative program, which called for reestablishment of a national bank, an increased tariff, and federally funded internal improvements.

The Whig party was furious. An angry mob gathered at the White House, threw rocks through the windows, and burned the president in effigy. To protest Tyler's rejection of the Whig political agenda, all members of the cabinet but one resigned. Tyler became a president without a party. "His Accidency" vetoed nine bills during his four years in office, more than any previous one-term president, frustrating Whig plans to recharter the national bank and raise the tariff while simultaneously distributing proceeds of land sales to the states. In 1843 Whigs in the House of Representatives made Tyler the subject of the first serious impeachment attempt, but the resolutions failed by a vote of 127 to 83.

Curiously, it was during John Tyler's tumultuous presidency that the nation's new two-party system achieved full maturity. Prior to Tyler's ascension to office, the Whig party had been a loose conglomeration of diverse political factions unable to agree on a party platform. Tyler's presidency increased unity among Whigs who found common cause in their opposition to his policies. Never before had party identity been so high or partisan sentiment so strong.

John Tyler's opponents mocked him as "His Accidency" because he was the first vice president to take office as president upon the death of his predecessor.

Who Were the Whigs?

The Jacksonians made a great effort to persuade voters to identify their own cause with Thomas Jefferson and their Whig opponents with Alexander Hamilton. A radical Jacksonian Democrat made the point bluntly. "The aristocracy of our country . . . continually contrive to change their party name," wrote Frederick Robinson. "It was first Tory, then Federalist, then no party, then amalgamation, then National Republican, now Whig." In spite of Democratic charges to the contrary, however, the Whigs were not

Chronology OF KEY EVENTS

1820   Land Act reduces price of public land to $1.25 per acre

1821   New York State Constitutional Convention eliminates property qualification for voting

1824   House of Representatives elects John Quincy Adams as sixth president

1825   President Monroe calls for voluntary removal of Native Americans in the east to lands west of the Mississippi River

1826   Disappearance of William Morgan touches off Anti-Masonic movement in New York State

1828   John C. Calhoun's "South Carolina Exposition" spells out the doctrine of nullification; Congress passes Tariff of Abominations; Andrew Jackson is elected seventh president

1830   Indian Removal Act provides funds to purchase Indian homelands in exchange for land in present-day Oklahoma and Arkansas; Webster-Hayne debate on land policy and nature of the union; Anti-Masons hold the first national party convention

1832   Jackson vetoes the bill to recharter the second Bank of the United States; John C. Cal-

houn becomes the first vice president to resign; South Carolina nullifies the federal tariff; United States defeats the Sauk and Fox Indians in the Black Hawk War

1833   Congress adopts "Compromise Tariff," lowering tariff rates, but also passes "Force Bill," authorizing Jackson to enforce federal law in South Carolina

1835   Roger B. Taney succeeds John Marshall as chief justice

1836   Jackson issues the Specie Circular; Martin Van Buren is elected eighth president

1837   Panic of 1837; *Charles River Bridge* v. *Warren Bridge* decides against monopoly privilege, rejecting the notion of implied rights in contracts and ruling that ambiguities in charters should be resolved in the favor of public welfare

1840   Congress passes Van Buren's Independent Treasury Act; William Henry Harrison, a Whig, is elected ninth president

1841   Harrison's death makes John Tyler the tenth president; Dorr Rebellion against suffrage restrictions in Rhode Island is put down

---

simply a continuation of the Federalist party. Like the Democrats, the Whigs drew support from all parts of the nation. Indeed, the Whigs often formed the majority of the South's representatives in Congress. Like the Democrats, the Whigs were a coalition of sectional interests, class and economic interests, and ethnic and religious interests.

Democratic voters tended to be small farmers, residents of less-prosperous towns, and the Scots-Irish and Catholic Irish. Whigs tended to be educators and professionals; manufacturers; business-oriented farmers; British and German Protestant immigrants; upwardly aspiring manual laborers; free blacks; and active members of Presbyterian, Unitarian, and Congregational churches. The Whig coalition included supporters of Henry Clay's American System, states' righters, religious groups alien-

ated by Jackson's Indian removal policies, and bankers and businesspeople frightened by the Democrats' antimonopoly and antibank rhetoric.

Whereas the Democrats stressed class conflict, Whigs emphasized the harmony of interests between labor and capital, the need for humanitarian reform, and leadership by men of talent. The Whigs also idealized the "self-made man," who starts "from an humble origin, and from small beginnings rise[s] gradually in the world, as a result of merit and industry." Finally, the Whigs viewed technology and factory enterprise as forces for increasing national wealth and improving living conditions.

In 1848 and 1852 the Whigs tried to repeat their successful 1840 presidential campaign by nominating military heroes for the presidency. The party won the 1848 election with General Zachary Taylor, an Indian fighter and hero of the Mexican War, who had boasted that he had never cast a vote in a presidential election. Like Harrison, Taylor confined his campaign speeches to uncontroversial platitudes. "Old Rough and Ready," as he was known, died after just 1 year and 127 days in office. Then, in 1852, the Whigs nominated another Indian fighter and Mexican War hero, General Winfield Scott, who carried just four states for his dying party. "Old Fuss and Feathers," as he was called, was the last Whig nominee to play an important role in a presidential election.

CONCLUSION

A political revolution occurred in the United States between 1820 and 1840. Those two decades saw the abolition of property qualification for voting and officeholding, the elimination of voting by voice, an increase in voter participation, and the emergence of a new party system. Unlike America's first political parties, the Federalists and Republicans, the Jacksonian Democrats and the Whigs were parties with grassroots organization and support in all parts of the nation.

Andrew Jackson, the dominant political figure of the period, spelled out the new democratic approach to politics. In the name of eliminating special privilege and promoting equality of opportunity, he helped institute the national political nominating convention, defended the spoils system, destroyed the second Bank of the United States, and opened millions of acres of Indian lands to white settlement. A strong and determined leader, Jackson greatly expanded the power of the presidency. When South Carolina asserted the right of a state to nullify the federal tariff, Jackson made it clear that he would not tolerate defiance of federal authority. No matter how one evaluates his eight years in the White House, there can be no doubt that he left an indelible stamp on the nation's highest office; indeed, on a whole epoch in American history.

SUGGESTIONS FOR FURTHER READING

Donald B. Cole, *The Presidency of Andrew Jackson* (1993), and Richard Latner, *The Presidency of Andrew Jackson* (1979). Provide general overviews of Jackson's presidency.

Daniel Feller, *The Jacksonian Promise* (1995). An up-to-date reinterpretation of the Jacksonian era.

Michael Holt, *Rise and Fall of the American Whig Party* (1999). A thorough reappraisal of Jackson's political opposition.

Daniel Walker Howe, *The Political Culture of the American Whigs* (1979). Examines the political ideologies of the Whig party.

Edward Pessen, *Jacksonian America*, rev. ed. (1978), and Harry L. Watson, *Liberty and Power* (1990). Offer insightful surveys of the Jacksonian era.

Robert Remini, *Andrew Jackson and the Course of American Freedom* (1981), and *Andrew Jackson and the Course of American Democracy* (1984). Major biographies of Andrew Jackson.

Peter Temin, *The Jacksonian Economy* (1969). Reexamines Jackson's economic and banking policies.

Anthony F. C. Wallace, *The Long, Bitter Trail: Andrew Jackson and the Indians* (1993). Analyzes Jackson's Indian policies.

Overviews and Surveys

John Ashworth, *Slavery, Capitalism, and Politics in the Antebellum Republic* (1995); James MacGregor Burns, *The Crosswinds of Freedom: The Vineyard of Liberty* (1982); Ronald P. Formisano, "Toward a Reorientation of Jacksonian Politics: A Review of the Literature, 1959–1975," *Journal of American History*, 63 (1976); Edward Pessen, *Jacksonian America: Society, Personality, and Politics*, rev. ed. (1978); Robert V. Remini, *The Revolutionary Age of Andrew Jackson* (1976); Arthur M. Schlesinger, Jr., *The Age of Jackson* (1945); Harry L. Watson, *Liberty and Power: The Politics of Jacksonian America* (1990).

Political Democratization

Henry Christman, *Tin Horns and Calico: A Decisive Episode in the Emergence of Democracy* (1945); Ronald Formisano, *Transformation of Political Culture: Massachusetts Parties, 1790s–1840s* (1983); Paul Goodman, *Toward a Christian Republic: Antimasonry and the Great Transition in New England* (1988); Merrill Peterson, ed., *Democracy, Liberty and Property: The State Constitutional Conventions of the 1820s* (1966); Lorman Ratner, *Anti-Masonry: The Crusade and the Party* (1969); W. P. Vaughn, *The Antimasonic Party in the United States, 1826–1843* (1983); Chilton Williamson, *American Suffrage: From Property to Democracy, 1760–1860* (1960).

The Rebirth of Parties

Lee Benson, *The Concept of Jacksonian Democracy: New York as a Test Case* (1961); Steven C. Bullock, *Revolutionary Brotherhood: Freemasonry and the Transformation of the American Social Order* (1996); James S. Chase, *Emergence of the Presidential Nominating Convention, 1789–1832* (1973); Donald B. Cole, *Jacksonian Democracy in New Hampshire, 1800–1851* (1970); Ronald Formisano, *The Birth of Mass Political Parties: Michigan, 1827–1861* (1971); Marvin E. Gettleman, *The Dorr Rebellion: A Study in American Radicalism, 1833–1849* (1973); M. J. Heale, *The Presidential Quest: Candidates and Images in American Political Culture, 1787–1852* (1982); Richard

Hofstadter, *The Idea of a Party System: The Rise of Legitimate Opposition in the United States, 1780–1840* (1969); Robert Kelley, *The Cultural Pattern in American Politics: The First Century* (1979); Peter D. Levine, *The Behavior of State Legislative Parties in the Jacksonian Era, New Jersey, 1829–1844* (1977); Shaw Livermore, *The Twilight of Federalism: The Disintegration of the Federalist Party, 1815–1830* (1962); Richard P. McCormick, *The Second American Party System* (1966), and *The Presidential Game: The Origins of American Presidential Politics* (1982); Edward Pessen, *Riches, Class, and Power Before the Civil War* (1973); Robert V. Remini, *The Election of Andrew Jackson* (1963), and *Martin Van Buren and the Making of the Democratic Party* (1959); Arthur M. Schlesinger, Jr., ed., *History of U.S. Political Parties, 1789–1860: From Factions to Parties* (1973); Arthur M. Schlesinger, Jr. and Fred L. Israel, eds., *History of American Presidential Elections, 1789–1968* (1971); Joel Silbey, *The American Political Nation, 1838–1893* (1991), and *The Partisan Imperative: The Dynamics of American Politics Before the Civil War* (1985); J. Mills Thornton III, *Politics and Power in a Slave Society: Alabama, 1800–1860* (1977); Harry L. Watson, *Jacksonian Politics and Community Conflict: The Emergence of the Second Party System in Cumberland County, North Carolina* (1981).

Andrew Jackson: The Politics of Egalitarianism

William L. Anderson, ed., *Cherokee Removal: Before and After* (1991); John Ashworth, *"Agrarians" and "Aristocrats": Party Political Ideology in the United States, 1837–1846* (1983); Jean H. Baker, *Affairs of Party: The Political Culture of Northern Democrats in the Mid-Nineteenth Century* (1983); Amy Bridges, *A City in the Republic: Antebellum New York and the Origins of Machine Politics* (1984); Matthew A. Crenson, *The Federal Machine: Beginnings of Bureaucracy in Jacksonian America* (1975); James C. Curtis, *Andrew Jackson and the Search for Vindication* (1976); Angie Debo, *And Still the Waters Run: The Betrayal of the Five Civilized Tribes* (1940); A. H. DeRosier, Jr., *The Removal of the Choctaw Indians* (1970); B. W. Dippie, *The Vanishing American: White Attitudes and U.S. Indian Policy* (1982); Cecil Eby, *"That Disgraceful Affair": The Black Hawk War* (1973); Richard Ellis, *The Union at Risk: Jacksonian Democracy, States' Rights, and the Nullification Crisis* (1987); Daniel Feller, *Public Lands in Jacksonian Politics* (1984); William W. Freehling, *Prelude to Civil War: The Nullification Controversy in South Carolina, 1816–1836* (1966); Michael D. Green, *The Politics of Indian Removal: Creek Government and Society in Crisis* (1982); Charles G. Haines and Foster H. Sherwood, *The Role of the Supreme Court in American Government and Politics, 1835–1864* (1957); Bray Hammond, *Banks and Politics in America: From the Revolution to the Civil War* (1957); Stanley I. Kutler, *Privilege and Creative Destruction: The Charles River Bridge Case* (1971); Richard Latner, *The Presidency of Andrew Jackson: White House Politics, 1829–1837* (1979); John M. McFaul, *The Politics of Jacksonian Finance* (1972); R. C. McGrane, *The Panic of 1837* (1924); William G. McLoughlin, *Cherokee Renascence in the New Republic* (1986); James H. Merrell, *The Indians' New World: Catawbas and Their Neighbors from European Contact Through the Era of Removal* (1989); Marvin Meyers, *The Jacksonian Persuasion* (1957); Roger L. Nichols, *Black Hawk and the Warrior's Path* (1992); M. D. Peterson, *Olive Branch and Sword: The Compromise of 1833* (1982); F. P. Prucha, *American Indian Policy in the Formative Years* (1962); Fritz Redlich, *The Molding of American Banking: Men and Ideas* (1951); Robert Remini, *The Legacy of Andrew Jackson* (1988); Hugh Rockoff, *The Free Banking Era* (1975); Ronald N. Satz, *American Indian Policy in the Jacksonian Era* (1975); Bernard Schwartz, *From Confederation to Nation: The American Constitution, 1835–1877* (1973); W. G. Shade, *Banks or No Banks: The Money Issue in Western Politics, 1832–1865* (1972); J. R. Sharp, *The Jacksonians versus the Banks* (1970); W. B. Smith and A. H. Cole, *Fluctuations in American Business, 1790–1860* (1935); Paul Studenski and Herman E. Krooss, *Financial History of the United States*, 2d ed. (1963); Peter Temin, *The Jacksonian Economy* (1969); Richard H. Timberlake, Jr., *The Origins of Central Banking in the United States* (1978); J. Van Fenstermaker, *The Development of American Commercial Banking, 1782–1837* (1965); Herman J. Viola, *Thomas L. McKenney: Architect of America's Early Indian Policy* (1974); Anthony F. C. Wallace, *The Long, Bitter Trail: Andrew Jackson and the Indians* (1993); John William Ward, *Andrew Jackson: Symbol for an Age* (1955); Philip Weeks, *Farewell, My Nation: The American Indian & the United States, 1820–1890* (1990); Leonard D. White, *The Jacksonians: A Study in Administrative History, 1829–1861* (1954); Jean Alexander Wilburn, *Biddle's Bank: The Crucial Years* (1967).

Rise of a Political Opposition

Thomas Brown, *Politics and Statesmanship: Essays on the American Whig Party* (1985); Daniel Walker Howe, *The Political Culture of the American Whigs* (1979); Lawrence Frederick Kohl, *The Politics of Individualism: Parties and the American Character in the Jacksonian Era* (1989); Thomas H. O'Connor, *Lords of the Loom: The Cotton Whigs and the Coming of the Civil War* (1968).

Biographies

Irving H. Bartlett, *Daniel Webster* (1978); Maurice G. Baxter, *One and Inseparable: Daniel Webster and the Union* (1984), and *Henry Clay and the American System* (1995); Norman D. Brown, *Daniel Webster and the Politics of Availability* (1969); Alfred A. Cave, *An American Conservative in the Age of Jackson: The Political and Social Thought of Calvin Colton* (1969); William N. Chambers, *Old Bullion Benton: Senator from the New West* (1956); Oliver Perry Chitwood, *John Tyler: Champion of the Old South* (1939); Freeman Cleaves, *Old Tippecanoe: William Henry Harrison and His Time* (1939); Donald B. Cole, *Martin Van Buren and the American Political System* (1984); Richard N. Current, *Daniel Webster and the Rise of National Conservatism* (1955), and *John C. Calhoun* (1963); James C. Curtis, *The Fox at Bay: Martin Van Buren and the Presidency, 1837–1841* (1970); Robert F. Dalzell, Jr., *Daniel Webster and the Trial of American Nationalism, 1843–1852* (1973); Martin Duberman, *Charles Francis Adams, 1807–1886* (1961); Robert G. Gunderson, *The Log Cabin Campaign*

(1957); Richard Hofstadter, *The American Political Tradition* (1948); Robert J. Morgan, *A Whig Embattled: The Presidency Under John Tyler* (1954); Jerome Mushkat and Joseph G. Raybeck, *Martin Van Buren* (1997); Paul C. Nagel, *John Quincy Adams* (1997); Sydney Nathans, *Daniel Webster and Jacksonian Democracy* (1973); John Niven, *John C. Calhoun and the Price of Union* (1988), and *Martin Van Buren: The Romantic Age of American Politics* (1983); Lynn Hudson Parsons, *John Quincy Adams* (1998); Robert V. Remini, *Andrew Jackson and the Course of American Empire, 1767–1821* (1977), *Andrew Jackson and the Course of American Freedom, 1822–1832* (1981), *Andrew Jackson and the Course of American Democracy, 1833–1845* (1984), and *Martin Van Buren and the Making of the Democratic Party* (1959); G. G. Van Deusen, *The Life of Henry Clay* (1937).

INTERNET RESOURCES

Jacksonian Era Medicine and Life

http://www.indianapolis.in.us/cp/jmed.html
Survival was far from certain in the Jacksonian Era. This site discusses some of the reasons and some of the possible cures of the times.

The University of Pennsylvania in 1830

http://www.upenn.edu/AR/1830/
This "virtual tour" shows what a fairly typical campus looked like and what student life was like at one of the larger universities in the Antebelllum Era.

1830s Clothing

http://www.connerprairie.org/clothing.html
See how clothing worn in the early republic was quite different from what you are wearing now.

KEY TERMS

American System [of Henry Clay]   (p. 265)

Tariff of Abominations   (p. 265)

Nullification   (p. 266)

Spoils System   (p. 268)

Removal [Indian Removal Policy]   (p. 269)

Second Bank of the United States   (p. 274)

Panic of 1837   (p. 276)

Whig Party   (p. 277)

REVIEW QUESTIONS

1. What changes took place in voting, nominating procedures, party organization, and campaign strategies between 1820 and 1840?

2. What new political parties emerged in the 1820s and 1830s? How did these parties differ?

3. What groups were denied political participation under Jacksonian democracy?

4. Why did settlers want to move Native Americans west of the Mississippi River? How did Native Americans try to resist removal? Why is the removal of the Native Americans from their homelands in the Southeast known as the Trail of Tears?

5. Why did South Carolina try to nullify the federal tariff? What was President Jackson's reaction? How was the controversy resolved?

6. Why was President Jackson opposed to the Second Bank of the United States? What actions did he take to weaken the bank?

7. How did President Jackson strengthen the presidency?

NOT LIKE
OTHER GIRLS

7 feet

50 feet

Ground Line

Scale 1/8 of an inch = 16 in

Plan for : Asylums Hospitals

schools

THE WORLD'S GRA

P.T. BARNUM

11

AMERICA'S FIRST AGE OF REFORM

"And a'n't I a woman?"

She was born into slavery around 1797 in New York State's Hudson River Valley, 80 miles from New York City. As a slave, she was known simply as "Isabella." But a decade and a half after escaping from bondage, she adopted a new name. As **Sojourner Truth,** she became a legend in the struggle to abolish slavery and extend equal rights to women.

The youngest of some 10 or 12 children, she grew up in a single room in a dark and damp cellar, sleeping on straw on top of loose boards. For 16 years, from 1810 to 1826, she served as a household slave in upstate New York, and was sold five times. One owner beat her so savagely that her arms and shoulders bore scars for the rest of her life. She bore a fellow slave five children, only to see at least three of her offspring sold away. In 1826, just a year before slavery was finally abolished in the state, she fled after her owner broke a promise to free her and her husband. She took refuge with a farm family that later bought her freedom.

A legend in the abolitionist and women's rights movements, Sojourner Truth was born into slavery around 1797 and escaped from bondage in 1826.

Isabella then moved to New York City, carrying only a bag of clothing and 25 cents. There she supported herself as a domestic servant. It was a period of intense religious excitement, and, although she lacked formal schooling, Isabella began to preach at camp meetings and on street corners.

In 1843, Isabella took on the name Sojourner Truth, convinced that God had called on her to wander the country and boldly speak out the truth. Her fame as a preacher, singer, and orator for abolition and women's rights

spread quickly and three incidents became the stuff of legend. During the late 1840s, when the black abolitionist Frederick Douglass expressed doubt about the possibility of ending slavery peacefully, she replied forcefully: "Frederick, is God dead?" Several years later, in a speech before a woman's rights convention in Akron, Ohio, in 1851, she demanded that Americans recognize that impoverished African American women were women too, reportedly saying: "I could work as much and eat as much as a man—when I could get it—and bear de lash as well! And a'n't I a woman?" And in 1858, when a hostile audience insisted that the six-foot tall orator spoke too powerfully to be a woman, she reportedly bared her breasts before them.

During the Civil War, she took an active role promoting the Union cause, collecting food and supplies for black troops and struggling to make emancipation a war aim. When the war was over, she traveled across the North, collecting signatures on petitions calling on Congress to set aside western land for former slaves. At her death in 1883, she could rightly be remembered as one of the nation's most eloquent opponents of discrimination in all forms.

The decades before the Civil War saw the birth of the American reform tradition. Reformers launched unprecedented campaigns to educate the deaf and the blind, rehabilitate criminals, extend equal rights to women, and abolish slavery. Our modern systems of free public schools, prisons, and hospitals for the infirm and the mentally ill are all legacies of this first generation of American reform.

SOURCES OF THE REFORM IMPULSE

What factors gave rise to the reform impulse and why was it unleashed with such vigor in pre–Civil War America? Reformers had many different reasons for wanting to change American society. Some hoped to remedy the distresses created by social disorder, violence, and widening class divisions. Others found motivation in a religious vision of a godly society on earth.

Social Problems on the Rise

During the early nineteenth century, poverty, lawlessness, violence, and vice appeared to be increasing at an alarming rate. In New York, the nation's largest city, crime rose far faster than in the overall population. Between 1814 and 1834, the city's population doubled, but reports of crime quadrupled. Gangs, bearing such names as Plug Uglies and Bowery B'hoys, prowled the streets, stealing from warehouses and private residences. Public drunkenness was a common sight. By 1835, there were nearly 3000 drinking places in New York—one for every 50 persons over the age of 15. Prostitution also generated concern. By 1850, a reported 6000 "fallen women" strolled the city streets. Mob violence evoked particular fear. In a single decade, 1834–1844, 200 incidents of mob violence occurred in New York. Adding to the sense of alarm were scenes of heart-wrenching poverty, such as children standing barefoot outside hotels, selling matches.

Social problems were not confined to large cities like New York. During the decades before the Civil War, newspapers reported hundreds of incidences of duels, lynchings, and mob violence. In the slave states and southwestern territories men frequently resolved quarrels by dueling. In one 1818 duel between two cousins, the combatants faced off with shotguns at four paces! Lynchings too were widely reported. In 1835, the citizens of Vicksburg, Mississippi, attempted to rid the city of gambling and prostitution by raiding gaming houses and brothels and lynching five gamblers. In urban areas, mob violence increased in frequency and destructiveness. Between 1810 and 1819 there were 7 major riots; in the 1830s there were 115.

A nation in which the vice president had to carry a gun while presiding over the Senate—lest senators attack each other with knives or pistols—seemed to confirm criticism by Europeans that democracy inevitably led to anarchy. Incidents of crime and violence led many Americans to ask how a free society could maintain stability and moral order. Americans sought to answer this question through religion, education, and social reform.

A New Moral Sensibility

More than anxiety over lawlessness, violence, and vice sparked the reform impulse during the first decades of the nineteenth century. America's revolutionary heritage, the philosophy of the Enlightenment, and religious zeal all contributed to a sensitivity to human suffering and a boundless faith in humankind's capacity to improve social institutions.

Many pre–Civil War reformers saw their efforts as an attempt to realize the ideals enshrined in the Declaration of Independence. Invoking the principles of liberty and equality set forth in the Declaration, abolitionists such as William Lloyd Garrison attacked slavery and feminists such as Elizabeth Cady Stanton called for equal rights for women.

The philosophy of the **Enlightenment,** with its belief in the people's innate goodness and with its rejection of the inevitability of poverty and ignorance, was another important source of the reform impulse. Those who espoused the Enlightenment philosophy argued that the creation of a more favorable moral and physical environment could alleviate social problems.

Religion further strengthened the reform impulse. Almost all the leading reformers were devoutly religious men and women who wanted to deepen the nation's commitment to Christian principles. Two trends in religious thought—religious liberalism and evangelical revivalism—strengthened reformers' zeal. **Religious liberalism** was an emerging form of humanitarianism that rejected the harsh Calvinist doctrines of original sin and predestination. Its preachers stressed the basic goodness of human nature and each individual's capacity to follow the example of Christ.

William Ellery Channing (1780–1842) was America's leading exponent of religious liberalism, and his beliefs, proclaimed in a sermon he delivered in Baltimore in 1819, became the basis for American Unitarianism. The new religious denomination stressed individual freedom of belief, a united world under a single God, and the mortal nature of Jesus Christ, whom individuals should strive to emulate. Channing's beliefs stimulated many reformers to work toward improving the conditions of the physically handicapped, the criminal, the impoverished, and the enslaved.

The Second Great Awakening

Enthusiastic religious revivals swept the nation in the early nineteenth century, providing further religious motivation for the reform impulse. On August 6, 1801, some 25,000 men, women, and children gathered in the small frontier community of Cane Ridge, Kentucky, in search of religious salvation. Twenty-five thousand was a fantastically large number of people at a time when the population of the whole state of Kentucky was a quarter million, and the state's largest city, Lexington, had only 1795 residents. The Cane Ridge camp meeting went on for a week. Baptists, Methodists, and ministers of other denominations joined together to preach to the vast throng. Within three years, similar revivals occurred throughout Kentucky, Tennessee, and Ohio. This great wave of religious fervor became known as the **Second Great Awakening.**

Gouging Fights and Backcountry Honor

NOBODY ever called them pretty. Eastern and European travelers to the American southern back- country employed many descriptive and emotive adjectives— disgusting, brutal, savage, uncivilized, disgraceful, barbaric, unsightly—but never once pretty. And, indeed, backcountry fights, whether called "gouging" matches, "rough-and-tumble" contests, or "no holds barred" battles, were not attractive affairs. Men fought all out, using fists, hands, feet, elbows, knees, teeth, and whatever other part of their anatomy promised to do bodily damage to their opponents. Capturing the temper of these battles, Anglican minister Charles Woodmason counseled, "I would advise you when You do fight Not to act like Tygers and Bears as these Virginians do—Biting one anothers Lips and Noses off, and *gouging* one another—that is, thrusting out one anothers Eyes, and kicking one another on the Cods, to the Great damage of many a Poor Woman."

The goal of a gouging match was the disfigurement of one's opponent. This could be accomplished in any number of ways, but the most popular was eye gouging. Fighters manicured their fingernails hard and sharp so that they could use them as a fulcrum to pry out their adversary's eye. On seeing a renowned fighter badly mauled, a passerby remarked, "'You have come off badly this time; I doubt?' 'Have I,' says he triumphantly, showing from his pocket at the same time an eye; which he had extracted during the combat, and preserved as a trophy."

Reading descriptions of these sanguinary contests provokes a series of questions. Who would engage in such activities? And why? Were the contests considered sports or manifestations of blood feuds? And what of the spectators and the law—did they enjoy and allow and condone such barbarities? Finally, what do the contests tell us about the society in which they flourished?

Gouging centered in the region of rivers and largely untamed backcountry south of the Ohio River. It was a land of dangers and violence and early deaths. Organized groups of Native Americans threatened settlers. Wild animals roamed the heavily wooded forests. Outlaws practiced their professions almost unchecked by the law. High infant mortality rates, short life expectancies, dangerous occupations, and random violence stood as grim reminders that life in this region of nature was, as philosopher Thomas Hobbes once noted, "solitary, poor, nasty, brutish, and short."

The men who disfigured each other in gouging matches had been hardened by their environment and their occupations. Many worked on the rivers as roustabouts, rivermen, or gamblers. Others were hunters, herders, or subsistence farmers. No plantations dotted their world; no landed aristocrats dominated them. As a leading historian of the subject commented, "the upland folk lived in an intensely local, kin-based society. Rural hamlets, impassable roads, and provincial isolations—not growing towns, internal improvements, or international commerce—characterized the backcountry."

The work these men performed was physically demanding and dangerous. Working on a Mississippi barge or trapping game in the backcountry exposed men to all the forces of nature and did not foster a gentle view of life. Death and pain were everywhere to be seen. Mark Twain remembered such men from his boyhood experiences in a raw river town: "Rude, uneducated, brave, suffering terrific hardships with sailorlike stoicism; heavy drinkers, coarse frolickers . . . , heavy fighters, reckless fellows, every one, elephantinely jolly, foul witted, profane, prodigal of their money, bankrupt at the end of the trip, fond of barbaric finery, prodigious braggarts." They were not Jacksonian men on the make or respectable churchgoers. Rather they were men who worked hard, played hard, and drank hard.

Since they spent most of their lives in the company of other men, much of their sense of self-worth came from how their companions viewed them. They did not use money or piety as yardsticks for measuring the worth of a man. Bravery, strength, conviviality, and a jealous sense of personal honor determined the cut of a man. The ability to drink, boast, and fight with equal ability marked a backcountry Renaissance man.

Question a man's honor and you questioned in the most profound sense his manhood. If aristocratic Southerners dueled over such slights, backcountry laborers gouged over them. Northerners found this touchy sense of honor perplexing. Philip Vickers Fithian, a New Jerseyite who traveled to the South in the 1770s, commented about the reason for one fight, "I suppose either that they are lovers, and one has in Jest or reality some way supplanted the other; or has in

a merry hour called him a *Lubber* or a *Thick-Skull*, or a *Buckskin*, or a *Scotsman*, or perhaps one has mislaid the other's hat, or knocked a peach out of his Hand, or offered him a dram without wiping the mouth of the Bottle." Any excuse, thought Fithian, could lead to mortal combat. But he misread the situation. In truth, any insult, no matter how slight, could be judged serious enough to provoke violence.

Once men exchanged angry words and angrier challenges, their combat provided entertainment for their companions. At the fights, drinking and boasting continued, and the line between participant and spectator was hazy. One fight often led to another and general melees were not uncommon. Were such contests sports? Probably not, but it was

not a question that anyone would have posed. Just as there was little distinction between participant and spectator, there was little difference between sport and battery.

Gouging matches were certainly not civilized affairs, and as civilized behavior and culture penetrated the backcountry, men ceased to settle their differences in such brutal contests. This is not to say that they stopped fighting. Rather they "defended their honor" in more "civilized" ways. Bowie knives, swords, and pistols replaced honed thumbnails and filed teeth as the weapons of choice. And these "affairs of honor" were held before a few solemn witnesses rather than a host of cheering friends.

But if gouging became a relic of another age, it remained a particu-

larly telling relic. It provides an important clue to the values of the southern backcountry. How men fought—just as how they worked or played—indicates much about their lives. The men who gouged led strenuous, often violent lives. They were not the sort of men to turn pale at the sight of blood or even at the sight of an eyeless eye socket. They admired toughness, fearlessness, and even meanness—not piety, gentleness, and sensitivity.

During an earlier time, it was considered an unmanly sign of fear for a person to carry a weapon. But more refined sensibilities reversed this notion. By the mid-nineteenth century weapon carrying had become an indication of manliness.

287

Americans turned to revival meetings in times of social and economic upheaval. These meetings, which stressed new-birth conversions, could last for days.

The revivals inspired a widespread sense that the nation was standing close to the millennium, a thousand years of peace and benevolence when sin, war, and tyranny would vanish from the earth. Evangelical leaders urged their followers to reject selfishness and materialism and repent their sins. To the revivalists, sin was no metaphysical abstraction. Luxury, high living, indifference to religion, preoccupation with worldly and commercial matters—all were denounced as sinful. If men and women did not seek God through Christ, the nation would face divine retribution. **Evangelical revivals** helped instill in Americans a belief that they had been chosen by God to lead the world toward "a millennium of republicanism."

Charles Grandison Finney (1792–1875), the "father of modern revivalism," led revivals throughout the Northeast. Finney became the North's leading revivalist. Despite his lack of formal theological training, he was remarkably successful in converting souls to Christ. Finney's message was that anyone could experience a redemptive change of heart and a resurgence of religious feeling. He prayed for sinners by name; he held meetings that lasted night after night for a week or more; he set up an "anxious bench" at the front of the meeting, where the almost-saved could receive special prayers. He also encouraged women to participate actively in revivals. If only enough people converted to Christ, Finney told his listeners, the millennium—Christ's reign on earth—would arrive within three years.

Revival meetings attracted both frontier settlers and city folk, slaves and masters, farmers and shop-keepers. The revivals had their greatest appeal among isolated farming families on the western and southern frontier and among upwardly mobile merchants, shopkeepers, artisans, skilled laborers in the expanding commercial and industrial towns of the North. They also drew support from social conservatives who feared that America would disintegrate into a state of anarchy without the influence of evangelical religion. Above all, revivals attracted large numbers of young women, who took an active role organizing meetings, establishing church societies, and editing religious publications.

Religious Diversity

The early nineteenth century was a period of extraordinary religious ferment. Church membership climbed steeply, until three-quarters of all Americans were affiliated with a church. The religious landscape grew increasingly diverse. A number of older denominations—notably the Baptists, Catholics, and Methodists—expanded rapidly while a host of new denominations and movements arose, including the African Methodist Episcopal church, the Disciples of Christ, the Mormons, and the Unitarian and Universalist churches.

During the late eighteenth century, church membership was low and falling. Deism—a movement that emphasized reason rather than revelation and denied that a divine creator interfered with the workings of the universe—and skepticism seemed to be spreading. A French immigrant claimed that "religious indifference is imperceptibly disseminated from one end of the continent to the other." Yet by 1830, foreign observers considered the United States the most religious country in the western world.

Religious revivals played a critical role in this outpouring of religion. In part, revivalism represented a response to the growing separation of church and state that followed the American Revolution. When states deprived established churches of state support (as did Virginia in 1785, Connecticut in 1818, and Massachusetts in 1833), Protestant ministers held revivals to ensure that America would remain a God-fearing nation. The popularity of revivals also reflected the hunger of many Americans for an emotional religion that downplayed creeds and rituals and instead emphasized conversion.

No religious group grew more rapidly during the pre–Civil War era or faced more bitter hostility than the Roman Catholic Church. From just 25,000 members and 6 priests in 1776, the Catholic church in America grew to 3 million members in 1860. With English, French, German, Irish, and Mexican mem-

As early
Five Poir
crime, fil
prostitut

result o
formers
to remo
thize ar
to refor
them in
Rev
ment le
tions in
antined
in a ca
prison
constru
ities ad
large w
rate cel
and ref
other. I
constru
stress
prison

bers, it was not only the nation's largest denomination, it was also America's first multicultural church. Concerned that many immigrants were only nominally Catholic, the Church established urban missions and launched religious revivals to strengthen Catholics' religious identity. Somewhat similar to the Protestant evangelical revivals, the Catholic revivals featured rousing sermons and encouraged piety, fervor, and devotion. By establishing its own schools and system of hospitals, orphanages, and benevolent societies, the Church sought to help Catholics preserve their faith in the face of Protestant proselytizing.

Prejudice and discrimination led African Americans to create their own churches. The first were established in Philadelphia, after the city's black Methodists were ordered to sit in a segregated gallery. Between 1804 and 1815, African Americans formed their own Baptist, Methodist, and Presbyterian churches in eastern cities. In 1816, the African Methodist Episcopal church, the first autonomous black denomination, was founded.

Another religious group that grew sharply before the Civil War was American Jewry. At the beginning of the nineteenth century, there were only about 2000 Jews in the United States, 6 Jewish congregations, no Jewish newspapers, and not a single rabbi. By 1860, when the number of American Jews had climbed to 150,000, Jewish newspapers reached readers in 1250 communities, and Jews had served in the legislatures of Georgia, Indiana, New York, North Carolina, and South Carolina. Jews faced less discrimination and hostility than Catholics, in part because the Jewish community was scattered and in

part because most Jews shed the distinctive dress, long sideburns, and other customs that set European Jews apart. Yet, although they adapted to American life in many ways, Jews vigorously resisted threats to their identity, strongly opposing state laws that limited public office to Christians, bans against commerce on the Christian Sabbath, and the recitation of Christian prayers in schools.

MORAL REFORM

The earliest reformers wanted to persuade Americans to adopt more godly personal habits. They set up associations to battle profanity and Sabbath breaking, to place a Bible in every American home, and to curb the widespread heavy use of hard liquor. By discouraging drinking and gambling and encouraging observance of the Sabbath, reformers hoped to "restore the government of God."

One of the most dramatic attempts at moral reform involved Magdalene societies, which sought in the 1830s and 1840s to rehabilitate prostitutes and discourage male solicitation. The New York Moral Reform Society had 15,000 members in 1837 and had branches in New England and upstate New York. Members walked into brothels and prayed for the prostitutes, publicized in the newspapers the names of men who patronized prostitutes, visited prostitutes in jails, and lobbied for state laws that would make male solicitation of prostitutes a crime.

The most extensive moral reform campaign, however, was that against drinking, which was an integral part of American life. Many people believed

The temperance movement of the 1830s and 1840s used religious revivalist tactics to frighten drinkers into taking the "pledge" to abstain from drinking.

Division Within the Antislavery Movement

Questions over strategy and tactics divided the antislavery movement. At the 1840 annual meeting of the American Anti-Slavery Society in New York, abolitionists split over such questions as women's right to participate in the administration of the organization and the advisability of nominating abolitionists as independent political candidates. Garrison won control of the organization, and his opponents promptly walked out. From this point on, no single organization could speak for abolitionism.

One group of abolitionists looked to politics as the answer to ending slavery and founded political parties for that purpose. The **Liberty party,** founded in 1839 under the leadership of Arthur and Lewis Tappan, wealthy New York City businessmen, and James G. Birney, a former slaveholder, called on Congress to abolish slavery in the District of Columbia, end the interstate slave trade, and cease admitting new slave states to the Union. The party also sought the repeal of local and state "black laws" in the North, which discriminated against free blacks, much as segregation laws would in the post-Reconstruction South. The Liberty party nominated Birney for president in 1840 and again in 1844. Although it gathered fewer than 7100 votes in its first campaign, it polled some 62,000 votes 4 years later and captured enough votes in Michigan and New York to deny Henry Clay the presidency.

In 1848 antislavery Democrats and Whigs merged with the Liberty party to form the Free Soil party. Unlike the Liberty party, which was dedicated to the abolition of slavery and equal rights for African Americans, the **Free Soil party** narrowed its demands to the abolition of slavery in the District of Columbia and the exclusion of slavery from the federal territories. The Free Soilers also wanted a homestead law to provide free land for western settlers, high tariffs to protect American industry, and federally sponsored internal improvements. Campaigning under the slogan "free soil, free speech, free labor, and free men," the new party polled 300,000 votes (or 10 percent) in the presidential election of 1848 and helped elect Whig candidate Zachary Taylor.

Other abolitionists, led by Garrison, took a more radical direction, advocating civil disobedience and linking abolitionism to other reforms such as women's rights, world government, and international peace. Garrison and his supporters established the New England Non-Resistance Society in 1838. Members refused to vote, to hold public office, or to bring suits in court. In 1854 Garrison attracted notoriety by publicly burning a copy of the Constitution, which he called "a covenant with death and an agreement with Hell" because it acknowledged the legality of slavery.

African Americans played a vital role in the abolitionist movement, staging protests against segregated churches, schools, and public transportation. In New York and Pennsylvania, free blacks launched petition drives for equal voting rights. Northern blacks also had a pivotal role in the "underground railroad," which provided escape routes for southern slaves through the northern states and into Canada. African-American churches offered sanctuary to runaways, and black "vigilance" groups in cities such as New York and Detroit battled slave catchers who sought to recapture fugitive slaves.

Fugitive slaves, such as William Wells Brown, Henry Bibb, and Harriet Tubman, advanced abolitionism by publicizing the horrors of slavery. Their firsthand tales of whippings and separation from spouses and children combated the notion that slaves were contented under slavery and undermined belief in racial inferiority. Tubman risked her life by making 19 trips into slave territory to free as many as 300 slaves. Slaveholders posted a reward of $40,000 for the capture of the "Black Moses."

Frederick Douglass was the most famous fugitive slave and black abolitionist. The son of a Maryland slave woman and an unknown white father, Douglass was separated from his mother and sent to work on a plantation when he was 6 years old. At the age of 20, in 1838, he escaped to the North using the papers of a free black sailor. In the North, Douglass became the first runaway slave to speak out against slavery. When many Northerners refused to believe that this eloquent orator could possibly have been a slave, he responded by writing an autobiography that identified his previous owners by name. Although he initially allied himself with William Lloyd Garrison, Douglass later started his own newspaper, *The North Star*, and supported political action against slavery.

By the 1850s, many blacks had become pessimistic about defeating slavery. Some African Americans looked again to colonization as a solution. In the 15 months following passage of the federal Fugitive Slave Law in 1850, some 13,000 free blacks fled the North for Canada. In 1854, Martin Delany (1812–1885), a Pittsburgh doctor who had studied medicine at Harvard, organized the National Emigration Convention to investigate possible sites for black colonization in Haiti, Central America, and West Africa.

Other blacks argued in favor of violence. Black abolitionists in Ohio adopted resolutions encouraging slaves to escape and called on their fellow citi-

Fugitive slave, abolitionist, and later spy for the Union during the Civil War Harriet Tubman is pictured here at the extreme left with some of the slaves she helped escape. She led at least 19 raids into slave territory to escort more than 300 slaves to freedom in the northern states and Canada. Frederick Douglass (right) gained public notice by giving a powerful speech against slavery. He opposed not only slavery but all forms of racial discrimination.

zens to violate any law that "conflicts with reason, liberty and justice, North or South." A meeting of fugitive slaves in Cazenovia, New York, declared that "the State motto of Virginia, 'Death to Tyrants,' is as well the black man's as the white man's motto." By the late 1850s, a growing number of free blacks had concluded that it was just as legitimate to use violence to secure the freedom of the slaves as it had been to establish the independence of the American colonies.

Over the long run, the fragmentation of the antislavery movement worked to the advantage of the cause. Henceforth, Northerners could support whichever form of antislavery best reflected their views. Moderates could vote for political candidates with abolitionist sentiments without being accused of radical Garrisonian views or of advocating violence for redress of grievances.

The Birth of Feminism

The women's rights movement was a major legacy of radical reform. At the outset of the century, women could not vote or hold office in any state, they had no access to higher education, and they were excluded from professional occupations. American law accepted the principle that a wife had no legal identity apart from her husband. She could not be sued, nor could she bring a legal suit; she could not make a contract, nor could she own property. She was not permitted to control her own wages or gain custody of her children in case of separation or divorce. Under many circumstances she was even deemed incapable of committing crimes.

Broad social and economic changes, such as the development of a market economy and a decline in the birthrate, opened employment opportunities for women. Instead of bearing children at two-year intervals after marriage, as was the general case throughout the colonial era, during the early nineteenth century women bore fewer children and ceased childbearing at younger ages. During these decades the first women's college was established, and some men's colleges first opened their doors to women students. More women were postponing marriage or not marrying at all; unmarried women gained new employment opportunities as "mill girls" and elementary school teachers; and a growing number of women achieved prominence as novelists, editors, teachers, and leaders of church and philanthropic societies.

THE PEOPLE SPEAK

Women's Rights: Seneca Falls Declaration and Resolutions (1848)

At the first convention in history dedicated to equal rights for women, held in Seneca Falls, New York, in 1848, the delegates adopted a "Declaration of Sentiments." Drafted by Elizabeth Cady Stanton and modeled on the Declaration of Independence, it listed a series of injuries that women had suffered at the hands of men and declared that women and men shared the same inalienable rights.

> We hold these truth to be self-evident: that all men and women are created equal. . . .
>
> The history of mankind is a history of repeated injuries and usurpations on the part of man toward woman, having in direct object the establishment of an absolute tyranny over her. To prove this, let facts be submitted to a candid world.
>
> He has never permitted her to exercise her inalienable right to the elective franchise.
>
> He has compelled her to submit to laws, in the formation of which she had no voice.
>
> He has withheld from her rights which are given to the most ignorant and degraded men—both natives and foreigners.
>
> Having deprived her of this first right of a citizen, the elective franchise, thereby leaving her without representation in the halls of legislation, he has opposed her on all sides.
>
> He has made her, if married, in the eye of the law, civilly dead.
>
> He has taken from her all rights in property, even to the wages she earns.
>
> He has made her, morally, an irresponsible being, as she can commit many crimes with impunity, provided they be done in the presence of her husband. In the covenant of marriage, she is compelled to promise obedience to her husband, he becoming, to all intents and purposes, her master—the law giving him power to deprive her of her liberty, and to administer chastisement.
>
> He has so framed the laws of divorce, as to what shall be the proper causes, and in case of separation, to whom the guardianship of children shall be given, as to be wholly regardless of the happiness of women—the law, in all cases, going into a false supposition of the supremacy of man, and giving all power into his hands.
>
> After depriving her of all rights as a married woman, if single, and the owner of property, he has taxed her to support a government which recognizes her only when her property can be made profitable to it.
>
> He has monopolized nearly all the profitable employments, and from those she is permitted to follow, she receives but a scanty remuneration. He closes against her all avenues to wealth and distinction which he considers most honorable to himself. As a teacher of theology, medicine, or law, she is not known. . . .
>
> He has endeavored, in every way that he could, to destroy her confidence in her own powers, to lessen her self-respect, and to make her willing to lead a dependent and abject life.

Source: Seneca Falls Declaration and Resolutions, 1848, in Susan B. Anthony, Elizabeth Cady Stanton, and Matilda Joslyn Gage, eds., *History of Woman Suffrage* (Rochester, 1889), 1: 75–80.

The two most striking characteristics of the Shaker communities were their dances and abstinence from sexual relations. The Shakers believed that religious fervor should be expressed through the head, heart, and mind, and their ritual religious practices included shaking, shouting, and dancing. Viewing sexual intercourse as the basic cause of human sin, the Shakers also adopted strict rules concerning celibacy. They attempted to replenish their membership by admitting volunteers and taking in orphans. Today, the Shakers have all but died out. Fewer than 20 members survived in the 1990s.

Another utopian effort was Robert Owen's experimental community at New Harmony, Indiana, which reflected the influence of Enlightenment ideas. Owen, a paternalistic Scottish industrialist, was deeply troubled by the social consequences of the industrial revolution. Inspired by the idea that people are shaped by their environment, Owen purchased a site in Indiana where he sought to establish common ownership of property and abolish religion. At New Harmony the marriage ceremony was reduced to a single sentence and children were raised outside of their natural parents' home. The community lasted just three years, from 1825 to 1828.

Some 40 utopian communities based their organization on the ideas of the French theorist Charles Fourier, who hoped to eliminate poverty through the establishment of scientifically organized cooperative communities called "phalanxes." Each phalanx was to be set up as a "joint-stock company," in which profits were divided according to the amount of

Officially named "The United Society of Believers in Christ's Second Appearing," the Shakers received their popular name from the movements they made during their religious dances.

money members had invested, their skill, and their labor. Fourier coined the term *feminism,* and in the phalanxes, women received equal job opportunities and equal pay, equal participation in decision making, and the right to speak in public assemblies. Although one Fourier community lasted for 18 years, most were unsuccessful.

The currents of radical antislavery thought inspired Frances Wright, a fervent Scottish abolitionist, to found Nashoba Colony in 1826, near Memphis, Tennessee, as an experiment in interracial living. She established a racially integrated cooperative community in which slaves were to receive an education and earn enough money to purchase their own freedom. Publicity about Fanny Wright's desire to abolish the nuclear family, religion, private property, and slavery created a furor, and the community dissolved after only four years.

Perhaps the most successful—and notorious—experimental colony was John Humphrey Noyes's Oneida Community. A lawyer who was converted in one of Charles Finney's revivals, Noyes believed that the millennium would occur only when people strove to become perfect through an "immediate and total cessation from sin."

In Putney, Vermont, in 1835 and in Oneida, New York, in 1848, Noyes established perfectionist communities that practiced communal ownership of property and "complex marriage." Complex marriage involved the marriage of each member of the community to every member of the opposite sex. Exclusive emotional or sexual attachments were forbidden, and sexual relations were arranged through an intermediary in order to protect a woman's individuality and give her a choice in the matter. Men were required to practice *coitus interruptus* (withdrawal) as a method of birth control, unless the group had ap-

proved of the couple's conceiving offspring. After the Civil War, the community conducted experiments in eugenics, the selective control of mating to improve the hereditary qualities of children. Other notable features of the community were mutual criticism sessions and communal child rearing. Noyes left the community in 1879 and fled to Canada to escape prosecution for adultery. As late as the early 1990s descendants of the original community could be found working at the Oneida silverworks, which became a corporation after Noyes's departure.

ARTISTIC AND CULTURAL FERMENT

In the late eighteenth century, many Americans wondered whether their country's infant democracy could produce great works of art. The revolutionary generation drew its models of art and architecture from the world of classical antiquity, especially the Roman republic. The new United States had few professional writers or artists. It lacked a large class of patrons to subsidize the arts. It published few magazines and housed only a single art museum. Above all, America seemed to lack the traditions out of which artists and writers could create great works.

Europeans treated American culture with contempt. They charged that America was too commercial and materialistic, too preoccupied with money and technology to produce great art and literature. "In the four quarters of the globe," asked one English critic, "who reads an American book? or goes to an American play? or looks at an American picture or statue?"

On August 31, 1837, a 34-year-old former Unitarian minister named Ralph Waldo Emerson (1803–1882) answered these critics. As he stood at the pulpit of the First Parish Church of Cambridge, Massachusetts—the very spot where Anne Hutchinson had been examined for heresy two centuries earlier—he delivered a talk, entitled "The American Scholar," that would be called America's "intellectual Declaration of Independence." In his address, Emerson urged Americans to cast off their "long apprenticeship to the learning of other lands" and abandon subservience to English models and create distinctly American forms of art rooted in the facts of American life.

Even before Emerson's call for a distinctly American culture, a number of authors had already begun to create literature emphasizing native scenes and characters. Washington Irving (1783–1859), who was probably the first American to support himself as a man of letters, demonstrated the possibility of creating art out of native elements in his classic tales

Henry David Thoreau said he went to live in solitude in the woods because he wished to "front only the essential facts of life."

The title page from the first edition of Thoreau's *Walden*, published in 1854.

During his 26 months at Walden Pond, he constructed his own cabin, raised his own food ("seven miles of beans"), observed nature, explored his inner self, and kept a 6000-page journal. He served as "self-appointed inspector of snow-storms and rain-storms," "surveyor of forest-paths," and protector of "wild-stock." He also spent a night in jail, for refusing to pay taxes as a protest against the Mexican-American War. This incident led him to write the classic defense of nonviolent direct action, "Civil Disobedience."

Another figure who sought to realize transcendentalist ideals in her personal life was Margaret Fuller (1810–1850), editor of the transcendentalist journal *The Dial*. Often mocked as an egotist, she once said: "I know all the people worth knowing in America, and I find no intellect comparable to my own." She did indeed possess one of nineteenth-century America's towering minds. She was the first woman to use the Harvard College library and later became one of the nation's first woman journalists,

writing for Horace Greeley's New York *Tribune*. A determined social reformer, she became a leading advocate of women's rights, publishing *Woman in the Nineteenth Century* in 1845. The book, in which she called for the complete equality of women, became a central work of the emerging women's rights movement. A partisan in Rome's revolution of 1849, she shocked Bostonians by taking an Italian revolutionary nobleman, 11 years her junior, as her lover, and bearing his child out of wedlock (they secretly married later). She died in a shipwreck off Long Island, at the age of 40, along with her husband and son. Edgar Allan Poe spoke for many Americans when he said of her: "Humanity is divided into men, women, and Margaret Fuller."

Another key figure in the transcendentalist circle was Bronson Alcott (1799–1888), a pioneer in the areas of child development and education. Often ridiculed—reviewers mockingly described one of his books as "clear as mud"—Alcott was far ahead of his time in his conception of education, which he viewed as a process of awakening and drawing out children's intellectual and moral capacities through dialogue, individualized instruction, nature study, and encouragement of creative expression through art and writing. Critics scoffed at his techniques, particularly his rejection of corporal punishment and his substitution of "vicarious atonement," a method of child discipline in which Alcott had naughty children spank him. When his own daughters misbehaved, Alcott went without dinner. Convinced that adults had a great deal to learn about children's physical, intellectual, and moral development, Alcott recorded 2500 pages of observations on the first years of his daughters' lives (including Louisa May, who later wrote *Little Women* and *Little Men*). He also published his dialogues with pupils on such controversial topics as the meaning of the Christian gospel and the processes of conception and birth.

Two dramatic attempts to apply the ideas of transcendentalism to everyday life were Brook Farm, a community located near Boston, and Fruitlands, a utopian community near Harvard, Massachusetts. In 1841, George Ripley, like Emerson a former Unitarian clergyman, established Brook Farm in an attempt to substitute transcendentalist ideals of "brotherly cooperation," harmony, and spiritual fulfillment for the "selfish competition," class division, and alienation that increasingly characterized the larger society. "Our ulterior aim is nothing less than Heaven on Earth," declared one community member. Brook Farm's residents, who never numbered more than 200, supported themselves by farming, teaching, and manufacturing clothing. The most famous member of the community was Nathaniel Hawthorne, who based his 1852 novel *The Blithedale Romance* on his experiences there. The community lasted in its original form just three years.

In 1843, Bronson Alcott and others attempted to form a "New Eden" at Fruitlands—a community where they could achieve human perfection through high thinking, manual labor, and dress and diet reform. Practices at Fruitlands included communal ownership of property, frequent cold water baths, and a diet based entirely on native grains, fruits, herbs, and roots. Residents wore canvas shoes and linen tunics, so as not to have to kill animals for leather or use slave-grown cotton. Division of labor

by gender, however, remained traditional. Responsibility for housekeeping and food preparation fell on Alcott's wife Abba. Asked by a visitor if there were any beasts of burden at Fruitlands, Abba Alcott replied: "There is one woman."

A Literary Renaissance

Emerson's 1837 plea for Americans to cease imitating Europeans, speak with their own voices, and create art drawn from their own experiences coincided with an extraordinary burst of literary creativity. Nathaniel Hawthorne, Herman Melville, Edgar Allan Poe, Harriet Beecher Stowe, and Walt Whitman, like Emerson and Thoreau, produced literary works of the highest magnitude, yet in their own time many of their greatest works were greeted with derision, abuse, or indifference. It is a tragic fact that with the sole exception of Harriet Beecher Stowe, none of pre–Civil War America's greatest writers was able to earn more than a modest income from his or her books (on Harriet Beecher Stowe, see pp. 390–391).

During his lifetime, Edgar Allan Poe (1809–1849) received far more notoriety from his legendary dissipation than from his poetry or short stories. The Boston-born son of two poor actors, Poe was raised by a Richmond, Virginia, merchant after his father abandoned the family and his mother died. For two years he went to the University of Virginia and briefly attended West Point, but drinking, gambling debts, and bitter fights with his guardian cut short his formal education. At the age of 24, he married a 13-year-old second cousin, who died a decade later of tuberculosis, brought on by cold and starvation. Found drunk and unconscious in Baltimore in 1849, Poe died at the age of 40.

Sorely underappreciated by contemporaries, Poe invented the detective novel; edited the *Southern Literary Messenger*, one of the country's leading literary journals; wrote incisive essays on literary criticism; and produced some of the most masterful poems and frightening tales of horror ever written. His literary techniques inspired a

Edgar Allan Poe, shown here in a self-portrait, is known for his haunting stories and poems, his literary theories, and his invention of the modern detective story.

tion Through Renaissance (1986); Mary Kupiec Cayton, Emerson's Emergence (1990); Ann Fabian, Card Sharps, Dream Books, & Bucket Shops: Gambling in Nineteenth-Century America (1990); Jon W. Finson, The Voices That Are Gone: Themes in Nineteenth-Century American Popular Song (1994) Len Gougeon, Virtue's Hero: Emerson, Antislavery, and Reform (1990); Neil Harris, The Artist in American Society: The Formative Years, 1790–1860 (1982), and Humbug: The Art of P. T. Barnum (1973); Richard Lebeaux, Young Man Thoreau (1977); Lawrence Levine, Highbrow/ Lowbrow: The Emergence of Cultural Hierarchy in America (1988) F. O. Matthiessen, American Renaissance (1941); Michael Meyer, Several More Lives to Live: Thoreau's Political Reputation in America (1977); Perry Miller, The Life of the Mind in America: From the Revolution to the Civil War (1965); Joel Myerson, ed., Critical Essays on Henry David Thoreau's Walden (1988); Anne C. Rose, Transcendentalism as a Social Movement, 1830–1850 (1981) and Voices of the Marketplace: American Thought and Culture, 1830–1860 (1995).

American Popular Culture

Ann Fabian, Card Sharps, Dream Books, & Bucket Shops: Gambling in Nineteenth-Century America (1990); Jon W. Finson, The Voices That Are Gone: Themes in Nineteenth-Century American Popular Song (1994); Neil Harris, Humbug: The Art of P. T. Barnum (1973); Lawrence Levine, Highbrow/Lowbrow: The Emergence of Cultural Hierarchy in America (1988); Russel B. Nye, Society and Culture in America, 1830–1860 (1974); Ronald J. Zboray, A Fictive People: Antebellum Economic Development and the American Reading Public (1993).

Biographies

Robert Abzug, Passionate Liberator: Theodore Dwight Weld and the Dilemma of Reform (1980); Lois Banner, Elizabeth Cady Stanton: A Radical for Woman's Rights (1980); Thomas J. Brown, Dorothea Dix (1998); Frank L. Byrne, Prophet of Prohibition: Neal Dow and His Crusade (1961); Charles Capper, Margaret Fuller: An American Romantic Life (1992); Charles Crowe, George Ripley: Transcendentalist and Utopian Socialist (1967); Hugh Davis, Joshua Leavitt: Evangelical Abolitionist (1990); Merton Dillon, Elijah P. Lovejoy, Abolitionist Editor (1961); Isabelle Webb Entrikin, Sarah Josepha Hale and Godey's Lady's Book (1946); Edward Farrison, William Wells Brown: Author and Reformer (1969); Betty Fladeland, James Gillespie Birney: Slaveholder to Abolitionist (1955); Frank O. Gatell, John Gorham Palfrey and the New England Conscience (1963); David L. Gollaher, A Voice for the Mad: The Life of Dorothea Dix (1995); Lawrence B. Goodheart, Abolitionist, Actuary, Atheist: Elizur Wright and the Reform Impulse (1990); Cyril Griffith, African Dream: Martin R. Delany and the Emergence of Pan-African Thought (1975); Keith J. Hardman, Charles Grandison Finney (1987); Ralph Volney Harlow, Gerrit Smith, Philanthropist and Reformer (1939); Joan D. Hedrick, Harriet Beecher Stowe, A Life (1993); Carolyn L. Karcher, The First Woman in the Republic: A Cultural Biography of Lydia Maria Child (1994); Gerda Lerner, The Grimké Sisters from South Carolina: Pioneers for Women's Rights and Abolition (1967); Katherine Du Pre Lumpkin, The Emancipation of Angelina Grimké (1974); Carleton Mabee, Sojourner Truth (1993); Helen E. Marshall, Dorothea Dix: Forgotten Samaritan (1937); Waldo E. Martin, Jr., The Mind of Frederick Douglass (1984); William McFeely, Frederick Douglass (1991); Milton Meltzer, Tongue of Flame: The Life of Lydia Maria Child (1965); Walter M. Merrill, Against Wind and Tide: A Biography of William Lloyd Garrison (1963); Jonathan Messerli, Horace Mann: A Biography (1972); Nell Painter, Sojourner Truth (1996); Jane H. Pease, Bound with Them in Chains (1972); Benjamin Quarles, Frederick Douglass (1948); David S. Reynolds, Walt Whitman's America (1995); A. H. Saxon, P. T. Barnum: The Legend and the Man (1989); Richard H. Sewell, John P. Hale and the Politics of Abolition (1965); Kathryn Kish Sklar, Catharine Beecher: A Study in American Domesticity (1973); James Brewer Stewart, Joshua R. Giddings and the Tactics of Radical Politics (1970), and Wendell Phillips, Liberty's Hero (1986); Benjamin P. Thomas, Theodore Weld, Crusader for Freedom (1950); John L. Thomas, The Liberator, William Lloyd Garrison (1963); Robert David Thomas, The Man Who Would Be Perfect: John Humphrey Noyes and the Utopian Impulse (1977); Nancy Tomes, A Generous Confidence: The Art of Asylum Keeping, Thomas Story Kirkbride and the Origins of American Psychiatry (1984); Albert J. Von Frank, The Trials of Anthony Burns (1998); Bertram Wyatt-Brown, Lewis Tappan and the Evangelical War Against Slavery (1969).

INTERNET RESOURCES

America's First Look into the Camera: Daguerreotype Portraits and Views, 1839–1862

http://memory.loc.gov/ammem/daghtml/daghome.html

The Library of Congress's daguerreotype collection consists of more than 650 photographs dating from 1839 to 1864. Portraits, architectural views, and some street scenes make up most of the collection.

Votes for Women: Selections from the National American Woman Suffrage Association Collection, 1848–1921

http://memory.loc.gov/ammem/naw/nawshome.html

This Library of Congress site contains 167 books, pamphlets, and other artifacts documenting the suffrage campaign.

By Popular Demand: "Votes for Women" Suffrage Pictures, 1850–1920

http://memory.loc.gov/ammem/vfwhtml/vfwhome.html

Portraits, suffrage parades, picketing suffragists, an anti-suffrage display, and cartoons commenting on the movement make up this Library of Congress site.

Women in America, 1820–1842

http://xroads.virginia.edu/~HYPER/DETOC/FEM/home.htm

This University of Virginia site takes a look at women in antebellum America.

Godey's Ladies Book Online
http://www.history.rochester.edu/godeys/
Here is online text of this interesting nineteenth century journal.

Important Black Abolitionists
http://www.loc.gov/exhibits/african/influ.html
An exhibit site, with pictures and text, that discusses some key African American abolitionists and their efforts to end slavery, from the Library of Congress.

The Alexis de Tocqueville Tour Exploring Democracy in America
http://www.tocqueville.org/
Text, images, and teaching suggestions are a part of this companion site to C-SPAN's recent programming on de Tocqueville.

KEY TERMS

Sojourner Truth   (p. 284)

Enlightenment   (p. 285)

Religious Liberalism   (p. 285)

William Ellery Channing   (p. 285)

Second Great Awakening   (p. 285)

Evangelical Revivalism (revivals)   (p. 288)

Charles Grandison Finney   (p. 288)

Temperance   (p. 290)

Insanity Defense   (p. 291)

Capital Punishment   (p. 291)

Imprisonment for Debt   (p. 291)

Horace Mann   (p. 292)

Prudence Crandall   (p. 292)

Dorothea Dix   (p. 293)

Thomas Hopkins Gallaudet   (p. 293)

Samuel Gridley Howe   (p. 293)

Colonization   (p. 294)

Paul Cuffe   (p. 294)

David Walker   (p. 294)

William Lloyd Garrison   (p. 294)

Liberty Party   (p. 296)

Free Soil Party   (p. 296)

Frederick Douglass   (p. 296)

Angelina and Sarah Grimké   (p. 298)

Elizabeth Cady Stanton   (p. 299)

Transcendentalists   (p. 303)

Ralph Waldo Emerson   (p. 303)

Henry David Thoreau   (p. 303)

REVIEW QUESTIONS

1. Describe the social and religious roots of the reform movements of the early nineteenth century.

2. In what ways did moral reformers try to change the behavior of early nineteenth-century Americans? How successful were they?

3. Describe the efforts of pre–Civil War reformers in each of the following areas: (a) educational reform; (b) the treatment of criminals; and (c) the treatment of the mentally ill.

4. Why did the abolition movement arouse resentment among many Northerners as well as many Southerners?

5. Why did a movement for women's rights emerge in the mid-nineteenth century? Identify the movement's achievements.

6. In what ways did American literature and art give expression to a distinctive national identity in the years before the Civil War?

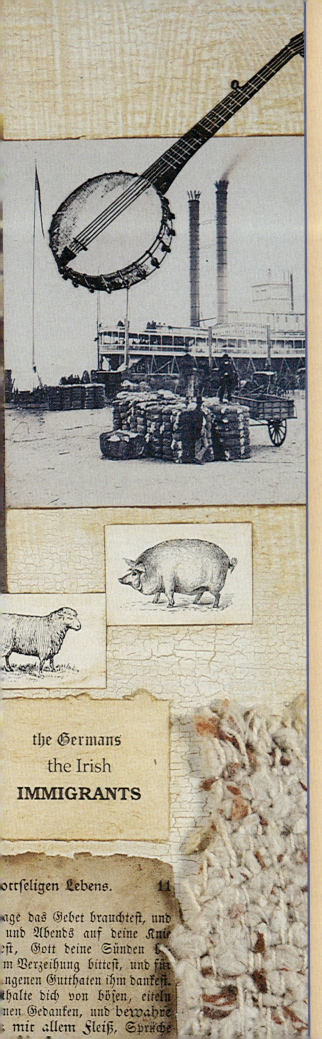

the Germans
the Irish
IMMIGRANTS

THE DIVIDED NORTH, THE DIVIDED SOUTH

319

"Some other means of cultivating their estates"

In the early 1790s, slavery appeared to be a dying institution. Slave imports into the New World were declining and slave prices were falling because the crops grown by slaves—tobacco, rice, and indigo—did not generate enough income to pay for their upkeep. In Maryland and Virginia, planters were replacing tobacco, a labor-intensive crop that needed a slave labor force, with wheat and corn, which did not. At the same time, leading Southerners, including Thomas Jefferson, denounced slavery as a source of debt, economic stagnation, and moral dissipation. A French traveler reported that people throughout the South "are constantly talking of abolishing slavery, of contriving some other means of cultivating their estates."

Then **Eli Whitney** of Massachusetts gave slavery a new lease on life. Even as a teenager, Whitney was considered a mechanical genius. At the age of 12, he produced a violin that "made tolerable good musick." At 15 he took over his father's workshop in Westborough, Massachusetts, and began manufacturing nails. By the time he was 18, he had begun to produce hat pins for women's bonnets and men's walking sticks. But young Whitney hoped to become something more than a clever mechanic, and at the age of 23 he abandoned his father's workshop and entered college.

In 1792, just after graduating from Yale, Whitney traveled south in search of employment as a tutor. His journey was filled with disasters. During the boat trip, he became seasick. Before he could recover, his boat ran aground on rocks near New York City. Then he contracted smallpox. The only good thing to happen during his journey was that he was befriended by a charming Southern widow named Catharine Greene, whose late husband, General Nathanael Greene, had been a leading general during the American Revolution. When he arrived in the South, Whitney discovered that his promised salary as a tutor had been cut in half. So he quit the job and accepted Greene's invitation to visit her plantation near Savannah, Georgia.

During his visit, Whitney became intrigued with the problem encountered by southern planters in producing short-staple cotton. The booming textile industry had created a high demand for the crop, but it could not be marketed until the seeds had been extracted from the cotton boll, a laborious and time-consuming process.

From a slave known only by the name Sam, Whitney learned that a comb could be used to remove seeds from cotton. In just ten days, Whitney devised a way of mechanizing the comb. Within a month, Whitney's cotton engine (gin for short) could separate fiber from seeds faster than 50 people working by hand.

Whitney's invention revitalized slavery in the South by stimulating demand for slaves to raise short-staple cotton. Between 1792, when Whitney arrived on the Greene plantation, and 1794, the price of slaves doubled. By 1825 field hands, who brought $500 apiece in 1794, were worth $1500. As the price of slaves rose, so too did the number of slaves. During the first decade of the nineteenth century, the number of slaves in the United States increased by 33 percent; during the following decade (after the African slave trade became illegal), the slave population grew another 29 percent.

As the institution of slavery expanded in the South, it declined in the North. In 1777, Vermont's constitution outlawed slavery, making it the first area in the New World to prohibit slavery. Judicial decisions freed slaves in Massachusetts and New Hampshire, and other northern states adopted gradual emancipation acts. By the beginning of the nineteenth century, the new republic was fatefully divided into a slave section and a free section.

While seeking employment in the South, Yankee schoolteacher Eli Whitney developed a simple machine for separating cotton from its seeds. The "cotton gin" met the increasing demand for cotton and breathed new life into the institution of slavery.

A DIVIDED CULTURE

By 1860 most Americans believed that the Mason-Dixon line divided the nation into two distinctive cultures: a commercial North and an agrarian South. This belief—that the cultures of the North and South were fundamentally different—was not a new idea on the eve of the Civil War. During the bitter political battles of the 1790s, New England Federalists pictured the South as a backward, economically stagnant society in which manual labor was degraded and wealth was dissipated in personal luxury. Many Southern Republicans countered by denouncing the corrupt, grasping, materialistic society of the North.

Many factors contributed to this sense of sectional difference. Diction, work habits, diet, and labor systems distinguished the two sections. One section depended on slave-based agriculture; the other emphasized commercial agriculture based on family farms and a developing industrial sector resting on wage labor.

The North was over 50 percent more populous than the South. Urban centers grew as European immigrants arrived in greater and greater numbers. Commerce, financial institutions, manufacturing, and transportation were developing rapidly. In contrast, the South had primitive transportation facilities, and it had smaller and fewer cities. Most important of all, a third of the South's population lived in slavery.

Despite these differences, the pre–Civil War North and South shared many important characteristics. Both regions were predominantly rural, both had booming economies, and both were engaged in speculation and trade. They shared western expansion, the enactment of democratic political reforms, and the same national political parties. Nevertheless, most Americans thought of their nation as divided into two halves, a commercial civilization and an agrarian civilization, each operating according to entirely different sets of values.

THE EMERGENCE OF A NEW INDUSTRIAL ORDER IN THE NORTH

To all outward appearances, life in the North in 1790 was not much different than in 1740. The vast majority of the people—more than 90 percent—still lived and worked on farms or in small rural villages. Less than 1 Northerner in 13 worked in trade or manufacturing.

Conditions of life remained primitive. The typical house—a single-story one- or two-room log or wood frame structure—was small, sparsely furnished, and afforded little personal privacy. Sleeping, eating, and work spaces were not sharply differentiated, and mirrors, curtains, upholstered chairs, carpets, desks, and bookcases were luxuries enjoyed only by wealthy families.

Even prosperous farming or merchant families lived simply. Many families ate meals out of a common pot or bowl, just as their ancestors had in the seventeenth century. Standards of cleanliness remained exceedingly low. Bedbugs were constant sleeping companions, and people seldom bathed or even washed their clothes or dishes.

Daily life was physically demanding. Most families made their own cloth, clothing, and soap. Because they lacked matches, they lit fires by striking a flint again and again with a steel striker until a spark ignited some tinder. Because there was no indoor plumbing, chamber pots had to be used and emptied. Homes were usually heated by a single open fireplace and illuminated by candles. Housewives hand-carried water from a pump, well, or stream and threw the dirty water or slops out the window. Family members hauled grain to a local grist mill or else milled it by hand. They cut, split, and gathered wood and fed it into a fireplace.

But by 1860, profound and far-reaching changes had taken place. Commercial agriculture had replaced subsistence agriculture. Household production had been supplanted by centralized manufacturing outside the home. And nonagricultural employment had begun to overtake agricultural employment: Nearly half of the North's population made a living outside the agricultural sector.

These economic transformations were all results of the industrial revolution, which affected every aspect of life. It raised living standards, transformed the work process, and relocated hundreds of thousands of people across oceans and from rural farms and villages into fast-growing industrial cities.

The most obvious consequence of this revolution was an impressive increase in wealth, per capita income, and commercial, middle-class job opportunities. Between 1800 and 1860, output increased 12-fold, and purchasing power doubled. New middle-class jobs proliferated. Increasing numbers of men found work as agents, bankers, brokers, clerks, merchants, professionals, and traders.

Living standards rose sharply, at least for the rapidly expanding middle class. Instead of making cloth and clothing at home, families began to buy them. Instead of hand milling grains, an increasing number of families began to buy processed grains. Kerosene lamps replaced candles as a source of light; coal replaced wood as fuel; friction matches replaced crude flints. Even poorer families began to cook their food on cast-iron cookstoves and to heat their rooms with individual-room heaters. The advent of railroads and the first canned foods brought year-round variety to the northern diet.

The industrial revolution led to rising standards of living that enabled white, middle-class families, like the one shown here, to enjoy new household comforts. Portraits and other artwork adorn the walls, bric-a-brac and knickknacks line the mantel. The fire in the fireplace provides heat, but the woman sews by the light of the kerosene lamp on the table. The middle-class wife and mother was expected to maintain a comfortable home that would provide her husband with rest and refuge from the pressures of work and business. Child rearing came to be guided by affection and patient instruction, rather than punishment and intimidation.

Physical comfort increased markedly. Padded seats, spring mattresses, and pillows became more common. By 1860 many urban middle-class families had central heating, indoor plumbing, and wall-to-wall carpeting.

Houses became larger and more affordable. The invention in the 1830s of the balloon frame—a lightweight house frame made up of boards nailed together—as well as prefabricated doors, window frames, shutters, and sashes resulted in larger and more reasonably priced houses. The cost of building a house fell by 40 percent, and two-story houses, with four or five rooms, became increasingly common.

A revolution in values and sensibility accompanied these changes in the standard of living. Standards of cleanliness and personal hygiene rose sharply. People bathed more frequently, washed their clothes more often, and dusted, swept, and scrubbed their houses more regularly. Standards of propriety also rose. The respectable classes began to blow their noses into handkerchiefs, instead of wiping them with their sleeves, and to dispose of their spittle in spittoons.

Northerners regarded all of these changes as signs of progress. A host of northern political leaders, mainly Whigs and later Republicans, celebrated the North as a region of bustling cities, factories, railroads, and prosperous farms and independent craftsmen—a stark contrast to an impoverished, backward, slave-owning South, suffering from soil exhaustion and economic and social decline.

Although the industrial revolution brought many material benefits, critics decried its negative consequences. Labor leaders deplored the bitter suffering of factory and sweatshop workers, the breakdown of craft skills, the vulnerability of urban workers to layoffs and economic crises, and the maldistribution of wealth and property. Conservatives lamented the disintegration of an older household-centered economy in which husbands, wives, and children had labored together. Southern writers, such as George Fitzhugh, argued that the North's growing class of free laborers were slaves of the marketplace, suffering even more insecurity than the South's chattel slaves, who were provided for in sickness and old age.

During the early nineteenth century, the industrial revolution transformed northern society, altering the way people worked and lived and contributing to growing sectional differences between the North and South. How and why did the industrial revolution occur when it did? What were its consequences? How did it fuel sectional antagonisms?

The Transformation of the Rural Countryside

In 1790 most farm families in the rural North produced most of what they needed to live. Instead of using money to purchase necessities, families entered into complex exchange relationships with relatives and neighbors and bartered to acquire the goods they

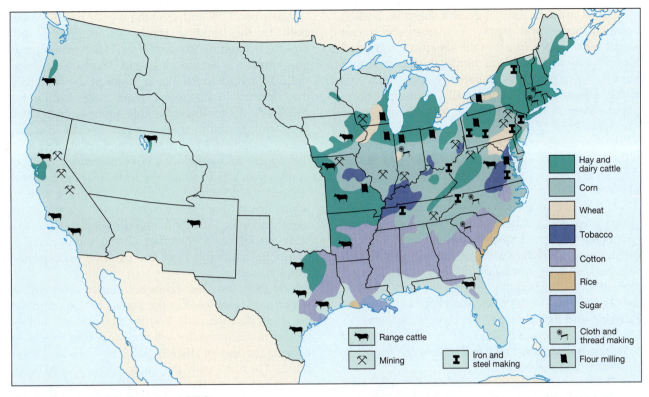

Agriculture and Industry, 1850

Legend:
- Hay and dairy cattle
- Corn
- Wheat
- Tobacco
- Cotton
- Rice
- Sugar
- Cloth and thread making
- Flour milling
- Range cattle
- Mining
- Iron and steel making

needed. To supplement their meager incomes, farm families often did piecework for shopkeepers and craftsmen. In the late eighteenth century these "household industries" provided work for thousands of men, women, and children in rural areas. Shopkeepers or master craftsmen supplied farm families with raw materials and paid them piece rates to produce such items as linens and farm utensils.

Between 1790 and the 1820s, a new pattern emerged. Subsistence farming gave way to commercial agriculture as farmers increasingly began to grow cash crops for sale and used the proceeds to buy goods produced by others. In New Hampshire farmers raised sheep for wool; in western Massachusetts they began to fatten cattle and pigs for sale to Boston; in eastern Pennsylvania they specialized in dairy products.

After 1820, the household industries that had employed thousands of women and children began to decline. They were replaced by manufacturing in city shops and factories. New England farm families began to buy their shoes, furniture, cloth, and sometimes even their clothes ready-made. Small rural factories closed their doors, and village artisans who produced for local markets found themselves unable to compete against cheaper city-made goods. As local opportunities declined, many long-settled farm

areas suffered sharp population losses. Convinced that "agriculture is not the road to wealth, nor honor, nor to happiness," thousands of young people left the fields for cities.

The Disruption of the Artisan System of Labor

In the late eighteenth century, the North's few industries were small. Skilled craftspeople, known as *artisans* or *mechanics*, performed most manufacturing in small towns and larger cities. These craftspeople manufactured goods in traditional ways—by hand in their own homes or in small shops located nearby—and marketed the goods they produced. Matthew Carey, a Philadelphia newspaperman, personified the early nineteenth-century artisan-craftsman. He not only wrote articles and editorials that appeared in his newspaper, he also set the paper's type, operated the printing press, and hawked the newspaper.

The artisan class was divided into three subgroups. At the highest level were self-employed master craftspeople. They were assisted by skilled journeymen, who owned their own tools but lacked the capital to set up their own shops, and by apprentices, teenage boys who typically worked for three years in exchange for training in a craft.

Urban artisans did not draw a sharp separation between home and work. A master shoemaker might make shoes in a 10-foot square shed located immediately in back of his house. A printer would bind books or print newspapers in a room below his family's living quarters. Typically, a master craftsperson lived in the same house with his assistants. The household of Everard Peck, a Rochester, New York, publisher, was not unusual. It included his wife, his children, his brother, his business partner, a day laborer, and four journeyman printers and bookbinders.

Nor did urban artisans draw a sharp division between work and leisure. Work patterns tended to be irregular and were frequently interrupted by leisure breaks during which masters and journeymen would drink whiskey or other alcoholic beverages. During slow periods or periodic layoffs, workers enjoyed fishing trips and sleigh rides or cockfights, as well as drinking and gambling at local taverns. Artisans often took unscheduled time off to attend boxing matches, horse races, and exhibitions by traveling musicians and acrobats.

The first half of the nineteenth century witnessed the decline of the artisan system of labor. Skilled tasks, previously performed by artisans, were divided and subcontracted to less expensive unskilled laborers. Small shops were replaced by large "machineless" factories, which made the relationship between employer and employee increasingly impersonal. Many master craftspeople abandoned their supervisory role to foremen and contractors and substituted unskilled teenage boys for journeymen. Words like *employer, employee, boss,* and *foreman*—descriptive of the new relationships—began to be widely used.

In the factory system of production, machines lowered the costs of producing goods, but workers faced increasing demands to tend more machines and put out greater numbers of items.

Between 1790 and 1850 the work process—especially in the building trades, printing, and such rapidly expanding consumer oriented manufacturing industries as tailoring and shoemaking—was radically reorganized. The changes in the shoemaking industry in Rochester, New York, during the 1820s and 1830s illustrate this process. Instead of producing an entire shoe, a master would fit a customer, rough-cut the leather uppers, and then send the uppers and soles to a boardinghouse, where a journeyman would shape the leather. Then, the journeyman would send the pieces to a binder, a woman who worked in her home, who would sew the shoes together. Finally, the binder would send the shoe to a store for sale to a customer. Tremendous gains in productivity sprang from the division and specialization of labor.

By 1850, the older household-based economy, in which assistants lived in the homes of their employers, had disappeared. Young men moved out of rooms in their master's home and into hotels or boardinghouses in distinct working-class neighborhoods. The older view that each worker should be attached to a particular master, who would supervise his behavior and assume responsibility for his welfare, declined. This paternalistic view was replaced by a new conception of labor as a commodity, like cotton, that could be acquired or disposed of according to the laws of supply and demand.

The Introduction of the Factory System

In 1789 the Pennsylvania legislature placed an advertisement in British newspapers offering a cash bounty to any English textile worker who would migrate to the state. Samuel Slater, who was just finishing an apprenticeship in a Derbyshire textile mill, read the ad. He went to London, booked passage to America, and landed in Philadelphia. There he learned that Moses Brown, a Quaker merchant, had just completed a mill in Pawtucket, Rhode Island, and needed a manager. Slater applied for the job and received it, along with a promise that if he made the factory a success he would receive all the business's profits, less the cost and interest on the machinery.

On December 21, 1790, the mill opened. Seven boys and two girls, all between the ages of 7 and 12, operated the little factory's 72 spindles. Slater soon discovered that these children, "constantly employed under the immediate inspection of a [supervisor]," could produce three times as much as whole families working in their homes. To keep the children awake and alert, Slater whipped them with a

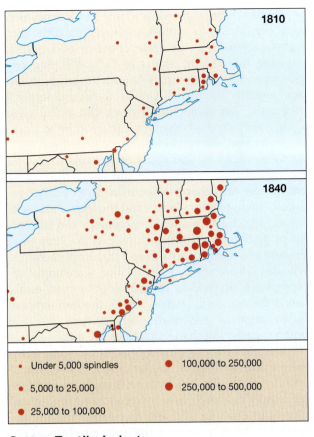

1810

1840

· Under 5,000 spindles

· 5,000 to 25,000

● 25,000 to 100,000

● 100,000 to 250,000

● 250,000 to 500,000

Cotton Textile Industry

leather strap or sprinkled them with water. On Sundays the children attended a special school Slater founded for their education.

The opening of Slater's mill marked the beginning of a widespread movement to consolidate manufacturing operations under a single roof. During the last years of the eighteenth century, merchants and master craftspeople who were discontented with the inefficiencies of their workforce created the nation's first modern factories. Within these centralized workshops, employers closely supervised employees, synchronized work to the clock, and punished infractions of rules with heavy fines or dismissal. In 1820, only 350,000 Americans worked in factories or mills. Four decades later, on the eve of the Civil War, the number had soared to 2 million.

For an inexpensive and reliable labor force, many factory owners turned to child labor. During the early phases of industrialization, textile mills and agricultural tool, metal goods, nail, and rubber factories had a ravenous appetite for cheap teenage laborers. In many mechanized industries, from a quarter to over half of the workforce was made up of young men or women under the age of 20.

During the first half of the nineteenth century, unmarried women made up a majority of the workforce in cotton textile mills and a substantial minority of workers in factories manufacturing ready-made clothing, hats, and shoes. Women were also employed in significant numbers in the manufacture of buttons, furniture, gloves, gunpowder, shovels, and tobacco.

Unlike farm work or domestic service, employment in a mill offered female companionship and an independent income. Wages were twice what a woman could make as a seamstress, tailor, or schoolteacher. Furthermore, most mill girls viewed the work as only temporary before marriage. Most worked in the mills fewer than four years, and frequently interrupted their stints in the mill for several months at a time with trips back home.

By the 1830s, increasing competition among textile manufacturers caused deteriorating working conditions that drove native-born women out of the mills. Employers cut wages, lengthened the workday, and required mill workers to tend four looms instead of just two. Hannah Borden, a Fall River, Massachusetts, textile worker, was required to have her loom running at 5 A.M. She was given an hour for breakfast and half an hour for lunch. Her workday ended at 7:30 P.M., 14½ hours after it had begun. For a 6-day workweek, she received between $2.50 and $3.50.

The mill girls militantly protested the wage cuts. In 1834 and again in 1836, the mill girls went out on strike. An open letter spelled out the workers' complaints: "sixteen females [crowded] into the same hot, ill-ventilated attic"; a workday "two or three hours longer . . . than is done in Europe"; and work-

Young women made up the bulk of the workforce in the early textile mills.

During the 1830s, rapid inflation and mounting competition for jobs encouraged the growth of unions. By 1836, an estimated 300,000 American workers were union members.

ers compelled to "stand so long at the machinery . . . that varicose veins, dropsical swelling of the feet and limbs, and prolapsus uter[us], diseases that end only with life, are not rare but common occurrences."

During the 1840s, fewer and fewer native-born women were willing to work in the mills. "Slavers," which were long, black wagons that criss-crossed the Vermont and New Hampshire countryside in search of mill hands, arrived empty in Rhode Island and Massachusetts mill towns. Increasingly, employers replaced the native-born mill girls with a new class of permanent factory operatives: immigrant women from Ireland.

Labor Protests

In 1806 journeyman shoemakers in New York City organized one of the nation's first labor strikes. The workers' chief demands were not higher wages and shorter hours. Instead, they protested the changing conditions of work. They staged a "turn-out" or "stand-out," as a strike was then called, to protest the use of cheap unskilled and apprentice labor and the subdivision and subcontracting of work. The strike ended when a court ruled that a labor union was guilty of criminal conspiracy if workers struck to obtain wages higher than those set by custom. The court found the journeyman shoemakers guilty and fined them $1 plus court costs.

By the 1820s, a growing number of journeymen were organizing to protest employer practices that were undermining the independence of workers, reducing them to the status of "a humiliating servile dependency, incompatible with the inherent natural equality of men." Unlike their counterparts in Britain, American journeymen did not protest against the introduction of machinery into the workplace. Instead, they vehemently protested wage reductions, declining standards of workmanship, and the increased use of unskilled and semiskilled workers. Journeymen charged that manufacturers had reduced "them to degradation and the loss of that self-respect which had made the mechanics and laborers the pride of the world." They insisted that they were the true producers of wealth and that manufacturers, who did not engage in manual labor, were unjust expropriators of wealth. In 1834 journeymen established the National Trades' Union, the first national organization of American wage earners. By 1836 union membership had climbed to 300,000.

Despite bitter employer opposition, some gains were made. In 1842, in the landmark case *Commonwealth* v. *Hunt*, the Massachusetts supreme court established a new precedent by recognizing the right of unions to exist. In addition to establishing the nation's first labor unions, journeymen also formed political organizations, known as Working Men's parties, as well as mutual benefit societies, libraries, educational institutions, and producers' and consumers' cooperatives. Working men and women published at least 68 labor papers, and they agitated for free public education, reduction of the workday, and abolition of capital punishment, state militias, and imprisonment for debt. Following the Panic of 1837, land reform was one of labor's chief demands. One hundred sixty acres of free public land for those who would actually settle the land was the demand, and "Vote Yourself a Farm" became the popular slogan.

The Movement for a Ten-Hour Day

Labor's greatest success was a campaign to establish a ten-hour workday in most major northeastern cities. In 1835 carpenters, masons, and stonecutters in Boston staged a seven-month strike in favor of a ten-hour day. The strikers demanded that employers reduce excessively long hours worked in the summer and spread them throughout the year. Quickly, the movement for a ten-hour workday spread to Philadelphia, where carpenters, bricklayers, plasterers, masons, leather dressers, and blacksmiths went on strike. Textile workers in Paterson, New Jersey, were the first factory operatives to strike for a reduction in work hours. Soon, women textile operatives in Lowell added their voices to the call for a ten-hour day, contending that such a law would "lengthen the lives of those employed, by giving them a greater opportunity to breathe the pure air of heaven" as well as provide "more time for mental and moral cultivation."

In 1840 the federal government introduced a ten-hour workday on public works projects. In 1847 New Hampshire became the first state to adopt a ten-hour day law. It was followed by Pennsylvania in 1848. Both states' laws, however, included a clause that allowed workers to voluntarily agree to work more than a ten-hour day. Despite the limitations of these state laws, agitation for a ten-hour day did result in a reduction in the average number of hours worked, to approximately 11½ by 1850.

The Laboring Poor

In January 1850, police arrested John McFeaing in Newburyport, Massachusetts, for stealing wood from the wharves. McFeaing pleaded necessity and a public investigation was conducted. Investigators found McFeaing's wife and four children living "in the extremity of misery. The children were all scantily supplied with clothing and not one had a shoe to his feet. There was not a stick of firewood or scarcely a morsel of food in the house, and everything betokened the most abject want and misery." McFeaing's predicament was not uncommon at that time.

The quickening pace of trade and finance during the early nineteenth century not only increased the demand for middle-class clerks and shopkeepers, it also dramatically increased demand for unskilled workers, who earned extremely low incomes and led difficult lives.

In 1851 Horace Greeley, editor of the New York *Tribune*, estimated the minimum weekly budget needed to support a family of five. Essential expenditures for rent, food, fuel, and clothing amounted to $10.37 a week. In that year, a shoemaker or a printer earned just $4 to $6 a week, a male textile operative $6.50 a week, and an unskilled laborer just $1 a week. The only manual laborers able to earn Greeley's minimum were blacksmiths and machinists.

Frequent unemployment compounded the problems of the unskilled. In Massachusetts upward of 40 percent of all workers were out of a job for part of a year, usually for four months or more. Fluctuations in demand, inclement weather, interruptions in transportation, technological displacement, fire, injury, and illness all could leave workers jobless.

Typically, a male laborer earned just two-thirds of his family's income. The other third was earned by wives and children. Many married women performed work in the home, such as embroidery and making artificial flowers, tailoring garments, or doing laundry. The wages of children were critical for a family's standard of living. Children under the age of 15 contributed 20 percent of the income of many working-class families. These children worked not because their parents were heartless, but because children's earnings were absolutely essential to the family's survival.

To provide protection against temporary unemployment, many working-class families scrimped and saved to buy a house or maintain a garden. In Newburyport, Massachusetts, many workers bought farm property on the edge of town. On New York City's East Side, many families kept goats and pigs. Ownership of a house was a particularly valuable source of security, since a family could always obtain extra income by taking in boarders and lodgers.

Immigration Begins

During the summer of 1845, a "blight of unusual character" devastated Ireland's potato crop, the basic staple in the Irish diet. A few days after potatoes were dug from the ground, they began to turn into a slimy, decaying, blackish "mass of rottenness." Expert panels, convened to investigate the blight's cause, suggested that it was a result of "static electricity" or the smoke that billowed from railroad locomotives or "mortiferous vapours" rising from un-

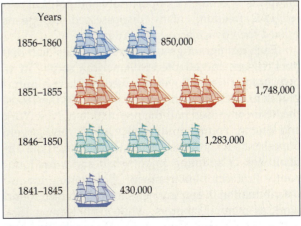

FIGURE 12.1
Total Immigration, 1841–1860

Years

1856–1860   850,000

1851–1855   1,748,000

1846–1850   1,283,000

1841–1845   430,000

derground volcanoes. In fact, the cause was a fungus that had traveled from America to Ireland.

"Famine fever"—dysentery, typhus, and infestations of lice—soon spread through the Irish countryside. Observers reported seeing children crying with pain and looking "like skeletons, their features sharpened with hunger and their limbs wasted, so that there was little left but bones, their hands and arms." Masses of bodies were buried without coffins, a few inches below the soil.

Over the next ten years, 750,000 Irish died and another 2 million left their homeland for Great Britain, Canada, and the United States. Freighters, which carried American and Canadian timber to Europe, offered fares as low as $17 to $20 between Liverpool and Boston—fares subsidized by English landlords eager to be rid of the starving peasants. As many as 10 percent of the emigrants perished while still at sea. In 1847, 40,000 (or 20 percent) of those who set out from Ireland died along the way. "If crosses and tombs could be erected on water," wrote the U.S. commissioner for emigration, "the whole route of the emigrant vessels from Europe to America would long since have assumed the appearance of a crowded cemetery."

At the beginning of the nineteenth century, only about 5000 immigrants arrived in the United States each year. During the 1830s, however, immigration climbed sharply as 600,000 immigrants poured into the country. This figure jumped to 1.7 million in the 1840s, when harvests all across Europe failed, and reached 2.6 million in the 1850s. Most of these immigrants came from Germany, Ireland, and Scandinavia, pushed from their homelands by famine, eviction from farmlands by landlords, political unrest, and the destruction of traditional handicrafts by factory enterprises. Attracted to the United States by the prospects of economic opportunity and political and religious freedom, many dispossessed Europeans braved the voyage across the Atlantic.

Each immigrant group migrated for its own distinct reasons and adapted to American society in its own unique ways. Poverty forced most Irish immigrants to settle in their port of origin. By the 1850s, the Irish comprised half the population of New York and Boston. Young, unmarried, Catholic, and largely of peasant background, the immigrants faced the difficult task of adapting to an urban and a predominantly Protestant environment. Confronting intense discrimination in employment, most Irish men found work as manual laborers, while Irish women took jobs mainly in domestic service. Discrimination had an important consequence: It encouraged Irish immigrants to become actively involved in politics. With a

Immigrants from Europe, hoping for economic opportunity and a better life in the United States, crowd the deck of a ship bound for America. Crop failures across Europe hit Ireland particularly hard as blight destroyed the potato crop—the single crop on which poor Irish farmers depended on for their livelihood—several times between 1845 and 1855. More than 1 million Irish died of starvation or disease during this time of the "Great Hunger." Almost 2 million emigrated, about 80 percent of them to the United States. Without any industrial skills or experience, many of the new immigrants could find work only in unskilled labor or domestic service.

strong sense of ethnic identity, high rates of literacy, and impressive organizational talents, Irish politicians played an important role in the development of modern American urban politics.

Unlike Irish immigrants, who settled primarily in northeastern cities and engaged in politics, German immigrants tended to move to farms or frontier towns in the Midwest and were less active politically. While some Germans fled to the United States to escape political persecution following the revolutions of 1830 and 1848, most migrated for quite a different reason: to sustain traditional ways of life. The industrial revolution severely disrupted traditional patterns of life for German farmers, shopkeepers, and practitioners of traditional crafts (like baking, brewing, and carpentering). In the Midwest's farmland and frontier cities, including Cincinnati and St. Louis, they sought to reestablish old German lifeways, setting up German fraternal lodges, coffee circles, and educational and musical societies. German immigrants carried important aspects of German culture with them, which quickly became integral parts of American culture, including the Christmas tree and the practice of Christmas gift giving, the kindergarten, and the gymnasium. Given Germany's

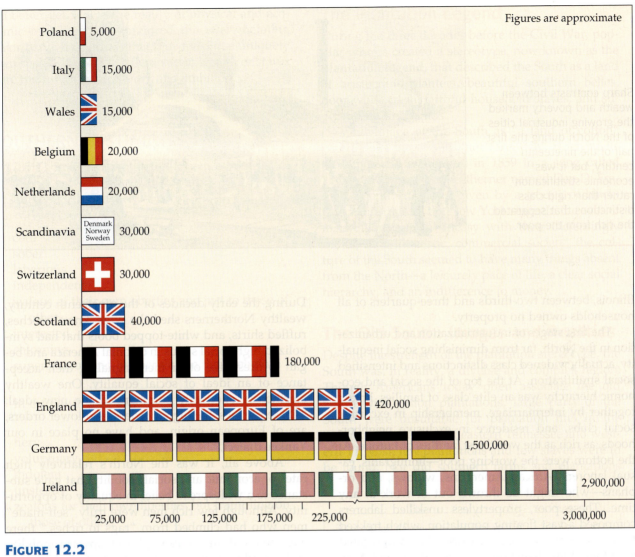

FIGURE 12.2
Immigration by Country of Origin, 1840–1860

strong educational and craft traditions, it is not surprising that German immigrants would be particularly prominent in the fields of engineering, optics, drug manufacture, and metal and tool making, as well as in the labor movement.

The Divided North

During the decades preceding the Civil War, it was an article of faith among Northerners that their society offered unprecedented economic equality and opportunity, free of rigid class divisions and glaring extremes of wealth and poverty. It was a land where even a "humble mechanic" had "every means of winning independence which are extended only to rich monopolists in England." How accurate is this picture of the pre–Civil War North as a land of opportunity, where material success was available to all?

In fact, the percentage of wealth held by those at the top of the economic hierarchy appears to have increased substantially before the Civil War. While the proportion of wealth controlled by the richest 10 percent rose from 50 percent in the 1770s to 70 percent in 1860, the real wages of unskilled northern workers stagnated or, at best, rose modestly. By 1860 half of all free whites held fewer than 1 percent of the North's real and personal property, while the richest 1 percent owned 27 percent of the region's wealth—a level of inequality comparable to that found in early nineteenth-century Europe and greater than that found in the United States today. In towns as different as Stonington, Connecticut, and Chicago,

Policing the Pre–Civil War City

DURING the mid-1830s, a wave of rioting without parallel in earlier American history swept the nation. In April 1834, in New York, three days of rioting pitting pro-Democrat against pro-Whig gangs erupted during municipal elections. In July, another New York mob stormed the house of a prominent abolitionist, carried the furniture into the street, and set it on fire. Over the next two days, a mob gutted New York's Episcopal African Church and attacked the homes of many of the city's African Americans. The state militia had to be called out to quell the disturbances.

Rioting was not confined to New York City. On August 11, 1834, a mob composed of lower-class men and boys sacked and burned a convent in Charlestown, Massachusetts, near the site of Bunker Hill, following a series of impassioned anti-Catholic sermons by the Reverend Lyman Beecher, the father of novelist Harriet Beecher Stowe. Two months later, a proslavery riot swept through Philadelphia, destroying 45 homes in the city's African American community.

Altogether there were at least 115 incidents of mob violence during the 1830s, compared to just 7 incidents in the 1810s and 21 incidents in the 1820s. *Niles' Register*, a respected newspaper of the time, reported that a "spirit of riot or a disposition to 'take the law into their own hands' prevails in every quarter." Abraham Lincoln, then a young Springfield, Illinois, attorney, echoed these sentiments. "Outrages committed by mobs," he lamented, had become "the everyday news of the times."

Mob violence during the 1830s had a variety of sources. A rate of urban growth faster than that in any previous decade was one major contributor to social turbulence during the 1830s. Urban populations grew by 60 percent and the sharp upsurge in foreign immigration heightened religious and ethnic tensions. The number of immigrants entering the country jumped from 5000 a year at the beginning of the century to over 50,000 annually during the 1830s.

Another source of violence came with abolitionism, which emerged at the beginning of the decade and produced a violent reaction. The belief that abolitionists favored miscegenation—interracial marriages of African Americans and whites—enflamed anti-African American sentiment. The mobs that attacked African American homes and churches, burned white abolitionists' homes and businesses, and disrupted antislavery meetings were often led by "gentlemen of property and standing." These old-stock merchants and bankers feared that abolitionist appeals to the middle class and especially to women and children threatened their patriarchal position in local communities and even in their own families.

The birth of a new two-party political system also contributed to a growing climate of violence. Mob violence frequently broke out on election days as rival Democratic and Whig gangs tried to steal ballot boxes and keep the opposition's voters from reaching local polling places.

Traditional methods of preserving public order proved totally inadequate by the 1830s. Earlier in time, the nation's cities were "policed" by a handful of unpaid, untrained, ununiformed, and unarmed sheriffs, aldermen, marshals, constables, and nightwatchmen. In New England towns, tithingmen armed with long black sticks tipped with brass patrolled streets searching for drunkards, disorderly children, and wayward servants.

These law officers were not a particularly effective deterrent to crime. Nightwatchmen generally held other jobs during the day and sometimes slept at their posts at night. Sheriffs, aldermen, marshals, and constables made a living not by investigating crimes or patrolling city streets but by collecting debts, foreclosing on mortgages, and serving court orders. Victims of crime had to offer a reward if they wanted these unpaid law officers to investigate a case.

This early system of maintaining public order worked in previous decades when the rates of serious crime were extremely low and citizens had informal mechanisms that helped maintain order. Most cities were small and compact and lacked any distinct working-class ghettoes. Shopkeepers usually lived at or near their place of business and apprentices, journeymen, and laborers tended to live in or near the house of their master. Under these circumstances, the poor and the working class were subject to close supervision by their social superiors. By the mid-1830s, however, this older pattern of social organization had clearly broken down. Class-segregated neighborhoods grew increasingly common. Youth gangs, organized along ethnic and neighborhood lines, proliferated. Older mechanisms of social control weakened.

After 1830, drunken brawls, robberies, beatings, and murders all in-

creased in number. Fear of crime led city leaders to look for new ways of preserving public order. Many municipal leaders regarded the new professional police force established in London in 1829 by the British Parliament as a model. London's police, nicknamed "bobbies" after Prime Minister Robert Peel, were trained, full-time professionals. They wore distinctive uniforms to make them visible to the public, patrolled regular beats, and lived in the neighborhoods they patrolled.

Initially, resistance to the establishment of professional police forces in American cities was intense. Taxpayers feared the cost of a police force. Local political machines feared the loss of the night watch as a source of political patronage. During the late 1830s and 1840s, rising crime rates overcame opposition to the establishment of a professional police force. Boston appointed the nation's first police officers in 1838.

In New York City, the turning point came in 1841 following the un-solved murder of Mary Rogers, who worked in a tobacco shop. On July 25, 1841, she disappeared. Three days later, the body of the "beautiful cigar girl" was found in a river. The coroner said she had died not from drowning but from being abused and murdered by a gang of ruffians. The case aroused intense passion in New York City, prompting vocal demands for an end to waterfront gangs. But the city's constables said that they would only investigate the murder if they were promised a substantial reward. The public was outraged. In 1844, the New York state legislature authorized the establishment of a professional police force to investigate crimes and patrol streets in New York City.

The life of a mid-nineteenth-century police officer was exceptionally hard. In many cities, members of gangs, like New York's Bowery B'hoys, Baltimore's Rip Raps, and Philadelphia's Schuylkill Rangers, actually outnumbered police officers. Young toughs regularly harrassed police officers. Many officers resisted wearing uniforms on the grounds that any distinctive dress made them readily identifiable targets for street gangs. In New York City, four officers were killed in the line of duty in a single year.

After 1850, in large part as a result of more efficient policing, the number of street disorders in American cities began to drop. Despite the introduction of the Colt revolver and other easily concealed and relatively inexpensive handguns during the middle years of the century, homicide rates, too, began to decline. By the eve of the Civil War, the nation's cities had become far less violent and far more orderly places than they had been two decades before.

devote their efforts exclusively to growing cotton or other cash crops, such as rice and tobacco. Unlike the slave societies of the Caribbean, which produced crops exclusively for export, the South devoted much of its energy to raising food and livestock.

The pre–Civil War South encompassed a wide variety of regions that differed geographically, economically, and politically. Such regions included the Piedmont, Tidewater, coastal plain, piney woods, Delta, Appalachian mountains, upcountry, and a fertile "black belt"—regions that clashed repeatedly over such political questions as debt relief, taxes, apportionment of representation, and internal improvements.

The white South's social structure was much more complex than the popular stereotype of proud aristocrats disdainful of honest work and ignorant, vicious, exploited poor whites. The old South's intricate social structure included many small slaveowners and relatively few large ones.

Actually, large slaveholders were extremely rare. In 1860 only 11,000 Southerners—three-quarters of one percent of the white population—owned more than 50 slaves; a mere 2358 owned as many as 100 slaves. However, although large slaveholders were few in number, they owned most of the South's slaves. Over half of all slaves lived on plantations with 20 or more slaves and a quarter lived on plantations with more than 50 slaves.

Slave ownership was relatively widespread. In the first half of the nineteenth century, one-third of all southern white families owned slaves, and a majority of white southern families either owned slaves,

had owned them, or expected to own them. These slaveowners were a diverse lot. A few were African American, mulatto, or Native American; one-tenth were women; and more than one in ten worked as artisans, businesspeople, or merchants rather than as farmers or planters. Few led lives of leisure or refinement. The average slaveowner lived in a log cabin rather than a mansion and was a farmer rather than a planter. The average holding varied between four and six slaves, and most slaveholders possessed no more than five.

White women in the South, despite the image of the hoop-skirted southern belle, suffered under heavier burdens than their northern counterparts. They married earlier, bore more children, and were more likely to die young. They lived in greater isolation, had less access to the company of other women, and lacked the satisfactions of voluntary associations and reform movements. Their education was briefer and much less likely to result in opportunities for independent careers.

The plantation legend was misleading in still other respects. Slavery was neither dying nor unprofitable. In 1860 the South was richer than any country in Europe except England, and it had achieved a level of wealth unmatched by Italy or Spain until the eve of World War II.

The southern economy generated enormous wealth and was critical to the economic growth of the entire United States. Well over half of the richest 1 percent of Americans in 1860 lived in the South. Even more important, southern agriculture helped finance early nineteenth-century American economic growth. Before the Civil War, the South grew 60 percent of the world's cotton, provided over half of all U.S. export earnings, and furnished 70 percent of the cotton consumed by the British textile industry. Cotton exports paid for a substantial share of the capital and technology that laid the basis for America's industrial revolution. In addition, precisely because the South specialized in agricultural production, the North developed a variety of businesses that provided services for the southern states, including textile and meat processing industries and financial and commercial facilities.

Impact of Slavery on the Southern Economy

Although slavery was highly profitable, it had a negative impact on the southern economy. It impeded the development of industry and cities and contributed to high debts, soil exhaustion, and a lack of technological innovation. The philosopher and poet Ralph Waldo Emerson said that "slavery is no

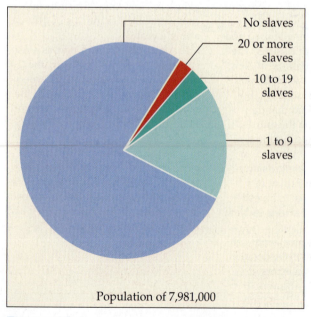

No slaves

20 or more slaves

10 to 19 slaves

1 to 9 slaves

Population of 7,981,000

FIGURE 12.4
Southern White Population, 1860

scholar, no improver; it does not love the whistle of the railroad; it does not love the newspaper, the mail-bag, a college, a book or a preacher who has the absurd whim of saying what he thinks; it does not increase the white population; it does not improve the soil; everything goes to decay." There appears to be a large element of truth in Emerson's observation.

The South, like other slave societies, did not develop urban centers for commerce, finance, and industry on a scale equal to those found in the North. Virginia's largest city, Richmond, had a population of just 15,274 in 1850. That same year, Wilmington, North Carolina's largest city, had only 7264 inhabitants, while Natchez and Vicksburg, the two largest cities in Mississippi, had fewer than 3000 white inhabitants.

Southern cities were small because they failed to develop diversified economies. Unlike the cities of the North, southern cities rarely became processing or finishing centers and southern ports rarely engaged in international trade. Their primary functions were to market and transport cotton or other agricultural crops, supply local planters and farmers with such necessities as agricultural implements, and produce the small number of manufactured goods, such as cotton gins, needed by farmers.

An overemphasis on slave-based agriculture led Southerners to neglect industry and transportation improvements. As a result, manufacturing and transportation lagged far behind in comparison to the North. In 1860 the North had approximately 1.3 million industrial workers, whereas the South had 110,000, and northern factories manufactured nine-tenths of the industrial goods produced in the United States.

The South's transportation network was primitive by northern standards. Traveling the 1460 overland miles from Baltimore to New Orleans in 1850 meant riding five different railroads, two stage-coaches, and two steamboats. Most southern railroads served primarily to transport cotton to southern ports, where the crop could be shipped on northern vessels to northern or British factories for processing.

Because of high rates of personal debt, Southern states kept taxation and government spending at much lower levels than did the states in the North. As a result, Southerners lagged far behind Northerners in their support for public education. Illiteracy was widespread. In 1850, 20 percent of all southern white adults could not read or write, while the illiteracy rate in New England was less than half of 1 percent.

Because large slaveholders owned most of the region's slaves, wealth was more stratified than in the North. In the Deep South, the middle class held a relatively small proportion of the region's property, while wealthy planters owned a very significant portion of the productive lands and slave labor. In 1850, 17 percent of the farming population held two-thirds

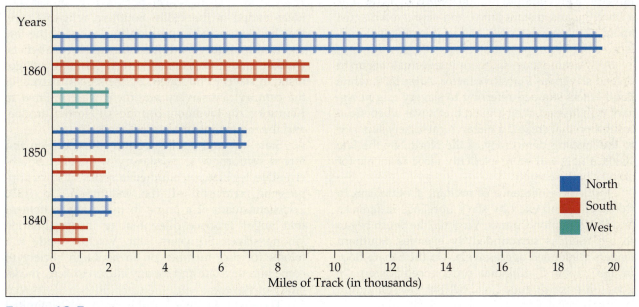

FIGURE 12.5
Railroad Growth, 1840–1860

An overemphasis on slave-based agriculture led Southerners to neglect transportation improvements.

of all acres in the rich cotton-growing regions of the South.

There are indications that during the last decade before the Civil War slave ownership was increasingly concentrated in fewer and fewer hands. As soil erosion and exhaustion diminished the availability of cotton land, scarcity and heavy demand forced the price of land and slaves to rise beyond the reach of most, and in newer cotton-growing regions, yeomen farmers were pushed off the land as planters expanded their holdings. In Louisiana, for example, nearly half of all rural white families owned no land. During the 1850s, the percentage of the total white population owning slaves declined significantly. By 1860, the proportion of whites holding slaves had fallen from about one-third to one-fourth. As slave and land ownership grew more concentrated, a growing number of whites were forced by economic pressure to leave the land and move to urban centers.

Growth of a Distinctive Southern Identity

Beginning in the 1830s, the South developed a new and aggressive sense of "nationalism" that was rooted in its sense of distinctiveness and its perception that it was ringed by enemies. The South began to conceive of itself more and more as the true custodian of America's revolutionary heritage. Southern travelers who ventured into the North regarded it as a "strange and distant land" and expressed disgust about its vice-ridden cities and its grasping materialism.

At the same time, southern intellectuals began to defend slavery as a positive factor. After 1830, white Southerners stopped referring to slavery as a necessary evil. Instead, they argued that it was a beneficial institution that created a hierarchical society superior to the leveling democracy of the North. By the late 1840s, a new and more explicitly racist rationale for slavery had emerged.

With the emergence of militant abolitionism in the North, sharpened by slave uprisings in Jamaica and Southampton County, Virginia, the South began to see itself as surrounded by enemies. Southern leaders responded aggressively. On the Senate floor in 1837, John C. Calhoun pronounced slavery "a good—a positive good" and set the tone for future southern proslavery arguments. Before the 1830s, southern statements on slavery had been defensive; afterward, they were defiant.

In the 1840s, a growing number of southern ministers, journalists, and politicians began to denounce the North's form of capitalism as "wage slavery."

The condition of free labor, they argued, was actually "worse than slavery," because slaveholders, unlike greedy northern employers, provide for their employees "when most needed, when sickness or old age has overtaken [them]." Northern workers, they declared, were simply "slaves without masters."

During the 1840s, more and more Southerners defended slavery on explicitly racial grounds. In doing so, they drew on new pseudoscientific theories of racial inferiority. Some of these theories came from Europe, which was seeking justification of imperial expansion over nonwhite peoples in Africa and Asia. Other racist ideas were drawn from northern scientists, who employed an elaborate theory of "polygenesis," which claimed that Africans and whites were separate species.

The Decline of Antislavery Sentiment in the South

During the eighteenth century, the South was unique among slave societies in its openness to antislavery ideas. In Delaware, Maryland, and North Carolina, Quakers freed more than 1500 slaves and sent them out of state. Scattered Presbyterian, Baptist, and Methodist ministers and advisory committees condemned slavery as a sin "contrary to the word of God." As late as 1827, the number of antislavery organizations in the South actually outnumbered those in the free states by at least four to one.

The South's historical openness to antislavery ideas ended in the 1830s. Southern religious sects that had expressed opposition to slavery in the late eighteenth century modified their antislavery beliefs. Quakers and Unitarians who were strongly antagonistic to slavery emigrated. By the second decade of the century, antislavery sentiment was confined to Kentucky, the Piedmont counties of North Carolina, and the mountains in eastern Tennessee.

State law and public opinion stifled debate and forced conformity to proslavery arguments. Southern state legislatures adopted a series of laws suppressing criticism of the institution. In 1830 Louisiana made it a crime to make any statement that might produce discontent or insubordination among slaves. Six years later, Virginia made it a felony for any member of an abolition society to come into the state and for any citizen to deny the legality of slavery.

The silent pressure of public opinion also limited public discussion of the slavery question. College presidents or professors suspected of sympathizing with abolitionists lost their jobs. Mobs attacked editors who dared to print articles critical of slavery. One Richmond, Virginia, editor fought eight duels in two years to defend his views on slavery. In Parkville, Missouri, and Lexington, Kentucky, crowds dismantled printing presses of antislavery newspapers. An "iron curtain" was erected against the invasion of antislavery propaganda.

Only once, in the wake of Nat Turner's famous slave insurrection in 1831, did a southern state openly debate the possibility of ending slavery. These debates in the Virginia legislature in January and February 1832 ended with the defeat of proposals to abolish slavery.

James G. Birney was one of many Southerners to discover that it was hopeless to work for slave emancipation in the South. Birney was born into a wealthy Kentucky slaveholding family, and, like many members of the South's slaveowning elite, was educated at Princeton. After graduation, he moved to Huntsville, Alabama, where he practiced law and operated a cotton plantation. In Huntsville, he developed qualms about slavery and began to work as an agent for the American Colonization Society. Soon, his doubts about slavery had grown into an active hatred for the institution. He returned to Kentucky, emancipated his slaves, and in 1835 organized the Kentucky Anti-Slavery Society.

In Kentucky, Birney quickly discovered that public opinion vehemently opposed antislavery ideas. A committee of leading citizens in Danville informed him that they would not permit him to establish an antislavery newspaper in the city. When Birney announced that he would go through with his plans anyway, the committee bought out the paper's printer, and the town's postmaster announced that he would refuse to deliver the newspaper. In a final effort to publish his paper, Birney moved across the Ohio River into Cincinnati, but a mob destroyed his press while the city's mayor looked on.

The defense of slavery after 1830 also led to hostility toward all social reforms. One southern newspaper editor declared that the South "has uniformly rejected the isms which infest Europe and the Eastern and Western states of this country." Many Southerners spoke proudly of rejecting the reforms that flourished in the North. The South, said one South Carolina scientist, was "the breakwater which is to stay that furious tide of social and political heresies now setting toward us from the shores of the old world." Only the temperance movement made headway in the South.

"Reforming" Slavery from Within

Many white Southerners felt genuine moral doubts about slavery. For the most part, however, these doubts were directed into efforts to reform the institution by converting slaves to Christianity, revising slave codes to make them less harsh, and making slavery conform to the ideal depicted in the Old Testament.

During the early eighteenth century, ministers from such denominations as the Quakers, Moravians, and Anglicans launched the first concerted campaigns to convert slaves in the American colonies to Christianity. Missionaries established schools and taught several thousand slaves to read and recite Scripture. They stressed that Christian slaves would make more loyal and productive workers, less likely to stage insurrections. The Great Awakening of the 1730s and 1740s stimulated renewed efforts to promote Christianization, but was not until the early nineteenth century that most slaveowners expressed concern for converting their slaves to Christianity.

There were also early nineteenth-century efforts to ameliorate the harshness of the early slave codes. The eighteenth-century codes permitted owners to punish slaves by castration and cutting off limbs. Slaveholders had no specific obligations for housing, feeding, or clothing slaves, and many observers reported seeing slaves half-clothed or naked. Few eighteenth-century masters showed any concern for slave marriages, families, or religion.

During the early nineteenth century, the southern states enacted new codes regulating the punishment of slaves and setting minimum standards for maintenance. State legislatures defined killing a

In a particularly cruel twist, an African slave is forced to whip a fellow slave as the white slave owner watches. Punishments and tortures that slaves might be forced to endure included, in addition to whipping, chaining, confinement, and branding.

prohibited from bringing suit to seek legal redress for violations of their rights.

The main goal of the slave codes, however, was to regulate slaves' lives. Slaves were forbidden to strike whites or use insulting language toward white people, hold a meeting without a white person present, visit whites or freed slaves, or leave plantations without permission. The laws prohibited whites and free blacks from teaching slaves to read and write, gambling with slaves, or supplying them with liquor, guns, or poisonous drugs. Most of the time, authorities loosely enforced these legal restrictions, but whenever fears of slave uprisings spread, enforcement tightened.

Slave Labor

Simon Gray was a slave. He was also the captain of a Mississippi River flatboat and the builder and operator of a number of sawmills. Emanuel Quivers, too, was a slave. He worked at the Tredegar Iron Works of Richmond, Virginia. Andrew Dirt was also a slave. He was an overseer.

Slaves performed all kinds of work. During the 1850s, half a million slaves lived in southern towns and cities, where they were hired out by their owners to work in ironworks, textile mills, tobacco factories, laundries, shipyards, and mechanics' homes. Other slaves labored as lumberjacks, as deckhands and fire tenders on river boats, and in sawmills, gristmills, and quarries. Many other slaves were engaged in construction of roads and railroads. Most slaves, to be sure, were field hands, raising cotton, hemp, rice,

tobacco, and sugar cane. But even on plantations not all slaves were menial laborers. Some worked as skilled artisans such as blacksmiths, shoemakers, or carpenters; others held domestic posts, such as coachmen or house servants; and still others held managerial posts. At least two-thirds of the slaves worked under the supervision of black foremen of gangs, called drivers. Not infrequently they managed the whole plantation in the absence of their masters.

For most slaves, slavery meant backbreaking field work on small farms or larger plantations. On the typical plantation, slaves worked "from day clean to first dark." Solomon Northrup, a free black who was kidnapped and enslaved for 12 years on a Louisiana cotton plantation, wrote a graphic description of the work regimen imposed on slaves: "The hands are required to be in the cotton field as soon as it is light in the morning, and, with the exception of ten or fifteen minutes, which is given them at noon to swallow their allowance of cold bacon, they are not permitted to be a moment idle until it is too dark to see, and when the moon is full, they often times labor till the middle of the night." Even then, the slaves' work was not over; it was still necessary to feed swine and mules, cut wood, and pack the cotton. At planting time or harvest time, work was even more exacting as planters required slaves to stay in the fields 15 or 16 hours a day.

To maximize productivity, slaveowners assigned each hand a specific set of tasks throughout the year. During the winter, field slaves ginned and pressed cotton, cut wood, repaired buildings and fences, and cleared fields. In the spring and summer, field hands

The dirt-floored, poorly ventilated, roughly built log one-room huts in which slaves lived were breeding grounds for disease. When slave owners realized they were losing the productive labor of their frequently ill slaves, they provided them with sturdier, better constructed cabins—still made of logs, but with wooden floors and glazed windows.

plowed and hoed fields, killed weeds, and planted and cultivated crops. In the fall, slaves picked, ginned, and packed cotton, shucked corn, and gathered peas. Elderly slaves cared for children, made clothes, and prepared food.

Labor on large plantations was as rigidly organized as in a factory. Under the gang system, which was widely used on cotton plantations, field hands were divided into plow gangs and hoe gangs, each commanded by a driver. Under the task system, mainly used on rice plantations, each hand was given a specific daily work assignment.

Because slaves had little direct incentive to work hard, slaveowners combined a variety of harsh penalties with positive incentives. Some masters denied disobedient slaves passes to leave the plantation or forced them to work on Sundays or holidays. Other planters confined disobedient hands to private or public jails, and one Maryland planter required a slave to eat the worms he had failed to pick off tobacco plants. Chains and shackles were widely used to control runaways. Whipping was a key part of the system of discipline and motivation. On one Louisiana plantation, at least one slave was lashed every four and one-half days. In his diary, Bennet H. Barrow, a Louisiana planter, recorded flogging "every hand in the field," breaking his sword on the head of one slave, shooting another slave in the thigh, and cutting another with a club "in 3 places very bad."

But physical pain alone was not enough to elicit hard work. To stimulate productivity, some masters gave slaves small garden plots and permitted them to sell their produce. Others distributed gifts of food or money at the end of the year. Still other planters awarded prizes, holidays, and year-end bonuses to particularly productive slaves. One Alabama master permitted his slaves to share in the profits of the cotton, peanut, and pea crops.

Material Conditions of Slave Life

Deprivation and physical hardship were the hallmarks of life under slavery. It now seems clear that the material conditions of slave life may have been even worse than those of the poorest, most downtrodden free laborers in the North and Europe. Although the material conditions for slaves improved greatly in the nineteenth century, slaves remained much more likely than southern or northern whites to die prematurely, suffer malnutrition or dietary deficiencies, or lose a child in infancy.

Plantation records reveal that over half of all slave babies died during their first year of life—a rate twice that of white babies. Although slave children's death rate declined after the first year of life, it remained twice the white rate. The average slave's small size indicates a deficient diet. At birth, over half of all slave children weighed less than 5 pounds—or what is today considered underweight. Throughout their childhoods, slaves were smaller than white children of the same age. The average slave children did not reach 3 feet in height until their fourth birthdays. At that age they were 5 inches shorter than a typical child today and about the same height as a child in present-day Bangladesh. At 17, slave men were shorter than 96 percent of present-day American men, and slave women were smaller than 80 percent of American women.

The slaves' diet was monotonous and unvaried, consisting largely of cornmeal, salt pork, and bacon. Only rarely did slaves drink milk or eat fresh meat or vegetables. This diet provided enough bulk calories to ensure that slaves had sufficient strength and energy to work as productive field hands, but it did not provide adequate nutrition. As a result, slaves were small for their ages, suffered from vitamin and protein deficiencies, and were victims of such ailments as beriberi, kwashiorkor, and pellagra. Poor nutrition and high rates of infant and child mortality contributed to a short average life expectancy—just 21 or 22 years compared to 40 to 43 years for whites.

The physical conditions in which slaves lived were appalling. Lacking privies, slaves had to urinate and defecate in the cover of nearby bushes. Lacking any sanitary disposal of garbage, they were surrounded by decaying food. Chickens, dogs, and pigs lived next to the slave quarters, and in consequence, animal feces contaminated the area. Such squalor contributed to high rates of dysentery, typhus, diarrhea, hepatitis, typhoid fever, and intestinal worms.

Slave quarters were cramped and crowded. The typical cabin—a single, windowless room, with a chimney constructed of clay and twigs and a floor made up of dirt or planks resting on the ground—ranged in size from 10 feet by 10 feet to 21 feet by 21 feet. These small cabins often contained five, six, or more occupants. On some plantations, slaves lived in single-family cabins; on others, two or more shared the same room. On the largest plantations, unmarried men and women were sometimes lodged together in barracklike structures. Josiah Henson, the Kentucky slave who served as the model for Harriet Beecher Stowe's Uncle Tom, described his plantation's cabins this way:

> We lodged in log huts. . . . Wooden floors were an unknown luxury. In a single room were huddled, like cattle, ten or a dozen persons, men, women, and chil-

"Our slave population is not only a happy one," said a Virginia legislator, "but it is a contented, peaceful, and harmless one."

In fact, there is no evidence that the majority of slaves were contented. One scholar has identified more than 200 instances of attempted insurrection or rumors of slave resistance between the seventeenth century and the Civil War. And many slaves who did not directly rebel made their masters' lives miserable through a variety of indirect protests against slavery, including sabotage, stealing, malingering, murder, arson, and infanticide.

Four times during the first 31 years of the nineteenth century, slaves attempted major insurrections. In 1800, a 24-year-old Virginia slave named **Gabriel,** who was a blacksmith, led a march of perhaps 50 armed slaves on Richmond. The plot failed when a storm washed out the road to Richmond, giving the Virginia militia time to arrest the rebels. White authorities executed Gabriel and 25 other conspirators.

In 1811 in southern Louisiana, between 180 and 500 slaves, led by Charles Deslondes, a free mulatto from Haiti, marched on New Orleans, armed with axes and other weapons. Slaveowners retaliated by killing 82 blacks and placing the heads of 16 leaders on pikes.

In 1822 **Denmark Vesey,** a former West Indian slave who had been born in Africa, bought his freedom, and moved to Charleston, South Carolina. There he devised a conspiracy to take over the city on a summer Sunday when many whites would be vacationing outside the city. Using his connections as a leader in the African Church of Charleston, Vesey drew support from skilled African-American artisans, carpenters, harnessmakers, mechanics, and blacksmiths as well as from field slaves. Before the revolt could take place, however, a domestic slave of a prominent Charlestonian informed his master. The authorities proceeded to arrest 131 African Americans and hang 37.

The best known slave revolt took place nine years later in Southampton County in southern Virginia. On August 22, 1831, **Nat Turner,** a trusted Baptist preacher, led a small group of fellow slaves into the home of his master Joseph Travis and killed the entire Travis household. By August 23, Turner's force had increased to between 60 and 80 slaves and had killed more than 50 whites. The local militia counterattacked and killed about 100 African Americans. Twenty more slaves, including Turner, were later executed. Turner's revolt sparked a panic that spread as far south as Alabama and Louisiana. One Virginian worried that "a Nat Turner might be in any family."

Slave uprisings were much less frequent and less extensive in the American South than in the West In-dies or Brazil. Outright revolts did not occur more often because the chances of success were minimal and the consequences of defeat catastrophic. As one Missouri slave put it, "I've seen Marse Newton and Marse John Ramsey shoot too often to believe they can't kill" a slave.

The conditions that favored revolts elsewhere were absent in the South. In Jamaica, slaves outnumbered whites ten to one, whereas in the South whites were a majority in every state except Mississippi and South Carolina. In addition, slaveholding units in the South were much smaller than in other slave societies in the Western Hemisphere. Half of all U.S. slaves worked on units of 20 or less; in contrast, many sugar plantations in Jamaica had more than 500 slaves.

The unity of the white population in defense of slavery made the prospects for a successful rebellion bleak. In Virginia in 1830, 100,000 of the state's 700,000 whites were members of the state militia. Finally, southern slaves had few havens to which to escape. The major exception was the swamp country in Florida, where former slave **maroons** joined with Seminole Indians in resisting the U.S. army.

Recognizing that open resistance would be futile or even counterproductive, most plantation slaves expressed their opposition to slavery in a variety of subtle ways. Most day-to-day resistance took the form of breaking tools, feigning illness, doing shoddy work, stealing, and running away. These acts of resistance most commonly occurred when a master or overseer overstepped customary bounds. Through these acts, slaves tried to establish a right to proper treatment.

Free African Americans

In 1860, 488,000 African Americans were not slaves. After the American Revolution, slaveowners freed thousands of slaves, and countless others emancipated themselves by running away. In Louisiana, a large free Creole population had emerged under Spanish and French rule, and in South Carolina a Creole population had arrived from Barbados. The number of free blacks in the Deep South increased rapidly with the arrival of thousands of light-colored refugees from the slave revolt in Haiti.

Free African Americans varied greatly in status. Most lived in poverty, but in a few cities, such as New Orleans, Baltimore, and Charleston, they worked as skilled carpenters, shoemakers, tailors, and millwrights. In the lower South, a few achieved high occupational status and actually bought slaves of their own. One of the wealthiest former slaves was William Ellison, the son of a slave mother and a

THE PEOPLE SPEAK

Slave Resistance

One of the first fugitive slaves to speak out publicly against slavery, Frederick Douglass electrified audiences with his firsthand accounts of slavery. Women's rights advocate Elizabeth Cady Stanton recalled her first glimpse of Douglass: "He stood there like an African prince, majestic in his wrath, as with wit, satire, and indignation he graphically described the bitterness of slavery and the humiliation of subjection." When many Northerners refused to believe that this eloquent orator could possibly have been a slave, he responded by writing an autobiography that identified his previous owners by name. Here, Douglass describes his battle with a brutal "slave-breaker."

If at any one time of my life . . . I was made to drink the bitterest dregs of slavery, that time was during the first six months of my stay with Mr. [Edward] Covey. We worked in all weather. It was never too hot or too cold. . . . The longest days were too short for him, and the shortest nights too long for him. I was somewhat unmanageable when I first went there, but a few months of this discipline tamed me. Mr. Covey succeeded in breaking me. I was broken in body, soul, and spirit. My natural elasticity was crushed, my intellect languished, the disposition to read departed, the cheerful spark that lingered about my eye died; the dark night of slavery closed in upon me; and behold a man transformed into a brute! . . .

You have seen how a man was made a slave; you shall see how a slave was made a man. On one of the hottest days of the month of August, 1833 . . . my strength utterly failed me; I was seized with a violent aching of the head, attended with extreme dizziness; I trembled in every limb. . . .

Mr. Covey . . . asked me what was the matter. I told him as well as I could, for I scarce had strength to speak. He then gave me a savage kick in the side, and told me to get up. I tried to do so, but fell back in the attempt. He gave me another kick. . . . At this moment I resolved to go to my master, enter a complaint, and ask his protection. In order to do this, I must that afternoon walk seven miles; and this undertaking. . . . I . . . started on my way, through bogs and briers . . . tearing my feet sometimes at every step. . . . I arrived at master's store. I then presented an appearance enough to affect any but a heart of iron. My hair was all clotted with dust and blood, my shirt was stiff with briers and thorns. . . . Master Thomas ridiculed the idea that there was any danger of Mr. Covey's killing me, and said . . . that I must go back to him, come what might. . . .

All went well till Monday morning. . . . Long before daylight, I was called to go and rub, curry, and feed the horses. I obeyed, and was glad to obey. But whilst thus engaged . . . Mr. Covey entered the stable with a long rope; and just as I was halfway out of the loft, he caught hold of my legs, and was about tying me. As soon as I found what he was up to, I gave a sudden spring. . . . But at this moment—from whence came the spirit I don't know—I resolved to fight; and suiting my action to the resolution, I seized Covey hard by the throat; and as I did so, I rose. He held on to me, and I to him. My resistance was so entirely unexpected, that Covey seemed taken all aback. He trembled like a leaf. This gave me assurance. . . .

The battle with Mr. Covey was the turning-point in my career as a slave. It rekindled the few expiring embers of freedom, and revived within me a sense of my own manhood. It recalled departed self-confidence, and inspired me again with a determination to be free.

Source: Frederick Douglass, *Narrative of the Life of Frederick Douglass, An American Slave* (Boston, 1845).

white planter. As a slave apprenticed to a skilled artisan, Ellison had learned how to make cotton gins, and at the age of 26 bought his freedom with his overtime earnings. At his death in 1861, he had acquired the home of a former South Carolina governor, a shop, lands, and 63 slaves worth more than $100,000.

Free people of color occupied an uneasy middle ground between the dominant whites and the masses of slaves. Legally, courts denied them the right to serve on juries or to testify against whites. Some, like William Ellison, distanced themselves from those black people who remained in slavery and even bought and sold slaves. Others identified with slaves and poor free slaves and took the lead in establishing separate African American churches.

In addition to the more than 250,000 free African Americans who lived in the South, another 200,000 of them lived in the North. Although they made up no more than 3.8 percent of the population of any northern state, free African Americans faced intense legal, economic, and social discrimination, which kept them desperately poor. They were prohibited from marrying whites and were forced into the lowest paying jobs. Whites denied them equal access to education, relegated them to segregated jails, ceme-

Although many free African Americans lived in poverty, some worked as skilled carpenters, tailors, millwrights, or sawyers.

teries, asylums, and schools, forbade them from testifying against whites in court, and, in all but four states—New Hampshire, Maine, Massachusetts, and Vermont—denied them the right to vote.

In the North as well as the South, most free African Americans faced economic hardship and substandard living conditions. Northern African Americans typically lived in tenements, sheds, and stables. An 1847 visitor described the typical black dwelling in Philadelphia as "a desolate pen," 6 feet square, without windows, beds, or furniture, possessing a leaky roof and a floor so low in the ground "that more or less water comes in on them from the yard in rainy weather." According to the *New York Express,* the principal residence of a free black in that city was a house with eight or ten rooms, "and in these are crowded not infrequently two or three hundred souls."

During the 1830s or even earlier, African Americans in both the North and South began to suffer from heightened discrimination and competition from white immigrants in both the skilled trades and such traditional occupations as domestic service. In the late 1850s, the plight of free African Americans worsened. In states such as South Carolina and Maryland, they faced a new crisis. White mechanics and artisans, bitter over the competition they faced from free people of color, demanded that the states legislate the reenslavement of African Americans. During the winter of 1859, politicians in the South Carolina legislature introduced 20 bills restricting the freedom of African Americans. None passed. The next summer, Charleston officials went house to house, demanding that free people of color provide documentary proof of their freedom and threatening to reenslave those who lacked evidence. A panic followed, and hundreds of free blacks emigrated to the North. Some 780 emigrated from South Carolina before secession; 2000 more left during the first month and a half of 1861.

CONCLUSION

In 1857 **Hinton Rowan Helper,** the son of a western North Carolina farmer, published one of the most politically influential books ever written by an American. Entitled *The Impending Crisis of the South,* the book argued that slavery was incompatible with economic progress. Using statistics drawn from the 1850 census, Helper maintained that by every possible measure, the North was growing far faster than the South and that slavery was the cause of the South's economic backwardness.

Helper's thesis was that southern slavery was inefficient and wasteful, inferior in all respects to the North's free labor system. Helper argued that slavery was incompatible with economic progress; it impoverished the South, degraded labor, inhibited urbanization, thwarted industrialization, and stifled innovation. A rabid racist, Helper accompanied a call for the abolition of slavery with a demand for black colonization overseas. He concluded his book with a call for the South's nonslaveholders to overthrow the region's planter elite.

Helper's book created a nationwide furor. A leading antislavery newspaper distributed 500 copies a day, viewing the book as the most effective propaganda against slavery ever written. Many Southerners burned it, fearful that it would divide the white population and undermine the institution of slavery.

By 1857, when Helper's book appeared, the North and South had become in the eyes of many Americans two distinct civilizations, with their own

Chronology
OF KEY EVENTS

1790 Samuel Slater opens the nation's first textile mill in Pawtucket, Rhode Island

1793 Eli Whitney obtains a patent for the cotton gin

1800 Gabriel slave insurrection is uncovered in Richmond, Virginia

1806 Journeyman shoemakers in New York stage one of the nation's first labor strikes

1811 Charles Deslondes's slave insurrection in southern Louisiana is suppressed

1822 Denmark Vesey's slave rebellion is uncovered in South Carolina

1831 Nat Turner's slave insurrection in Southhampton County, Virginia

1832 Virginia legislature defeats proposal to abolish slavery

1834 National Trades' Union is organized; Massachusetts mill girls stage their first strike

1837 Panic of 1837 begins

1838 Boston establishes the nation's first modern police force

1840 Ten-hour day is established for federal employees

1842 Massachusetts supreme court, in *Commonwealth* v. *Hunt*, recognizes unions' right to exist

1844 Methodist church divides over slavery issue

1845 Potato blight strikes Ireland; Baptists split over the slavery issue

1848 Revolutions in Europe; Free Soil party is organized to oppose expansion of slavery into new territories

1857 Hinton Helper publishes *The Impending Crisis of the South*

distinctive sets of values and ideals: one increasingly urban and industrial, the other committed to slave labor. Although the two sections shared many of the same ideals, ambitions, and prejudices, they had developed along diverging lines. In increasing numbers, Northerners identified their society with progress and believed that slavery was an intolerable obstacle to innovation, self-improvement, and commercial and economic growth. A growing number of Southerners, in turn, regarded their rural and agricultural society as the true embodiment of republican values. The great question before the nation was whether it could continue to exist half slave, half free.

SUGGESTIONS FOR FURTHER READING

William J. Cooper, Jr., *The South and the Politics of Slavery* (1978) and Cooper and Thomas E. Terrill, *The American*

South (1990) are valuable studies of the pre–Civil War South.

Peter Kolchin, *American Slavery, 1619–1877* (1993) offers an insightful overview of slavery.

Sean Wilentz, *Chants Democratic: New York City and the Rise of the American Working Class, 1788–1850.* (1984) provides extensive information on the antebellum northern working class.

Overviews and Surveys

Daniel Boorstin, *The Americans: The National Experience* (1965); Russel B. Nye, *Society and Culture in America, 1830–1860* (1974); Edward Pessen, *Jacksonian America: Society, Personality, and Politics*, rev. ed. (1978).

The Emergence of a New Industrial Order in the North

Hal S. Barron, *Those Who Stayed Behind: Rural Society in Nineteenth-Century New England* (1984); Mary H. Blewett,

INDIAN OF OREGON.

ILLINOIS C

ONE MILLION

40, 80 & 160 a

NOT S

THE WHOLE L

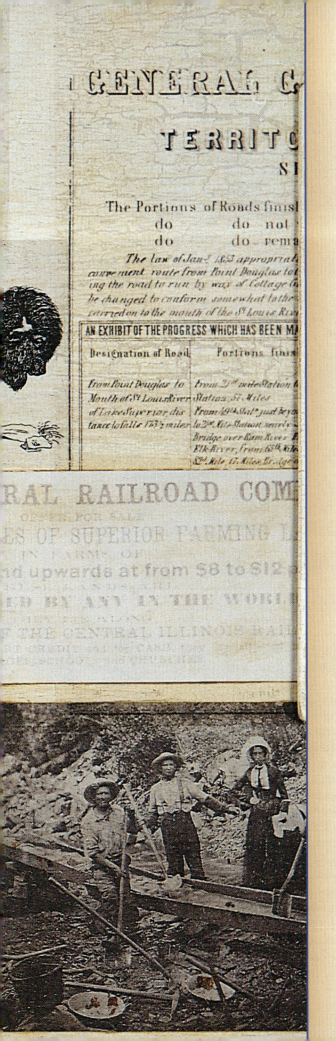

13

CULTURES COLLIDE IN THE FAR WEST

"Vampires, in the guise of men"

In 1920 an enormously popular figure burst onto the Hollywood screen. Zorro, a California version of Robin Hood, was Hollywood's first swashbuckling hero. Played by some of Hollywood's biggest stars—including Douglas Fairbanks, Sr., and Tyrone Power—Zorro was a gifted horseman and master of disguise. He wore a mask, wielded a cape and a sword with panache, and announced his presence by slashing the letter Z on a wall. Like the legendary English outlaw, he robbed from the rich and gave to the poor—but he had a crucial difference: he was Hispanic. In more than a dozen feature films and a long-running Walt Disney television series, Don Diego Vegas, the son of a prominent wealthy California *alcalde* (administrator and judge), deeply resents the exploitation of California's peasants. He adopts the secret identity of Zorro, robs tax collectors, and returns the money to the poor.

Zorro was the fictional creation of a popular novelist named Johnston Culley. But the figure he portrayed—the social bandit protecting the interests of ordinary Mexicans (and later Mexican Americans) in the Southwest—was based on reality. Especially after Americans moved into the Southwest, many Mexicans struggled to preserve their culture, economy, and traditional rights. Some Mexicans in Texas and California—such as the legendary Joaquín Murieta—turned to banditry as a way to resist exploitation and avenge injustice. Though called *bandidos*, these figures did not rob banks or stage coaches; instead, they sought to protect the rights and interests of poorer Mexicans and Mexican Americans.

One of the most famous social bandits was Juan Nepomuceno Cortina of Texas. Born in 1824 to a wealthy, established family, Cortina fought for Mexico in its war with the United States, between 1846 and 1848. After the war, he saw many Mexicans reduced to second-class citizenship, mistreated by local police officers and Texas Rangers, and cheated out of their cattle and land. "Flocks of vampires, in the guise of men," he wrote, robbed Mexicans "of

Joaquín Murieta turned to banditry to avenge the mistreatment of Mexicans in California.

their property, incarcerated, chased, murdered, and hunted [them] like wild beasts." In July 1859, he saw a marshal in Brownsville beating a Mexican farmhand. Cortina ordered the marshal to stop, and when he refused, shot him in the shoulder. Then, in September, Cortina and other Mexicans raided Brownsville, proclaimed a Republic of the Rio Grande, and raised the Mexican flag. A force consisting of Texas Rangers and the United States Army eventually forced Cortina and his supporters to retreat into Mexico. Cortina would later serve as governor of the Mexican state of Tamaulipas.

Until recently, American popular culture presented the story of America's westward expansion largely from the perspective of white Americans. Countless western novels and films depicted the westward movement primarily through the eyes of explorers, missionaries, soldiers, trappers, traders, and pioneers. Theodore Roosevelt captured their perspective in a book entitled *The Winning of the*

West, an epic tale of white civilization conquering the western wilderness. But there are other sides to the story. To properly understand America's surge to the Pacific, one must understand it from multiple perspectives, including the viewpoint of the people who already inhabited the region: Mexicans and Native Americans.

THE HISPANIC AND NATIVE AMERICAN WEST

When Americans ventured westward, they did not enter uninhabited land. Large parts of the Far West were inhabited by Native Americans and Mexicans, who had lived on those lands for hundreds of years and established their own distinctive ways of life.

Spanish America

Until 1821, Spain ruled the area that now includes the states of Arizona, California, Colorado, Nevada, New Mexico, Texas, and Utah. Spanish explorers, priests, and soldiers first entered the area in the early sixteenth century, half a century before the first English colonists arrived at Jamestown. Between 1528 and 1800 Spain established imperial claims and isolated outposts in an area extending from Mexico to Montana and from California to the Mississippi River. Spain established permanent settlements in the region partly as a way to keep out other European powers. In the late sixteenth century, Spain planted a colony in New Mexico and a century later built the first settlements in what is now Arizona and Texas. In the late eighteenth century, fears of British and Russian occupation of the Pacific Coast led Spain also to establish outposts in California.

Unlike England or France, Spain did not actively encourage settlement or economic development in its northern empire. Instead, Spain concentrated much of its energies in Mexico. Spain restricted manufacturing and trade and discouraged migration to regions north of Mexico. In 1821, the year Mexico gained its independence, Spanish settlement was concentrated in just four areas: in southern Arizona, along California's coast, in New Mexico, and in Texas. Santa Fe, Spain's largest settlement, had only 6000 Spanish inhabitants, and San Antonio a mere 1500.

Despite these small numbers, Spain would leave a lasting cultural imprint on the entire region. Such institutions as the rodeo and the cowboy (the *vaquero*) had their roots in Spanish culture. Place names, too, bear witness to the Spanish heritage: Los Angeles, San Diego, and San Francisco were founded by Spanish explorers and priests. To this day, Spanish architecture—adobe walls, tile roofs, wooden beams, and intricate mosaics—continues to characterize the Southwest. By introducing horses and livestock, Spanish colonists and missionaries transformed the southwestern economy and that area's physical appearance. As livestock devoured the region's tall, native grasses, a new and distinctively southwestern environment arose, one of cactus, sagebrush, and mesquite.

The first American cowboys borrowed the clothing and customs of Mexican cowhands known as *vaqueros*.

Between 1769 and 1823, Spain built 21 missions between San Diego and San Francisco. Here Native Americans perform a dance at the San Francisco mission in 1816.

California Missions

Mission life reached its peak of development in California.

The Mission System

The Spanish clergy, particularly Jesuits and Franciscans, played a critical role in settling the Southwest using the mission system. Their missions were designed to spread Christianity among, and establish control over, native populations. In some areas, they forced Indians to live in mission communities, where the priests taught them weaving, blacksmithing, candle-making, and leather-working, and forced them to work in orchards, workshops, and fields for long hours. The missions were most successful in New Mexico (despite an Indian revolt in 1680) and California and far less successful in Arizona and Texas.

Mission life reached its peak in California, an area Spain did not begin to colonize until 1769. Spain built 21 missions between 1769 and 1823, extending from San Diego northward to Sonoma. By 1830, 30,000 of California's 300,000 Native Americans worked on missions, where they harvested grain and herded 400,000 cattle, horses, goats, hogs, and sheep.

Impact of Mexican Independence

By the early nineteenth century, resistance to Spanish colonial rule was growing. In 1810, Miguel Hidalgo y Costilla, a Mexican priest, led a revolt against

Spain, which, although short-lived, represented the beginning of Mexico's struggle for independence. Mexican independence was finally achieved in 1821.

The War of Independence marked the beginning of a period of far-reaching change in the Southwest. Among the most important consequences of the collapse of Spanish rule was the opening of the region to American economic penetration. Mexican authorities in New Mexico and Arizona allowed American

After it won its independence from Spain, Mexico secularized the missions and divided the land into ranchos. This painting shows a master of a rancho in the Mexican Southwest.

traders to bring American goods into the area and trappers to hunt for beaver. Texas and California were also opened to American commerce and settlement. By 1848, Americans made up about half of California's non-Indian population.

Mexican independence also led to the demise of the mission system. After the revolution the missions were "secularized"—broken up and their property sold or given away to private citizens. In 1833–1834, the Mexican government confiscated California mission properties and exiled the Franciscan friars. As a result, mission properties fell into private hands. By 1846, mission land and cattle had passed into the hands of 800 private landowners called *rancheros*, who controlled 8 million acres of land in units called *ranchos*, which ranged in size from 4500 to 50,000 acres. These ranchos were run like feudal estates. They were worked by Native Americans, who were treated like slaves. Indeed, the death rate of Native Americans who worked on ranchos was twice that among southern slaves.

Native Americans

In 1840, before large numbers of pioneers and farmers crossed the Mississippi, at least 300,000 people lived in the Southwest, on the Great Plains, in California, and on the northwest Pacific Coast. This population was divided into more than 200 nations whose lifestyles ranged from sedentary farming to nomadic hunting and gathering. Their social organization was equally diverse, each nation having its own language, religious beliefs, kinship patterns, and system of government.

The best-known of the western Indians are the 23 Indian tribes—including the Cheyenne and Sioux—who lived on the Great Plains and hunted buffalo, antelope, deer, and elk for subsistence. For many present-day Americans, the Plains Indians, riding on horseback, wearing warbonnets, and living in tepees, are regarded as the typical American Indians. In fact, however, the Plains Indians first acquired the horse from the Spanish in the sixteenth century. Not until the middle of the eighteenth century did these tribes have a large supply of horses and not until the early to mid-nineteenth century did most Plains Indians have firearms.

South and west of the Plains, in the huge, arid region that is now Arizona and New Mexico, sophisticated farmers, like the Hopi, Zuni, and other Pueblo groups, coexisted alongside migratory hunters, like the Apaches and Navajos. In the Great Basin, the harsh barren region between the Sierra Nevada and the Rocky Mountains, nations like the Paiutes and

Comanche Chasing Buffalo with Bows and Lances, by George Catlin. Catlin lived in many different nations of the Plains and produced an important record of Native American life, both in his book *Letters and Notes on the Manners, Customs and Condition of the North American Indians*, published in 1841, and in hundreds of sketches, engravings, and paintings.

the Gosiutes lived on berries, nuts, roots, insects, and reptiles.

More than 100,000 Native Americans lived in California when the area was acquired by the United States in 1848. Most lived in small villages in the winter but moved during the rest of the year gathering wild plants and seeds, hunting small game, and fishing in the ocean and rivers.

The large number of tribes living along the northwest Pacific Coast developed an elaborate social hierarchy based on wealth and descent. These people found an abundant food supply in the sea, coastal rivers, and forests. They took salmon, seal, whale, and otter from the coastal waters and hunted deer, moose, and elk in the forests.

Impact of Contact

Contact with white traders, trappers, and settlers caused a dramatic decline in Native American populations. In California, disease and deliberate campaigns of extermination on the part of settlers killed 70,000 Native Americans between 1849 and 1859. In the Great Basin, trappers shot Gosiutes and Paiutes for sport. In Texas, the Karankawas and many other nations in the area largely disappeared. Further west, Comanche, Kiowa, and Apache warriors bitterly resisted white encroachment on their land.

Nations in the Pacific Northwest and northern Plains struggled desperately to slow the pioneers' surge westward. The Nez Perce and Flathead nations expelled American missionaries from their lands, and the Snake, Cheyenne, Shasta, and Rogue River nations tried futilely to cut emigrant roots. The fed-

Tejanos at the Alamo

GENERAL Antonio López de Santa Anna, backed by some 2400 Mexican troops, put the Alamo under siege on February 23, 1836. On that day Santa Anna ordered the hoisting of a red flag, meaning "no quarter," or no mercy toward potential prisoners of war. This only hardened the resolve of the Alamo's small contingent of defenders, including the legendary Jim Bowie, Davy Crockett, and William Barret Travis. Also inside the Alamo were men like Juan Seguin and Gregorio Esparza. They represented a handful of Tejano defenders. As native residents of Texas (named the province of Tejas in 1691 by the conquering Spanish), they despised Santa Anna for having so recently overthrown the Mexican Constitution of 1824 in favor of dictatorship.

San Antonio was a center of the Tejano population of Texas. Juan Seguin's father, Don Erasmo, was a wealthy local rancher who in earlier years had encouraged the opening of the Mexican province of Coahuila y Tejas to nonnatives from the United States. Most of the Americans settled far to the east of San Antonio, but those who traveled to the Tejano settlements knew Don Erasmo as a generous host who entertained lavishly at his *hacienda*, "Casa Blanca." His son Juan was also locally prominent and had helped immeasurably in driving Mexican troops under General Martin Perfecto de Cós, Santa Anna's brother-in-law, out of San Antonio late in 1835. His reward was a commission as a captain of Texas cavalry.

Much less is known about Gregorio Esparza. He lived with his wife and four children in San Antonio when Juan Seguin recruited him for his cavalry company. When Santa Anna's advance troops appeared on February 23, Esparza quickly gathered up his family and rushed for protection behind the thick walls of the old Spanish mission known locally as the Alamo.

The Alamo defenders were in an all but impossible position, especially with Santa Anna tightening his siege lines every day. Inside the Alamo, the defenders looked to Jim Bowie for leadership, but he was seriously ill with pneumonia. So they accepted orders from William Barret Travis. With 1000 troops, Travis had argued, the Alamo would never fall. His numbers, however, were hardly more than 150. As a result, Travis regularly sent out couriers with urgent messages for relief. His words were direct. He would never "surrender or retreat." He would "die like a soldier who never forgets what is due to his own honor and that of his country." For those at the Alamo, the alternatives were now "Victory or death."

Late in February Travis, who would gain only 32 troops as reinforcements, prepared yet another appeal, this time addressed to Sam Houston, commander-in-chief of the Texas army. Time was running out, Travis wrote. "If they overpower us," he explained, "we hope posterity and our country will do our memory justice. Give me help, oh my country!" Travis handed the message to Juan Seguin, who borrowed Jim Bowie's horse and rode off with his aide, Antonio Cruz, under the cover of a driving rainstorm. They eventually found Houston, far to the east, but there was nothing anyone could do now to save those defenders still with Travis.

Early on the morning of March 6, 1836, the Alamo fell to 1800 attacking Mexican soldiers. The fighting was so brutal that 600 of Santa Anna's troops lay dead or wounded before the last of the 183 defenders faced mutilation from countless musket balls, bayonet thrusts, or summary executions after the battle. Gregorio Esparza was torn to shreds as the Mexicans reached the church inside the courtyard. Only women, children, Colonel Travis's slave Joe, and one Tejano, who claimed that he was a prisoner, survived. Later that day Mrs. Esparza got permission to bury her husband with Christian rites. Santa Anna issued orders to have the bodies of all other defenders heaped into piles and set on fire.

During the next several weeks Santa Anna's troops pushed steadily eastward with the goal of destroying another Texas army being hastily assembled by Sam Houston. The Seguins, father and son, played key parts in providing resistance. Don Erasmo worked furiously to collect needed food supplies, and Juan led troops in harassing and delaying the Mexican column, all of which aided in the staging of Houston's stunning victory over Santa Anna at the Battle of San Jacinto on April 21, 1836—the day the Republic of Texas secured its independence.

As the Texas Revolution gained momentum in late 1835 and early 1836, Tejanos had to choose which side to support. Some hoped that uniting with the Americans would force Santa Anna to renounce his dictatorship in favor of the liberal 1824 constitution. Few Tejanos actually favored independence because they knew that Americans held them in

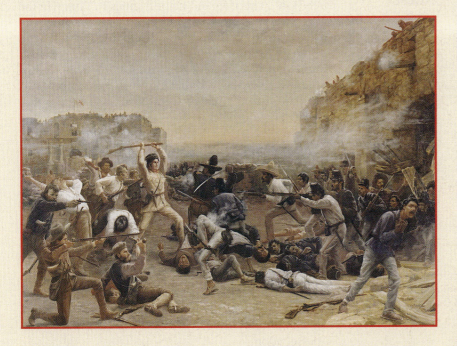

like depraved, violent, less-than-human creatures as personified by Santa Anna at the Alamo and by Mexican troops later at Goliad, where nearly 400 captured rebels were systematically shot to death. Wrote one American veteran of the Texas Revolution late in life: "I thought that I could kill Mexicans as easily as I could deer and turkeys." He apparently did so while shouting: "Remember the Alamo! Remember Goliad!"

This veteran, like so many others looking back at the days of the Texas Revolution, only recalled selected portions of the Alamo story. They talked of the bravery of Bowie, Crockett, and Travis but ignored the courage of Tejanos like Don Erasmo and Juan Seguin and Gregorio Esparza. Nor did they remember that Juan Seguin received an honorable military discharge before serving as mayor of San Antonio until 1842, when Anglo rumormongers accused him of supporting an attempted military invasion from Mexico. To save himself, Seguin had to flee across the border. Eventually he returned to his native Texas and quietly lived out his days far removed from the public limelight. No doubt Seguin wondered whether he had made the right decision in not joining the side of Santa Anna, especially as he experienced the racial and cultural malice directed at Mexican Americans as the United States surged forward toward the Pacific. Although his thoughts are not known, it is fortunate that his story and those of other Tejano resisters have not been forgotten. Surely they too deserve remembrance as heroes of the Alamo and the Texas Revolution.

contempt. This caused men like Gregorio Esparza's brother to join Santa Anna's army and fight against the Alamo defenders. He suspected that heavy-handed rule under the Mexican dictator could not be worse and might well be better than living under culturally and racially intolerant Americans.

From the very outset, Americans entering Texas spoke of Tejanos and Mexicans as debased human beings, comparable in many ways to Native American "savages" blocking the westward movement of white European civilization. In 1831 colonizer Stephen F. Austin wrote: "My object, the sole and only desire of my ambitions since I first saw Texas, was to . . . settle it with an intelligent, honorable, and enterprising people." Four years later Austin still wanted to see Texas "Americanized, that is, settled by a population that will harmonize with their neighbors on the East, in language, political principles, common origin, sympathy, and even interest." The success of the Texas Revolution, from Austin's point of view, would ensure that Americans pouring into the region would not be ruled by what they considered an inferior native populace.

Increasingly, before and after 1836, American migrants employed terms of racial and cultural derision to describe the native Tejanos. They were the most "lazy, indolent, poor, starved set of people as ever the sun shined upon"; they were "slaves of popish superstitions and despotism"; and they would "spend days in gambling to gain a few bits" rather than "make a living by honest industry." With their mixture of blood from Spanish, Native American, and African parents, the native populace represented a "mongrel" race, a "swarthy looking people much resembling . . . mulattoes."

Worse yet, according to the Americans, they behaved at times

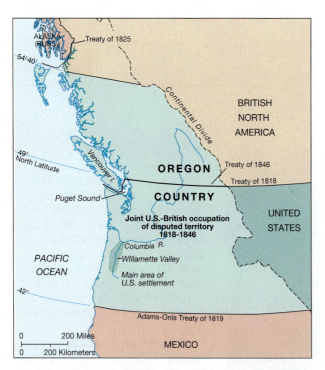

Oregon Country, Pacific Northwest Boundary Dispute

The United States and Great Britain nearly came to blows over the disputed boundary in Oregon.

two years later Secretary of State John Quincy Adams warned Russia that the United States would oppose any Russian attempts to occupy the territory.

But U.S. politicians, merchants, and fur traders were unsuccessful in promoting American settlement of Oregon. In the end, it was neither commerce nor politics, but religion that led to American settlement of the region.

The first missionaries arrived in Oregon in 1834. The most famous were Marcus Whitman, a young doctor, and his wife Narcissa Prentiss Whitman, who were sent west in 1836 by the Methodists. The couple founded a mission near present-day Walla Walla, Washington, and persisted in their efforts to convert Native Americans to Christianity until 1847, when a severe epidemic of measles broke out in the area. Many Native Americans blamed the epidemic on white missionaries, and the Whitmans and 12 others were murdered.

Before his death, Marcus Whitman made an epic 3000-mile journey to Boston, during which he publicized the attractions of the Pacific Northwest and the need to offset British influence in the region. On his return trip to Oregon in 1843, Whitman guided nearly 900 immigrants along the Oregon trail. By the mid-1840s, 6000 Americans had moved to Oregon.

The rapid influx of land-hungry Americans into Oregon in the mid-1840s forced Britain and the United States to decide the status of Oregon. In the presidential election of 1844, the Democratic party demanded the "re-occupation" of Oregon and the annexation of the entire Pacific Northwest coast up to the edge of Russian-held Alaska, which was fixed at 54°40'. This demand helped James K. Polk win the presidency in 1844.

In truth, Polk had little desire to go to war with Britain. As an ardent proslavery Southerner, he did not want to add new free states to the Union. Furthermore, he believed that the northernmost portions of the Oregon country were unsuitable for agriculture. Therefore, in 1846—despite the expansionist slogan "54°40' or fight!"—he readily accepted a British compromise to extend the existing United States–Canadian boundary along the 49th parallel from the Rocky Mountains to the Pacific Ocean.

The Mormon Frontier

Pioneers migrated to the West for a variety of reasons. Some moved west in the hope of economic and social betterment, others out of a restless curiosity and an urge for adventure. The Mormons migrated for an entirely different reason—to escape religious persecution.

The Mormon church had its beginnings in upstate New York, which was a hotbed of religious fervor. Methodist, Baptist, Presbyterian, and Universalist preachers all eagerly sought converts. Fourteen-year-old **Joseph Smith, Jr.**, the son of a farmer, listened closely to these preachers but was uncertain which way to turn.

In the spring of 1820, Smith went into the woods near Palmyra, New York, to seek divine guidance. According to his account, a brilliant light revealed "two personages," who announced that they were God the Father and Christ the Savior. They told him that all existing churches were false and that the true church of God was about to be reestablished on earth.

In 1823, Smith had another revelation that told him of the existence of buried golden plates that contained a lost section from the Bible describing a tribe of Israelites that had lived in America. Smith wrote that he unearthed the golden plates and four years later translated them into English. The messages on the plates were later published as the *Book of Mormon*.

By the 1830s Smith attracted several thousand followers from rural areas of the North and the frontier Midwest. The converts were usually small farmers, mechanics, and traders who had been displaced by the growing commercial economy and who were

Saints [Mormons] *Driven from Jackson County, Missouri*, by C. C. A. Christensen. Mormon settlements in Missouri were repeatedly attacked and destroyed by mobs between 1832 and 1839, when the Mormons moved to Illinois.

repelled by the rising tide of liberal religion and individualism in early nineteenth-century America.

Because Smith said that he conversed with angels and received direct revelations from God, local authorities threatened to indict him for blasphemy. He and his followers responded by moving to Ohio, where they built their first temple and experimented with an economy planned and controlled by the church. From Ohio, the Mormons moved to Missouri. There, proslavery mobs attacked the Mormons, accusing them of inciting slave insurrections. Fifteen thousand Mormons fled Missouri after the governor proclaimed them enemies who "had to be exterminated, or driven from the state."

In 1839, the Mormons resettled along the east bank of the Mississippi River in Nauvoo, Illinois, which soon grew into the second largest city in the state. Both Illinois Whigs and Democrats eagerly sought support among the Mormons, who usually voted as a bloc. In exchange for their votes, the state legislature awarded Nauvoo a special charter that made the town an autonomous city-state, complete with its own 2000-man militia.

But trouble arose again. A dissident group within the church published a newspaper denouncing the practice of polygamy and attacking Joseph Smith for trying to become "king or lawgiver to the church." On Smith's orders, city officials destroyed the dissidents' printing press. Under the protection of the Illinois governor, Smith and his brother were then confined to a jail cell in Carthage, Illinois. Late

in the afternoon of June 27, 1844, a mob broke into Smith's cell, shot him and his brother, and threw their bodies out of a second-story window.

Why did the Mormons seem so menacing? Anti-Mormonism was rooted in a struggle for economic and political power. Individualistic frontier settlers felt threatened by Mormon communalism. By voting as their elders told them to and controlling land as a bloc, Mormons seemed to have an unfair advantage in the struggle for wealth and power.

Mormonism was also denounced as a threat to fundamental social values. Protestant ministers railed against it as a threat to Christianity because Mormons rejected the legitimacy of the established churches and insisted that the *Book of Mormon* was sacred Scripture, equal in importance to the Bible. The Mormons were also accused of corrupt moral values. Before the church changed its rules in 1890, some Mormons practiced polygyny, which they saw as an effort to reestablish the patriarchal Old Testament family. Polygamy also served an important social function by absorbing single or widowed women into Mormon communities. Contrary to popular belief, it was not widely practiced. Altogether, only 10 to 20 percent of Mormon families were polygamous and nearly two-thirds involved a man and two wives.

After Joseph Smith's murder, the Mormons decided to migrate across a thousand miles of unsettled prairie and desert in search of a new refuge outside the boundaries of the United States. In 1846 a new

(1977); W. R. Swagerty, ed., *Scholars and the Indian Experience: Critical Reviews of Recent Writings in the Social Sciences* (1984); Wilcomb Washburn, *The Indian in America* (1975); David J. Weber, *The Mexican Frontier, 1821–1846: The American Southwest Under Mexico* (1982).

The Surge Westward

Stephen Ambrose, *Undaunted Courage: Meriwether Lewis, Thomas Jefferson, and the Opening of the American West* (1996); Gloria G. Cline, *Exploring the Great Basin* (1963); William Cronon, *Nature's Metropolis: Chicago and the Great West* (1991); R. L. Duffus, *The Santa Fe Trail* (1930); John Mack Faragher, *Women and Men on the Overland Trail* (1979); William H. Goetzmann, *Army Exploration in the American West, 1803–1863* (1959), and *Exploration and Empire: Explorer and Scientist in the Winning of the West* (1966); Julie Roy Jeffrey, *Frontier Women: The Transmississippi West, 1840–1880* (1979); Michael P. Malone, ed., *Historians and the American West* (1983); Dale L. Morgan, *Jedediah Smith and the Opening of the West* (1953); Sandra L. Myres, *Westering Women and the Frontier Experience, 1800–1915* (1982); Francis Parkman, *The Oregon Trail* (1849); Gerald Rawling, *The Pathfinders* (1964); Glenda Riley, *The Female Frontier* (1988); Lillian Schlissel, *Women's Diaries of the Westward Journey* (1982), and with Byrd Gibbens and Elizabeth Hampsten, *Far from Home: Families of the Western Journey* (1989); Joanna Stratton, *Pioneer Women* (1981); Richard Slotkin, *The Fatal Environment: The Myth of the Frontier in the Age of Industrialization* (1985); John Unruh, *The Plains Across: The Overland Emigrants and the Trans-Mississippi West* (1979); David J. Wishart, *The Fur Trade of the American West* (1979).

Manifest Destiny

Leonard J. Arrington, *Great Basin Kingdom* (1958), and with Davis Bitton, *The Mormon Experience* (1979); Gunther Barth, *Instant Cities: Urbanization and the Rise of San Francisco and Denver* (1975); William C. Binkley, *The Texas Revolution* (1952); John L. Brooke, *The Refiner's Fire: The Making of Mormon Cosmology* (1994); Robert Calvert and Arnoldo De León, *The History of Texas* (1990); Randolph Campbell, *Sam Houston and the American Southwest* (1993); Malcolm Clark, Jr., *Eden Seekers: The Settlement of Oregon, 1818–1862* (1981); Robert B. Flanders, *Nauvoo: Kingdom on the Mississippi* (1965); Norman F. Furniss, *The Mormon Conflict, 1850–1859* (1960); Robert Gottlieb and Peter Wiley, *America's Saints: The Rise of Mormon Power* (1984); Norman A. Graebner, *Empire on the Pacific* (1955); Klaus Hansen, *Quest for Empire: The Political Kingdom of God and the Council of Fifty in Mormon History* (1967); Sam W. Haynes and Christopher M. Morris, eds., *Manifest Destiny and Empire* (1997); Robert F. Heizer and Alan J. Almquist, *The Other Californians: Prejudice and Discrimination Under Spain, Mexico, and the United States* (1971); Marvin S. Hill and James B. Allen, eds., *Mormonism and American Culture* (1972); Frederick Merk, *Fruits of Propaganda in the Tyler Administration* (1971), *The Oregon Question: Essays in Anglo-American Diplomacy and Politics* (1967); and *Slavery and the Annexation of Texas* (1972);

William Mulder and A. Russell Mortensen, eds., *Among the Mormons: Historic Accounts by Contemporary Observers* (1958); David M. Pletcher, *The Diplomacy of Annexation: Texas, Oregon, and the Mexican War* (1973); Earl Pomeroy, *The Pacific Slope: A History* (1965); Jan Shipps, *Mormonism: The Story of a New Religious Tradition* (1985); Wallace Stegner, *The Gathering of Zion: The Story of the Mormon Trail* (1964); Anders Stephanson, *Manifest Destiny* (1995); Philip Taylor, *Expectations Westward: The Mormons and the Emigration of Their British Converts in the Nineteenth Century* (1966); Grant Underwood, *The Millenarian World of Early Mormonism* (1993).

War with Mexico

K. Jack Bauer, *The Mexican War, 1846–1848* (1974); Walton Bean, *California: An Interpretive History*, 3d ed. (1978); Warren A. Beck and David A. Williams, *California: A History of the Golden State* (1972); Paul H. Bergeron, *The Presidency of James K. Polk* (1987); Gene M. Brack, *Mexico Views Manifest Destiny, 1821–1846: An Essay on the Origins of the Mexican War* (1975); Kinley J. Brauer, *Cotton Versus Conscience: Massachusetts Whig Politics and Southwestern Expansion, 1843–1848* (1967); William R. Brock, *Parties and Political Conscience, 1840–1850* (1979); Seymour V. Connor and Odie B. Faulk, *North America Divided: The Mexican War, 1846–1848* (1971); Eric Foner, "The Wilmot Proviso Revisited," *Journal of American History*, 56 (1969); Paul W. Gates, ed., *California Ranchos and Farms, 1846–1862* (1967); Richard Griswold Del Castillo, *Treaty of Guadalupe Hidalgo* (1990); Neal Harlow, *California Conquered: War and Peace on the Pacific, 1846–1850* (1982); J. S. Holliday, *The World Rushed In* (1981); Robert Johannsen, *To the Halls of the Montezumas: The Mexican War in the American Imagination* (1985); Rudolph M. Lapp, *Blacks in Gold Rush California* (1977); James M. McCaffrey, *Army of Manifest Destiny: The American Soldier in the Mexican War* (1992); Frederick Merk, "Dissent in the Mexican War," Samuel E. Morison et al., eds., in *Dissent in Three American Wars* (1970); Robert Ryal Miller, *Shamrock and Sword: Saint Patrick's Battalion in the U.S.-Mexican War* (1989); C. W. Morrison, *Democratic Politics and Sectionalism: The Wilmot Proviso Controversy* (1967); Rodman W. Paul, *California Gold: The Beginning of Mining in the Far West* (1947), and *Mining Frontiers of the Far West, 1848–1880* (1963); R. H. Peterson, *Manifest Destiny in the Mines: A Cultural Interpretation of Anti-Mexican Nativism in California, 1848–1853* (1975); Andrew F. Rolle, *California: A History*, 4th ed. (1987); Alexander Saxton, *The Indispensable Enemy: Labor and the Anti-Chinese Movement in California* (1971); John H. Schroeder, *Mr. Polk's War: American Opposition and Dissent* (1973); Kevin Starr, *Americans and the California Dream, 1850–1915* (1973); John E. Weems, *To Conquer a Peace: The War Between the United States and Mexico* (1974); Richard Bruce Winders, *Mr. Polk's Army* (1997).

Biographies

Leonard J. Arrington, *Brigham Young: American Moses* (1985); Richard L. Bushman, *Joseph Smith and the Beginnings of Mormonism* (1984); K. Jack Bauer, *Zachary Taylor* (1985); John S. D. Eisenhower, *Agent of Destiny: The Life and Times of General Winfield Scott* (1997); Sam Haynes, *James K. Polk and the Expansionist Impulse* (1996); Charles G. Sellers, *James K. Polk: Continentalist* (1966).

INTERNET RESOURCES

Pioneering the Upper Midwest: Books from Michigan, Minnesota, and Wisconsin, ca. 1820–1910
http://memory.loc.gov/ammem/umhtml/umhome.html
This Library of Congress site looks at first-person accounts, biographies, promotional literature, local histories, ethnographic and antiquarian texts, colonial archival documents, and other works from the seventeenth to the early twentieth century. It covers many topics and issues that affected Americans in the settlement and development of the upper Midwest.

The Mexican-American War Memorial Homepage
http://sunsite.unam.mx/revistas/1847
Images and text explain the causes, courses, and outcomes of the Mexican-American War.

On the Trail in Kansas
http://www.ukans.edu/carrie/kancoll/galtrl.htm
This Kansas Collection site holds several good primary sources with images concerning the Oregon Trail and America's early movement westward.

The Era of the Mountain Men
http://www.xmission.com/~drudy/amm.html
Private letters can speak volumes about the concerns and environment of the writers and recipients. Letters from early settlers west of the Mississippi River are offered on this site.

The Donner Party
http://members.aol.com/danmrosen/donner/index.htm
This site includes logs from the infamous party that resorted to extreme measures to survive. It also has images of the region.

National Museum of the American Indian, 1846–1996
http://www.si.edu/organiza/museums/amerind/start.htm
The Smithsonian Institution maintains this site providing information about this museum.

KEY TERMS

General Antonio López de Santa Anna   (p. 363)

James K. Polk   (p. 365)

Joseph Smith, Jr.   (p. 368)

Brigham Young   (p. 370)

Treaty of Guadalupe Hidalgo   (p. 374)

Wilmot Proviso   (p. 376)

REVIEW QUESTIONS

1. Describe the role of each of the following in the settlement of the Far West: (a) trappers and traders; (b) government explorers; and (c) missionaries.

2. Why did Anglo American settlers in Texas rebel against the Mexican government?

3. What is the meaning of the phrase "manifest destiny"? Explain why Americans expanded west of the Mississippi River during the 1840s.

4. Why did the United States and Mexico go to war in 1846? Why did the war arouse bitter controversy?

THE HOUSE DIVIDED

The "slave power" conspiracy

IN MEMORY OF DEPARTED WORTH.

GEN. W.ᵐ H. HARRISON.

Late President of the United States

Born at Berkley, Charles City Co. Va. Feb. 9, 1773.
DIED at Washington City, D. C. April 4, 1841,
Aged 68 Years.

"*Sir,*—I wish you to understand the true principles of the Government. I wish them carried out. I ask nothing more."
[Dying words of Harrison

In 1864, New York economist John Smith Dye argued that the slave power had secretly poisoned two presidents—William Henry Harrison and Zachary Taylor—and had conspired to murder three others.

Early in 1864, a New York economist named John Smith Dye published a book entitled *The Adder's Den or Secrets of the Great Conspiracy to Overthrow Liberty in America.* In his volume, Dye set out to prove that for more than 30 years a ruthless southern "slave power" had engaged in a deliberate, systematic plan to subvert civil liberties, pervert the Constitution, and extend slavery into the western territories.

In Dye's eyes, the entire history of the United States was the record of the South's repeated plots to expand slavery. An arrogant and aggressive "slave power," he maintained, had entrenched slavery in the Constitution, caused financial panics to sabotage the North's economy, dispossessed Indians from their native lands, and fomented revolution in Texas and war with Mexico in order to expand the South's slave empire. Most important of all, he insisted, the southern slaveocracy had secretly assassinated two presidents by poison and unsuccessfully attempted to murder three others.

According to Dye, this campaign of political assassination began in 1835 when John C. Calhoun, outraged by Andrew Jackson's opposition to states' rights and nullification, encouraged a deranged man named Richard Lawrence to kill Jackson. This plot failed when Lawrence's pistols misfired. Six years later, in 1841, Dye argued, a successful attempt was made on William Henry Harrison's life. After he refused to cooperate in a southern scheme to annex Texas, Harrison died of symptoms resembling arsenic poisoning. This left John Tyler, a strong defender of slavery, in the White House.

The next president to die at the hands of the slave power, according to Dye, was Zachary Taylor. A Louisiana slave owner who had commanded American troops in the Mexican War, Taylor had shocked Southerners by opposing the extension of slavery into California. Just 16 months after taking office, Taylor died suddenly of acute gastroenteritis, caused, claimed Dye, by arsenic poisoning. (A 1991 postmortem examination of Taylor's remains disproved this theory.) He was succeeded by Vice President Millard Fillmore, who was more sympathetic to the southern cause. Just three years later, Dye maintained, an attempt was made on Millard Fillmore's successor, Franklin Pierce, a New Hampshire Democrat whom the slave power considered unreliable. On the way to his inauguration, Pierce's railroad car derailed and rolled down an embankment. The president and his wife escaped injury, but their 12-year-old son was killed. From that point on, Pierce toed the southern line.

According to Dye, the next attempt came on February 23, 1857. President-elect James Buchanan, a Pennsylvania Democrat, was dining at Washington's National Hotel. Buchanan had won the Democratic presidential nomination in the face of fierce southern opposition, and, in Dye's view, the slaveocracy wanted to remind Buchanan who was in charge. Southern agents sprinkled arsenic on the lump sugar used by Northerners to sweeten their tea. Because Southerners drank coffee and used granulated sugar, no Southerners were injured. According to Dye, 60 Northerners, including the President, were poisoned and 38 died. Frightened by this brush with death, Buchanan became a reliable tool of the slave power.

In fact, no credible evidence supports any of John Smith Dye's sensational allegations. Historians have uncovered no connection between John C. Calhoun and the assassination attempt on Andrew Jackson; nor have they found any proof that Harrison's and Taylor's deaths resulted from poisoning or that southern agents derailed Pierce's train; nor have they located any evidence at all that 60 Northerners were poisoned at the dinner for President-elect Buchanan. Yet even if his charges were without foundation, Dye was not alone in interpreting events in conspiratorial terms. His book *The Adder's Den* was only one of the most extreme examples of conspiratorial charges that had been made by abolitionists since the late 1830s.

By the 1850s, a growing number of Northerners had come to believe that an aggressive southern slave power had seized control of the federal government and threatened to subvert republican ideals of liberty, equality, and self-rule. At the same time, an increasing number of Southerners had begun to believe that antislavery radicals dominated northern politics and would "rejoice" in the ultimate consequences of abolition—race war and racial amalgamation that would surely follow emancipation. Sectional animosities were becoming increasingly ideological and inflamed, moving the torn nation closer to secession and civil war.

During the 1850s, the American political system was incapable of containing the sectional disputes between the North and South that had smoldered for more than half a century. One major political party—the Whigs—collapsed. Another—the Democrats—split into northern and southern factions. With the breakdown of the party system, the issues raised

by slavery exploded. The bonds that had bound the country for more than seven decades began to unravel.

THE CRISIS OF 1850

In 1849 an expedition of Texas slaveowners and their slaves arrived in the California gold fields. As curious prospectors looked on, the Texans staked out claims and put their slaves to work panning for gold. White miners considered it unfair that they should have to compete with slave labor. They held a mass meeting and resolved "that no slave or Negro should own claims or even work in the mines." They ordered the Texans out of the gold fields within 24 hours.

Three days later, the white miners elected a delegate to a convention that had been called to frame a state constitution for California and to apply for admission to the Union. At the convention, the miners' delegate proposed that "neither slavery nor involuntary servitude" should ever "be tolerated" in California. The convention adopted his proposal unanimously.

In California white miners refused "to swing a pick side by side with the Negro." Their delegate to the California constitutional convention of 1849 proposed that "neither salvery nor industry servitude . . . shall ever be tolerated in this state."

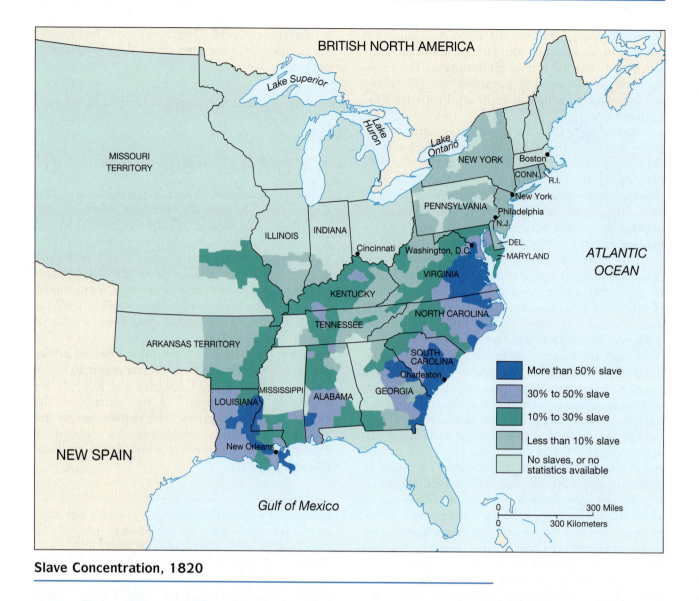

Slave Concentration, 1820

Map legend:
- More than 50% slave
- 30% to 50% slave
- 10% to 30% slave
- Less than 10% slave
- No slaves, or no statistics available

California's application for admission to the Union as a free state in September 1849 raised the question that would dominate American politics during the 1850s: would slavery be allowed to expand into the West or would the West remain free soil? It was the issue of slave expansion—and not the morality of slavery—that would make antislavery a respectable political position in the North, polarize public opinion, and initiate the chain of events that would lead the United States to civil war.

California's application for statehood made slavery's expansion an unavoidable political issue. Southerners feared that California's admission as a free state would upset the sectional balance of power. The free states already held a commanding majority in the House of Representatives because they had a much greater population than did the slave states. Therefore, the political power of

proslavery Southerners depended on maintaining a balance of power in the Senate. Since the Missouri Compromise, Congress had paired the admission of a free state and a slave state. In 1836 and 1837, Congress had admitted Arkansas as a slave state and Michigan as a free state. In 1845 Florida and Texas had joined the Union as slave states, but Congress restored the sectional balance by admitting Iowa as a free state in 1846 and Wisconsin in 1848. If California was admitted as a free state, there would be 16 free states and only 15 slave states. The sectional balance of power in the Senate would be disrupted, and the South feared that it would lose its ability to influence political events.

The instability of the Democratic and Whig parties, and the growing political power of northern opponents of slave expansion, further dimmed chances of a peaceful compromise. When the

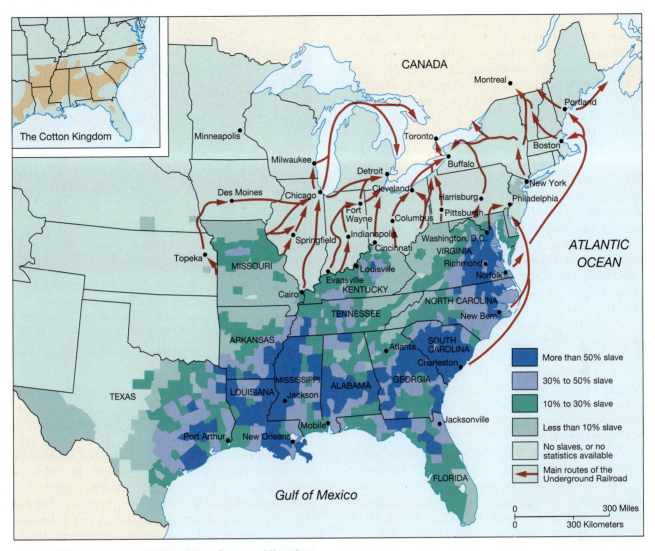

The Cotton Kingdom

Slave Concentration, 1860/The Cotton Kingdom

As shown here, northern African Americans were providing escape routes for slaves along the underground railroad. Slaveowning Southerners feared that the end of slavery would reduce their economic and political status in the Union.

Thirty-first Congress convened in December 1849, neither the Democrats nor the Whigs had a stable majority. Southern Whigs were deserting their party in droves, and northern and southern Democrats were badly split. The parties were so divided that it took 3 weeks and 63 ballots simply to elect the Speaker of the House.

In the North, opponents of the westward expansion of slavery made striking gains, particularly within the Democratic party. Coalitions of Democrats and Free Soilers in Connecticut, Illinois, Indiana, Massachusetts, New York, Ohio, Vermont, and Wisconsin elected congressmen determined to prevent southern expansion. Every northern state legislature,

except Iowa's, asserted that Congress had the power and duty to exclude slavery from the territories.

Southern hotspurs talked openly of secession. Robert Toombs of Georgia declared that if the North deprived the South of the right to take slaves into California and New Mexico, "I am for disunion." Such bold talk inched the South closer to secession.

The South's Dilemma

Why were the South's political leaders so worried about whether slavery would be permitted in the West when geography and climate made it unlikely that slavery would ever prosper in the area? The answer lies in the South's growing awareness of its minority status in the Union, of the elimination of slavery in many other areas of the Western Hemisphere, and of the decline of slavery in the upper South. For more and more Southerners, the region's future depended on whether the West was opened or closed to slavery.

By 1850, New World slavery was confined to Brazil, Cuba, Puerto Rico, a small number of Dutch colonies, and the American South. British slave emancipation in the Caribbean had been followed by an intensified campaign to eradicate the international slave trade. In areas such as Brazil and Cuba, slavery could not long survive once the slave trade was cut off, because the slave populations of these countries had a skewed sex ratio and were unable to naturally reproduce their numbers. Only in the American South could slavery survive without the Atlantic slave trade.

Exacerbating southern fears about slavery's future was a sharp decline in slavery in the upper South. Between 1830 and 1860, the proportion of slaves in Missouri's population fell from 18 to 10 percent; in Kentucky from 24 to 19 percent; in Maryland from 23 to 13 percent. The South's leaders feared that in the future the upper South would soon become a region of free labor.

By mid-century, the South's slaveowners faced a further dilemma. Within the region itself, slave ownership was increasingly concentrated in fewer and fewer hands. Abolitionists were stigmatizing the South as out of step with the times. Many of the South's leading politicians feared that these criticisms of slavery would weaken lower-class white support for slavery.

The desire to ensure the support for slavery among poorer whites led some Southereners to agitate for reopening the African slave trade, believing that nonslaveholding Southerners would only support the institution if they had a chance to own slaves themselves. But most Southern leaders believed the best way to perpetuate slavery was through westward expansion, and they wanted concrete assurance that Congress would not infringe on the right to take slaves into the western territories. Without such a guarantee, declared an Alabama politician, "This union cannot stand."

The Compromise of 1850: The Illusion of Sectional Peace

Ever since David Wilmot had proposed in 1846 that slavery be prohibited from any territory acquired from Mexico, opponents of slavery had argued that Congress possessed the power to regulate slavery in

Seventy-three-year-old Henry Clay pleads his case for sectional compromise. The Senate chamber was so crowded when he made his speech that the temperature reached 100 degrees.

all of the territories. Ardent proslavery Southerners vigorously disagreed.

Politicians had repeatedly but unsuccessfully tried to work out a compromise. One simple proposal had been to extend the Missouri Compromise line to the Pacific Ocean. Thus, slavery would have been forbidden north of 36°30' north latitude but permitted south of that line. This proposal attracted the support of moderate Southerners but generated little support outside the region. Another proposal, supported by two key Democratic senators, Lewis Cass of Michigan and Stephen Douglas of Illinois, was known as squatter sovereignty or **popular sovereignty.** It declared that the people actually living in a territory should decide whether or not to allow slavery.

Henry Clay, the aging statesman known as the "Great Compromiser," for his efforts on behalf of the Missouri Compromise and the Compromise Tariff of 1832 (which resolved the nullification crisis), once again appealed to Northerners and Southerners to place national patriotism ahead of sectional loyalties. He believed that compromise could be effective only if it addressed all the issues dividing the two regions. He proposed that California be admitted as a free state; that territorial governments be established in New Mexico and Utah without any restrictions on slavery; that Texas relinquish its claims to land in New Mexico in exchange for federal assumption of Texas's unpaid debts; that Congress enact a stringent and enforceable fugitive slave law; and that the slave trade—but not slavery—be abolished in the District of Columbia.

Clay's proposal ignited an eight-month debate in Congress and led John C. Calhoun to threaten Southern secession. On March 4, 1850, Calhoun, the "Sentinel of the South," offered his response to Clay's compromise proposal. Calhoun was dying of tuberculosis and was too ill to speak publicly, so his speech was read by a colleague. He warned the North that the only way to save the Union was to "cease the agitation of the slave question," concede "to the South an equal right" to the western territories, return runaway slaves, and accept a constitutional amendment that would protect the South against northern violations of its rights. In the absence of such concessions, Calhoun argued, the South's only option was to secede.

Three days later, Daniel Webster, the North's most spellbinding orator, abandoned his previous opposition to the expansion of slavery into the western territories and threw his support behind Clay's compromise. "Mr. President," he began, "I wish to speak today not as a Massachusetts man, nor as Northern man, but as an American. . . . I speak today for the preservation of the Union. Hear me for my cause." The 68-year-old Massachusetts Whig called on both sides to resolve their differences in the name of patriotism. The North, he insisted, could afford to be generous because climate and geography ensured that slavery would never be profitable in the western territories. He concluded by warning his listeners that "there can be no such thing as a peaceable secession."

Webster's speech provoked a storm of outrage from northern opponents of compromise. Senator William H. Seward of New York called Webster a "traitor to the cause of freedom." But Webster's speech did have one important effect. It reassured moderate Southerners that powerful interests in the North were committed to compromise.

Still, opposition to compromise was fierce. Whig President Zachary Taylor argued that California, New Mexico, Oregon, Utah, and Minnesota should all be admitted to statehood before the question of slavery was addressed—a proposal that would have given the North a 10-vote majority in the Senate. William H. Seward, speaking for abolitionists and other opponents of slave expansion, denounced the compromise as conceding too much to the South and proclaimed that there was a "higher law" than the Constitution, a law that demanded an end to slavery. At the same time, many Southern extremists bridled at the idea of admitting California as a free state. In July, northern and southern senators opposed to the very idea of compromise joined ranks to defeat a bill that would have admitted California to the Union and organized New Mexico and Utah without reference to slavery.

Compromise appeared to be dead. A bitterly disappointed and exhausted Henry Clay dejectedly left the Capitol, his efforts apparently for naught. Then with unexpected suddenness the outlook changed. On the evening of July 9, 1850, President Taylor died of gastroenteritis, five days after taking part in a Fourth of July celebration dedicated to the building of the Washington Monument. Taylor's successor was Millard Fillmore, a 50-year-old New Yorker who was an ardent supporter of compromise.

In Congress, leadership in the fight for a compromise passed to Stephen Douglas, a Democratic senator from Illinois. An arrogant and dynamic leader, 5 feet 4 inches in height, with stubby legs, a massive head, bushy eyebrows, and a booming voice, Douglas was known as the "Little Giant." Douglas abandoned Clay's strategy of gathering all issues dividing the sections into a single "omnibus" bill. Instead, he introduced Clay's proposals one at a time. In this way, he was able to gather support from varying coalitions of Whigs, Democrats, Northerners, and Southerners on each issue. At the same time, banking and business interests as well as speculators in Texas bonds lobbied and even bribed members of Congress to support compromise. Despite these manipulations, the compromise proposals never succeeded in gathering solid congressional support. In the end, only 4 senators and 28 representatives voted for every one of the measures. Nevertheless, they all passed.

As finally approved, the compromise admitted California as a free state, allowed the territorial legislatures of New Mexico and Utah to settle the question of slavery in those areas, set up a stringent federal law for the return of runaway slaves, abolished the slave trade in the District of Columbia, and gave Texas $10 million to abandon its claims to territory in New Mexico east of the Rio Grande.

The compromise created the illusion that the territorial issue had been resolved once and for all. "There is rejoicing over the land," wrote one Northerner, "the bone of contention is removed; disunion, fanaticism, violence, insurrection are defeated." Sectional hostility had been defused; calm had returned. But, as one southern editor correctly noted, it was "the calm of preparation, and not of peace."

The Fugitive Slave Law

The most divisive element in the Compromise of 1850 was the **Fugitive Slave Law,** which permitted any African American to be sent South solely on the affidavit of anyone claiming to be his or her owner. As a result, free African Americans were in danger of being placed in slavery. The law also stripped runaway slaves of such basic legal rights as the right to a jury trial and the right to testify in one's own defense. The law further stipulated that accused runaways stand trial in front of special commissioners, not a judge or a jury, and that the commissioners be paid $10 if a fugitive was returned to slavery but only $5 if the fugitive was freed—a provision that many Northerners regarded as a bribe to ensure that any African American accused of being a runaway would be found guilty. Finally, the law required all U.S. citizens and U.S. marshals to assist in the capture of escapees. Anyone who refused to aid in the capture of a fugitive, interfered with the arrest of a slave, or tried to free a slave already in custody was subject to a heavy fine and imprisonment.

The Fugitive Slave Law kindled widespread outrage in the North and converted thousands of Northerners to the free soil doctrine that slavery should be barred from the western territories. "We went to bed one night old-fashioned, conservative, compromise, Union Whigs," wrote a Massachusetts factory owner, "and waked up stark mad Abolitionists."

Efforts to enforce the new law provoked wholesale opposition. Riots directed against the law broke out in many cities. In Christiana, Pennsylvania, in 1851, a gun battle broke out between abolitionists and slave catchers, and in Wisconsin, an abolitionist editor named Sherman M. Booth freed Joshua Glover, a fugitive slave, from a local jail. In Boston,

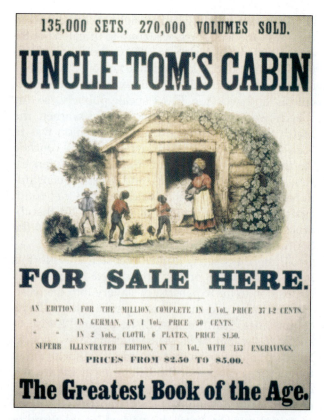

Apologists for slavery denounced *Uncle Tom's Cabin* as inaccurate. Harriet Beecher Stowe responded by writing *The Key to Uncle Tom's Cabin*, which provided documentary proof of the abuses she described in her novel.

Copyright © Collection of The New-York Historical Society.

No part of the Compromise of 1850 drew more outrage from Northerners than the Fugitive Slave Law. An Ohio congressman defiantly stated: "Let the President drench our land of freedom in blood; but he will never make us obey that law."

federal marshals and 22 companies of state troops were needed to prevent a crowd from storming a courthouse to free a fugitive named Anthony Burns.

Eight northern states attempted to invalidate the law by enacting "personal liberty" laws that forbade state officials from assisting in the return of runaways and extended the right of jury trial to fugitives. Southerners regarded these attempts to obstruct the return of runaways as a violation of the Constitution and federal law.

The free black communities of the North responded defiantly to the 1850 law. Northern blacks provided about 1500 fugitive slaves with sanctuary along the Underground Railroad to freedom. Others established vigilance committees to protect blacks from hired kidnappers who were searching the North for runaways. And 15,000 free blacks, convinced that they could never achieve equality in America, emigrated to Canada, the Caribbean, and Africa after adoption of the federal law.

One northern moderate who was repelled by the Fugitive Slave Law was a 41-year-old Maine

Harriet Beecher Stowe.
Gift of I.N. Phelps Stokes, Edward S. Hawes, Alice Mary Hawes, Marion Augusta Hawes/Metropolitan Museum of Art.

mother of six named Harriet Beecher Stowe. In 1852 she published *Uncle Tom's Cabin,* the single most widely read attack on slavery ever written. Stowe had learned about slavery while living in Cincinnati, Ohio, across from slaveholding Kentucky. Her book awakened millions of Northerners to the moral evil of slavery. Southerners denounced Stowe as a "wretch in petticoats," but in the North the book sold a million copies in sixteen months. No novel has ever exerted a stronger influence on American public opinion. Legend has it that when President Lincoln met Mrs. Stowe during the Civil War, he said, "So this is the little woman who made this big war."

DISINTEGRATION OF THE PARTY SYSTEM

As late as 1850, the two-party system was, to all outward appearances, still healthy. Every state, except for South Carolina, had two effective political parties. Both the Democratic party and the Whigs were able to attract support in every section and in every state in the country. Voter participation was extremely high, and in presidential elections neither party was able to gain more than 53 percent of the popular vote. Then, in the space of just five years, the two-party system began to disintegrate in response to two issues: massive foreign immigration and the reemergence of the issue of the expansion of slavery.

The Know Nothings

The most momentous shift in party sentiment in American history took place in the early 1850s following the rise of a party vigorously opposed to immigrants and Catholics. This party, which was known as the American party or **Know Nothing Party,** crippled the Whig party, weakened the Democratic party, and made the political system incapable of resolving the growing crisis over slavery.

Hostility toward immigrants and Catholics had deep roots in American culture. The Protestant religious revivals of the 1820s and 1830s stimulated a "No Popery" movement. Prominent northern clerics, mostly Whig in politics, accused the Catholic Church of conspiring to overthrow democracy and subject the United States to Catholic despotism. Popular fiction offered graphic descriptions of priests seducing women during confession and nuns cutting unborn infants from their mothers' wombs and throwing them to dogs. A popular children's game was called "break the Pope's neck." Anti-Catholic sentiment culminated in mob rioting and in the burning of churches and convents. In 1834, for example, a Philadelphia mob rampaged through Irish neighborhoods, burning churches and houses.

A massive wave of immigration from Ireland and Germany after 1845 led to a renewed outburst of antiforeign and anti-Catholic sentiment. Between 1846 and 1855, more than three million foreigners arrived in America. In cities such as Chicago, Milwaukee, New York, and St. Louis, immigrants actually outnumbered native-born citizens. Nativists—ardent opponents of immigration—capitalized on deep-seated Protestant antagonism toward Catholics, working-class fear of economic competition from cheaper immigrant labor, and resentment among native-born Americans of the growing political power of foreigners. Nativists charged that Catholics were responsible for a sharp increase in poverty, crime, and drunkenness and were subservient to a foreign leader, the Pope.

To native-born Protestant workers, the new immigrants posed a tangible economic threat. Economic slumps in 1851 and 1854 resulted in severe unemployment and wage cuts. Native workers blamed Irish and German immigrants for their plight. The immigrants also posed a political threat. Concentrated in the large cities of the eastern seaboard, Irish immigrants voted as blocs and quickly built up strong political organizations.

One example of anti-Catholic hostility was the formation of a secret fraternal society made up of native-born Protestant working men. This secret society, "The Order of the Star Spangled Banner," soon formed the nucleus of a new political party known as

Physicians and Planters, Prescription for Slave Medical Care

"SO perverse and stubbornly foolish are these people," one slaveholder wrote of his bondsmen, "they are either running into the hospital without cause or braving such a disease as cholera, by concealing the symptoms." Maintenance of slaves' health presented masters with diverse dilemmas. In the continual battle of wills between slaves and their owners over the amount and type of work to be performed, pretending to be sick became a form of "striking" for some slaves. Due to the state of medicine at the time, however, other slaves feared the cure more than the disease. Determining who really was sick was a tricky but crucial matter. Complicating the task were issues of profits, humanitarianism, and racism. Sick slaves could produce few profits; dead slaves none. At the same time, to provide healthy living conditions and constant medical care cost money, which cut into profits. Most masters liked to see themselves as paternalists who took good care of their "slave children." Planters and physicians consequently spent much time trying to determine appropriate responses to slave illnesses.

Feigning illness was an art that some slaves learned through trial and error. Some complaints worked better than others, as the Virginia slave James L. Smith discovered. He detested shooing crows from the cornfield but knew that if he acted sick "they will give me something that will physic me to death." That something was frequently ipecac, which induced vomiting. In response to an earlier stomach complaint Smith's mistress had "made me drunk with whiskey"—a state he had not enjoyed. So he finally decided to claim

to have injured his leg and stayed in his room, eating less, to give his claim credibility. Two weeks later, after the crows had deserted the cornfield for the cherry orchard, Smith "began to grow better very fast."

For the same reason that Smith avoided certain imaginary complaints, a number of slaves concealed symptoms of real diseases. Most masters called in the doctor only after the failure of home remedies—many of which had unpleasant and occasionally fatal side effects. Treatment by a physician was not always better. Nineteenth-century medical science was still primitive and had cures for only a handful of conditions. Otherwise doctors resorted to the use of excessive drugs and diuretics, leeching and bloodletting, purging and sweating, all of which caused discomfort and often weakened the body's ability to fight the disease. Many slaves therefore preferred to treat themselves with herbal cures that had been quietly passed down through the generations. Some home remedies in the slaves' quarters were superior to those of whites and were occasionally reported in medical journals. Others, however, were based on superstition, and conjurers sometimes caused treatable diseases to progress to irreversible states. For some slaves the decision to conceal an illness was an act of independence. Even though an unannounced illness meant they had to continue to work while sick, some slaves preferred that to surrendering their bodies to the care of white owners and physicians.

Once planters had overcome the hurdle of determining which slaves were ill, they then had to decide on a course of action. Here humanitarian

and profit concerns frequently intersected. Slaveowners were concerned about slaves' health for essentially three reasons: protecting their financial investment, preventing the spread of illness to themselves and their families, and concern for the slaves as human beings. The decision of when to call in a doctor was difficult even for those with the best intentions. To his overseer, Thomas Jefferson specified certain illnesses for which physicians should be summoned as they could provide "certain relief," but insisted that "in most other cases they oftener do harm than good."

For many reasons home care was the first resort of most planters in all cases except those in which the value of professional care was obvious. Treatments for some illnesses were fairly standardized, well known, and easily performed by laymen. Many planters questioned the need to pay a doctor to treat such maladies. Through various suppliers, they obtained such commonly used drugs as calomel, castor oil, ipecac, laudanum, opium, camphor, and quinine. They consulted various household medical guides about proper dosages. Frequently the home cures worked as well as or better than professional services. Often, however, planters misdiagnosed. Even if the improper treatment made the condition no worse, it prolonged the course of the illness until too late for effective treatment.

Some slaveholders consciously waited until everything else had failed before they called in a doctor. Planter Robert Garter of Virginia sent a dying patient to a physician with a note: "I do not wish to continue prac-

tice any longer on Peter—and now I deliver him to you." Such actions infuriated doctors, who were then blamed for their low cure rates. On some plantations where the doctor was not summoned until death was at hand, slaves superstitiously began to link the doctor's arrival with life's departure, giving them another reason to conceal their symptoms.

There were limits to paternalism. The growing knowledge of the impact of environment on health did not induce many planters to improve the living quarters or diets of their bondsmen. That cut into profits too drastically for the perceived benefits. Hence inadequate diets, clothing, and shelter dramatically decreased slaves' health. Economic and humane considerations were offset by a racism that placed less value on slave life. Landon Carter administered rattlesnake powder to his slaves during

an attack of "bilious fever." It seemed to help but produced unpleasant side effects. "I wish my own fears did not prevent my giving it to my Children," Carter wrote in his diary—displaying a willingness to "experiment" on slaves that was not uncommon for physicians or planters. Slaves had no authority to refuse any kind of treatment.

African Americans were sometimes treated differently from whites because of perceived physiological differences. A number of the perceptions were accurate assessments distilled from experience. Physicians could not help but note variations in the susceptibility to specific diseases or in the response to treatment between the two groups. Modern researchers have found physiological bases for some of their observations, such as the effect of the sickle-cell trait—more common in African

Americans than in the rest of the population—on some malarial viruses. At the time, however, those differences were often used and exaggerated as justification for both slavery and inadequate health care. Some asserted that African American bodies were uniquely suited for hard labor as well as slavery—a proposal not supported by mortality statistics.

Samuel W. Cartwright of Louisiana was a leading medical apologist for slavery. He argued that African Americans were intellectually inferior because dark pigmentation was more than skin deep. "Even the negro's brain and nerves," he wrote, "are tinctured with a shade of pervading darkness." To support his claims of African American bodies and minds being built for slavery, Cartwright explained all "unslave-like" behavior as diseases peculiar to African Americans. Careless habits were a symptom of what he called *Dysaetesia Aethipica.* Slaves who ran away were affected with *Drapetomania.* He could not accept that either could be rational forms of resistance to slavery. The health care of slaves illustrates the interplay of medicine and public values. Physicians became apologists for slavery and built lucrative careers on treating "Negro illnesses." Although slaves often sought to control their medical destinies through secret self-treatment, ultimate authority over their bodies rested in the property rights of their owners. Those owners most frequently acted on the basis of self-interest, which sometimes, but not always, coincided with benevolence. Few valued African American life as highly as white. Medical care, like most other life-and-death matters, was controlled by the white establishment.

After Philadelphia's Catholic bishop convinced the city's board of education in 1844 to use both the Catholic and Protestant versions of the Bible in schools, a vicious anti-Catholic riot erupted.

the Know Nothing or the American party. The party received its name because when members were asked about the workings of the party, they were supposed to reply, "I know nothing."

The sudden growth of the **Know Nothing party** is one of the most extraordinary stories in American political history. In the North, the Know Nothings drew support from many native-born Protestants hostile toward Catholics and immigrants. In the South and in the border states, the party attracted voters disturbed by the mounting sectional disputes over slavery. Throughout the country, the Know Nothings capitalized on a popular longing for new political leaders.

By 1855 the Know Nothings had captured control of the legislatures in New England, except in Vermont and Maine, and were the dominant opposition party to the Democrats in New York, Pennsylvania, Maryland, Virginia, Tennessee, Georgia, Alabama, Mississippi, and Louisiana. In the presidential election of 1856, the party supported Millard Fillmore and won more than 21 percent of the popular vote and 8 electoral votes. In Congress, the party had 5 senators and 43 representatives. Between 1853 and 1855, the Know Nothings replaced the Whigs as the nation's second largest party.

Respectable public opinion spoke out vehemently against the dangers posed by the party. In 1855 an Illinois Whig politician named Abraham Lincoln denounced the Know Nothings in eloquent terms:

I am not a Know-Nothing. How could I be? How can any one who abhors the oppression of Negroes be in favor of degrading classes of white people? Our progress in degeneracy appears to me pretty rapid, as a nation we began by declaring "all men are created equal." We now practically read it, "all men are created equal, except Negroes." When the Know-Nothings get control, it will read "all men are created equal, except Negroes, and foreigners, and Catholics." When it comes to this I should prefer emigrating to some country where they make no pretense of loving liberty—to Russia, for example, where despotism can be taken pure and without the base alloy of hypocrisy.

By 1856, however, the Know Nothing party was already in decline. Many Know Nothing officeholders were relatively unknown men with little political experience. In the states where they gained control, the Know Nothings proved unable to enact their legislative program, which included a 21-year residency period before immigrants could become citizens and vote, a limitation on political officeholding to native-born Americans, and restrictions on the sale of liquor.

After 1855 the Know Nothing party was supplanted in the North by a new and explosive sectional party, the Republicans. By 1856 northern workers felt more threatened by the southern slave power than by the Pope and Catholic immigrants. At the same time, fewer and fewer Southerners were willing to support a party that ignored the question of the expansion of slavery. As a result, the Know Nothing party rapidly dissolved.

Nevertheless, the Know Nothings left an indelible mark on American politics. The Know Nothing movement eroded loyalty to the national political parties, helped destroy the Whig party, and undermined the capacity of the political system to contain the divisive issue of slavery.

Young America

For nearly four years following the Compromise of 1850, agitation over the question of the expansion of slavery abated. Most Americans were weary of the continuing controversy and turned their attention away from politics to focus instead on railroads, cotton, and trade. The early 1850s were dominated by dreams of greater American influence abroad—in areas such as Asia, the Caribbean, and Central America. Majestic clipper ships raced from New York to China in as few as 104 days. Steamship and railroad promoters launched ambitious schemes to build transit routes across Central America to link California and the Atlantic Coast.

In 1853 Commodore Matthew Perry sailed into Tokyo Bay with two steam frigates and two sailing ships, ending Japan's era of isolation from the western world. The whole world appeared to be opening up to American influence.

Franklin Pierce, a New Hampshire Democrat elected as the nation's fourteenth president in 1852, tried to unite the country with an aggressive program of foreign expansion called "Young America." He sought to annex Hawaii, expand American influence in Honduras and Nicaragua, and acquire new territory from Mexico and Spain. He announced that

his administration would not be deterred "by any timid forebodings of evil" raised by the slavery question. But each effort to expand the country's boundaries only provoked new sectional disputes because any acquisition would have posed the question of its status with regard to slavery.

Pierce was the first "doughface" president. He was, in the popular phrase, "a Northern man with Southern principles." Many Northerners suspected that Pierce's real goal was the acquisition of new territory for slavery. This suspicion was first raised in 1853, when the president instructed James Gadsden, his minister to Mexico, to purchase as much Mexican territory as possible, to provide a route for a southern railroad from New Orleans to California.

Cuba was the next object of Pierce's ambitions. Southern slaveholders coveted Cuba's 300,000 slaves. Other Americans wanted to free Cuba's white population from Spanish rule. In 1854 Pierce instructed his ambassador to Spain to offer $130 million for Cuba, but Spain refused the offer. That same year, at a meeting in Ostend, Belgium, three of Pierce's diplomatic ministers (including a future Democratic president, James Buchanan) sent a dispatch, later titled the Ostend Manifesto, to the secretary of state. It urged the military seizure of Cuba if Spain continued to refuse to sell the island. The Ostend Manifesto outraged Northerners, who regarded it as a brazen attempt to expand U.S. slavery in defiance of Spain's sovereign rights.

Commodore Matthew Perry's display of armor and technology led Japan to accept the Treaty of Kanagawa, opening Japanese ports to American trade. These drawings were done by artists dispatched by Japanese officials to keep a visual record of Perry's activities.

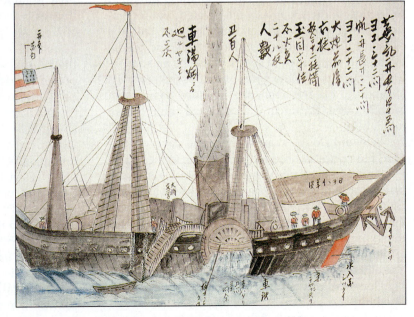

The Kansas-Nebraska Act

In 1854, less than four years after the Compromise of 1850, a piece of legislation was introduced in Congress that revived the issue of the expansion of slavery, shattered all illusions of sectional peace, and reordered the political landscape by destroying the Whig party, dividing the Democratic party, and creating the Republican party. Ironically, the author of this legislation was Senator Stephen A. Douglas, the very man who had pushed the earlier compromise through Congress—and a man who had sworn after the passage of the Compromise of 1850 that he would never make a speech on the slavery question again.

As chairman of the Senate Committee on Territories, Douglas proposed that the area west of Iowa and Missouri—which had been set aside as a permanent Indian reservation—be organized as the Nebraska territory and opened to white settlement. Douglas had sought to achieve this objective since 1844, but southern congressmen had objected because Nebraska was located in the northern half of the Louisiana Purchase where the Missouri Compromise prohibited slavery. To forestall southern opposition, Douglas's original bill ignored both the Missouri Compromise and the status of slavery in the Nebraska territory. It simply provided that Nebraska, when admitted as a state, could enter the Union "with or without slavery," as its "constitution may prescribe."

Southern senators, however, demanded that Douglas add a clause specifically repealing the Missouri Compromise and stating that the question of slavery would be determined on the basis of popular sovereignty. Douglas relented to southern pressure. In its final form, Douglas's bill created two territories, Kansas and Nebraska, and declared that the Missouri Compromise was "inoperative and void." With solid support from southern Whigs and southern Democrats and the votes of half of the northern Democratic congressmen, the measure passed. On May 30, 1854, President Pierce signed the measure into law.

Why did Douglas risk reviving the slavery question? His critics accused him of yielding to the southern pressure because of his presidential ambitions and a desire to enhance the value of his holdings in Chicago real estate and western lands. They charged that the Illinois senator's chief interest in opening up Kansas and Nebraska was to secure a right-of-way for a transcontinental railroad that would make Chicago the transportation center of mid-America.

Douglas's supporters, on the other hand, pictured him as a statesman laboring for western development and a sincere believer in popular sover-eignty as a solution to the problem of slavery in the western territories. Douglas had long insisted that the democratic solution to the slavery issue was to allow the people who actually settled a territory to decide whether slavery would be permitted or forbidden. Popular sovereignty, he believed, would allow the nation to "avoid the slavery agitation for all time to come." Moreover, he believed that because of climate and geography slavery could never be extended into Kansas and Nebraska anyway.

To understand why Douglas introduced the **Kansas-Nebraska Act,** it is important to realize that by 1854 political and economic pressure to organize Kansas and Nebraska had become overwhelming. Midwestern farmers agitated for new land. A southern rail route had been completed through the Gadsden Purchase in December 1853, and promoters of a northern route for a transcontinental railroad viewed territorial organization as essential. Missouri slaveholders, already bordered on two sides by free states, believed that slavery in their state was doomed if they were surrounded by a free territory. All wanted to see the region opened to settlement.

Revival of the Slavery Issue

Neither Douglas nor his southern supporters anticipated the extent and fury of northern opposition to the Kansas-Nebraska Act. Opponents denounced it as "a gross violation of a sacred pledge." They burned so many figures of Douglas from trees, the Illinois senator joked, "I could travel from Boston to Chicago by the light of my own effigy."

Douglas predicted that the "storm will soon spend its fury," but it did not subside. Northern Free Soilers regarded the Missouri Compromise line as a "sacred compact" that had forever excluded slavery from the northern half of the Louisiana Purchase. Now, they feared that under the guise of popular sovereignty, the southern slave power threatened to spread slavery across the entire western frontier.

No single piece of legislation ever passed by Congress had more far-reaching political consequences. The Kansas-Nebraska Act brought about nothing less than a dramatic realignment of the two-party system. Conservative Whigs abandoned their party and joined the Democrats, while northern Democrats with free soil sentiments repudiated their own elected representatives. In the elections of 1854, 44 of the 51 northern Democratic representatives who voted for the act were defeated.

The chief beneficiary of these defections was a new political organization, the Republican party. A combination of diverse elements, it stood for the belief that slavery must be barred from the western ter-

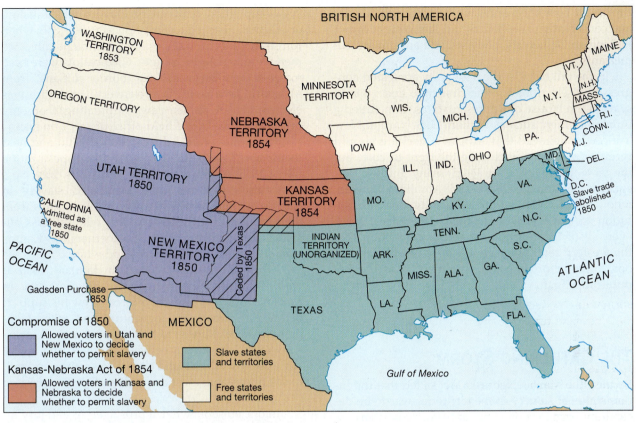

Compromise of 1850/Kansas-Nebraska Act

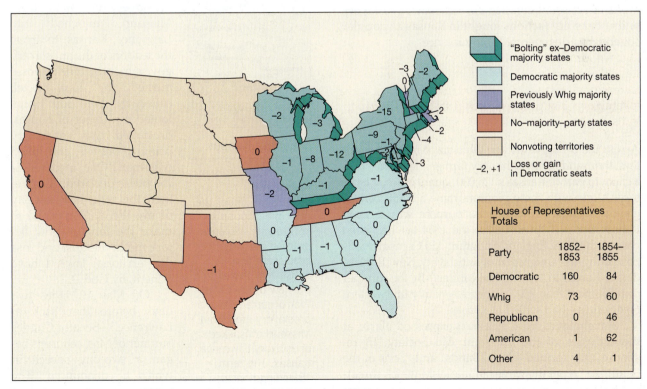

Gains and Losses in the Congressional Election of 1854

The sectional rift grew even sharper after the Kansas-Nebraska Act.

ritories. It contained antislavery radicals, moderate and conservative Free Soilers, old-line Whigs, former Jacksonian Democrats, nativists, and antislavery immigrants.

In the fall of 1854, the new party contested congressional elections for the first time and won 46 seats in the House of Representatives. It included a number of men, such as William H. Seward of New York, who believed that African Americans should receive civil rights, including the right to vote. But the new party also attracted many individuals, such as Salmon P. Chase and Abraham Lincoln, who favored colonization as the only workable solution to slavery. Despite their differences, however, all of these groups shared a conviction that the western territories should be saved for free labor. "Free labor, free soil, free men," was the Republican slogan.

THE GATHERING STORM

Because the Kansas-Nebraska Act stated that the future status of slavery in the territories was to be decided by popular vote, both antislavery northerners and proslavery southerners competed to win the region for their section. Because Nebraska was too far north to attract slave owners, Kansas became the arena of sectional conflict. For six years, proslavery and antislavery factions fought in Kansas as popular sovereignty degenerated into violence.

"Bleeding Kansas" and "Bleeding Sumner"

Across the drought-stricken Ohio and Mississippi valleys, thousands of land-hungry farmers hoped to stake a claim to part of Kansas's 126,000 square miles of territory. Along with these pioneers came a small contingent of settlers whose express purpose was to keep Kansas free soil. Even before the 1854 act had been passed, the New England Emigrant Aid Company was promoting the emigration of antislavery New Englanders to Kansas to "vote to make it free." By the summer of 1855, more than 9000 pioneers—mainly midwestern Free Soilers—had settled in Kansas.

Slaveholders from Missouri expressed alarm at the activities of the Emigrant Aid Society. In response, they formed "Social Bands" and "Sons of the South" to "repel the wave of fanaticism which threatens to break upon our border." One Missouri lawyer told a cheering crowd that he would hang any "free soil" emigrant who came into Kansas.

Competition between proslavery and antislavery factions reached a climax on May 30, 1855, when Kansas held territorial elections. Although only 1500 men were registered to vote, 6000 ballots were cast, many of them by proslavery "border ruffians" from Missouri. As a result, a proslavery legislature was elected, which passed laws stipulating that only proslavery men could hold office or serve on juries.

Free Soilers called the election a fraud and held their own "Free State" convention in Topeka in the fall of 1855. At this convention, delegates drew up a constitution that not only prohibited slavery in Kansas but also barred free African Americans from the territory. Like the Free Soilers who settled California and Oregon, most northerners in Kansas wanted the territory to be free and white.

When Congress convened in January 1856, it was confronted by two rival governments in Kansas. President Franklin Pierce threw his support behind the proslavery legislature and asked Congress to admit Kansas to the Union as a slave state.

Violence broke out between northern and southern settlers over rival land claims, town sites, and railroad routes—and, most dangerous of all, the question of slavery.

In one episode, when a proslavery grand jury indicted several members of the Free Soil Topeka government for high treason, 800 proslavery men, many from Missouri, marched into Lawrence, Kansas, to arrest the leaders of the antislavery government. The posse burned the local hotel, called the Free Soil Hotel, looted a number of houses, destroyed two antislavery printing presses, and killed one man. One member of the posse declared: "Gentlemen, this is the happiest day of my life. I determined to make the fanatics bow before me in the dust and kiss the territorial laws. I have done it, by God."

On May 19, 1856—two days before the "sack of Lawrence"—Senator Charles Sumner of Massachusetts began a two-day speech in which he denounced "The Crime Against Kansas." In his speech, Sumner charged that there was a southern

Bleeding Kansas

When the territory of Kansas was established under the principle of popular sovereignty, violence erupted between proslavery and antislavery forces. A preview of the Civil War occurred when a proslavery mob from Missouri ransacked antislavery Lawrence, Kansas. The term "Bleeding Kansas" became a battle cry for antislavery advocates.

Between May and September 1856, terrorism and guerrilla warfare swept across Kansas, leaving 200 dead and $2 million in property damage. In one incident, Kansas Free Soilers fired on a proslavery settlement at the Battle of Hickory Point.

conspiracy to make Kansas a slave state. He proceeded to argue that a number of southern senators, including Senator Andrew Butler of South Carolina, stood behind this conspiracy. Launching into a bitter personal diatribe, Sumner accused Senator Butler of taking "the harlot, Slavery," for his "mistress" and proceeded to make fun of a medical disorder from which Senator Butler suffered. At the rear of the Senate chamber, Stephen Douglas muttered: "That damn fool will get himself killed by some other damned fool."

Two days later, Senator Butler's nephew, Congressman Preston Brooks of South Carolina, entered a nearly empty Senate chamber. Brooks was convinced that he had a duty to "avenge the insult to my State." Sighting Sumner at his desk, Brooks charged at him and began striking the Massachusetts senator over the head with a cane. He swung so hard that the cane broke into pieces. Brooks caned Sumner, rather than challenging him to a duel, because he regarded

the Senator as his social inferior. Thus, he wanted to use the same method slaveholders used to chastise slaves. Although it took Sumner three years to recover from his injuries and return to his Senate seat, he promptly became a martyr to the cause of freedom in the the North, where a million copies of his "Crime Against Kansas" speech were distributed. In the South, Brooks was hailed as a hero. Merchants in Charleston bought the congressman a new cane, inscribed "Hit him again." A vote to expel Brooks from Congress failed because every Southern representative but one voted against the measure. Instead, Brooks was censured. He promptly resigned his seat and was immediately reelected.

The caning of Sumner had repercussions in strife-torn Kansas. John Brown, a devoted Bible-quoting Calvinist who believed he had a personal responsibility to overthrow slavery, announced that the time had come "to fight fire with fire" and "strike terror in the hearts of proslavery men." The next day, in reprisal for the "sack of Lawrence" and the assault on Sumner, Brown and six companions dragged five proslavery men and boys from their beds at Pottawatomie Creek, split open their skulls with a sword, cut off their hands, and laid out their entrails.

A war of revenge erupted in Kansas. Columns of proslavery Southerners ransacked free farms, while they searched for Brown and the other "Pottawatomie killers." Armed bands looted enemy stores and farms. At Osawatomie, proslavery forces attacked John Brown's headquarters, leaving a dozen men dead. John Brown's men killed four Missourians, and proslavery forces retaliated by blockading the free towns of Topeka and Lawrence. Before it was over, guerilla warfare in eastern Kansas left 200 dead.

The Election of 1856

The presidential election of 1856 took place in the midst of Kansas's civil war. President Pierce hoped for renomination to a second term in office, but northern indignation over the Kansas-Nebraska Act led the Democrats to seek out a less controversial candidate. On the seventeenth ballot, northern and western Democrats succeeded in winning the nomination for James Buchanan, a 65-year-old Pennsylvania bachelor, who had been minister to Great Britain during the struggle over the Kansas-Nebraska bill. The dying Whig party and the southern wing of the Know Nothing party nominated former President Millard Fillmore.

The Republican party held its first national convention in Philadelphia and adopted a platform

Clutching a pen in one hand and a copy of his "Crime Against Kansas" speech in the other, Senator Charles Sumner attempts to defend himself against an attack by South Carolina Congressman Preston Brooks.

denying the authority of Congress and of territorial legislatures "to give legal existence to slavery" in the territories. The convention nominated the dashing young explorer and soldier John C. Frémont for president as young Republicans chanted, "Free Speech, Free Soil and Frémont." Frémont was a romantic figure who had led more than a dozen major explorations of the Rocky Mountains and Far West. After accepting the Republican nomination, he declared that Kansas should be admitted to the Union as a free state. This was his only public utterance during the entire 1856 campaign. A few weeks later, the northern wing of the Know Nothing party threw its support behind Frémont.

The election was one of the most bitter in American history and the first in which voting divided along rigid sectional lines. The Democratic strategy was to picture the Republican party as a hotbed of radicalism. Democrats called the Republicans the party of disunion and described Frémont as a "black abolitionist" who would destroy the union. Republicans responded by accusing the Democrats of being accomplices in a conspiracy to extend slavery.

Although Buchanan garnered only 45 percent of the popular vote because of the presence of Fillmore, he narrowly carried five northern states, giving him a comfortable margin in the electoral college. Buchanan won 174 electoral college votes to 114 for Frémont and 8 for Fillmore.

The election results showed how polarized the nation had become. The South, except for Maryland, voted solidly Democratic. Frémont did not receive a single vote south of the Mason-Dixon line. At the same time, the northernmost states were solidly Republican.

In their first presidential campaign, the Republicans had made an extraordinarily impressive showing. Eleven free states voted for Frémont. If only two more states had voted in his favor, the Republicans would have won the election.

The Supreme Court Speaks

In his inaugural address, Buchanan declared that "the great object of my administration will be to arrest . . . the agitation of the slavery question in the North." He then predicted that a forthcoming Supreme Court decision would once and for all settle the controversy over slavery in the western territories. Two days after Buchanan's inauguration, the high court handed down its decision.

On March 6, 1857, the Supreme Court finally decided a question that Congress had evaded for decades: whether Congress had the power to pro-

In the sweeping Dred Scott (left) decision, Chief Justice Roger Taney (right) sought to resolve the constitutional questions raised by slavery. The decision, which remained a major source of controversy until the eruption of the Civil War, intensified divisions between proslavery and antislavery factions.

hibit slavery in the territories. Repeatedly, Congress had declared that this was a constitutional question that the Supreme Court should settle. Now, for the first time, the Supreme Court offered its answer.

The case originated in 1846, when a Missouri slave, **Dred Scott,** sued to gain his freedom. Scott argued that while he had been the slave of an army surgeon, he had lived for four years in Illinois, a free state, and Wisconsin, a free territory, and that his residence on free soil had erased his slave status. By a 7–2 margin, the Court ruled that Dred Scott had no right to sue in federal court, that the Missouri Compromise was unconstitutional, and that Congress had no right to exclude slavery from the territories.

All nine justices rendered separate opinions, but Chief Justice Taney delivered the opinion that expressed the position of the Court's majority. His opinion represented a judicial defense of the most extreme proslavery position.

The chief justice made two sweeping rulings. The first was that Dred Scott had no right to sue in federal court because neither slaves nor free blacks were citizens of the United States. At the time the Constitution was adopted, the chief justice wrote, blacks had been "regarded as beings of an inferior order" with "no rights which the white man was bound to respect."

Second, Taney declared that Congress had no right to exclude slavery from the federal territories since any law excluding slave property from the territories was a violation of the Fifth Amendment prohibition against the seizure of property without due process of law. For the first time since *Marbury* v. *Madison* in 1803, the Court declared an act of Congress unconstitutional. The Missouri Compromise was unconstitutional, the Court declared, because it prohibited slavery north of 36°30'. Newspaper headlines summarized the Court's rulings: "SLAVERY ALONE NATIONAL—THE MISSOURI COMPROMISE UNCONSTITUTIONAL—NEGROES CANNOT BE CITIZENS—THE TRIUMPH OF SLAVERY COMPLETE."

In a single decision, the Court sought to resolve all the major constitutional questions raised by slavery. It declared that the Declaration of Independence and the Bill of Rights were not intended to apply to African Americans. It stated that the Republican party platform—barring slavery from the western territories—was unconstitutional. And it ruled that Stephen Douglas's doctrine of "popular sovereignty"—which stated that territorial governments had the power to prohibit slavery—was also unconstitutional.

Republicans reacted with scorn. The decision, said the *New York Tribune*, carried as much moral weight as "the judgment of a majority of those congregated in any Washington barroom." Radical abolitionists called for secession. Many Republicans—including an Illinois politician named Abraham Lincoln—regarded the decision as part of a slave power conspiracy to legalize slavery throughout the United States.

The Dred Scott decision was a major political miscalculation. In its ruling, the Supreme Court sought to solve the slavery controversy once and for all. Instead the Court intensified sectional strife, undercut possible compromise solutions to the divisive issue of the expansion of slavery, and weakened the moral authority of the judiciary.

The Lecompton Constitution: "A Swindle and a Fraud"

Late in 1857, President Buchanan faced a major test of his ability to suppress the slavery controversy. In September, proslavery forces in Kansas met in Lecompton, the territorial capital, to draft a constitution that would bring Kansas into the Union as a slave state. Recognizing that a proslavery constitution would be defeated in a free and fair election, proslavery delegates withheld the new state charter from the territory's voters. Instead, they offered voters a referendum on whether they preferred "the constitution with slavery" or "the constitution without slavery." In either case, however, the new constitution guaranteed slave ownership as a sacred right. Free Soilers boycotted the election and, as a result, "the constitution with slavery" was approved by a 6000-vote margin.

President Buchanan—afraid that the South would secede if Kansas were not admitted to the Union as a slave state—accepted the proslavery Lecompton constitution as a satisfactory application of the principle of popular sovereignty. He then demanded that Congress admit Kansas as the sixteenth slave state.

Stephen Douglas was aghast. "A small minority" of proslavery men in Kansas, he said, had "attempted to cheat and defraud the majority by trickery and juggling." Appalled by this travesty of the principle of popular sovereignty, Douglas broke with the Buchanan administration.

After a rancorous debate, the Senate passed a bill that admitted Kansas as a slave state under the Lecompton constitution. But the House of Representatives rejected this measure and instead substituted a compromise, known as the English bill, which allowed Kansans to vote on the proslavery constitution. As a thinly veiled bribe to encourage Kansans to ratify the document, the English bill offered Kansas a huge grant of public land if it approved the Lecompton constitution. In 1858, while federal troops guarded the polls, Kansas voters overwhelmingly rejected the proslavery constitution.

The bloody battle for Kansas had come to an end. Free Soilers took control of the territorial legislature and repealed the Kansas territorial slave code. Stripped of any legal safeguards for their slave property, most Kansas slaveowners quickly left the territory. When the federal census was taken in 1860, just two slaves remained in Kansas.

But the nation would never be the same. To antislavery Northerners, the Lecompton controversy showed that the slave power was willing to subvert democratic processes in an attempt to force slavery on a free people. In Kansas, they charged, proslavery forces had used violence, fraud, and intimidation to expand the territory open to slavery. To the more extreme opponents of slavery in the North, the lesson was clear. The only way to preserve freedom and democratic procedures was to destroy slavery and the slave power through force of arms.

CRISIS OF THE UNION

In 1858, Senator William H. Seward of New York examined the sources of the conflicts between the North and the South. Some people, said Seward, thought the sectional conflict was "accidental, unnecessary, the work of interested or fanatical agitators, and therefore ephemeral." But Seward believed that these people were wrong. The roots of the conflict went far deeper. "It is an irrepressible conflict," Seward said, "between opposing and enduring forces."

By 1858, a growing number of Northerners were convinced that two fundamentally antagonistic societies had evolved in the nation, one dedicated to freedom, the other opposed. They had come to believe that their society was locked in a life-and-death struggle with a southern society dominated by an aggressive slave power, which had seized control of the federal government and imperiled the liberties of free people. Declared the *New York Tribune:* "We are not one people. We are two peoples. We are a people for Freedom and a people for Slavery. Between the two, conflict is inevitable."

At the same time, an increasing number of Southerners expressed alarm at the growth of anti-slavery and anti-South sentiment in the North. They were convinced that Republicans would not only insist on halting slavery's expansion but would also seek to undermine the institution where it already existed. As the decade closed, the dominant question of American political life was whether the nation's leaders could find a peaceful way to resolve the differences separating the North and South.

The Lincoln-Douglas Debates

The critical issues dividing the nation—slavery versus free labor, popular sovereignty, and the legal and political status of African Americans—were brought into sharp focus in a series of dramatic forensic duels during the 1858 election campaign for U.S. senator from Illinois. The campaign pitted a little-known lawyer from Springfield named Abraham Lincoln against Senator Stephen A. Douglas, the front-runner for the Democratic presidential nomination in 1860. (Senators, at the time, were elected by state legislators, and Douglas and Lincoln were actually campaigning for candidates from their party for the state legislature.)

The contest received intense national publicity. One reason for the public attention was that the political future of Stephen Douglas was at stake. Douglas had openly broken with the Buchanan administration over the proslavery Lecompton constitution and had joined with Republicans to defeat the admission of Kansas to the Union as a slave state. Now, many wondered, would Douglas assume the leadership of the free soil movement?

The public knew little about the man the Republicans selected to run against Douglas. Lincoln had been born on February 12, 1809, in a log cabin and grew up on the wild Kentucky and Indiana frontier. At the age of 21, he moved to Illinois, where he worked as a clerk in a country store, became a local postmaster and a lawyer, and served four terms in the lower house of the Illinois General Assembly. A Whig in politics, Lincoln was elected in 1846 to the U.S. House of Representatives, but his stand against the Mexican War had made him too unpopular to win reelection. After the passage of the Kansas-Nebraska Act in 1854, Lincoln reentered politics, and in 1858 the Republican party nominated him to run against Douglas for the Senate.

Lincoln accepted the nomination with the famous words: "'A house divided against itself cannot stand.' I believe this Government cannot endure permanently half-slave and half-free." He did not believe the Union would fall, but he did predict that it would cease to be divided. Lincoln proceeded to argue that Stephen Douglas's Kansas-Nebraska Act and the Supreme Court's Dred Scott decision were part of a conspiracy to make slavery lawful "in all the States, old as well as new—North as well as South."

For 4 months Lincoln and Douglas crisscrossed Illinois, traveling nearly 10,000 miles and participating in seven face-to-face debates before crowds of up to 15,000.

During the course of the debates, Lincoln and Douglas presented two sharply contrasting views of the problem of slavery. Douglas argued that slavery was a dying institution that had reached its natural limits and could not thrive where climate and soil were inhospitable. He asserted that the problem of slavery could best be resolved if it were treated as essentially a local problem. Lincoln, on the other hand, regarded slavery as a dynamic, expansionistic institution, hungry for new territory. He argued that if Northerners allowed slavery to spread unchecked, slaveowners would make slavery a national institution and would reduce all laborers, white as well as black, to a state of virtual slavery.

The sharpest difference between the two candidates involved the issue of African Americans' legal rights. Douglas was unable to conceive of African Americans as anything but inferior to whites, and he was unalterably opposed to their citizenship. "I want citizenship for whites only," he declared. Lincoln said that he, too, was opposed to granting free blacks full legal rights. But he insisted that African Americans were equal to Douglas and "every living man" in their right to life, liberty, and the fruits of their own labor.

The debates reached a climax on a damp, chilly August 27. At Freeport, Illinois, Lincoln asked Douglas to reconcile the Supreme Court's Dred Scott decision, which denied Congress the power to exclude slavery from a territory, with popular sovereignty. Could the residents of a territory "in any lawful way" exclude slavery prior to statehood? Douglas replied that the residents of a territory could exclude

The question of the legal status of slavery in the territories was the major issue Illinois senatorial candidates Stephen A. Douglas and Abraham Lincoln discussed in their series of seven debates in 1858. Lincoln lost the Senate race to Douglas, nicknamed the "Little Giant" in reference to his short stature but outstanding oratorical skills. The debates, however, helped bring Lincoln to national prominence, and two years later he defeated Douglas for the presidency.

slavery by refusing to pass laws protecting slave-holders' property rights. "Slavery cannot exist a day or an hour anywhere," he declared, "unless it is supported by local police regulations."

Any way he answered, Douglas was certain to alienate northern Free Soilers or proslavery Southerners. The Dred Scott decision had given slave owners the right to take their slavery into any western territories. Now Douglas said that territorial settlers could exclude slavery, despite what the Court had ruled. Douglas won reelection, but his cautious statements antagonized Southerners and northern Free Soilers alike.

In the final balloting, the Republicans outpolled the Democrats. But the Democrats had gerrymandered the voting districts so skillfully that they kept control of the state legislature.

Although Lincoln failed to win a Senate seat, his battle with Stephen Douglas had catapulted him into the national spotlight and made him a serious presidential possibility in 1860. As Lincoln himself noted, his defeat was "a slip and not a fall."

Harpers Ferry

On August 19, 1859, John Brown, the Kansas abolitionist, and Frederick Douglass, the celebrated African American abolitionist and former slave, met in an abandoned stone quarry near Chambersburg, Pennsylvania. For three days, the two men discussed whether violence could be legitimately used to free the nation's slaves. The Kansas guerrilla leader asked Douglass if he would join a band of raiders who would seize a federal arsenal and spark a mass uprising of slaves. "When I strike," Brown said, "the bees will begin to swarm, and I shall need you to help hive them."

As Robert E. Lee's marines broke through the brick walls of John Brown's stronghold at Harpers Ferry, Brown "felt the pulse of his dying son with one hand and held his rifle with the other," and commanded his men with the utmost composure.

THE PEOPLE SPEAK

John Brown Defends His Raid on Harpers Ferry (1859)

At the very end of his trial in a Virginia court for treason, conspiracy, and murder, John Brown delivered a five-minute speech in which he defended his raid on Harpers Ferry.

I have, may it please the Court, a few words to say.

In the first place, I deny everything but what I have all along admitted: of a design on my part to free slaves. I intended certainly to have made a clean thing of that matter, as I did last winter, when I went into Missouri and there took slaves without the snapping of a gun on either side, moving them through the country, and finally leaving them in Canada. I designed to have done the same thing again on a larger scale. That was all I intended. I never did intend murder, or treason, or the destruction of property, or to exercise or incite slaves to rebellion, or to make insurrection.

I have another objection, and that is that it is unjust that I should suffer such a penalty. . . . Had I so interfered in behalf of the rich, the powerful, the intelligent, the so-called great . . . it would have been all right. Every man in this Court would have deemed it an act worthy of reward rather than punishment.

This Court acknowledges . . . the validity of the law of God. I see a book kissed, which I suppose to be the Bible, or at least the New Testament, which teaches me that all things whatsoever I would that men should do to me, I should do even so to them. It teaches me, further, to remember them that are in bonds as bound with them. I endeavored to act up to that instruction. I say I am yet too young to understand that God is any respecter of persons. I believe that to have interfered as I have done . . . in behalf of His despised poor, I did no wrong, but right. Now, if it is deemed necessary that I should forfeit my life for the furtherance of the ends of justice, and mingle my blood further with the blood of my children and with the blood of millions in this slave country whose rights are disregarded by wicked, cruel, and unjust enactments, I say let it be done.

Source: John Brown, "Last Statement to the Court," in *The Life and Execution of Captain John Brown, Known as "Old Brown of Ossawatomie"* (New York, 1859).

"No," Douglass replied. Brown's plan, he knew, was suicidal. Brown had earlier proposed a somewhat more realistic plan. According to that scheme, Brown would have launched guerrilla activity in the Virginia mountains, providing a haven for slaves and an escape route into the North. That scheme had a chance of working, but Brown's new plan was hopeless.

Up until the Kansas-Nebraska Act, abolitionists were averse to the use of violence. Opponents of slavery hoped to use moral suasion and other peaceful means to eliminate slavery. But by the mid-1850s, the abolitionists' aversion to violence had begun to fade. In 1858 William Lloyd Garrison complained that his followers were "growing more and more warlike." On the night of October 16, 1859, violence came, and John Brown was its instrument.

Brown's plan was to capture the federal arsenal at Harpers Ferry, Virginia (now West Virginia), and arm slaves from the surrounding countryside. His long-range goal was to drive southward into Tennessee and Alabama, raiding federal arsenals and inciting slave insurrections. Failing that, he hoped to ignite a sectional crisis that would destroy slavery.

At eight o'clock Sunday evening, October 16, John Brown led a raiding party of approximately 21 men toward Harpers Ferry, where they captured the lone night watchman and cut the town's telegraph lines. Encountering no resistance, Brown's raiders seized the federal arsenal, an armory, and a rifle works along with several million dollars worth of arms and munitions. Brown then sent out several detachments to round up hostages and liberate slaves.

But Brown's plans soon went awry. As news of the raid spread, many townspeople and local militia companies cut off Brown's escape routes and trapped his men in the armory. Twice, Brown sent men carrying flags of truce to negotiate. On both occasions, drunken mobs, yelling "Kill them, kill them," gunned the men down.

Two days later U.S. Marines, commanded by Colonel Robert E. Lee and Lieutenant J. E. B. Stuart, arrived in Harpers Ferry. Brown and his men took refuge in a fire engine house and battered holes through the building's brick wall to shoot through. A hostage later described the climactic scene: "With one son dead by his side and another shot through, he felt the pulse of his dying son with one hand and held his rifle with the other and commanded his men . . . encouraging them to fire and sell their lives as dearly as they could."

Later that morning, Colonel Lee's marines stormed the engine house and rammed down its doors. Brown and his men continued firing until the leader of the storming party cornered Brown and knocked him unconscious with a sword. Five of Brown's party escaped, ten were killed, and seven, including Brown himself, were taken prisoner.

A week later, John Brown was put on trial in a Virginia court, even though his attack had occurred on federal property. During the six-day proceedings, Brown refused to plead insanity as a defense. He was found guilty of treason, conspiracy, and murder, and was sentenced to die on the gallows.

The trial's high point came at the very end when Brown was allowed to make a five-minute speech. His words helped convince thousands of Northerners that this grizzled man of 59, with his "piercing eyes" and "resolute countenance," was a martyr to the cause of freedom. Brown denied that he had come to Virginia to commit violence. His only goal, he said, was to liberate the slaves. "If it is deemed necessary," he told the Virginia court, "that I should forfeit my life for the furtherance of the ends of justice and mingle my blood . . . with the blood of millions in this slave country whose rights are disregarded by wicked, cruel, and unjust enactments, I say let it be done."

Brown's execution was set for December 2. Before he went to the gallows, Brown wrote one last message: "I . . . am now quite certain that the crimes of this guilty land will never be purged away but with blood." At 11 A.M., he was led to the execution site, a halter was placed around his neck, and a sheriff led him over a trapdoor. The sheriff cut the rope and the trapdoor opened. As the old man's body convulsed on the gallows, a Virginia officer cried out: "So perish all enemies of Virginia!"

Across the North, church bells tolled, flags flew at half-mast, and buildings were draped in black bunting. Ralph Waldo Emerson compared Brown to Jesus Christ and declared that his death had made "the gallows as glorious as the cross." William Lloyd Garrison, previously the strongest exponent of nonviolent opposition to slavery, announced that Brown's death had convinced him of "the need for violence" to destroy slavery. He told a Boston meeting that "every slave holder has forfeited his right to live" if he opposed immediate emancipation.

Prominent northern Democrats and Republicans, including Stephen Douglas and Abraham Lincoln, spoke out forcefully against Brown's raid and his tactics. Lincoln expressed the views of the Republican leadership when he denounced Brown's raid as an act of "violence, bloodshed, and treason" that deserved to be punished by death. But southern whites refused to believe that politicians like Lincoln and Douglas represented the true opinion of most Northerners. These men condemned Brown's "invasion," observed a Virginia senator, "only because it failed."

Chronology
OF KEY EVENTS

1846 Wilmot Proviso, banning slavery from any territory acquired from Mexico, is proposed

1850 Compromise of 1850

1852 Harriet Beecher Stowe publishes *Uncle Tom's Cabin*

1853 Gadsden Purchase from Mexico

1854 Ostend Manifesto calls on the United States to acquire Cuba from Spain; Commodore Matthew Perry negotiates a treaty opening Japan to American trade; Kansas-Nebraska Act reignites sectional controversy over slavery; "Bleeding Kansas" begins; conventions of Free Soilers form the Republican party

1856 "Sack of Lawrence"—proslavery Missourians loot and burn several buildings in Lawrence, Kansas; "Bleeding Sumner"—Congressman Preston Brooks of South Carolina beats Senator Charles Sumner of Massachusetts with a cane; John Brown's raid on Pottawatomie Creek, Kansas

1857 Dred Scott decision

1858 Kansas voters reject the Lecompton constitution; Lincoln-Douglas debates

1859 John Brown's raid at Harpers Ferry

CONCLUSION

For 40 years the debate over the extension of slavery had divided North and South. National leaders had tried on several occasions to reach a permanent, workable solution to the problem, without success. With the collapse of the Whigs and the rise of the Republicans, the American political process could no longer contain the fierce antagonisms and mutual distrust that separated the two regions.

In 1859, John Brown's raid convinced many white Southerners that a majority of Northerners wished to free the slaves and incite a race war. Southern extremists, known as "fire-eaters," told large crowds that John Brown's attack on Harpers Ferry was "the first act in the grand tragedy of emancipation, and the subjugation of the South in bloody treason." After Harpers Ferry, Southerners increasingly believed that secession and creation of a slaveholding confederacy were now the South's only options. A Virginia newspaper noted that there were "thousands of men in our midst who, a month ago, scoffed at the idea of a dissolution of the Union as a madman's dream, but who now hold the opinion that its days are numbered." The final bonds that had held the Union together had come unraveled.

SUGGESTIONS FOR FURTHER READING

Tyler Anbinder, *Nativism and Slavery: The Northern Know Nothings and the Politics of the 1850s* (1992) and William E. Gienapp, *Origins of the Republican Party* (1987). Analyze shifts in voting patterns in the 1850s.

William J. Cooper, Jr., *Liberty and Slavery* (1983). Examines white southern attitudes on the eve of the Civil War. Eric Foner, *Free Soil, Free Labor, Free Men* (1970). Explores northern attitudes.

Don E. Fehrenbacher, *The Dred Scott Case* (1978). Thoroughly examines this landmark Supreme Court decision.

William W. Freehling, *The Road to Disunion* (1990); Bruce Levine, *Half Slave and Half Free: The Roots of the Civil War* (1992); David M. Potter, *The Impending Crisis* (1976); and Kenneth M. Stampp, *America in 1857* (1990). Explore the causes of the Civil War.

Overviews and Surveys

Philip D. Curtin, *The Rise and Fall of the Plantation Complex* (1990); David Brion Davis, *The Slave Power Conspiracy and the Paranoid Style* (1970); Eric Foner and Olivia Mahoney, *A House Divided: America in the Age of Lincoln* (1990); William W. Freehling, *The Road to Disunion: Secessionists at Bay, 1776–1854* (1990); Michael Holt, *The Political Crisis of the 1850s* (1978); James M. McPherson, *Ordeal by Fire* (1982); William L. Neumann, *America Encounters Japan: From Perry to MacArthur* (1963); Allan Nevins, *The Ordeal of the Union* (1947), and *The Emergence of Lincoln,* 2 vols. (1950); Roy F. Nichols and Eugene H. Berwanger, *The Stakes of Power, 1845–1877,* rev. ed. (1982); John Niven, *The Coming of the Civil War, 1837–1861* (1990); David Potter, *The Impending Crisis, 1848–1861* (1976); James A. Rawley, *Secession: Disruption of the American Republic, 1844–1861* (1990); Joel H. Silbey, *The American Political Nation, 1838–1893* (1991), and *The Partisan Imperative: The Dynamics of American Politics Before the Civil War* (1985); Kenneth Stampp, *The Imperiled Union* (1980).

The Crisis of 1850

William L. Barney, *The Road to Secession: A New Perspective on the Old South* (1972); John Barrywell, *Love of Order: South Carolina's First Secession Crisis* (1982); Stanley W. Campbell, *The Slave Catchers: Enforcement of the Fugitive Slave Law, 1850–1860* (1970); William J. Cooper, *Liberty and Slavery* (1983), and *The South and the Politics of Slavery, 1828–1856* (1978); Barbara J. Fields, *Slavery and Freedom on the Middle Ground* (1985); Holman Hamilton, *Prologue to Conflict: The Crisis and Compromise of 1850* (1964); Joseph G. Rayback, *Free Soil: The Election of 1848* (1970).

Disintegration of the Party System

Thomas Alexander, *Sectional Stress and Party Strength* (1967); Carleton Beales, *Brass Knuckles Crusade: The Great Know-Nothing Conspiracy* (1960); Ray Allen Billington, *The Protestant Crusade, 1800–1860* (1938); Eric Foner, *Free Soil, Free Labor, Free Men: The Ideology of the Republican Party* (1970); Paul W. Gates, *Fifty Million Acres: Conflicts over Kansas Land Policy, 1854–1890* (1954); William E. Gienapp, *Origins of the Republican Party* (1987); Charles G. Hamilton, *Lincoln and the Know-Nothing Movement* (1954); Michael F. Holt, *Forging a Majority: The Formation of the Republican Party in Pittsburgh, 1848–1860* (1969); James C. Malin, *The Nebraska Question, 1852–1854* (1953); Stuart C. Miller, *The Unwelcome Immigrant* (1969); John R. Mulkern, *The Know-Nothing Party in Massachusetts* (1990); Alice Nichols, *Bleeding Kansas* (1954); Roy F. Nichols, "The Kansas-Nebraska Act: A Century of Historiography," *Mississippi Valley Historical Review,* 43 (1956); W. Darrell Overdyke, *The Know-Nothing Party in the South* (1950); James A. Rawley, *Race and Politics: "Bleeding Kansas" and the Coming of the Civil War* (1969); Joel H. Silbey, *The Shrine of Party: Congressional Voting Behavior, 1841–1852* (1967), and *The Transformation of American Politics, 1840–1860* (1967); Thomas P. Slaughter, *Bloody Dawn: The Christiana Riot and Racial Tensions in the Antebellum North* (1991); Mark W. Summers, *The Plundering Generation: Corruption and the Crisis of the Union* (1987).

The Gathering Storm

Dale Baum, *The Civil War Party System: The Case of Massachusetts, 1848–1876* (1984); Robert M. Cover, *Justice Accused* (1975); Don E. Fehrenbacher, *The Dred Scott Case: Its Signifi-*

cance in American Law and Politics (1978); Paul Finkelman, An Imperfect Union: Slavery, Federalism and Comity (1981); Eric Foner, Free Soil, Free Labor, Free Men: The Ideology of the Republican Party before the Civil War (1970); A. Leon Higginbotham, Jr., In the Matter of Color: Race and the American Legal Process (1978); Michael F. Holt, Forging a Majority: The Formation of the Republican Party in Pittsburgh, 1848–1860 (1969); Stanley I. Kutler, The Dred Scott Decision (1967); Stephen E. Maizlish, The Triumph of Sectionalism: The Transformation of Ohio Politics (1983); William Lee Miller, Arguing About Slavery (1996); Thomas D. Morris, Free Men All: The Personal Liberty Laws of the North (1974); Michael A. Morrison, Slavery and the American West (1997); Arthur M. Schlesinger, Jr., and Fred L. Israel, eds., History of U.S. Political Parties (1973); Hans L. Treffouse, The Radical Republicans (1969); Edward L. Widmer, Young America: The Flowering of Democracy in New York City (1998).

Crisis of the Union

Jules Abels, Man on Fire: John Brown and the Cause of Liberty (1971); Elizabeth Ammons, ed., Critical Essays on Harriet Beecher Stowe (1979); Hannah Page Wheeler Andrews, Time and Variations: Uncle Tom's Cabin as Book, Play, and Film (1979); R. O. Boyer, The Legend of John Brown (1973); Don E. Fehrenbacher, Prelude to Greatness: Lincoln in the 1850s (1962); Paul Finkelman, ed., His Soul Goes Marching On: Responses to John Brown (1995); Charles H. Foster, The Rungless Ladder: Harriet Beecher Stowe and New England Puritanism (1970); Thomas F. Gossett, Uncle Tom's Cabin and American Culture (1985); Theodore R. Hovet, The Master Narrative: Harriet Beecher Stowe's Subversive Story of Master and Slave (1988); Henry V. Jaffa, Crisis of the House Divided: An Interpretation of the Issues in the Lincoln-Douglas Debates (1959); Ellen Moers, Harriet Beecher Stowe and American Literature (1978). Truman Nelson, The Old Man: John Brown at Harper's Ferry (1973); Benjamin Quarles, Allies for Freedom: Blacks and John Brown (1974), and Blacks on John Brown (1972); Edward J. Renehan, Jr., The Secret Six (1995); Jeffrey Rossbach, Ambivalent Conspirators: John Brown, the Secret Six, and a Theory of Slave Violence (1982); Louis Ruchames, ed., John Brown: The Making of a Revolutionary (1969); Kenneth M. Stampp, America in 1857 (1990); David Zarefsky, Lincoln, Douglas, and Slavery (1990).

Biographies

John R. Adams, Harriet Beecher Stowe (1989); Richard Current, The Lincoln Nobody Knows (1963); David Herbert Donald, Lincoln (1995); Robert W. Johannsen, Stephen A. Douglas (1973); William S. McFeely, Frederick Douglass (1991); Samuel Eliot Morison, "Old Bruin": Commodore Matthew C. Perry, 1794–1858 (1967); William L. Neumann, America Encounters Japan: From Perry to MacArthur (1963); John Niven, John C. Calhoun and the Price of Union (1988); Stephen B. Oates, To Purge This Land with Blood: A Biography of John Brown, 2d ed. (1984), and With Malice Toward None: The Life of Abraham Lincoln (1977); William E. Parrish, David Rice Atchison of Missouri (1961); Robert V. Remini, Henry Clay: Statesman for the Union (1991); Damon Wells, Stephen Douglas: The Last Years, 1857–1861 (1971).

INTERNET RESOURCES

Daniel Webster: Dartmouth's Favorite Son
http://grafton.dartmouth.edu:8005/~dw/
Dartmouth College provides texts and images concerning famous alumnus Daniel Webster.

Secession Era Editorials Project
http://history.furman.edu/~benson/docs/
Furman University is digitizing editorials about the secession crisis and already includes scores of them on this site.

John Brown Trial Links
http://www.law.umkc.edu/faculty/projects/ftrials/Brown.html
For information about the trial of John Brown, this site provides a list of excellent links.

Abraham Lincoln and Slavery
http://odur.let.rug.nl/~usa/H/1990/ch5_p6.htm
This site discusses Lincoln's views and action concerning slavery, especially the Lincoln-Douglas debates.

Bleeding Kansas
http://www.ukans.edu/carrie/kancoll/galbks.htm
Contemporary and later accounts of America's rehearsal for the Civil War make up this University of Kansas site.

KEY TERMS

Popular Sovereignty   (p. 388)

Fugitive Slave Law   (p. 389)

Know Nothing Party   (p. 391)

Kansas-Nebraska Act   (p. 396)

Dred Scott   (p. 400)

REVIEW QUESTIONS

1. Why did California's application for statehood cause heated debate in Congress?

2. In what ways did Southerners benefit from the Compromise of 1850? In what ways did Northerners benefit?

3. Why did the Fugitive Slave Law anger many Northerners?

4. What issue led to the formation of the Republican party?

5. How was the issue of slavery to be decided in Kansas and Nebraska? Why did the status of slavery in Kansas become a divisive issue during the 1850s?

6. What did the Supreme Court rule in the Dred Scott decision? What was the ruling's significance?

7. What were the major differences in the attitudes of Abraham Lincoln and Stephen Douglas toward slavery?

8. Why did John Brown's raid convince many Southerners that their states should secede from the Union?

A NATION SHATTERED BY CIVIL WAR, 1860–1865

"We will make our stand"

Looking eastward from Sharpsburg into the mountains of western Maryland, General Robert E. Lee uttered the fateful words: "We will make our stand." Behind him was the Potomac River and to his front was Antietam Creek. Having invaded Union territory in early September 1862, Lee dispersed his Army of Northern Virginia, some 50,000 strong, across the countryside to capture strategic points such as Harpers Ferry and to rally the citizens of this border slaveholding state behind the Confederate cause. Now he issued orders for his troops to reassemble with all haste at Sharpsburg. A major battle was in the making. General George B. McClellan's Army of the Potomac, numbering nearly 100,000 soldiers, was rapidly descending upon Lee's position.

Early on the morning of September 17, the great battle began. As the day progressed, Union forces attacked in five uncoordinated waves, which allowed Lee to maneuver his heavily outnumbered troops from point to point, warding off federal assaults. As usual, Lee calculated his opponent's temperament correctly. McClellan was too timid to throw every-

thing into the battle at once. As darkness fell, the Confederates still held their lines. Lee knew, however, that if McClellan attacked again the next morning, the southern army might well be annihilated.

Among those rebel troops who had marched into Maryland was 25-year-old Thomas Jefferson Rushin. He had grown up secure in his social station as the second son of Joel Rushin, a prospering west Georgia cotton planter who owned 21 slaves. Thomas was anxious to show those far-off "Black Republican" Yankees that Southern gentlemen would never shrink from battle in defense of their way of life. He enlisted in Company K of the Twelfth Georgia Volunteers in June 1861. At 5:30 A.M. on September 17, 1862, Sergeant Rushin waited restlessly north of Sharpsburg—where the first Union assault occurred.

As dawn beckoned, Rushin and his comrades first heard skirmish fire, then the booming of cannons. Out in an open field they soon engaged Yankee troops appearing at the edge of a nearby woods. The Twelfth Georgia Volunteers stood their ground until they pulled back at 6:45 A.M. By the time that order came, 62 of the Georgians lay dead or wounded, among them the lifeless remains of Thomas Jefferson Rushin.

To the south of Sharpsburg, the battle would soon heat up. At 9:00 A.M. General Ambrose E. Burnside's Union soldiers prepared to cross a stone bridge over Antietam Creek. On the other side was sharply rising ground, on top of which troops in gray waited, ready to shoot at any person bold enough to venture onto what became known as Burnside Bridge.

The Eleventh Connecticut Volunteers were among those poised for the advance. Included in their number was 18-year-old Private Alvin Flint, Jr., who had enlisted a few months before in Company D. He was from Hartford, where his father, Alvin, Sr., worked in a papermaking factory. Flint's departure from home was sorrowful because his mother had just died of consumption. A few weeks later he received word that his younger sister had succumbed to the same disease.

Flint's own sense of foreboding must have been overwhelming as he charged toward the bridge. In an instant, he became part of the human carnage, as minié balls poured down from across the bridge. Bleeding profusely from a mortal wound, he died before stretcher-bearers from the Ambulance Corps could reach him.

Flint had not known that his father and younger brother had recently joined another Connecticut regiment, affording Alvin, Sr., the chance to visit the

The human toll of the Civil War was overwhelming for contemporaries and remains so for later generations. Thomas Jefferson Rushin (left) and Alvin Flint, Jr. (right), were young casualties of the Battle of Antietam.

battlefield a month later in search of his son's remains. Deeply distressed, his father wrote the *Hartford Courant* and decried the loss of "my boy" who "was brutally murdered" because of this "hellish, wicked rebellion." "Oh how dreadful was that place to me," he wrote in agony, where his son "had been buried like a beast of the field!"

Fifty-three-year-old Alvin Flint, Sr., gave up, returned to his regiment, and marched toward Fredericksburg, Virginia, where another major battle took place in December 1862. A month later the two remaining Flints died of typhoid fever, a disease then raging through the Army of the Potomac.

As the human toll mounted higher and higher, Civil War battlefields became hallowed ground. Southerners named these sites after towns while Northerners named them for nearby landmarks like rivers and streams. In the South the Battle of Sharpsburg symbolized a valiant stand against overwhelming odds. In the North the Battle of Antietam represented a turning point in the war because Union troops, at last, controlled the field of combat after Lee, astonished that McClellan did not continue the fight, ordered a retreat back into Virginia on the evening of September 18.

Different names for the same battle could not change the results. With 23,000 dead and wounded soldiers, Antietam turned out to be the bloodiest one-day action of the Civil War. Before the slaughter ended in 1865, total casualties reached 1.2 million people, including 620,000 dead—more than the total number of United States troops who lost their lives in World Wars I and II combined. Back in April 1861, when the Confederates fired on Fort Sumter, no one foresaw such carnage. No one imagined bodies as "thick as human leaves" decaying in fields around Sharpsburg, or how "horrible" looking would be "the faces of the dead."

The coming of the Civil War could be compared to a time bomb ready to explode. The fundamental issue was slavery, or more specifically whether the "peculiar institution" would be allowed to spread across the American landscape. Southerners feared that northern leaders would use federal authority to declare slavery null and void throughout the land. The South made its stand on the principle of states' rights and voted to secede. The North, in response, went to war to save the Union, but always lurking in the background was the issue of permitting the continued existence of slavery. The carnage of the war settled the matter. A few days after Antietam, President Abraham Lincoln announced the Emancipation Proclamation, which transformed the Civil War into a struggle to end slavery—and the way of life it supported—as a means of destroying Confederate resistance and preserving the federal Union.

FROM SECESSION TO FULL-SCALE WAR

On April 23, 1860, the Democratic party gathered in Charleston, South Carolina, to select a presidential candidate. No nominating convention faced a more difficult task. The delegates argued bitterly among themselves, and many southern delegates walked out of the convention. The breaking up of the Democratic party cleared the way for Lincoln's election, which in turn provoked the secession of seven southern states by February 1861. As the Union fell apart, all Americans watched closely to see how "Honest Abe," the "Railsplitter" from Illinois, would handle the secession crisis.

Electing a New President

Even before the Democratic convention met, evidence was abundant that the party was crumbling. Early in 1860 Jefferson Davis of Mississippi introduced a series of resolutions in the U.S. Senate calling for federal protection of slavery in all western territories. More extreme **fire-eaters,** such as William L. Yancey of Alabama, not only embraced Davis's proposal but announced that he and others would leave the convention if the party did not defend their inalienable right to hold slaves and nominate a Southerner for president. After the convention rejected an extreme proslavery platform, delegates from eight southern states walked out.

Those who remained tried to nominate a candidate, but after dozens of ballots no one received a two-thirds majority. So the delegates gave up and agreed to reconvene in Baltimore in another six weeks. That convention also failed to produce a consensus. Finally, in two separate meetings, northern delegates named Stephen A. Douglas as their candidate, and southern delegates chose John C. Breckinridge of Kentucky.

To confuse matters further, a short-lived party, the Constitutional Unionists, emerged. This coalition of former Whigs, Know Nothings, and Unionist Democrats adopted a platform advocating "no political principle other than the Constitution of the country, the union of the states, and the enforcement of the laws." The Constitutional Unionists nominated John

This 1860 cartoon shows Abraham Lincoln, "the fittest of all candidates," outdistancing his opponents.

Bell of Tennessee, who enjoyed some support in the border states and drew votes away from both Douglas and Breckinridge, thereby making it easier for the sectional Republican party to carry the election.

When the Republicans gathered in Chicago during mid-May, they were very optimistic, especially with the Democrats hopelessly divided. Delegates constructed a platform with many promises, including high tariffs in an appeal to gain the support of northern manufacturers and a homestead law in a bid to win the backing of citizens wanting free farmland. On the slave expansion issue there was no hint of compromise. "The normal condition of all the territory of the United States is that of freedom," the platform read, and no federal, state, or local legislative body could ever "give legal existence to slavery in any territory." The platform, however, did not call for an end to slavery in states where that institution already existed.

To ensure victory, Republican party regulars sought a candidate, as one of them stated, "of popular origin, . . . who had no record to defend and no radicalism of an offensive character." This left out Senator William H. Seward, the front-runner, who was widely known as a strong antislavery advocate. Seward fell short of a majority on the first ballot. Then the skilled floor managers of Abraham Lincoln, the local favorite from Illinois—the Republican party had failed to carry this state in 1856—started what became a landslide for their candidate.

The 1860 presidential campaign took place in a lightning-charged atmosphere of threats and fears bordering on hysteria. Rumors of slave revolts, town burnings, and the murder of women and children swept the South. Newspapers reported the imminence of John Brown–style invasions and of slaves

Election of 1860

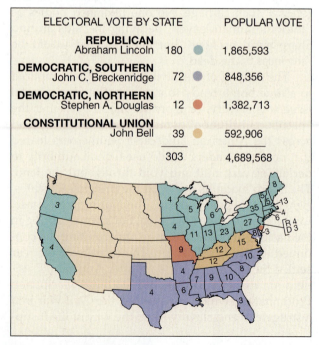

ELECTORAL VOTE BY STATE			POPULAR VOTE
REPUBLICAN Abraham Lincoln	180	●	1,865,593
DEMOCRATIC, SOUTHERN John C. Breckenridge	72	●	848,356
DEMOCRATIC, NORTHERN Stephen A. Douglas	12	●	1,382,713
CONSTITUTIONAL UNION John Bell	39	●	592,906
	303		4,689,568

stockpiling strychnine to poison water supplies. In one Alabama town, a mob hanged a stranger, thinking him to be an abolitionist. Across the South militia companies armed themselves and started to drill just in case that "black-hearted abolitionist fanatic" Lincoln won the election.

According to custom, Lincoln stayed home during the campaign and let others speak for him. His supporters inflamed sectional tensions by bragging that slavery would never survive their candidate's presidency. Stephen Douglas, desperately trying "to save the Union," announced, "I will go South." He embarked on the first nationwide speaking tour of a presidential nominee. Once under way, southern Democrats asked Douglas to withdraw from the election in favor of Breckinridge, whom they thought had a better chance to beat Lincoln. Douglas refused, asserting that only he could defeat the Republican candidate.

On election day, November 6, 1860, Lincoln won only 39.9 percent of the popular vote, but he received 180 electoral college votes, 57 more than the combined total of his opponents. The vote was purely sectional; Lincoln's name did not appear on the ballots of 10 southern states. Even when totaling all the popular votes against him, Lincoln still would have won in the electoral college by 17 votes because he carried the most populous states—all in the North. His election dramatically demonstrated to Southerners their minority status.

Secession Rends the Union

Lincoln said to a friend during the campaign that Southerners "have too much good sense, and good temper, to attempt the ruin of the government." He told others he would support a constitutional amendment protecting slavery where it already existed, but Southerners believed otherwise. The choice for the South, as the Mississippi secession convention framed the alternatives, was either to "submit to degradation, and to the loss of [slave] property worth four billions," or to leave the Union. No matter what, "the South will never submit" was the common refrain. Secession, then, meant liberation from the oppression of Black Republicans.

South Carolina led the way when its legislature, in the wake of Lincoln's victory, unanimously called for a secession convention. On December 20, 1860, the delegates voted 169 to 0 to leave the Union. The rationale had long since been developed by John C. Calhoun. State authority was superior to that of the

Secession

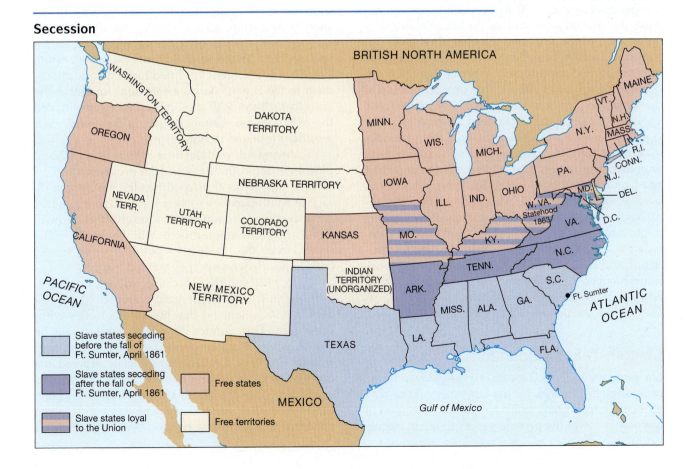

nation, and as sovereign entities, states could as freely leave as they had freely joined the Union. South Carolina, as the delegates proclaimed, had "resumed her position among the nations of the world."

By early February 1861 the states of Georgia, Florida, Alabama, Mississippi, Louisiana, and Texas had also voted for secession. Representatives from the seven states first met in Montgomery, Alabama, on February 8 and proclaimed a new nation, the Confederate States of America. They elected Jefferson Davis provisional president and wrote a plan of government, which they modeled on the federal Constitution except for their emphasis on states' rights. The southern government would consist of an executive branch headed by a president, a two-house Congress, and a Supreme Court. The Confederate constitution limited the president to a single six-year term, required a two-thirds vote of Congress to admit new states or enact appropriations bills, and forbade protective tariffs and government funding of internal improvements.

For some Northerners, such as newspaper editor Horace Greeley of the *New York Tribune*, the intelligent course was to let the "wayward sisters" of the South "depart in peace." A more conciliatory approach, as suggested in December 1860 by Senator John J. Crittenden of Kentucky, was to enshrine the old Missouri Compromise line of 36°30' in a constitutional amendment that would also promise no future restrictions on slavery where it existed. Neither alternative appealed to Lincoln. Secession was unconstitutional, he maintained, and appeasement, especially any plan endorsing the spread of slavery, was unacceptable. "On the territorial question," he stated, "I am inflexible." These words killed the Crittenden Compromise.

President-elect Lincoln, pressured from all sides to do something, decided instead to do nothing until after his inauguration. He had continued to hope that pro-Unionist sentiment in the South would win out over secessionist feelings. Also, eight slave states remained in the Union and controversial statements might have pushed some or all of them into the Confederate camp. Lincoln would make his moves prudently, indeed so carefully that some leading Republicans misread him as a bumbling, inept fool. William Seward, his future secretary of state, even politely offered to run the presidency on Lincoln's behalf.

Lincoln Takes Command

On February 11, 1861, Lincoln left his beloved home of Springfield, Illinois, for the last time. All the way to the nation's capital, as his special train stopped in town after town, the president-elect spoke in vague,

conciliatory terms. Between stops, he worked on his inaugural address, which embodied his plan.

On March 4, Lincoln raised his hand and swore to uphold the Constitution as the nation's sixteenth president. Then he read his inaugural address, with its powerful but simple message. The Union was "perpetual," and secession was illegal. To resist federal authority was both "insurrectionary" and "revolutionary." As president, he would support the Union by maintaining possession of federal properties in the South. Then Lincoln appealed to the southern people: "We are not enemies, but friends." And he warned: "In your hands, my dissatisfied countrymen, and not in mine, is the momentous issue of civil war. . . . You can have no conflict without yourselves being the aggressors."

Even as he spoke, Lincoln knew the seceding states had taken possession of all federal military installations within their borders—with the principal exceptions of Fort Sumter, guarding the entrance to Charleston harbor, and Fort Pickens along the Florida coast at Pensacola. The next day Lincoln received an ominous report. Major Robert Anderson, in command of Fort Sumter, was running out of provisions and would have to abandon his position within six weeks unless resupplied.

Lincoln had a month to back off or decide on a showdown. He consulted his cabinet, only to get sharply conflicting advice. Finally, he sent an emissary to South Carolina to gather intelligence. At the end of March he received a distressing report. South Carolinians, the agent informed him, had "no attachment to the Union" and were anxious for war. Now Lincoln realized how grossly he had overestimated the extent of pro-Union feeling in the South. The president resolved to stand firm.

Knowing full well the implications of his actions, Lincoln ordered the navy to take provisions to Fort Sumter. Just before the expedition left, he sent a message to South Carolina's governor, notifying him that "if such attempt be not resisted, no effort to throw in men, arms, or ammunition, will be made." The rebels, from the president's point of view, would have to decide whether they wanted war.

Before the supply expedition arrived, Confederate General P. G. T. Beauregard presented Major Anderson with a demand that he and his troops withdraw from Fort Sumter. Anderson replied that he would do so if not resupplied. Knowing that help was on the way, Confederate officials ordered the cannonading of Fort Sumter. The firing commenced at 4:30 A.M. on April 12, 1861. Thirty-four hours later, Major Anderson surrendered. On April 15, Lincoln announced that an "insurrection" existed and called for 75,000 volunteers to put down the South's rebellion. The Civil War had begun.

An Accounting of Resources

The firing on Fort Sumter caused both jubilation and consternation. Most citizens thought a battle or two would quickly end the conflict, so they rushed to enlist, not wanting to miss the action. The emotional outburst was particularly strong in the South where up to 200,000 enthusiasts tried to join the fledgling Confederate military machine. Several thousand had to be sent home, since it was impossible to muster them into the service in so short a time with even the

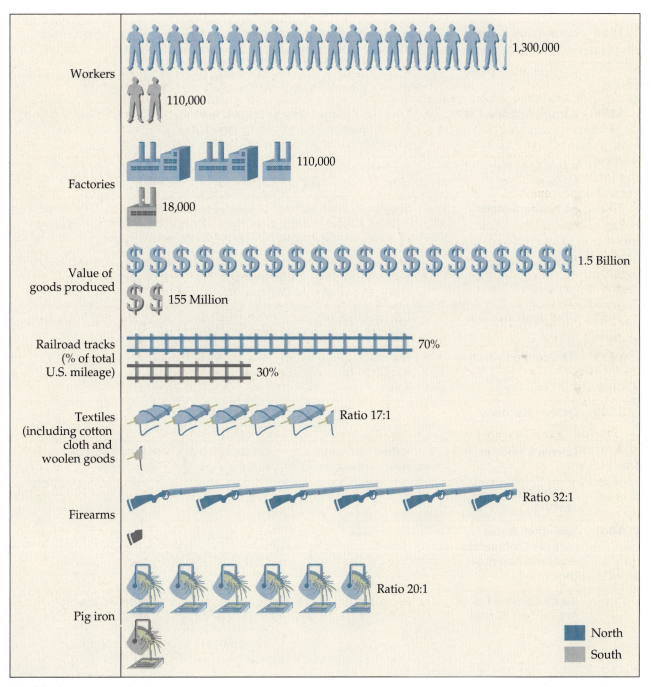

FIGURE 15.1
Resources, North and South

THE ROAD TO WAR

CIVIL WAR

1850	**Compromise of 1850**	Series of acts which appear to settle sectional strife over slavery; most controversial feature was a strict law for the return of fugitive slaves.
1852	*Uncle Tom's Cabin*	Harriet Beecher Stowe's novel, which sells a million copies in 18 months, arouses antislavery sentiment in the North.
	Know Nothing Party	Anti-Catholic, anti-immigrant party grows largely at the expense of the Whig party, weakening the party system.
1854	**Kansas-Nebraska Act**	Organizes Kansas and Nebraska territories and provides that slavery in those territories will be decided on the basis of popular sovereignty; reopens issue of slavery in the territories.
	Republican Party formed	Founded by opponents of the Kansas-Nebraska Act, the party is committed to halting slavery's westward expansion.
1856	**"Bleeding Sumner"**	Senator Charles Sumner of Massachusetts denounces "The Crime Against Kansas"; three days later, Representative Preston Brooks of South Carolina beats him unconscious with a cane.
	"Bleeding Kansas"	Proslavery Kansans attack Lawrence, center of free soil settlers; a band led by John Brown avenges the "Sack of Lawrence" by killing five people at Pottawatomie Creek.
1857	**Dred Scott decision**	Declares the Missouri Compromise unconstitutional and holds that Negroes are not citizens of the United States.
1859	**Harpers Ferry Raid**	An armed group led by John Brown seizes the federal arsenal at Harpers Ferry, Virginia; Brown is subsequently executed for treason.
1860	**Democratic party splits**	Northern Democrats nominate Stephen Douglas for president; Southern Democrats nominate John Breckinridge.
	Lincoln's election	Republican candidate Abraham Lincoln, committed to halting the westward spread of slavery, wins election.
	South Carolina secedes	The Union begins to disintegrate.
1861	**Ten other states secede; Confederate States of America forms**	Compromise efforts fail.
	South Carolina troops fire on Fort Sumter	President Lincoln responds by declaring a state of insurrection and calls for 75,000 volunteers to put down the rebellion.

bare essentials of war—uniforms, weapons, camp equipment, and food rations.

Professional military men like Lieutenant Colonel Robert E. Lee, who had experienced combat in the Mexican War, were less enthusiastic. "I see only that a fearful calamity is upon us," he wrote. Lee was anxious "for the preservation of the Union," but he felt compelled to defend the "honor" of Virginia, should state leaders vote for secession. If that happened, he would resign his military commission and "go back in sorrow to my people and share the misery of my native state."

On April 17, Virginians seceded in direct response to Lincoln's declaration of an insurrection. By late May, North Carolina, Tennessee, and Arkansas had also voted to leave the Union, meaning that 11 states containing a population of nearly 9 million people, including 3.5 million slaves, ultimately proclaimed their independence. On the other hand, four slaveholding states bordering the North—Delaware, Maryland, Kentucky, and Missouri—equivocated about secession. Lincoln understood that sustaining the loyalty of the border states was critical. Besides making it more difficult for the Confederates to carry the war into the North, their presence gave the Union, with 23 million people, a decisive population edge, a major asset should a prolonged military struggle ensue.

Set in this frame, Robert E. Lee's gloom reflected more than a personal dilemma about conflicting loyalties; it also related to a realistic appraisal of what were overwhelming northern advantages going into the war. The value of northern property was twice that of the South; the banking capital advantage was 10 to 1, and it was 8 to 1 in investment capital. The North could easily underwrite the production of war goods, whereas the South would have to struggle, given its scarce capital resources and an industrial capacity far below that of the North. In 1861 there were just 18,000 Confederate manufacturing establishments employing 110,000 workers. By comparison, the North had 110,000 establishments utilizing the labor of 1.3 million workers.

By other crucial resource measures, such as railroad mileage, representing the capacity to move armies and supplies easily, the Union was far ahead of the Confederacy. The North had 22,000 miles of track, as compared to 9000 for the South. In 1860 U.S. manufacturers produced 470 locomotives, only 17 of which were built in the South. That same year the North produced 20 times as much pig iron, 17 times the clothing, and 32 times as many firearms. Indeed, Northern factories manufactured nearly 97 percent of all firearms, a major reason that the Confederacy could not absorb all those enthusiasts who wanted to

Despite the South's valiant efforts to produce war goods, the advantage of material resources in the North took its toll. This photograph shows the equipment used by General Grant during his Southern campaigns.

enlist in the spring of 1861. The South went to war with a serious weapons shortage.

What is remarkable is that the South, despite this imbalance, performed so well in the early going and that the North fared so poorly. Among the South's assets, at least in 1861, was sheer geographic size. As long as the Confederacy maintained a defensive military posture, the North would have to demonstrate an ability to win more than an occasional battle. It would have to conquer a massive region. This factor alone emboldened Southern leaders. In analogies alluding to the American Revolution, they discussed how the British, with superior resources, had failed to reconquer the colonies. If Southerners maintained their resolve, something more likely to happen when soldiers were defending homes and families, nothing, it appeared, could extinguish their desire for national independence.

In addition, the South held an initial advantage in generalship. When secession occurred, regular army officers, some of them trained at West Point, had to decide which side to serve. Most, like Robert E. Lee, stood with their states. There were about 300 available West Pointers, and some 120 joined the Confederate army. Of those senior in age, the South

treated after two inconclusive fights north of the Chickahominy. What ensued was the Battle of the Seven Days (June 25–July 1) in which combined casualties reached 30,000, two-thirds sustained by the Confederates. Still, Lee's offensive punches prevailed—and saved Richmond. McClellan soon boarded his troops on waiting transport ships and returned to Washington.

The aggressive Lee, meanwhile, sensed other opportunities. In defending Richmond the rebels had abandoned their advanced post at Manassas Junction. A Union force numbering 45,000 under General John Pope moved into position there. Having just come in from the western theater, Pope was as blind to danger as McClellan was cautious. He thought the enemy a trifle and kept exhorting his officers to "study the probable lines of retreat of our opponents." What Pope did not factor in was the audacity of Lee, who, once sure of McClellan's decision to retreat, wheeled about and rushed northward straight toward Pope.

Lee broke all the rules by dividing his force and sending Jackson's corps in a wide, looping arc around Pope. On August 29, Jackson began a battle known as Second Bull Run (Second Manassas). When Pope turned to face Jackson, Lee hit him from the other side. The battle raged for another day and ended with Union troops again fleeing for Washington. Combined casualties were 19,000 (10,000 for the North).

Even with another monstrous body count, the Army of the Potomac had gained nothing in over a year's campaigning. A tired, frustrated Lincoln said: "We might as well stop fighting." The president knew he had to get the war off dead center, and he was already devising plans to do so, which included an emancipation proclamation. Lee gave Lincoln the opportunity to announce that document when he led his victorious army into Maryland in early September, moving toward Antietam and yet another rendezvous with McClellan.

Federal Breakthrough in the West

The two Union western commanders, Henry W. Halleck and Don Carlos Buell, also suffered from "the slows." Neither responded to Lincoln's pleas for action. Halleck, however, was not afraid to let his subordinates take chances. Brigadier General Ulysses S. Grant had a good idea about how to break through 50,000 Confederate troops—under the overall command of General Albert Sidney Johnston—spread thinly along a 150-mile line running westward from Bowling Green, Kentucky, to the Mississippi River. The weak points were the two rebel forts, Henry and Donelson, guarding the Tennessee and Cumberland rivers in far northern Tennessee.

ANTIETAM

"We Will Make Our Stand"

As George B. McClellan moved his Army of the Potomac into Maryland during September 1862, in pursuit of Robert E. Lee's Army of Northern Virginia, a Union soldier stumbled upon cigars lying in a field wrapped in a piece of paper. The paper was a copy of Lee's orders regarding his invasion of Maryland. The Confederate general had divided his force to strike at such vulnerable federal posts as Harpers Ferry.

McClellan now had the opportunity to destroy separate components of Lee's army. The methodical Union general did speed up his advance but not at a fast enough pace to take advantage of circumstances.

Learning of McClellan's discovery, Lee issued urgent orders for his units to reassemble at Sharpsburg. Most critical were "Stonewall" Jackson's soldiers, who had easily captured Harpers Ferry and a Union garrison of 12,000 on September 15. Had McClellan attacked Lee on the 16th before Jackson's troops covered the 15 miles from Harpers Ferry to Sharpsburg, he might have crushed his opponent. As usual, McClellan acted slowly, preferring to refine his battle plan for the 17th.

There was nothing wrong with the plan. The idea was to throw the weight of Union troops against Lee's left flank, north of Sharpsburg. Meanwhile, General Ambrose E. Burnside was to create a diversion by crossing the stone bridge over Antietam Creek southeast of town, thereby pinning down rebels that could be shifted to support Lee's left flank.

The Union army, however, never got its punches coordinated. Three assaults on Lee's left, from dawn until late morning, proved futile. Then the battle shifted toward the center, where soldiers fought along a sunken farm road, since known as Bloody Lane. In the early afternoon, Burnside finally got his troops across the bridge. They threatened to crush Lee's right flank before a column of Confederates rushing north from Harpers Ferry cut off their thrust.

Antietam was the bloodiest day of the war. Once again, President Lincoln was furious with McClellan's unaggressive generalship, and he eventually removed him from command. More important, the appearance of a Union victory, based on Lee's retreat back into Virginia, gave Lincoln what he needed, the opportunity to announce his Emancipation Proclamation.

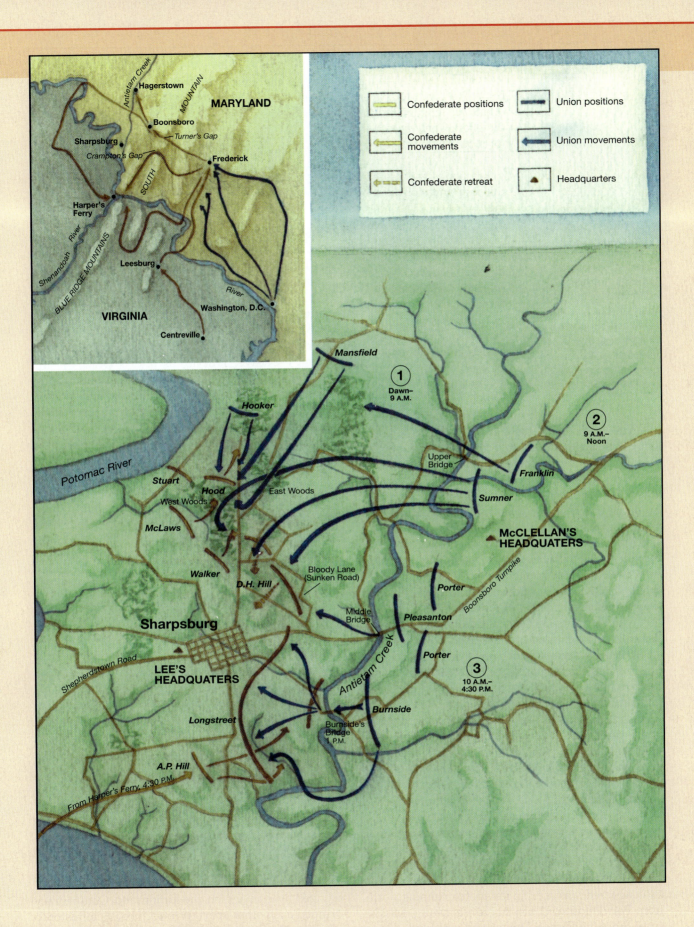

MARYLAND

Antietam Creek
Hagerstown
MOUNTAIN
Boonsboro
— Turner's Gap
Sharpsburg
Crampton's Gap
Frederick
SOUTH
Harper's Ferry
Shenandoah River
BLUE RIDGE MOUNTAINS
Leesburg
River
Washington, D.C.
VIRGINIA
Centreville

Confederate positions	Union positions
Confederate movements	Union movements
Confederate retreat	Headquarters

Mansfield

1 Dawn– 9 A.M.

2 9 A.M.– Noon

Hooker

Upper Bridge

Franklin

Potomac River

Stuart

Hood

East Woods

Sumner

West Woods

McClellan's Headquaters

McLaws

Walker

D.H. Hill

Bloody Lane (Sunken Road)

Porter

Boonsboro Turnpike

Sharpsburg

Middle Bridge

Pleasanton

Porter

3 10 A.M.– 4:30 P.M.

Lee's Headquaters

Antietam Creek

Shepherdstown Road

Longstreet

Burnside

Burnside's Bridge 1 P.M.

A.P. Hill

From Harper's Ferry, 4:30 PM

Ulysses S. Grant was criticized for his command tactics early in the war, but Lincoln remained supportive of him throughout. Grant later became the eighteenth president of the United States.

Grant sensed that a combined land and river offensive might reduce these forts, thereby cutting through the rebel defensive line and opening states such as Tennessee to full-scale invasion. Working with Flag Officer Andrew H. Foote, who commanded the Union gunboats, the Federals captured both forts in February 1862. Grant even earned the nickname "Unconditional Surrender" when he told the Fort Donelson commander to choose between capitulation or annihilation, which netted the Union side 15,000 rebel prisoners.

After puncturing the Confederate line, Grant's army of 40,000 poured into Tennessee, following after Johnston, who retreated all the way to Corinth in northern Mississippi. Cautioned by Halleck "to strike no blow until we are strong enough to admit no doubt of the result," Grant settled his army in at Pittsburgh Landing, 25 miles north of Corinth along the Tennessee River—with advanced lines around a humble log church bearing the name Shiloh. There he waited for reinforcements marching south under Buell. Flushed with confidence, Grant did not bother to order a careful posting of picket guards.

When Johnston received additional troops under Beauregard, he decided to attack. At dawn on April 6, 40,000 rebels overran Grant's outer lines, and for two days the battle raged before the Federals drove off the Confederates. The Battle of Shiloh (Pittsburgh Landing) resulted in 20,000 combined casualties. General Johnston died the first day from a severe leg wound, which cost the South a valued commander. Grant, so recently hailed as a war hero, now faced severe criticism for not having secured his lines. Some even claimed that he was dead drunk when the rebels first struck, undercutting—at least for the moment—thoughts of elevating him to higher command.

With other Union victories along the Mississippi corridor, and with Farragut's capture of New Orleans, the Union western offensive was making headway. The only portion of the Mississippi River yet to be conquered was a 110-mile stretch running north from Port Hudson, Louisiana, to Vicksburg, Mississippi. Since the rebels had powerful artillery batteries trained on the river, Union gunboats could not pass through this strategic zone and complete the dissec-

tion of the Confederacy. General Grant would redeem his reputation in 1863 by conquering Vicksburg after a prolonged siege.

TO AND FROM EMANCIPATION: THE WAR ON THE HOME FRONT

Rarely a man of humor, Jefferson Davis laughed when he read a letter from a young woman demanding that her soldiering boyfriend be sent home to wed her. Even though "I is willin" to marry him, she wrote, the problem was "Jeem's capt'in," who "ain't willin" to let him leave the front. She begged Davis to intervene, promising that "I'll make him go straight back when he's done got married and fight just as hard as ever." Thinking it good for morale, Davis ordered the leave. True to his bride's word, "Jeem," once married, did return to his unit in one of thousands of incidents involving ordinary citizens who were trying to maintain the normal rhythms of life in the midst of a terrible war.

Keeping up morale—and the will to endure at all costs—was a major challenge for both sides, once citizens at home accepted the reality of a long and bloody conflict. How civilian leaders in the North and the South handled these problems had a direct bearing on the outcome of the conflict. Northern leaders, drawing on greater resources, proved more adept at finding solutions designed to keep up morale while breaking the southern will to continue the war.

An Abundance of Confederate Shortages

With their society lacking an industrial base, southern leaders realized the great need to secure material aid from Europe, just as the American colonists had received vital foreign support to sustain their rebellion against Britain. Overconfident secession enthusiasts expected Europe's dependence on cotton to assure them unofficial assistance, if not diplomatic recognition as an independent nation. "Cotton," predicted the *Charleston Mercury*, "would bring England to her knees." It did not. A glut then existed in the European marketplace, and British textile manufacturers after 1861 turned to Egypt, India, and Brazil as sources for new supplies of cotton.

Some British leaders saw advantages to a prolonged war in which the Union and Confederacy ripped each other apart. Wrote Lincoln's minister to Russia, "I saw at a glance where the feeling of England was. They hoped for our ruin! They are jealous of our power. They care neither for the South nor the North." In addition, Britain had long since abandoned slavery, and leaders had moral qualms about publicly recognizing a slave power. Having so little to gain except the possible destruction of the rising—and still much-hated—American nation, the English government chose to remain on the sidelines. Queen Victoria announced her country's neutrality in May 1861.

Despite concerted southern diplomatic efforts, other European nations followed Britain's lead and officially ignored the Confederacy. Some of these countries depended heavily on northern grain crops to help feed their populace. Grain rather than "king cotton" was most vital to their national well-being.

The Confederacy, however, received small amounts of clandestine aid from Europe. In 1862 English shipyards constructed two commerce raiders, the *Florida* and the *Alabama*, before protests from the Lincoln administration ended such activity. By 1865 blockade runners had transported an estimated 600,000 European-produced weapons into southern ports. The Richmond government also obtained about $710 million in foreign loans, secured by promises to deliver cotton; but the tightening Union naval blockade made the exportation of cotton difficult, discouraging further European loans because of the mounting risk of never being paid back.

From the very outset, Union naval superiority was a critical factor in isolating the South. There was a moment of hope in March 1862, when a scuttled U.S. naval vessel, the *Merrimack*, now covered with iron plates, given a huge ram, and renamed the CSS *Virginia*, steamed out into Norfolk Bay and battered a fleet of wooden Union blockade vessels. Losing engine power, the *Virginia* retreated, then returned the next day to discover a new adversary, the USS *Monitor*, also clad in iron and ready to fight. The *Virginia* held its own in the ensuing battle but finally backed away, as if admitting that whatever the South tried, the North could counter it effectively. The Confederacy simply lacked the funds to build a naval fleet of any consequence, a disadvantage that allowed the Union navy to dominate the sea lanes.

The effects of cutting the South off from external support were profound. By the spring of 1862 citizens at home were experiencing many shortages—and getting mad about it. Such common items as salt, sugar, and coffee had all but disappeared, and shoes and clothing were at a premium. In 1863 bread riots broke out in several southern cities, including Richmond, where citizens demanded basic food amid shouts of, "we are starving." Shortages abetted rapid inflation, as did the overprinting of Confederate dollars. The central government put a total of $1.5 billion into circulation to help pay for the war.

Although neither the *Monitor* (foreground) nor the *Merrimack* (*CSS Virginia*) won a decisive victory when they met, they helped introduce a new era in naval warfare by demonstrating the superior capacity of ironclads over wooden vessels.

Between 1861 and 1865 prices spiraled upward on the average of 7000 percent.

Once it was obvious that cotton would not bring significant foreign support, Jefferson Davis tried to turn adversity to advantage by urging citizens to raise less cotton and grow more food. Farm women, thrown into new roles as heads of households with husbands and older sons off at war, did so, but then Richmond-based tax collectors appeared and started seizing portions of these crops—wheat, corn, and peas—to feed the armies. For struggling wives, this was too much. Many wrote their husbands and begged them to come home. Some did, thus aggravating an increasing desertion problem.

Most Southerners, in trying to comprehend so many difficulties, blamed their central government. When the Confederate Congress, for example, enacted a conscription act in April 1862—the first draft law in U.S. history—because of rapidly declining enlistments, a North Carolina soldier wrote: "I would like to know what has been done to the main principle for which we are now fighting—*States' Rights!*—Where is it? . . . When we hear men comparing the despotism of the *Confederacy* with that of the Lincoln government—*something must be wrong.*" The fault lay with power-hungry leaders like Davis, many argued, not with a political philosophy inherently at odds with the need for effective, centralized military planning to defeat the North's war machine.

In the months that followed, accusations of political high-handedness in Richmond could be heard everywhere. The draft law, for example, allowed individuals to purchase substitutes, and with rapid inflation, avoiding service became solely a wealthy man's prerogative. When the central government in October 1862 exempted from the draft all those managing 20 or more slaves, ordinary citizens were furious with their planter leaders. Some

ing on a distinction between legitimate dissent in support of the nation and willful attempts to subvert the Union. Most agree that Lincoln, given the tense wartime climate, showed sensitivity toward basic rights. At the same time he clearly tested the limits of presidential powers.

Some of his political opponents, mostly Peace Democrats who favored negotiating an end to the war and letting the South leave the Union, regularly described Lincoln as a doer of all evil. These **Copperheads,** as their detractors called them, had some support in the Midwest. They rallied around individuals such as Congressman Clement L. Vallandigham of Ohio. In 1863 Union military officials arrested him on nonspecific charges, but Lincoln ordered him set free and banished to the South. Vallandigham then moved to Canada where he conducted a vigorous election campaign to become governor of Ohio, which he decisively lost. Lincoln wisely ignored the matter, hoping that Vallandigham and other Peace Democrats, who most of all liked to bewail the **Emancipation Proclamation,** could not muster enough popular support to undermine the Union cause.

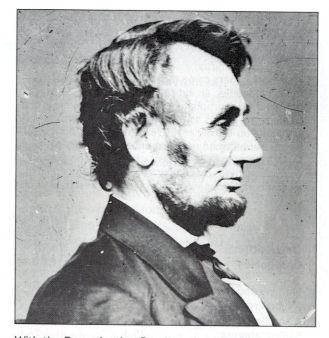

With the Emancipation Proclamation, Abraham Lincoln provided a new rationale for the war beyond the original goal of preserving the Union.

Issuing the Emancipation Proclamation

Abraham Lincoln believed fervently in the ideals of the Declaration of Independence, which gave Americans "the right to rise" out of poverty, as he described his own experience, and "get through the world respectably." He also admired the Declaration's emphasis on human liberty, which made chattel slavery inconsistent with the ideals of the Revolution. Slavery, he wrote as early as 1837, was "founded both on injustice and bad policy."

After becoming president, Lincoln promised not to interfere with slavery in established southern states. When warfare began, he seemed to move with indecisive steps toward emancipation. His only war aim, he claimed well into the spring of 1862, was to save the Union. When in August 1861 General John C. Frémont, then heading federal military operations in Missouri, declared an end to slavery in that state, the president not only rescinded the proclamation but severely rebuked Frémont by removing him from command in Missouri.

For a person who despised slavery, Lincoln held back in resolving the emancipation question for many reasons. First, he did not want to drive slaveholding border states such as Missouri into the Confederacy. Second, he worried about pervasive racism; white Northerners had willingly taken up arms to save the Union, but he wondered whether they would keep fighting to liberate the slave population. Third, if he moved too fast, he reasoned, he

might lose everything, including the Union itself, should northern peace advocates seize upon popular fears of emancipation and create an overwhelming demand to stop the fighting in favor of southern independence. Fourth, he had personal doubts as to whether black Americans and white Americans could ever live together in freedom.

For all these reasons Lincoln moved cautiously, allowing people and events to decide the issue. He did not seek close identity with radical Republicans in Congress, led by Charles Sumner and Benjamin Wade in the Senate and Thaddeus Stevens in the House, men who built a strong coalition in favor of ending slavery. When these same radicals scoffed at his proposals for compensated emancipation at $500 a head, or for colonization in Central America or Liberia, he stated, "I can only go just as fast as I can see how to go." Lincoln did support a series of radical-sponsored bills adopted by Congress in the spring and early summer of 1862. One act abolished slaveholding in the nation's capital and western territories; and a second bill, the Confiscation Act, freed all slaves belonging to rebel masters fighting against the Union.

By the summer of 1862, Lincoln had finally made up his mind. The war's death toll, he now reasoned, had become too great; all the maiming and killing had to have some larger purpose, transcending the primary objective of preserving the Union. For Lincoln, the military contest had become a test to see whether the republic, at long last, had the capacity to live up to the ideals of the American Revolution. This could be determined only by announcing the Emancipation Proclamation.

Lincoln knew he was gambling with northern morale at a time when Union victories were all but nonexistent, when enlistments were in decline, and when war weariness had set in. He was aware that racists, such as the person who wrote and called him a "god-damned black nigger," would spread their poison far and wide. So the president waited for the right moment, such as after an important battlefield triumph, to quiet his critics, who would surely say that emancipation was a desperate measure designed to cover up presidential mismanagement of the war.

As a shrewd politician, Lincoln began to prepare Northerners for what was coming. He explained to readers of Horace Greeley's *New York Tribune* in late August: "If I could save the Union without freeing *any* slave, I would do it; and if I could save it by freeing *all* the slaves, I would do it; and if I could save it by freeing some and leaving others alone, I would also do that." Sidestepping any pronouncement of high ideals in public, the president would treat his assault on slavery as a war measure designed to ensure total military victory.

On September 22, 1862, five days after the Battle of Antietam, Lincoln announced his preliminary Emancipation Proclamation, which called on Southerners to lay down their arms and return to the Union by year's end or to accept the abolition of slavery. Getting no formal response, on January 1, 1863, he declared all slaves in the Confederacy "forever free." The final document called emancipation "an act of justice, warranted by the Constitution upon military necessity." Out of necessity, too, slavery could continue to exist in the four Union border states—to ensure a united front against the rebels.

In private, Lincoln referred to the horrible carnage at Antietam as "an indication of Divine will" that had forever "decided the question" of emancipation "in favor of the slaves." He did not see how slavery, even in the loyal border states, could long outlast the war, and he happily envisioned a republic now moving forward toward the realization of its ideals.

Lincoln did something else in the wake of Antietam. He fired George McClellan for not using his superior troop strength to destroy Lee's army when the opportunity had so clearly presented itself. In trying to save soldiers' lives, Lincoln reasoned, McClellan's timidity would actually cost thousands more in the days ahead. So the president kept searching for a commander with the capacity to bring down the Confederacy in a war now dedicated to abolishing slavery as a means to preserve the Union.

Emancipation Tests Northern Resolve

Reaction to the preliminary proclamation varied widely. With Democrats in Congress calling for Lincoln's impeachment, some cabinet members urged the president to reconsider. They also feared repercussions in the upcoming November elections. The Republicans did lose seats, but they still controlled Congress, despite the efforts of many Democrats to smear "Black Republican" candidates. Certainly, too, frustration with so many battlefield reverses, as much as news of the proclamation, hurt the Republicans at the polls.

Others, however, criticized Lincoln for not going far enough. Abolitionists chided him for offering only half a loaf, and female activists like Susan B. Anthony and Elizabeth Cady Stanton formed the Woman's Loyal National League, dedicated to the eradication of slavery in all the states. Foreign opinion generally applauded Lincoln, although a few commentators made caustic remarks about a curious new "principle" that no American would henceforth be allowed to own slaves "unless he is loyal to the United States."

In the Confederacy, the planter elite played on traditional racist attitudes and used the proclamation to rally citizens wavering in their resolve. Here was proof, shouted planter leaders, that every indignity the South had suffered was part of a never-ending abolitionist plot to stir up slave rebellions and "convert the quiet, ignorant black son of toil into a savage incendiary and brutal murderer."

Back in the North, African Americans were jubilant. Wrote Frederick Douglass, "We shout for joy that we live to record this righteous decree." Standing outside the White House on New Year's Day, 1863, a group of African Americans sang praises to the president, shouting that "they would hug him to death" if he would "come out of that palace" and greet them. For African Americans the Civil War meant liberation at last.

Up until this point, black Americans had found the war frustrating. Federal officials had blocked their attempts to enlist. Not wanting to stir up racial violence, Lincoln had danced around the issue. Most early African American enlistments were in the navy. Finally, in 1862, Secretary of War Edwin M. Stanton, with the president's backing, called for the enlistment of African Americans—North and South—in land forces. In a model program, Colonel Thomas Wentworth Higginson, one of the financial sponsors of radical abolitionist John Brown, worked with former slaves in the Sea Island region of South Carolina, an area under Union control, to mold them into a well-trained regiment (the 1st South Carolina Volunteers). They fought effectively in the coastal region running south to Florida.

THE PEOPLE SPEAK

Frederick Douglass Calls upon African Americans to Take up Arms Against the Confederacy (1863)

Escaping to the North in 1838, former slave Frederick Douglass gained widespread fame as a leading black abolitionist. For years he spoke out passionately against the institution of chattel slavery, and he rejoiced at the news of Lincoln's Emancipation Proclamation. Douglass then took an activist's role in encouraging African Americans to join Union military forces. He became an unofficial recruiter for Robert Gould Shaw's Massachusetts 54th Infantry, the first black regiment organized in the North, in which two of his own sons served. In his recruiting appeal that follows, Douglass offered many reasons why African Americans should enlist and fight in a war now being waged, he hoped, as much to end slavery as to save the Union:

> When the first rebel cannon shattered the walls of [Fort] Sumter and drove away its starving garrison, I predicted that the war then and there inaugurated would not be fought out entirely by white men. Every month's experience during these dreary years has confirmed that opinion. A war undertaken and brazenly carried on for the perpetual enslavement of colored men, calls logically and loudly for colored men to help suppress it. Only a moderate share of sagacity was needed to see that the arm of the slave was the best defense against the arm of the slaveholder. Hence with every reverse to the national arms, with every exulting shout of victory raised by the slaveholding rebels, I have implored the imperiled nation to unchain against her foes, her powerful black hand. Slowly and reluctantly that appeal is beginning to be heeded. Stop not now to complain that it was not heeded sooner. It may or may not have been best that it should not. This is not the time to discuss that question. Leave it to the future. When the war is over, the country is saved, peace is established, and the black man's rights are secured, as they will be, history with an impartial hand will dispose of that and sundry other questions. Action! Action! not criticism, is the plain duty of this hour. Words are now useful only as they stimulate to blows. The office of speech now is only to point out when, where, and how to strike to the best advantage. There is no time to delay. The tide is at its flood that leads on to fortune. From East to West, from North to South, the sky is written all over, "Now or never."
>
> Liberty won by white men would lose half its luster. "Who would be free themselves must strike the blow." "Better even die free, than to live slaves." This is the sentiment of every brave colored man amongst us. There are weak and cowardly men in all nations. We have them amongst us. They tell you this is the "white man's war"; that you will be "no better off after than before the war"; that the getting of you into the army is to "sacrifice you on the first opportunity." Believe them not; cowards themselves, they do not wish to have their cowardice shamed by your brave example. Leave them to their timidity, or to whatever motive may hold them back. I have not thought lightly of the words I am now addressing you. The counsel I give comes of close observation of the great struggle now in progress, and of the deep conviction that this is your hour and mine. In good earnest then, and after the best deliberation, I now for the first time during this war feel at liberty to call and counsel you to arms. By every consideration which binds you to your enslaved fellow-countrymen, and the peace and welfare of your country; by every aspiration which you cherish for the freedom and equality of yourselves and your children; by all the ties of blood and identity which make us one with the brave black men now fighting our battles in Louisiana and in South Carolina, I urge you to fly to arms, and smite with death the power that would bury the government and your liberty in the same hopeless grave. . . .

Source: Douglass's Monthly, March 1863, Rochester, New York.

The success of Higginson's troops broke down some racial stereotypes by demonstrating that African Americans could master the art of war. No regiment proved that more dramatically than the 54th Massachusetts Infantry. Like all other black regiments, the 54th trained separately from white units and received its commands from white officers. This regiment prepared itself for combat during the spring of 1863 under 25-year-old Robert Gould Shaw, the scion of a wealthy Boston antislavery family. Then the unit shipped out to the front lines in coastal South Carolina.

On July 18, 1863, the 54th Massachusetts Infantry led an early evening assault against an army more than twice its numbers that was defending Fort Wagner, a major bastion protecting Charleston harbor for the Confederacy. Eventually repulsed after fierce fighting, the 54th experienced more than a 40 percent casualty rate that evening. Shaw, who had complete confidence in his troops, was shot dead in the charge. After the battle the rebel defenders tried to mock Shaw, even in death as a Confederate stated, by burying him in a common grave "with his niggers!" Their attempted insult failed. Shaw became a mar-

Despite an excellent record in combat, black soldiers often found themselves the victims of discrimination. Black regiments were kept separate from white units and were commanded by white officers.

tyred war hero in the North, and his surviving troops, wrote one of them, swore "Revenge for our galant Curnel." The 54th still expected "to Plant the Stars and Stripes on the Sity of Charleston" or die in the effort, this soldier declared with conviction.

Before the war ended, 179,000 African Americans had served in the Union army (10 percent of total land forces), and another 29,000 in the navy (25 percent of total naval forces). About 135,000 were former slaves, delighted to be free at last of their masters. Some 44,000 died fighting to save the Union and to defend the prize of freedom for black Americans. Twenty-four received the Congressional Medal of Honor for extraordinary bravery in battle. Among them was Sergeant William H. Carney of the 54th Massachusetts, whose citation praised him for grabbing the regimental flag after its bearer was shot down and leading the troops forward into the outer works of Fort Wagner. Carney, a runaway slave from Virginia, then planted the flag and engaged in hand-to-hand combat. Severely wounded, he reluctantly retreated with

flag in hand, not suspecting that he would become the first African American Medal of Honor recipient in the Civil War—and in American history.

Because of the Emancipation Proclamation, African Americans could "march through . . . fine thoroughfares," explained one black observer, as "Negro soldiers!—with banners flying." Still, as they marched, they received lower pay until protests ended such discrimination in 1864; and they quite often drew menial work assignments, such as digging latrines and burying the dead after battle. Emancipation, African Americans soon realized, was just the beginning of a monumental struggle that lay ahead—beyond the Civil War—to overcome the prejudice and hatred that had locked them in slavery for over two centuries.

BREAKING CONFEDERATE RESISTANCE, 1863–1865

During the spring of 1863, Union war sentiment sagged to a low point. Generals kept demanding

Although outnumbered nearly two to one, the Confederates soundly defeated the northern army under the command of General Joseph Hooker at the Battle of Chancellorsville in May, 1863. The four days of fighting cost each side thousands of casualties. A major loss for the Southerners was General Thomas A. "Stonewall" Jackson, who was accidentally wounded by his own troops and died of pneumonia a few days later.

Pickett's Charge at Gettysburg

FOR two days the death toll mounted, but nothing conclusive had yet happened in the Battle of Gettysburg. Late on the evening of July 2, 1863, General Robert E. Lee made the momentous decision. The next afternoon, on the third day of fighting, 13,000 troops under the command of Major General George E. Pickett would attack the center of the Union line, which stretched for 3 miles south of Gettysburg along Cemetery Ridge, a mile to the east of Lee's 5-mile line along Seminary Ridge. His soldiers, Lee believed with pride, could do anything. The question was whether, in the face of concentrated enemy fire, they could drive off their adversaries and achieve a victory so crushing that it would result in independence for the South.

Late on the morning of July 3, Pickett's officers and men started to assemble under the cover of woods along Seminary Ridge. The fear of death lurked among them, but they spoke of courage and the need "to force manhood to the front." In numerous engagements they had seen their comrades die in ghastly ways from metal hurled by Yankee weapons. They suppressed thoughts of death as best they could and prayed for God's help in girding themselves up for battle.

Like their commanders, these "Johnny Rebs" were battle-hardened veterans who knew what to expect as they marched across the open fields toward Cemetery Ridge. At first, solid shot from enemy artillery, fired mostly from cannons called Napoleons, would fly at them from up to a mile away. As they moved closer, within 400 yards or so, enemy cannons would unleash canisters, or large tin cans filled with lethal cast-iron pellets. Once in flight, the cans fell away, and the pellets ripped human beings to shreds. Within 200 yards, if not before, "Billy Yanks" would start firing their rifled muskets, the basic infantry weapon of the Civil War. With grooves inside the barrel, the rifled musket shot the minié ball, really an elongated bullet, up to 400 yards or more with accuracy. For Civil War soldiers, all of these weapons made the offensive charge a deadly proposition.

To reduce enemy firepower, Lee ordered a heavy cannonade to weaken the Union center. He hoped to knock out enemy artillery units and cause mayhem among the massed infantry on Cemetery Ridge. The bombardment began at 1:00 P.M. and lasted for over one and a half hours. Federal cannons quickly responded in what proved to be the greatest artillery barrage of the Civil War. One officer compared the noise to "that from the falls of Niagara." Another stated "that the earth shook as if in fright." When Southern officers spotted Union cannoneers pulling their artillery pieces back to greater cover, they concluded that much damage had been done. They were wrong. Sensing that so great a cannonade would be followed by an infantry attack, Brigadier General Henry J. Hunt, artillery chief for the Army of the Potomac, had ordered his units to regroup and reload with canister shot.

As the battlefield fell silent, another drama played itself out. Lieutenant General James Longstreet, Lee's valuable deputy, was adamantly opposed to the assault, believing it would only produce a senseless slaughter. Still, as Pickett's corps commander, his responsibility was to order the charge. A little after 2:30 P.M., Pickett rode up to Longstreet and said: "General, shall we advance?" Longstreet looked away and made no reply. The handsomely dressed Pickett, described by one officer as a "desperate-looking character" with long, flowing locks of hair, saluted and stated grandly: "I am going to lead my division forward, sir."

Soon Pickett was riding among the assembled regiments and shouting: "Up men and to your posts! Don't forget today that you are from old Virginia." The afternoon was excruciatingly hot, and the soldiers had been lying down to protect themselves from the Union cannonade. Now with officers urging them into line, the men were soon ready to leave the woods and press forward with red battle flags unfurled before them. Even before the advance, a few soldiers fell to the ground, suffering from "seeming sunstroke," but more likely from fear. As for the rest, wrote a rebel lieutenant, they formed a "beautiful line of battle."

From the Union vantage point on Cemetery Ridge, officers and soldiers whispered back and forth that "the enemy is advancing." The waiting Yankees "grew pale" as they crouched behind stone fences and hastily constructed earthworks. Pickett's front stretched for half a mile, and the rebels moved forward in three battle lines, "man touching man, rank pressing rank, and line supporting line." At first, Union artillery fire was sporadic, cutting only occasional holes in Pickett's proud lines. When soldiers fell, torn to bits

by cannon balls, those beside them closed ranks, as if nothing had happened.

While the Confederates advanced, Union infantry troops held their fire, reported Major General Winfield S. Hancock, whose corps took the brunt of Pickett's Charge. Then when Pickett's front line closed to about 300 yards, Union officers gave the command to fire. Hunt's artillery belched forth with canister shot, and a hailstorm of minié balls flew through the air. Rebel officers suddenly realized how little damage Lee's cannon barrage had done. They had been deceived by Hunt's decision to pull back his cannons. There was no serious weakness in the Union line.

Still the Confederates came on, now at double-quick step, determined to break through or to die honorably in the attempt. Rebel soldiers leveled their muskets, yet few got off shots before being struck down. Only 5000 men reached the stone wall, where they temporarily breached the Union line. Those who made it were shot, stabbed by bayonets, captured, or driven back in hand-to-hand combat. In little more than 20 minutes Pickett's Charge was all over. Wrote General Hancock afterward, the Confederates

"were repulsed . . . and sought safety in flight or by throwing themselves on the ground to escape our fire. Their battle flags were ours and the victory was won."

Retreating as best they could, fewer than half of the rebels got back to Seminary Ridge. Pickett, a survivor among the officers, rode up to Lee in tears and shouted that his division had been massacred. Lee replied softly: "Never mind, general; all this has been *my* fault. It is *I* who have lost this fight, and you must help me out of it in the best way you can." Then Lee rode among the broken soldiers, soothing them by saying over and over again: "All this will come right in the end. . . . All good men must rally."

Gettysburg was the high mark of human carnage during the Civil War. Combined Union and Confederate losses of 50,000 or more after three days of battle were greater than total British and American casualties in eight years of fighting during the War for American Independence. The huge increase in human carnage reflected many changes in the conduct of war over the previous 80 years. Armies had grown dramatically in size, and significant technological improvements in weaponry, as repre-

sented in the expanded range and accuracy of the rifled musket over its smoothbore predecessor, turned Civil War battlefields into deadly killing zones.

Soldiers of Robert E. Lee's generation had been trained in the advantages of offensive tactical maneuvers. The massed charge of infantry troops during the Mexican War of 1846–1848, in which Lee and many other high-ranking Civil War officers fought, had worked in storming positions without great loss of life. This was before the United States had fully adopted the rifled musket, which occurred during the 1850s.

After Gettysburg, Lee never attempted another massed charge of soldiers. His army fought primarily on the defensive until its surrender in April 1865. And as Union troops buried slain rebels after Lee's retreat on July 4, they spoke of how the Confederates had "advanced magnificently, unshaken by shot and shell" into the jaws of death. Certainly, too, more than one Yankee reflected on the irony of the words painted on a sign hanging from a tree on Cemetery Hill: "All persons found using firearms in these grounds will be prosecuted with the utmost rigor of the law."

433

THE MAN WITH THE (CARPET) BAGS.

The bag in front of him, filled with others' faults, he always sees. The one behind him, filled with his own faults, he never sees.

16

THE NATION RECONSTRUCTED: NORTH, SOUTH, AND THE WEST, 1865–1877

445

Day of Jubilo: Slaves Confront Emancipation

ROOTED in Africa, the oral tradition became one of the tools slaves used to maintain a sense of self-worth. Each generation heard the same stories, and story-telling did not die with slavery. The day that slaves first learned of their emancipation remained vivid in their own minds and later in those of their descendants. The great-grandchildren of a strong-willed woman named Caddy relished the family account of her first taste of freedom:

> Caddy threw down that hoe, she marched herself up to the big house, then she looked around and found the mistress. She went over to the mistress, she flipped up her dress and told the white woman to do some thing. She said it mean and ugly. This is what she said: *Kiss my ass!*

Caddy's reaction was not typical. There was no typical response. Reminiscences of what was called the "Day of Jubilo" formed a tapestry as varied as the range of personality. Some, however, seem to have occurred more frequently than others. Many former slaves echoed one man's description of his and his mother's action when their master announced their emancipation: "Jes like tarpins or turtles after 'mancipation. Jes stick our heads out to see how the land lays."

Caution was a shrewd and realistic response. One of the survival lessons in slavery had been not to trust whites too much. This had been reinforced during the war when Union troops moved through regions proclaiming emancipation only to de-part, leaving blacks at the mercy of local whites. One elderly slave described the aftermath to a Union correspondent. "Why, the day after you left, they jist had us all out in a row and told us they was going to shoot us, and they did hang two of us; and Mr. Pierce, the overseer, knocked one with a fence rail and he died the next day. Oh, Master! we seen stars in de day time."

Environment played a role in slaves' reactions to the Day of Jubilo. Urban slaves frequently enjoyed more freedom than plantation slaves. Even before emancipation such black social institutions as schools and churches emerged in many cities. When those cities were liberated, organized celebrations occurred quickly. In Charleston 4000 black men and women paraded before some 10,000 spectators. Two black women sat in one mule-drawn cart while a mock auctioneer shouted, "How much am I offered?" In the next cart a black-draped coffin was inscribed with the words "Slavery is Dead." Four days after the fall of Richmond blacks there held a mass rally of some 1500 people in the First African Church.

Knowledge of their freedom came in many forms to the slaves. Rural slaves were less likely to enjoy the benefits of freedom as early as urban slaves. Many heard of the Emancipation Proclamation through the slave grapevine or from Union soldiers long before its words became reality for them. Masters sometimes took advantage of the isolation of their plantations to keep their slaves in ignorance or to make freedom seem vague and frightening. Their ploys usually failed, but learned patterns of deference made some former slaves unwilling to challenge their former masters. Months after emancipation one North Carolina slave continued to work without compensation, explaining to a northern correspondent, "No, sir; my mistress never said anything to me that I was to have wages, nor yet that I was free; nor I never said anything to her. Ye see I left it to her honor to talk to me about it, because I was afraid she'd say I was insultin' to her and presumin', so I wouldn't speak first. She ha'n't spoke yet." There were, however, limits to his patience; he intended to ask her for wages at Christmas.

Numerous blacks described the exuberance they felt. One elderly Virginia man went to the barn, jumped from one stack of straw to another, and "screamed and screamed!" A Texan remembered, "We all felt like horses" and "everybody went wild." Other blacks recalled how slave songs and spirituals were updated, and "purty soon ev'ybody fo' miles around was singin' freedom songs."

Quite a few slaves learned of freedom when a Union officer or Freedmen's Bureau agent read them the Emancipation Proclamation—often over the objections of the master. "Dat one time," Sarah Ford declared, "Massa Charley can't open he mouth, 'cause de captain tell him to shut up, dat he'd do the talkin'." Some masters, however, still sought to have the last word. A Louisiana planter's wife announced immediately after the Union officer departed, "Ten years from today I'll have you all back 'gain."

Fear did not leave all slaves as soon as their bondage was lifted. Jenny Proctor of Alabama recalled that her fellow slaves were stunned by the news. "We didn' hardly know what he means. We jes' sort of huddle 'round together like scared rabbits, but after we knowed what he mean, didn' many of us go, 'cause we didn' know where to of went." James Lucas, a former slave of Jefferson Davis, explained, "folks dat ain' never been free don' rightly know de *feel* of bein' free. Dey don' know de meanin' of it."

Former slaves quickly learned that one could not eat or wear freedom. "Dis livin' on liberty," one declared, "is lak young folks livin' on love after they gits married. It just don't work." They searched for the real meaning of liberty in numerous ways. Some followed the advice of a black Florida preacher, "You ain't none 'o you, gwinter feel rale free till you shakes de dus ob de Ole Plantashun offen you feet," and moved. Others declared their independence by legalizing their marriages and taking new names or publicly using surnames they had secretly adopted while in slavery. "We had a real sho' nuff weddin' wid a preacher," one recalled. "Dat cost a dollar." When encouraged to take his old master's surname, a black man declared, "Him's nothing to me now. I don't belong to he no longer, an' I don't see no use in being called for him." Education was the key for others. "If I nebber does do nothing more while I live," a Mississippi freedman vowed, "I shall give my children a chance to go to school, for I considers education next best ting to liberty."

Most came to a good understanding of the benefits and limits of their new status. One explained, "Why, sar, all I made before was Miss Pinckney's, but all I make now is my own." Another noted, "You could change places and work for different men." One newly freed slave wrote his brother, "I's mighty well pleased tu git my eatin' by de 'sweat o' my face, an all I ax o' ole masser's tu jes' keep he hands off o' de Lawd Almighty's property, fur *dat's me*." A new sense of dignity was cherished by many. An elderly South Carolina freedman rejoiced, "Don't hab me feelins hurt now. Used to hab me feelins hurt all de times. But don't hab em hurt now, no more." Charlie Barbour exulted over one thing: "I won't wake up some mornin' fer fin' dat my mammy or some ob de rest of my family am done sold." Most agreed with Margrett Millin's answer when she was asked decades later whether she had liked slavery or freedom better. "Well, it's dis way. In slavery I owns nothin'. In freedom I's own de home and raise de family. All dat cause me worryment and in slavery I has no worryment, but I takes de freedom."

Appendix

The Declaration of Independence

In Congress, July 4, 1776

The Unanimous Declaration of the Thirteen United States of America

When, in the course of human events, it becomes necessary for one people to dissolve the political bonds which have connected them with another, and to assume, among the powers of the earth, the separate and equal station to which the laws of nature and of nature's God entitle them, a decent respect to the opinions of mankind requires that they should declare the causes which impel them to the separation.

We hold these truths to be self-evident: That all men are created equal; that they are endowed by their Creator with certain unalienable rights; that among these are life, liberty, and the pursuit of happiness; that, to secure these rights, governments are instituted among men, deriving their just powers from the consent of the governed; that whenever any form of government becomes destructive of these ends, it is the right of the people to alter or to abolish it, and to institute new government, laying its foundation on such principles, and organizing its powers in such form, as to them shall seem most likely to effect their safety and happiness. Prudence, indeed, will dictate that governments long established should not be changed for light and transient causes; and accordingly all experience hath shown that mankind are more disposed to suffer, while evils are sufferable, than to right themselves by abolishing the forms to which they are accustomed. But when a long train of abuses and usurpations, pursuing invariably the same object, evinces a design to reduce them under absolute despotism, it is their right, it is their duty, to throw off such government, and to provide new guards for their future security. Such has been the patient sufferance of these colonies; and such is now the necessity which constrains them to alter their former systems of government. The history of the present King of Great Britain is a history of repeated injuries and usurpations, all having in direct object the establishment of an absolute tyranny over these states. To prove this, let facts be submitted to a candid world.

He has refused his assent to laws, the most wholesome and necessary for the public good.

He has forbidden his governors to pass laws of immediate and pressing importance, unless suspended in their operation till his assent should be obtained; and, when so suspended, he has utterly neglected to attend to them.

He has refused to pass other laws for the accommodation of large districts of people, unless those people would relinquish the right of representation in the legislature, a right inestimable to them, and formidable to tyrants only.

He has called together legislative bodies at places unusual, uncomfortable, and distant from the depository of their public records, for the sole purpose of fatiguing them into compliance with his measures.

He has dissolved representative houses repeatedly, for opposing, with manly firmness, his invasions on the rights of the people.

He has refused for a long time, after such dissolutions, to cause others to be elected; whereby the legislative powers, incapable of annihilation, have returned to the people at large for their exercise; the state remaining, in the mean time, exposed to all the dangers of invasions from without and convulsions within.

He has endeavored to prevent the population of these states; for that purpose obstructing the laws for naturalization of foreigners; refusing to pass others to encourage their migration hither, and raising the conditions of new appropriations of lands.

He has obstructed the administration of justice, by refusing his assent to laws for establishing judiciary powers.

He has made judges dependent on his will alone, for the tenure of their offices, and the amount and payment of their salaries.

He has erected a multitude of new offices, and sent hither swarms of officers to harass our people and eat out their substance.

He has kept among us, in times of peace, standing armies, without the consent of our legislatures.

He has affected to render the military independent of, and superior to, the civil power.

He has combined with others to subject us to a jurisdiction foreign to our constitution, and unacknowledged by our laws, giving his assent to their acts of pretended legislation:

For quartering large bodies of armed troops among us;

For protecting them, by a mock trial, from punishment for any murder which they should commit on the inhabitants of these states;

For cutting off our trade with all parts of the world;

For imposing taxes on us without our consent;

For depriving us, in many cases, of the benefits of trial by jury;

For transporting us beyond seas, to be tried for pretended offenses;

For abolishing the free system of English laws in a neighboring province, establishing therein an arbitrary government, and enlarging its boundaries, so as to render it at once an example and fit instrument for introducing the same absolute rule into these colonies;

For taking away our charters abolishing our most valuable laws, and altering fundamentally the forms of our governments;

For suspending our own legislatures, and declaring themselves invested with power to legislate for us in all cases whatsoever.

He has abdicated government here, by declaring us out of his protection and waging war against us.

He has plundered our seas, ravaged our coasts, burned our towns, and destroyed the lives of our people.

He is at this time transporting large armies of foreign mercenaries to complete the works of death, desolation, and tyranny already begun with circumstances of cruelty and perfidy scarcely paralleled in the most barbarous ages, and totally unworthy the head of a civilized nation.

He has constrained our fellow-citizens, taken captive on the high seas, to bear arms against their country, to become the executioners of their friends and brethren, or to fall themselves by their hands.

He has excited domestic insurrection among us, and has endeavored to bring on the inhabitants of our frontiers the merciless Indian savages, whose known rule of warfare is an undistinguished destruction of all ages, sexes, and conditions.

In every stage of these oppressions we have petitioned for redress in the most humble terms; our repeated petitions have been answered only by repeated injury. A prince, whose character is thus marked by every act which may define a tyrant, is unfit to be the ruler of a free people.

Nor have we been wanting in our attentions to our British brethren. We have warned them, from time to time, of attempts by their legislature to extend an unwarrantable jurisdiction over us. We have reminded them of the circumstances of our emigration and settlement here. We have appealed to their native justice and magnanimity; and we have conjured them, by the ties of our common kindred, to disavow these usurpations, which would inevitably interrupt our connections and correspondence. They, too, have been deaf to the voice of justice and of consanguinity. We must, therefore, acquiesce in the necessity which denounces our separation, and hold them, as we hold the rest of mankind, enemies in war, in peace friends.

We, therefore, the representatives of the United States of America, in General Congress assembled, appealing to the Supreme Judge of the world for the rectitude of our intentions, do, in the name and by the authority of the good people of these colonies, solemnly publish and declare, that these United Colonies are, and of right ought to be, FREE AND INDEPENDENT STATES; that they are absolved from all allegiance to the British crown, and that all political connection between them and the state of Great Britain is, and ought to be, totally dissolved; and that, as free and independent states, they have full power to levy war, conclude peace, contract alliances, establish commerce, and do all other acts and things which independent states may of right do. And for the support of this declaration, with a firm reliance on the protection of Divine Providence, we mutually pledge to each other our lives, our fortunes, and our sacred honor.

JOHN HANCOCK

BUTTON GWENNETT	THS. NELSON, JR.	RICHD. STOCKTON
LYMAN HALL	FRANCIS LIGHTFOOT LEE	JNO. WITHERSPOON
GEO. WALTON	CARTER BRAXTON	FRAS. HOPKINSON
WM. HOOPER	ROBT. MORRIS	JOHN HART
JOSEPH HEWES	BENJAMIN RUSH	ABRA. CLARK
JOHN PENN	BENJA. FRANKLIN	JOSIAH BARTLETT
EDWARD RUTLEDGE	JOHN MORTON	WM. WHIPPLE
THOS. HEYWARD, JUNR.	GEO. CLYMER	SAML. ADAMS
THOMAS LYNCH, JUNR.	JAS. SMITH	JOHN ADAMS
ARTHUR MIDDLETON	GEO. TAYLOR	ROBT. TREAT PAINE
SAMUEL CHASE	JAMES WILSON	ELBRIDGE GERRY
WM. PACA	GEO. ROSS	STEP. HOPKINS
THOS. STONE	CAESAR RODNEY	WILLIAM ELLERY
CHARLES CARROLL OF CARROLLTON	GEO. READ	ROGER SHERMAN
GEORGE WYTHE	THO. M'KEAN	SAM'EL. HUNTINGTON
RICHARD HENRY LEE	WM. FLOYD	WM. WILLIAMS
TH. JEFFERSON	PHIL. LIVINGSTON	OLIVER WOLCOTT
BENJA. HARRISON	FRANS. LEWIS	MATTHEW THORNTON
	LEWIS MORRIS	

Secretary of War	John H. Eaton	1829–1831
	Lewis Cass	1831–1837
	Benjamin Butler	1837
Attorney General	John M. Berrien	1829–1831
	Roger B. Taney	1831–1833
	Benjamin Butler	1833–1837
Postmaster General	William Barry	1829–1835
	Amos Kendall	1835–1837
Secretary of Navy	John Branch	1829–1831
	Levi Woodbury	1831–1834
	Mahlon Dickerson	1834–1837

The Van Buren Administration (1837–1841)

Vice President	Richard M. Johnson	1837–1841
Secretary of State	John Forsyth	1837–1841
Secretary of Treasury	Levi Woodbury	1837–1841
Secretary of War	Joel Poinsett	1837–1841
Attorney General	Benjamin Butler	1837–1838
	Felix Grundy	1838–1840
	Henry D. Gilpin	1840–1841
Postmaster General	Amos Kendall	1837–1840
	John M. Niles	1840–1841
Secretary of Navy	Mahlon Dickerson	1837–1838
	James Paulding	1838–1841

The William Harrison Administration (1841)

Vice President	John Tyler	1841
Secretary of State	Daniel Webster	1841
Secretary of Treasury	Thomas Ewing	1841
Secretary of War	John Bell	1841
Attorney General	John J. Crittenden	1841
Postmaster General	Francis Granger	1841
Secretary of Navy	George Badger	1841

The Tyler Administration (1841–1845)

Vice President	None	
Secretary of State	Daniel Webster	1841–1843
	Hugh S. Legaré	1843
	Abel P. Upshur	1843–1844
	John C. Calhoun	1844–1845
Secretary of Treasury	Thomas Ewing	1841
	Walter Forward	1841–1843
	John C. Spencer	1843–1844
	George Bibb	1844–1845
Secretary of War	John Bell	1841
	John C. Spencer	1841–1843
	James M. Porter	1843–1844
	William Wilkins	1844–1845
Attorney General	John J. Crittenden	1841
	Hugh S. Legaré	1841–1843
	John Nelson	1843–1845
Postmaster General	Francis Granger	1841
	Charles Wickliffe	1841
Secretary of Navy	George Badger	1841
	Abel P. Upshur	1841
	David Henshaw	1843–1844
	Thomas Gilmer	1844
	John Y. Mason	1844–1845

The Polk Administration (1845–1849)

Vice President	George M. Dallas	1845–1849
Secretary of State	James Buchanan	1845–1849
Secretary of Treasury	Robert J. Walker	1845–1849
Secretary of War	William L. Marcy	1845–1849
Attorney General	John Y. Mason	1845–1846
	Nathan Clifford	1846–1848
	Isaac Toucey	1848–1849
Postmaster General	Cave Johnson	1845–1849
Secretary of Navy	George Bancroft	1845–1846
	John Y. Mason	1846–1849

The Taylor Administration (1849–1850)

Vice President	Millard Fillmore	1849–1850
Secretary of State	John M. Clayton	1849–1850
Secretary of Treasury	William Meredith	1849–1850
Secretary of War	George Crawford	1849–1850
Attorney General	Reverdy Johnson	1849–1850
Postmaster General	Jacob Collamer	1849–1850
Secretary of Navy	William Preston	1849–1850
Secretary of Interior	Thomas Ewing	1849–1850

The Fillmore Administration (1850–1853)

Vice President	None	
Secretary of State	Daniel Webster	1850–1852
	Edward Everett	1852–1853
Secretary of Treasury	Thomas Corwin	1850–1853
Secretary of War	Charles Conrad	1850–1853
Attorney General	John J. Crittenden	1850–1853
Postmaster General	Nathan Hall	1850–1852
	Samuel D. Hubbard	1852–1853
Secretary of Navy	William A. Graham	1850–1852
	John P. Kennedy	1852–1853
Secretary of Interior	Thomas McKennan	1850
	Alexander Stuart	1850–1853

The Pierce Administration (1853–1857)

Vice President	William R. King	1853–d. 1853
Secretary of State	William L. Marcy	1853–1857
Secretary of Treasury	James Guthrie	1853–1857
Secretary of War	Jefferson Davis	1853–1857
Attorney General	Caleb Cushing	1853–1857
Postmaster General	James Campbell	1853–1857
Secretary of Navy	James C. Dobbin	1853–1857
Secretary of Interior	Robert McClelland	1853–1857

The Buchanan Administration (1857–1861)

Vice President	John C. Breckinridge	1857–1861
Secretary of State	Lewis Cass	1857–1860
	Jeremiah S. Black	1860–1861
Secretary of Treasury	Howell Cobb	1857–1860
	Philip Thomas	1860–1861
	John A. Dix	1861
Secretary of War	John B. Floyd	1857–1861
	Joseph Holt	1861
Attorney General	Jeremiah S. Black	1857–1860
	Edwin M. Stanton	1860–1861

Postmaster General	Aaron V. Brown	1857–1859
	Joseph Holt	1859–1861
	Horatio King	1861
Secretary of Navy	Isaac Toucey	1857–1861
Secretary of Interior	Jacob Thompson	1857–1861

The Lincoln Administration (1861–1865)

Vice President	Hannibal Hamlin	1861–1865
	Andrew Johnson	1865
Secretary of State	William H. Seward	1861–1865
Secretary of Treasury	Samuel P. Chase	1861–1864
	William P. Fessenden	1864–1865
	Hugh McCulloch	1865
Secretary of War	Simon Cameron	1861–1862
	Edwin M. Stanton	1862–1865
Attorney General	Edward Bates	1861–1864
	James Speed	1864–1865
Postmaster General	Horatio King	1861
	Montgomery Blair	1861–1864
	William Dennison	1864–1865
Secretary of Navy	Gideon Welles	1861–1865
Secretary of Interior	Caleb B. Smith	1861–1863
	John P. Usher	1863–1865

The Andrew Johnson Administration (1865–1869)

Vice President	None	
Secretary of State	William H. Seward	1865–1869
Secretary of Treasury	Hugh McCulloch	1865–1869
Secretary of War	Edwin M. Stanton	1865–1867
	Ulysses S. Grant	1867–1868
	Lorenzo Thomas	1868
	John M. Schofield	1868–1869
Attorney General	James Speed	1865–1866
	Henry Stanbery	1866–1868
	William M. Evarts	1868–1869
Postmaster General	William Dennison	1865–1866
	Alexander Randall	1866–1869
Secretary of Navy	Gideon Welles	1865–1869
Secretary of Interior	John P. Usher	1865
	James Harlan	1865–1866
	Ovrille H. Browning	1866–1869

The Grant Administration (1869–1877)

Vice President	Schuyler Colfax	1869–1873
	Henry Wilson	1873–d. 1875
Secretary of State	Elihu B. Washburne	1869
	Hamilton Fish	1869–1877
Secretary of Treasury	George S. Boutwell	1869–1873
	William Richardson	1873–1874
	Benjamin Bristow	1874–1876
	Lot M. Morrill	1876–1877
Secretary of War	John A. Rawlins	1869
	William T. Sherman	1869
	William W. Belknap	1869–1876
	Alphonso Taft	1876
	James D. Cameron	1876–1877
Attorney General	Ebenezer Hoar	1869–1870
	Amos T. Ackerman	1870–1871
	G. H. Williams	1871–1875

	Edwards Pierrepont	1875–1876
	Alphonso Taft	1876–1877
Postmaster General	John A. J. Creswell	1869–1874
	James W. Marshall	1874
	Marshall Jewell	1874–1876
	James N. Tyner	1876–1877
Secretary of Navy	Adolph E. Borie	1869
	George M. Robeson	1869–1877
Secretary of Interior	Jacob D. Cox	1869–1870
	Columbus Delano	1870–1875
	Zachariah Chandler	1875–1877

The Hayes Administration (1877–1881)

Vice President	William A. Wheeler	1877–1881
Secretary of State	William M. Evarts	1877–1881
Secretary of Treasury	John Sherman	1877–1881
Secretary of War	George W. McCrary	1877–1879
	Alex Ramsey	1879–1881
Attorney General	Charles Devens	1877–1881
Postmaster General	David M. Key	1877–1880
	Horace Maynard	1880–1881
Secretary of Navy	Richard W. Thompson	1877–1880
	Nathan Goff, Jr.	1881
Secretary of Interior	Carl Schurz	1877–1881

The Garfield Administration (1881)

Vice President	Chester A. Arthur	1881
Secretary of State	James G. Blaine	1881
Secretary of Treasury	William Windom	1881
Secretary of War	Robert T. Lincoln	1881
Attorney General	Wayne MacVeagh	1881
Postmaster General	Thomas L. James	1881
Secretary of Navy	William H. Hunt	1881
Secretary of Interior	Samuel J. Kirkwood	1881

The Arthur Administration (1881–1885)

Vice President	None	
Secretary of State	F. T. Frelinghuysen	1881–1885
Secretary of Treasury	Charles J. Folger	1881–1884
	Walter Q. Gresham	1884
	Hugh McCulloch	1884–1885
Secretary of War	Robert T. Lincoln	1881–1885
Attorney General	Benjamin H. Brewster	1881–1885
Postmaster General	Timothy O. Howe	1881–1883
	Walter Q. Gresham	1883–1884
	Frank Hatton	1884–1885
Secretary of Navy	William H. Hunt	1881–1882
	William E. Chandler	1882–1885
Secretary of Interior	Samuel J. Kirkwood	1881–1882
	Henry M. Teller	1882–1885

The Cleveland Administration (1885–1889)

Vice President	Thomas A. Hendricks	1885–d. 1885
Secretary of State	Thomas F. Bayard	1885–1889
Secretary of Treasury	Daniel Manning	1885–1887
	Charles S. Fairchild	1887–1889
Secretary of War	William C. Endicott	1885–1889
Attorney General	Augustus H. Garland	1885–1889

Secretary of Agriculture	Clinton P. Anderson	1945–1948
	Charles F. Brannan	1948–1953
Secretary of Commerce	Henry A. Wallace	1945–1946
	W. Averell Harriman	1946–1948
	Charles W. Sawyer	1948–1953
Secretary of Labor	Lewis B. Schwellenbach	1945–1948
	Maurice J. Tobin	1948–1953
Secretary of Defense	James V. Forrestal	1947–1949
	Louis A. Johnson	1949–1950
	George C. Marshall	1950–1951
	Robert A. Lovett	1951–1953

The Eisenhower Administration (1953–1961)

Vice President	Richard M. Nixon	1953–1961
Secretary of State	John Foster Dulles	1953–1959
	Christian A. Herter	1959–1961
Secretary of Treasury	George M. Humphrey	1953–1957
	Robert B. Anderson	1957–1961
Attorney General	Herbert Brownell, Jr.	1953–1958
	William P. Rogers	1958–1961
Postmaster General	Arthur E. Summerfield	1953–1961
Secretary of Interior	Douglas McKay	1953–1958
	Fred A. Seaton	1956–1961
Secretary of Agriculture	Ezra T. Benson	1953–1961
Secretary of Commerce	Sinclair Weeks	1953–1958
	Lewis L. Strauss	1958–1959
	Frederick H. Mueller	1959–1961
Secretary of Labor	Martin P. Durkin	1953
	James P. Mitchell	1953–1961
Secretary of Defense	Charles E. Wilson	1953–1957
	Neil H. McElroy	1957–1959
	Thomas S. Gates, Jr.	1959–1961
Secretary of Health, Education, and Welfare	Oveta Culp Hobby	1953–1955
	Marlon B. Folsom	1955–1958
	Arthur S. Flemming	1958–1961

The Kennedy Administration (1961–1963)

Vice President	Lyndon B. Johnson	1961–1963
Secretary of State	Dean Rusk	1961–1963
Secretary of Treasury	C. Douglas Dillon	1961–1963
Attorney General	Robert F. Kennedy	1961–1963
Postmaster General	J. Edward Day	1961–1963
	John A. Gronouski	1963
Secretary of Interior	Stewart L. Udall	1961–1963
Secretary of Agriculture	Orville L. Freeman	1961–1963
Secretary of Commerce	Luther H. Hodges	1961–1963
Secretary of Labor	Arthur J. Goldberg	1961–1962
	W. Willard Wirtz	1962–1963
Secretary of Defense	Robert S. McNamara	1961–1963
Secretary of Health, Education, and Welfare	Abraham A. Ribicoff	1961–1962
	Anthony J. Celebrezze	1962–1963

The Lyndon Johnson Administration (1963–1969)

Vice President	Hubert H. Humphrey	1965–1969
Secretary of State	Dean Rusk	1963–1969
Secretary of Treasury	C. Douglas Dillon	1963–1965
	Henry H. Fowler	1965–1969
Attorney General	Robert F. Kennedy	1963–1964
	Nicholas Katzenbach	1965–1966
	Ramsey Clark	1967–1969
Postmaster General	John A. Gronouski	1963–1965
	Lawrence F. O'Brien	1965–1968
	Marvin Watson	1968–1969
Secretary of Interior	Stewart L. Udall	1963–1969
Secretary of Agriculture	Orville L. Freeman	1963–1969
Secretary of Commerce	Luther H. Hodges	1963–1964
	John T. Connor	1964–1967
	Alexander B. Trowbridge	1967–1968
	Cyrus R. Smith	1968–1969
Secretary of Labor	W. Willard Wirtz	1963–1969
Secretary of Defense	Robert F. McNamara	1963–1968
	Clark Clifford	1968–1969
Secretary of Health, Education, and Welfare	Anthony J. Celebrezze	1963–1965
	John W. Gardner	1965–1968
	Wilbur J. Cohen	1968–1969
Secretary of Housing and Urban Development	Robert C. Weaver	1966–1969
	Robert C. Wood	1969
Secretary of Transportation	Alan S. Boyd	1967–1969

The Nixon Administration (1969–1974)

Vice President	Spiro T. Agnew	1969–1973
	Gerald R. Ford	1973–1974
Secretary of State	William P. Rogers	1969–1973
	Henry A. Kissinger	1973–1974
Secretary of Treasury	David M. Kennedy	1969–1970
	John B. Connally	1971–1972
	George P. Shultz	1972–1974
	William E. Simon	1974
Attorney General	John N. Mitchell	1969–1972
	Richard G. Kleindienst	1972–1973
	Elliot L. Richardson	1973
	William B. Saxbe	1973–1974
Postmaster General	Winton M. Blount	1969–1971
Secretary of Interior	Walter J. Hickel	1969–1970
	Rogers Morton	1971–1974
Secretary of Agriculture	Clifford M. Hardin	1969–1971
	Earl L. Butz	1971–1974
Secretary of Commerce	Maurice H. Stans	1969–1972
	Peter G. Peterson	1972–1973
	Frederick B. Dent	1973–1974
Secretary of Labor	George P. Shultz	1969–1970
	James D. Hodgson	1970–1973
	Peter J. Brennan	1973–1974
Secretary of Defense	Melvin R. Laird	1969–1973
	Elliot L. Richardson	1973
	James R. Schlesinger	1973–1974
Secretary of Health, Education, and Welfare	Robert H. Finch	1969–1970
	Elliot L. Richardson	1970–1973
	Caspar W. Weinberger	1973–1974

Secretary of Housing and Urban Development	George Romney	1969–1973
	James T. Lynn	1973–1974
Secretary of Transportation	John A. Volpe	1969–1973
	Claude S. Brinegar	1973–1974

The Ford Administration (1974–1977)

Vice President	Nelson A. Rockefeller	1974–1977
Secretary of State	Henry A. Kissinger	1974–1977
Secretary of Treasury	William E. Simon	1974–1977
Attorney General	William B. Saxbe	1974–1975
	Edward Levi	1975–1977
Secretary of Interior	Rogers Morton	1974–1975
	Stanley K. Hathaway	1975
	Thomas Kleppe	1975–1977
Secretary of Agriculture	Earl L. Butz	1974–1976
	John A. Knebel	1976–1977
Secretary of Commerce	Frederick B. Dent	1974–1975
	Rogers Morton	1975–1976
	Elliot L. Richardson	1976–1977
Secretary of Labor	Peter J. Brennan	1974–1975
	John T. Dunlop	1975–1976
	W. J. Usery	1976–1977
Secretary of Defense	James R. Schlesinger	1974–1975
	Donald Rumsfeld	1975–1977
Secretary of Health, Education, and Welfare	Caspar W. Weinberger	1974–1975
	Forrest D. Mathews	1975–1977
Secretary of Housing and Urban Development	James T. Lynn	1974–1975
	Carla A. Hills	1975–1977
Secretary of Transportation	Claude S. Brinegar	1974–1975
	William T. Coleman	1975–1977

The Carter Administration (1977–1981)

Vice President	Walter F. Mondale	1977–1981
Secretary of State	Cyrus R. Vance	1977–1980
	Edmund Muskie	1980–1981
Secretary of Treasury	W. Michael Blumenthal	1977–1979
	G. William Miller	1979–1981
Attorney General	Griffin Bell	1977–1979
	Benjamin R. Civiletti	1979–1981
Secretary of Interior	Cecil D. Andrus	1977–1981
Secretary of Agriculture	Robert Bergland	1977–1981
Secretary of Commerce	Juanita M. Kreps	1977–1979
	Philip M. Klutznick	1979–1981
Secretary of Labor	F. Ray Marshall	1977–1981
Secretary of Defense	Harold Brown	1977–1981
Secretary of Health Education, and Welfare	Joseph A. Califano	1977–1979
	Patricia R. Harris	1979
Secretary of Health and Human Services	Patricia R. Harris	1979–1981
Secretary of Education	Shirley M. Hufstedler	1979–1981

Secretary of Housing and Urban Development	Patricia R. Harris	1977–1979
	Moon Landrieu	1979–1981
Secretary of Transportation	Brock Adams	1977–1979
	Neil E. Goldschmidt	1979–1981
Secretary of Energy	James R. Schlesinger	1979–1979
	Charles W. Duncan	1979–1981

The Reagan Administration (1981–1989)

Vice President	George Bush	1981–1989
Secretary of State	Alexander M. Haig	1981–1982
	George P. Shultz	1982–1989
Secretary of Treasury	Donald Regan	1981–1985
	James A. Baker, III	1985–1988
	Nicholas Brady	1988–1989
Attorney General	William F. Smith	1981–1985
	Edwin A. Meese, III	1985–1988
	Richard Thornburgh	1988–1989
Secretary of Interior	James Watt	1981–1983
	William P. Clark, Jr.	1983–1985
	Donald P. Hodel	1985–1989
Secretary of Agriculture	John Block	1981–1986
	Richard E. Lyng	1986–1989
Secretary of Commerce	Malcolm Baldridge	1981–1987
	C. William Verity, Jr.	1987–1989
Secretary of Labor	Raymond Donovan	1981–1985
	William E. Brock	1985–1988
	Ann Dore McLaughlin	1988–1989
Secretary of Defense	Caspar W. Weinberger	1981–1988
	Frank Carlucci	1988–1989
Secretary of Health and Human Services	Richard Schweiker	1981–1983
	Margaret Heckler	1983–1985
	Otis R. Bowen	1985–1989
Secretary of Education	Terrel H. Bell	1981–1985
	William J. Bennett	1985–1988
	Lauro F. Cavazos	1988–1989
Secretary of Housing and Urban Development	Samuel Pierce	1981–1989
Secretary of Transportation	Drew Lewis	1981–1983
	Elizabeth Dole	1983–1987
	James L. Burnley, IV	1987–1989
Secretary of Energy	James Edwards	1981–1982
	Donald P. Hodel	1982–1985
	John S. Herrington	1985–1989

The Bush Administration (1989–1993)

Vice President	J. Danforth Quayle	1989–1993
Secretary of State	James A. Baker, III	1989–1992
	Lawrence Eagleburger	1992–1993
Secretary of Treasury	Nicholas F. Brady	1988–1993
Attorney General	Richard Thornburgh	1989–1991
	William Barr	1991–1992
Secretary of Interior	Manuel Lujan, Jr.	1989–1993
Secretary of Agriculture	Clayton K. Yeutter	1989–1991
	Edward Madigan	1991–1993

Name	Terms of Service	Appointed by	Name	Terms of Service	Appointed by
Abe Fortas	1965–1970	Johnson	**William H. Rehnquist**	1986–	Reagan
Thurgood Marshall	1967–1991	Johnson	Antonin Scalia	1986–	Reagan
Warren E. Burger	1969–1986	Nixon	Anthony M. Kennedy	1988–	Reagan
Harry A. Blackmun	1970–1994	Nixon	David H. Souter	1990–	Bush
Lewis F. Powell, Jr.	1971–1988	Nixon	Clarence Thomas	1991–	Bush
William H. Rehnquist	1971–1986	Nixon	Ruth Bader Ginsberg	1993–	Clinton
John Paul Stevens	1975–	Ford	Stephen G. Breyer	1994–	Clinton
Sandra Day O'Connor	1981–	Reagan			

Chief Justices in bold type

[1]The date on which the justice's took their judicial oath is here used as the date of the beginning of service, for until that oath is taken they are not vested with the prerogatives of their office. Justices, however, receive their commissions ("letters patent") before taking their oath—in some instances, in the preceding year.

[2]Acting Chief Justice; Senate refused to confirm appointment.

Admission of States to the Union

State	Date of Admission	State	Date of Admission
1. Delaware	December 7, 1787	26. Michigan	January 26, 1837
2. Pennsylvania	December 12, 1787	27. Florida	March 3, 1845
3. New Jersey	December 18, 1787	28. Texas	December 29, 1845
4. Georgia	January 2, 1788	29. Iowa	December 28, 1846
5. Connecticut	January 9, 1788	30. Wisconsin	May 29, 1848
6. Massachusetts	February 6, 1788	31. California	September 9, 1850
7. Maryland	April 28, 1788	32. Minnesota	May 11, 1858
8. South Carolina	May 23, 1788	33. Oregon	February 14, 1859
9. New Hampshire	June 21, 1788	34. Kansas	January 29, 1861
10. Virginia	June 25, 1788	35. West Virginia	June 20, 1863
11. New York	July 26, 1788	36. Nevada	October 31, 1864
12. North Carolina	November 21, 1789	37. Nebraska	March 1, 1867
13. Rhode Island	May 29, 1790	38. Colorado	August 1, 1876
14. Vermont	March 4, 1791	39. North Dakota	November 2, 1889
15. Kentucky	June 1, 1792	40. South Dakota	November 2, 1889
16. Tennessee	June 1, 1796	41. Montana	November 8, 1889
17. Ohio	March 1, 1803	42. Washington	November 11, 1889
18. Louisiana	April 30, 1812	43. Idaho	July 3, 1890
19. Indiana	December 11, 1816	44. Wyoming	July 10, 1890
20. Mississippi	December 10, 1817	45. Utah	January 4, 1896
21. Illinois	December 3, 1818	46. Oklahoma	November 16, 1907
22. Alabama	December 14, 1819	47. New Mexico	January 6, 1912
23. Maine	March 15, 1820	48. Arizona	February 14, 1912
24. Missouri	August 10, 1821	49. Alaska	January 3, 1959
25. Arkansas	June 15, 1836	50. Hawaii	August 21, 1959

Territorial Expansion of the U.S.

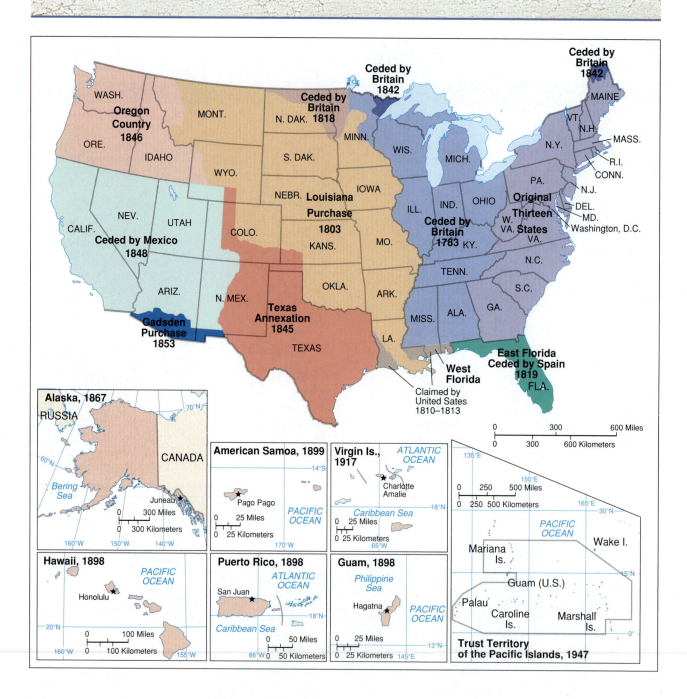

Louisiana Purchase	1803	Hawaii	1898
Florida	1819	Puerto Rico	1898
Texas	1845	Guam	1898
Oregon	1846	American Samoa	1899
Mexican Cession	1848	U.S. Virgin Islands	1917
Gadsden Purchase	1853	Pacific Islands Trust Territory	1947
Alaska	1867		

U.S. Population, 1790–1990

Year	Population	Percent Increase	Population Per Square Mile	Sex (rounded to nearest million) Male	Female	Median Age
1790	3,929,214		4.5	NA	NA	NA
1800	5,308,483	35.1	6.1	NA	NA	NA
1810	7,239,881	36.4	4.3	NA	NA	NA
1820	9,638,453	33.1	5.5	5	5	16.7
1830	12,866,020	33.5	7.4	7	6	17.2
1840	17,069,453	32.7	9.8	9	8	17.8
1850	23,191,876	35.9	7.9	12	11	18.9
1860	31,443,321	35.6	10.6	16	15	19.4
1870	39,818,449	26.6	13.4	19	19	20.2
1880	50,155,783	26.0	16.9	26	25	20.9
1890	62,947,714	25.5	21.2	32	31	22.0
1900	75,994,575	20.7	25.6	39	37	22.9
1910	91,972,266	21.0	31.0	47	45	24.1
1920	105,710,620	14.9	35.6	54	52	25.3
1930	122,775,046	16.1	41.2	62	61	26.4
1940	131,669,275	7.2	44.2	66	66	29.0
1950	150,697,361	14.5	50.7	75	76	30.2
1960	179,323,175	18.5	50.6	88	91	29.5
1970	203,302,031	13.4	57.4	99	104	28.0
1980	226,545,805	11.4	64.0	110	116	30.0
1985	237,839,000	5.0	64.0	117	123	31.3
1990	249,975,000	1.1	70.3	121	127	32.6

NA = Not available.

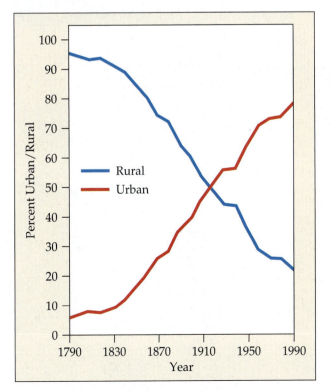

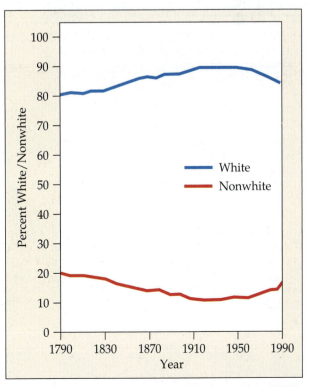

Ethnic Diversity of the U.S., 1990

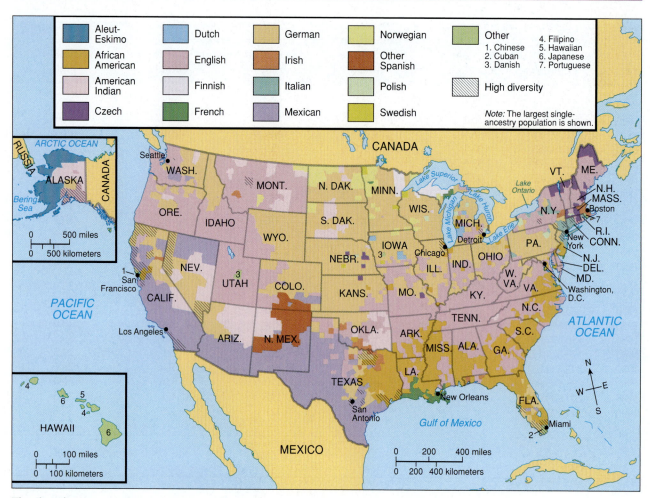

The classifications on this map suggest the pluralism of American society but fail to reflect completely the nation's ethnic diversity.

Data from U.S. Department of Commerce, Bureau of the Census, U.S. Summary Files, Population and Housing, 1990.

ARCTIC OCEAN

GREENLAND

Beaufort
Sea

ALASKA (U.S.)

C A N A D A

ICELAND

Bering
Sea

Gulf
of Alaska

Baffin
Bay

Hudson
Bay

Labrador
Sea

Great
Lakes

UNITED STATES

ATLANTIC
OCEAN

MOROCCO

Hawaiian Islands
(U.S.)

MEXICO

Gulf
of Mexico

SEE CARIBBEAN INSET

WESTERN
SAHARA

BELIZE

PACIFIC
OCEAN

GUATEMALA
EL SALVADOR

Caribbean Sea

CAPE
VERDE

MAURITANIA

BURK

SENEGAL
THE GAMBIA
GUINEA-BISSAU

M

GUINEA

COLOMBIA

FRENCH GUIANA
(FR.)

SIERRA LEONE
LIBERIA

Galapagos
Islands
(EQ.)

ECUADOR

SURINAME

CÔTE
D'IVOIRE

KIRIBATI

PERU

BRAZIL

SÃO TO
PRI

TOKELAU

SAMOA
AM.
SAMOA
TONGA

COOK
ISLANDS

FRENCH
POLYNESIA

BOLIVIA

PARAGUAY

ATLANTIC
OCEAN

CHILE

URUGUAY

ARGENTINA

Falkland
Islands
(U.K.)

South
Georgia
(U.K.)

UNITED
STATES

BAHAMAS

| 0 | 300 | 600 mi |
| 0 | 300 | 600 km |

ATLANTIC OCEAN

CUBA

Turks & Caicos Is.
(U.K.)

Cayman
Is. (U.K.)

HAITI

DOMINICAN
REPUBLIC

PUERTO
RICO

Virgin Is.(U.S.)

ANTIGUA &
BARBUDA

JAMAICA

ST. CHRISTOPHER
AND NEVIS

GUADALOUPE

HONDURAS

Caribbean Sea

DOMINICA

MARTINIQUE

Weddell
Sea

ST. LUCIA

NICARAGUA

CURACAO

ST. VINCENT AND
THE GRENADINES

BARBADOS

| 0 | 1500 | 300 |
| 0 | 1500 | 3000 km |

GRENADA

COSTA
RICA

PANAMA

COLOMBIA

VENEZUELA

TRINIDAD
AND TOBAGO

GUYANA

A N T A R C T I C A

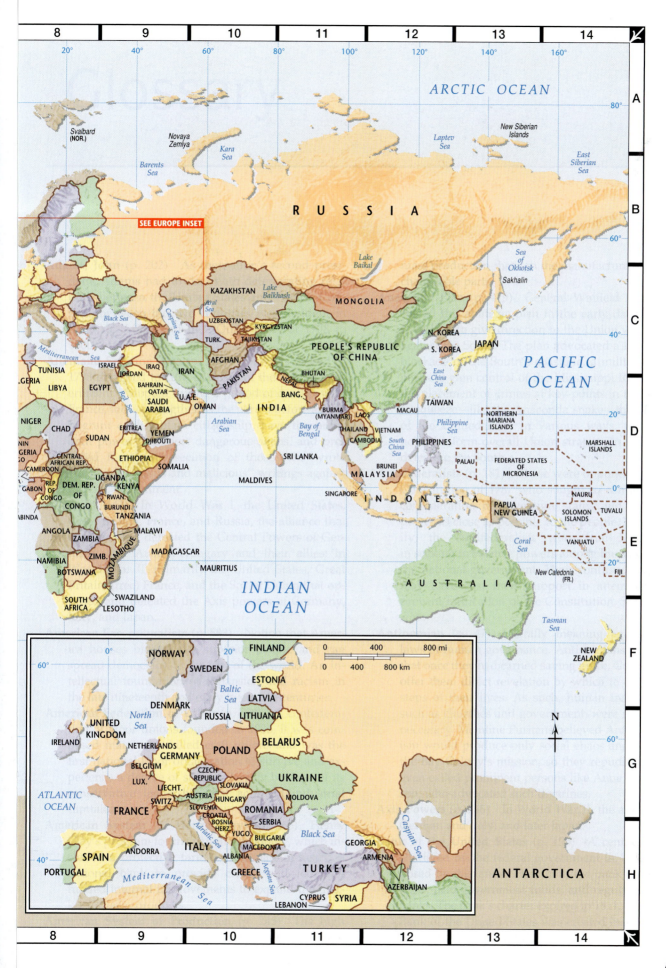

Bay of Pigs Fiasco (p. 850) A plan to assassinate Cuban leader Fidel Castro and liberate Cuba with a trained military force of political exiles. The limited 1961 invasion was an unmitigated military failure and actually strengthened Castro's position in Cuba.

Beat Generation (p. 814) A cultural style and artistic movement of the 1950s that rejected traditional American family life and material values and celebrated African-American culture. They tapped an underground dissatisfaction with mainstream American culture.

Big Stick Diplomacy (p. 629) The proclaimed foreign policy of Theodore Roosevelt, it was based on the proverb, "Speak softly and carry a big stick," and advocated the threat of force to achieve the United States' goals, especially in the Western Hemisphere.

Bill of Rights (p. 193) The first ten amendments to the U.S. Constitution, which protect the rights of individuals from the powers of the national government. Congress and the states adopted the ten amendments in 1791.

Billy Yank (p. 419) This appellation was used to refer to common soldiers serving in Union armies during the Civil War. See *Johnny Reb.*

Birds of Passage (p. 518) Immigrants who never intended to make the United States their home. Unable to make a living in their native countries, they came to America, worked and saved, and returned home. About 20 to 30 percent of immigrants returned home.

Black Codes (p. 453) Laws passed by Southern state legislatures during Reconstruction, while Congress was out of session. These laws limited the rights of former slaves and led Congress to ratify the Fourteenth Amendment.

Black Power (p. 886) A rallying cry for more militant blacks advocated by younger leaders like Stokely Carmichael and H. Rap Brown, beginning in the mid-1960s. It called for African Americans to form their own economic, political, and cultural institutions.

Black Tuesday (p. 692) October 29, 1929, the day of the stock market crash that initiated the Great Depression.

Bonus Army (p. 706) Group of unemployed World War I veterans who marched on Washington, D.C., in June 1932 to ask for immediate payment of their war pensions.

Brain Trust (p. 708) Close advisors to President Franklin Delano Roosevelt during the early days of his first term whose policy suggestions influenced much New Deal legislation.

Brown* v. *Board of Education of Topeka (p. 807) Supreme Court decision of 1954 that overturned the "separate but equal doctrine" that justified Jim Crow laws. Chief Justice Earl Warren argued that "separate educational facilities are inherently unequal."

Burr, Aaron (p. 206) Thomas Jefferson's first vice president, who killed Alexander Hamilton in a duel in 1804.

Cabinet (p. 173) This term refers to the heads of the executive departments.

Calhoun, John C. (p. 236) As vice president, Calhoun anonymously expounded the doctrine of nullification, which held that states could prevent the enforcement of a federal law within their boundaries.

Calvinism (p. 22) Broadly influential Protestant theology emanating from the French theologian John Calvin, who fled to Switzerland, where he reordered life in the community of Geneva according to his conception of the Bible. Calvinism emphasized the power and omnipotence of God and the importance of seeking to earn saving grace and salvation, even though God had already determined (the concept of predestination) who would be eternally saved or damned.

Camp David Accords (p. 918) An historic 1979 peace agreement negotiated between Egypt and Israel at the U.S. presidential retreat at Camp David, Maryland. Under the pact, Israel agreed to return captured territory to Egypt and to negotiate Palestinian autonomy in the West Bank and Gaza Strip.

Capital Punishment (p. 291) During the early nineteenth century, a movement arose to end the death penalty.

Carpetbaggers (p. 460) People who moved to the South during or following the Civil War and became active in politics, they helped to bring Republican control of southern state governments during Reconstruction and were bitterly resented by most white Southerners.

Carter, Jimmy (p. 823) Georgia governor in 1970, and president in 1976. His progressive racial views reflected an emergent South less concerned with racial distinctions and more concerned with economic development and political power.

Cautious Revolutionaries (p. 162) Sometimes called reluctant revolutionaries, these leaders lacked a strong trust in the people to rise above their own self-interest and provide for enlightened legislative policies (see *public virtue*). At the time of the American Revolution, they argued in favor of forms of government that could easily check the popular will. To assure political stability, they believed that political decision making should be in the hands of society's proven social and economic elite. John Dickinson, John Adams (very much an eager revolutionary), and Robert Morris might be described as cautious revolutionaries. See *radical revolutionaries.*

Central Powers (p. 646)   In World War I, Germany and Austria-Hungary and their allies.

Channing, William Ellery (p. 285)   America's leading exponent of religious liberalism, Channing was one of the founders of American Unitarianism.

The China Lobby (p. 773)   An informal group of media leaders and political pundits who criticized the communist takeover of China, claiming the United States could have prevented it.

City upon a Hill (p. 44)   Phrase from John Winthrop's sermon, "A Model of Christian Charity," in which he challenged his fellow Puritans to build a model, ideal community in America that would serve as an example of how the rest of the world should order its existence. Here was the beginning of the idea of America as a special, indeed exceptional society, therefore worthy of emulation by others. The concept of American exceptionalism has dominated American history and culture down to the present.

Civil Rights Act of 1964 (p. 883)   Landmark legislation that prohibited discrimination on the basis of race, sex, religion, or national origin in employment and public facilities such as hotels, restaurants, and playgrounds. It established the Equal Employment Opportunity Commission.

Clay, Henry (p. 236)   As Speaker of the House of Representatives, Senator, and unsuccessful candidate for the presidency, he was an advocate of the "American System," which called for a protective tariff, a national bank, and federally funded internal improvements. See *American system (of Henry Clay).*

Colonization (p. 294)   The effort to encourage masters to voluntarily emancipate their slaves and to resettle free blacks in Africa.

Columbian Exchange (p. 30)   The process of transferring plants, animals, foods, diseases, wealth, and culture between Europe and the Americas, beginning at the time of Christopher Columbus and continuing throughout the era of exploration and expansion. The exchange often resulted in the devastation of Native American peoples and cultures, so much so that the process is sometimes referred to as the "Columbian collision."

Committee on Public Information (CPI) (p. 653)   U.S. propaganda agency of World War I.

Committees of Correspondence (p. 119)   As American leaders became increasingly anxious about a perceived British imperial conspiracy to deprive them of their liberties, they set up networks of communication among the colonies. Beginning in 1773 colonial assemblies began to appoint committees of correspondence to warn each other about possible

abuses. In some colonies, such as Massachusetts, local communities also organized such committees, all with the intention of being vigilant against arbitrary acts from British officials.

Common Sense (p. 138)   This best-selling pamphlet by Thomas Paine, first published in 1776, denounced the British monarchy, called for American independence, and encouraged the adoption of republican forms of government. Paine's bold words thus helped crack the power of reconciliationist leaders in the Second Continental Congress who did not believe the colonies could stand up to British arms and survive as an independent nation.

Compromise of 1877 (p. 473)   A bargain made between southern Democrats and Republican candidate Rutherford B. Hayes after the disputed presidential election of 1876. The southern Democrats pledged to let Hayes take office in return for his promise to withdraw the remaining federal troops from the southern states. The removal of the last troops in 1877 marked the end of Reconstruction.

Coney Island (p. 540)   Popular site of New York amusement parks opening in 1890s, attracting working class Americans with rides and games celebrating abandon and instant gratification.

Copperheads (p. 428)   Not every person living in the North during the Civil War favored making war against the Confederacy. Such persons came to be identified as Copperheads. Often affiliated with the Democratic party and residing in the Midwest, Copperheads favored a negotiated peace settlement that would allow the South to leave the Union. Some of them were arbitrarily thrown into jail without proper *habeas corpus* proceedings after publicly advocating their views.

Court Packing (p. 720)   President Franklin Delano Roosevelt's controversial plan to appoint Supreme Court justices who were sympathetic to his views, by offering retirement benefits to the sitting justices.

Coverture (p. 57)   Coverture is closely connected with patriarchy because this concept contends that the legal identity of women is subordinated first in their fathers and, then, in their husbands, as the sanctioned heads of households. See *patriarchal.*

Coxey's Army (p. 569)   A movement founded by Jacob S. Coxey to help the unemployed during the depression of the 1890s, it brought out-of-work people to Washington, D.C., to demand that the federal government provide jobs and inflate the currency.

Crandall, Prudence (p. 292)   A Quaker schoolteacher, Crandall sparked controversy when she opened a school for the education of free blacks.

Cuban Missile Crisis (p. 850)   The conflict in 1962 prompted by Soviet installation of missiles on Cuba

First 100 Days (p. 707) President Franklin Delano Roosevelt's first 100 days in office, when he proposed and Congress passed fifteen major bills that reshaped the U.S. economy.

First Continental Congress (p. 121) This body was the most important expression of intercolonial protest activity up to 1774. Called in response to Parliament's Coercive Acts, the delegates met in Philadelphia for nearly two months. More radical delegates dominated the deliberations. Before dissolving itself, the Congress called for ongoing resistance, even military preparations to defend American communities, and a second congress, should King and Parliament not redress American grievances.

Flapper (p. 681) Term for a liberated woman who bucked conventional ideas of propriety in dress and manners during the 1920s.

Flexible Response (p. 856) Approach to foreign policy of the Kennedy administration based on developing and maintaining conventional, counterinsurgency (antiguerilla), and nuclear forces so that the United States would be able to choose from among these options in response to communist threat anywhere in the world.

Fourteen Points (p. 661) President Woodrow Wilson's formula for peace after World War I.

Free Soil Party (p. 296) An antislavery political party founded in 1848.

Freedmen's Bureau (Bureau of Refugees, Freedmen, and Abandoned Lands) (p. 450) An organization established by Congress on March 3, 1865 to deal with the dislocations of the Civil War. It provided relief, helped settle disputes, and founded schools and hospitals.

Freedom of Information Act (p. 914) This law allows the public and press to request declassification of government documents.

Freedom Riders (p. 879) Civil rights activists who in 1961 demonstrated that despite a federal ban on segregated travel on interstate buses, segregation prevailed in parts of the South.

Friedan, Betty (p. 892) Author of *The Feminine Mystique,* the 1963 book that articulated the discontent among white middle-class housewives in the "Baby Boom" era. She founded the National Organization for Women (NOW) in 1966.

Fugitive Slave Law (p. 389) The most controversial element of the Compromise of 1850, the Fugitive Slave Law provided for the return of runaway slaves to their masters.

Gabriel (p. 344) A Virginia slave and blacksmith who organized an attempted assault against Richmond in 1800.

Gallaudet, Thomas Hopkins (p. 293) Founder of the nation's first school to teach deaf mutes to read and write and communicate through hand signals.

Garrison, William Lloyd (p. 294) The leader of radical abolitionism, Garrison sought immediate freedom for slaves without compensation to their owners.

Goldwater, Barry (p. 831) Presidential candidate in 1964, Goldwater spearheaded an emergent conservative drive out of the South and West. Unhappy with the nation's path toward liberalism, Goldwater called for more limited taxes, a reduction in legislation aiding farmers and organized labor, and a reduction of federal spending.

Good Neighbor Policy (p. 730) During the administration of President Franklin D. Roosevelt, the U.S. policy of not interfering in the internal affairs of hemispheric neighbors.

Gorbachev, Mikhail (p. 925) The last leader of the Soviet Union, Gorbachev adopted policies of *glastnost* (political liberalization) and *perestroika* (economic reform).

Gospel of Wealth (p. 485) The belief that God ordains certain people to amass money and use it to further God's purposes, it justified the concentration of wealth as long as the rich used their money responsibly.

Grand Alliance (p. 745) In World War II, the alliance between the United States, Great Britain, and France.

Great Awakening (p. 86) Spilling over into the colonies from a wave of revivals in Europe, the Awakening placed renewed emphasis on vital religious faith, partially in reaction to more secular, rationalist thinking characterizing the Enlightenment. Beginning as scattered revivals in the 1720s, the Awakening grew into a fully developed outpouring of rejuvenated faith by the 1740s. Key figures included Jonathan Edwards and George Whitefield. The Awakening's legacy included more emphasis on personal choice, as opposed to state mandates about worship, in matters of religious faith.

Great Migration (p. 657) The mass movement of African Americans from the South to the North during World War I.

Great Society (p. 836) The liberal reform program of President Lyndon Johnson. The program included civil rights legislation, increased public spending to help the poor, Medicare and Medicaid programs, educational legislation, and liberalized immigration policies.

Greenback Party (p. 558) A political party founded in 1874 to promote the issuance of legal tender paper currency not backed by precious metals in order to inflate the money supply and relieve the suffering of people hurt by the era's deflation, most of its members merged with the Populist party.

Greenbacks (p. 425)   To help fund the military forces used against the Confederacy during the Civil War, the federal Congress issued a paper currency known as greenbacks. Even though greenbacks had no backing in specie (hard currency), this currency held its value fairly well because of mounting confidence the Union would prevail in the war. See also *specie*.

Grimké, Angelina, and Sarah (p. 298)   Born to a wealthy South Carolina slaveholding family, these sisters became leaders in the abolitionist and women's rights movements.

Gulf of Tonkin Resolution (p. 855)   Following two reported attacks on the *U.S.S. Maddox* in 1964, American president Lyndon B. Johnson asked for and received this authorization from Congress to "take all necessary measures" to repel attacks, prevent aggression, and protect American security. It allowed Johnson to act without Congressional authorization on military matters in Vietnam.

Half-Way Covenant (p. 55)   Realizing that many children of the Massachusetts Bay Colony's first generation were not actively seeking God's saving grace and full church membership, the question was how to keep the next generation of children active in church affairs. The solution, agreed to in 1662, was to permit the baptism of children and grandchildren of professing saints, thereby according them half-way membership. Full church membership still would come only after individuals testified to a conversion experience. This compromise on standards of membership was seen as a sign of declension. See *declension*.

Hamilton, Alexander (p. 194)   The first secretary of the treasury and a leader of the Federalist party. As secretary of the treasury, he devised a plan for repaying the nation's debts and promoting economic growth. This plan included funding and assumption of the national and state debts at face value, establishment of the Bank of the United States, and tariffs on imported goods. Hamilton died following a duel with Aaron Burr in 1804.

Harlem Renaissance (p. 688)   Self-conscious African American cultural, literary, and artistic movement centered in Harlem in New York City during the 1920s.

Hartford Convention (p. 227)   Convention held in late 1814 and early 1815 by New Englanders opposed to the War of 1812, which recommended Constitutional amendments to weaken the power of the South and to restrict Congress's power to impose embargoes or declare war.

Haymarket Square riot (p. 507)   A violent encounter between police and protestors in 1886 in Chicago, which led to the execution of four protest leaders, it scared the public with the specter of labor violence and demonstrated government's support of industrialists over workers.

Headright (p. 39)   As an economic incentive to encourage English settlement in Virginia and other English colonies during the seventeenth century, sponsoring parties would offer 50 acres of land per person to those who migrated or who paid for the passage of others willing to migrate to America. Because of Virginia's high death rate and difficult living conditions, headrights functioned as an inducement to help bolster the colony's low settlement rate.

Helper, Hinton Rowan (p. 346)   The North Carolina-born author of *The Impending Crisis of the South*, a book that argued that slavery was incompatible with economic progress.

Hessians (p. 140)   Six German principalities provided 30,000 soldiers to Great Britain to fight against the American rebels during the War for Independence. More than half of these troops-for-hire came from Hesse-Cassel. Hessian thus would serve as the generic term for all German mercenaries fighting in the war, whether or not they came from Hesse-Cassel.

Holy Experiment (p. 71)   Tolerance of religious diversity was at the core of William Penn's vision for a colony in America. As such, the colony of Pennsylvania represented a "holy experiment" for Penn. He encouraged people of all faiths to live together in harmony and to maintain harmonious relations with Native Americans in the region. The residents of early Pennsylvania never fully embraced Penn's vision, but the colony was open to religious dissenters and became a model for the diversity that later characterized America.

Hooverizing (p. 652)   Herbert Hoover's program as director of the Food Administration to conserve food during World War I.

Hoovervilles (p. 701)   Shanty-towns of the Great Depression, named after President Herbert Hoover.

House Un-American Activities Committee (HUAC) (p. 781) investigated subversive right- and left-wing movements. During the Cold War, it was best known for its two investigations of the American film industry.

Howe, Samuel Gridley (p. 293)   Founder of the nation's first school for the blind.

Hudson Highlands Strategy (p. 147)   The British tried to execute this strategy early in the War for American Independence but never successfully implemented it. The idea was to gain control of the Hudson River-Lake Champlain corridor running north from New York City and south from Montreal, Canada. Had the British done so, the effect would

Malcolm X (p. 885)   Spokesman for the Nation of Islam, a black religious and political organization that advocated black-owned businesses and castigated "white devils." He achieved notoriety as a public speaker and recruiter of boxer Muhammad Ali to the organization. He left the Nation of Islam in 1964 to form the Organization of Afro-American Unity in 1964, and was assassinated in 1965.

Manhattan Project (p. 755)   The secret government program to develop an atomic bomb during World War II.

Mann, Horace (p. 292)   The early nineteenth century's leading educational reformer, Mann led the fight for government support for public schools in Massachusetts.

Manumission (p. 178)   The freeing or emancipation of chattel slaves by their owners, which became more common in the upper South in the wake of so much talk during the American Revolution about human liberty. George Washington was among those planters who provided for the manumission of his slaves after the death of his wife Martha.

Marbury v. Madison (p. 216)   This landmark 1803 Supreme Court decision, which established the principle of judicial review, marked the first time that the Court declared an act of Congress unconstitutional.

Maroons (p. 344)   Escaped slaves who formed communities of runaways.

Marquis of Queensberry Rules (p. 536)   Standardized boxing rules of the late nineteenth century, creating structured three minute rounds with one minute rest periods, outlawing wrestling throws and holds, and specifying the number of rounds.

Marshall Plan (p. 770)   A massive foreign aid program to Western Europe of $17 billion over four years, beginning in 1948. Named after Secretary of State George Marshall, the program restored economic prosperity to the region and stabilized its system of democracy and capitalism.

Marshall, John (p. 215)   Appointed Chief Justice in 1801, Marshall expanded the Supreme Court's power and prestige and established its power to determine the constitutionality of the acts of other branches of government and to declare unconstitutional acts null and void. He defended the supremacy of the federal government over state governments and held that the Constitution should be construed broadly and flexibly.

Matrilineal (p. 9)   Unlike European nations that were male-based, or patrilineal, in organization, many Native American societies structured tribal and family power and authority through women. Quite often use rights to land and personal property passed from mother to daughter, and the eldest women chose male chiefs. Matrilineal societies thus placed great importance on the capacities of women to provide for the long-term welfare of their tribes.

McCullough v. Maryland (p. 239)   A landmark 1819 Supreme Court decision establishing Congress's power to charter a national bank and declaring unconstitutional a tax imposed by Maryland on the bank's Baltimore branch.

Mercantilism (p. 67)   An economic system built on the assumption that the world's supply of wealth is fixed and that nations must export more goods than they import to assure a steady supply of gold and silver into national coffers. Mercantile thinkers saw the inflow of such wealth as the key to maintaining and enhancing national power and self-sufficiency. Within this context, the accumulation and development of colonies was of great importance, since colonies could supply scarce raw materials to parent nations and serve as markets for finished goods.

Meredith, James (p. 880)   Black student who courageously sought admission into all-white University of Mississippi in 1962. His enrollment sparked a riot instigated by a white mob that attacked federal marshals and national guard troops, leaving 2 dead and 375 injured. Meredith attended the university and eventually graduated.

Military Reconstruction Act (p. 456)   A law passed after the South's refusal to accept the Fourteenth Amendment in 1867, it nullified existing state governments and divided the South into five military districts headed by military governors.

Modern Republicanism (p. 794)   also called "dynamic conservatism," President Eisenhower's domestic agenda advocated conservative spending approaches without drastically cutting back New Deal social programs.

Monroe Doctrine (p. 241)   In this 1823 statement of American foreign policy, President James Monroe declared that the United States would not allow European powers to create new colonies in the Western Hemisphere or to expand the boundaries of existing colonies.

Monroe, James (p. 235)   The president of the United States during the Era of Good Feelings.

Muckrakers (p. 611)   Investigative journalists during the Progressive Era, they wrote sensational exposés of social and political problems that helped spark the reform movements of their day.

Mugwumps (p. 554)   A reform faction of the Republican party in the 1870s and 1880s, they crusaded for honest and effective government and sometimes supported Democratic reform candidates.

National American Woman Suffrage Association (NAWSA) (p. 556)   An organization formed in

1890 from two factions of the suffrage movement, it sought a constitutional amendment to grant women the right to vote throughout the nation, eventually leading to the Nineteenth Amendment.

National Association for the Advancement of Colored People (NAACP) (p. 618, 687) Organization established in 1909 to fight for African-American civil rights through legal action.

National Origins Act of 1924 (p. 523, 686) Law that restricted immigration to 2 percent for any given nationality, based on the total amounts from the 1890 census. Use of the 1890 census effectively restricted immigrants from eastern and southern Europe.

National Recovery Administration (NRA) (p. 709) The federal government's plan to revive industry during the Great Depression through rational planning.

National Security Paper Number 68 (NSC-68) (p. 773) Influential National Security Council document arguing communism was a monolithic world movement directed from the Kremlin and advocating a massive military buildup to counteract the encroachment of communism.

National System of Interstate and Defense Highways Act (p. 795) 1956 legislation creating national highway system of 41,000 miles, costing $26 billion and taking 13 years to construct. It solidified the central role of the automobile in American culture.

Nationalists (p. 164) These revolutionary leaders favored a stronger national government than the one provided for in the Articles of Confederation. They believed that only a powerful national government, rather than self-serving states, could deal effectively with the many vexing problems besetting the new nation. George Washington, Alexander Hamilton, and James Madison were prominent nationalists.

Nativism (p. 521) A backlash against immigration by white native-born Protestants. Nativism could be based on racial prejudice (professors and scientists sometimes classified Eastern Europeans as innately inferior), religion (Protestants distrusted Catholics and Jews), politics (immigrants were often associated with radical political philosophies), and economics (labor leaders resented competition).

Naturalism (p. 531) Literary style of the late nineteenth and early twentieth century, where the individual was seen as a helpless victim in a world in which biological, social, and psychological forces determined his or her fate.

Navigation System (p. 68) To effect mercantilist goals, King and Parliament legislated a series of Navigation Acts (1651, 1660, 1663, 1673, 1696) that established England as the central hub of trade in its emerging empire. Various rules of trade, as embodied in the Navigation Acts, made it clear that England's colonies in the Americas existed first and foremost to serve the parent nation's economic interests, regardless of what was best for the colonists.

Neutrality (p. 643) U.S. policy of impartiality during World Wars I and II.

New Deal (p. 706) President Franklin Delano Roosevelt's program designed to bring about economic recovery and reform during the Great Depression.

New Lights (p. 87) As the Great Awakening spread during the 1730s and 1740s, various religious groups fractured into two camps, sometimes known as the New Lights and Old Lights. The New Lights placed emphasis on a "new birth" conversion experience—gaining God's saving grace. They also demanded ministers who had clearly experienced conversions themselves. See *Old Lights.*

The New Look (p. 798) President Eisenhower's adjustment to the doctrine of containment. He advocated saving money by emphasizing nuclear over conventional weapons, on the premise that the next major world conflict would be nuclear.

"New South" (p. 500) The ideology following Reconstruction that the South could be restored to its previous glory through a diversified economy, it was used to rally Southerners and convince outside investors to underwrite regional industrialization by extolling the resources, labor supply, and racial harmony of the South.

Nineteenth Amendment (p. 684) Passed in 1920, the Constitutional guarantee of women's right to vote.

Nixon Doctrine (p. 863) President Nixon argued for "Vietnamization," the notion that the South Vietnamese would carry more of the war's combat burden. This plan never reached full realization because of the South Vietnamese inability to carry on the war effort without American troops.

Non-Intercourse Act (p. 221) An 1809 statute which replaced the Embargo of 1807. It forbade trade with Britain, France, and their possessions, but reopened trade with other countries.

Nonseparatists (p. 42) Religious dissenters from England who wanted to purify, rather than separate from, what they viewed as the corrupted, state-supported Anglican church, or Church of England. By and large, the Puritans were nonseparatists, and some of them banded together to form a utopian community of believers in America. The Massachusetts Bay Colony was to be a model society that would show how godly societies and churches were to be properly organized. See *separatists.*

Northwest Passage (p. 20) During the Age of Exploration, adventurers from England, France, and the

Netherlands kept seeking an all-water route across North America. The goal was to gain access to Oriental material goods and riches while avoiding contact with the developing Spanish empire farther to the south in Central and South America.

Nullification (p. 266)   The doctrine, devised by John C. Calhoun, that a state has the power to "nullify" federal legislation within its borders.

Oil Crisis (p. 916)   Oil supply disruptions and soaring oil prices that the United States experienced in 1973 and 1979. In 1973, Middle Eastern nations imposed an embargo on oil shipments to punish the West for supporting Israel in that year's Arab-Israeli war. A second oil shock occurred when the Iranian Revolution disrupted oil shipments to the western nations.

Old Lights (p. 87)   As the Great Awakening spread during the 1730s and 1740s, various religious groups fractured into two camps, sometimes known as the Old Lights and the New Lights. The Old Lights were not very enthusiastic about the Awakening, particularly in terms of what they viewed as popular excesses in seeking after God's grace. Old Light ministers emphasized formal schooling in theology as a source of their religious authority, and they emphasized good order in their churches. See *New Lights.*

O'Malley, Walter (p. 828)   Penny-pinching owner of baseball's Dodgers who oversaw their 1958 move from Brooklyn to Los Angeles. Unhappy with the deterioration of Brooklyn's neighborhoods and lured by the economic promise of California, the Dodgers' move west illustrated the profound westward demographic shift in modern America.

Open Door Note (p. 600)   Policy set forth in 1899 by Secretary of State John Hay preventing further partitioning of China by European powers, and protecting the principle of free trade.

Operation Just Cause (p. 924)   An American military intervention in Panama in December 1989, which was launched after Panama's leader, Manuel Noriega, who was indicted on drug-related charges, invalidated civilian elections and declared a state of war with the United States.

Panic of 1837 (p. 276)   A financial depression that lasted until the early 1840s.

Parks, Rosa (p. 808)   African-American seamstress and active NAACP member arrested for refusing to give up her seat to a white patron in Montgomery, Alabama, prompting a huge bus boycott led by Martin Luther King, Jr.

Patriarchal (p. 51)   Patriarchal social and political systems are denoted by power and authority residing in males, such as in the father of the family. Such authority then passes from father to son through the generations, and males, in general, control decision making. See *coverture.*

Patrons of Husbandry (p. 564)   An organization founded in 1867 to aid farmers through its local granges, it was responsible for state laws regulating railroads, established cooperatives to help with marketing problems, and provided a social outlet for rural areas.

Pearl Harbor (p. 737)   The main base of the U.S. Pacific fleet, which Japan attacked on December 7, 1941, forcing the United States to enter World War II.

Pendleton Act (p. 558)   A law passed in 1883 to eliminate political corruption in the federal government, it outlawed political contributions by appointed officeholders and established the Civil Service Commission to administer competitive examinations for covered government jobs.

Permanent Immigrants (p. 519)   Immigrants coming to America to settle permanently, often due to ethnic and religious persecution at home.

Perpetual Servitude (p. 56)   Indentured servitude represented temporary service for a specified period, usually from four to seven years, to a legally designated owner. Perpetual servitude meant being owned by some other person for life—and ultimately, even through the generations. In the early days of Virginia, both English subjects and African Americans were indentured servants, but over time blacks would be subjected to perpetual servitude as chattels, defined as the movable property of their all-powerful masters and without legal rights of any kind.

Ping-Pong Diplomacy (p. 864)   Communist China's chairman Mao Tse-tung sent a table tennis team to the world championships in Nagoya, Japan, and then invited an American team to compete in Japan in 1971. This small gesture paved the way for President Nixon's visit to China in February 1972.

Plantation Legend (p. 331)   A stereotype, created by popular pre-Civil War writers, that depicted the South as a region of aristocratic planters, beautiful Southern belles, poor white trash, and faithful household slaves.

Platt Amendment (p. 595)   1901 amendment to the Army Appropriation Bill, limiting Cuban independence by giving the United States two naval bases on Cuba and the right to intervene in Cuban affairs if the American government felt Cuban independence was threatened.

Plessy v. Ferguson (p. 501)   A Supreme Court decision in 1896 that ruled "separate but equal" facilities for African Americans were constitutional under the Fourteenth Amendment, it had the effect of legalizing segregation and led to the passage of much discriminatory legislation known as Jim Crow laws.

Political Slavery (p. 117)   During the 1760s and 1770s many colonial leaders believed that if they did not keep resisting unwanted British policies, they would fall into a state of political slavery in which they had no liberties. As such, they would be akin to chattel slaves in their midst. Comprehending how potentially tyrannical chattel slavery was spurred on many colonists to defend American liberties, even to the point of open rebellion.

Polk, James K. (p. 365)   As president of the United States during the Mexican War, Polk increased American territory by a third.

Popular Sovereignty (p. 388)   The principle, incorporated into the Compromise of 1850 and the Kansas-Nebraska Act, that the people living in the western territories should decide whether or not to permit slavery.

Populist (People's) Party (p. 556)   A political party established in 1892 primarily by remnants of the Farmers' Alliance and Greenback Party, it sought to inflate the currency with silver dollars and to establish an income tax; some of its platform was adopted by the Democrats in 1896 and it died out after the defeat of joint candidate William Jennings Bryan.

Pragmatism (p. 610)   A distinctly American philosophy proposed by William James, it contends that any concept should be tested and its validity determined by its outcome and that the truth of an idea is found in the conduct it dictates or inspires.

Price Revolution (p. 23)   The large influx of gold and silver into Europe from Spanish America during the sixteenth century, along with increased demand for limited supplies of goods, set off a threefold rise in prices (the "great inflation") that caused profound economic turmoil, social disruption, and political instability among European peoples and nations.

Progressive (Bull Moose) Party (p. 626)   A political party established in 1912 by supporters of Theodore Roosevelt after William H. Taft won the Republican presidential nomination. The party proposed a broad program of reform but Bull Moose candidate Roosevelt and Republican nominee lost to the Democratic candidate, Woodrow Wilson.

Prohibition (p. 684)   The ban of the production, sale, and consumption of alcoholic beverages. The Eighteenth Amendment to the U.S. Constitution, adopted in 1919, established prohibition. The amendment was repealed in 1933, with adoption of the Twenty-first Amendment.

Protestant Reformation (p. 21)   A religious reform movement formally begun in 1517 when the Ger-man friar Martin Luther openly attacked abuses of Roman Catholic doctrine. Luther contended that the people could read scripture for themselves in seeking God's grace and that the Bible, not church doctrine, was the ultimate authority in human relationships. Luther's complaints helped foster a variety of dissenting religious groups, some of which would settle in America to get away from various forms of oppression in Europe.

Public Virtue (p. 162)   A cornerstone of good citizenship in republican states, public virtue involved the subordination of individual self-interest to serving the greater good of the whole community. Revolutionary leaders believed that public virtue was essential for a republic to survive and thrive. If absent, governments would be torn apart by competing private interests and succumb to anarchy, at which point tyrants would emerge to offer political stability but with the loss of dearly won political liberties.

Radical Republicans (p. 451)   A faction of the Republican party during Reconstruction, they favored forcing the South to make fundamental changes before readmission to the Union. Eventually they won control because of Southerners' refusal to accept more lenient plans for Reconstruction.

Radical Revolutionaries (p. 162)   At the time of the American Revolution, they argued in favor of establishing more democratic forms of government. Radical revolutionaries had a strong trust in the people, viewed them as inherently virtuous (see *public virtue*), and believed that citizens could govern themselves. Samuel Adams, Thomas Jefferson, and Thomas Paine might be described as radical revolutionaries. See *cautious revolutionaries*.

Rage Militaire (p. 128)   Meaning a passion for arms, the rage militaire characterized the attitudes of American colonists as the war with Great Britain began in 1775. When the ravages and deprivations of warfare became more self-evident, however, this early enthusiasm gave out. In 1776 Thomas Paine criticized the "summer soldiers and sunshine patriots" among the colonists who seemed so eager to fight at the beginning of the War for Independence but who so quickly dropped out as the dangers of engaging in warfare increased.

Rationalism (p. 83)   A main tenet of the Enlightenment era, meaning a firm trust in the ability of the human mind to solve earthly problems, thereby lessening the role of—and reliance on—God as an active force in the ordering of human affairs.

Reagan Doctrine (p. 922)   President Ronald Reagan's 1985 pledge of American aid to insurgent movements attempting to overthrow Soviet-backed regimes in the Third World.

Redemptioners (p. 79)   The redemptioner labor system was similar to that of indentured servitude in providing a way for persons without financial means to get to America. Normally, the family had to locate someone to pay for its passage in return for a set number of years of labor. If no buyer could be found, then ships captains could sell the family's labor, most likely on less desirable terms for the family, to recoup the costs of passage. Thousands of Germans migrated to America as redemptioners in the eight-eenth century.

Referendum   *See* Intiative and Referendum

Reform Darwinists (p. 610)   Sociologists who rejected the determinism of the Social Darwinists, they accepted evolutionary theory but held that people could shape their environment rather than only be shaped by it and accepted human intervention in society.

Religious Liberalism (p. 285)   A religious viewpoint that rejected the Calvinist doctrines of original sin and predestination and stressed the basic goodness of human nature.

Remember the *Maine!* (p. 593)   A national catch phrase following the mysterious 1898 explosion of the U.S. battleship *Maine* in Havana harbor that inflamed public opinion, leading to the Spanish-American War.

Removal (Indian Removal Policy) (p. 269)   A policy of resettling eastern Indian tribes on lands west of the Mississippi River.

Renaissance (p. 14)   Beginning in the 1400s, the European Renaissance represented an intellectual and cultural flowering in the arts, literature, philosophy, and the sciences. One of the most important tenets of the Renaissance was the belief in human progress, or the betterment of society.

Republican Motherhood (p. 174)   This definition of motherhood, emanating from the American Revolution, assigned mothers the task of raising dutiful children, especially sons, who would be prepared to serve the nation in disinterested fashion (see *public virtue)*. Mothers thus acquired the special charge of assuring that future generations could uphold the tenets of republicanism. This expanded role for mothers meant that women, not men, would be responsible for the domestic sphere of life.

Republicanism (p. 162)   At the time of the American Revolution, republicanism referred to the concept that sovereignty, or ultimate political authority, is vested in the people—the citizens of the nation. As such, republican governments not only derive their authority from the consent of the governed but also predicate themselves on the principles of rule by law and legislation by elected representatives.

Republicans (p. 196)   A political party founded by James Madison and Thomas Jefferson to combat Alexander Hamilton's fiscal policies.

Rock and Roll (p. 813)   Musical style new to the 1950s, combining black rhythm and blues with white country music. Listened to mostly by young Americans and embodied by Elvis Presley, the music softly challenged notions of sexual propriety and racial division.

Roderigue Hortalez & Cie. (p. 146)   Prior to its formal involvement in the War for Independence, the French government supplied the American rebels with critically needed war goods through a bogus private trading firm known as Roderigue Hortalez & Cie. French officials did so because they hoped to see the power of Great Britain reduced but without becoming directly engaged in the war itself. Once the Franco-American alliance came into being in 1778, the French could abandon such ruses in favor of open support of their rebel allies.

Rosenberg, Julius and Ethel (p. 779)   American radicals accused of passing atomic secrets to the Soviets during World War II. Although the death penalty was not mandatory for their crime, their 1953 execution reflected the national anti-communist hysteria.

Sagebrush Rebellion (p. 839)   Failed movement led by conservative Western politicians to cede federal control of western land to individual states, promoting private ownership and commercial development.

Salisbury, Lord (p. 589)   Imperious British prime minister who rejected American intervention in an 1895 border dispute between Venezuela and British Guiana, prompting an American threat of military involvement. Salisbury ultimately reversed his position and allowed a commission to arbitrate the dispute.

Salutary Neglect (p. 78)   This term signifies England's relatively benign neglect of its American colonies from about 1690 to 1760. During these years King and Parliament rarely legislated constraints of any kind and allowed the colonists much autonomy in provincial and local matters. In turn, the colonists supported the parent nation's economic and political objectives. This harmonious period came to an end after the Seven Year's War when King and Parliament began asserting more control over the American colonists through taxes and trade regulations.

Santa Anna, General Antonio López de (p. 363)   The Mexican general and president whose defeat at the Battle of San Jacinto in 1836 permitted Texas to gain its independence.

Scalawags (p. 461)   Southern white Republicans during Reconstruction, they came from every class and had a variety of motives but were pictured by their opponents as ignorant and degraded.

Scopes Trial (p. 686) Trial against John Scopes in 1925 for teaching Charles Darwin's theory of evolution in a Tennessee public school; also called the "Monkey Trial."

Scott, Dred (p. 400) A Missouri slave, Scott sued for his freedom on the grounds that his master had taken him onto free soil. The Supreme Court ruled in 1857 that Scott was not a citizen and that Congress had no power to exclude slavery from the federal territories.

Second Bank of the United States (p. 274) A national bank chartered in 1816 to hold government funds, ease the transfer of money across state lines, and regulate private banks. Its federal charter expired in 1836.

Second Continental Congress (p. 132) This body gathered in Philadelphia during May 1775 after the shooting war with Great Britain had started. The second Congress functioned as a coordinating government for the colonies and states in providing overall direction for the patriot war effort. It continued as a central legislative body under the Articles of Confederation until 1789 when a new national legislature, the federal Congress as established under the Constitution of 1787, first convened.

Second Great Awakening (p. 285) A wave of religious fervor and revivalism that swept the United States from the early nineteenth century through the Civil War.

Second New Deal (p. 713) The second stage of President Franklin Delano Roosevelt's economic recovery and reform program, launched January 4, 1935.

Separatists (p. 42) Religious dissenters from England who believed that the state-supported Anglican church, or Church of England, was too corrupt to be reformed. Thus, like the Pilgrims, they often migrated elsewhere to form their own religious communities. See *nonseparatists*.

Settlement House Movement (p. 615) A reform movement growing out of Jane Addams' Hull House in the late nineteenth century, it led to the formation of community centers in which mainly middle-class women sought to meet the needs of recent immigrants to urban centers.

Seward, William Henry (p. 582) Secretary of State for Abraham Lincoln and Andrew Johnson, and advocate of a vigorous expansionism. He is perhaps best known for the purchase of Alaska from Russia in 1867 for $7.2 million, an act labeled "Seward's Folly."

Sharecropping (p. 463) A system of labor to replace slavery that allowed landless farmers to work the land of others for a share of the crops they produced. It was favored by freedpeople over gang labor but sometimes led to virtual peonage.

Shaysites (p. 169) Beset by a hard-hitting economic depression after the War for American Independence, these farmers from western Massachusetts finally rose up in rebellion against their state government in 1786 because they had failed to obtain tax relief. One leader of the uprising was Daniel Shays, from whom the Shaysites derived their name.

Sherman Antitrust Act (p. 561) A law passed in 1890 to break up trusts and monopolies, it was rarely enforced except against labor unions and most of its power was stripped away by the Supreme Court, but it began federal attempts to prevent unfair, anticompetitive business practices.

Sit-in (p. 878) A form of nonviolent protest in which civil rights activists occupy seats in a segregated establishment.

Slave Codes (p. 339) Legal codes that defined the slaveholders' power and the slaves' status as property.

Smith, Joseph, Jr. (p. 368) The founder of the Mormon Church, Smith was murdered in Illinois in 1844.

Smog (p. 831) The chemical-laden fog caused by automobile engines, a serious problem in southern California. Like nuclear waste and the shrinking water supply, it reflects the problems associated with the rapid demographic shift to the West in modern times.

Social Darwinism (p. 485) An ideology based upon the evolutionary theories of Charles Darwin, it justified the concentration of wealth and lack of governmental protection of the weak through the ideas of natural selection and survival of the fittest.

Social Gospel (p. 610) A movement among Christian theologians, it applied Christian doctrines to social problems and advocated creating living conditions conducive to saving souls by tackling the problems of the poor.

Social Security Act (p. 713) New Deal legislation enacted in 1935 to provide monthly stipends for workers aged 65 or older and to provide assistance to the indigent elderly, blind and handicapped persons, and dependent children who did not have a wage-earning parent. The act also established the nation's first federally funded system of unemployment insurance.

Southern Strategy (p. 150) Once France formally entered the War for Independence in 1778 on the American side, the British had to concern themselves with protecting such vital holdings as their sugar islands in the Caribbean region. Needing to disperse their troop strength, the idea of the Southern strategy was to tap into a perceived reservoir of loyalist numbers in the southern colonies. Reduced British forces could employ these loyalists as troops in subduing the rebels and as civil officials in reestablishing royal governments. The plan failed for many reasons, including a shortfall of loyalist support and an inability to hold ground once conquered in places like South Carolina.

Specie (p. 100)   A term for hard coin, such as gold or silver, that can also back and give a fixed point of valuation to paper currencies.

Spirituals (p. 343)   Religious songs composed by enslaved African Americans.

Spoils system (p. 268, 558)   The policy of awarding political or financial help with a government job. Abuses of the spoils system led to the passage in 1883 of the Pendleton Act, which created the Civil Service Commission to award government jobs on the basis of merit.

Sputnik (p. 800)   Russian satellite that successfully orbited the earth in 1957, prompting Americans to question their own values and educational system. The hysteria over Soviet technological superiority led to the 1958 National Defense Education Act.

Stagflation (p. 916)   The economic conditions of slow economic growth, rising inflation, and flagging productivity that characterized the American economy during the 1970s.

Stalin, Joseph (p. 745)   Soviet premier in the 1930s and 1940s, known for his violent purges of internal political enemies and his suspicion of Western leaders, an ideology guided by two major German invasions into Russia.

Stamp Act Congress (p. 109)   This intercolonial body of political leaders from nine colonies met for a few days in October 1765 to consider ways to protest the Stamp Act. The delegates drafted a petition declaring that Parliament should not tax Americans, since they were not represented in that legislative body. The Congress showed that the colonies, when aggrieved, could act in unity, an important precedent for further intercolonial resistance efforts in years to come.

Stanton, Elizabeth Cady (p. 299)   Organizer of the first women's rights convention in Seneca Falls, New York, in 1848, Stanton led the struggle for woman suffrage.

Strategic Arms Limitation Treaty of 1972 (SALT I) (p. 865)   Arms control treaty signed by President Nixon and Soviet premier Leonid Brezhnev. Although it only froze the deployment of relatively inconsequential intercontinental ballistic missiles, this first treaty would lead to more comprehensive arms reduction treaties in the future.

Strict Construction (p. 194)   The view that the powers of the national government are limited to those described in the U.S. Constitution.

Students for a Democratic Society (SDS) (p. 890)   Founded in Port Huron, Michigan in 1962, the rad-

ical organization aimed to rid American society of poverty, racism, and violence through an individually oriented approach called participatory democracy. By 1968, the organization had over 100,000 followers and was responsible for demonstrations at nearly 1000 colleges.

Taft-Hartley Act (p. 777)   Legislation in 1947 that reflected the conservative post-war mood. It outlawed the closed shop, gave presidential power to delay strikes with a "cooling-off" period, and curtailed the political and economic power of organized labor.

Tariff of Abominations (p. 265)   An 1828 protective tariff opposed by many Southerners.

Temperance (p. 290)   The pre-Civil War reform movement which sought to curb the drinking of hard liquor.

Tet Offensive (p. 856)   As American military and political leaders suggested victory in Vietnam was in sight, North Vietnam launched an offensive in January 1968 against every major South Vietnamese target. Although the United States repelled the Tet Offensive, it prompted waves of criticism from those who felt the government had been misleading the American people.

Thoreau, Henry David (p. 303)   A pencilmaker, poet, and author of the influential essay "Civil Disobedience," Thoreau sought to realize transcendentalist ideals in his personal life.

Tory (p. 139)   In England during the eighteenth century the Tory Party was closely identified with the king's interests and monarchism, or in the minds of many American patriots, with tyrannical government. As the Revolution dawned, tory became a term of derision applied to those colonists who sought to maintain their allegiance to the British crown. They preferred to think of themselves as loyalists, since they were not rebelling against but were still supporting British imperial authority in America.

Total War (p. 436)   As opposed to limited war, total war usually denotes a military conflict in which warfare ultimately affects the entire population, civilian as well as military. The American Civil War, at least in its latter stages, might serve as an example of total war because of the destruction of both military and civilian resources in the South by Union armies operating under General Grant and especially General Sherman during 1864 and 1865.

Transcendentalists (p. 303)   A group of New England intellectuals who glorified nature and believed that each person contains god-like potentialities.

Treaty of Guadalupe Hidalgo (p. 374)   The peace treaty ending the Mexican War gave the United States California, Nevada, New Mexico, Utah, and parts of Arizona, Colorado, Kansas, and Wyoming in exchange for $15 million and assumption of $3.25 million in debts owed to Americans by Mexico.

Treaty of Versailles (p. 664)   The treaty that ended World War I.

Truman Doctrine (p. 769)   A speech by President Truman in March 1947 that set the course of U.S. foreign policy for the next generation, painting international affairs as a struggle between free democratic governments and tyrannical communist governments, and advocating American intervention to protect democratic governments.

Trust (p. 490)   A form of business organization that created a single board to trustees to oversee competing firms, the term came to apply when any single entity had the power to control competition within a given industry, such as oil production.

Truth, Sojourner (p. 284)   A leading orator in the abolitionist and women's rights movements, Sojourner Truth was born into slavery in New York's Hudson River Valley and escaped in 1826.

Turner, Nat (p. 344)   A black Baptist preacher who led a revolt against slavery in Southampton County in southern Virginia in 1831.

Twenty-Fourth Amendment (p. 884)   This amendment, adopt-ed in 1964, barred a poll tax in federal elections.

Vertical Integration (p. 490)   The practice of controlling every phase of production by owning the sources of raw materials and often the transportation facilities needed to distribute the product, it was a means of gaining a competitive edge over rival companies.

Vesey, Denmark (p. 344)   A former West Indian slave who organized an attempted rebellion against slavery in Charleston, South Carolina, in 1822.

Vice-Admiralty Courts (p. 103)   The English government established these courts in its North American colonies to deal with issues of maritime law, including smuggling. If judges condemned vessels for smuggling, they would share in profits from the sale of such craft and their cargoes. Judges made all rulings without juries and thus could clearly benefit from their own decisions, which caused many colonists to view these courts as centers of despotic imperial power. The Stamp Act of 1765 stated that colonists who did not pay stamp duties could be tried in vice-admiralty courts, which became another colonial grievance—in this case the prospect of being convicted and sent to jail without a jury trial, a violation of fundamental English liberties.

Virtual Representation (p. 105)   King George III's chief minister, George Grenville, employed this concept in 1765 in relation to the Stamp Act. He insisted that all colonists were represented in Parliament by virtue of being English subjects, regardless of where they lived. Grenville was attempting to counter the colonists' position that King and Parliament had no authority to tax them, since the Americans had no duly elected representatives serving in Parliament.

Voting Rights Act of 1965 (p. 884)   This law prohibited literacy tests and sent federal examiners to the South to register voters.

Wagner Act (National Labor Relations Act) (p. 712)   New Deal legislation enacted in 1935 guaranteeing the right of workers to form unions and bargain collectively. The act established the National Labor Relations Board (NLRB) to settle union-management disputes over unfair labor practices.

Walker, David (p. 294)   The free black author of *An Appeal to the Colored Citizens of the World,* which threatened violence if slavery was not abolished.

Wallace, George (p. 861)   Alabama governor who ran for president in 1968 as a third-party candidate on the American Independent ticket. His message rejecting forced racial integration, the activities of radical college students, and the perceived national drift toward the left appealed to many working class Americans, and he received 13.5 percent of that election's vote.

War of 1812 (p. 227)   War between Britain and the United States. Causes included British interference with American shipping, impressment of seamen, a desire to end British aid to Indians, and an American desire for expansion.

War Powers Act (p. 914)   This 1973 law required presidents to win specific authorization from Congress to engage U.S. forces in foreign combat for more than 90 days.

War Production Board (p. 738)   The board established in January 1942 to help mobilize the U.S. economy for war production.

Washington, George (p. 92)   As the nation's first president, Washington helped define the powers of the presidency, demonstrated in the Whiskey Rebellion that the national government would enforce federal law, cleared the Ohio country of Indians, and attempted to preserve American neutrality during the war between Britain and France.

Watergate Break-In (p. 912)   During the 1972 presidential campaign, burglars, tied to the Nixon White House, were caught installing eavesdropping devices in Democratic Party headquarters in the Watergate Complex in Washington, D.C. Revelations of White House efforts to obstruct the investigation of the break-in, of financial irregularities, and the use of government agencies for partisan purposes led President Nixon to resign in 1974.

Webster, Daniel (p. 236)   A noted orator, Webster opposed the War of 1812 and the protectionist tariff of 1816 after his election to the House of Representatives. He later became a staunch nationalist and defender of tariff protection.

Whig Party, Whigs (p. 117, 277)   During the eighteenth century in England the Whig Party was a loosely organized coalition of political leaders that opposed any hint of arbitrary authority that might emanate from the monarchy and royally appointed officials in government. Like the radical whig pamphleteers, they also viewed themselves as defenders of liberty, which is one reason why many American leaders, even though not organized as a political party, called themselves whigs. During the 1830s and 1840s in the United States, there was a Whig party that opposed the policies of Andrew Jackson, Martin Van Buren, and other members of the Democratic Party.

Whitney, Eli (p. 245, 320)   The inventor of the cotton gin, Whitney pioneered a system of mass production of interchangeable parts. Whitney's cotton gin, which separated cotton from its seeds, met the growing demand for cotton from the textile industry and breathed new life into the institution of slavery.

Wilmot Proviso (p. 376)   An amendment to an 1846 appropriations bill that would have forbade slavery from any territory acquired from Mexico. The amendment passed the House twice but was defeated in the Senate.

Woman's Christian Temperance Union (WCTU) (p. 614)   An organization led by Frances Willard to stop the abuse of alcohol, it joined forces with other groups in the movement for the prohibition of alcohol to reduce such problems as wife abuse.

Women's Army Corps (WAC) (p. 741)   The auxiliary women's unit to the U.S. army.

Workmen's Compensation Laws (p. 620)   Legislation establishing mandatory insurance to be carried by employers to cover on-the-job injuries to their workers, it was a reform that provided protection to workers while also lowering the risk to employers.

Writs of Assistance (p. 107)   Blanket search warrants used by English customs collectors in the colonies to try to catch suspected smugglers. These writs did not require any form of prior evidence to justify searches, which the colonies viewed as yet another imperial violation of fundamental English liberties.

Yalta Conference (p. 748)   The meeting between President Franklin Roosevelt, British prime minister Winston Churchill, and Soviet premier Joseph Stalin at Yalta in the Russian Crimea in February 1945 to determine the post-World War II world order.

Yellow Journalism (p. 591)   Sensationalistic press accounts of the volatile Cuban situation in the 1890s, led by William Randolph Hearst's *New York Journal* and Joseph Pulitzer's *New York World*. Helped mobilize pro-interventionist public opinion prior to the Spanish-American war.

Young, Brigham (p. 370)   The leader of the Mormon church following Joseph Smith's murder, Young led the Mormon exodus from Illinois to the Great Salt Lake.

Zimmermann Telegram (p. 649) Telegram from German Foreign Minister Arnold Zimmermann to the German ambassador to Mexico pledging a Mexican-German alliance against the United States, which brought the United States into World War I.

CREDITS

Page abbreviations are as follows: (T)top, (C)center, (B)bottom, (L)left, (R)right.

Left page of title page spread: Suffragettes: Culver, Family photo: Collection of Michael Staats, FDR: Corbis/Bettmann, Nat Love: Library of Congress.
Right page of title page spread: Tom Torlino: Arizona Historical Society, Sojourner Truth: Sophia Smith Collection, Smith College, Northampton, MA, detail of Harrison campaign handkerchief: New York Historical Society.
ix Courtesy of the Library of Congress

CHAPTER OPENERS

Chapter 1 Spanish in New World and European War Dogs: Theodor deBry, *America*, 1617/ Laudonnnie with Indian Chief: Print Collection/Miriam & Ira D. Wallach Division of Arts, Prints & Photography/New York Public Library, Astor, Lenox & Tilden Foundations / Ad for Virginia Settlers: New York Public Library, Astor Lenox & Tilden **Chapter 2** Johnson Treaty with the Iroquois: New York Historical Society / View of New Amsterdam, Quaker Synod: New York Public Library, Astor, Lenox & Tilden Foundations / Photo: Ken Burris **Chapter 3** Braddock's defeat: The Granger Collection / Alexander de Batz, "Members of the Illinois Tribe": Peabody Museum/Harvard University / John Singleton Copley, "Head of a Negro": From the Collection of the Detroit Institute of Arts, Founders Society/Gibbs-Williams Fund / Benjamin West, "Penn's Treaty with the Indians": Pennsylvania Academy of the Fine Arts / Benjamin Franklin: Historical Society of Pennsylvania **Chapter 4** Act newspaper: *Pennsylvania Journal*, October 31, 1765 / Boston Long Wharf: Courtesy Henry Francis duPont Winterthur Museum / George Washington at Trenton: Library of Congress / Map of Fort Clinton: New York Historical Society / Philadelphia at time of revolution: North Wind Picture Archives **Chapter 5** Boston Long Wharf: Courtesy Henry Francis duPont Winterthur Museum / Navigation Treaty: New York Historical Society / James Madison portrait: Gilcrease Museum / Washington at Valley Forge: Courtesy Valley Forge Historical Society / George Washington: Metropolitan Museum of Art, Bequest of Grace Wilkes, 1922 / Joseph Brant: New York Public Library, Astor, Lenox & Tilden Foundation **Chapter 6** Continental currency: Smithsonian Institution / "Fairview Inn": Maryland Historical Society / *New Cleared Farm in the New World*: New York Public Library, Astor, Lenox & Tilden Foundations / Conestoga wagon: Shelburne Museum / Stagecoach: Library of Congress / "Signing of the Constitution": National Historical Park Collections, Eastern National Parks & Monuments Association **Chapter 7** Benjamin West, "Conference of the Treaty of Paris": Courtesy the Henry Francis du Pont Winterthur Museum / Alexander Hamilton: Copyright Yale University Art Gallery / John Quincy Adams: Historical Society of Pennsylvania **Chapter 8** "Burning of New York": Library of Congress / Dolly Madison: Pennsylvania Academy of the Fine Arts / Thomas Jefferson: Metropolitan Museum of Art, Bequest of Cornelia Crugar / Jefferson campaign broadside: New York Historical Society / James Madison: Gilcrease Museum / Tenskwatawa (the Prophet): Library of Congress **Chapter 9** Cotton gin: Corbis/Bettmann Archive / Robert Fulton: Collection of Michael Staats / Cotton mill: Library of Congress / "Mississippi River at St. Louis": St. Louis Museum of Art, Collection of Arthur Ziern, Jr. **Chapter 10** Harrison campaign handkerchief: New York Historical Society / Manchester factory: Library of Congress / Currier & Ives, "Preparing for Market": Copyright Yale University Art Gallery / Mabel Brady Garvan Collection / "Cherokee Phoenix": American Antiquarian Society / "Rafting Downstream": Indiana University Art Museum, Transfer from IU Collections to Museum **Chapter 11** Asher B. Durand, "In the Catskills": Walters Art Gallery / Edgar Allan Poe: Manuscripts Dept./Lilly Library, Indiana University, Bloomington, IN / Harriet Tubman: Library of Congress **Chapter 12** Steamboats on the Mississippi: Historic New Orleans Collection, Rochester, NY: George Eastman House, International Museum of Photography / Women working in cotton mill, Freed blacks in Richmond: Library of Congress / Middle-class livingroom: The Granger Collection / Immigrants aboard ship: Corbis / Lucretia Mott,

Elizabeth Cady Stanton: Sophia Smith Collection, Smith College, Northampton **Chapter 13** Daguerreotype of two girls: Collection of Michael Staats / Illinois Central Railroad poster: Newberry Library / Miners: California State Library / Chief Joseph: Library of Congress / Mormons sitting in front of their covered wagons: Western History Department/Denver Public Library / William S. Jewett, "The Promised Land—The Grayson Family": Berry-Hill Galleries, NY **Chapter 14** Civil War soldier, Abraham Lincoln, Northern supplies: Library of Congress / The Lincoln–Douglas debates: AP/Wide World Photos / Anti-Slave-Catchers' poster: New York Public Library, Astor, Lenox & Tilden Foundations / "Monitor & Merrimac": Chicago Historical Society **Chapter 15** Robert E. Lee, Abraham Lincoln / "Storming of Fort Wagner": Library of Congress / Battery A, 2nd Colored Artillery: Chicago Historical Society **Chapter 16** Black Elk: Smithsonian Institution / Geronimo: National Archives / Carpetbagger: Culver Pictures Inc. / Black schoolroom, Ruins of Richmond

CHAPTER 1

4 The Granger Collection **7R** Courtesy of the Library of Congress **7** Hillel Burger/Peabody Museum, Harvard University **8** Tony Linck **9** North Wind Picture Archives **11** Corbis **13** Hulton Getty/Liaison Agency, Inc. **14** Copyright © The British Museum **16** The New York Public Library, Rare Book Division **18** The Granger Collection **19** The Granger Collection **21** Philadelphia Museum of Art **21** National Portrait Gallery, London **21** National Portrait Gallery, London **22** Musee Historique de la Reformation **24** National Portrait Gallery, London **25** The Granger Collection **27** Hulton Getty/Liaison Agency, Inc.

CHAPTER 2

36 North Wind Picture Archives **38** The Granger Collection **39** Copyright © The British Museum **41** Copyright © National Maritime Museum Picture Library, London, England **41** National Portrait Gallery, London **43** Colonial Williamsburg Foundation **44** Pilgrim Society **44** American Antiquarian Society **46** Courtesy Massachusetts Historical Society, Boston **47** The Granger Collection **48** Brown County Library **49** The New York Public Library, Rare Book Division **49** The Huntington Library **50** Peabody Essex Museum **53** Abby Aldrich Rockefeller Folk Art Center **54** Brown Brothers **56** Ellett Tazewell **57** The Granger Collection **59** Abby Aldrich Rockefeller Folk Art Center

CHAPTER 3

66 Bernard Gallagher **68** Courtesy of the Library of Congress **72** Pennsylvania Academy of the Fine Arts **72** Abby Aldrich Rockefeller Folk Art Center **76** Peabody Essex Museum **83** The Granger Collection **85** The Granger Collection **86** Courtesy of Mr. and Mrs. Wharton Sinkler Collection/Philadelphia Museum of Art **87** Courtesy of the Library of Congress **87** National Portrait Gallery, London **88** Brown University **89** Paul Mellon Collection/National Gallery of Art, Washington, D.C. **92** Courtesy of the Library of Congress **93** The Granger Collection

CHAPTER 4

100 Spencer Collection/New York Public Library, Astor, Lenox & Tilden Foundations **102** Royal Academy of Arts **103** Anderson, Elmer G. (American, active c. 1935). Pa. German Painted Wooden Box, c. 1937, watercolor and graphite on paper, . 463 x . 369 (18 1/4 x 14 1/2). Index of American Design, Copyright © 2000 Board of Trustees, National Gallery of Art, Washington, D.C. **106** Courtesy of the Library of Congress **107** Courtesy Massachusetts Historical Society, Boston **108** Courtesy of the Library of Congress **109** Shelburne Museum **110** Courtesy of the Library of Congress **115** I. N. Phelps Stokes Collection/Miriam & Ira D. Wallach Division of Art, Prints & Photographs Division/New York Public Library, Astor, Lenox, and Tilden Foundations **116** Revere, Paul, Boston Massacre, 1770. U.S., 1735–1818. Engraving after Henry Pelham, hand-colored by Christian Remick (1726-after 1783) Sight: 10-1/4 x 8-5/8 in. Gift of Watson Grant Cutter. Courtesy, Museum of Fine Arts, Boston **117** Rhode Island Historical Society **121** North Wind Picture Archives

Index

Abenaki Indians, 66

Abolitionism, 273, 294–297; arguments of, 295, 346; and colonization movement, 294, 296; divisions within, 296–297; and Emancipation Proclamation, 429; public reaction to, 295, 332; in revolutionary period, 175–178; in South, 175–178, 320, 336–337; and violence, 404, 405; and women's rights movement, 298, 299

Abortion, 177

Adams, Abigail, 172, 173, 202, 203, 204

Adams, Charles Francis, 426

Adams, John, 113, 132, 154; and Abigail, 172–173; appointment of judgeships, 215, 216; in Britain, 168; and Declaration of Independence, 139; presidency of, 202–205; and quasi war with France, 203–204

Adams, John Quincy, 235–236, 252–253, 261; and Adams-Onis Treaty, 241; election of 1828, 266; and Oregon country, 368; presidency of, 264–265; on slavery debates, 264; and Texas annexation, 365

Adams, Samuel, 100–101; and Boston massacre, 117, 118; and First Continental Congress, 121; in resistance to British, 106, 107–108, 111, 113, 114, 131; and Second Continental Congress, 132; views on government, 162, 183

Adams, Samuel (father), 100

Adams-Onis Treaty, 241

The Adder's Den (Dye), 384–385

Africa, 15, 57, 58; colonization to, 294, 296; slave trade in, 15, 57, 59

African Americans. *See also* Free blacks; Racism; Slavery; Slaves: in abolitionist movement, 294, 296–297; in American Revolution, 134–138, 144; Black Codes, 453–454; in Civil War, 429–431, 436; in colonies, 36–37, 78, 79; and colonization movement, 294, 296; education, 179, 292–293, 450, 464; in government, 461, 462–463; labor system after Civil War, 446, 453, 454, 463–464; land ownership, 450, 453, 463; legal status/rights, 451, 453–454, 455; literature, 307; medical care, 392–393; music, 343; in New Spain, 19–20; and poor whites, 464; population growth, 78, 79; after Reconstruction, 472, 473; in Reconstruction, 440, 446, 447–450, 453–456, 458–466, 474; religion of, 89, 178, 179, 289, 337, 343, 464; in revolutionary era, 161, 175–179; and segregation, 178–179, 430, 431, 463, 464; sharecropping, 463–464;

stereotypes, 312–313; violence against, 454, 465, 466; voting rights, 260, 346, 451, 453, 455, 456, 458–459, 465

African Free School, 179

African Methodist Episcopal Church, 178, 179, 250, 289, 464

Agriculture: and Columbian exchange, 30; commercial, 323; early nineteenth-century, 242, 245, 323; Native American, 5–6; sharecropping, 463–464; in South, 334, 335–336, 463–464

Alabama (ship), 425

Alamo, the, 364, 366

Albany Plan of Union, 92, 122

Alcott, Abba, 305

Alcott, Bronson, 302, 305

Alcott, Louisa May, 305

Alexander VI (pope), 16

Alien Act, 204

Alien and Sedition acts, 204–205

Alien Enemies Act, 204

Allan, Ethan, 133

Allen, Richard, 178, 179

Allerton, Mary Norris, 52

American Anti-Slavery Society, 296, 299, 313

American Party (Know Nothings), 391–395, 399, 400

American Philosophical Society, 86

American Revolution, 101; beginning of, 129–132; British military buildup, 140–141; Bunker Hill, 118, 133–134, 136–137; Continental army, 128, 129, 132, 142–146, 149, 150, 152, 155; Declaration of Independence and, 138–140; events leading to, 100–123, 129–132; expansion of, 133–138; French assistance in, 146–147; Lexington and Concord, 131, 132, 134–135; in North, 131, 132, 133–137, 140–144, 147–149; peace settlement, 154–155; Second Continental Congress and, 132–133; in South, 134–138, 138, 150–153; surrender at Yorktown, 153–154; Valley Forge, 128, 129, 149

"The American Scholar" (Emerson), 301

American Society for the Promotion of Temperance, 290

American system, 265

American system of production, 245

American Woman Suffrage Association, 458, 459

Amherst, Jeffrey, 93

Amish, 79

Anaconda Plan, 419–421

Anderson, Robert, 414, 439

Andros, Edmund, 74, 75

Anglican church. *See* Church of England

Annapolis (Maryland), 168, 179

Anthony, Susan B., 429, 458, 459

Anti-Mason movement, 260–261, 277

Antietam, battle of, 410–411, 422–423, 429

Antifederalists, 181, 182–183

Antinomian crisis, 47–48

Antiwar movement(s): Civil War, 428, 436; Mexican-American War, 373, 374

Antrobus, John, 343

Apache Indians, 357, 468

Apes, William, 307

Appeal to the Colored Citizens of the World (Walker), 295

Appomattox, surrender at, 438

Arapaho Indians, 8, 469

Arawak Indians, 15–16

Arizona, 355, 356–357, 376

Arizona Territory, 376

Arkansas, 451, 452

Army, U.S. *See* Union army

Arnold, Benedict, 112, 133, 148, 152, 153

Arrillaga, Mariano Paredes y, 371

Art, early nineteenth-century, 301, 307–308

Articles of Confederation, 164; financial problems under, 164, 165–169; plans to revise, 166–167, 168, 179, 180; ratification of, 165

Artisans, 323–324; free black, 344, 346

Astor, John Jacob, 365

Astor Place Riot, 310

Asylums, 293

Atahualpa, 18

Atlanta (Georgia), 436

Attucks, Crispus, 116

Austin, Stephen F., 362, 363, 364, 367

Autobiographies, by minority authors, 307

Avilés, Pedro Menéndez de, 23

Azores, 15

Aztecs, 6, 7, 17–18

Backus, Isaac, 88

Bacon, Nathaniel, 73

Bacon's rebellion, 73–74

Bahamas, 15–16

Balboa, Vasco Nuñez de, 17

Baldwin, Luther, 204–205

Ballard, Martha, 52

Baltimore (Maryland), 226, 248, 258, 344, 427

bandidos, 354

Bank of the United States, 194–195, 215; second, 236, 237, 239–240, 274–275

Banking system: under Jackson, 274–276; and National Banking acts, 426

Banneker, Benjamin, 178

Davis, David, 473

Davis, Jefferson, 339, 411, 449, 459; as Confederate president, 414, 418, 421, 424, 425, 434, 436

Davis, Joseph, 339

Dawes, William, 131

Dawes Severalty Act, 471

Day, Benjamin H., 309

Day of Jubilo, 448

De La Warr, Lord, 38

de Soto, Hernando, 12, 18

de Vaca, Cabeza, 18

Dead Indian Act, 471

Deaf people, 293

Deane, Silas, 146

Death Comes to the Archbishop (Cather), 307

Debt, 105; imprisonment for, 291; national (*See* National debt)

Decatur, Stephen, Jr., 217, 240

Declaration of Independence, 138–140, 170; events leading to, 138–139

Declaratory Act, 111

Declension, 55–56

Deism, 86, 288

Delany, Martin R., 296, 307

Delaware, 71, 138, 178

Delaware Indians, 71, 102, 172, 200

Democratic party. *See also specific elections*: after Civil War, 451; Jacksonian, 265, 278, 332; and Know Nothings, 391, 394; and national Reconstruction policies, 451–458, 465, 467; North-South split in, 411, 451; Peace Democrats, 428, 436; in Reconstruction South, 461–465; and slavery expansion issue, 386, 387, 389, 396; southern, 451; and Whigs, 277

Democratic republicanism, 267

Demographic transition, 176

Depression(s): after American Revolution, 168; Panic of 1819, 248, 261–264; Panic of 1837, 275–276; Panic of 1873, 467

Dermer, Thomas, 4

Deslondes, Charles, 344

Detroit (Michigan), 222, 223

Dias, Bartholomeu, 15

Dickens, Charles, 242, 309

Dickinson, John, 111, 114, 132, 133, 138, 164, 179, 180

Diet, of slaves, 341

Dime novels, 309

Dinwiddie, Robert, 92

Dirt, Andrew, 340

Discourse of Western Planting (Hakluyt), 23–24

Disease(s). *See also* Medical care: of African Americans, 341, 392, 393, 437; cholera, 262–263; in Civil War, 411, 437; in colonies, 37; in Europe, 11, 18; inoculation for, 86; and Native Americans, 4, 5, 10, 16, 18, 30, 224; on Oregon Trail, 362; of slaves, 341, 392, 393; yellow fever, 198–199

Dissenters. *See* Baptists; Pilgrims; Puritans; Quakers

Divine right, 40

Dix, Dorothea, 293, 437

"Dixie" (song), 331

Domestic novels, 309–310

Doniphan, A. W., 372

Donner party, 358

Douglas, Stephen A., 388, 389, 396, 399, 401; on Brown's raid, 405; debates with Lincoln, 402–403; and election of 1860, 411, 413

Douglass, Frederick, 251, 284, 296, 297, 299, 307, 345; and black suffrage, 458; and Brown's raid, 403–404; call to arms, 430; and Emancipation Proclamation, 429, 430; on freedmen, 450; life of, 296

Dragging Canoe (Chincohacina), 150

Drake, Francis, 23, 25

Dred Scott decision, 400–401, 402–403, 451

Drinking, in 1830s-40s, 285, 289–290

Driven from Jackson County, Missouri (Christensen), 369

Du Bois, W. E. B., 461

Dudingston, William, 118

Dueling, 285

Dunmore, Lord (John Murray), 134–138

Dustan, Hannah, 66–67

Dutch: in American Revolution, 150; in New World, 28, 69, 73, 75; in slave trade, 36; trade, 28, 69, 74, 150, 168

Dutch West India Company, 28, 69

Dwight, Timothy, 206

Dye, John Smith, 384, 385

Dyer, Mary, 70

East India Company, 119

Eaton, Peggy, 272–273

Economic growth. *See also* Industrialization: American system and, 265; Civil War and, 426–427; Hamilton's financial program for, 193–195; in 1790s, 192; South and, 334–336, 338, 426–427; Taney Court and, 276; after War of 1812, 234, 236, 241–248

Economic recession. *See* Depression(s)

Economic stratification: after American Revolution, 171; in colonies, 81–82; Jacksonian view of, 268; in North, pre–Civil War, 329–330; in South, pre–Civil War, 335–336

Education: of African Americans, 179, 292–293, 450, 463, 464; Bronson Alcott and, 305; late eighteenth-century, 192; in Massachusetts Bay Colony, 46–47; of Native Americans, 471; public, 46–47, 292, 463; reforms, pre–Civil War, 292–293; segregation of, 463; in South, 335, 338, 450, 463; universities, 88, 293, 338, 464; of women, 174–175, 293

Edwards, Jonathan, 86–87

Election(s): of 1796, 202; of 1800, 205–206; of 1804, 220; of 1824, 264; of 1828, and Jackson's campaign, 266; of 1832, 274; of 1836, 277; of 1840, and Harrison's campaign, 258–259, 277; of 1844, 365, 368; of 1846, 374; of 1848, 278–279; of 1852, 278, 279; of 1854, 397, 398; of 1856, 394, 399–400; of 1858, and Lincoln-Douglas debates, 402–403; of 1860, 411–413, 412–413; of 1862, 429; of 1864, 436; of 1866, 455–456; of 1868, 458; of 1872, 467; of 1876, 472–473; early nineteenth-century, 259, 332; violence related to, 332, 465

Electoral system, 181, 206, 264

Eleventh Amendment, 216

Eliot, John, 49

Elites. *See also* Gentleman-planters: and attacks on privilege, in 1820s, 260–261; colonial, 81–83, 85; and Constitution, 182–183; Jacksonians and, 267–268; revolutionary-era, 162, 163

Elizabeth I, Queen of England, 21, 23, 24, 25

Ellison, William, 344–345

Emancipation proclamation (Dunmore's), 134–138

Emancipation Proclamation (Lincoln's), 411, 428–429; impact of, 429–431

Emerson, Ralph Waldo, 301, 302, 306, 311, 335, 376, 405

Emmanuel (slave), 37

Emmett, Dan D., 331

Enclosure movement, 23

encomienda system, 19

Enforcement Acts, 465

England. *See* Britain

English colonies, 37–60; Enlightenment in, 83–86; Glorious Revolution in, 74–75; government by England, 74, 76–78, 82–83, 102, 103–106; immigration to, 78–79, 82, 83; imperial wars in, 89–95; motives for immigration to, 23–24, 30; pastimes, 84–85; population growth, 78–80; resistance to British, 106–123; social stratification, 80–83; trade, 28–29, 37, 67–68, 73, 77–78

Enlightenment, the, 83–86, 176, 285

Entertainment, colonial, 84–85

Enumerated goods, 68, 73

Equiano, Olaudah, 57, 80–81

Era of Good Feelings, 234–253

Eratosthenes, 14

Eric the Red, 10

Ericson, Leif, 10, 11

Erie Canal, 242–243

Esparza, Gregorio, 366

Essay Concerning Human Understanding (Locke), 83

Ether, 245

Ethiopian regiment, 138

Ethnocide, of Native Americans, 471

Eugenics, 301

Europe: Black Death in, 11; and Civil War, 425, 426; claims in North America, 1750-1763, 90, 102; emigration from, 83; Middle Ages, 10–11; and Monroe Doctrine, 241; nation-states in, 15; population growth, 10–11; Price Revolution in, 23; Protestant Reformation in, 21–22; Renaissance, 14; trade with Orient, 11–14

Europeans: and Columbian exchange, 30; exploration by, 14, 15–16, 17; fighting style, 12–13; in Middle Ages, 10–11; in slave trade, 57; social stratification, 80; view of Native Americans, 9–10, 12–13

Evangelical revivalism, 214, 285–288

Evans, Oliver, 244

Executive privilege, 201

Expansionism. *See also* Westward expansion: southern, 338–339; Young America program (1850s), 395

Exploration: Dutch, 28; English, 20; European, 14, 15–16, 17; French, 20, 89; of Ohio river regions, 172; Portuguese, 15, 16; Spanish, 15, 16–18, 20; Viking, 10; of West, 359–360

Fallen Timbers, battle of, 197, 200, 224

Families: in Chesapeake colonies, 51, 54, 55, 56; elite, 81–83; and fall in birth rate, 176; Puritan, 51–54; slave, 342–343

Fannin, James, 364

Wild, Elizabeth, 54
Wilderness, battle of the, 436
Wilkinson, James, 219, 220
Willard, Emma Hart, 293
Willard, Samuel, 51
William of Orange, 75, 76
Williams, Roger, 47, 48
Wilmot, David, 376
Wilmot Proviso, 376–377
Wilson, Woodrow, 215
Wingina, 25
The Winning of the West (Roosevelt), 354–355
Winthrop, John, 44, 47–48, 49
Witchcraft hysteria, 75–76
Wolfe, James, 93, 95
Woman in the Nineteenth Century (Fuller), 304
Women: and birth control, 176–177; in Chesapeake colonies, 51, 54, 55; in Civil War, 437; colonial, 39, 51–54, 55, 66–67, 70; early nineteenth-century, 297–298, 327; education of, 174–175, 293; employment of, 54, 234, 235, 325–326, 327; household work, 327; legal status/rights, 55; Native American, 9; novels by, 309–310; pioneer, 362; pregnancy and childbirth, 52–53; prostitution, 285, 289; Puritan, 51–54; Quaker, 70; revolutionary-era, 115, 144–146, 160–161, 163, 172–175; slave, 342, 343; in South, 334, 425; in Virginia colony, 39; voting rights, 163, 164, 259–260, 299, 458, 459, 462–463
Women's movement: early, 297–299, 300, 304; and Seneca Falls Declaration and Resolutions, 300; for suffrage, 458–459
Wood, Jethro, 246
Woodmason, Charles, 286
Woolen Act, 77

Worcester v. Georgia, 269
Working class, 327. *See also* Poverty; Unskilled workers
Working Men's parties, 326
Wounded Knee massacre, 471
Wright, Frances, 298, 301
Writs of assistance, 107
Wyandot Indians, 238

XYZ Affair, 203

Yancey, William L., 411, 426
Yellow fever, 198–199
Yorktown, battle of, 153–154
Young, Brigham, 370
Young America program, 395

Zorro, 354
Zuni Indians, 8, 357, 468